LEARNING LEGAL RULES

A Students' Guide to Legal Method and Reasoning

LEARNING LEGAL RULES

A Students' Guide to Legal Method and Reasoning

Ninth Edition

James Holland LLB, PhD, Barrister (Middle Temple)

Emeritus Professor of Employment Law
University of the West of England, Bristol

Julian Webb BA, LLM, LLD, FRSA

Professor of Law
University of Melbourne, Australia

Foreword to the First Edition by the Rt Hon Lord Templeman MBE

OXFORD
UNIVERSITY PRESS

OXFORD
UNIVERSITY PRESS

Great Clarendon Street, Oxford, OX2 6DP,
United Kingdom

Oxford University Press is a department of the University of Oxford.
It furthers the University's objective of excellence in research, scholarship,
and education by publishing worldwide. Oxford is a registered trade mark of
Oxford University Press in the UK and in certain other countries

Sixth edition 2006
Seventh edition 2010
Eighth edition 2013
Impression: 4

Public sector information reproduced under Open Government Licence v2.0
(http://www.nationalarchives.gov.uk/doc/open-government-licence/open-government-licence.htm)

Published in the United States of America by Oxford University Press
198 Madison Avenue, New York, NY 10016, United States of America

British Library Cataloguing in Publication Data
Data available

Library of Congress Control Number: 2015957926

ISBN 978-0-19-872843-6

Printed in UK by
Bell & Bain Ltd, Glasgow.

*This book is dedicated to the memories of our respective parents
Julie and Jim Holland, and Lucy and Sidney Webb*

Contents

Foreword to the First Edition

The Rt Hon Lord Templeman MBE,
Lord of Appeal in Ordinary

This book answers all the questions which a student of the law ought to ask and pro-pounds answers to questions which every lawyer and every judge should ask himself from time to time.

The lawyer is a manipulator of words; this is an assertion and not a criticism. Language is the means of disclosing facts, expressing ideas, and applying principles. The ultimate solution of any legal problem is to be found in the application of basic principles to ascer-tained facts. The difficulties which obstruct the ultimate solution lie in the selection of appropriate principles and the rejection of irrelevant facts. The practice of the law is an art and not a science because the applicability of principle and the analysis of complicated facts depend on the language employed. The judge resembles a conductor of a nineteenth-century symphony. The conductor and the judge must establish the main themes, elimi-nate discordant sounds, and present a harmonious whole. Modern litigation, like a twentieth-century symphony, suffers from the obscurity of themes and the tyranny of discordant sounds. In this book the authors set out to teach the art of conducting the law.

For the student the first task is to become well acquainted with the instruments of English law and Community law, namely, primary legislation, delegated legislation, judi-cial authorities, and textbooks. The first three chapters introduce all these sources of the law. The fourth [now fifth—all subsequent chapter references are to the 9th edn] chap-ter deals with the interplay of law, fact, and language. The authors illustrate the fact that the flexibility of words affords a danger to logic as well as an effective aid to explana-tion. Rhetoric and jargon may disguise principle and obscure uncomfortable fact. The [sixth] and [seventh] chapters are invaluable guides to the dissection and application of precedents—those themes which enable the lawyer and the judge to determine the pres-ence or absence of compatible variations. The [ninth] and [eleventh] chapters manfully grapple with the different problems of construing English and Community legislation. The differences are substantial; Articles 30 and 35 of the Treaty of Rome, prohibiting quantitative restrictions on imports and exports, enabled the European Court of Justice to establish a free trade regime which could only have been established by about four English statutes containing 500 sections and 15 Schedules and hundreds of statutory instruments. The interplay of United Kingdom law and Community law is explored, not always in agreement with the House of Lords. Finally, in Chapter [12] the art of reconciling fact, principle, and language in English law and in Community law is explained and illustrated.

The book is aimed at law students but is valuable to the citizen who knows no law, the lawyer who has forgotten some law and a judge who fears that a just result may be buried under torrents of oral and written words. The book should enable all its readers to guard against asking a silly question and thus provoking a silly answer. The language of the book is clear and the style interesting and thought-provoking.

The authors make a new contribution to legal literature and, at the same time, illuminate and recognise old controversies.

Templeman
House of Lords

Preface to the Ninth Edition

In writing the preface to our first edition, over twenty-five years ago, we said our primary aim was to provide a practical, user-friendly and critical introduction to legal method and reasoning; to demystify the subject. That is still very much our intention today.

Why you should read this book

If you are studying law it is extremely easy to get focused on the substantive aspects of the subject—the concepts, rules, and principles that go to make up contract, tort, crime, etc. There is a risk that, in the process, we lose sight of the glue that holds all these things together:

1. that the substantive law is constructed within the context of a set of institutions that make up the legal system, and

2. that these institutions themselves make and develop the law within the framework of a further set of values, rules and principles that determine the legitimate limits of law-making, interpretation, and application.

This book is intended to help you develop both the knowledge and reasoning skills that will support your understanding of this context, and thus also support and enhance your performance in your substantive law subjects. Legal method does not exist in isolation. In reality, it is a key part of your toolkit for making sense of how law works. The most common problem a law student faces is not *'what are the rules?'* but rather *'how do I make use of the rules?'* This requires that you develop the abilities that are the core focus of this book:

- to **find** and **'make sense'** of the primary and secondary sources of law (see **Chapters 1–3**);

- to **interpret** and **apply** *authorities*; and by the term 'authorities' we mean primarily the *legislation* and reported *cases* that can be found in a law library (see **Chapters 6–11**);

- to **construct** arguments both about the *facts* of a case, and as to *how* and *why* a particular authority should or should not be applied in a given situation (see chiefly **Chapters 5–7, 9**, and **12**);

- to **write** clearly and in an appropriate (legal) style, making reference to authority as necessary, and **citing** sources in the proper academic form (see **Chapter 4**).

In supporting you to develop these skills, and acquire the requisite knowledge, we have tried to stress not just what the rules and principles *are*, but to understand *why* they are as they are, and what *consequences* they have. We remember our own frustrations as undergraduates trying to make sense of legal method (though when we were students explicit courses on legal method were the exception rather than the norm, which made the job even harder). When we started to write *Legal Rules* we therefore set out to try to answer the sorts of questions we had as students. We hope you will find that useful.

Although the most common comment we hear about *Learning Legal Rules* is that it is clear and user-friendly, we sometimes hear the complaint that we make legal method more complicated than it needs to be. We don't think that is true. The reality is that any topic can be addressed at a number of levels. A lot of general 'English legal system' books deal, in a single chapter, with topics that take us two or three chapters to address. Equally, there are even more specialist texts that take a whole book to cover a topic that we cover in a couple of chapters. In other words, we have tried to steer a middle course, between the very detailed knowledge required by the specialist (i.e. the advocate arguing technical points of precedent and interpretation in the higher courts) and the oversimplification of some more generalist student texts. We don't believe understanding is achieved by oversimplification. The reality is that legal method and reasoning can be quite complex, and we want you to achieve an adequately complex understanding of how they work. In the same way that you would not expect your doctor to 'give up' on the difficult bits, lawyers have to face up to the complexities of legal argument and acquire the skill and knowledge to deal with them.

How to use this book

Learning Legal Rules can be used either to support a course of study in legal method, or as a self-teaching guide to the subject. We are aware that many people study law by independent or distance-learning methods, and have tried to anticipate their needs, in addition to those of students on traditional full- or part-time courses. We would, however, say that the course of study laid down in this book cannot be wholly followed without access to, at least, a basic library containing some primary sources (law reports and statutes) and a good Internet connexion!

We have also sought to organise the contents in a sequence that supports you to build your knowledge sequentially from **Chapters 1–12**. On the whole it makes sense, therefore, not to read the later chapters until you have worked through the earlier material. Having said that, there are two chapters which are more heavily theoretical than the rest (**Chapters 5** and **12**). These may not be appropriate material for all courses at either first degree or postgraduate level, and so we have tried to ensure that the material in them may be disregarded (or taken far more selectively) without destroying the sense of the rest of the text.

In order to make the text easier to follow, we have avoided the use of footnotes. All case references appear in the text. References to books and articles in the text are cited using what is called the Harvard reference system. This gives the name of the author followed by date of publication and (if appropriate) the page number, thus, 'Smith (1986: 123)'. The full citation of references is listed at the end of each chapter. Some of those references are marked with an asterisk (*). This indicates a text which we consider particularly suitable for further reading; though you should (where possible) be guided by your teachers with regard to what additional reading is required for your course.

This book is also supported by an Online Resource Centre (which can be accessed at www.oxfordtextbooks.co.uk/orc/holland_webb9e/). The website is regularly updated, and contains a variety of resources for both students and lecturers. These include: a test bank of multiple-choice questions and answers with feedback; updates on recent cases and legislation; ideas for seminars and lecturers; and additional web links.

As part of our step-by-step approach to the mechanics of legal reasoning, we have included a range of practical exercises which are designed to enable you to gain experience in, as well as knowledge of, the area. Learning by experience really is the key to understanding legal method. If you are following a formal course in legal method and/ or legal system, do make the most of the opportunities to learn by experience that seminars or tutorials provide. Whether or not you are following such a course, the paper and online exercises that go with this book will provide you with an opportunity to deepen your understanding of the topics discussed.

Changes from the Eighth Edition

As ever we are grateful to those users (lecturers and students from around the world) who have given us feedback on the strengths and weaknesses of the last edition. In the light of this feedback we have made a number of changes. Indeed, legal method itself has changed substantially since we wrote the first edition and continues to evolve. In 1991 it was not even a recognised law subject in many law schools; now it is a given. We have sought to reflect these changes as to how legal skills, and particularly legal method, have been viewed in each new edition. In this edition, **Chapter 1** has been revised to offer a slightly shorter and more focused Introduction; **Chapter 2** has been substantially rewritten to emphasise the importance of online and digital resources within the context of a growing demand for law graduates who are fully 'digitally literate'. The section in **Chapter 4** on plagiarism has been extended at the request of a number of lecturers around the globe. **Chapter 10** has been updated and revised to take account of the latest debates over the future of the Human Rights Act and **Chapter 11** on European Legal Method has been shortened. All chapters have been updated and we are grateful to the many helpful comments we have received on the text generally. We have sought to state the law as it stood at 31 December 2015.

In writing this ninth edition we have sought to preserve the strengths of previous editions. It is still our firm belief, as we noted in 1991, that the study of law is challenging but also immensely rewarding and enjoyable; we hope that you will find it so.

James Holland
Julian Webb
January 2016

Acknowledgements

This book has been shaped and influenced by the contributions and support of many friends and colleagues over the years. Our particular, and continuing, thanks are due to Professor Adrian Chandler, Carol Crowdy, Dr Rachel Fenton, and Julie Hamley at UWE, Bristol, Professor Lisa Webley at Westminster Law School, and to Professor Geoffrey Samuel of the University of Kent for continuing access to and updates of his translations of material from the work of Bergel and Villey, cited in **Chapter 12**. At Warwick University, Dr James Harrison and Helen Riley were instrumental in developing the current MELS course, which in turn had an influence on previous editions. We would also like to acknowledge Jo Kendal's research assistance at UWE in previous editions, and Joanna Ramsay, our editor at Oxford University Press, not least for her enthusiasm, professionalism, and perseverance in attempting to keep us to deadlines. And we could not forget the assistance of those university and college teachers and students from countries around the world who have shared their experiences of using *Learning Legal Rules* with us over various editions: thank you too. In particular, as regards this edition, we are grateful to Maureen Maksymiw at Nottingham Trent University for her fascinating comments on the different advertisements that appeared in the case of *Carlill v Carbolic Smoke Ball Company* (covered in Chapter 7).

We have an enduring debt to two key people. The first is Alistair MacQueen (1944-2008). Alistair was one of the founders of Blackstone Press (the original publishers of this work) and the man who really was responsible for *Learning Legal Rules* seeing the light of day. Our second debt is owed to the Rt Hon Lord Templeman MBE, former Lord of Appeal in Ordinary, for agreeing to write the Foreword to this book, and for the continuing interest he showed in the text throughout its entire history from that point until his death in the summer of 2014, aged 94. We believe Sydney was the first sitting Law Lord to write such a piece for an undergraduate text and he insisted on reading and sometimes debating every word in the book before he would lend his name to it. As per his reputation in practice, described below, we did not get off lightly. His obituaries last year demonstrated how loved and admired he was across the legal world. *The Daily Telegraph* put it this way: 'Off the bench, Sydney Templeman was a genial character entirely lacking in pomposity; on it, however, he could be distinctly fierce.... His peremptoriness resulted in his being affectionately known as "Syd Vicious" by some of the barristers who appeared before him.'

Sydney believed fervently in every student having the chance to fulfil his or her own potential and, to this effect, he established and funded scholarships for UK and overseas students as well as prestigious prizes in a number of Law Schools in the UK. At UWE, Bristol he also frequently judged moots and gave talks to students on life as a judge and on how legal method related to real-world legal argument. He is sadly missed both in academia and practice, especially by the authors of this book

The authors and publishers also wish to thank the following for permission to reprint copyright material: RELX (UK) Limited, trading as LexisNexis for extracts from the *All England Law Reports*; the Incorporated Council of Law Reporting for England and Wales for permission to reproduce *DPP* v *Bull* [1994]; Thomson Reuters (Professional) UK for permission to reproduce extracts from *Pierrel SpA and others* v *Ministero della Sanità* [1995] from the *Common Market Law Reports* along with screenshots from westlaw.co.uk; and Reed Elsevier (UK) Limited, trading as LexisNexis, for screenshots of their online services.

Table of Cases

1

Understanding the Law

1.1 Introduction

Law is everywhere. It governs our work, the products we buy and sell, our relation-ships, and even helps shape the physical environment in which we live. This first chapter sets out to introduce some fundamentals that will underpin your under-standing of law and 'legal method'—that is, those core principles and techniques that underpin the process of legal reasoning. We do this by, first, introducing you to the idea of 'law' and some of the major functions of law, and then by looking at the main sources of law that you will become familiar with as you work through this book: pri-marily *legislation* as well as other less 'formal' categories of legal rules, and *case law* as it is developed by the courts. We will also look at the institutions responsible for making and shaping those laws—chiefly Parliament and the courts—and consider the impact of Europe on English (and United Kingdom) law. So, let's start at the very beginning.

1.2 What is Law?

At first glance this seems a very simple, if not a rather strange, question to ask. After all, as the poet W.H. Auden said, 'The law is The Law' and we tend to know it when we see it. But it is also a question that philosophers and legal theorists have expended many pages in trying to answer. Why do you think that is? And what answers do you think they might have come up with?

Some of the philosophers' answers, reduced to their most basic form, are:

- law is a system of rules laid down by a body or person with the power and authority to make law;
- law is what legislators, judges, and lawyers 'do';
- law is a tool of oppression used by the ruling class to advance its own interests; and
- law is a system of rules grounded on fundamental principles of morality.

Each of these characterisations has the capacity to tell us something useful about the nature of 'law' and how it operates—at least within Western legal systems; whether each (or any of them) offers 'the truth' about law is a different question, and not one that we intend to dwell on here. We think 'what is law' is a useful question for at least three reasons.

First, at its simplest, understanding law presupposes the ability to find and read the law. This in turn assumes that we know how to identify it in the first place, which leads us back, in a sense, to that fundamental question: 'what is law?'

Secondly, even asking the question obliges us to think about how we conceptualise complex phenomena like 'law'. Being able to conceptualise something and describe it in language is a crucial step on the path to understanding that thing and the ideas and beliefs which shape and are shaped by it.

Our third reason for asking the question also flows from this: namely, that understanding in turn helps us to determine how we should make sensible or reasoned choices about what constitutes law in any given situation. This too can be a complex issue for legal theory, but it is also of real significance, for example, in assessing the perennial problem of whether and how we can determine if a law is 'good' or 'bad'; and if it is bad, what we can (or should) do about it. We will touch on some basic issues of conceptualisation in **Chapters 3** and **5**, entitled 'Reading the Law' and 'Law, Fact, and Language' respectively. But for the moment we will focus on something a little more concrete.

1.3 A Sample Legal Problem

A friend who is a shopkeeper has recently received a consignment of camping and other knives, including a small number of flick-knives. She is concerned that the police may take action if she were to display and sell these flick-knives to the public, and asks you for advice. In considering this problem, we are going to ask you two questions:

1. Why might the sale of flick-knives be a matter for law in the first place?

2. How can you find out if she would be breaking the law?

These look like very different kinds of question. Asking *why* something might be a matter for law requires us to think about the role and purposes of law—what it *ought* to do. It might also imply that there are some things law should not do, or activities it ought not interfere with. We will look at this question first, under the heading the 'functions of law'. Our second question seems much more mechanical: how do we find the law? But that in turn assumes certain knowledge and skills: sufficient knowledge to identify, first, the different kinds of rules that are recognised as 'law' in the relevant legal system; secondly, the appropriate search skills to find the rules and principles you need; and, thirdly, enough understanding of what the rules actually mean (and how they are likely to be applied) to advise. As we shall see in the course of this book, finding and understanding the law is not quite as straightforward as it sounds, but a good starting point is to be aware of the range of rules that are developed by the important institutional sources we have already mentioned. We will come back to this in sections **1.6**, **1.7**, and **1.10**.

1.4 The Functions of Law

Thinking functionally about law is an important part of studying because it helps us to focus beyond what law *is*, to what law *does* and *why* it may be an appropriate tool of social policy. Learning law is not just a rote exercise; it is not just about learning the rules (despite the title of this book!). In learning law we need also to pay attention to the bigger picture of what law in general is *for*. This is one of the things that can make understanding the law both exciting and important. Moreover it is not just a social policy question, it can take us into some quite deeply philosophical territory—if you take a module in legal theory or philosophy of law, you will certainly look at some of those larger issues, though these philosophical questions can be raised in virtually any substantive subject too.

For our present purposes it is enough to note that a functional perspective emphasises the extent to which law performs a range of 'coercive', 'protective', and 'facilitative' roles. The coercive function of law is the one with which we are most familiar, where law acts as a power over our conduct, notably in criminal law matters, though the coercive force of law can also be much more subtle than fining someone or throwing them in prison! The flip side of such coercion is that law also serves to protect and defend the rights and interests of legal persons, and to stabilise social conduct and expectations (for example by blocking conflict, or diverting it into an acceptable—i.e. institutionalised—form). Law—and lawyers—also perform an important enabling (facilitating) role in society. Law in this latter sense makes a whole range of interpersonal, business, and even inter-state transactions possible: from getting married, to selling a house, buying products for a business, liquidating a company, through to constructing a bilateral or multilateral trade agreement between states.

Linked to this is the rather obvious point that specific laws also tend to be made for a particular *purpose*. Such purposes may well be significant considerations in interpreting and applying the law. To that extent the functional question, 'what is *this* law for?' can be of real practical importance. This is a theme to which we will return at a number of points in this book.

1.4.1 Maintenance of Public Order and Safety

The law is often regarded as a critical part of the 'glue' that holds the fabric of society together, and protects us from the risks of social disorder and anarchy. The criminal law, in particular, is important in this respect, since it defines those behaviours which are regarded as sufficiently antisocial or potentially damaging to the public good to be outlawed and punishable by the state. At the same time, there is a real risk that the state itself can use the law to legitimate its rule and to suppress dissent by force. This abuse of law can be seen in many repressive regimes, and it is therefore considered important that political and legal authority in the state are kept reasonably separate and subject to a range of checks and balances, for example, by ensuring that lawyers, the police, and courts are independent of executive government.

1.4.2 The Protection of Individual Rights and Liberties

An important function of law in liberal democratic societies is that it should curb the capacity of the state and other powerful social actors to infringe the rights and liberties of individual citizens. This is often encapsulated in notions like the 'rule of law' which requires that no person or organisation be above the law, and 'freedom under the law', which implies that individual autonomy can only be constrained by a legitimate exercise of law. The protection of fundamental rights and liberties such as the right to a fair trial, the freedom of speech, and of lawful protest are important in constraining potential abuses of state power. Increasingly, in the context of the international and national human rights movements, the language of (negative) civil liberties and freedoms is being superseded by a language of positive, enforceable, rights such as the right not to be discriminated against because of one's sex, race, age, sexual orientation, or disability.

This dimension of the law presents the courts with many of their most complex and politically and/or morally challenging problems. One such example is the case of the conjoined twins, referred to pseudonymously in proceedings as 'Jodie' and 'Mary': see *In re A (Children) (Conjoined Twins: Surgical Separation)* [2000] EWCA Civ 254; [2001] Fam 147. The case involved the fate of conjoined twins, joined at the abdomen, but sharing a common blood supply. From the medical evidence it was clear that both babies would die within a matter of months if not separated. If they were separated it was equally certain that Mary would die during or very shortly following the procedure, while Jodie had a very strong chance of survival and, subsequently, a reasonable quality of life. While doctors were willing to undertake the surgery, the parents felt, on religious grounds, unable to consent to an operation that would actively take the life of one of their children. The medical team also needed to know that they would not be prosecuted for murder if the operation went ahead.

The case was without legal precedent, and raised fundamental questions of human rights, family law, and criminal law. In a unanimous judgment the Court of Appeal allowed the operation to go ahead, but the complexity of the issues were such that the three judges came to that conclusion by quite different routes.

1.4.3 The Organisation and Control of the Political Sphere

Although we often think of law and politics as necessarily distinct systems, the reality is more complex, as law performs an important part in preserving the political structure and processes, and politics plays an increasing role in shaping the law, not least through the extensive annual legislative programme of Parliament.

In many countries the relationship between law and state is defined primarily by a written constitution. The UK, by contrast, is distinctive in retaining an unwritten constitution, but this does not mean that there is no constitutional law, nor that the courts lack any authority over the political and legislative process. Moreover, major legislative reforms such as the European Communities Act 1972, the Human Rights Act 1998, the various devolution Acts, and the Constitutional Reform Act 2005 all point to ways in which our constitutional arrangements are becoming increasingly embedded in written—statute—law. We will touch on a number of these developments in the course of this chapter, and later in the book.

1.4.4 The Regulation of Economic Activity

Within the dominant ethos of market capitalism, law plays an important function in facilitating and encouraging national and international trade in goods and services. It does this by creating legal frameworks and conditions for facilitating trade, and by establishing principles of risk allocation and dispute resolution for when things go wrong. At the same time, the law also plays a role in restricting the activities of economic entities, and protecting citizens, states, and the environment itself—for example, from unsafe labour practices, abuses by an entity of a dominant market position, and other forms of unfair exploitation. Achieving a balance between these aims is often extremely difficult, and, as the recent banking crisis has shown, regulatory failure can have massive economic and social impact.

1.4.5 The Regulation of Human Relationships

The law serves to legitimate and control various aspects of personal relationships. This includes laws on marriage and civil partnership; setting principles governing the distribution of family property on relationship dissolution or death; regulating parent–child relationships, and those situations where the state and the courts may take measures to protect the welfare of a child, even against the rights of the parent. The law may also play some part in regulating our most intimate relationships, by setting limits to what constitutes lawful sexual activity, and regulating both abortion and assisted reproduction.

1.4.6 The Preservation of a Moral Order

Closely related to the law's role in regulating both public order and human relationships is another idea: that the law plays an important role in the reproduction and enforcement of certain moral principles and values. Both laws and moral principles share a characteristic that legal philosophers describe as 'normativity'—that is, they describe behavioural 'norms', or statements of what we *ought* to do. However, laws become distinct from purely moral norms by virtue of acquiring a particular material form (as statute or case law) developed within and legitimated by the institutional framework of a 'legal system'. This does not mean that laws have no moral content, or that law necessarily lacks moral functions and values. There are, of course, many specific areas of law which try to reflect a current moral consensus within society—for example, laws protecting freedom of religion, and others which attempt to control certain 'immoral' behaviours such as the public display of pornography, or racist 'hate speech'. Beyond these sorts of specifics, however, some would also argue that the law itself is grounded upon certain core moral values—a commitment, for example, to ideals of order, justice, and individual freedom (Stein and Shand, 1974). The rise of 'human rights' similarly can be regarded as a predominantly moral discourse that has sought to embed notions of human dignity and fundamental rights within national legal systems. In these ways the law itself, in its ideal form, can be regarded as a means of realising value, and an institution of civil society that is dedicated to human flourishing.

When talking about the relationship between law and the moral order, it is hard not to address the difficult question of the relationship between law and religion. Most legal traditions reflect a strong faith-based history—whether Christian, Islamic, Hindu, or other. Even in supposedly secular Western states such as the UK there are often quite strong vestiges of the society's historically dominant religious tradition within the law. However, at the same time, the relationship between law and religion is itself a significant source of potential conflict within the law.

Modern liberal democracies, like the UK, are, in theory, predicated on the principle of tolerance and a commitment to the moral neutrality of the state. But as these societies become more pluralistic, the drawing of legal boundary lines between morally acceptable and unacceptable behaviour may become harder to achieve in consensus terms.

The state can be drawn more and more into faith-based disputes, or disputes between secularism and faith-based values.

In this context it may be that the law will increasingly be obliged to choose between defending the state's secularity—at the risk of appearing intolerant to certain faith-based communities—or playing a more active role in protecting religious freedoms, almost paradoxically, as part of the state's commitment to a pluralist society. Either way, this process will create challenges for the social legitimacy of law and legal decision-making. Indeed, in the context of growing religious fundamentalisms, which often reject the liberal ideal of the secular and tolerant state, the relationship between law, state, and religion may be becoming one of the key issues internationally for both legal and political theory, and state practice in the early twenty-first century (see, e.g., An-Na'im, 2008; Bradney, 2009).

1.4.7 The Regulation of International Relations

International relations are governed primarily by a form of law called public international law. This creates rules, for example, for the recognition of states as legal entities, the setting of their territorial boundaries, and the conduct of diplomacy between them. Wars and armed conflict are also governed by international legal rules; principles of international humanitarian law exist to protect those caught up in conflict, and, increasingly, those accused of war crimes and other crimes against humanity are liable to be judged before international tribunals according to standards set by international criminal law. At the interstate level, international trade is also increasingly regulated, chiefly by the World Trade Organization in Geneva, but also by regional trade systems such as the European Union (which is the most closely harmonised, and most like a regional legal system of all the trading blocs), the North American Free Trade Area (NAFTA), and the Association of South East Asian Nations (ASEAN) Free Trade Area. These bodies exist as negotiating *fora*, and offer systems of dispute resolution for trade disputes between states within their jurisdiction.

1.4.8 Why Thinking Functionally Matters

A good academic, and often a good practising lawyer too, needs to be able to think critically about the law, what it can, and also what it *ought* to do. Examining its social, political, economic, or moral role and consequences opens up a whole range of arguments and issues that we might not consider if our thinking stopped at just a technical analysis of the rules themselves. As we shall see later, particularly in **Chapters 9, 10, and 11**, thinking about law in this kind of 'purposive' way is also something judges do when they are making a decision, or interpreting legislation. But for now we return to the question of what law is, by looking at how it differs from other forms of regulation and what we can call 'social rules'.

1.5 Regulation: Legal Rules and Social Rules

One of the words that kept cropping up in the last section was 'regulation'. Law is commonly used to regulate aspects of individual and institutional behaviour; indeed legislation in particular is sometimes seen as a paradigm form of regulation. But law is not the only means of regulating.

The term regulation can be seen as encompassing 'all forms of social control, whether intentional or not, and whether imposed by the state or other social institutions' (Morgan and Yeung, 2007: 3–4). If we think about it, law does not operate in isolation from other forms of regulation. Any society is governed by a mass of other rules which are not laws in the formal sense, but merely private rules or more general social conventions—perceptions of 'proper' behaviour. These are also means of regulating social conduct, but the focus on regulation reminds us that societies have a choice about what and how they regulate. Thus, while most of us would accept that anyone stealing the possessions of another, or possibly someone selling flick-knives, should be liable to a penalty under the criminal law, we might be surprised to see someone in court for eating peas off their knife! Regulating table manners is not really so important to our society as to require the force of law.

Thinking about law as one of a number of possible ways of regulating thus helps us understand what is distinctive about law, and the way it relates to other social rules, thus:

(i) Laws tend to perform the important regulatory functions that often could not be performed (at all or as well) by other kinds of rule.

(ii) Law may be particularly important because of its formal character and the specialist sanctions or remedies that are not available to other forms of regulation.

(iii) The choice of formal or less formal mechanisms employed may well reflect different priorities, or different social values, regarding the behaviour in question.

(iv) The use of law and legal sanction is also symbolic: it sends out a powerful message about what society *does value*.

Decisions about regulatory tools and approaches may also reflect judgements about the effectiveness of different forms of regulation. In some contexts regulation may be much more effective if it makes little or no use of law. Economic policy may thus be used to regulate market behaviour; or design principles may be applied in such a way as to regulate the ways in which buildings or roads, etc. are used. Consider, for example, how traffic-calming measures, or putting pedestrians and car users into a shared space, may control drivers' speed more effectively than (just) a speed limit. Governments and regulators are becoming more aware of how different kinds of rules, together with a variety of other regulatory tools, can be used purposefully, recognising that, in some settings, it may be sufficient to guide or steer conduct, rather than deploy the full force of traditional legal regulation.

Generally, laws are identifiable by the fact that they take a form which distinguishes them from other social rules and conventions. Their form tells us that they are derived from an 'institutional' source that is socially recognised (and some would say accepted) as having the power to create law. Only rules so created can be said to be *legally binding* upon the individual, or even upon the state itself. Thus our first step in finding the law governing the sale of flick-knives would be to discover whether any of the legal institutions have had anything to say on the matter. In this and the following sections we turn our attention more specifically to the forms and sources of English law.

In English law there are currently four main institutional sources which we shall consider: Parliament, the courts, the European Union, and the European Convention on Human Rights (ECHR). By taking them as our starting point, we are defining legal material by concentrating on the 'law-makers'. This is a rather narrow basis, but it does emphasise the importance of what are often called the 'primary' sources, and distinguishes them from 'secondary' or literary sources of law that provide only a commentary on or analysis of the rules (see **Chapter 2**).

1.6 Parliament and Legislation

Parliament is significant for three reasons. First, it is the originator of what is probably the single most important modern source of law—that is, **statute law**. Secondly, through its legislative powers, Parliament is able to give law-making powers to other bodies, such as local councils, government departments, and other agencies. This results in a form of law that is called **subordinate** or **delegated legislation**. Thirdly, Parliament's delegatory powers are being widely used to create less formalised regulatory systems which operate within a framework of formal rules created by statute.

1.6.1 The Importance of Legislation

It is critical that you understand what legislation is and how it operates. Legislation matters because statutes are constitutionally the highest form of law in the UK legal systems, and, practically speaking, because most new laws over the last 100 or so years have had their basis in legislation. Against this background you should not be surprised to find quite a lot of legislation governing the display and sale of flick-knives, for example.

The growth in legislation has been a key feature of the modern English legal system. It reflects the extent to which social life has become more complex, and government has extended its control over our activities, both in the areas of business and commerce, and in the social sphere, where many important fields, such as employment, child care, and social security law, owe their modern existence almost exclusively to statute.

This has meant that over the last fifty to sixty years the amount of legislation in force has grown significantly. This reflects two processess: first, a tendency of law to accumulate, because 'old' laws are not necessarily removed at the same rate that new ones are created, and, secondly, a higher level of legislative activity by Parliament than in the past. If we look at the nature of that legislative activity, however, it is not simply that we are seeing more Acts of Parliament every year. In fact, the number of Acts being passed per parliamentary session actually peaked in the 1970s (see Miers, 1986; cf. Cracknell and Clements, 2012). So what is happening to make the statute book continue to expand?

(i) The amount of statute law, judged by the number of *pages* of legislation passed has still tended to grow decade on decade. Miers (1989) has thus shown that the volume of primary legislation rose steadily from an average of 745 pages per session in the 1950s to 1,525 pages in the 1980s. By the end of the 2000s, that average had increased to 3,224 (our figure, based on data in Cracknell and Clements, 2012).

(ii) This has also been accompanied by a growth in the amount and length of secondary legislation. We return to this in section **1.6.3**.

So what this tells us is not that there is simply more legislation, but that the way in which legislation is being designed and used is changing. Acts are becoming longer and perhaps therefore more complex, and, at the same time, more and more law-making is being channelled through delegated legislation.

1.6.2 Statute Law

A statute is a document which contains laws made by Parliament. Statutes are also referred to as *Acts of Parliament*. You will learn more about their design in **Chapter 3**.

Statutes are now found in virtually all fields of law and govern all sorts of activities. Many statutes affect our lives without us even knowing about them. For instance, how is the date of Easter calculated? For the answer to that one has to turn to a strange Act of 1750—the Calendar (New Style) Act. This Act determined many calendar calculations, including leap years and Easter. The strangest provision, however, came with the calendar itself. In 1750 Britain used the old Julian calendar. Many other countries had switched to the more accurate Gregorian calendar. There was a difference of eleven days between these calendars. When it was the end of September here, it was October elsewhere. A change had to be made. The question was: how? The Act provided the answer by stating that 2 September 1752 was to be followed by 14 September 1752. Eleven days were thus simply deemed not to exist! This clearly illustrates the power and authority that legislation has. Unfortunately, in this case, it also led to riots in the streets; not least because some people were not getting birthdays in September 1752, and everyone was suddenly eleven days older!

Statutes are created directly by Parliament, following procedures laid down in both the House of Commons and the House of Lords. A statute becomes law only after it has been introduced into Parliament as a 'Bill', been approved by both Houses of Parliament, and has satisfied the formality of obtaining the Royal Assent. Once an Act has been passed it is unimpeachable, so far as English law is concerned. As Lord Campbell put it in *Edinburgh & Dalkeith Railway* v *Wauchope* (1842) 8 Cl & F 710: 'no Court of Justice can inquire into the mode in which it was introduced into Parliament, nor into what was done previous to its introduction, or what passed in Parliament during its progress'.

Lord Campbell's statement still rings broadly true today. There is no single United Kingdom court with the power equivalent to, say, the American Supreme Court to declare domestic legislation unconstitutional and therefore invalid. This absence of constitutional review reflects a principle called *parliamentary sovereignty*, or sometimes 'supremacy'. This is the idea that Parliament is the primary law-maker, and that an Act of Parliament is the supreme form of English law. The supremacy of Parliament is important for legal method, since it creates a division between law-making and judicial functions in the state. According to this view, the role of judges is to interpret the law, not make it (though as we shall see in the course of this book, the reality is rather more complicated than this simple idea suggests). But the doctrine of parliamentary sovereignty does mean that English judges are wary of exercising their powers in any way that may seem to usurp the legislative role of Parliament. Many cases that come before the courts involve questions about the application of statute law. Generally these create no constitutional issues, because the questions for the court are ones of *interpretation*—what is the scope or effect of a particular provision? More problematic for the courts are those cases which raise questions about the *validity* of an Act.

Generally, the basic principle, that the courts cannot challenge the validity of an Act that has been properly made, stands. However, a very small number of modern cases suggests that the normal principles of parliamentary sovereignty may be restricted in respect of certain fundamental 'constitutional principles' (see *R (Jackson and Others) v Attorney-General* [2005] UKHL 56; [2006] 1 AC 262) and/or a limited category of 'constitutional statutes', including the Act of Union 1707, the European Communities Act 1972, the Human Rights Act 1998, and the Scottish and Welsh Devolution Acts (see *H v Lord Advocate* [2012] UKSC 24; [2013] 1 AC 413; also *Thoburn v Sunderland City Council* [2002] EWHC 195 (Admin); [2003] QB 151, discussed later in this chapter).

The ambit of any such powers is uncertain, and none of the judicial opinions on which these views are based actually constitute binding authority. But it is nonetheless significant that in two of these cases—*Jackson* and *H*—the possibility of a judicially constrained sovereignty is openly considered by members of the highest court in the UK. This in itself signals a perceptible shift in judicial thinking about the relationship between the courts and Parliament in the twenty-first century.

1.6.3 Delegated Legislation

Acts of Parliament are not only a major source of law in their own right; they provide a legitimate means whereby Parliament can pass on, or delegate, its law-making powers to another body or person. Parliament's power of delegation has in fact been widely used for many years, but because its exercise is much less visible than the act of legislating, it is easy to lose sight of the importance of delegated legislation. The volume of secondary legislation is in fact considerable: 11,888 UK statutory instruments were made in 2009 alone (Cracknell and Clements, 2012). Statutory instruments are not just quantitatively important. It is worth remembering that, in practice, the operation of whole areas of law, such as social security and immigration, is dependent upon a network of regulations, which will be of greater day-to-day significance than much of the statute law. As most of this book focuses on primary legislation and case law, we will look at delegated legislation in some detail here.

Delegated legislation takes primarily one of two forms, called *secondary* or *tertiary legislation*. Be aware, however, that terminology in this area is not entirely consistent. You may also come across the concept *quasi-legislation*, which seems to cover a broad spectrum of rules (what we will here refer to as tertiary legislation and 'soft law') that are not directly enforceable by the courts.

The most important secondary legislation is published as a **statutory instrument (SI)** (individual instruments may also be called *Regulations*). The term SI derives from the Statutory Instruments Act 1946, s. 1, which provides:

(1) Where by this Act or any Act passed after the commencement of this Act power to make, confirm or approve orders, rules, regulations or other subordinate legislation is conferred on His Majesty in Council or on any Minister of the Crown then, if the power is expressed—

(a) in the case of a power conferred on His Majesty, to be exercisable by Order in Council;

> (b) in the case of a power conferred on a Minister of the Crown, to be exercisable by statutory instrument,
>
> any document by which that power is exercised shall be known as a 'statutory instrument'....

Most secondary legislation is published in the form of an ordinary SI. However, there are a number of specialised forms of secondary legislation of which it is useful to be aware. These are:

- Orders in Council, which are orders issued under statutory authority by the Crown on the advice of the Privy Council. They can be used for a wide variety of functions, but tend to be used for administrative and governance matters for which SIs are not deemed appropriate. For example, the transfer of specific ministerial powers from the UK government to ministers of the devolved governments in Wales and Scotland was completed by Orders in Council.

- Legislative Reform Orders (LROs) were created by the Legislative and Regulatory Reform Act 2006 and enable ministers, subject to certain safeguards, to amend primary legislation by SI. The intention is that LROs are used to reduce regulatory burdens without having to resort to amending legislation.

- Remedial Orders: where a UK court or the European Court of Human Rights has found a specific UK statutory provision to be incompatible with a Convention right, a minister may, where this is possible, amend or repeal the offending provision by remedial order.

The Statutory Instruments Act 1946 also lays down a number of clear rules about the form or style that SIs must adopt, and SIs, in theory at least, are subject to parliamentary oversight. In practice, however, many are not actually 'laid before Parliament'—a technical term, meaning that copies are given to Parliament to scrutinise—as the level of scrutiny depends on the enabling legislation.

Delegation always requires the express authority of an Act of Parliament, which, in respect of any delegated legislation created under its authority, will be referred to as the *parent or enabling Act*. The parent Act will not only give authority to the process of delegation, but also will set the parameters of the delegated power.

Where a public body attempts to act outside the authority of the powers delegated to it by Parliament, or fails to follow proper or prescribed procedures in the exercise of its power, then the courts may intervene and declare such actions unlawful because they are *ultra vires*, meaning 'beyond the powers'. Thus, in *R v Secretary of State for Health, ex parte United States Tobacco International Inc* [1992] 1 QB 353, the Secretary of State made a regulation banning the use of oral snuff, which the US Tobacco Company had imported into the UK for many years. The Secretary of State based the ban upon the scientific opinion of a committee set up to advise the government, but declined to disclose the text of that advice to the company. The Divisional Court (now called the Administrative Court) quashed the decision on the basis that failure to disclose the advice was, in the circumstances, procedurally unfair and hence unlawful.

Statutes can also delegate law-making authority to a wide range of government ministers, public agencies, and even private organisations or corporations. The rules made by such bodies are now commonly referred to as 'tertiary legislation'. The word 'tertiary' is somewhat confusing, because it seems to suggest that this type of law is at a level below secondary legislation. It isn't. It is still a direct delegation from Parliament, and so at the same 'level' as secondary legislation, but the style of the regulation is different, and there is no expectation of parliamentary scrutiny. These two points represent the key distinctions between statutory instruments and tertiary legislation, though in practice, as we noted previously, the *actual* level of scrutiny of SIs and tertiary legislation may often not be very different.

If properly authorised by statute, and made in the correct form, tertiary legislation has the full force of law, albeit often only for narrowly prescribed purposes. A good example of this is Code of Practice 'C' governing the detention and questioning of persons held at a police station. Codes of Practice governing the conduct of police are made by the Home Office under powers contained in the Police and Criminal Evidence Act 1984 (PACE). Code of Practice 'C' is not directly enforceable in the courts, by virtue of PACE, s. 67. This means that breaches of the Code are not themselves breaches of law; however, the Act does allow them to be used by a court to justify excluding any item of evidence that has been improperly obtained by the police (see, e.g., *R v Samuel* [1988] QB 615; [1988] 2 All ER 135).

Tertiary legislation goes by a wide variety of names. Common titles include 'codes of practice', 'directions', and 'statutory guidance' or just 'guidance'. Be aware that these terms may also be used to describe things that are *not* tertiary legislation—see the section on 'soft law', following, where we discuss how you can tell the difference.

The term tertiary legislation is also used in the context of European Union Law, where it has a very specific but different meaning from that used here—see further section **1.10.2**.

1.6.4 'Soft Law'

Legislation may also enable other bodies to issue a variety of 'soft law'. This term is used to describe a range of measures that are less formal than tertiary legislation and often non-binding in their effect. Such measures tend to be administrative in character, providing guidance to officials or sometimes advice and information to citizens. Despite its relatively informal character, soft law is recognised as an important source of rights and duties, and such policy statements may be sufficiently clear or 'hard-edged' to be justiciable in the sense that they are open to interpretation by the courts, even if not enforceable as 'hard law'. As Lord Steyn put it in *Re McFarland* [2005] UKHL 17; [2004] 1 WLR 1289 at [24]:

> ...in respect of the many kinds of 'soft laws' with which we are now familiar, one must bear in mind that citizens are led to believe that the carefully drafted and considered statements truly represent government policy which will be observed in decision-making unless there is good reason to depart from it. It is an integral part of the working of a mature process of public administration. Such policy statements are an important source of individual rights and corresponding duties. In a fair and effective public law system such policy statements must be interpreted objectively in accordance with the language employed by the Minister. The citizen is entitled to rely on the language of the statement, seen as always in its proper context. The very reason for making the statement is to give guidance to the public. The decision-maker, here a Minister, may depart from the policy but until he has done so, the citizen is entitled to ask in a court of law whether he fairly comes within the language of the publicly announced policy.... This is not to say that policy statements must be construed like primary

or subordinate legislation. It seems sensible that a broader and wholly untechnical approach should prevail. But what is involved is still an interpretative process conducted by a court which must necessarily be approached objectively and without speculation about what a particular minister may have had in mind.

The distinction between soft law and more formal regulation is not always straightforward. Neither the stated intention of the rulemaker, nor the name of the measure will be determinative. Codes of practice, circulars, guidance, etc., may be either tertiary legislation, or soft law. Their legal nature and effect can only be determined by examining the material in question within its whole context (including the legal powers under which it was made), to assess whether or not it has the character of a rule or is just information, advice or guidance as to how the requirements of a rule might be met: *R (on the application of Alvi)* v *Secretary of State for the Home Department* [2012] UKSC 33; [2012] 1 WLR 2208. Thus, in the *Alvi* case it was held that the Occupation Codes of Practice, which set detailed qualification standards for skilled migrant workers seeking entry to the UK, contained material which was not just guidance, but which would properly constitute 'rules' under the Immigration Act 1971, s. 3(2). However, since a fair reading of s. 3(2) required that rules be laid before Parliament and in this case the codes of practice had not been so laid, it was not open to the Secretary of State to treat them as part of the Immigration Rules, and hence as a ground for rejecting an application (see paras. 62, 107–8).

Guidance by statutory or public bodies may sometimes combine elements of soft law with more formal tertiary legislation. 'Public Notices' which are published by HM Revenue and Customs (HMRC) exemplify this approach. They often combine tertiary legislation together with non-legislative guidance to taxpayers.

Obviously where guidance combines these functions it is important that it is clear to users which bits are obligatory and which are not; consequently enabling powers may set down in some detail how guidance documents are designed and presented. Thus, where a Public Notice includes tertiary legislation, those sections having the force of law are required to appear in bold text, placed within a text box on the Notice.

In summary, then, we have seen how both statute and, with it, delegated legislation have expanded over the last thirty to forty years. This creates a challenge for those seeking to know and use the law: there is quite simply a lot more of it, and it is more widely distributed across a range of legal instruments. Consequently, in advising our friend about her business, we need to look not just for statute law, but whether Parliament has delegated relevant authority to make regulations about flick-knives, and then exercised that power to make regulations, and/or authorised any other bodies to issue guidelines or other controls.

Practically, the ability to delegate carries great advantages to the government, and sometimes to the legal system, for example in times of emergency, or whenever we need to be able to change the law quickly and easily. Thus, during an outbreak of foot and mouth disease in 2007, regulations controlling the movement of cattle were made at 5 p.m. on 5 December and came into effect at 6 p.m. on the same day—see the Export and Movement Restrictions (Foot-and-Mouth Disease) (No. 2) Regulations 2007. Delegated legislation can also deal with rapidly changing technical detail, or variations in local conditions, more effectively than statute law. However, as we have seen, Parliament does not maintain the same level of supervision over delegated as compared to primary legislation, so there is concern that those advantages are bought at some cost to the constitution.

Soft law and informal rules similarly are adaptable and can provide a flexible way of providing authoritative advice and guidance to citizens and officials. They can be instrumental in guiding officials in the use of their discretion, and can actually impose significant restraints upon it. The risk of soft law, however, lies in the extent to which public power is thus being exercised from within less public places: (semi-)autonomous government agencies and the private sector, and according to rules found in guides and manuals rather than statute books and published regulations. These are not necessarily beyond the reach of the supervisory powers of Parliament and the courts, but the scope for judicial oversight and intervention tends, by definition, to be less.

1.7 The Courts

Although legislation is extremely important, it cannot operate in isolation. Legislation requires implementation. On a day-to-day basis that is the function of a wide variety of officials, whose job is either itself to carry out Parliament's commands or else to make sure that other organisations or private individuals are doing so. In this process, questions may be raised about the effect of a particular piece of legislation. Often these will involve technical questions of *interpretation*. Officials are constantly engaged in interpreting both primary and secondary legislation, but sometimes we require a more authoritative statement of what the law means. That process of interpretation is usually undertaken by the courts.

The courts, moreover, are not only important as interpreters of legislation, they are also the second major source of English law in their own right, through the development of the **common law**, a term which we first need to define.

1.7.1 The Meaning of 'Common Law'

This term is used in two ways:

To distinguish common law from statute: 'Common law' is used to describe all those rules of law that have evolved through court cases (as opposed to those which have emerged from Parliament) over the past 800 years. Despite the growth of statute, English law is still generally understood in common law terms. By this we mean that the way in which we think about law, and categorise laws, is still heavily influenced by the old common law *forms of action* which determine what types of problem we now call 'contract', 'tort', etc.

To distinguish common law from other legal systems: Comparative lawyers have long used the term 'legal families' to group together legal systems which share certain common features. More recently, the term 'legal tradition' has become more popular as a way of thinking comparatively about different legal systems and cultures (see, e.g., Glenn, 2010).

Tradition in this setting emphasises both the influence of (legal) history—the continuing presence of the past in shaping the law—and the complex, dynamic nature of legal culture. The philosopher Alasdair MacIntyre (1998) summarises this idea of a 'living tradition' as 'an historically extended, socially embodied argument, and an argument precisely about the goods that constitute that tradition'. In other words, 'tradition' becomes a way of understanding and explaining the norms and values that make up a particular conception of the legal world, and the ways in which that legal world embraces both continuity and change.

In the Western world, there are two dominant 'traditions' which we call civil and common law, though there are a number of legal systems, such as the Scottish, which reflect elements of both traditions. The term 'common law' is thus used as a means of defining all those legal systems in the world whose laws are derived from the English system. We use the term 'English' rather than 'British' with good cause. For reasons of history, not only Scotland, but also Northern Ireland, and even the Isle of Man and Channel Islands, have evolved as separate legal systems from England and Wales (the Channel Islands, for instance, are part of Great Britain but not part of the UK or the EU). Although much of the legislation passed by the Westminster Parliament now governs the whole of the United Kingdom, there remain substantial differences in law and the legal processes that apply in the different jurisdictions that make up the British Isles; indeed with devolution of powers to Scotland and Wales, the differences are increasing.

The common law world remains extensive; it includes the federal laws of the United States of America, and most existing or former members of the British Commonwealth, such as Australia, Canada, India, New Zealand, and Singapore, though in many such systems the English influence may coexist with elements of local customary law or even with other legal traditions, such as Islamic law or Hindu law (see, e.g., Glenn, 2010). This does not mean that these countries have all developed uniform responses to particular legal problems. To survive transplanting, the common law has had to respond to the different needs and conditions of each jurisdiction. This has often meant departing from the established (English) rules. Such variation is generally seen not so much as a dilution of the common law, but rather as a sign of its capacity to adapt (see, e.g., *per* Lord Diplock in *Cassell* v *Broome* [1972] AC 1027 at 1127; [1972] 1 All ER 801 at 871; *per* Lord Lloyd in the New Zealand case of *Invercargill City Council* v *Hamlin* [1996] 1 All ER 756, at 764–5). Courts, legislators, and lawyers in the common law world still share a more or less common approach to legal reasoning, and, as Lord Lloyd put it in *Invercargill*, a willingness to learn from each other. For example, it is not that uncommon, particularly in areas where the law is uncertain, for judges to refer to decisions from several common law jurisdictions, thereby enabling them to analyse a range of potential solutions to the problem.

1.7.2 The Contrast with 'Civil Law'

The term civil law describes those systems which have developed out of the Romano-Germanic legal tradition of continental Europe. It is the civil law tradition which dominates within the present European Union. Only two Member States, the Republic of Ireland and the United Kingdom, subject to the caveat regarding Scotland, belong to the common law world as such. (One other Member State, Cyprus, shares some of the common law tradition, but is best seen as a mixed system, rather like Scotland.) As large sections of this book will be concerned with comparative issues between English and 'European' law, we will come back to the differences between the common law and civil law traditions at various points, but for now we return to the other meaning of common law as a source of judge-made English law.

1.7.3 The Court Structure

To understand how the common law works, we need to understand the English court structure and its role in making *precedent*. We begin with two basic distinctions: one is the difference between *trial* and *appellate* courts; the other is between *civil* and *criminal* courts.

The function of trial courts, such as the county court, is to hear cases 'at first instance': that is, to make a ruling on the issues of fact and law (this is a distinction that we shall discuss in detail in **Chapters 3** and **5**) that arise in the case. This distinguishes them from appellate courts, whose function it is to reconsider the application of legal principles to a case that has already been heard by a lower court. Some appeal courts also have jurisdiction to reconsider disputed issues of fact—i.e. disputes about the events leading to the legal action. Thus, any one case may well be heard by more than one court before the issues are finally resolved. Rights of appeal can be a complex subject in their own right, governed by a whole set of procedural rules; the detail of these falls outside the scope of this book, and we shall only outline the general principles that apply.

Trial and appellate functions are often combined within one court; the system is not simple enough for us to say that court X is solely a trial court, while court Y is purely appellate.

Civil and criminal law are significantly different in their aims, and employ different legal procedures. This latter point is particularly true of rules of evidence, for example. 'Evidence' describes the legal rules which control what facts may be proved, and the manner of their proving, before the courts. If you were to study the law of evidence, you would soon be struck by the greater evidential restrictions governing criminal as opposed to civil cases.

Criminal law describes those wrongs—*offences*—which are sufficiently important for society, usually through the intervention of the state, to outlaw as crimes, and to impose special penalties on the wrongdoer (such as a fine or term of imprisonment). If you haven't studied law before, this is probably what you most immediately think of when you think about 'law', whereas, in reality, the criminal law is a relatively small part of the totality of English law.

The term civil law (as opposed to 'civil (romano-germanic) law' as already considered) is also used to describe all those areas of law which are not criminal. Areas that govern the relationship between legal persons—i.e. individuals and corporations—such as contract, employment, or tort (itself an umbrella term used to describe a whole variety of specific wrongs (not 'offences', which is a term reserved for criminal matters) and areas such as negligence, libel, and trespass are all classed as civil law. In civil law matters the injured party will, if they succeed, be entitled to a 'remedy'. This will most commonly be in the form of financial compensation for the harm suffered, and where that compensation is awarded by the court it is called 'damages'.

By and large there is a fairly clear distinction between those courts having civil law and those having criminal law responsibilities (what lawyers call *jurisdiction*). **Figures 1.1** and **1.2** provide a basic guide to the structure of the English civil and criminal court systems.

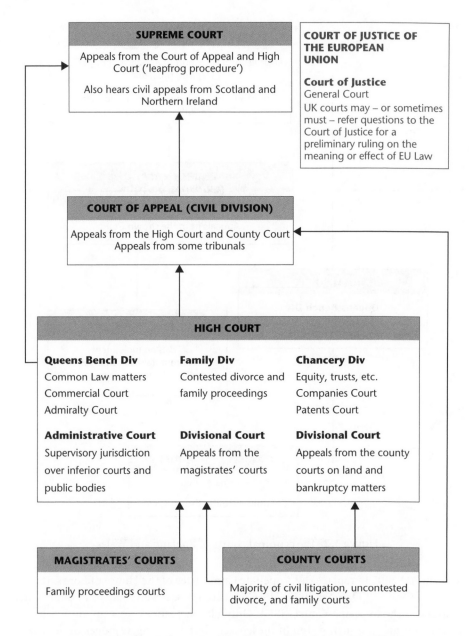

Figure 1.1 The civil courts of England and Wales, and the CJEU

The judicial figures given are taken from the latest source available (as at 31 July 2015) and details can be found on the website for the Judiciary of England and Wales (at www.judiciary.gov.uk/publications/judicial-statistics-2015/).

The Supreme Court of the United Kingdom

The Supreme Court is at the top of the hierarchy of English courts. It is the final court of appeal in civil and criminal matters in England, Wales, and Northern Ireland, and for civil appeals from Scotland. The Court was created by the Constitutional

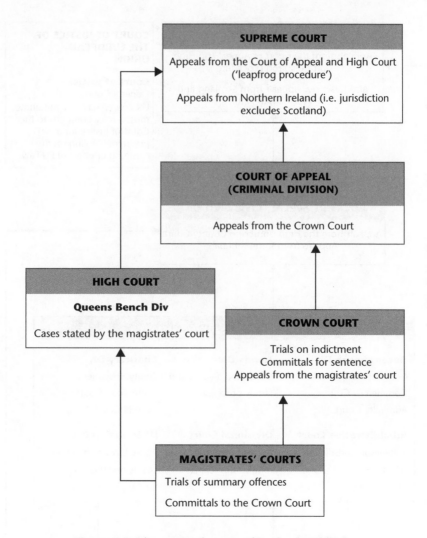

Figure 1.2 The criminal courts of England and Wales

Reform Act 2005 to replace the Appellate Committee of the House of Lords. It commenced work on 1 October 2009. The Court comprises twelve judges in total, called Justices of the Supreme Court (JSC). Only eleven Justices were appointed by the time it commenced sitting. Ten of these were already sitting as judges in the House of Lords, including the first President of the Supreme Court, Lord Phillips of Worth Matravers.

There has already been a substantial change in the composition of the Supreme Court as a total of eight of the original Justices, including the President, retired between 2010 and 2013. The current President of the Court is Lord Neuberger, who took up the role in September 2012, having been first appointed to the House of Lords in 2007. Baroness Hale of Richmond, who, in January 2004 had become the first woman to be appointed to the Supreme Court, is Deputy President of the Supreme Court, and remains its only female Justice.

The majority of appeals to the Supreme Court come from the Court of Appeal in England and Wales. Although it may also hear appeals direct from the High Court by a special procedure (called 'leapfrog') such cases are rare.

Cases in the Supreme Court are normally heard by five judges, or, exceptionally, by as many as seven or nine judges if the case is felt to raise issues of special importance. *HM Treasury v A and Others*, the very first case to be heard before the Supreme Court on 5 October 2009, was thus one of three joined appeals listed to be heard by a bench of seven Justices. For earlier examples, see *Pepper* v *Hart* [1992] 3 WLR 1032; [1993] 1 All ER 42 and *R* v *Bow Street Metropolitan Magistrate, ex parte Pinochet Ugarte (No. 3)* [1999] 2 All ER 97.

The Supreme Court only hears appeals in respect of cases which raise points of law of 'general public importance'—that means that there must be some significant area of doubt regarding the operation of a rule of law before the Court will hear the case. Such cases are relatively few, and, like its predecessor the House of Lords, it receives in the region of 200 applications a year, but tends to hear only around sixty or so full appeals in a year. This does not represent the whole work of the Court and its Justices, since the Justices must also sit to hear applications for permission to appeal to the Supreme Court, and also undertake most of the judicial work of the Privy Council (discussed later in the chapter).

Procedure in the Supreme Court is governed by a set of regulations called the Supreme Court Rules 2009, and by 'Practice Directions' set down by the Court itself. These can all be accessed from the Supreme Court website (at www.supremecourt.gov.uk).

Historically the office of Lord Chancellor carried the status of head of the judiciary, and included the right to sit as a judge in the House of Lords. Following the passing of the Constitutional Reform Act 2005 the judicial functions of the Lord Chancellor were transferred to the Lord Chief Justice, who is now the senior judicial figure in England and Wales and also Head of Criminal Justice (but does not sit in the Supreme Court). The present incumbent, Lord Thomas of Cwmgiedd was appointed in October 2013, having previously been President of the Queen's Bench Division.

The Court of Appeal

The Court of Appeal, together with the High Court, constitute what are called the Senior Courts of England and Wales. The Court of Appeal itself is split into two Divisions, Civil and Criminal. The Civil Division will hear appeals from the High Court and county courts. Cases are heard by a minimum of two, but normally three, judges called Lords Justices of Appeal. For some years the first woman to be appointed (Dame Elizabeth Butler-Sloss, now retired) was also referred to as 'Lord Justice', but she (and the others) are referred to now as 'Lady Justice'. Female judges will tell you, however, that they are often referred to in all manner of ways. Thus, female District Judges should be called 'Ma'am', but 'Sir', 'Your Worshipfulness', 'Madam', and even 'Lovey', all betray various confusions or prejudices. The title Lord (or Lady) Justice is written as 'LJ' following the judge's name—hence 'Smith LJ'. The Civil Division is headed by a senior judge known as the Master of the Rolls, who is also Head of Civil Justice in England and Wales. He (as yet there has never been a female Master of the Rolls) is referred to by whatever title is appropriate with the suffix 'MR'. The present incumbent is thus Lord Dyson MR.

There are presently no judges in the Court of Appeal with black or Asian ethnic origins. As of July 2015, of the thirty-eight Lords Justices of Appeal, eight (21 per cent) were women.

The Criminal Division will hear criminal appeals against either conviction or sentence from the Crown Court. Criminal cases will normally be heard by at least two or three judges drawn from among the Lord Chief Justice, the Lords Justices of Appeal, and the Judges of the High Court.

The High Court

This is the most complex of the courts to understand. The best way to grasp how it operates is to consider the trial functions of the various elements.

You can see in **Figure 1.1** that the Court is subdivided into three divisions, each of which has a separate jurisdiction to hear cases at first instance (i.e. trials). These divisions are the **Queen's Bench**, which deals with the main areas of common law, such as contract and tort, and some criminal and public law matters; **Family**, which deals with matrimonial cases and the wardship and adoption of children; and the **Chancery** Division, which deals chiefly with certain property, corporate, and tax matters. That seems simple enough, but now it begins to get more complicated. The English courts have long been important in the development and adjudication of both 'local' and international commercial disputes, not least because of Britain's (and particularly London's) historical importance as a centre of international trade and commerce. Because commercial law itself and the demands of court users have become increasingly complex and specialised, there has been a growing need for specialisation within the two divisions which have significant commercial law jurisdictions: Queen's Bench and Chancery. As a consequence, a number of specialist, commercial, trial courts have been created *within* each of those divisions, with judges being assigned specifically to those courts. The oldest of these is the Admiralty Court, which existed originally as a separate common law court in its own right, but was, in the late nineteenth century, amalgamated into a rather curious hybrid, the Probate, Divorce, and Admiralty (PDA) Division. The functions of the old PDA division were dispersed across all three divisions when the present system was created. The other specialist courts are of relatively recent creation. Their location and jurisdictional responsibilities are represented in **Table 1.1**.

Each division has its judicial 'head', normally appointed from among the Lords Justices of Appeal. The head of the Chancery Division is now called the Chancellor of the High Court. The present incumbent is Sir Terence Etherton. The Family Division is led by a President, currently Sir James Munby. The head of the Queen's Bench Division was, historically, the Lord Chief Justice, however the Constitutional Reform Act relieved him of that role by creating a new post of President, currently occupied by Sir Brian Leveson.

In addition to these first instance jurisdictions, each division has appellate functions performed by a 'Divisional Court'. A Divisional Court will normally be presided over by two or three judges. The Divisional Courts of the Chancery and Family Divisions have jurisdiction over certain appeals from the county and magistrates' courts. The main function of the Divisional Court of the Queen's Bench Division has been to exercise what is called the 'supervisory jurisdiction' of the High Court; that is, the power

Table 1.1 Specialist courts of the High Court

Chancery Division	Queen's Bench Division
Bankruptcy and Companies Court Personal actions for bankruptcy. Compulsory liquidation of companies and other matters arising under Insolvency and Companies Acts.	**Admiralty Court** Deals principally with the legal consequences of collisions at sea, salvage, and damage to cargoes.
Patents Court Deals with a range of intellectual property matters, not just patents. Hears appeals from decisions of the Comptroller-General of Patents, Designs and Trade Marks.	**Commercial Court** Wide jurisdiction over banking, international credit, and international trade matters, including shipping contracts that are not within the Admiralty Court's jurisdiction. Judges of the Commercial Court also have jurisdiction to arbitrate commercial disputes.
Intellectual Property Enterprise Court (IPEC) Replaces the Patents County Court in dealing with intellectual property matters (copyright, patent, and trade mark infringements and breach of confidence) where damages recoverable are below £500,000. Higher value claims continue to go to the specialist Patents Court.	**Technology and Construction Court** Specialist jurisdiction over building and engineering disputes, and computer litigation. Cases may be heard in London or at a number of regional court centres.

to oversee the quality and legality of decision-making in inferior courts and tribunals. It also (occasionally) hears criminal appeals '*by way of case stated*' on points of law from the magistrates' courts and Crown Court. Following recommendations in the Bowman Review of the judicial review process, the Divisional Court of the Queen's Bench Division was renamed the 'Administrative Court' in October 2000.

At first instance cases are heard by usually a single puisne (pronounced 'puny') judge, referred to as 'Mr Justice . . . ' and written as, e.g., 'Brown J.' (plural—'JJ.'). As of July 2015, there were only three High Court judges who declared themselves to be from a black or minority ethnic background (representing 3 per cent of the total (and down from 4.5 per cent in 2012). Twenty-one judges (20 per cent) out of the total of 106 sitting in the High Court were women. They have conventionally been called 'Mrs Justice', regardless of marital status, however Dame Alison Russell on her appointment in 2014 became the first British High Court judge to be permitted to adopt the style 'Ms Justice'.

The county court

Whereas the High Court can trace its ancestry back to Norman times, the county courts are essentially nineteenth-century creations. Two types of judges sit in the county courts: Circuit Judges (the more senior) and District Judges. Work is divided among these judges on a set of procedural rules which are outside the ambit of this book. An appeal from the decision of a District Judge (the right to appeal is based on limited grounds) will go to a Circuit Judge. An appeal from the decision of a Circuit Judge goes to the Court of Appeal.

The High Court and the county court deal with the same sort of legal issues. The difference is that the High Court deals generally with the more legally complex and/or higher monetary value claims. Major changes to the procedure of the High Court and the county courts were introduced on 26 April 1999, following recommendations in Access to Justice (1996)—often referred to as the 'Woolf Report', after its author, the then Master of the Rolls, Lord Woolf. While much of the detailed application of these rules goes beyond the scope of this book, we will briefly consider some of the consequences in **section 1.8**.

The Crown Court

This court deals almost exclusively with criminal trials and appeals. Most of its case load involves the trial at first instance of the more serious criminal offences, such as homicides, serious physical and sexual assaults, and property offences involving loss or damage of a 'high value'. It is in this context that the Crown Court remains the only court in the English system in which a judge regularly sits with a jury. The function of the judge is to advise the jury on the law; the jury, however, remains the sole tribunal of fact, and it is for the jury alone to decide whether an accused is guilty or innocent as charged. The Crown Court has an appellate function whereby it also hears appeals (without a jury) from the magistrates' courts on issues of fact or law.

The magistrates' courts

Magistrates' courts are purely courts of first instance. The bulk of their case load involves the trial of less serious criminal offences (in fact over 90 per cent of all criminal cases are tried by magistrates), though the courts also have a civil jurisdiction over some licensing, tax arrears, and matrimonial matters. The magistrates' court is unique in that the great majority of cases are heard before Justices of the Peace—lay persons with little formalised legal training, though they are advised on the legal issues by a legally qualified Justices' Clerk. Legally qualified magistrates may sit alone to hear cases: they were formerly called stipendiaries but now have the title of District Judge (Criminal).

Administrative tribunals and other courts

In addition to the formal courts, there is a plethora of administrative tribunals, many of which have been created only since the Second World War (though some, like the Commissioners of the Inland Revenue, are far older). They control a vast range of activities from the issuing of passenger licences to airlines, through employment disputes, to adjudicating on parking fines or the award of social security entitlement. The tribunal system has been significantly restructured and rationalised by the Tribunals, Courts and Enforcement Act 2007, bringing many individual tribunals within the structure of a standardised 'First-Tier Tribunal' with rights of appeal to an 'Upper Tribunal', which has taken over the appellate jurisdiction of the Administrative Court in respect of a large number of tribunals. One very important set of tribunals still sits outside this structure. These are the Employment Tribunals (until 1998 known as 'Industrial Tribunals'). Appeals from these tribunals go to a specialist appeal forum known as the Employment Appeal Tribunal, and from there any appeal goes to the Court of Appeal.

In England and Wales there are a number of other local or special courts in existence, which are rather too specialised to merit discussion here. However, you should be aware of three other courts which, formally speaking, are not a regular part of the English court system, but are still of considerable importance to it. These courts are the Court of Justice of the European Union, the European Court of Human Rights, and the Privy Council.

The **Court of Justice of the European Union (CJEU)** is the final authority on points of interpretation of European Union law. The Court actually comprises three courts: the Court of Justice, the 'General Court', and the EU Civil Service Tribunal. We discuss these in greater detail in **Chapter 11**. For our purposes the Court of Justice is the most important court in the CJEU structure. It exercises a range of judicial oversight powers over EU institutions and legislation, and courts in the EU Member States can refer points of European law to it for clarification and ruling (see further **section 1.10** and **Figure 1.1**).

The **European Court of Human Rights** is the international court created by, and with power to adjudicate cases involving the application of, the European Convention on Human Rights. It is a wholly separate institution from the CJEU, and the two should not be confused. Again we discuss the nature and role of this court more fully later, this time in **Chapter 10**.

The **Judicial Committee of the Privy Council** (normally abbreviated to just 'Privy Council') acts as the final court of appeal for a number of UK dependent territories and independent Commonwealth states, though its jurisdiction has been steadily eroded by continuing UK and international reforms. Today it tends to hear anywhere between around thirty and fifty cases a year, mostly from the Commonwealth Caribbean and the Channel Islands. It has a number of rather esoteric functions in the English legal system, relating to matters such as Admiralty cases and appeals from the disciplinary decisions of the General Medical Council. Its jurisdiction was extended in 1998 to include adjudicating on the 'legislative competence' of the devolved governments of Scotland, Wales, and Northern Ireland, though these powers have now been transferred to the UK Supreme Court.

Cases before the Privy Council are normally heard by the Justices of the Supreme Court. Senior judges from other Commonwealth states are entitled to sit, but that right is not always exercised. Given the status of the judges, Privy Council decisions may carry some considerable weight within the English legal system (see the discussion in **Chapter 6**), as well as being binding in the jurisdictions for which it remains the final court of appeal.

1.7.4 Precedent and the Common Law

The common law has not, as a system of rules, evolved from the totality of case law. It would be physically impossible to maintain records of and develop principles from every decision of every court that has ever heard a case. Rather, the origins of the common law can be traced back to the practice which developed in medieval England, whereby records of arguments used in the Royal courts were kept and circulated, at first unofficially, among the judges, student advocates, and practitioners. This practice gradually hardened into an officially sanctioned system of *precedent*, whereby important cases were recorded and subsequently used as authority for specific rules of law. As a reflection of that original practice, precedent is still created only by the superior courts—the High Court, Court of Appeal, and Supreme Court. Some of the major tribunals have separately created their own internal systems of precedent, and where rights of appeal to the courts exist, they will also be bound to follow the precedents set by those courts. Precedent is, in theory, binding on all inferior courts (and tribunals). These include, chiefly, the Crown Court, magistrates' courts, and county courts; the details of our system of precedent will be discussed at much greater length in **Chapters 6** and 7.

So, in advising our friend we would almost certainly have to take some account of case law, either because the legal rules concerned are actually a creation of the common law, or because the courts have considered the operation and effect of some relevant statutory provision. In advising her, we would not only have to know what cases (if any) existed, but also, by reference to the doctrine of precedent, assess what impact those cases might have on any future proceedings against her, which leads us onto our next point: what might those proceedings involve?

1.8 The Importance of Procedural Law

When someone goes to court, there are two kinds of law that need to be taken into account in managing their case. The first is what we call the **substantive law**, that is, the specific rules which tell us what the law of contract or crime says about selling flick-knives (to continue with our example). The second is the **procedural law**, which lays down the process by which a case is brought before the court, and how it is tried. Thus the procedural law will prescribe the process by which a claim is made or criminal action commenced, and the pre-trial steps required (under judicial supervision) to bring it to trial. Procedural and evidential rules also set some parameters on the conduct of trials and on what evidence may be admitted.

The procedural law tends to operate differently in civil disputes and criminal prosecutions. Generally procedural and evidential rules tend to be rather more restrictive in criminal cases, not least because an individual's liberty is often at stake. The rules are contained in two main sources: the Civil Procedure Rules 1998 and the Criminal Procedure Rules 2015, which are supplemented by Practice Directions issued from time to time by the courts, under powers to regulate their own procedure.

The details of procedural law are not widely taught in English law schools before the stage of professional training, but a basic knowledge of how cases come to court, and the systemic assumptions underpinning that process, is useful in understanding how and why cases get to court (and sometimes into the law reports) in the way they do. Moreover, because the continuing development of the common law system depends to a significant extent on cases getting into the superior courts, the processes by which cases get before those courts are important for legal method, because they will also help determine the future shape of the common law, and the pace of change.

1.8.1 The Adversarial Process

One thing procedurally that virtually all common law civil and criminal courts (it is much less true of tribunals) have in common is the assumption of what is commonly called an *adversarial process*. This was described by Justice (1974: 18) as:

> a fight, a pitting of strengths and wits against each other, a display of aggression mitigated only by the ritual of a complex set of rules and conventions.

This notion of 'trial by battle' is deeply embedded, both historically and psychologically, within the common law tradition. It has created a system in which, traditionally, it is the parties themselves who make the running in any case. It is they, not the judge, who select the facts and the legal issues upon which a case is to be fought. This is reflected in both the role of the judge and the ethical obligations borne by the advocates.

Traditionally, the role of the judge is thus, in theory, restricted to being a passive umpire, overseeing proceedings and ensuring that the trial is pursued according to the rules of the legal game. Judicial neutrality is, of course, a fundamental principle. Judges are expected to remove themselves (or risk being removed) from hearing cases in which they have a personal interest, or where, viewed objectively, they have acted in a manner that demonstrates actual or apprehended bias or prejudice. Of course, this does not mean that the judge is a silent bystander; he is quite at liberty to interject, for example, to direct a witness to answer questions, to test the quality of the legal arguments being put forward, to seek clarification of some point of fact or law, or to prevent an improper line of questioning. And judges can legitimately be quite robust or forthright in their language without that of itself leading to a finding of bias.

Unlike the judge, the advocate's role in common law systems is, it follows, essentially partisan. Their job is to represent their client, though this too is subject to certain ethical limitations: most notably, the lawyer's partisanship is qualified and balanced by duties to the court and, to a lesser extent, third parties and the profession at large. Professional codes of conduct in the UK thus make it a disciplinary matter actively to mislead the court or other parties to the proceedings, though the boundaries of such obligations may themselves be a matter of some debate (see generally Herring, 2014: ch. 4).

Even so, it is sometimes said that the system is of limited efficacy. The promise of adversarialism is a pragmatic commitment to procedural fairness, which may in practice be significantly undermined by resources and other inequalities between parties. Defenders of the system nonetheless argue that the law is doing the best it can. In *Air Canada* v *Secretary of State for Trade (No. 2)* [1983] 1 All ER 910, Lord Wilberforce put it in these terms (at 919):

> In a contest purely between one litigant and another, such as the present, the task of the court is to do . . . justice between the parties . . . There is no higher or additional duty to ascertain some independent truth. It often happens, from the imperfection of evidence, or the withholding of it, sometimes by the party in whose favour it would tell if presented, that an adjudication has to be made which is not and is known not to be, the whole truth of the matter; yet if the decision has been in accordance with the available evidence, and with the law, justice will have been fairly done.

This traditional adversarial approach differs somewhat from the *inquisitorial* procedure in the majority of civil law systems, though those differences are often overstated.

The inquisitorial process is typified by a far more pro-active judicial role than we would expect to find in a true adversarial system.

There is not an assumption in civilian systems that the court's function is to vindicate the winner, to establish that one party has a legal right. Rather there is a more open and free-ranging search for 'truth'. This difference in perception affects the substantive procedures used. Because there is no perceived battle between two sides, there is less need to control inquisitorial proceedings by restrictive procedural and evidential rules (a point we shall explore in more detail in **Chapter 5**). Whether it is more effective at finding the truth is debatable. While it is common to draw quite a stark contrast between these two types of process, in reality that is rather artificial. There have always been legal institutions in common law countries (including England) which adopt a form of inquisitorial process. Equally, there are civilian legal systems (such as Italy) where adversarial procedure is more in evidence. Moreover, trends towards greater judicial control and 'case management' of proceedings in England and Wales also potentially narrow the gap (see, eg, Partington, 2015: 204–7).

1.8.2 Legal Method and the Limits of the Trial

Most infringements of the law never get before a court, either because they are never identified as such, or never pursued, or resolved by less formal means. Moreover, contrary to common belief that societies are becoming more litigious, long-term studies of trends in both England and the US indicate that there is actually proportionately *less* civil litigation than fifty or sixty years ago (Kritzer, 2004; Genn, 2009), Procedural changes in England and Wales since the late 1990s have, in the words of one leading commentator, converted the trial and rendering of judgment in the civil courts into a 'solution of last resort' (Roberts, 2009: 458). This has been achieved by, for example, front-loading the costs of going to trial, reframing the objective of pre-trial proceedings as being to promote settlement, and actively diverting cases to mediation.

In criminal matters, the trial has not been de-centred from the legal process to anything like the same degree, but it should be borne in mind that the great majority—around 98 per cent—of criminal cases are dealt with at the lowest level of the system, by magistrates' courts, and most proceed no further. Moreover, many matters in the criminal justice system are resolved by the decision to plead guilty, or by 'plea bargains': agreements (or a kind of 'settlement') between prosecution and defence that also result in a guilty plea, and thus obviate the need for a full trial (see, e.g., Sanders *et al.*, 2010).

Trials are thus only the tip of a (potential) disputes iceberg; and appeal cases, which shape the rules discussed in this book, are in turn only a fraction of a fraction of that total activity. Why is this rather self-evident fact important for legal method?

First, the growth in a settlement culture, whilst in many respects a good thing, does involve a substitution of private for public forms of dispute resolution. Negotiated and mediated settlements are usually confidential to the parties and, by definition, there is no adjudication of a claim. Some commentators have raised concerns about the wider implications of this shift from public to private ordering. In the USA, for example, Professor Owen Fiss (1984) has argued that more private resolution of disputes reduces the power of law to articulate public values, to bring, in Fiss's words, 'a recalcitrant reality closer to our chosen ideals'. It might even be argued that too great a reliance on private and alternative forms of dispute settlement potentially reduces the opportunity for courts to establish points of principle through the public deciding of cases and the development of precedent.

Secondly, if we think about the cases that get to the higher courts, we cannot avoid seeing case-law development as other than a relatively *ad hoc* and possibly even inefficient process (though that latter assertion is difficult to confirm empirically). The evolution of legal rules through court decisions depends on a number of variables, not least:

- The 'right' legal claims arising. Common law development can be seen as a bit of a lottery. The way the law evolves depends on the factual matrices and 'strength' of the cases coming to court. However, we have no idea when or whether the 'right' cases will emerge from the primordial soup of human (mis)conduct. Unless the issue is serious enough to justify legislation, the (lower) courts may consequently be stuck with 'bad' law for a considerable period, until the right case comes along.

- The resources of the parties. Even if we do have a potential case with the appropriate facts, that case will only become a precedent if the parties have the power, resources, and willingness to pursue the issues through the appellate courts.

- The prevailing 'judicial practice'. As we shall see (in **Chapters 6** and **12**), precedent is not simply a matter of courts blindly following a set of concrete rules or principles. Rather, it is best understood as a 'judicial practice' (see, e.g., Gearey *et al.*, 2013: ch. 6); that is, an activity that is shaped by the interplay of rules and principles in the context of a particular judicial culture. Though judicial cultures tend to be relatively stable, they will vary not just over time but possibly between courts in the hierarchy, and even between cases, as regards, for example, the extent of judicial activism or creativity that is permissible and appropriate.

Thirdly, it also reminds us that, while the rules and principles explained in this book are incredibly important for understanding how the higher reaches of 'the law' work, and how the law itself evolves according to its own logic, this is only part of the story. Much of the legal process operates at 'street level', below the radar of the higher courts. You do need to be aware that the law in books and the law in action can be surprisingly different creatures, and that you will be seeing only a part of the picture from a doctrinal analysis of law.

Before we close this chapter, there are two areas of European law with an increasing impact on the English legal system and legal method, which we need also to consider.

1.9 English Law and the European Convention on Human Rights

The ECHR is an international treaty which was created in the aftermath of the Second World War. It has been signed by most European governments, including the UK, as a statement of their commitment to the protection of certain fundamental human rights, such as freedom from torture and slavery, freedom of religion, freedom of expression, and the right to a fair trial. The ECHR is not one of the EU treaties and is not part of European Union law. Its political governing body is a separate organisation called the Council of Europe. There is a separate EU Charter of Fundamental Rights which was introduced precisely because the EU institutions were not bound by the ECHR (see Opinion 2/94 of the Court of Justice: *Accession by the Community to the European Convention for the Protection of Human Rights and Fundamental Freedoms* [1996] ECR I–1759).

Whether or not individuals can enforce their rights under the ECHR within their own legal systems depends on the rules and structures of each legal system. Many, though not all, Western European legal systems are framed so that treaty obligations entered into by their governments are automatically incorporated into domestic (i.e. national) law. In that situation, a citizen could pursue a Convention right through the domestic courts. The legal position in Britain is different. Here, international legal rights can be directly enforced only where the treaty has been expressly incorporated into law. This normally requires an Act of Parliament. Although the courts and Parliament sometimes made reference to the ECHR in defining the scope of rights and duties under English law, there had been, prior to 1998, no express incorporation. Consequently, British citizens seeking redress under the ECHR had to rely exclusively on an international institution called the European Court of Human Rights at Strasbourg. There have been a significant number of such cases on a variety of issues, including the freedom of the press; the rights of transsexuals to have public documents such as passports and birth certificates changed to record their 'reassigned' rather than 'genetic' sex; the detention and trial of 'political' prisoners in Northern Ireland; and the use of corporal punishment in schools. Indeed, the British government had a relatively poor track record before the Court, having been found in violation of the ECHR in a total of fifty cases (see Greer, 1999: 5); this has been one of the key reasons why the political pressure for incorporation of the ECHR into English law steadily increased, though for many years neither Labour nor Conservative governments had supported the move to incorporation as part of government policy.

That changed in 1996 when the Labour Party published an influential policy paper called *Bringing Rights Home*, proposing measures for the incorporation of the ECHR. This policy came to be reflected in Labour's 1997 election manifesto and its first legislative programme after that election. Consequently, after a sometimes rather bumpy ride through Parliament, the Human Rights Bill received the Royal Assent in November 1998. In addition, the original legislation devolving powers to the new Scottish and Welsh assemblies also contained provisions requiring those bodies to legislate consistently with the rights contained in the ECHR. The Human Rights Act 1998 (HRA) came into force in England on 2 October 2000. We shall explore the role of the Act in greater detail in **Chapter 10**.

Politically and legally the passing of the HRA has been a landmark moment in English law, fundamentally reshaping legal discourse and the legal accountability of the state to maintain human rights standards. Anyone following media debates about human rights will be aware that the HRA generates strong opinions both for and against. This is not new. Lord McCluskey, in his 2000 Reith lecture, for example, warned that 'we are going to have to struggle to avoid being buried in new claims of right' (*Guardian*, 8 May 2000). In fact, the feared deluge of claims has not really materialised, with debates focusing far more on the kinds of claims being allowed than the volume. Nevertheless, as we shall see further in **Chapter 10**, there have been growing calls for reform of the Human Rights Act, with members of both the last coalition and present Conservative government pushing for the Act's replacement by a 'British Bill of Rights' more independent of the ECHR. When, or indeed whether, such legislation will be introduced is, at the time of writing, uncertain. For us, as lawyers, the HRA has created a whole new set of concepts and rights which must be understood and developed through practice in courts and tribunals. As we will see, the Act has had a notable impact on that part of legal culture we call 'legal method'. At the same time, there are things that the HRA will not do, partly because of the internal limits and restrictions built into the Act (see further **Chapter 10**), and partly because there is much that the ECHR itself does not do. Human rights remain a developing area of law, and many of our conceptions of fundamental rights have evolved and changed since the Convention was drafted nearly fifty years ago. There are newer forms of human rights, some of which are not yet fully recognised or understood, and about which the ECHR is largely silent (see Rainey *et al.*, 2014: 7; Macklem, 2015). These include:

- the group rights of minority peoples;
- economic rights (so our seller of flick-knives could not use the HRA to argue that laws restricting trade in particular goods are an unwarranted restriction of her right to engage in a particular business) and cultural rights; and
- so-called 'third generation' rights, which include the recognition of individual and community rights over the environment.

Nevertheless, as we shall see in **Chapter 10**, just as the influence of EU law has gradually overtaken this book (as we predicted it would in the first edition), so too issues of human rights have taken on an increasingly pervasive role in shaping British law.

1.10 English Law and the European Union

The European Union is a political and legal organisation of twenty-eight Member States (at present; Croatia was the latest to join in 2013—full membership details can be found on the *Europa* website, listed in **Chapter 2**). It was founded as the European Economic Community (EEC) by the original six members (France, Germany, Italy, and the Benelux countries—Belgium, the Netherlands, and Luxembourg), and given international legal status by the Treaty of Rome in 1957. The European Union grew out of the EEC, and was formally established by the Treaty of Maastricht on 1 November 1993. The United Kingdom has been a member of the European Community/Union since 1 January 1973. For over forty years, therefore, there has been a gradual but substantial mingling of European and English concepts within the legal system. The days are thus gone when anyone studying law in this country could afford to concentrate only on English law and the English legal system. To this end we have dedicated **Chapter 11** of this book to the European influence and 'European Legal Method', though we have also sought to make some specific comparisons with civil law practices and institutions in each chapter. We have also, as here, tried to incorporate specific references to European Union institutions and legal method where we have thought it helpful in appreciating the context in which our law now operates.

As a general point, our leaving the 'European Union dimension' until the penultimate chapter should not be seen as relegating the topic to an afterthought. The European influence has been far too important for that. European law is generally taught as a subject in its own right in British law schools, and usually as a compulsory subject at that. However, it is also of much wider significance to the English legal system, because of the constitutional relationship that currently exists between the European Union and Britain. It is not like studying, say, contract law where you might decide in your examination revision to ignore Chapter 8 on illegality. Experience has shown us, however, that a student (on whatever course and at whatever level) who is new to legal studies needs to become accustomed to and comfortable with English legal system and method before investigating other systems too deeply. In this chapter we shall simply introduce you to some basic EU concepts, which will be developed more fully in the penultimate chapter.

1.10.1 The Legal Foundations of the EU

Following the Treaty of Lisbon (2007) the three foundational texts of the EU are the Treaty on European Union (the amended 1992 Maastricht Treaty), the Treaty on the Functioning of the European Union (TFEU), which is the new name for the Treaty Establishing the European Community (the original Treaty of Rome), and the EU Charter of Fundamental Rights, which will have the same legal value as the Treaties.

The Treaty of Rome created the institutions which enable the Community to function. Today these are the European Commission; the Council of the European Union, also called the Council of Ministers; the European Parliament; and the Community court, discussed earlier.

1.10.2 EU Legislation

EU legislation can also be defined as primary, secondary, or tertiary. The various treaties are the EU's primary legislation. They have shaped EU institutions and established a framework of rights and duties between Member States. The TFEU is unusual in that it contains a number of provisions which give individuals (as opposed to nation states) substantive legal rights. A particularly important and well-known example is Article 157, which lays down a general principle that men and women are entitled to equal pay for work of equal value. This has been used in the UK to give rights to equal pay to women who have fallen outside the protection of our own sex discrimination laws (see *Garland* v *British Rail Engineering Ltd* [1983] 2 AC 751; [1982] 2 All ER 402).

Apart from the substantive provisions of the Treaty, there are three types of secondary legislation emanating from the European Commission or Council of Ministers:

Regulations: These are directly applicable in each Member State and take precedence over any conflicting provisions of domestic (i.e. national) law.

Directives: These are binding upon each Member State 'as to result', but not as regards methods of 'implementation'. What this means is that each state is obliged to pass such laws as are necessary to give effect to a particular Directive, and then usually within a specified period of time. The Commission may commence proceedings against a state for failure to implement within the required period, but generally a Directive may not be enforced by or against private organisations or citizens *before* it is implemented.

Decisions: These are binding only upon the Member State(s) or individual(s) to whom they are addressed; they thus tend to have a much narrower field of application than either Regulations or Directives. They take effect from the date at which they are noti-fied to the addressee. You should be careful not to confuse decisions as referred to here, as a species of legislation, with the case-law decisions of the CJEU.

Finally, the European Commission is authorised under Articles 290 and 291 TFEU to make tertiary legislation. This is a form of delegated legislation, since the specific power must be conferred on the Commission by EU secondary legislation. Typically, tertiary legislation is used to make and update technical rules and annexes, or to fill in the operational detail needed to effect the law.

1.10.3 The European Dimension of English Law

The EU is not unusual in owing its existence to an international agreement. Many mul-tinational organisations of states are created in this way. What makes the EU unique is that the Treaty itself creates rights and obligations which are enforceable not only within the institutions of the EU (just considered), but before the national courts of each Member State.

In English law the enforceability of the Treaties and of legislation emanating from the EU Institutions (such as Directives) is guaranteed by the European Communities Act 1972—an Act of the Westminster Parliament. Although the effects of that Act are still debated by European Union and British constitutional lawyers, it seems increas-ingly to be accepted that, by passing the Act, Parliament has ceded some of its sovereign power to the EU. In July 1990, for instance, following a reference to the ECJ, the House of Lords prevented the Secretary of State for Trade from implementing provisions of the Merchant Shipping Act 1988; see *R v Secretary of State for Transport ex parte Factortame (No. 2)* [1991] 1 AC 603; [1991] 1 All ER 70.

The House of Lords, in delivering the reasons for its decision, concentrated upon the issues of granting 'interim relief' until the question finally came to court. By so doing their Lordships avoided the necessity of discussing the implications of their decision to disapply the Act. This case is undoubtedly of constitutional significance. Prior to the decision in *Factortame (No. 2)* no English court, in modern times, had accepted that it had the power to disapply an Act of Parliament. Indeed, in the original *Factortame* case the House of Lords had expressly denied that such power existed—see [1990] 2 AC 85; [1989] 2 All ER 692. Although the issue in the *Factortame* cases was a rather techni-cal, preliminary point regarding the powers of the court to grant 'interim relief' (that is, to give a provisional remedy to a claimant to protect his interests until the case is heard on the substantive issue), the effect of *Factortame (No. 2)* is far more general. It is now incontestable that, in cases where there is a conflict between principles of directly enforceable Community law and national law, Community law must prevail, regardless of the source of that domestic law. To EU lawyers, this is hardly a shock, since it reflects one of the founding principles of the EU legal order—the principle of supremacy of EU law. As Lord Bridge explained in *Factortame (No. 2)* ([1991] 1 All ER 70, at 108):

[the principle of supremacy] was certainly well established in the jurisprudence of the Court of Justice long before the United Kingdom joined the Community. Thus whatever limitation of its sovereignty Parliament accepted when it enacted the European Communities Act 1972 was entirely voluntary. Under the terms of the 1972 Act it has always been clear that it was the duty of a United Kingdom court, when delivering final judgment, to override any rule of national law found to be in conflict

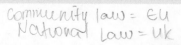

> with any directly enforceable rule of Community law....Thus there is nothing in any way novel in according supremacy to rules of Community law in those areas to which they apply and to insist that, in the protection of rights under Community law, national courts must not be inhibited by rules of national law from granting interim relief in appropriate cases is no more than a logical recognition of that supremacy.

Another more recent case illustrates the constitutional significance of the 1972 Act: *Thoburn* v *Sunderland City Council* [2002] EWHC 195; [2003] QB 151; [2002] 4 All ER 156. The case concerned the conflict between the Weights and Measures Act 1985, s. 1 and, among other Statutory Instruments, the Units of Measurement Regulations 1994 (which had implemented Council Directive 80/181 Art. 1, as amended by Council Directive 89/617 and which were stated to be made in the exercise of powers conferred by s. 2(2) and (4) of the European Communities Act 1972). The 1985 Act had permitted the continued use of imperial and metric measures in selling goods loose in bulk (e.g. bananas on a market stall). However, the 1994 Regulations meant that the continued use of imperial measures for trade in such goods was permitted only until 31 December 1999. Thereafter the use of the pound as a primary indicator of weight was forbidden. The arguments before the court related to the doctrine of implied repeal and, in particular, whether the 1985 Act had impliedly repealed the European Communities Act 1972, s. 2(2) to the extent that the latter empowered the provision of subordinate legislation which was inconsistent with it.

Lord Justice Laws held that the 1985 Act had not impliedly repealed s. 2(2). Section 2(2) is what is sometimes called a 'Henry VIII' clause (a reference to ideas of absolute monarchy): it allows secondary legislation to override primary legislation for the purposes of implementing EU law. The appropriate analysis of the relationship between EU and domestic law, said Laws LJ, required regard to be given to the following propositions:

1. each specific right and obligation provided under EU law was by virtue of the 1972 Act incorporated into domestic law and took precedence. Anything within domestic law which was inconsistent with EU law was either abrogated or had to be modified so as to avoid inconsistency;

2. the 1972 Act was a constitutional statute which could not be impliedly repealed.

You may recall that we touched on the controversial notion of a 'constitutional statute' earlier (see section **1.6.2**). Laws LJ indicated in *Thoburn* that these were Acts which governed the relationship between the state and the individual and enlarged or diminished fundamental constitutional rights. These types of statute, he suggested, could never be impliedly repealed. As noted, further discussion of this topic is outside the scope of this book, but it is fair to say that this statement remains controversial.

The *Factortame* and *Thoburn* cases illustrate how English and European case law has developed in response to the legal order established by the EU. But it is important to remember that that legal order is also capable of undergoing change. The scope of EU law today is significantly greater than forty years ago, when the UK joined the Community.

One implication of this is that, for the lawyer, it has become more difficult to identify clear points of demarcation between national and EU law, and to find areas of national law which are wholly unaffected by EU law. As we shall see in **Chapter 11**, even areas such as criminal law and family law are increasingly being shaped more by a European influence. To what extent this trend will continue is, of course, moot in the current climate. The majority political consensus around EU membership is under considerable strain, and the possibility that the UK will leave the EU (the so-called 'Brexit' option) cannot be discounted. The present Government included a commitment to hold a national referendum on EU membership in their 2015 election manifesto. The Prime Minister, David Cameron, has indicated that this should take place before the end of 2017.

Even if the referendum does result in a vote to leave the EU, quite how this will be achieved, over what time period, and with what legal consequences will take some working out. Membership of the EU was never designed on the assumption that members might one day want to leave the club. It will be a complicated process (see, e.g., Lang, 2014), not least because so many of the UK's obligations under international trade law are subsumed within its EU membership, and these relationships, and the UK's future relationship with the EU itself, would require substantial (re)negotiation. In short, EU law will not be consigned to the history books overnight.

For the present, to return to our flick-knife example, if our concern was whether there are any controls on the importation of flick-knives, or whether this was an unfair restraint on cross-border trade, then we might well have to consider EU law. Nevertheless, despite the continuing expansion of European law into new areas, the question as raised would be unlikely to require research into the European dimension.

CONCLUSION

In this chapter we have explored the functions of law, the variety of forms that law takes, and have glimpsed some of the ways in which English law is being shaped by external influences. In solving any legal problem, including the one set at the beginning of this chapter, we need to be aware of these many dimensions of English law. Any advice we give must take into account the kind of issue with which we are dealing. Is it a question of criminal or civil law? Have we considered all relevant Acts (if any), and checked on the existence of any subordinate legislation? What about case law? Are there any human rights implications? Have the courts said anything about the matter, either in interpreting a relevant statute or in applying rules of common law? Does the problem have an EU dimension? It is only by appreciating this context that we can, ultimately, find the relevant law to solve our problem. In practice, of course, you quickly overcome the need to run through the kind of checklist we have just presented. Your knowledge and understanding of substantive areas of law will help to make the job of researching legal issues much simpler. Even so, no one can retain sufficient detailed knowledge to make legal research redundant. The next chapter is intended to help you develop the basic research skills necessary to find the law on any basic legal problem.

CHAPTER REFERENCES

An-Na'im, A. (2008), *Islam and the Secular State: Negotiating the Future of Shari'a* (Cambridge, MA: Harvard University Press).

Bradney, A. (2009), *Law and Faith in a Sceptical Age* (London: Routledge).

CRACKNELL, R. and CLEMENTS, R. (2012), 'Acts and Statutory Instruments: The Volume of Legislation 1950–2012', Standard Note SN/SG/2911, House of Commons Library (available at www.parliament.uk/briefing-papers/SN02911).

EWING, K.D. (1999), 'The Human Rights Act and Parliamentary Democracy', 62 *Modern Law Review*, 79.

FISS, O. (1984), 'Against Settlement', 93 *Yale Law Journal*, 1073.

GEARY, A., MORRISON, W., and JAGO, R. (2013), *The Politics of the Common Law: Perspectives, Rights, Processes, Institutions* (2nd edn, Abingdon: Routledge).

GENN, H. (2009), *Judging Civil Justice* (Cambridge: Cambridge University Press).

GLENN, H.P. (2010), *Legal Traditions of the World* (4th edn, Oxford: Oxford University Press).

HERRING, J. (2014), *Legal Ethics* (Oxford: Oxford University Press).

JUSTICE (1974), *Going to Law: A Critique of English Civil Procedure* (London: Stevens).

KRITZER, H.M. (2004), 'Disappearing Trials? A Comparative Perspective', 1 *Journal of Empirical Legal Studies*, 735.

LANG, A.T.F. (2014), 'The Consequences of Brexit: Some Complications From International Law'. LSE Law: Policy Briefing Paper No. 3. Available at SSRN: http://ssrn.com/abstract=2482323.

MACINTYRE, A. (1988), *Whose Justice? Which Rationality?* (Notre Dame, IN: University of Notre Dame Press).

MACKLEM, P. (2015), 'Human Rights in International Law: Three Generations or One?' 3 *London Review of International Law*, 61.

MIERS, D. (1986), 'Legislation, Linguistic Adequacy and Public Policy', *Statute Law Review*, 90.

——— (1989), 'Legislation and the Legislative Process: A Case for Reform?', *Statute Law Review*, 26.

MORGAN, B. and YEUNG, K. (2007), *An Introduction to Law and Regulation: Text and Materials* (Cambridge: Cambridge University Press).

PARTINGTON, M. (2015), *An Introduction to the English Legal System 2015–16* (Oxford: Oxford University Press).

RAINEY, B., WICKS, E., and OVEY, C. (2014), *Jacobs, White and Ovey: The European Convention on Human Rights* (6th edn, Oxford: Oxford University Press).

ROBERTS, S. (2009), '"Listing Concentrates the Mind": The English Civil Court as an Arena for Structured Negotiation', 29 *Oxford Journal of Legal Studies*, 457.

SANDERS, A., YOUNG, R., and BURTON, M. (2010), *Criminal Justice* (4th edn, Oxford: Oxford University Press).

STEIN, P. and SHAND, J. (1974), *Legal Values in Western Society* (Edinburgh: Edinburgh University Press).

2

Finding the Law

Let's begin by considering again the problem of the shopkeeper, which we introduced in **Chapter 1**. We now know that the answer to her question is likely to lie somewhere in either existing legislation, or in case law, or perhaps in a combination of the two. We also know that there is a vast amount of that primary material to be searched.

How do we go about finding the law on a particular issue? That is a question of developing the appropriate research skills to do the job. Research skills matter, particularly for new lawyers, not just at university or college, but when working in a wide range of trainee and paralegal roles. Indeed, it is no exaggeration to say that research skills are a key element of both academic and professional learning. For example, for those of you who do go into practice, you will have an ethical obligation to represent your clients competently and with appropriate skill and diligence. Competence expressly includes the ability to do effective research, or as the Solicitors Regulation Authority's *Competence Statement* puts it, to use '*appropriate* methods and resources to undertake research' (our emphasis). The point is not an insignificant one. A recent and substantial review of legal education and training, commissioned by the main legal services regulators, reported concerns that:

* Trainee lawyers appear generally to be unfamiliar with paper-based resources by comparison with digital resources
* Trainees depend too much on one-hit searching and thus do not check their findings thoroughly and contextually
* Trainees use Google extensively, and their searches tend to be shallow and brief
* Trainees also appear to lack the skills to organise their research.

(LETR Report, 2013: 45)

An aim of this and the following chapters is therefore to set you on the right path, and help you avoid at least some of those problems.

When we were writing the first edition of this book back in 1990, 'research skills' pretty much meant the ability to use a physical law library. Even in the wake of developing commercial platforms (Lexis, the precursor to LexisNexis, for example, was launched in 1973) and despite the growth in specialist legal informatics during the 1980s and early 90s (Bing, 2010), we could still quite confidently proclaim that 'law is above all else a library-based subject'. In a sense that is still true, but today the 'library' and the associated research skills involved in finding and using legal information have moved substantially from physical to virtual space.

This process of digitisation has not simply been about converting print media into an electronic form. Consequently, the skills, tools, and processes we are talking about in this and the next chapter need to be thought of not simply as discrete 'legal research skills', but as part of a broader package of (particularly digital) information *literacy*. By 'information literacy' we mean the set of capabilities necessary for learning and working in an information-rich, digital society—see further section **2.2**. Though, as the LETR Report reminds us, we cannot ignore paper entirely (yet).

This chapter thus starts out by outlining how not just access to information, but information itself, and legal information in particular, is changing and why that matters. It then explores the skills and capabilities you need to develop to function effectively in this environment, before discussing the specific kinds of sources you need to be familiar with, and some of the research tools you will use in legal settings.

2.1 Law and Legal Information in a Digital Society

Let's begin with what may seem like a bit of a digression, though it serves to put what follows in context. The massive growth of computer processing power over the last thirty years has been at the heart of the information revolution. It is this that has enabled us to digitise and move large amounts of information (text, sound, images, or any combination thereof) around the globe.

The public launch of the World Wide Web in 1992 opened up the potential for individuals and small businesses to use communication technologies which a few years previously had been the preserve of governments and large corporations, and, only a few years before that, had simply not existed. In 1994, there were fewer than 3,000 websites (LaFrance, 2015); twenty-one years later the figure is over 943 million. E-commerce has become big business and robotics and artificial intelligence (AI) are out of the lab and changing (often quite imperceptibly) the way we live and work.

2.1.1 The Implications for Law

Even a relatively traditional field like law is not immune from this transformation. New information technologies are changing the subject matter of law itself. Digital media have created new challenges, for example for intellectual property law, for data security and protection, and for the criminal law in responding to a wide range of electronic crime (from online theft and fraud, through control of extreme internet porn, to policing the online activities of terrorist groups). Financial regulatory systems are having to come to terms with digital currencies such as bitcoin. The military applications of robotics, for example in constructing semi-autonomous and autonomous weapon systems have profound implications for the laws of war, and so on. Scientific and technological innovations are thus creating many of the most interesting and cutting-edge challenges for today's lawyers and legal systems.

Technology is also changing the way lawyers work, and even the kinds of job that exist in the legal services market (Susskind, 2013). Large-scale litigation has been transformed by the ability to digitise and organise vast swathes of documents and share them through electronic disclosure protocols; the use of visual and audio evidence in the courts is increasingly widespread; private systems of online dispute resolution are expanding. Firms are investing in legal artificial intelligence to standardise and auto-mate more of their routine transactional work. New hybrid roles are emerging that combine legal and other technical know-how in, for example, knowledge and process engineering, project management, or legal risk management: it is not just about being a solicitor, barrister, or paralegal.

In sum, technology is having a profound impact on the substantive law, the practice of law, and also, more subtly, on how we think conceptually about the subject (see, e.g., Parker, 2011; Sherwin, 2011). As Marshall McLuhan didn't quite say, the medium really does change the message. This has important implications for how we think about legal information and legal research.

2.1.2 Information in the Digital Society

Let's start with the obvious: digitisation has led to an information explosion of unimagi-nable proportions. As Professor Richard Susskind (2013: 10) observes, quoting Google's Eric Schmidt, we now create in every two days as much information as existed 'from the dawn of civilization up to 2003'.

Of course not all of that is legal material, or even material about law; but a lot is, and the amount is growing all the time. In part this reflects the underlying trend for primary legal information (cases, statutes, regulations, and other sources of law) to expand, and never contract. Payne (1983) put it more graphically:

> The Ten Commandments consist of 120 words, the Magna Carta 63 Clauses and the American Declaration of Independence 500 words. The Common Market regulations concerning duck eggs run to no fewer than 120,000 words!

But it also reflects (and has facilitated) an explosion of information *about* law. Information put out by courts and advice agencies, publications from law firms, research and policy documents prepared by government, regulatory bodies and interest groups; academic articles, working papers, and conference proceedings; media reports; and all sorts of self-publishing through blogs and other social media. All of these might, to a greater or lesser degree, be considered research resources.

The sheer amount of information, however, is only one part of the story. Two other crucial things have happened that make digitisation significant for our present purposes.

First, digitisation has, to an extent, democratised access to and control over infor-mation and, in the process, changed the nature of information itself. This is particu-larly true of web-based information, which is fundamentally non-hierarchical and (in quality terms) loosely controlled. As Tim Berners-Lee, the inventor of the World Wide Web acknowledges, this facet is fundamental to the design principles and architecture of the web:

> the Web is about anything being connected with anything. It is a vision that provides us with new freedoms, and allows us to grow faster than we could when we were fettered by hierarchical classification systems into which we bound ourselves.
>
> (Berners-Lee, 2000: 1)

In some respects this makes the web an amazing resource, and in other ways it makes it incredibly unhelpful, particularly for academic and professional work where the quality and authenticity of research resources matter. In sum the main problems are:

- There is no all-seeing editor. To put it crudely, anyone with basic resources can publish on the web and basic web architecture does not help us distinguish an idiot from an Einstein. This does not mean that self-published content is intrinsically poor (there are some extremely good legal blogs—or 'blawgs'—for example), but you do need to develop robust criteria for evaluating them.

- Document history and provenance can be difficult to ascertain. The web is not intrinsically interested in authorship, or whether a document is an original or a copy, real or fake, draft or final version.

- As scale increases, depth of research declines. If you have only ten 'hits' it is pretty easy to search all of them. It is a different matter if your search returns 164,000 items. Remember that search algorithms tend to use a wide range of indices in ranking pages: popularity and 'freshness' of the source, relevance to the search and (technical) page quality indicators tend to be significant. These may provide only a weak proxy for the intrinsic quality of the page content.

Secondly, digitisation has also radically blurred the distinction between users and producers of information. This has been a particular function of the kinds of Web 2.0 technologies we associate with social media. It creates a couple of significant challenges in academic and professional contexts:

- It has changed our relationship to the ownership and authorship of information. Digital information often occurs as a public resource, something we can share freely and readily on Facebook or Instagram. This is, however, a bit of a myth. Outside the digital commons, where authors actively reduce or give up their ownership rights, all information belongs to someone. In the academic and professional worlds acknowledging ownership ('attribution') is important, and the failure to do so has consequences. At university or college such behaviour may be considered 'plagiarism', a kind of cheating that might lead to you failing a module, or even your whole degree (we revisit this in **Chapter 4**). At work it may be embarrassing (a number of law firms, for example, have had to apologise and remove material after lifting content from other firms' websites!) or have disciplinary consequences.

- It has changed the nature of authorship in all sorts of ways. For example, it increases the capacity and, perhaps, the tendency to respond instantaneously to events. This can be great for currency, sometimes less good for quality. Web technologies also facilitate collaborative authoring, with Wikipedia a well-known example. Collaboration fundamentally blurs the line between users and producers, and can be a highly creative and valuable process, but it can also pose risks for other users. The quality of the content depends fundamentally on the skills, knowledge, and interest of the community editing that content. As we see with Wikipedia itself, public content may be provisional, and even disputed; quality and accuracy can be very variable between topics and even within single pages, consequently academic advice is generally against relying on Wikipedia as an authoritative source. In sum, you need to look carefully at who is authoring anything, in what context and with what quality controls in place.

So, in the light of all this, what sort of skills should you be aiming to develop?

2.2 Developing Your Information and Research Skills

Developing your own information literacy and research skills involves a mix of domain (i.e. legal) knowledge, plus functional IT, research, and communication skills. Visually we can represent it as shown in **Figure 2.1**. We will say a little about each element here.

2.2.1 Five Core Capabilities

Domain knowledge is an obvious requirement, and it is not just about 'knowing' some law, it is about developing ways of constructing (or deconstructing) legal problems. To be an effective researcher, you need to develop some sense of how lawyers think about legal issues (i.e. the terminology and concepts they use, how legal information is structured and classified, what might be more standard or creative solutions, etc.). This does mean that, to start with, legal research can be really slow and frustrating as you try to find your way around the material. Persevere—it becomes easier with experience.

Understanding your relationship to the problem may also help define the kind and level of research you need to undertake. What is your standpoint? (Learner, legal

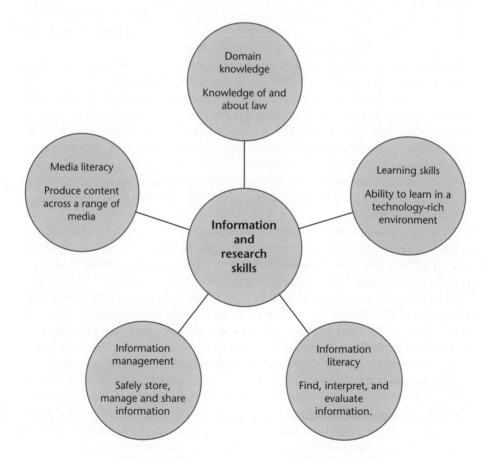

Figure 2.1 Information and research skills

adviser, friend…) What is your task, and your objective? Are you reading to fill in the background of a subject, to enhance your own understanding, or to provide a detailed study of some issue or point of law? Are you producing a letter of advice or an academic essay? Each of these locations and activities may require rather different research strategies (we develop this further in **Chapter 3**), and may influence your choice of sources.

Learning skills: information literacy builds on a good platform of general learning skills. Part of being at university involves learning how to learn in ways that prepare you for the next stages of your career. In particular, it requires developing greater independence as a learner, i.e.:

- actively and critically engaging with material;
- taking responsibility for finding things out rather than waiting to be taught;
- reflecting on your own learning and how you might close any gaps you identify.

The approach we take in this book is particularly geared to helping you develop those skills. That is why we ask questions and include self-tests. It is why we do not pretend that everything is really simple, and include material that is designed to stretch you as a learner.

Information literacy is the primary business of this and the next chapter. It involves finding, reading, and understanding the law. You should also be aware that finding the law increasingly requires a reasonable level of ICT literacy: a basic knowledge of computers, and some understanding of how digital information is stored and retrieved. This will help you construct more effective information searches.

Information management: once you have your information you need to consider how to organise it and store it safely and securely. Dumping everything into a single default documents folder becomes a recipe for overwhelm. Think about how you want to organise your file space, whether it is a hard drive or cloud-based application. Develop good habits in naming files, so you can easily identify the contents. Think about version control: include version numbers or dates in filenames so you can readily see which is the latest version of a file. Keep secure backups of documents separate from your main PC or laptop hard drive, and back up regularly. These days, as excuses go, 'the computer ate my essay' is generally going to garner about as much sympathy as 'the dog ate my essay'!

Media literacy is, at a minimum about communicating the outcomes of your research. It is still something that plays little real part in legal education, and much of it falls outside the scope of this book. By media literacy we mean the capability to select and use a range of media in ways that are appropriate for your audience and your activity.

At law school many of your assessments and related tasks will involve written communication skills. Most of them may take the form of conventional essays and exams (and we focus on these in **Chapter 4**). Some law schools have opened up their assessment to include multiple forms of writing (professional communications, reflective journals, blogs, etc.), and to allow multimedia use—making videos, dramatic performances, blogs, apps, and so on. These opportunities are really useful. Writing for or speaking in different formats will sharpen your communication and presentation skills, provided you really focus on understanding how these different formats, and different audiences, influence the way in which you engage people in what you are doing. Look out for extra courses or student societies that will give you access to these sorts of experience.

The remainder of this chapter is about getting you on the path to finding and researching the law.

2.2.2 Getting Started: The Sources

Lawyers have essentially two types of library and information sources: what we call **literary** and **primary** sources. These may be further subdivided. Accordingly, we have split the following discussion into four constituent parts, covering:

(a) literary sources;

(b) case law;

(c) legislation; and

(d) EU law.

2.3 Literary Sources

The term 'literary sources' is used to describe books *about* law, as opposed to those books *of* law, which contain 'official' copies of legislation or case reports. It thus includes student textbooks, books for practitioners, and articles from professional and academic journals and newspapers. We might also include new media—blogs and commentary on websites—in this category.

We start with literary sources because the simplest way to begin researching a problem is often to find a book about it. This is also going to seem more familiar to you at the start of your law career than going to the cases and statutes themselves (though that is important, as we shall see). Literary sources are sometimes also referred to as *secondary* sources, to distinguish them from those books of law, which are *primary* sources. Be careful that you don't confuse the term 'secondary', meaning literary, with other uses of the term, particularly in relation to secondary legislation.

2.3.1 Books and Journals

In terms simply of quantity, textbooks are the main literary source of law. We conventionally make a distinction between academic and practitioner texts. That distinction is a bit arbitrary, as many books may be as useful to the practitioner as to the academic lawyer, but, to generalise, academic texts tend to be less concerned with matters of procedure, and to offer a more critical perspective on the law than practitioner texts. Many academic texts now take a specifically *contextual approach* to law; that is, an approach that attempts to place law in a social, political, or economic perspective, rather than just concentrating on what we call *black-letter* law—i.e. the rules themselves. Accordingly, the answers you find may well reflect the function of the text and the perspective of the author on the subject.

Law journals also take a wide variety of forms. Some, such as the *Law Society Gazette*, are primarily practitioner journals, which will contain articles of interest to legal practitioners on matters of substantive law or practice management; they will also normally maintain an element of updating, with short case notes and information about recent or planned legislation. Many of the more 'heavyweight' journals, such as the *Law Quarterly Review*, appeal to both practitioner and academic audiences. Of these, the majority have some kind of specialist focus—hence we have titles like the *Journal of Business Law*, *Industrial Law Journal*, and *Journal of Social Welfare and Family Law*. Others, such as the *Modern Law Review, Oxford Journal of Legal Studies*, and *Journal of Law and Society*, have a broad coverage of subject matter, but a primarily academic outlook. Most of the main journals have adopted a similar format, with each containing a number of leading articles and book reviews, sometimes alongside shorter articles on cases or new legislation.

2.3.2 Finding Literary Sources

As a starting point in your studies you will almost certainly be given guidance on what texts are required for the course, though for most purposes you will be expected to read more widely than just the required or recommended text. So, sooner rather than later, you will be required to look for other sources (both textbooks and journal articles) from which to work. There are a number of ways of going about this.

- *Check your reading or study guide.* Most lecturers include additional readings and references in their course materials. These will often include alternative and 'key' sources.

- *Start with your textbook:* this is one strategy, but not necessarily the best one. Textbooks will tend to focus on the primary and most important secondary literature, and so are certainly helpful. But they may also be quite selective, particularly in referencing other textbooks ('the competition'!), and they inevitably get out of date so will not necessarily include the latest works.

- *Access the library catalogue.* All university libraries have an online catalogue of their collection. This will enable you to search by keywords (usually title and/or subject based) and by author, and will link you to available online content from your library. This is a good starting point, but still a fairly limited technique for in-depth searching, as catalogues contain relatively general search terms, so it is unlikely you would find, for example, any references to the law on flick-knives this way! Catalogues also do not reference specific journal articles.

Most university libraries have access to extensive digital book collections, as well as a print collection. If you are not used to using digital books they are worth exploring. Digital platforms increasingly have the capacity to change *how* we interact with information. For example the more sophisticated e-book readers are more than just reading platforms. They enable us to interact with the text in a multiplicity of ways: bookmarking, adding marginalia and 'sticky notes' (as you might with hardcopy), but also cutting and pasting and linking to other online resources in ways that were never possible with paper sources.

Journal articles and notes can be a very useful resource for a number of purposes, including:

- researching recent developments, which may not have made it into your textbooks;
- identifying different opinions about the purpose and/or effects of a particular legal principle; and
- finding empirical research about the way the law works in the 'real world'.

Searching for journal articles now is best done through electronic resources, of which there are a number, including Westlaw, LexisLibrary, and Lawtel (discussed later), though none of these has a complete set of even the most commonly cited academic journals. For example, none of these databases carries the *Cambridge Law Journal* or *Legal Studies*. There are, however, various other databases to which many law libraries subscribe, including:

HeinOnline: a US-based database containing a very extensive full-text library of journal articles, mostly from North America, but including some UK and Australasian academic journals as well. It also holds copies of English case reports from 1212–1865. Because all its content is converted into pdf format, it is not as up to date as Ingenta or the publishers' own sites.

Commercial online resources: all the major publishing groups provide full-text online access to their journals, and often a range of online books as well. You will only have full-text access to those journals and e-books for which your library has a subscription. Non-subscription items can be purchased for a fee. The major databases include Oxford Journals, Ingentaconnect, Taylor & Francis Online, and Wiley Online Library. None of these are purely law-specific, and all are limited in the sense that they only carry their own publications, so you cannot use them to search 'across the board'.

JSTOR: this is a large and multi-disciplinary not-for-profit archive project. It does not carry the most recently published issues of journals (usually those for the last three to five years), but users can link from the JSTOR archive to the publisher's site or sometimes to another online source. Its law collection overlaps with and is much smaller than Hein, but it includes archive copies of the *Modern Law Review*, *Cambridge Law Journal*, *Harvard Law Review*, *Legal Studies*, *Oxford Journal of Legal Studies*, and *Yale Law Journal* and may be useful, especially if you do not have access to HeinOnline.

In addition to these specific sites, you can use a number of published indexes to search for journal articles by subject or other keywords. These do not necessarily give you direct access to the full text of the article, but can be a useful way of building up a bibliography for further research. There are three that may be of value to you:

The Legal Journals Index: This, the most useful, commenced publishing in 1986, and contains full details of all the legal journals published in the United Kingdom, and so provides an extremely important research resource. It is published online as part of the Westlaw database and can be searched by 'free text' or by subject keyword.

Index to Legal Periodicals and Index to Foreign Legal Periodicals: These are both American publications and are available in paper and electronic forms. The former is an index to all American journals, plus a selection from Britain, the Republic of Ireland, and the Commonwealth from 1981 to date. In the electronic version, details of articles in UK, Irish, North American, and Australasian legal journals for 1908–1981 are held in a separate database called 'Index to Legal Periodicals Retrospective'. The Index to Foreign Legal Periodicals indexes articles on international and comparative law, and on the municipal law of all countries which do not appear in the Index to Legal Periodicals.

2.3.3 Citations

When textbooks and articles make reference to other journal publications, they will do so using relatively standardised modes of referencing or 'citation'. You need to be able to understand and use proper systems of citation both to find and reference legal materials.

In law there is no internationally, or even nationally, agreed system of citation, though the differences in various forms of citation tend to be fairly small. References may be *in-line*, that is, they are incorporated in the text itself, using author-date systems of citation, such as the Harvard system, or, more commonly, references appear in footnotes or endnotes. Footnotes and endnotes tend to adopt the structure shown in **Figure 2.2**.

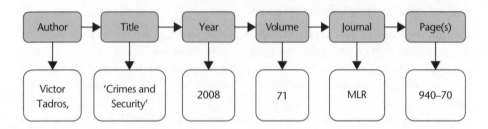

Figure 2.2 Construction of a journal citation

Be aware that different citation systems may require variations on this format. There is some move in the UK to encourage standardisation around 'OSCOLA'—the Oxford University Standard for Citation of Legal Authorities—which has been adopted by a number of law schools. The full standard and a quick guide can be downloaded at www.law.ox.ac.uk/publications/oscola.php.

In-line, author–date systems, such as Harvard, are less commonly used in law. They do not use footnotes, but refer to sources in the text by author and year of publication, thus: 'Tadros (2008)'. The full reference is then reserved to the bibliography. This contains essentially the same information as a footnote, but in a different sequence; thus this reference would appear as Tadros, V. (2008) 'Crimes and Security', *Modern Law Review*, 71(6), 940–70. Note that the Harvard citation includes not just the volume but also the issue or part number—here (6), which is often excluded from conventional law citations. Traditionally, when not using the Harvard form of citation, certain standard abbreviations are used in citing journal names. Thus, as the example demonstrates, the *Modern Law Review* is cited as MLR. *Public Law* is cited as PL, and so on. Each citation depends on the form adopted by the particular journal, so it takes a while to get used to the different citations. Do be precise in their use. This is not just a matter of pedantry, it is a way of ensuring that we are all 'speaking the same language' and that references can be easily traced. We will come back to the importance of citation in **Chapter 4**. A guide to legal abbreviations has been written by Donald Raistrick (2008); and a list of the main abbreviations in use is also contained on the website that accompanies this book.

2.3.4 How Authoritative are Literary Sources?

Literary sources do not really contain 'the law'; they contain the author's interpretation of it. This is reflected in the way, historically, the courts have used them.

By and large, the courts have been reluctant to place reliance on secondary sources in coming to decisions—though exceptionally, *Halsbury's Laws* (see section **2.3.5**) have long been cited before the courts. Indeed, at one time, it was the practice that no living author could be cited in court—a rather curious rule, which seemed to suggest that death gives an author authority that he or she may never have had when alive! This restriction has largely fallen into disuse, and some well-established texts are now quite widely cited.

Academic journal articles are increasingly being cited, not as authoritative texts, but as being influential on the court's decision. Thus in *R v A* [2001] UKHL 25; [2001] 2 AC 45, their Lordships referred to a number of academic analyses of the procedural rules governing the bringing of evidence of a complainant's previous sexual experiences in the trial of various sex offences.

2.3.5 Legal Encyclopedias

Encyclopedias are usually designed to provide a reasonably complete statement of the law in a relatively concise form. They come in a variety of shapes and sizes. Many of them are subject-specific—so, for example, there are encyclopedias on consumer protection, social welfare law, employment law, and so on. Most of these are large loose-leaf volumes designed mainly for legal practitioners. Other significant multi-volume sets for practitioners include the *Encyclopedia of Forms and Precedents* and *Halsbury's Statutes*.

One of the most valuable starting points, particularly if you are researching a topic about which you have little or no existing knowledge, is the legal encyclopedia called *Halsbury's Laws of England*. This is available in hard-copy format and online as part of the LexisLibrary service (discussed later). The online search facility makes using the electronic version very simple. Searching is not so straightforward with the paper version. As this is an important source, and one which in practice you may well have to consult in paper form, we have included a brief guide to searching in *Halsbury's* among our online resources.

2.4 Cases

The operation of our system of precedent is dependent upon us being able to find out what the courts have said about any given question. This means that we must have a record of the courts' decisions. These records are referred to as 'law reports'.

Whenever possible you are recommended to look at actual reports of cases rather than just to accept the interpretation given in textbooks. This section is intended to give you some guidance to the English system of law reporting, and then to help you to find and update specific cases.

2.4.1 Law Reporting

The tradition of law reporting is very ancient in the English legal system, though many of these early reports are now regarded as highly unreliable. In essence the law reports can be divided into two historical phases, pre- and post-1865.

Before 1865, there were two main sources of case reports:

Year books Established about 1285, these continued in existence until 1535. They were probably derived from the notes of cases taken by student advocates. Consequently they are not consistently reliable: would you want to rely on your notes as law reports? They are often difficult to read and make relatively little sense to anyone except a legal historian.

Private reports Sometimes called 'nominate reports' because each series is named after the lawyer who compiled them. Hundreds of reports appeared in this era. The same case could be reported by a range of reporters, and in such cases it is not unusual for the contents, even the decision, to vary as between reports! The significance of these reports, however, lay in the evolution of more precise methods of recording judgments, e.g. in about 1765 Burrow's Reports introduced the idea of a 'Headnote' (a summary of the facts, decision, and reasoning—a device which is used in every report today). Some were good, e.g. Coke's Reports [1600–58]; others were not so, e.g. Espinasse's Reports [1793–1807], of whom it was said: he was deaf; he heard only half of what went on in court, and reported the other half. These reports are now collected together in *The English Reports*. Cases from the nominate reports are still cited, though increasingly rarely. Some of the most important have also been reprinted in a series called the All England Law Reports Reprint (cited as All ER Rep), which contains a selection of cases from between 1558 and 1935, and most important ones have been digitised and appear on LexisNexis or Westlaw.

Even after 1865, there remains no single 'official' (in the sense of state sponsored) source of law reports in the English legal system. This is yet another respect in which our system differs from much of continental Europe. For example, in France there are separate criminal and civil series of the *Bulletin des arrêts de la Cour de Cassation* (the final court of appeal in most civil matters) dating back to 1798, while in Germany there are about twelve current sets of official law reports; these tend to be published separately by reference to the particular court in which the cases were heard. Thus, e.g., the Federal Supreme Court (*Bundesgerichtshof*) and Federal Constitutional Court (*Bundesverfassungsgericht*) reports constitute separate series.

In England, in 1865, a body called the Incorporated Council of Law Reporting (ICLR) introduced what is now recognised as the 'official' source of law reports. The Council is still responsible for these today, though there are a number of other organisations which publish various law reports, as well as a body of case law that is never published. We shall consider each of these in turn.

The Law Reports and alternatives

The so-called 'Law Reports' consist of Queen's Bench Reports (abbreviated to QB), Chancery (Ch), Family (Fam), the Industrial Cases Reports (ICR), and Appeal Cases (AC). This broadly reflects the division of work between the superior courts, as Queen's Bench, Chancery, and Family Reports will contain reports of both High Court and Court of Appeal decisions. The ICR, as the name implies, covers employment law in the Employment Appeal Tribunal and above. Appeal Cases contain chiefly Supreme Court, House of Lords, and Privy Council cases. The Council also publishes the Weekly Law Reports (WLR), which are published ahead of the main series and are relied upon by many practitioners.

There are other reputable reports not published by the Council. The All England Law Reports (All ER), published by Butterworths, is a prime example. These are probably the most widely used alternative. Indeed, many smaller law libraries in the UK and abroad rely purely on the All England Law Reports, which are also available electronically through LexisLibrary, discussed below. The Incorporated Council of Law Reporting also publishes the Law Reports in an online version, (though behind a paywall) and free electronic case summaries. Originally called the Daily Law Reports, these are now published on the ICLR website (see section **2.7.2**) as the Weekly Law Reports (Daily)—WLR (D). Both the Weekly Law Reports and the All England Reports are published in weekly paper parts as well as annual bound volumes. Electronic versions of all the law reports are available from a range of other sources, discussed in section **2.7**.

The Law Reports are generally preferred to other reports in the case of any conflict, and, in terms of court practice, represent the authoritative version of a judgment, which must be used where available—see the *Practice Direction (Citation of Authorities)* (2012) issued by the Lord Chief Justice and published on the judiciary website (at www.judiciary.gov.uk/publications-and-reports/practice-directions/2012/lcj-practice-direction-citation-authorities-2012). This preference is because judgments in the Law Reports are revised either by the judges themselves or with their cooperation.

This should ensure that they are a more reliable source of what was said. However, the opportunity for correction enables a judge sometimes to introduce changes to the text which may reflect what he meant to say, rather than what he actually said. This is perhaps a rather more controversial practice, though in some cases it has enabled judges to amend or clarify their reasoning in the light of criticisms directed at the unreported transcript—see, e.g., Lord Denning's judgment in *Ghani* v *Jones* [1970] 1 QB 693, and Jackson (1970: 3).

Conflicts between the various law report versions of a case are comparatively rare, but not wholly unknown. For an example you might like to look at the reports of *Davies* v *Swan Motor Co. (Swansea) Ltd* [1949] 2 KB 291, at 319; [1949] 1 All ER 620, at 629, where there is a small but confusing discrepancy in the reporting of the judgment of Evershed LJ. See if you can spot it!

Specialist reports

There are many and varied specialist reports such as the Criminal Appeal Reports, Reports of Patents Cases, and Industrial Cases Reports. These are of considerable assistance to subject specialists. A list of the majority of such reports can be found in Raistrick (2008).

Unreported cases

Cases in the inferior courts are not routinely reported. Cases in the higher courts and tribunals may be reported because those are formally 'courts of record', i.e. courts which are required to maintain a full transcript of proceedings. Historically limited resources meant that not all cases could be reported, and decisions had to be made by the editors as to which cases would appear in the printed volumes. Sometimes they got it wrong. This happened in 1973, for example, with the case of *Mesher* v *Mesher*, which introduced a new kind of 'property adjustment order' for use in divorce cases. Initially the case had been picked up only by *The Times* (a point that seems to have been forgotten as the case was widely cited as unreported). Even so, the Mesher Order (as it was called) became very popular with the divorce courts, with the result that the case was belatedly reported in the All England Law Reports in 1980 (see *Mesher* v *Mesher and Hall (Note)* [1980] 1 All ER 126). Practically speaking, the higher up the structure one goes, the more likely that a case will be reported. All decisions of the Supreme Court and the Privy Council are thus reported as a matter of course. However, reporting today is rather less critical as digitisation has significantly reduced the proportion of unreported cases.

As a matter of general principle the citing of unreported cases is discouraged. The 2012 Practice Direction states at para. 10:

> Where a judgment has not been reported, reference may be made to the official transcript if that is available, not the handed-down text of the judgment, as this may have been subject to late revision after the text was handed down. Official transcripts may be obtained from, for instance, BAILII (http://www.bailii.org/). An unreported case should not usually be cited unless it contains a relevant statement of legal principle not found in reported authority.

Clearly, there is some merit to the core of this argument, to the effect that lawyers should only cite cases that actually lay down or explain a principle of law.

2.4.2 How to Cite a Case

Cases are cited by their name and their 'neutral citation' and/or location in the law reports. Taken together, these provide a means of identification as unique as a fingerprint. The name of any case in English law is normally based upon the parties involved—hence some of the case names we have already seen, such as *Mesher* v *Mesher* or *R* v *Shivpuri*. The case reference is more properly called its **citation**. For the paper volumes of the law reports the most common form of citation of any case will be made up of the following elements:

YEAR	VOLUME (if any)	REPORT	PAGE
[1989]	2	QB	123

This tells us that the case is to be found in volume 2 of the Queen's Bench Law Reports for 1989, beginning at page 123. There is one significant variation on that, which affects the style of citing dates and volume numbers. Some series of law reports in the last century, and a few modern sets, have consecutively numbered volumes, year by year—e.g. the case of *Bowker* v *Rose* which is reported only in (1978) 122 Sol Jo 147. Theoretically, the date there is not significant—we could find that case merely by knowing that it is in volume 122 of the *Solicitor's Journal*. For that reason, where the set of reports is consecutively numbered, the date is cited in round brackets. If the date is in square brackets, it is vital to the finding of that case, because the volume number will only refer to volumes *within that particular year*.

With the growing use of online sources, the courts needed a system of citation that could cope with the fact that cases were being published online from transcripts more quickly than they could appear in the traditional law reports The system that was devised adopts what is termed a 'neutral' form of citation, and came into operation in 2001.

Every case before a court of record is given a neutral citation that takes a similar form to conventional citations, thus:

[YEAR]	Court	Ref No

The identifiers for each court, which form the core of the neutral citation, are as follows:

- UKSC for the UK Supreme Court;
- UKHL for the House of Lords;
- UKPC for the Privy Council;
- EWCA for the Court of Appeal followed by 'Civ' or 'Crim' respectively for the Civil and Criminal Divisions; and
- EWHC for the High Court (followed by the abbreviation for the Division of the High Court, or 'Admin' for the Administrative Court).

Though these are the most important for our purposes, they are not the only citations. The system has also been adopted by the courts in Scotland and Northern Ireland, and for a number of specialist courts and tribunals not included here. The result is that we now have a uniform, UK-wide system of neutral citations for all electronically reported case law.

To see how the system works, let's say we have a case of *Smith v Jones*, which is the tenth case in 2014 to be decided by the Court of Appeal (Civil Division). It will thus appear as: *Smith v Jones* [2014] EWCA Civ 10. The official number (here, 10) will now always have to be cited on at least one occasion whenever a reference is made to *Smith v Jones* in later cases. The judgment itself will also be organised by paragraph (not page) numbers. These will appear identically in both the electronic and printed forms of the report. The paragraph numbers do not start and stop with each judge's judgment, but run throughout the case report sequentially, thereby both facilitating searching in electronic form, and enabling comparison of electronic and paper versions. If reference is to be made to, say, paragraph 59, in our fictitious case, the citation becomes: *Smith v Jones* [2014] EWCA Civ 10 at [59]. Multiple paragraph references will take the form of: *Smith v Jones* [2014] EWCA Civ 10 at [1], [7], and [30]-[42].

Once the judgment has been reported in the printed reports the neutral citation will appear in front of the law reports citation described earlier in this chapter: thus, *Smith v Jones* [2014] EWCA Civ 10 at [42]; [2014] QB 113 at [42]; [2014] 1 All ER 88 at [42]. The Law Reports produced by the Incorporated Council of Law Reporting are, as we noted earlier, still judicially preferred in the High Court and Court of Appeal, and should be cited where available. This was confirmed in the 2012 Practice Direction, discussed previously.

The style of citing cases is, as with journal citations, rigidly adhered to. You may find the system rather complex and confusing at first, but it will soon become familiar. We have already indicated the main reports, with their abbreviations. If you need help, fuller lists of specialist, and of American and Commonwealth, reports with their abbreviations can be found in Raistrick (2008).

2.5 Legislation

Legislation, you will recall, can be divided chiefly into Acts of Parliament and statutory instruments. The publication of each of these is a separate activity, so separate search techniques are required.

2.5.1 Acts of Parliament: The Sources

Before we begin, one important thing you need to know about an Act is the way in which it is cited. Like cases, Acts of Parliament have a unique signature. This is not based solely upon their name (or **short title** to use the technical term), however. Many different Acts share a common name—for example, there are presently five statutes in force bearing the title 'Criminal Justice Act'. This means that the year in which the Act became law will be crucial in identifying it. Additionally, every Act passed has a 'chapter number' which may also be used in its identification. In practice, it is quite possible to find legislation by reference to the year and chapter number alone. The citation of an Act as '1988 c. 33', for example, could refer only to the Criminal Justice Act 1988.

Until comparatively modern times, Acts were not formally given short titles (though such titles were quite widely used on an informal basis) so that all legislation was identified by chapter number and **regnal year** (that is, a number assigned to the year in which it was passed, counting it from the first year of that monarch's reign). Hence, the famous Poor Law Amendment Act passed in 1834 was properly cited as '4 & 5 Will. IV c. 76'. This indicates that it was the 76th statute passed in the Parliamentary session which overlapped the fourth and fifth years of William IV's reign.

The tradition of citing regnal years gradually declined after the Second World War, and the system was formally dropped in 1963. Since there are numerous older Acts of Parliament still in force, the old system of citation cannot be wholly disregarded. However, do remember that when writing about any statutes it is conventional now to refer to them, wherever possible, by their short title and date only.

Acts of Parliament are published in a variety of paper series and online. The initial responsibility for publication lies with the Stationery Office which, as the government printer, is required to publish individual copies of all statutes as they are passed. These are ultimately brought together in the annual bound editions of the *Public General Acts and Measures*. All statutes passed since 1988 are also published online through the National Archives (at www.legislation.gov.uk/). The site contains either the full text of the Acts as originally passed, or revised versions which incorporate later amendments. The majority of legislation is held in revised format, but revisions are by no means entirely up to date, so it is important that you check for warnings where there are revisions pending. As these versions may be less current than LexisLibrary and Westlaw (which contain fully annotated versions of legislation), and the site has relatively limited search functionality by comparison with those others, you should, if you have access to Lexis or Westlaw, use one of those in preference.

In addition to the government printer's versions, there are a number of other paper series which are worth knowing about. The most widely available of these are the *Law Reports: Statutes*, *Halsbury's Statutes*, and *Current Law Statutes Annotated*.

Law Reports: Statutes

This rather incongruously named collection is also published by the Incorporated Council of Law Reporting—hence the title. The contents are not annotated or revised, and so they do not provide anything different from the Stationery Office copies.

Halsbury's Statutes of England

This provides a partner series to *Halsbury's Laws*, containing an annotated version of all legislation presently in force, organised by subject. It is therefore the main resource for discovering whether legislation exists on any topic.

Current Law Statutes Annotated

All Acts are published in a loose-leaf format soon after coming into force. Of these, those which the editors judge to be sufficiently important are annotated by someone who is a specialist in that area of law. The annotations are not part of the Act, and do not, of course, have any legal effect, though they can be very useful in explaining the background, scope, and operation of the Act. During the course of each year, bound volumes of the *Current Law Statutes Annotated* are published; they are printed in order, according to the chapter numbers of the Acts.

2.5.2 Tracing the Legislative History of an Act

Since the House of Lords' decision in *Pepper* v *Hart* [1993] 1 All ER 42, the courts have also been entitled to refer to the Official Reports of proceedings in Parliament (Hansard) as an aid to construction in cases where the language of the Act is unclear (we discuss the parameters of this principle further in **Chapter 9**). This means that lawyers today also need to be familiar with the research techniques necessary to make sense of the legislative history of an Act. The potential scale of this change is indicated by the fact that *Pepper* v *Hart* affects not only Acts passed since 1993, but *all* Acts in force.

Every Parliamentary Bill has to go through both the Commons and the Lords before receiving the royal assent and becoming law. In this process, the Bill will normally be introduced by its promoter at the so-called second-reading stage, where you may find some general statements about purpose or legislative intent; it will also be debated before both Houses, sometimes briefly, sometimes in some detail. It will also be analysed clause by clause in standing committee—this is often the most useful part of the process for our purposes, as in *Pepper* v *Hart* itself. You need to check all of these stages. The following research strategy should work in most cases (see Tunkel, 1993: 18 for further information and alternative approaches).

For established legislation, the best starting point is an annotated version of the Act, though none of these are guaranteed to make the job entirely simple, as much depends on the quality of annotation, which is sometimes variable. Westlaw includes specifically what it refers to as 'Pepper v Hart Notes' amongst its annotatations. LexisLibrary uses *Halsbury's Statutes* annotations which may also contain references to legislative history. Amongst paper sources, it follows that *Halsbury's Statutes* may be useful, although the *Current Law Statutes* version of the Act will give you all the Hansard references to debates in both Commons and Lords. It will also generally (though not always, especially with older Acts) refer to the discussion in standing committee. Once you have identified the relevant debates, etc. these can be followed up through Hansard. This is published online at the UK Parliament website (see **Table 2.2**) with separate pages for the House of Commons and House of Lords. The online version only includes debates in the Commons from 1988–9, and in the House of Lords since 1994–5; for earlier debates, you have to use the paper volumes. These are bound in separate volumes for the Commons and the Lords, by parliamentary session rather than calendar year. The main Hansard Commons series does not include reports of standing committees. These are published as a separate series.

2.5.3 Statutory Instruments

Statutory instruments (SIs) are also published by the Stationery Office, separately, in the annual bound volumes of *Statutory Instruments* (entitled, until 1948, *Statutory Rules and Orders*), and in electronic form on the legislation.gov.uk website (from 1987) as well as on Lexis and Westlaw.

The main alternative (paper) source for SIs is *Halsbury's Statutory Instruments*, a multiple-volume set organised by subject, with a Current Service containing instruments passed since the publication of the bound volumes. *Halsbury's* contains information on all instruments in force, though not necessarily in a full-text form.

Note that SIs also have their own mode of reference, which is made up of their title, the year in which they were passed, and the instrument number. So, for example, we have the UK Borders Act 2007 (Code of Practice on Children) Order 2008, SI 2008/3158.

2.5.4 Legislation of the Scottish Parliament and Welsh Assembly

Under the devolution Acts, the Scottish Parliament and Welsh Assembly each have the power to create legislation in their own right. The Scottish Parliament can create primary and secondary legislation. The primary legislation is known as 'Acts of the Scottish Parliament' (the Scotland Act 1998, s. 28(1)). These are published independently of the laws passed by the Westminster Parliament, and are available electronically as well as in paper form. They generally fall outside the scope of this book, since Acts of the Scottish Parliament extend only to the law of Scotland, not England and Wales.

Under the original devolution Act, the Welsh Assembly could only make secondary legislation. However, Part 3 of the Government of Wales Act 2006 extended the powers of the National Assembly for Wales (as it is now properly called) and gave it the power to pass primary legislation on matters within its legislative competence. Within Wales this has the same authority as an Act of the UK Parliament. Between 2006 and 2011 these legislative acts were called 'Assembly Measures'. Following a referendum on 3 March 2011, the National Assembly for Wales was granted further primary law-making powers. The twenty areas in which the Assembly now has competence are listed in Schedule 7 to the Government of Wales Act 2006. Primary legislation passed by the Assembly under these extended powers are known as Assembly Acts.

Assembly legislation in force is printed with authoritative versions in both Welsh and English. Together with all Welsh statutory instruments, they are published electronically on the Welsh government website and on the legislation.gov.uk website—see www.legislation.gov.uk/browse/wales. Assembly Bills, with information on their progress, can be accessed online from the Welsh government website (at http://wales.gov.uk/legislation/?lang=en).

2.6 EU Law

Because the EU has separate law-making institutions from the United Kingdom, it is hardly surprising that much EU law is found in locations distinct from those we have so far discussed.

However, elements of EU law can often be found in the kind of sources we have already considered. Both *Halsbury's Laws* and *Halsbury's Statutes* have volumes specifically on European Union law, for example.

In addition to occasional articles in the journals already considered, there are quite a number of journals which specialise in EC law matters. These include the *European Law Review, Common Market Law Review,* and *Legal Issues of European Integration.* Articles on the Community may also be found in the main journals of International Law, such as the *International and Comparative Law Quarterly.* These all appear in the *Legal Journals Index.*

The various English law reports increasingly contain cases concerned with EU law— where the English courts are considering the application of EU law either *ab initio,* or in response to a preliminary ruling of the CJEU. Furthermore, it is becoming more common to find decisions of the Court of Justice (particularly, though not exclusively, those involving the UK) reported in the usual English law reports—.

Despite this, there are a number of specific sources of EU law with which you ought to be familiar.

2.6.1 European Court Reports

The European Court Reports (cited as ECR) are the official reports published by the ECJ. The Reports are available in all the Community languages, including English, but the demands of producing multiple translations of every case do mean that there are substantial delays between the Court handing down its decision and that case being reported. In the early 1990s, the time lag was such that even the first reports—in French—were taking over a year to appear in the ECR. Since 1994, steps have been taken to reduce delays by excluding the Report of the Hearing from the published version, and also by excluding most staff cases heard by the General Court from publication in the ECR.

Following the creation of the Court of First Instance (now the General Court) in 1989, the ECR has been divided into two parts: ECR I, which reports decisions of the Court of Justice, and ECR II, which contains decisions of the General Court.

2.6.2 Common Market Law Reports (CMLR)

The CMLR are an 'unofficial' series published weekly in English by the European Law Centre. They cover cases before the CJEU, and before national courts within the EU. Although unofficial, the relative speed of publication makes them largely preferable to the ECR.

Both series are indexed by subject and case name or number. The case number is an important feature of ECJ decisions. The proper mode of citation is to give the case *number* first, followed by its name, and then the citation of any report. Thus for example, one of the leading cases on the impact of EU membership on national sovereignty is properly cited as Case 6/64 *Costa v Ente Nazionale per l'Energia Elettrica (ENEL)* [1964] ECR 585. The case number, it can be seen, contains two elements: the actual number at which the case was listed (here, no. 6) and the year in which the application or reference was made (64—indicating 1964). Since the creation of the Court of First Instance (CFI), a further element has been introduced into the citation of cases. Now all case numbers have the prefix 'C–' or 'T–'. This indicates that the case was listed, respectively, either before the ECJ or the CFI/General Court.

Note also that the year contained in the case number will not be the same year that judgment was given, or that the case was reported. For example, the reference for a preliminary ruling in *R v Secretary of State, ex parte Factortame Ltd* was made in 1989. The case therefore received the number C–213/89. Judgment by the Court, however, was not handed down until June 1990. In fact, several years may elapse between the reference and the case being heard. You should also be aware that some English textbooks do not adopt the full European mode of citation, and either disregard the case number or place it after the names of the parties.

2.6.3 Online Access to EU Cases

EU cases can also be retrieved electronically from the Court of Justice's 'Curia' website (at http://curia.europa.eu/ and from Lexis or Westlaw. The Curia site can be accessed in all of the official languages, and contains full-text versions of judgments from both the Court of Justice and General Court from 17 June 1997 (though formally speaking until 2011, only the paper reports of cases in the General Court constituted the official version of judgments). Earlier case law can also be accessed from the Eur-Lex site (discussed in the next section). From its homepage the Curia website enables you to browse recent decisions and search for specific cases by official case number, or by the names of parties. It does allow keyword searching, but this is not obvious—you have to click the advanced search icon on the homepage, and it will take you to a separate search page to do that.

Commercial systems like LexisLibrary and Westlaw offer more powerful search tools. In Westlaw, for example, you can search for both UK and EU cases together by keyword within the general UK database.

2.6.4 The *Official Journal*

The *Official Journal* (OJ) is the primary organ of legal information within the EU. It is published almost daily and thus provides an extremely current source of legal information. Mastering the OJ is one of the major challenges of researching EU law, though it is much simpler to search online than via the paper version. The *Journal* is made up of several sections, of which the most important are referred to as the *L*, *C*, *and CE Series*. The *L Series* contains a record of all Community legislation, whereas the *C Series* covers a wide range of information generally falling under the heading of 'Communications'. The *CE Series* commenced publication in January 2008. It contains the preparatory acts in the legislative process and is only available electronically

Table 2.1 Sections of the *Official Journal*

L Series	Section I	Legislation whose publication is obligatory under the EC or Euratom Treaties—i.e. regulations, directives, and decisions of the Parliament and Council addressed to all Member States.
	Section II	Legislation whose publication is not mandatory under the EC or Euratom Treaties, chiefly—Commission or Council decisions and recommendations.
	Section III	Legislative acts (e.g. decisions, common positions, and declarations) adopted under the EU Treaty.
C Series	Section I	Resolutions, recommendations, and opinions of the EU institutions.
	Section II	Information from EU institutions and bodies.
	[Section III	Preparatory acts—i.e. proposals for legislation, including the draft text and explanatory memoranda—now published separately under the tab 'preparatory acts' on the EUR-Lex homepage].
	Section IV	Formal notices from the EU institutions and other bodies, and notices from Member States.
	Section V	Announcements from the Institutions (e.g. on changes to administrative procedures, announcements on competition policy; commencement of proceedings, orders, and summaries of judgments before the ECJ and CFI; staff vacancies, etc.).

in the EUR-Lex database. The full text of the OJ *L* and *C Series* is freely available on the EUR-Lex website (at http://eur-lex.europa.eu/en/index.htm). Their current coverage is explained in **Table 2.1**.

Journal references to legislation are usually cited by year, series, issue number, and page. For example, the 1985 Product Liability Directive is found at [1985] OJ L210/29—meaning *L Series*, issue number 210, of 7 August 1985 at page 29 (note that the date of the citation is to the OJ reference, not the date that the Act was passed). Cases reported in the *C Series* of the *Journal* are usually cited in the same form, thus, [1990] OJ C146/9 refers to Case C–70/88 *European Parliament* v *Council of the European Community*. The OJ is quite a useful source of basic information on Court decisions, as the summaries usually appear substantially in advance of any full reports.

2.6.5 Citing EU Legislation

The system for citing EU legislation looks different from what we are familiar with in the UK, though the underlying principle is similar. Each piece of legislation has its own identifiers, based on the year it became law and its own unique 'act number' (rather like the chapter number of a UK Act or the reference number of an SI). So, for example, the important Equal Treatment Directive of 1976 (on sex discrimination) is cited as 'Directive 76/207' (i.e. number 207 of 1976). The same format applies to decisions and recommendations. That numerical sequence, however, is reversed in respect of regulations, hence we speak of 'Regulation 1408/71', not 71/1408.

Full references will also indicate the institutional source of the legislation. Thus, for example, directives, decisions, and recommendations under the authority of the EC Treaty use, depending on their age, e.g. the suffix 'EC' or 'EEC'—thus Directive 76/207/EEC, but Directive 2009/36/EC. Regulations, strictly speaking are cited in the form 'Commission Regulation (EC) No. 312/2009' or 'Council Regulation (EC)...'.

2.6.6 Other Legislative Sources

The texts of the Treaties and of all international agreements entered into by the EU are available on the EUR-Lex site. This also contains a searchable directory of all EU legislation currently in force. Lawtel, LexisLibrary, and Westlaw also carry full text EU legislation, and there are also specialist subscription services, such as Justis CELEX which are built around the official EU multilingual CELEX database.

2.7 Online Resources

Computerised and online legal information retrieval systems have developed substantially since the 1970s and are a key part of the legal research toolkit. The advantages of such systems are fairly obvious. They have the potential to store, with relative ease, large quantities of information in electronic form, which can be searched thoroughly and accessed far more quickly than by traditional means.

The amount of computer-based legal information has grown exponentially since the early 1980s. The earliest systems to develop were those which required dedicated online searching, i.e. using a special terminal to connect, via the public telephone network, to a commercial database in another location. Today, these kinds of subscription service have been integrated into PC-based Internet technologies, and supplemented by a growing number of public information services that are freely available across the web.

2.7.1 Commercial Systems

The main online legal information systems available in the UK are LexisLibrary, Westlaw, and Lawtel; the same or similar services exist in many other common law jurisdictions. Their core coverage of primary legal materials is quite similar, but they vary in the range of other resources on offer. If you are studying law at university your library will almost certainly offer you dedicated training in the systems to which you have access, so we have not included detailed guides in this chapter (they also tend to date quite quickly). We have, however, included some basic guides in our online resource centre.

Figure 2.3 LexisLibrary homepage

LexisLibrary

The LexisNexis database, marketed in the UK as **LexisLibrary** (see **Figure 2.3**), offers full-text legal information retrieval to a range of sources, including:

- over 600,000 UK law reports;
- UK statutes in force, consolidated, giving access to over 86,000 Acts;
- over 290 practitioner texts (predominantly Butterworths/LexisNexis titles), and a range of 126 full text journals, including titles from Oxford and Cambridge University Presses, Hart/Bloomsbury, and DeGruyter;
- *Halsbury's Laws of England.*

The extent of one's access is determined by the range of services to which a user has subscribed. The user interface can be customised and it provides a good platform for searching multiple kinds of content. The basic search techniques draw substantially on Boolean search methodology, which we discuss later.

Westlaw

Westlaw, like LexisLibrary, is originally a US-based service and also provides access to an extensive full-text retrieval system (see **Figure 2.4**). Features of the Westlaw UK system include:

- over 400,000 UK law reports in full text;
- UK statutes in force, consolidated, plus full coverage of devolved legislation;
- access to Sweet & Maxwell's Common Law Library and a selection of practitioner texts;
- full-text access to 110 journals—from Sweet & Maxwell, Oxford and Cambridge University Presses, Bloomsbury Professional, and Emerald;
- access to journal abstracts via the Legal Journals Index and Financial Journals Index; and
- national, regional, and international news and business updates.

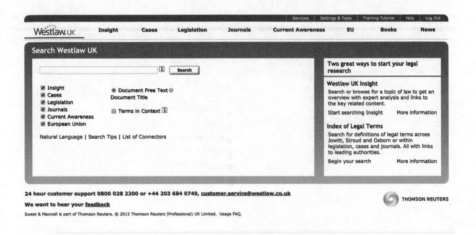

Figure 2.4 Westlaw homepage

Both LexisLibrary and Westlaw also have very extensive US, Commonwealth, and international case libraries, and as noted previously, EU resources. Both allow 'natural language' as well as keyword searching (discussed later).

Lawtel

Lawtel has a more limited database and relies more on summaries, with the result that some aspects of the system are far more geared to updating and preliminary rather than in-depth research. The main data available include:

- links to the original (i.e. not consolidated) text of statutes passed since 1987, and section-by-section information on the commencement, amendment, and repeal of statutes from 1984;

- summaries of cases (60,000+), both unreported and from the main generalist and some specialist law reports (from 1980 on), with links to full-text transcripts for the High Court, Court of Appeal, and Privy Council from 1990, and for the House of Lords/UK Supreme Court from 1980;

- full text of all parliamentary Bills from 1997/98;

- publication details of all Command Papers from 1997/98 with links to full-text versions where available; details of government Green and White Papers from 1992/93; and

- summaries of articles published in a range of key practitioner journals.

2.7.2 Free Online Legal Information

The massive improvements in both communications and database technology over the last decade have unleashed the potential for storing and sharing large quantities of legal information across the web. The global Legal Information Institutes (LII) network, which started in the US, Australia, and the Netherlands in the 1990s in particular has become a central pillar of what is known as the Free Access to Law Movement and the WorldLII collaborative portal now provides access to over 800 databases from 40 countries. In fact, the quality and quantity of free legal information is improving very rapidly, to the extent that, as long ago as 2008, the American Bar Association's *Legal Technology Survey Report* found that, for the first time slightly more lawyers in the US were making use of free legal information retrieval than subscription services. This does not yet mean that we can obtain from public sites everything that is available commercially, nor does it mean that searchability is necessarily as easy or sophisticated, but public access has nonetheless improved considerably in terms of quality and quantity. We will look at what is available, first, in terms of primary sources, and then secondary sources.

Primary sources

Table 2.2 provides details of some key free legal information providers, particularly useful for UK law students. The basic reliability of information from these sites is as good as the commercial sites, though it will lack the add-ons that you pay for—essentially annotation, updating, and the slicker interface and search functionality.

Table 2.2 Useful 'free' websites for legal research

Legislation:	www.legislation.gov.uk/	Full text of all public Acts of the UK Parliament from 1988. Acts of the Scottish Parliament (1999–) and Northern Ireland Assembly (2000–), and Welsh Assembly Acts (2011—) and Measures (2007–11). UK SIs from 1987; Northern Irish statutory orders (1991–), Scottish and Welsh SIs (1999–).
	www.bailii.org	The British and Irish Legal Information Institute's full text database of UK statutes (1988–), Northern Irish statutes (1945–), Irish statutes (Republic) (1922–), Acts of the Scottish Parliament and Welsh Assembly Measures. Also a range of English, Scottish, Irish, and Welsh SIs.
	http://services.parliament.uk/bills/	Full text of Bills presented before Parliament in the current session, and Bills from previous sessions since 2001–2.
Case law:	www.bailii.org	Full text of decisions of the Supreme Court (2009–), HL, PC, CA (all complete from 1996–) and the High Court (from various start dates). Also decisions of the Scottish Court of Session (1998–) and High Court (1998–), and of the Northern Ireland Court of Appeal (1998–). ECJ decisions since 1954; all CFI/GC decisions. A range of reported tribunal decisions. Content is being added regularly to earlier years.

Table 2.2 continued

	www.supremecourt.uk www.publications. parliament.uk/pa/ld/ ldjudgmt.htm	Full text of Supreme Court decisions (from October 2009). Full text versions of all House of Lords' judgments from 14 November 1996–30 July 2009.
	www.iclr.co.uk	Incorporated Council of Law Reporting site, containing its 'WLR Daily' feature. This service, updated daily Monday–Friday provides summaries of important new decisions of the ECJ, HL, CA, and High Court prior to their appearing in the published Law Reports series.
	www.curia.europa.eu	Court of Justice of the European Communities: contains documentation relating to the ECJ, all cases decided by the ECJ and CFI since June 1997, and a weekly list of recent proceedings (opinions and judgments).
	www.echr.coe.int	European Court of Human Rights: searchable full-text database of cases. Also has full text of the Rules of the Court and the ECHR and its Protocols.
UK Parliament:	www.parliament.uk/	Gateway to House of Lords and House of Commons websites, with information on their functions and activities, and access to the Information Offices of both Houses. Can also be used to access parliamentary publications.
	www.publications. parliament.uk/pa/ pahansard.htm	Full text of the House of Lords Hansard (debates, oral and written questions) from November 1995. Full text of House of Commons Hansard (debates, oral and written questions); complete from the start of session in November 1988.
Other useful sources:	www.worldlii.org	899 databases of legal information from 123 countries and territories including the UK and Ireland (based on the BAILII databases), the USA, Canada, Hong Kong, South Africa, Australasia, and the South Pacific. Also provides access to over 20,000 journal articles, chiefly from Australasia.
	www.direct.gov.uk	Gateway to a vast range of sites created by UK central government departments (including the Ministry of Justice and the Home Office), government agencies and local authorities. Of variable utility.

www.justice.gov.uk/	UK government's Ministry of Justice site: contains useful information on law reform, the administration of justice, court rules, and Ministry-supported research publications.
http://europa.eu	Gateway to the multilingual EU website. Contains information, statistics, and extensive documentation on the EU, its legislation, and institutions, including the courts.
www.judiciary.gov.uk/	Judiciary of England and Wales site. Includes statistics, judicial biographies, practice directions, and guidance.

Secondary sources

It is also becoming easier to access some secondary sources online, though coverage is far more patchy and *ad hoc*, and you need to take steps to verify the quality of what you have found.

Useful websites worth considering, include:

- Social Science Research Network (SSRN) at http://ssrn.com: the SSRN is a large multi-disciplinary searchable database containing abstracts of around 635,000 scholarly working papers and forthcoming papers and an Electronic Paper Collection currently containing over 523,000 downloadable full-text documents in Adobe Acrobat pdf format. A Legal Scholarship Network Research Paper series forms a significant part of this database, with the Network primarily made up of contributing Law Schools. There is a predominance of US material, but a significant number of leading law schools from the UK and other jurisdictions are using SSRN to profile their research. It includes both externally published work and institutional 'working papers'.

- WorldLII (see **Table 2.2**) includes a limited range of journals in full text. The material is predominantly from Australia and New Zealand, and includes virtually all of the university-based law reviews in those jurisdictions, plus a small amount of material from Europe and Asia-Pacific.

- ResearchGate and Academia: these are used by growing numbers of academics to publicise and self-publish their work. There is no editorial or institutional quality control, though a high proportion of the papers uploaded are drafts or final versions of published work. It is most easily searched by author name or keyword, though publications may also show up via more refined Google searches.

- Institutional repositories and research centres: for more specialist work, where you are concentrating on a specific research topic, or want to follow up the work of a particular individual or research centre, it is worth checking their university webpages, as some full-text publications may be accessible there.

None of these strategies will give you the range or depth of material you would find via commercial databases, largely because of the copyright restrictions imposed by some journal publishers. There is also no specialist search engine that is particularly effective at distinguishing academic publications from other material, though Google

Scholar can be helpful in identifying published research for which free access copies are also available. If you are not familiar with Google Scholar, you can access it by typing 'scholar' in the Google search box. For easy access you can also install a Scholar 'button' from the settings page into your browser.

There is thus much more public access to legal information than there used to be, and it is increasingly stable: most of these sites and URLs have not changed since the last edition in 2013, and many have now been in existence for fifteen to twenty years, which is an eternity in IT terms. We are thus already at a point where public knowledgeability of law is determined far more by access to computer resources than to conventional library materials.

2.7.3 Search Techniques

Most online systems (commercial and public) have little in the way of organising or indexing, other than into broadly thematic but large-scale libraries of data. So what most systems use is a technique of searching by matching keywords or phrases entered by the user to the text contained in the database.

In technical terms this involves a system of what is called 'Boolean searching' (Leith, 1991). This engages fairly simple word-matching techniques, so that, for example, if you search for cases containing the word 'knife', that is precisely what you will get—all cases in which the word knife appears, regardless of its legal significance. You will likely be familiar with this problem already from your experience of using generic search engines like Google or Bing. This is probably the greatest practical limitation of such systems, as it means they are not very effective if you are trying to research concepts, particularly concepts which are difficult to define.

An example of such is 'good faith', which is an important concept relating to contract law. However, it is extremely difficult to define, is not always identified by name, and arises in a range of legal contexts, as well as being a term that may be used colloquially. As a result it is almost impossible to construct an effective Boolean search related to that concept.

Against this, these systems do have the advantage of being *interactive*. It is not necessary to get one's search terms exactly right first time; it is quite possible to modify a search request in response to the information that one has received from the system already. In developing search terms, it is important to note that various systems use particular words to enable you to structure your request with some degree of precision. These special words are normally referred to as *connectors* or *logical operators*. This means that those particular terms will not actually be searched for, but will tell the system how your search terms relate to each other. The main connectors can be described diagrammatically as shown in **Figure 2.5**.

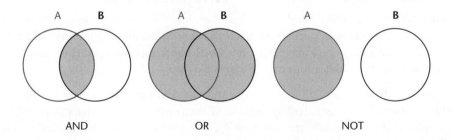

Figure 2.5 Logical operators

As you can see, there are essentially three ways in which search terms can be connected; we have identified them by the most commonly used connectors AND, OR, and NOT (the precise terms used and variety of connectors will vary from system to system):

- AND will search documents for terms A and B, and will retrieve those only where *both* terms are discovered (here represented by the shaded area in the two circles). LexisLibrary and Westlaw also have a rather more sophisticated proximity connector which enables you to specify the maximum number of words you want separating your search terms, e.g. 'cat w/3 dog' in LexisLibrary will retrieve only those documents where 'cat' occurs within three or fewer words either side of 'dog'; similarly 'cat/s dog' in Westlaw will find documents where cat and dog are in the same sentence (whereas AND will retrieve any documents where both your research terms occur, regardless of proximity).
- OR will retrieve all documents containing *either or both* search terms A and B.
- NOT enables you to search for term A, but *excludes* documents which also contain word B.

The technicality of Boolean searching undoubtedly limits the research utility of electronic systems, and may well be one reason why it is estimated that Boolean searching alone may retrieve as little as 25 per cent of the relevant information from a system (Poynder, 1994). A number of search engines such as Google and information retrieval systems, including LexisLibrary and Westlaw, have developed a facility for *natural language searching*, which enables you to enter search terms in 'natural language' or 'free text' as it is sometimes called—in other words 'plain English', if you prefer. The process of keyword selection and pattern matching is then completed by the software. Natural language searching is not necessarily superior to Boolean. Most natural language systems simply convert into Boolean by selecting those words that appear to be searchable. The selection mechanism can be relatively crude, so a natural language search can actually throw up more irrelevant material than a well-constructed Boolean search.

2.7.4 Verifying Electronic Sources

If you are drawing on material from sites other than credible commercial or public legal information services, you need to think carefully about whether that material is likely to be accurate and from a credible source, and therefore something you should rely on. You need to be able to evaluate whether you have something written by the idiot or by Einstein, or someone somewhere between the two. There is no absolutely foolproof test of quality, but the following checks are common sense, and will help in most cases:

- Who is the author? If the paper doesn't have a name, that may be a warning in itself, though it is not determinative as some publications are 'staff papers' written under the name of the employing institution. Equally, even if a paper has a person's name and their institutional (e.g. university) affiliation, how do you know whether they are a student or a professor? If there is a name, search against it: what do they do? Where are they employed? What else have they published?

- Who is the publisher? Has the paper been published by a reputable publisher or institution? Or is it self-published? If so it may be risky to rely on it without further contextual information about the author and the paper's provenance. For example, is it a pre-publication draft? If so can you find anything to indicate the published version exists? Can you get the final published version?

- What else can you find out from the paper itself? Read it, don't just cherry-pick the bit you like! Does it make sense? Is it well-written? Does it reference other work or relevant legal sources that you might expect to see?

- What can you learn from its context? What other kinds of material are on the same website? Are there links to other sites? If there is an 'about us' section, what does it tell you about the organisation?

- Has it been referred to by anyone else? Put the title into Google Scholar and see if it comes up with any citations. Don't worry too much if the number is relatively small, most academic work gets read chiefly by closest collaborators, immediate family, your worst enemy, and the occasional pet hamster. (Except, of course, where the pet hamster is a co-author: see A.K. Geim and H.A.M.S. ter Tisha, 'Detection of earth's rotation with a diamagnetically levitating gyroscope' (2001) *Physica* B 294–5, 736-9. You can get away with things like that when you are a Nobel prizewinner.)

CONCLUSION

In this chapter we have introduced you to some of the challenges of research in a digital age; to the core dimensions of information literacy, and to the main resources and techniques required to undertake both conventional paper and electronic legal research. Research skills are critical. They are emphasised both in the Quality Assurance Agency's 'Benchmark' statement of skills required of the law degree, and in the requirements of the Solicitors Regulation Authority and Bar Standards Board at the professional stage of training, and there are concerns about students' performance in this area. But you will not get proficient in these skills just by reading this book. We have provided you with a start, and some reference resources to dip into if you get stuck; that is all. As with all skills, mastery lies in action, not reading! Get familiar with your library, use the training available, and get comfortable with the technology—the days are now long gone when any lawyer—academic or practising—can afford to be a technophobe.Finally, before moving on to **Chapter 3**, you will find a couple of exercises based upon some of the material in this chapter, and intended to help you to test your research skills.

EXERCISE 1 Flick-knives for sale

If you were wondering whether you would ever find the answer to the problem we have used to develop the themes of this book, now is *your* chance to find out. See if you can find answers to the following questions. If you can, you will have the basic material to advise our fictitious friend.

continued

EXERCISE 1 *continued*

Q QUESTIONS

(a) Using the paper or online version of *Halsbury's Laws*, find the volume number and paragraph containing information on criminal liability for the display and sale of flick-knives.

(b) Using any appropriate research strategy, what is the current **statutory** provision governing that liability?

(c) Can you find any **cases** on the interpretation of that provision?

(d) Using your research, what is your advice?

A ANSWERS

(a) In this case a simple online search for 'flick knives' or 'flick knife' will give you three options: 'hire of chattells'; 'carrying offensive weapons in a public place', and (bingo!) 'manufacture and sale, etc., of arms and offensive weapons'. The same result can be achieved using the paper index. Both refer you to vol. 11(1), para. 705 (2006 reissue). Be aware that a simple search like this doesn't always produce results, or, more likely, it will produce too many results, most of which are not relevant. In that situation you need to refine your search (and that sometimes means doing some initial research to discover more or more effective keywords that you could use).

(b) Volume 11 of *Halsbury's* refers you to the Restriction of Offensive Weapons Act 1959 s. 1(1), as amended. The latest amendment noted in that volume refers to the Criminal Justice Act 1988. On the electronic version, you can click on the section and it will take you to the source statute within LexisLibrary. If you scroll that page to the heading 'Amendment', it shows that the section has not been further amended since 1988. Searching online for related commentary will also quickly disclose that a separate offence exists of selling knives to persons under eighteen under s. 141A of the Criminal Justice Act 1988, but that knives expressly covered by s. 1 of the 1959 Act are excluded from that provision (meaning that sale to a person under 18 would be charged under the 1959 Act, s. 1, not s. 141A of the 1988 Act).

(c) Volume 11(1) para. 705 mentions no cases; that is misleading, they do exist! Interestingly, if you search from s. 1 for related cases online, it only comes up with one case, *British Car Auctions* v *Wright* (1972), which cites *Fisher* v *Bell*, but is not otherwise on point. This just goes to show that the online systems are not foolproof. However, if you go to s. 1 again and click on related commentary, it will lead you to *Blackstone's Criminal Practice*, and this cites a number of cases: *Lawrence* (1971) 57 Cr App R 64, *Allamby* [1974] 1 WLR 1494, *Gibson v Wales* [1983] 1 WLR 393, and *Simpson* [1983] 1 WLR 1494.

(d) Your advice should take into account that, though initially it was not an offence to offer a flick-knife for sale (*Fisher* v *Bell*), the Act has been amended. As a result it is now an offence not only to sell, but also to have on display or in one's possession, a flick-knife for sale.

EXERCISE 2 Researching the web

Using web-based legal resources, where would you find the following:

Q QUESTIONS

(a) The latest reported decision on circumstances in which a court may make a declaration of incompatibility under section 4, Human Rights Act 1998.

(b) The text of the Criminal Procedure Rules 2015.

(c) Statistics on the number of ethnic minority judges in England & Wales.

(d) Information on the progress of Bills in the current session of Parliament.

(e) The names of the Advocates General of the European Court of Justice.

(f) The decision of the House of Lords in *Pepper* v *Hart* [1993].

(g) Citations of *Pepper* v *Hart* in UK cases decided after 1 January 2003.

(h) References to the case 202/89 *European Commission* v *United Kingdom* in later decisions of the ECJ.

(i) An authoritative version of Article 62 of the Treaty of Rome.

(j) An authoritative version of Article 3 of the European Convention on Human Rights.

For obvious reasons we have not given the answers here—you will find them on our Online Resource Centre.

CHAPTER REFERENCES

BERNERS-LEE, T. (2000), *Weaving the Web* (New York: HarperCollins).

BING, J. (2010), 'Let There Be LITE: A Brief History of Legal Information Retrieval' 1 *European Journal of Law & Technology*, No. 1. Available at http://ejlt.org/article/view/15.

JACKSON, R. (1970), 'Police Search—Law Reports—Law Reform by Precedent', *Cambridge Law Journal* 1.

LAFRANCE, A. (2015), 'Raiders of the Lost Web' *The Atlantic*, 14 October 2015. Available at http://www.theatlantic.com/technology/archive/2015/10/raiders-of-the-lost-web/409210/

LEITH, P. (1991), *The Computerised Lawyer* (London: Springer-Verlag).

LETR REPORT (2013), *Setting Standards: The Future of Legal Services Education and Training Regulation in England and Wales* (Coventry: Legal Education and Training Review). Available at http://letr.org.uk/the-report/index.html.

PARKER, J. (2011), 'The Soundscape of Justice' 20 *Griffith Law Review*, 962.

PAYNE, R. (1983), 'Lawtel: A Prestel-based Legal Retrieval Service', in *The Progress in Legal Information Systems in Europe* (Strasbourg: Council of Europe).

POYNDER, R. (1994), 'Beyond Boolean', *Information World Review*, July/August, 14.

RAISTRICK, D. (2008), *Index to Legal Citations and Abbreviations* (3rd edn, London: Sweet & Maxwell).

SHERWIN, R.K. (2011), *Visualizing Law in the Age of the Digital Baroque: Arabesques and Entanglements* (New York: Routledge).

*SUSSKIND, R. (2013), *Tomorrow's Lawyers: An Introduction to Your Future* (Oxford: Oxford University Press).

TUNKEL, V. (1993), 'Legal Research after *Pepper* v *Hart*', 90 *Law Society's Gazette*, 12 May 1993, 17.

3

Reading the Law

In this chapter we focus on another important dimension of legal information literacy: the ability to read critically and with understanding. This is a fundamental precursor to the third major arm of literacy (discussed in **Chapter 4**), the ability to produce academic and, ultimately, professional communications appropriate to your audience.

Much of this book is concerned with principles of interpretation—both of legislation and of cases. At its heart, any process of interpretation is one of reading. Reading is an activity that can be carried on at different levels. If you have ever studied literature, you will be familiar with the idea of reading as a search for layers of meaning. For example, one does not find in Dickens's *Hard Times* just the story of the characters involved, but also a powerful critique of mid-Victorian social values, and a particular attack on the doctrine of utilitarianism which dominated that age.

Legal texts can similarly be seen as displaying layers of meaning. These layers broadly correspond to the three questions that we might ask about a legal text, what we call the *What, How & Why* of law, that is:

(a) *What* kind of law is it?

(b) *How* does it affect existing law?

(c) *Why* was it made?

At the first level (*what*), the form of the document itself tells us something about it. If, for example, it takes the form of an Act of Parliament, we know that it takes precedence over case law.

At another level (*how*) we must work out what it is actually about; this is a matter of constructing meaning from the text. Again, the way in which legal documents are put together can sometimes help us in this task, but also hinder (see further **Chapter 8**).

At a third level, legal texts contain a deeper meaning, which may help us to answer the question *why* the law has developed in such a way. Legislation has a history which may reflect particular economic, political, or social values. Court decisions may also reflect a variety of underlying influences, for example: the values which the legal system has traditionally served; the prejudices of a particular judge; or the perceived internal logic of the case-law system. Asking *why* may involve an element of historical analysis (e.g. to see how a law has developed over the years—though note that, traditionally, reading the law has been treated as a largely ahistorical process), or a consideration of governmental or judicial policy making. This will help us to understand the reasoning behind the court's decision in a case, or why an Act with those particular provisions was passed at that particular time.

In this chapter, we shall consider primarily the questions *what* and *why*. In looking at the structure of legal rules, we may occasionally trespass on the territory of *how*, though that will generally be left to later chapters. In so doing, we have broken this chapter down into three sections: reading legislation; reading cases; and reading literary sources.

3.1 Reading Legislation

In this section we will look at two kinds of legislation in depth: UK Acts of Parliament and EU regulations and directives.

3.1.1 Acts of Parliament

Once a bill has received the royal assent it becomes an Act of Parliament. An Act (note that the word 'Act' when used in this sense is always capitalised) is a public document and must be published by The Stationery Office; it will also, as we have seen, be published in a variety of other sources. A copy of such an Act is reproduced in **Figure 3.1**.

3.1.2 The Elements of an Act of Parliament

Any modern Act of Parliament will take the following form (each number here corresponds to that on **Figure 3.1**):

(1) short title;

(2) citation;

(3) long title;

(4) date of royal assent;

(5) sections; and

(6) marginal note.

In addition to these, copies of the statutes may also contain:

(a) enacting formula;

(b) textual amendments and annotations;

(c) date of commencement; and

(d) schedules and tables.

We shall now consider each of these in the order in which they appear in the Act. The numbers or letters in bold text after each heading refer to the illustration.

Long and short titles (3) & (1)

Modern Acts will have both a **long** and **short title**:

- the long title describes the general scope of the Act; and
- the short title is for convenience of citation.

Early Acts were enacted without a short title, and therefore tended formally to be known by their long titles. Thus, the famous Bill of Rights 1689 was originally known as *An Act*

| (1) | PUBLIC LAVATORIES (TURNSTILES) ACT 1963 (c. 32) | (2) |

Ss. 1,2

| (3) | An Act to make it the duty of local authorities to abolish turnstiles in public lavatories and sanitary conveniences. | |

| (4) | [31st July 1963] | |

Abolition of turnstiles.

| (6) | 1.—(1) Every turnstile in any part of a public lavatory or public sanitary convenience controlled or managed by a local authority, or in any entrance or exit of such a public lavatory or convenience, shall be removed not later than six months after the passing of this Act; and after the passing of this Act no turnstile shall be installed in, or in any entrance or exit of, any such public lavatory or convenience. | (5) |

(2) It shall be the duty of local authorities to ensure that the provisions of this Act are complied with notwithstanding anything in any other Act, whether public or local.

(3) If any local authority in England and Wales fail to discharge a duty imposed on them by the foregoing provisions of this section, that duty shall be enforceable, on the application of [¹the Secretary of State], by mandamus.

(4) There shall be paid out of moneys provided by Parliament any increase attributable to this Act in the sums of payable by way of Rate-deficiency Grant or Exchequer Equalisation Grant under the enactments relating to local government in England and Wales or in Scotland.

1972 c. 70.
1939 c. 40.

| (b) | (5) In this section the expression "local authority" means, in England and Wales, a local authority within the meaning of [²the Local Government Act 1972], a local authority within the meaning of the London Government Act 1939 or the Common Council of the City of London and, in Scotland, the council of a county, the town council of a burgh or a district council. | |

Short title and extent.

2.—(1) This Act may be cited as the Public Lavatories (Turnstiles) Act 1963.

(2) This Act shall not extend to Northern Ireland.

¹ Words substituted by virtue of (W.) S.I. 1965/319, arts. 2(1), 10(1)(a), Sch. 1
Pt. I and (E.) 1970/1681, arts. 2(1), 6(3)
² Words substituted by virtue of Local Government Act 1972 (c. 70), s. 272(2)

| | | (b) |

Figure 3.1 A Public General Act from Statutes in Force

Declaring the Rights and Liberties of the Subject and Settling the Succession of the Crown. It only formally acquired the short title of the Bill of Rights by virtue of a later enact-ment—the Short Titles Act 1896—which created short titles for a number of impor-tant earlier statutes. Very occasionally the short title of an Act may be changed by later legislation. This has happened recently with the Supreme Court Act 1981, which has been renamed the 'Senior Courts Act 1981' by the Constitutional Reform Act 2005, following the renaming of the Supreme Court of Judicature (the High Court and Court of Appeal) as the Senior Courts of England and Wales. This was done to avoid confusion with the UK Supreme Court.

As neither the short nor the long title provides more than the most general indication of what the Act is about, they are of very little help in deducing the scope or meaning of legislation. By contrast, older Acts contain a *Preamble*, following after the long title, which introduces the legislation, often in some detail, and usually explains why it had been passed. This device is not used in modern statutes. The Preambles to the older Acts are used as an aid to interpreting those particular Acts (see **Chapter 9**). This difference may seem rather odd; why should a preamble be of use when the long title is not? The answer lies in the fact that they serve diverse functions.

Consider, for example, an Act you may meet in the law of contract: the Unfair Contract Terms Act 1977 (referred to here as UCTA). The short title does not tell you, in fact, that the Act is concerned with exclusion clauses in contracts. The long title is not much more help.

> An Act to impose further limits on the extent to which under the Law of England and Wales and Northern Ireland civil liability for breach of contract, or for negligence or other breach of duty, can be avoided by means of contract terms or otherwise, and under the Law of Scotland civil liability can be avoided by means of contract terms.

In this way, they are perhaps analogous to the label on a jam jar. If you look at a jar, you will usually find the title in large letters on the front—STRAWBERRY JAM—but that does not really tell you what is in the jar. It does no more than broadly identify the product to us. You need to look much more closely to find that the jar does not just contain strawberries and sugar, but also, say, pectin, citric acid, and sodium citrate, and often a collection of 'E numbers' as well. So it is with an Act. To find out what it is really about you need to look at the contents (i.e. the operative sections) in detail. By comparison, preambles served to give the courts some notice of parliamentary intent, though even then, this was often in rather vague terms.

This does not mean that the long title is wholly useless; it will give you a general indication of the scope of the Act and, together with the contents list which sometimes precedes it (usually headed *Arrangement of Sections*), it can be helpful in establishing a sense of the Act's contents and structure when *skim reading* (see section **3.3.3**).

One other innovation that has developed since 1999 (but not shown here) is the creation of 'Explanatory Notes' to accompany Bills presented to Parliament. These notes are rather like an extended preamble, and may be helpful in understanding the context and purpose of the Act. As such, they may be used as a limited aid to interpretation. Lord Steyn endorsed reference to explanatory notes in *R* v *Chief Constable of South Yorkshire Police ex parte LS and Marper* [2004] UKHL 39, in the following terms:

> Explanatory Notes are not endorsed by Parliament. On the other hand, in so far as they cast light on the setting of a statute, and the mischief at which it is aimed, they are admissible in aid of construction of the statute. After all, they may potentially contain much more immediate and valuable material than other aids regularly used by the courts, such as Law Commission Reports, Government Committee reports, Green Papers, and so forth.

Citation (2)

Statutes obviously have their short title and the year of their creation cited, but, as we explained in the previous chapter, they also have what is known as a **Chapter number**. If a Statute was the fiftieth to be passed in 1977 then it will have that number. This is a means of reference only and is therefore neither very helpful nor exciting.

Royal assent (4)

No statute is law until assented to (i.e. formally agreed to) by the Monarch. The date of assent is given in the statute—in UCTA it is 26 October 1977. Frequently this is the date on which the Act becomes law. However, the Act may state that all or part of it will come into effect at a later date (in UCTA's case this was 1 February 1978) or at a date to be appointed by the appropriate minister. Different parts of the Act can thus come into effect at different times. Obviously this may have important practical consequences for the advice lawyers give. Inevitably it can make life very complicated, where you need to know which rules have already come into force, which have an agreed date for their introduction, and which do not.

Enacting formula (a)

Although not always reproduced in *Statutes in Force* (they are missing from our example), these are introductory words which appear in every Act stating that both Houses of Parliament and the Monarch have passed the Act. The form of words used is identical in every case, and is of long historical standing. They are of little practical legal significance, though the publication of the Act with these words is taken as conclusive evidence that the Act has been passed and is good law. Because of their different legislative competence Acts of the Scottish Parliament and Welsh Assembly Acts and Measures have differently worded enacting formulae, but the underlying principle is the same: it creates the presumption that the legislation is properly made.

The enacting formula normally follows directly after the long title. In online versions of the statutes (at www.legislation.gov.uk) these are now jointly referred to as 'Introductory Text'.

Sections (5)

All Acts are divided into sections—these are usually cited in an abbreviated form as s. 1 or s. 2, or (in the plural) ss. 2 and 3. Sometimes it may be possible to perceive a logical development of concepts as the sections progress, but this is not always the case, so you may, in resolving a single problem, find yourself starting at s. 1, which is qualified by something in s. 3, which contains terms defined in s. 45 and repeals part of an earlier enactment listed in sch. 4! We provide further discussion and specific examples of how statutes are organised in **Chapter 8**.

Each section will often be divided into **subsections**—cited as section 1(1) or section 1(4). After subsections we can have **paragraphs**—cited as section 1(1)(a) or section 1(2)(g); and even **sub-paragraphs**, as in section 1(1)(a)(i). Section 3 of UCTA has such a division. If you have ever tried to draft the rules of a committee or a game, you will appreciate that this device can be used to split up ideas or clarify particular points. Thus, each separate section of an Act may deal with a separate issue (though these sections may often remain closely related), and each subsection (etc.) within a section may express a different aspect of that issue. For example, if you have a definition section, it may be that the phrase to be defined has more than one statutory meaning, in which case you could use a different subsection for each meaning.

Often, you will also find that groups of sections dealing with the same point have *headings* and that very large groupings are divided into *parts*. These titles are of little value as an interpretative aid; they are essentially a form of indexing. At best they will indicate some general thematic coherence among the sections under that heading.

Marginal notes (6)

Most Acts display marginal notes as a kind of quick reference mechanism to help you find the section you want.

Amendments and annotations (b)

In *Statutes in Force*, and the revised statutes on legislation.gov.uk, it is normal for any amendments to an Act made subsequent to its passing to be incorporated into the text. As in the illustrated Act, the amendments are shown within square brackets in *Statutes in Force*, and by a different text colour on legislation.gov.uk. These amendments are cited as being part of the Act, and have the full force of law. Any footnotes or commentary annotated to an Act (as, e.g., in *Current Law Statutes Annotated*) do not form part of the Act and, of course, have no direct legal effect.

Date of commencement (c)

Acts will normally have a specific commencement section near to the end of the statute. It may either state that the Act, or parts of the Act, will come into force on a specific date or dates, or that it comes into force on a date to be fixed by the relevant government minister. On the latter occasions the normal form of words runs more or less as follows:

> this Act shall come into force on such day as the Secretary of State may by order appoint; and different days may be so appointed for different provisions or different purposes of the same provision...

This gives the minister *carte blanche* in deciding what comes into force and when.

Schedules (d)

Schedules (the term may be abbreviated to 'sched.' or 'sch.') can be found at the end of most Acts of Parliament. Schedules are parts of an Act that provide more detail regarding sections or groups of sections. Sometimes they give examples of how to calculate things contained in the Act, such as pensions, tax assessments, and so on; sometimes they simply expand upon phrases; sometimes they define phrases; or sometimes they contain detailed amendments of earlier legislation. As such, they may be quite detailed, perhaps even exceeding the length of the rest of the Act. Each provision within a schedule is called a **paragraph**, and there may also be **sub-paragraphs**. So, a provision is properly cited in the form 'sch. 1, para. 3(a)'.

A schedule, normally the last, tells you which earlier Acts the present statute repeals. This is important because, generally speaking, once an Act is passed it remains in force until repealed by another Act. This is why vestiges of the Witchcraft Acts were still in force as late as 1951 and why other such anachronisms remain 'on the Statute book'. By an odd quirk it also meant that, in English law, the USA did not gain its independence until 1963!

Note, here, that though lawyers sometimes talk of Acts being 'obsolete', there is no formal basis upon which an Act could be disapplied by the courts simply because it has become old or out of date. At most it can be argued that a statute should not apply to a novel situation, because that situation was not within the original legislative intent; this reflects what is sometimes called *the principle of contemporary exposition*: see *Aerated Bread Co. Ltd* v *Gregg* (1873) LR 8 QB 355. In this case Blackburn J. refused to apply provisions of the Bread Act 1836 regarding 'fancy bread' to the plaintiff's product, because at the time the Act was passed, the term had a very specific meaning, which could not be applied to the disputed product some thirty-six years later.

Some obsolete legislation is periodically repealed by the passing of Statute Law Revision Acts or Legislative Reform Orders, which are purely administrative measures intended to tidy up the statute book.

3.1.3 European Legislation

As we noted in **Chapter 1**, European legislation comprises a combination of treaty articles, regulations, directives, and decisions. In style these follow a broadly similar pattern. In terms of EU legislative acts (note: not capitalised), this structure reflects the Rules of Procedure for drafting laid down by the European Council—see Council Decision 2006/683/EC, Euratom (OJ L 285, 16.10.2006, p. 47)—which require the following components:

(a) title of the legislative act;

(b) enacting formula;

(c) reference to the 'legal basis' of the legislation;

(d) a statement of reasons;

(e) the 'enacting terms'; and

(f) signatures.

EU legislative acts may vary from two or three pages to very lengthy, technical, documents. We have not produced an actual facsimile here, however, we will discuss the main points, and particularly the points of difference from UK legislation, that it may help you to be aware of:

(a) **Title**: The title of each legislative act states its legal form (regulation, directive, decision), its unique identifier, date of adoption, and a narrative description of its subject matter, akin to what we, in the English context, would think of as the long title, thus:

DIRECTIVES

DIRECTIVE 2009/12/EC OF THE EUROPEAN PARLIAMENT AND OF THE COUNCIL

of 11 March 2009

on airport charges

There is no formal equivalent in EU legislation to the UK concept of a 'short title'. Note also that the formal date of adoption will commonly be different from the date the legislative act as a whole, or the dates at which different specific provisions, come into force. The latter will be spelled out as part of the enacting terms:

(b) **Enacting formula**: This takes a very different form from UK legislation. It has two simple parts, bracketed around elements (c) and (d) below: it starts by identifying the law-maker, and then uses the words, 'has adopted' to indicate the process of enactment. So, for example:

> THE COUNCIL OF THE EUROPEAN UNION . . .
> HAS ADOPTED THIS REGULATION

(c) **Legal basis:** all EU legislation must have a basis in one of the founding treaties. Without such a basis it would not be valid law. Consequently it is necessary to identify the relevant treaty under which each legislative act is made, thus:

> Having regard to the Treaty establishing the European Community, and in particular Articles 60 and 301 thereof

The legal basis will also often make reference to other legislative acts and opinions that provide the legal context within which this legislative act will sit:

(d) **Statement of reasons:** this is akin to the preamble in a UK Act, or what we call the recitals of a treaty. It helps to provide a context for interpretation by explaining how and why the act has come about, and in particular explains the legislative background or history of the legislation. This may include references to earlier proposals and consultation documents. These are called *travaux préparatoires* ('working papers' or 'preparatory texts') which may help identify why the legislation was introduced, and thence how it should be applied. This explicit mapping out of the background makes that legislative history transparent to anyone reading the legislation, and therefore easier to research. It is introduced by the word 'Whereas'.

(e) **Enacting terms:** i.e. the substantive, operative, provisions of the act. These are conventionally organised as 'Articles' (broadly equivalent to our 'sections') and in larger and more complex pieces of legislation, these are grouped into thematically organised parts variously called 'Chapters', 'Titles', or (confusingly for us) 'Sections'. At the detailed level, the actual style of drafting is rather different from what we are used to in the UK. Articles are written in more 'everyday' language (so far as possible), and in a more narrative style—generally with less subdivision into subsections and paragraphs than in English legislation. This reflects the strong influence of civil law drafting traditions on EU practice (see **Chapter 8**).

(f) **Signatures:** every piece of legislation is signed by an authorised signatory of the relevant law-making institution or institutions, e.g. the President of the Commission or Council, or the relevant commissioner responsible for that part of the Commission's legislative programme.

The complexity of the EU legislative process is quite considerable (see Robinson, 2008). Although each legislative act is drafted and revised in only one authoritative language—usually English or French—it must normally be translated into all of the official languages of the EU. Strict guidelines therefore exist on the layout and formatting of legislation, and on language usage in the official languages. Nevertheless, there have been longstanding concerns about the quality (Robinson, 2008: 182–6) and quantity of legislation. An extensive simplification and codification process began in 2005. This reduced the EU 'statute book' by some 5,000 pages in the first four years. Moreover, data suggest that the volume of new legislation being passed has also slowed since the early 2000s. Even so, it has been estimated that (using data to 2012) the EU still approves a lot of legislation: on average 80 directives, 1,200 regulations, and 700 decisions per year (Toshkov, n.d.).

3.2 Reading Cases

In this section we will look first at the form of English reports and then of European Union cases.

3.2.1 English Law Reports

Like statutes, modern English law reports tend to follow a standard format, similar to the illustration (see **Figure 3.2**) from *Finnegan v Clowney Youth Training Programme Ltd* [1990] 2 All ER 546. Running down the pages, you will find:

(1) The name of the case.

(2) The court in which it was heard.

(3) The names of the judge(s) presiding.

(4) The hearing date(s).

(5) The headnote.

(6) Notes of cross-references to *Halsbury's*.

(7) A list of cases referred to.

(8) Details of the appeal.

(9) The names of counsel appearing in the case.

(10) The judgment(s) (not shown).

(11) Letters in the margin.

Some of these are quite self-explanatory, so we will be selective in the points we discuss.

The name of the case (1)

It was said in **Chapter 2** that English case names follow the names of the parties involved. In this respect, common law case citations tend to differ from the forms adopted in many civilian systems, which often adopt a more anonymous, administrative title, based usually on the court, and a case number or date, though this is not always so. The French, for example, use both styles. Cases before the *Cour de Cassation* are cited by giving an abbreviated version of the division concerned (*civile, criminelle, sociale, commerciale*),

Finnegan v Clowney Youth Training Programme Ltd

(1)

a

HOUSE OF LORDS (2)

LORD BRIDGE OF HARWICH, LORD GRIFFITHS, LORD ACKNER, LORD OLIVER OF AYLMERTON AND LORD LOWRY

(3)

2 APRIL, 17 MAY 1990   (4)

b

Northern Ireland – Employment – Discrimination against a woman – Provision in relation to retirement – Female employees required to retire at 60 whereas men retiring at 65 – Northern Ireland and English legislation identical – English legislation passed before adoption of EEC equal treatment directive whereas Northern Ireland legislation passed subsequent to directive – Whether Northern Ireland provision passed to implement directive – Whether Northern Ireland c *provision to be construed differently from English provision – Whether unlawful discrimination for women to be required to retire earlier than men – Whether necessary to refer question to European Court – Sex Discrimination (Northern Ireland) Order 1976, art 8(2)(4) – Council Directive (EEC) 76/207, art 5(1).*

European Economic Community – National legislation – Construction – Construction of legislation d *relating to death or retirement – Determination of case not dependent on question of Community law – Whether court should make reference to European Court.*

In February 1986 the employee, who was employed by the employer as a supervisor, was told that she would be required to retire on 1 April 1986 following her sixtieth birthday on 22 March. Her request to be allowed to continue working beyond her sixtieth
(5) birthday was refused and her employment was duly terminated on 1 April. The employee e made a complaint to an industrial tribunal alleging that she had been unlawfully discriminated against by the employer on the grounds of sex, contrary to art 8(2)ᵃ of the Sex Discrimination (Northern Ireland) Order 1976, in that she had been forced to retire at the age of 60 whereas male employees retired at 65. The employer relied on art 8(4)ᵇ of the 1976 order, which f provided that art 8(2) did not apply to provisions relating to death or retirement. The tribunal upheld the complaint and awarded the employee compensation, on the ground that art 8(2) and (4) had to be construed consistently with art 5(1)ᶜ of Council Directive (EEC) 76/207 (the equal treatment directive), which prohibited discrimination in working conditions, including conditions governing dismissal, on grounds of sex. The employer appealed to the g Court of Appeal in Northern Ireland, which allowed the appeal on the ground, inter alia, that art 8(2) of the 1976 order was to be given the same meaning as identical legislation in England which had been construed as permitting discrimination in retirement ages. The employee appealed to the House of Lords, contending, inter alia, that the English legislation was distinguishable since it had been passed before the equal treatment directive was adopted whereas the 1976 order had not been made until after the adoption of the directive, so that the order had to be construed in the light of the directive. The employee also requested h the court to seek a preliminary ruling from the Court of Justice of the European Communities (11) under art 177 of the EEC Treaty on the question which arose on the appeal.

Held — (1) Since art 8(4) of the 1976 order was in identical terms and in an identical context to the English legislation it must have been intended to have identical effect and should not be presumed to have been made for the purpose of implementing the equal

---

a   Article 8(2), so far as material, provides: 'It is unlawful for a person, in the case of a woman employed by him at an establishment in Northern Ireland, to discriminate against her . . . (b) by dismissing her, or subjecting her to any other detriment.'
b   Article 8(4) provides: 'Paragraphs . . . (2) do not apply to provision in relation to death or retirement.'
c   Article 5(1) is set out at p 548 *h*, post

Figure 3.2 An English Law Report

HL   **Finnegan v Clowney Youth Training Ltd**   **547**

---

a treatment directive, notwithstanding that the order was made subsequently to that directive. It followed that although the employee's compulsory retirement at the age of 60 was a contravention of art 8(2) of the 1976 order, since it discriminated against her on the grounds of sex, it was a provision in relation to death or retirement which fell within the exception permitted by art 8(4) and therefore did not constitute unlawful discrimination. The employee's dismissal therefore did not contravene art 8(2). The appeal would accordingly be dismissed
b (see pp 551 *a b d* to *f h* to p 552 *b*, post); *Duke v GEC Reliance Ltd* [1988] 1 All ER 626 applied; *Marshall v Southampton and South West Hampshire Area Health Authority (Teaching)* Case 152/84 [1986] 2 All ER 584 considered.

(2) Since it was for the United Kingdom courts to interpret the 1976 order and since the equal treatment directive did not have direct effect between citizens the determination of the appeal did not depend on any question of Community law. Accordingly, a reference
c to the European Court under art 177 was not necessary (see p 551 *h* to p 552 *b*, post).

Notes
For discrimination against employees, see 16 Halsbury's Laws (4th edn) paras 771·2, 771·5, and for cases on the subject, see 20 Digest (Reissue) 588-593, *4495-4515*.
For Community provisions on equal treatment of employees, see 52 Halsbury's Laws (4th
d edn) paras 21·13, 21·17.   (6)
For references to the Court of Justice of the European Communities for a preliminary ruling, see 51 ibid paras 3·79-3·81.
For the EEC Treaty, art 177, see 50 Halsbury's Statutes (4th edn) 325.
Article 8 of the Sex Discrimination (Northern Ireland) Order 1976 corresponds to s 6 of the Sex Discrimination Act 1975. For s 6 of the 1975 Act, see 6 ibid 702.
e

Cases referred to in opinions
Burton v British Railways Board Case 19/81 [1982] 3 All ER 537, [1982] QB 1080, [1982] 3 WLR 387, [1982] ECR 555, CJEC.
Duke v GEC Reliance Ltd [1988] 1 All ER 626, [1988] AC 618, [1988] 2 WLR 359, HL.
f Litster v Forth Dry Dock and Engineering Co Ltd [1989] 1 All ER 1134, [1990] AC 546, [1989] 2 WLR 634, HL.   (7)
Marshall v Southampton and South West Hampshire Area Health Authority (Teaching) Case 152/84 [1986] 2 All ER 584, [1986] QB 401, [1986] 2 WLR 780, [1986] ECR 723, CJEC.
Note [1966] 3 All ER 77, [1966] 1 WLR 1234, HL.
g Pickstone v Freemans plc [1988] 2 All ER 803, [1989] AC 66, [1989] 2 WLR 634, HL.
von Colson and Kamann v Land Nordrhein-Westfalen Case 14/83 [1984] ECR 1891.

Appeal
Frances Finnegan (the employee) appealed with leave of the Court of Appeal in Northern Ireland against the decision of that court (Hutton LCJ and Mac Dermott LJ) on 28 November
h 1988 allowing the appeal of the respondent, Clowney Youth Training Programme Ltd (the employer), by way of case stated by an industrial tribunal (J E Maguire chairman) sitting at Belfast on 23 November 1987 in respect of its decision that the employer had unlawfully discriminated against the employee on grounds of sex, contrary to the provisions of art 8 of the Sex Discrimination (Northern Ireland) Order 1976, SI 1976/1042, in compulsorily (8)
j retiring the employee at 60 when comparable male employees were allowed to work until the age of 65. The facts are set out in the opinion of Lord Bridge.

Patrick Coghlin QC and *Seamus Treacy* (both of the Northern Ireland Bar) for the employee. (9)
Patrick Markey QC and *Brian Kennedy* (both of the Northern Ireland Bar) for the employer.

Their Lordships took time for consideration.

Figure 3.2 Continued

the date of the decision, and its location in the relevant case reports. Conversely, decisions of the *Conseil d'Etat* are cited by case name.

By comparison, the more consistent English system sounds simple, but, as is so often the case, that impression is misleading; there is a wide array of forms that the case name can take. However, these forms can tell us quite a lot about the nature of the case.

In *civil* cases the normal mode of citation is the name of the person bringing the case or appeal (**claimant**, formerly *plaintiff*, or **appellant**) first followed by the name of the **defendant** (or **respondent** in an appeal): thus, '*Smith* v *Jones*'. The 'v' means *versus*, that is 'against' (reflecting the adversarial nature of the process); it is usually spoken as 'and', hence 'Smith and Jones'—spoken citations can thus sound confusing if there are more than two parties, as you will have a multiplicity of 'ands', one of which is a 'v'! If Jones were to lose his case and appeal, the form of citation should switch to '*Jones* v *Smith*'. For an apparently unfathomable reason this does not always happen. Four other forms of civil citations crop up with some regularity.

First, in shipping cases (a number of which come up in contract and commercial law), it is a convention to abbreviate the case name to that of the ship involved, so, for example, the case of *Compania Financiera Soleada SA, Netherlands Antilles Ships Management Corp. and Dammers and van der Heide's Shipping and Trading Co.* v *Hamoor Tanker Corp. Inc.* (1981) is mercifully known as *The Borag*. That abbreviation will be sufficient to find the case in most books or citators.

Secondly, cases may appear in the form '*Re Smith*' (where '*Re*' roughly means 'concerning'). This form arises in some property cases, particularly those relating to trusts or the estates of deceased persons. It is also used in cases where the court is considering its wardship jurisdiction (where the court effectively takes ultimate control over the affairs of a child). In the latter cases the name of the child will not normally be disclosed, and the case citation will appear as '*Re M*', for example. They are usually indexed under the name referred to, not under '*Re*'. (There are also other situations where the court will grant the parties anonymity to protect their privacy, so that parties are identified only by an initial letter, in the form of '*A* v *B*'.)

Thirdly, you may come across cases cited as '*In B*' or '*In E*'. These cases arise in the law relating to wills and estates. '*In B*' stands for '*In Bonis*' (in the goods of). '*In E*' stands for '*In the Estate of*'. The distinction arose because, prior to the 1897 Land Transfer Act, personal representatives could only deal with a deceased's goods, not their land. The citations reflect this. The equivalent cases nowadays use the form '*Re*', so it is increasingly unlikely that you will come across this form of citation.

Lastly, another form appears where the Administrative Court has exercised its public law jurisdiction judicially to review the administration or an inferior court. These cases were for a long time cited in the form '*R* v *Bloggs, ex parte Smith*', though with the move to anglicise English legal terminology the form of citation has changed, thus: *R (on the application of Smith)* v *Bloggs*. This is the only context when the Crown ('*R*') is commonly cited in civil proceedings. It reflects the fact that technically the action has been taken by the Crown, on the application of some other party, under what are, historically, the *prerogative* powers of the Crown. The term *ex parte* properly denotes someone who is outside the proceedings. In this situation it seems rather peculiar, though strictly correct, as it identifies the person who made the application for judicial review. *Criminal* cases are normally cited as '*R* v *Smith*'. The '*R*' stands for *Rex* or *Regina* (Latin for king and queen) denoting the state's role as **prosecutor**; the accused is normally cited as the

defendant. The oral form of the citation is 'the Crown against Smith', although it is usually abbreviated to just *Smith*.

Once again, there is a variety of alternative forms. Some criminal prosecutions can be commenced only with the approval of one of the government's law officers—the Attorney-General (A-G) or the Director of Public Prosecutions (DPP). In such cases that official's title will appear instead of the Crown as prosecutor. Some cases, notably those which commenced in the magistrates' courts before the Crown Prosecution Service was set up in 1985, bore the name of the (police) prosecutor (see, e.g., *Albert* v *Lavin* [1982] AC 546; [1981] 3 All ER 878). This principle still applies in those very rare cases where a member of the public brings a private prosecution.

The court and presiding judge(s) (2) and (3)

These are perhaps of greater significance than you might at first think. Given that our system of precedent depends upon a ranking of courts, we need to know whereabouts in the 'batting order' this particular case is placed. Furthermore, in cases before the Supreme Court (or House of Lords before that), Court of Appeal, and a Divisional Court of the High Court, it is normal to have more than one judge presiding. Sometimes the number, and even the status, of the judges presiding will influence the weight of that decision.

The headnote (5)

This does three things. First, it provides a brief statement of the **material facts** of the case. By facts we are talking about the description of events leading up to the case (see further **Chapters 5** and **7**); the term *material* denotes those facts which the judge considered important in deciding the case (we discuss the concept of materiality in detail in **Chapter 7**). Secondly, it will normally indicate the legal issues (usually called the **questions of law**) to be considered by the court. Thirdly, the headnote contains a summary of the court's decision on the issues of fact and law (as appropriate), including details of any *dissenting* judgment (where one or more judges disagree with the majority view).

It will also frequently give some indication of the effect of this decision on existing case law. This is indicated by the use of the following terms in conjunction with the citation of the relevant case:

Affirmed: this indicates that the court has agreed with the decision of a lower court in respect of the *same* case.

Applied: this means that a court has regarded itself as bound by an earlier decision, and has therefore employed the same reasoning in the instant case. The alternative would have been to *distinguish* the earlier case (see the relevant heading later in this section).

Approved: this is used where a higher court states that another case before a lower court was correctly decided.

Considered: this seems to be something of a residual category. If the court has discussed a reported case (particularly one decided by a court of equal status) but not reached any dramatic conclusion about its application, then it will probably appear as 'considered'.

Distinguished: an earlier case will be distinguished where a court has no power (or no wish) to overrule it, but does not want to apply it either. The court will therefore find some ground for saying it is different, and should not be followed. Distinguishing is an important category as it provides one of the main mechanisms by which the common law refines the scope of legal principles. Distinguishing may be restrictive or non-restrictive. Where it is *restrictive*, the act of distinguishing will materially affect the scope of the earlier authority; where it is *non-restrictive*, the court is simply saying that there is a material difference, but not one that will affect the ambit of the rule for the future. For example, in *Rickards* v *Lothian* [1913] AC 263, Rickards was the landlord and manager of property occupied by Lothian and other tenants. Lothian ran a bookselling business on the second floor. One night, water overflowing from a tap left running on the fourth floor ran down into Lothian's premises, causing considerable damage to his stock. It was established that the accident was not caused by Rickard's negligence. Lothian consequently sought to bring an action under the tort of *Rylands* v *Fletcher* (1868) LR 3 HL 330 which, regardless of fault, makes the occupier of land liable for damage caused to another by the 'escape' from his property of anything likely to do harm, provided that the use of the land was 'non-natural'. Hence in *Rylands* v *Fletcher* itself, the claim was founded on the 'escape' of water from a reservoir constructed on the defendant's land—this construction being declared a non-natural use of the land. By contrast, in *Rickards* v *Lothian*, although there was an escape of water, the Privy Council held that the provision of a bathroom with running water was *not* a non-natural use of the defendant's property. Consequently this case could be distinguished from *Rylands* v *Fletcher* on its material facts, precisely because there was no non-natural user in the later case. This was, therefore, a **non-restrictive** distinction.

Now, suppose the facts had been slightly different. Assume that instead of an escape of water, the damage in *Rickards* had been caused maliciously by a trespasser who set fire to the property. This would clearly be a non-natural use, but the court might, arguably, still not allow Lothian to recover, because the case could again be distinguished from *Rylands* v *Fletcher*. In *Rylands*, the non-natural use was authorised by the owner, in our new version of *Rickards*, it was not. If the court was so to hold, this would be an example of **restrictive** distinguishing. We would now say that liability under the principle in *Rylands* v *Fletcher* was restricted to those cases where the use was authorised by the owner or occupier of the land.

Overruled: this is used to show where a court has rejected and invalidated an earlier decision of a court of lower (or sometimes equal) status to itself. The power to overrule is thus limited by a court's position in the hierarchy. Sometimes, as an alternative to overruling, you will see the comment '**Not followed**'. This is used where the decision in question is persuasive authority, for example, from another jurisdiction. 'Not followed' does not affect the status of the precedent within its own jurisdiction, but it will certainly cast doubt on the value of that decision within the jurisdiction that has declined to follow it.

Reversed: this is the opposite of affirmed. It means that the higher court has decided that the lower court in the *same* case came to the wrong decision.

Although the headnote is intended as a summary of the whole case, it is not authority for anything within the case. It is simply a *résumé* provided by the publishers of the report. Though they are usually fairly reliable, mistakes are sometimes made. For example, in *O'Grady* v *Saper* [1940] 3 All ER 527, which concerned an appeal from an action originally brought against an employer in respect of unpaid wages during the employee's absence for sickness, the headnote reads:

> *Held*, the facts proved showed by implication that there was no agreement that the respondent should be paid wages while absent through illness and he was not entitled to recover.

This significantly distorts the contractual point which was made in that case. What the Court actually said was that the respondent (the employee) could not recover because there was an implied contractual term that he was *not* to be paid wages during any sick leave. So be careful in relying upon the headnote of a case—it certainly should not be used as a substitute for reading the judgments.

List of cases (7)

Most law reports will contain two separate lists. The first is a list of cases cited by the judge(s) in the judgment. That list is useful if you are trying to discover how the courts have subsequently used a particular decision. In other words, it provides a list of possible precedents used in that case. The second list (if there is one) will refer to additional cases cited in argument by counsel. Since the judge has not cited them, they are obviously of much less significance, but they can sometimes be worth considering if you are undertaking detailed research into the rationale of a decision, as they may show up points that the judge has apparently ignored or rejected, but without referring to the case in the written judgment.

Details of the appeal (8)

Here the report gives a short history of the case, stating the parties, the previous hearing(s) of the case, and usually the legal findings which form the basis of the appeal.

There are a number of basic points regarding appeal terminology that we can deal with here. In most cases, the case will refer simply to an 'appeal', which may be an appeal on a point of law, or fact, or both depending upon the jurisdiction of the court. However, there are three particular procedures that you may confront quite frequently, which require a little more explanation:

(a) Appeal by way of case stated: this most commonly arises in appeals from the magistrates' court to the High Court, either where the applicant believes the magistrates have made an error of law (e.g. misinterpreted a statute) or acted outside their jurisdiction. The magistrates state a case by submitting to the High Court a statement of facts found by the justices, together with the question(s) of law or jurisdiction on which guidance is sought. The High Court may then come to its own decision on the issue, or refer the case back to the magistrates for reconsideration in the light of the High Court's opinion. Further rights of appeal exist on a case stated. These lie directly to the Supreme Court in criminal cases. A good example of the whole appeal process is provided by the case of *Albert* v *Lavin*, already mentioned. The law report includes the form of words used by the magistrates to state a case concerning police powers of arrest for a breach of the peace. In civil cases the appeal is normally to the Court of Appeal. In *Finnegan* v *Clowney Youth Training Programme Ltd* the appeal shows that a case was stated by an industrial tribunal to the Court of Appeal in Northern Ireland. This particular procedure is unique to the Northern Irish system; though there are a number of contexts in which an English civil case can be stated for the High Court, these tend to be rare.

(b) Interim application: in civil proceedings an interim application (formerly called an interlocutory application) is an application to the court for some kind of temporary order that will take effect until the case comes to a full trial at a later date. Such applications most commonly arise as requests for an *injunction* (an order requiring the other party to do, or stop doing, something). They are thus meant to preserve the *status quo* until the trial. Interim applications will normally be heard by a single judge in the High Court, with a right of appeal to the Court of Appeal.

(c) 'Leapfrog appeal': under the Administration of Justice Act 1969 Part II, a civil case may exceptionally move from the High Court direct to the Supreme Court. This is colloquially referred to as a 'leapfrog appeal'. It may only be used where:

(i)   the case involves a point of law of general public importance relating to the interpretation of primary or secondary legislation; and

(ii) the High Court is bound on that point of law by a precedent of the Court of Appeal or Supreme Court; and

(iii) the Supreme Court grants leave to appeal.

The procedure seems to be used in only a few cases (see Drewry, 1973).

The names of counsel (9)

Historically, the only lawyers entitled to appear before the High Court and above were barristers. Changes to the rules in the Courts and Legal Services Act 1990, s. 27, extended rights of audience to solicitors who have undergone additional advocacy training.

In the majority of cases before the higher courts, each side will be represented by two barristers, a leader and a junior counsel. Until late 1977, this was a formal requirement where the leader was a 'QC' (Queen's Counsel). Now a QC may appear alone, though she or he can decline to do so.

The judgments (10)

The judgments are the most important part of any case, and as we shall see in **Chapters 6** and **7**, they are crucial to the operation of the English doctrine of precedent. It is normally the practice that, where there is more than one judge sitting, each is entitled to deliver his own opinion on the case. The first judgment given tends to be that of the senior judge presiding. However, do not assume that because it is first it is therefore the 'main' or 'leading' judgment. Indeed, where there are multiple judgments, it can be dangerous to assume that any one has precedence over the others—though sometimes you can get an intuitive sense that one judgment is the most significant, perhaps because the other judges refer to it extensively, or because it seems to be the most comprehensive or to provide the best analysis. The judges following may then either give a full judgment of their own, either supporting or dissenting from the decision of one or more of the other speakers, or give a brief *concurring* judgment, which may be no more than 'I agree'. The chief exception to this practice is the Privy Council, where a unanimous or majority opinion is presented by one judge alone, and only dissenting voices from that have a separate right to be heard. It is notable, however, that, following a steady decline since the early 1990s, the number of single judgments issued by the Supreme Court has increased, to a point where, by 2013, single judgments constituted 55 per cent of decisions (Paterson, 2015).

So far as the formalities of judgments are concerned, there appear to be none of any real significance, though there are many points of style, particularly in respect of forms of address. Titles are always given—a matter of style which is normally followed in academic writing, though the judges are also strong on ritual courtesy. A fellow judge is seldom anything less than 'learned' even where the discussion of his judgment strongly suggests that the speaker considers him to have the reasoning powers of a codfish.

The style of judgments tends to be quite individual. Some judges adopt a clear narrative pattern; Lord Denning was a prime, in his later decisions one might say an extreme, example of this style, whereby the facts and the law are woven into a continuous 'story'. Others have a far more formal style, which can produce some very dense prose indeed. A more recent innovation by some judges is to break up the text with headings and sub-headings, which can much improve the clarity of the argument. Levity is unusual but not unknown. Court of Appeal judge Sir Alan Ward became something of a legend in this regard. His opening lines in one particular unreported case have rapidly passed into legal folklore: 'This case involves a number of—and here I must not fall into Dr Spooner's error—warring bankers' (Regan, 2014).

Sadly, Sir Alan retired in 2014 (an event, we hasten to add, not in any way linked to the judgment above), leaving the Court of Appeal a slightly more predictable place.

One final feature of English cases, which differentiates our process from that of most other countries, has been the high proportion of *ex tempore*, or 'off the cuff', judgments. It has been common practice in the High Court, though less common in the Court of Appeal, for judgment to be given either immediately after the conclusion of argument, or following a brief adjournment. There are certainly anecdotal indications that the practice is becoming less common as more and more of the relatively straightforward cases are dealt with by county courts, or diverted to alternative dispute resolution, meaning that it tends to be the more complex cases that come to trial. Where the judge is not prepared to give his or her decision *ex tempore*, judgment is said to be **reserved** for presentation at a later date. The House of Lords always reserved its decisions, and the Supreme Court follows this practice. In the lower courts it is for the judges to decide.

Where a judgment in the law reports has been reserved, that is usually indicated, at a point just preceding the judgment(s), by the abbreviation '*Cur. adv. vult*'. This is short for *Curia advisari vult*, meaning 'the court wishes to be advised'. Judgments in the House of Lords were preceded, as here, by the more mundane: 'Their Lordships took time for consideration'. These editorial devices do not, of course, appear in the official transcript, though reservation can be inferred from any difference between the hearing and judgment dates.

Letters in the margin (11)

These are a useful addendum to the page number, which may be cited in the form 'p. 123a'. (Note also that, conventionally, the 'p.' denoting the page can be dropped when citing pages of the law reports.) Taken together they can be used to locate more accurately a piece of text which is being referred to in court, in the headnote to a law report, or in an essay, and so on. As we noted in **Chapter 2**, with the rising use of online sources, it is now the normal practice that paragraphs are numbered continuously throughout the published version of the judgments. This reduces the significance of the pagination and marginal lettering when citing cases.

3.2.2 European Reports

As we also noted in **Chapter 2**, decisions of the Court of Justice of the European Union (CJEU) are reported in two main series of English language reports the *European Court Reports* (ECR) and the *Common Market Law Reports* (CMLR). There are slight but mostly insignificant differences in the way in which these two sets of reports are laid out. For our purposes, therefore, it is sufficient to focus on just one version—the CMLR. To do this we have chosen Case C–83/92 *Pierrel SpA v Ministero della Sanità* [1995] 1 CMLR 53, a decision on a point of conflict between Italian law and Community law governing the marketing of pharmaceuticals (see **Figure 3.3**); the issues in the case are not significant for our purposes, the structure of the report is. Rather than take you through each element of the report, we have highlighted only the significant differences from an English law report:

(1) the boxes;

(2) the court and chamber;

(3) the personnel;

(4) date of judgment;

(5) the headnote;

(6) advocates appearing;

(7) Advocate-General's Opinion (not shown); and

(8) the judgment.

The boxes (1)

This is a particular feature of the CMLR. The CMLR include cases from courts of national as well as international jurisdiction, and the publishers therefore needed to develop a system which would make it clear to readers in any country what the status of a decision was. This is the system they devised. The box on the left indicates the class of court as follows (variations reflect the structure in place at the time the case was reported):

ECJ—the Court of Justice of the EC

CFI—the Court of First Instance of the EC

EFTA—the Court of the European Free Trade Association

For courts of national jurisdiction, the CMLR identify decisions according to the level of the court in the national hierarchy. Level I thus indicates a court of first instance, or trial court; Level II covers all intermediate courts (like the English Court of Appeal); and Level III indicates a final court of appeal (e.g. the Supreme Court). The use of this system enables us roughly to gauge and compare the relative significance of decisions of national courts on points of EU law.

The box on the right of the page indicates the court's jurisdiction, e.g. 'EEC' for courts with jurisdiction across the Communities, or 'UK–England' for English courts, etc.

(1)   (1)

| ECJ* | | EEC | 1993
                                                               —
PIERREL SpA AND OTHERS *v.* MINISTERO DELLA SANITÀ   *Pierrel SpA*
                  (Case C–83/92)   *v.*
                                                          Ministero
                                                         della Sanità
BEFORE THE COURT OF JUSTICE OF THE EUROPEAN COMMUNITIES (2)   —
                  (5th CHAMBER)   European
                                                          Court of
                                                           Justice

(*Presiding*, Moitinho de Almeida PC; Joliet and Rodríguez (3)
                         Iglesias JJ.)
            Herr Carl Otto Lenz, *Advocate General.*

                                   7 December 1993 (4)

    Reference from Italy by the Consiglio di Stato under **Article 177**
                              EEC.

Provisions considered:
    Dir. 65/65
    Dir. 75/319
    Dir. 83/570
    Dir. 92/27

> **Regulation of trade. Pharmaceuticals.** Article 21 of the (5)
> Pharmaceuticals Specialties Directive 65/65 means that the
> suspension or revocation of a marketing authorisation for a
> proprietary medicinal product may be decided only on the
> grounds laid down in that directive or other relevant provi-
> sions of Community law. [23]
>> CLIN-MIDY SA *v.* BELGIAN STATE (301/82): [1984] E.C.R.
>> 251, [1985] 1 C.M.L.R. 443, *confirmed.*
>
> **Regulation of trade. Pharmaceuticals.** National rules,
> according to which marketing authorisations for proprietary
> medicinal products which are not used within a specified
> period are to lapse, breach the Pharmaceuticals Specialties
> Directive 65/65, as amended. [30]

 * This box indicates the court or, for national systems, the class of court which
delivered this judgment. The box on the right indicates the country or jurisdiction
to which the court belongs.

The Court *interpreted* the Pharmaceuticals Specialties Directive 65/65, as amended and
supplemented by Directives 75/319, 83/570 and 92/27, *in the context of* Italian legislation
which provided that authorisations to market proprietary medicines lapsed if they were
not used within 18 months *to the effect that* the grounds laid down by the directives for the
revocation or suspension of such authorisations (which did not include failure to use them
within a specified period) were exhaustive, *that* the lapse of an authorisation was analogous
to a revocation since they both resulted in termination, and so *that* the Italian legislation
breached the directive, it being irrelevant that it had been amended after the national
court's **Article 177** reference.

Figure 3.3 A Decision of the ECJ

Professor Luigi Ferrari Bravo, Head of the Department of Contentious Diplomatic Affairs at the Ministry of Foreign Affairs, assisted by *Oscar Fiumara* and *Francesco Guicciardi*, Avvocati dello Stato, for the Italian Government.

Luis Ines Fernandes, Director of the Legal Department of the Directorate-General for the European Communities at the Ministry for Foreign Affairs, *Maria Luisa Duarte*, Legal Adviser at the Directorate-General for the European Communities, and *Cláudio Monteiro*, Legal Adviser at the Directorate-General for Medicinal Products, for the Portuguese Government as *amicus curiae*.

Antonio Aresu, of the Legal Service of the E.C. Commission, and *Virginia Melgar*, a national official seconded to the Legal Service, for the Commission as *amicus curiae*.

The following case was referred to in the judgment:

1. CLIN-MIDY SA v. BELGIAN STATE (301/82), 26 January 1984: [1984] E.C.R. 251, [1985] 1 C.M.L.R. 443.

The following further cases were referred to by the Advocate General:

2. GUNA SRL v. E.C. COUNCIL (C–437/92), not yet decided.

3. ANGELOPHARM GmbH v. FREIE UND HANSESTADT HAMBURG (C–212/91), 25 January 1994: [1994] 1 E.C.R. 171, [1994] 3 C.M.L.R. 573.

4. MARLEASING SA v. LA COMERCIAL INTERNACIONAL DE ALIMENTACIÓN SA (C–106/89), 13 November 1990: [1990] 1 E.C.R. 4135, [1992] 3 C.M.L.R. 305.

The following additional cases were referred to in argument:

5. ALGERA v. COMMON ASSEMBLY (7/56 & 3–7/57), 12 July 1957: [1957–58] E.C.R. 39.

6. RE THE MARKETING OF MEDICINES: E.C. COMMISSION v. ITALY (C–145/82), 15 March 1983: [1983] E.C.R. 711, [1984] 1 C.M.L.R. 148.

TABLE OF PROCEEDINGS	PAGE
Opinion of Lenz A.G., 15 July 1993	58
Judgment of the European Court of Justice, 7 December 1993	64
Language of the proceedings: Italian	

Figure 3.3 Continued

The court and chamber (2)

The formal title of the court is given together with, where appropriate, the chamber in which it is heard. This is not a reference to the English practice of hearing some (mostly interim) applications in private in the judge's office (called 'chambers'); rather it refers to the procedural process of assigning the case to a particular group of judges. Each of the EU courts is divided into chambers, with each chamber having its own President, elected by the judges. In most of their cases the Court of Justice and General Court sit as a regular chamber of three or five judges, or as a Grand Chamber of fifteen judges, or, very exceptionally as a 'plenary' (full) court. The Court itself determines whether to hear proceedings in plenary session or as a chamber, and, if the latter, whether comprising a panel of three, five, or fifteen judges (the last being referred to as a 'Grand Chamber'). In the Court of Justice this decision is taken by the Court at the close of the written proceedings, and after the Advocate General has been heard. It is based simply on an assessment of the importance or difficulty of the issues raised. Member States and any Community institutions involved in the proceedings can require the trial to be conducted before the full Court. The General Court, also with a total of twenty-eight judges, operates in a very similar fashion, though it has only very rarely exercised its power to sit as a plenary court.

The personnel (3)

There are a number of key personnel within the CJEU. In addition to the judges, there are the eleven Advocates General and the Registrar of the CJEU. We will consider each of these roles in turn.

There are twenty-eight judges at present: one from each Member State. Under the terms of the Treaties, the judges are appointed for a renewable term of six years on the basis either of substantial professional expertise and seniority (the first option), or on the basis of academic scholarship (the second option). The alternative nature of these qualifications is particularly significant in the British or Irish context where, unlike most continental jurisdictions, academics *per se* are not eligible for domestic judicial appointment. To date, however, the UK has not nominated a judge who would not satisfy the first option, though two of the judges have also held chairs at British universities. David Edward, for example, was both a Scottish QC and Salveson Professor of European Institutions at Edinburgh University before his appointment, first to the CFI, and then, in 1992, to the ECJ.

Each chamber of the Court has a President elected, by its members, annually in the case of chamber of three judges, or for a three-year term where there are five judges in the chamber (in practice, this means that each judge serves as President in rotation). The Court of Justice also has an overall President and Vice-President who are elected for a (renewable) three-year term. The President of the Court presides at plenary hearings and has ultimate responsibility for the judicial administration of the court. Other than the presidents, all judges rank equally, though seating positions in court are determined by 'seniority in office'—in effect, length of service as a judge.

Each case has assigned to it a *Judge-Rapporteur*. This is a judge nominated by the President of one of the smaller chambers to undertake the preparatory inquiry phase once an application has been lodged with the court. The *Judge-Rapporteur*'s role is akin to that of the investigating magistrate in civilian court procedure, i.e. to undertake an inquiry and produce a report on the case for the Court to consider (see the CJEU website for a brief outline of its procedures: http://curia.europa.eu/jcms/jcms/Jo2_7024/). This report is used by the Court to determine procedure for the hearing of the matter—e.g. what witnesses (if any) may be called, whether the case is heard by the chamber to which it was assigned, or by a chamber of five judges or plenary court. The *Judge-Rapporteur* is also normally present at oral hearings, and is entitled to put questions to the advocates.

The *Advocates General* are perhaps the most distinctive element of the proceedings, having no equivalent in common law procedure. Advocates General are very much a part of the court, and subject broadly to the same conditions of appointment, tenure, salary, etc. as the judges (indeed, over the years, a number of Advocates General have become judges, and *vice versa*). In a sense, then, in true civilian style both Advocates General and judges are part of the same Community *magistrature*. In much the same way, in France we see a functional distinction between judges of the *siège* (i.e. those who sit in judgment 'on the bench') and judges of the *parquet* (the 'floorboards') who take responsibility for the prosecution of cases, but this does not alter the fact that both are part of the career judiciary. The analogy is not exact, of course, as the Court of Justice has no direct equivalent of the *parquet*, and it has been suggested that their role more clearly reflects the court's early links (both procedural and personal) with the French *Conseil d'Etat* (see further Vranken, 1996: 40–8).

The idea of an Advocate General is a familiar one in continental legal systems. The Advocate General is an 'adviser' to the court, performing a task which might be likened to 'sifting' through the law on behalf of the Court in each case. In practice this has meant that the Advocate General has tended to play an important part in the proceedings. He receives all the details of the case from the parties, investigates the law relating to the issues raised, and delivers his opinion on the case to the Court as to what decision it should reach. He sits with the judges on the Bench (opposite the Registrar) but plays no part in their deliberations. He delivers his opinion after the case has been heard by the court, and often at a later hearing. This can be highly influential on the reasoning of the court. We discuss the nature and role of the Advocate-General's opinion in more detail later in the chapter.

The procedure governing cases before the General Court is slightly different. There is no general requirement of an Advocate General to prepare the case, and no formal or permanently established body of Advocates General for the General Court. When the Court sits in plenary session, a judge of the General Court will normally be appointed to act as Advocate General. In addition, under the Court's rules of procedure, an Advocate General may be appointed to assist the Court where the case is to be heard before a chamber, and the legal difficulty or factual complexity of the case so requires. In practice, however, this power is seldom used (see Biavati, 2011: 79). Where appointed, an Advocate General has the same functions before the General Court as before the Court of Justice.

Note that since 1982 there is no hyphen in the spelling of Advocate General, except when referring to the possessive case, thus: the Advocate General said…but the Advocate-General's opinion was…The plural of an Advocate General is Advocates General. This distinction is not a popular question on game shows.

Last, there is the *Registrar*, who is in charge of the court Registry (i.e. its administrative arm) and deals with the procedure and administration of the court. His role is perceived as something more important than the title would imply under our system—he even sits with the judges in court, but takes no part in the decision. There are also two Assistant Registrars who take day-to-day responsibility for the administrative and judicial sides of the Registry's work respectively.

Date of judgment (4)

Again this is self-explanatory; note, however, that, unlike the English law reports, no separate hearing dates are given. Note too that the CJEU always reserves its judgments.

The headnote (5)

The form of a headnote differs substantially from that used in English law reports. Opening with a reference to the procedure whereby the case reached the Court (here, an Art. 177—now Art. 267—Reference) and citations of the relevant Community legislation, it then identifies the subject matter of the case, together with references to key paragraphs in the judgment (in square brackets) and refers to any authority cited in the judgment—but *not* authorities referred to by the Advocate General.

The advocates (6)

Parties before the CJEU must normally be represented by a lawyer. In addition, in reference proceedings, legal representatives from other Member States having an interest in the ruling may submit observations to the Court in both the written and oral proceedings. The Commission also always submits observations in reference proceedings. In the *Pierrel* case, you can see that observations were received from the Commission and from the Portuguese government.

Advocate-General's Opinion (not shown)

The Advocate-General's opinion is often an important part of the case, and one that has no direct counterpart in the English legal system. In his opinion the Advocate General will normally go through the facts, the law, and various authorities (including case law and academic commentary), and usually in far more detail than does the judgment of the court. Practically speaking, therefore, it makes a lot of sense to read the opinion before the judgment, as that will (especially if the opinion is followed by the court) give you significant insights into the development and rationale of the law.

The Advocate-General's opinion is not part of the court's judgment and is in no sense 'binding' either on the Court to which it is presented or on any other later court. It may, however, be referred to and used as a kind of persuasive authority in later cases before the CJEU. Thus, for example, in T–3/90 *Prodifarma v Commission* [1991] ECR II-11154, the Advocate-General's opinion in a previous Court of Justice decision was taken up by the Court of First Instance. It is also quite common practice for Advocates General to cite each other's opinions. The division between the Advocate-General's opinion and the judgment has become rather more blurred by the modern practice of the judges in some cases simply adopting the opinion in its entirety by 'direct reference'. For an example of the practice, see Case C–284/91 *Suiker Export v Belgium* [1992] ECR I-5473.

Whatever the procedure, estimates (albeit now rather dated) suggest that the Advocate-General's opinion is followed in something like 70 to 85 per cent of cases (Vranken, 1996: 61). Note, however, that there are also some indications of a gradual reduction in the importance of the Advocate-General's opinion. The increased maturity of the Court of Justice's jurisprudence, and the development of a settled body of relevant precedents has somewhat diminished the need for an opinion in all cases. Consequently, after the Treaty of Nice, it was decided that the need for a mandatory Advocate-General's opinion would be removed in respect of those cases that raise no novel questions of law (see Art. 20(5) of the CJEU Statute).

The judgment (not shown)

There are two particular points to note about the style of judgments of the Court of Justice and the General Court.

First, all decisions are *collegial*. A decision is reported as a decision of the court, without the individual (or idiosyncratic!) voices we often associate with English judgments. Collegiality also means that, following the civilian tradition, there is no provision for dissenting judgments. Decisions will follow the majority reasoning if unanimity cannot be achieved, but, unlike the common law approach, no record of the minority view is retained to trouble posterity. That said, the European courts work very hard to achieve unanimity, and this sometimes means that decisions reflect a 'lowest common denominator of conflicting opinions' (Edward, 2004: 124). Though collegiality may thus set limits on the development of EU law, or the CJEU's creativity, that is not necessarily a 'bad thing', and it can also be argued that collegiality might be the only way in which a court such as the CJEU could work:

> The principle of collegiality is an incentive to judicial modesty, as it is intended to be, and it is well adapted to the needs of a court that has to work in the multilingual, multinational and multicultural environment of the European Union. The individual Judges cannot be criticised for disloyalty to the interests of their own country nor, correspondingly, can the member states find an excuse for not accepting the Court's judgment on the ground that 'their' Judge did not vote for it.
>
> (Edward, 2004: 124)

Secondly, it follows that the form and style of the decision are also rather different from those found in English law reports. To start with, the judgment is presented in the form of numbered paragraphs, a practice which has only relatively recently been adopted by English courts. These provide a reference point when citing the decision. Note also that the actual ruling of the Court always appears at the end of the judgment. It is often quite short, and is identified by the opening phrase 'On those grounds...' from the French *pour ces motifs*. There are some other relatively minor stylistic differences between reports which can reflect the age of the case (the principles governing the format for judgments were relaxed in 1978) or small variations in 'house-style' between the ECR and CMLR. They are not significant for our purposes. Now to a more substantial issue.

The contents of the judgment also appear distinctive to lawyers of the common law tradition. But this is not just a matter of style—it reflects the different legal cultures involved, and particularly assumptions about the judicial function. Unlike the rather more rhetorical approach of many English judges, the language used by the CJEU tends to be more measured, if not downright flat. This is sometimes said to reflect the compromise nature of many decisions and is a consequence of the collegiality principle. If a camel is a horse designed by committee, European judgments can sometimes be the judicial equivalent of the camel. Judgments are also relatively short. This is not least because they commonly lack the detailed factual and legal analysis which is the feature of many English judgments and of the Advocate-General's opinion. Relatively few cases may be cited in support of the decision (though references to case law have become much more common) and older judgments rarely made any direct reference to the opinions of Advocates General—not even the opinion given in that case (though as we have seen, that too is changing).

This is not to say that EC decisions suffer from a lack of rigour or rationalisation: they are presented in a very logical, developmental form in which point follows point in a seemingly inexorable sequence. This form of presentation can sometimes make European decisions easier to read and understand than their English counterparts, but it does mean that points of uncertainty or argument get rather lost in what is packaged as a rational, deductive process (we explore some of the reasons behind this approach in **Chapter 12**). It can also mean that the Court is often reluctant to explore the implications or boundaries of the law beyond the issues directly raised by the case at hand. This contrasts with English practice, where judges will frequently speculate on the scope or implications of a particular ruling. Lawyers asking the question *'what if...'* of the CJEU will seldom find guidance in the judgment. Arguably this has meant that the Court has actually generated a lack of legal certainty through an unwillingness to provide fuller reasoning of its decisions in cases like *Francovich* (see, e.g., Bebr, 1992) and *Faccini Dori* (see our discussion of these cases in **Chapter 11**).

3.2.3 A Beginning, not an End

Thus far we have provided you with a basic road map to the structure of the law reports. The detail may seem rather dull, at worst, a bit overwhelming to start with. You will get used to it, provided you practise the skills of going back to these original sources, and not just relying on summaries in textbooks. Textbooks are useful (otherwise we wouldn't have written one), but there are times when you need to understand the nuances and the detail that you get from the original source material. Reading and observing how the judges actually structure their arguments can also help you learn how to compose and organise legal argument.

So far all we have given you is some basic tools to help you find your way around a case:

- to identify its position in the hierarchy of decision-making;
- to find the structural features that the editors of law reports have introduced to help you to identify the issues, locate the case in the existing law and understand the principles that the court has adopted or developed in its reasoning; and
- to understand some of the technical terminology used, and its significance.

These tools by themselves will not be enough to enable you to make full sense of a law report. You do need to understand something about the substantive law in the area discussed by your case (that's where textbooks and articles really do play a part), and you also need to understand the principles and practices of legal reasoning, which we will come back to in the later chapters of this book. But you also need to develop a further set of reading and analytical skills that will support you in dealing with materials of the length and technical complexity that you will encounter in law. That is what we will turn to next, and though we focus on using these skills in the context of books and articles, the basic principles can help you with complex primary sources too.

3.3 Reading Books and Articles

How do you read a book or article?

This may seem like a silly question, but it is not. Educational research has shown that many of us are very inefficient in the way we approach academic reading. Given the time pressures you will face as a student, it is vital that you develop an efficient technique. One that is worth trying is commonly called **SQ3R** (see, e.g., Williams, 1989: 4–5). It describes a sequence of five steps you should follow when looking at books and articles: Survey, Question, Read, Recall, and Review.

3.3.1 Survey

Start by getting a 'feel' for the publication and its potential usefulness. You can do this by looking at the elements outlined in the following sections.

The title

Yes, we are starting with the obvious, but mind that it is not so obvious that you overlook it! The title may tell you a lot about the author's aims. Consider, for example, what you might be able to tell about the contents from the following (real) book titles:

The Law of Contract

A Casebook on Contract

Nutshells—Contract Law

The Rise and Fall of Freedom of Contract

Contract Law—Questions and Answers

Understanding Contract Law

Sourcebook on Obligations and Legal Remedies

Similarly, phrases in titles or subtitles like 'a student's guide', 'a critical approach', or 'handbook' can also help indicate the level of difficulty or type of approach being taken.

The 'blurb', editorial, or abstract

Books almost invariably have a brief summary of their aims or arguments on the back cover or inside the jacket (if hardback). This is often written—or at least revised—by the author and should provide a reasonable indication of what the book is about, though do not forget that it is also written with the aim of selling the book! Similarly, some, though by no means all, journals either contain an editorial summarising the contents of the particular issue or require authors to provide a brief summary or 'abstract' of their article which gives a guide to the contents. This may provide a useful framework around which you can organise your own notes from your reading.

The date of publication

In a book this is given on either the face or obverse of the title page. In a constantly changing field such as law, recency of publication is important. Most law books will become progressively more out of date as time goes on. Always check the date of publication and be prepared to update accordingly. If the book is more than three or four years old, it is often worth checking a publisher's catalogue to see if there is a later edition or finding a more up-to-date alternative. With journal articles, the problem is more acute. These are not generally updated by revised versions and it can be difficult to check for accuracy other than by returning to primary sources. The older the article, the more careful you may have to be. Having said that, there is no general rule that can tell us when a piece of legal writing is past its 'sell by' date.

Contents page

A quick check of the contents page can also give a useful overview, not just of the bare contents of a book, but of how the material is structured and used. It is a curious reflection on academic cultures that many North American law journals will publish much longer articles than their British or European counterparts. In the USA particularly,

articles of 25,000 words or more are not uncommon. It is perhaps unsurprising therefore that in the American journals major articles will normally have their own table of
contents.

Preface

A lot of readers will skip the preface or introduction and just focus on the main text of
a book. This is often a bad idea. Most prefaces, etc. are written by authors expressly as a
way of explaining the thinking behind their books.

3.3.2 Question

Worthwhile reading requires more than staring at the page and trying to soak up the
contents like a sponge. You *must* ask yourself questions both before and during your
reading. Consider first your objectives in reading the text: what is it you want from this
book or article?

- Are you looking for an overview of a topic?
- Are you trying to answer a specific question or legal problem?
- Are you looking for a critical perspective on the law or the context in which it has
  evolved?

  Use these to focus and cross-check your reading.

3.3.3 Read

Think about how you have been using this book. Have you read everything we have written? Has your reading been all at the same speed, or to the same depth? In fact, it is highly
unlikely that you have read every word, and even if you have you will have varied the
depth and pace of your reading. You are almost certainly using a range of reading techniques already, according to the purpose for which you have been reading at the time. It
is worth thinking about how you might harness those techniques to make yourself a more
efficient and productive reader. In practice we suggest there are three stages to effective
reading:

(a) *Skim* the text for an overview. This can often be best achieved by taking the text
a paragraph at a time. When skim reading it is often sufficient to read just the opening
sentence or two of each paragraph. Let us explain why. Most well-constructed paragraphs can be split into three elements (this idea is useful in developing your writing
skills too): an opening sentence or two, incorporating the 'topic sentence'; an explanatory or discursive middle element; and a closing sentence, which commonly serves to
develop the topic sentence as well as to complete the paragraph. The topic sentence is
crucial; it provides the main idea of the paragraph and all other sentences develop it
and are dependent on it to some degree. Consider the following paragraph as an example (we have given each sentence a number, in brackets, for reasons which will become
apparent in a moment):

Lord Woolf has proposed fundamental and radical changes to the way litigation should be conducted.
[1] His diagnosis is that civil justice is in crisis because (among other things) it takes too long, costs
too much money and, even when people win, they are unhappy with the process. [2] Although this

analysis is far from new, I agree with it. **[3]** I also agree with Lord Woolf that radical change is needed, not cosmetic surgery. **[4]** However, reforming the civil justice system for the better 'ain't easy'. **[5]** This is why, despite some sixty reports in England on aspects of civil procedure since 1851, there has been no lasting solution to the twin problems of cost and delay. **[6]** The same is true of North America. **[7]** Our predecessors were neither foolish dullards nor acting in bad faith; reform is simply very difficult. **[8]** The challenge is not simply to propose change: it is to propose reforms which significantly improve the current position. **[9]** (Watson, 1996: 63)

Here the topic sentence is the first sentence: it tells us that the subject of the paragraph is Lord Woolf's proposals for the reform of civil justice. The later sentences relate back to the topic sentence (TS), albeit at different levels, to expand on or explain the theme it introduces. By identifying the TS, we can quickly spot the focus of that paragraph and thus decide whether to ignore it or return to it for a further reading and analysis. In longer paragraphs it can sometimes be helpful to skim the last sentence or two as well, to help us see where the argument is going.

(b) It follows, then, that the second stage is to *identify* those elements of the text which need to be read in detail. Do not make notes at this stage, other than to identify the bits to which you will return. You need to concentrate on understanding the text at the level of an overview first. Only once you have done this are you really ready for the next stage.

(c) *Read in detail.* This is never the first stage in effective reading. Indeed, you will often find that there is material you will never have to read in detail because by surveying the text and skim reading you can establish that *it is of absolutely no use to you whatsoever.* If you start by reading in detail, you risk wasting time on something that is of little or no practical help, whatever its intrinsic worth may be!

Reading in detail will usually involve two distinct processes:

(i) reading for understanding; and

(ii) reading critically.

Again we will take each of these ideas in turn.

You can really know something only if you understand it. Reading for understanding is therefore a central part of the learning process. Often you will find understanding does not come easily. The ideas represented in a piece of writing may be complex; sometimes they may not be clearly expressed. It may be necessary for you to work hard at unpicking the meaning. Here again, it is often helpful to work through the text a paragraph at a time. If you can make sense of the structure and order of the writer's ideas at this level, you will have a better chance of grasping their meaning. There are better ways of doing this than staring at the page and waiting for inspiration.

Think back to what we said about paragraph organisation in the section on skim reading. You will recall that we said that all sentences in a paragraph relate back to the topic sentence (TS), but at different levels. So there will be sentences which are directly subordinate to the topic sentence (Level 2 sentences), but also other sentences which illustrate or modify the Level 2 sentences and so are subordinate to them (Level 3 sentences) and, in more complex paragraphs, so on. Maughan and Maughan (2015) have shown how we might use a tree diagram more effectively to identify this relationship and thereby to extract the meaning from a paragraph (see **Figure 3.4**).

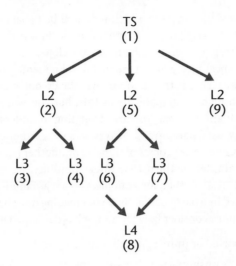

Figure 3.4. Topic and subordinate sentences

We suggest that this technique can help us to untangle long and complex paragraphs. We can, however, start with a straightforward example, using the extract from Garry Watson's paper quoted earlier. If we apply their approach here, we get a structure that looks like this (the numbers in brackets correspond to the sentence numbers in the text):

Thus Sentence 1, the TS, introduces the main theme:

> *Lord Woolf has proposed radical reforms.*

This is developed by Sentence 2 (L2):

> *Woolf says reform is necessary because of delays etc.*

which is then modified by Sentences 3 and 4 (L3):

> *I agree with Lord Woolf.*

Sentence 5 (L2) returns to the topic sentence to qualify it:

> *But reforming civil justice is not easy.*

The statement in Sentence 5 is then justified by Sentences 6 and 7 (L3):

> *Just look at the impact of previous attempts in the UK and N. America*

and Sentence 8 (L4) then emphasises the point by saying, in effect:

> *and it was not for want of trying.*

Lastly, Sentence 9 returns to the TS with a final modification that is crucial to the later development of the argument:

> *Proposing radical reform is one thing: making a difference is another.*

It is quite possible that you would analyse this, or any paragraph, slightly differently from us. That is because it is ultimately your interpretation of what the writer is saying, and which sentence is subordinate to which may well be debatable. That relationship is not really important for our purposes. What is important is that you can see a logical structure to the paragraph which establishes, develops, and ultimately modifies or transforms a basic theme. Once you can see that development, it becomes much easier to understand what the writer is trying to achieve. We do not suggest that you need to work through everything as systematically as this, but you would probably find this technique helpful with any material you are struggling to understand. Note also that in our analysis we have used paraphrases of Watson's text, rather than verbatim quotations. This too is deliberate—the process of translating another person's words into your own is also an important step on the path to understanding.

If your purpose is critical, in that, for example, you are attempting to analyse or challenge the ideas presented by a particular author, your reading must be directed to that purpose. In that case you must consider how the author has developed his argument. Has he:

(a) made any unsupported or unrecognised assumptions?

(b) reached conclusions unsupported by his argument?

(c) ignored counter-arguments that exist?

Often, a comparison of different texts can help you sort out the range of arguments and counter-arguments which exist. Do not fall into the trap of being dependent upon a single book or article when constructing any kind of critical analysis. Literary sources may also be of assistance if you are attempting some critical analysis of a case or statutory provision.

Lastly, always remember, when reading, what your purpose is. If you are unsure, stop, think, and read again.

3.3.4 Recall

In the recall phase you are really trying to test yourself on what the text was about. It is at this point that you should begin to make notes.

Note-taking is an integral part of effective, detailed reading. Simply photocopying text and going through it with a highlighter is a poor substitute for the kind of mental processing of information that takes place when making notes on your source material. Whether making handwritten notes is more effective than using a laptop or tablet may be moot. Research into the cognitive processing of lectures tends to suggest that typing and handwriting lecture notes result in appreciably different learning outcomes. Experiments show that those who write out notes by hand tend to have a stronger conceptual understanding and are more successful in applying and integrating the material than laptop users. Though the latter are able to take more verbatim notes, they may, consequently, process the material less, leading to lower retention of the information (see, e.g., May, 2014).

Do *not* take verbatim notes as you read. Read first, then make your notes. Obviously longer pieces of text need to be broken down into manageable chunks for this technique to work—no one can make meaningful notes on a whole book at one, two, or even three sittings! But why not make notes as you read? We advise against this for three reasons. First, it is difficult to assess just how critical any part of the text is before you have completed the whole; you are therefore more likely to misrepresent your source this way. Secondly, delaying note-taking encourages you to think about what you have read.

Thirdly, it reduces the likelihood of one kind of *plagiarism*, that is, of quoting someone else's work without attribution. This is an academic cardinal sin, and can be a ground for failure under the academic regulations of every law degree we have come across. However, it can be very easy to confuse quoted or paraphrased material from your own notes if you are not careful about maintaining that distinction. If you must take down verbatim extracts, make sure it is clear to you what is quoted material and what is not. Williams (1989: 30) also suggests the following guidelines for good note-taking practice:

(a) *Record your source:* Make sure that you keep a note of the full reference for your source material. You will need this for any works you cite in your bibliography, and you may need to locate it again. Note the author(s), the title, publisher, or journal name, year, and page reference(s). If it is a library book, it can save time later if you note the library (shelving) classification too. If you are doing an extended piece of project work, where you are likely to have a large number of references, it may be helpful to note each reference on individual index cards which can be stored as a permanent record. Alternatively, there are a number of cheap 'shareware' computer programs which can enable you to produce an electronic index of references that can be downloaded to a document file for word processing, or you may use specialist bibliographic software like *Zotero* (see www.zotero.com)—which is a free, web-based research database tool—or commercial equivalents such as *Endnote*, to which you may have access via your university network.

(b) *Show the main ideas clearly:* What are the key points/arguments to come out of the text? Identify them! Show also how the main ideas are linked and what supporting points are used for each.

(c) *Be brief:* Do not take copious notes unless you have to. It may be better to take brief notes at first, and come back to the source later if more detail proves necessary.

(d) *Be selective:* Avoid lengthy illustrations, asides, etc. If an example helps you to understand a point, outline it briefly. Make a note of the page reference of any examples you are uncertain about using.

(e) *Leave notes well spaced on the page:* This enables you to fill in with more detail later on (if necessary).

3.3.5 Review

Williams (1989: 5) also suggests that the review process has two elements. One is retrospective, the other prospective. First, you can quickly review the first four stages of **SQ3R** to check your progress:

- *Survey* the whole text to remind yourself of the structure.
- *Question*—what was your purpose? What were the specific questions to which you wanted answers?
- *Read* the text by skimming only. Are there any points you have missed?
- *Recall*—check your notes. Are there any gaps? Have you found answers to your questions?

From here you need, lastly, to think about what you will do with your notes. It may be that they will serve a one-off purpose, contributing to an essay, say. Even so, it is worth putting them aside for a day or two, to see if they still make sense or whether they need further revision or correction. However, it is more likely that they will form part of your knowledge bank for the future (for end-of-year examinations perhaps), in which case you will need to consider what future strategies of review and refinement you intend to adopt as part of your preparation for that event.

EXERCISE 3 SQ3R squared

Ask yourself the question, 'How can the SQ3R method improve my study skills?'. Now, using SQ3R, work through the relevant sections of this chapter, and see what answer you come up with.

Of course, we are not going to give you an answer to this one—that is for you to decide! Having said that, the technique is tried and trusted, and most people should get something of value from it. You should consider trying out SQ3R on an assignment. Do not be put off just because it may take you longer than your conventional research and reading methods. The time invested should pay off in the long run, both in terms of greater conceptual understanding as you progress through your course and in terms of better (and, hopefully, easier) preparation for examinations.

 CONCLUSION

In this chapter we have provided you with a set of concepts and tools to enable you better to understand both primary and secondary legal sources. There is perhaps a danger at this stage of having replaced the myth that the law can be found in one book with another, more sophisticated version, which says that law is simply about constructing a solution from a variety of written sources. Provided your research is adequate, and you understand how to go about reading what you have found, you will come up with the answer. To an extent there is some truth in that, but the reality is rather more uncertain.

In practice, the process of reading the law does not operate in a vacuum; it is not an arid activity, but one that is applied in real legal disputes. Going to law is not simply a case of lawyers dusting down the appropriate statutes and cases, and reading them (though that will inevitably be part of it); it is, at its heart, a process of reconstructing disputed events ('the facts') and proposing a legal solution to them. The implications of this reality on *our* reading of the law is, in part, the subject of **Chapter 5**, but before we get there, we turn our attention from the process of reading to writing.

EXERCISE 4 Attempting the impossible

Before attempting this exercise you are advised to read and make notes on:

(a) The case of *R v Shivpuri* [1986] 2 All ER 334—an important case in both criminal law and legal method. You are advised to use the All England report, as the answers make specific reference to that version.

(b) The introductory parts and s. 1 of the Criminal Attempts Act 1981.

continued

EXERCISE 4 *continued*

Make sure that you understand the basic context of the dispute—i.e. what the case was about; why it was before the particular court hearing the case; what that court decided; and why. Once you have done so, you should be ready to test your compre-hension against the following questions.

Q QUESTIONS

1. Starting with the Criminal Attempts Act, let us check your basic information:

(a) What is its full citation?

(b) When did it receive the royal assent?

(c) What is the subject of Part I of the Act?

2. Is the short title (Answer YES or NO to each of the points):

(a) An accurate statement of what the Act is about?

(b) Capable of assisting our interpretation of the Act?

3. Answer TRUE or FALSE to each of the points:
Section 1 of the Act:

(a) makes it a statutory offence to attempt to commit an indictable offence;

(b) seeks to exclude from criminal attempts any significant steps towards a crime where the offence is in fact impossible to complete;

(c) includes within the definition of an attempt any acts of an accused which he believes would involve the commission of a crime, but which, if completed, would not, in reality, be criminal.

4. Turning to *R* v *Shivpuri*:

(a) Which court's decision appears in the report cited?

(b) In which court(s) had the case appeared previously?

5. Which of the statements that follow contain(s) a material (i.e. important) fact (there may be more than one)?

(a) The accused believed he was carrying heroin or cannabis.

(b) The substance in the suitcase was not a prohibited drug.

(c) The full offence of 'dealing' could not be committed.

6. Which of the statements that follow reflect(s) the legal issue(s) at the root of the appeal? Again, there *may* be more than one right answer:

(a) Whether a merely 'preparatory' action constitutes an attempt in English law.

(b) Whether it is possible to be convicted of attempting to commit an offence where the facts make its actual commission impossible.

(c) Whether the requirement that the accused acted 'knowingly' means that the pros-ecution must prove that the accused *knew* it was a particular controlled drug.

continued

7. Do the judges all agree on the outcome of the case (YES or NO)?

8. Was that outcome:

(a) That the appeal was upheld on the question of attempting the impossible?

(b) That the appeal was dismissed because the judge had wrongly advised (*misdi-rected*) the jury?

(c) That the appeal was dismissed on the question of attempting the impossible?

(d) That the appeal was dismissed on *both* issues (i.e. attempting the impossible and on the misdirection of the jury?)

9. What was *Shivpuri*'s impact on the standing of the earlier decision in *Anderton* **v *Ryan*? Did it:**

(a) Overrule it?

(b) Apply it?

(c) Distinguish it?

1. (a) It is cited as the Criminal Attempts Act 1981, c. (i.e. *chapter*) 47.

   (b) It received the royal assent on 27 July 1981 (the date given just below the long title).

   (c) Simply 'Attempts etc'! This is to distinguish it from the repeal of the so-called 'sus' laws created under the Vagrancy Act 1824, which form the subject of Part II (see the 'Arrangement of Sections' and long title).

2. (a) is correct; it is a brief but accurate description.

   (b) No is the correct answer here: if you got this wrong, think back to the 'Strawberry Jam' analogy used earlier in this chapter.

3. (a) **TRUE:** this is the combined effect of subsections (1) and (4)—the latter restricts liability only to *indictable* (i.e. serious) criminal offences.

   (b) **FALSE:** this statement actually reverses the effect of subsection (2) which deals with cases of 'factual impossibility'—e.g. the situation where A attempts to poison B with a substance which is, in fact, harmless.

   (c) **TRUE:** this is the most difficult to work out. Subsection (3) is concerned with the intention of the accused. So long as the accused intends to commit the offence, it does not matter that, because of some mistake on his part about the law, what he does is not a crime. A widely cited example is the situation where A has sexual intercourse with B, believing her to be under the legal age of consent. Technically, A has committed the offence of attempting unlawful sexual intercourse, even though B is not in fact 'under age'.

4. (a) The House of Lords.

   (b) The Crown Court and Court of Appeal—see 335I.

continued

EXERCISE 4 *continued*

5. This comes close to being a trick question! All three of (a), (b), and (c) would have been material questions of fact. That this is the case with (a) and (b) should be reasonably evident. The accused's belief and the nature of the substance are both material to the question of attempting the impossible; they are both matters which are proved by evidence. Item (c) is rather more difficult. The *definition* of an offence is a matter of law; but that is not the point here. Here the issue is one of *proving* that the accused could not commit the offence. That, we suggest, is a matter of fact.

6. (b) and (c) are both correct. Statement (b) is probably the more obvious answer, but the issue identified by (c) also arises, e.g. at 339b *per* Lord Bridge. (a) is incorrect; though this point has arisen in a number of cases, it was not critical here—see e.g. Lord Bridge, at 342g.

7. Yes is the right answer, though they do not necessarily arrive at the same outcome for the same reasons. If you got this one wrong it is probably because you have confused the *result* of the appeal with the *reasoning* used by the judges to come to their decision (see further the answer to Question 9). They should always be kept separate in your mind.

8. (d) is the correct answer. The misdirection point is less obviously a ground of the appeal, but it is raised by the defence and discussed by the House of Lords. They held that though there had been a technical misdirection, it had caused no miscarriage of justice, and so could be disregarded under their Lordships' statutory powers—see Lord Bridge, at approximately 341d–h.

9. The correct answer is (a). The decision of the House was unanimous in this respect; though Lords Hailsham and MacKay state that they would have been content to distinguish *Anderton* v *Ryan* (see 337b and 345h), they do not actually dissent from the judgment given by Lord Bridge.

 CHAPTER REFERENCES

Bebr, G. (1992), 'Case Law', 29 *Common Market Law Review*, 577.

Biavati, P. (2011), *European Civil Procedure* (Alphen aan den Rijn, The Netherlands: Wolters Kluwer).

Drewry, G. (1973), 'Leapfrogging—And a Lord Justice's Eye View of the Final Appeal', 89 *Law Quarterly Review*, 260.

Edward. D. (2004), 'Luxembourg in Retrospect: A New Europe in Prospect', 16 *European Business Journal*, 120.

Maughan, C. and Maughan, M. (2015), 'Legal Writing', in J. Webb *et al.*, *Lawyers' Skills* (20th edn, Oxford: Oxford University Press).

May, C. (2014), 'A Learning Secret: Don't Take Notes With a Laptop', *Scientific American*, 3 June 2014. Available at http://www.scientificamerican.com/article/a-learning-secret-don-t-take-notes-with-a-laptop/.

Paterson, A. (2015), '*Final Judgment* Revisited' 21 *European Journal of Current Legal Issues*, No.1. Available at http://webjcli.org/article/view/418/531.

REGAN, D. (2014), 'Ward of Court', *New Law Journal*, 19 September 2014. Available at http://www.newlawjournal.co.uk/nlj/content/ward-court.

ROBINSON, W. (2008), 'Drafting of EU Acts: A View from the European Commission', in C. Stefanou and H. Xanthaki (eds) *Legislative Drafting: A Modern Approach* (Aldershot: Ashgate).

TOSHKOV, D. (n.d.), '55 years of EU Legislation', online presentation, Available at http://www.dimiter.eu/Eurlex.html.

VRANKEN, M. (1996), 'Role of the Advocate General in the Law-making Process of the European Community', 25 *Anglo-American Law Review*, 39.

WATSON, G. (1996), 'From an Adversarial to a Managed System of Litigation: A Comparative Critique of Lord Woolf's Interim Report', in R. Smith (ed.), *Achieving Civil Justice* (London: Legal Action Group), 63.

*WILLIAMS, K. (1989), *Study Skills* (Basingstoke: Macmillan).

4

From Reading to Writing

The processes of reading and note-taking will often be the precursor to a specific writing task—an essay or examination script. In this chapter we will consider briefly the techniques involved in basic academic legal writing, an aspect of one of the key skills required by employers, namely, written communication. There are many good, specialist, books on the market which cover general academic skills such as oral communication, mooting, team work, etc. (we have listed some at the end of the chapter), but here we want to introduce you to some of the basic requirements for producing what is still the most common form of assessment: written pieces of work.

4.1 Writing Legal Essays

Writing legal essays is essentially about three things:

- conveying *information*;
- constructing an *argument* based on the information you have acquired;
- *applying* the information and the arguments to the essay title or the problem posed.

4.1.1 Conveying Information

Any essay you are asked to write will require you to tell the reader what you know about the subject under discussion. In conveying that information there are three cardinal rules, set out as follows.

Cardinal rule 1: be accurate

Try to be as precise as possible in the information you put down. Vagueness is a sure sign of a lack of understanding or insufficient thought. If it is not possible to give an accurate statement of the principles involved (perhaps because the law is in a muddle), then say that there is no single answer and *clearly distinguish any alternatives that seem to exist*.

Accuracy is also about clarity of meaning. Style is important because a good style enhances the clarity of your exposition and your arguments can be only as good as your ability to express them. Do not ignore the fact that language has its own rhythm, and this can often guide you to sentences or phrases which do not work. Some people find that reading work aloud helps in this, because if a phrase sounds wrong it probably is wrong. Some people test out their work on friends who know nothing about the subject to see if the essay is clear enough.

An example of a very good writing style (even when the decisions are questionable) can be found in most of Lord Denning's judgments. He tended to favour a mixture of short and long sentences (with the balance in favour of short sentences). This creates a pattern which most people find attractive to read. Here is one of Lord Denning's more famous openings (from the case of *Hinz* v *Berry* [1970] 2 QB 40):

> It happened on 19 April 1964. It was bluebell time in Kent. Mr and Mrs Hinz, the plaintiff, had been married some ten years, and they had four children, all aged nine and under. The youngest was one. The plaintiff was a remarkable woman. In addition to her own four, she was foster mother to four other children. To add to it, she was two months pregnant with her fifth child.

Forget about the content: look at the patterns created and how they draw you into the narrative. Here is another example (from a case called *Thornton* v *Shoe Lane Parking* [1971] 2 QB 163). The passage centres on the point at which a contract is formed when driving up to an automated ticket machine. Lord Denning starts by referring to existing authorities that dealt in general terms with terms appearing on tickets. Again, look at the use of short and long sentences:

> These cases were based on the theory that the customer, on being handed the ticket, could refuse it and decline to enter into a contract on those terms. He could ask for his money back. That theory was, of course, a fiction. No customer in a thousand ever read the conditions. If he had stopped to do so, he would have missed the train or the boat. None of those cases has any application to a ticket which is issued by an automatic machine. The customer pays his money and gets a ticket. He cannot refuse it. He cannot get his money back. He may protest to the machine, even swear at it; but it will remain unmoved. He is committed beyond recall. He was committed at the very moment when he put his money into the machine. The contract was concluded at that time. It can be translated into offer and acceptance in this way. The offer is made when the proprietor of the machine holds it out as being ready to receive the money. The acceptance takes place when the customer puts his money into the slot.

A similar style can be found in the judgments of Laddie J. (e.g. here in a case called *Series 5 Software Ltd* v *Clarke* [1996] 1 All ER 853). Note how the learned judge mixes short and longer sentences, as needed, to explain the points:

> The basic outline of the dispute between the parties is as follows. The plaintiff is a company which is engaged in the development, production and sale of computer software for use in the printing and publishing industry. It commenced trading in June, 1992. Its main product is a software system called 'QC 2000' which enables print shops to quote, manage and schedule their production. It claims that it employed Mr Jenkinson, the fifth defendant, in February, 1995 as a technician, Mr Clarke, the first defendant, in June, 1995 as a sales manager and Mr Wheeler, the fourth defendant, as a computer programmer. The employment did not last long. By letters of August 25, 1995 all the defendants resigned. The three defendants say that this was because they had all been treated very shabbily. Their salaries were paid with cheques which were not honoured or they simply were not paid at all. There is little dispute as to this….

An example of how to refer to case law in a simple manner can be found in Dillon LJ's judgment in *Interfoto Picture Library Ltd* v *Stiletto Visual Programmes Ltd* [1989] QB 433, at 438:

> Counsel for the plaintiffs submits that *Thornton* v *Shoe Lane Parking Ltd* [1971] 2 Q.B. 613 was a case of an exemption clause and that what their Lordships said must be read as limited to exemption clauses

and in particular exemption clauses which would deprive the party on whom they are imposed of statutory rights. But what their Lordships said was said by way of interpretation and application of the general statement of the law by Mellish LJ in *Parker* v *South Eastern Railway Co.*, 2 C.P.D. 416, 423–424 and the logic of it is applicable to any particularly onerous clause in a printed set of conditions of the one contracting party which would not be generally known to the other party. Condition 2 of these plaintiffs' conditions is in my judgment a very onerous clause.

This has two long sentences and one short sentence, but clearly lays out a pattern, a structure which is easy to follow. His Lordship sets up the proposition (put by counsel), disagrees with this by reference to his interpretation of the authorities, and then sets about applying that analysis to the facts. Note also that in **Exercise 12** in **Chapter 7** we give some examples of how cases can be cited in essays.

It is equally important to avoid jargon or words you do not understand. Do not be like the famous Mrs Malaprop, with her 'nice derangement of epitaphs'. If in doubt, use a dictionary or a thesaurus if you want to bring in alternative vocabulary.

Cardinal rule 2: be relevant

Do not introduce something you know or suspect to be irrelevant into an answer. There is a great temptation to throw every possible bit of information you have at the question, and hope that some of it is right (what many lecturers call a 'shotgun' approach). This does not look impressive, as it again suggests a lack of forethought. Keeping to what is relevant is not magic; it is simply a question of familiarity with and understanding of your material. If you have taken the time to analyse the question, and thought out what is expected of you, there should be no need to adopt such an approach.

Cardinal rule 3: be concise

In our experience, lecturers do not award marks on the basis of the number of pages filled. It is obviously impossible for us to state what the 'average' acceptable length of an essay is, as criteria vary from course to course and year to year. You should always be guided by your tutors as to what is required. If you are given an indication of the appropriate length, then any significant shortfall normally indicates that something is missing.

Brevity is not, ultimately, just about the number of words you use; it is about how you use them. Again, it is a matter of clarity. Clarity is best achieved by short sentences and the proper use of paragraphs. You can add interest and explain related ideas by using some longer sentences but remember that a sentence should always make sense, and that each separate issue you discuss deserves its own paragraph.

A common misuse of sentences seems to be the 'hanging sentence', for example:

- *'Whereas the claimant has a good case. Therefore he should be advised to bring a claim.'*
  The first 'sentence' does not make sense: it goes nowhere and is technically not a sentence at all.

Here is another example:

- *'As counsel failed in her professional capacity to secure the company's costs. Then surely she should pay the costs herself as she was engaged as a competent and qualified person.'*
  You might just be able to run these together (with some amendments) to make one sentence, but, as they stand, neither 'sentence' does its job.

A sentence is a complete idea, capable of standing on its own. Forgive us for also making the basic point that a sentence begins with a capital letter and ends with a full stop. In addition, it must contain a main clause which usually has a subject, verb, and object, though it may contain much more. In our first example the student probably meant to write something like: 'The claimant appears to have a good case and should be advised to bring a claim'.

Sentences full of long words do not impress unless they convey a meaning not otherwise possible. Lawyers, perhaps more than any other profession, have a reputation for pomposity. It is a reputation that is not wholly undeserved.

4.1.2 Language

Formal legal writing is still perceived to be very different from everyday English. Indeed, there are those who suspect that its connexions with the English language are little more than coincidental. This is because, at its worst, it not only uses technical terms outside the general language, but also uses forms of language and phrasing that are archaic, and often redundant—documents full of jargon interspersed with the occasional 'whatsoever', 'wheresoever', 'heretofore', and 'hereafter'. In a brilliant parody, James D. Gordon III (1991: 1689) offers a classic example of such 'legalese'; a lawyer's translation of the phrase, 'I give you this orange':

> Know all men by these presents that I hereby give, grant, bargain, sell, release, convey, transfer, and quitclaim all my right, title, interest, benefit and use whatever in, of, and concerning this chattel, otherwise known as an orange, or citrus orantium, together with all the appurtenances thereto of skin, pulp, pip, rind, seeds and juice, to have and to hold the said orange together with its skin, pulp, pip, rind, seeds and juice for his own use and behoof, to himself and his heirs in fee simple forever, free from all liens, encumbrances, easements, limitations, restraints or conditions whatsoever, and all prior deeds, transfers or other documents whatsoever, now or anywhere made to the contrary notwithstanding, with full power to bite, cut, suck or otherwise eat the said orange or to give away the same, with or without its skin, pulp, pip, rind, seeds or juice.

Fortunately, this kind of 'supernatural incantation' (to borrow Gordon's phrase) is becoming far less common in legal practice, where there is a growing tendency to simplify documents and to move towards a system of 'plain English' drafting (see Watson-Brown, 2009). Although mastery of technical legal language is a requisite for both the study and practice of law, jargon used for its own sake has no place in the law school. Do not let your choice of words turn your work into a parody of legal language.

However, there is no escaping the fact that legal language is littered with Latin and Norman-French words: *ratio decidendi*, *stare decisis*, *autrefois acquit*, puisne judges, to name but a few. Many of these have, quite rightly, been abandoned—at least when talking to clients. However, that is a recent development and the law reports are full of such terms, so when you read a report from, say, 1950 you will encounter these and it is best to have a working knowledge of what they mean. Oddly enough, the one Latin term most lawyers come across very early in their studies (*mens rea*) does not mean what most textbooks say it means ('guilty mind') but just means 'mind thing' and the Romans never used this as a legal term anyway.

Legal jargon can also arise in unexpected quarters. A question once asked of one of the authors by an employment tribunal judge in Truro in an unfair dismissal case ('Are you asking me to read that *eiusdem generis* with the rest of the section so as to incorporate a notion of *mens rea?*') would not have been well received with a response of: 'I have no idea what you are talking about'. The case later went to the Court of Appeal on the question of whether one should use the criminal law concept of *mens rea* in employment misconduct cases.

All this need not be as terrifying as it first appears: we use Norman-French and Latin words every day. In a legal setting the following are all of Norman-French derivation yet they are used widely: accused, defendant, perjury, judgment, jury, arson, and dungeon. In a non-legal setting we have words such as bacon, pork, and beef (which, when out in the fields and not on the table, retain their Saxon names of pig and cow). Latin phrases such as *caveat emptor, ad nauseam, per se*, and *et cetera* are used frequently in ordinary conversation. English developed from a whole range of languages—chiefly, Latin, Ancient Greek, Norman-French, the Germanic and Scandinavian languages, and later Hindi and Urdu—adopting and adapting them when necessary. This is one of its great strengths.

4.1.3 Constructing an Argument

Essay writing is about constructing an *argument* based on the information you have acquired. Essay questions inevitably ask you to structure your material in one way or another. The clue usually lies in the first or last words of the question: 'Consider critically'; 'Discuss'; 'Evaluate', and so on. The greatest failing of all is to miss the significance of those words and simply 'write all you know' about a topic without bringing any critical faculty into play. 'Discuss' is the most general of these: anything else tends to narrow the field of enquiry.

The key thing to remember about argument in academic writing is that there are certain conventional rules about what constitutes a 'good argument'. If you have had little or no previous experience of this type of writing, it is something you will certainly need to think about, and practise. There are many useful publications on study skills, and we have listed some of them at the end of this chapter. We can briefly summarise the techniques here.

Authority

When lawyers use the word 'authority' we are referring to *legal* authority, i.e. cases and legislation (including European sources) together with academic sources, such as textbooks and journals. A good legal argument requires authority: it is insufficient to rely on your own value judgements or 'common sense'. **Any arguments you advance must be supported by authority from primary source (cases, legislation) or at least secondary sources (legal academic literature). Primary sources take precedence over secondary sources.**

Your own value judgements do not constitute evidence of how things work. To be blunt: your opinion does not matter unless it is backed by authority. Value judgements also personalise the debate, so that your arguments will lack a sense of objectivity. You may bring an element of value judgement into play in a conclusion, for example, where you have to choose between two established alternative arguments, but even then you should indicate why one argument is to be preferred. Your preference should be supportable on rational grounds, not just on the basis that 'I think it is the better answer' or 'this is fairer'. Common sense is of no more worth than one person's value judgement.

An argument is not necessarily true because the proponent believes most other people would support it. For instance, it is 'common knowledge' that before Christopher Columbus discovered America everyone thought the world was flat. First, he did not discover America (even from a European perspective) and secondly, at the time of his journey in 1492 very few people thought the world was flat—and had not thought so since the time of the Ancient Greeks. He was trying to sail around the world to find a quicker route to Japan; that is how he raised the money for the voyage, so a flat world would have been a problem. Nevertheless, possibly under the influence of the lyric 'They all laughed at Christopher Columbus when he said the world was round' (in the song 'They all laughed' by Ira and George Gershwin), there is the commonly held belief that our ancestors were a little on the stupid side. So much for generally held beliefs.

Having a plan

A good argument is built up carefully. In developing that argument it is important to have a plan of where you are going and, to persuade most people, arguments need to be developed gradually. A good essay comprises three elements:

- introduction;
- discussion; and
- conclusion.

Your *introduction* should explain what you are setting out to do. Your *discussion* should display the relevant information, derived from the appropriate sources, and show clearly on what side of the argument each piece falls. The *conclusion* should sum up the main points you have made and make clear your conclusions regarding the question asked. Keep these separate functions clearly in mind. Do not fall into the trap of presenting a lengthy ramble through the detail of the law, followed by a final paragraph containing a number of disparate critical remarks. That does not constitute an argument.

We return to this theme in **Exercise 12** in **Chapter 7**. There we have set out how an essay may be written using the structure described earlier and how you would cite relevant authorities. As the 'essay' concerns points discussed in **Chapters 6** and **7** we have left this fuller account until you have read those chapters.

Use of visual aids

You may find it helpful when planning an answer to reduce your plan to a diagrammatic form. Space precludes us from exploring the options in any depth, but you should be aware that there are a number of techniques you can use, including flowcharts and 'decision trees', which help you to construct a logical framework for ideas or processes, and 'mind maps' (see Buzan, 2002), which provide, it is said, a less formally structured way into a problem, and therefore a less restrictive and more powerful way of identifying the issues and making connexions between ideas. For examples of how each of these can be used to support legal problem solving, see Maughan and Webb (2005: ch. 10). **Figure 4.1** is a simple flowchart which could be used to examine the question of offer and acceptance in the law of contract.

A final word of warning: good planning and good writing technique can never wholly disguise a lack of content. It can, however, enable you to use your knowledge to its best effect. Failure to abide by the basic rules can be met with the kind of indignity once

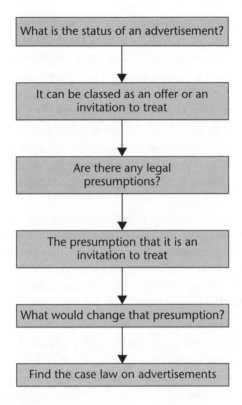

Figure 4.1 Law of contract: offer and acceptance

meted out to an attorney by the United States Supreme Court. The Court returned a brief with the instruction that a whole new set of papers be filed in a form that was 'logically arranged...concise and free from burdensome, irrelevant and immaterial matter...' (*Gilchrist* v *Interborough Rapid Transit Co.* (1929) 279 US 159). Back in the UK, in 2008, one judge referred to a prosecutor who kept saying 'grievous bodily harm' instead of 'grievous bodily harm' as 'an illiterate idiot'. We hope that none of your work receives a similar response.

4.1.4 Applying the Information

We will explore this more fully in the next section as regards the key topic of 'problem questions' but the idea of 'application' also relates to writing what may be termed 'pure essays' (the ones that have a quote or statement followed by 'Discuss' or something similar). The basic rule with these essays is to try to relate your answer throughout the text to the statement posed (i.e. do not write everything you know about a topic and then have a conclusion which starts, 'So, as can be seen, the statement is true...'). Here are some preliminary matters you need to note which concern all legal problems and essay questions set at academic stage:

- There is always a potential problem of proving the facts (a question of evidence). With such questions, however, unless you are actually studying the law of evidence, this is not something you need to worry about. All these questions are posed on the basis that the facts can be proven, so if you start examining all the problems of proof you will not be answering the question. Don't worry for the moment as to how we know that 'Patrick wanted to kill the neighbour's cat'. If the question says he did, then he did.

- Pure essay questions tend to present you with an extract from a book or judgment and ask you to comment on this. More marks are gained by relating your answer to the quotation than to your general description of the area of law in question.

- The question might ask you to discuss X's possible guilt. It could ask something different, e.g. 'what possible defences may she have to a charge of murder?' or 'For what crimes might X be charged?'. Although covering similar ground, these questions raise slightly different points and it is that question that should be answered specifically.

- In problems based on contract, negligence, and other civil matters it is quite common for the examiner to ask you to advise one client on his or her potential liability. If this is so, structure your answer to do this and do not just describe the legal position generally. Imagine, for instance, you are giving advice to a real client sitting in front of you. He or she wants their problem answered, not a general lecture on the law of trespass. Questions on criminal law tend to be more straightforward: is X guilty or not?

Here is an example of how to relate your essay to a title which reads: '*Most employers now believe that the law of unfair dismissal has gone too far in providing all employees with statutory rights which restrict the managerial prerogative of employers. Discuss.*' The statement asks for comment on a specific issue, not for a rambling exposition of the law on unfair dismissal. The comment is deliberately provocative and reflects how many employers mistakenly perceive the law on unfair dismissal to be biased in the employees' favour (the irony being that most employees think it is balanced in the employers' favour). So, one comment (early on) could be:

Before we discuss the merits of the claims made in the essay title we should note that the statement contains a common fallacy: it is based on the premise that *all* employees have the right to claim unfair dismissal. This is not true: in most cases only those employed for two years or more gain this right.

Another example might be:

When the statement in issue refers to 'managerial prerogative' it begs the question: what is 'managerial prerogative'? If it means that employers should have the right to dismiss without reason or justification, then it is certainly the case that the law restricts their freedom.

4.2 Answering Legal Problems

In studying law many of you will encounter what law teachers call 'problem questions' for the first time. Most students find these the best part of studying law because, to a limited extent, you are trying to apply the law to the facts as if in real life. Indeed, as we noted earlier, a good way to approach these questions is to imagine a real client asking you for advice (and then to imagine how, if you were the client, that advice addresses your concerns). The basic techniques of introduction and discussion which we have already considered apply to problems as much as essays, but you must be aware of the fact that you are dealing with a different kind of question.

The essence of any problem question is that it requires you to analyse some fictitious situation and consider questions of legal liability that it creates. The precise scope of your answer will depend on what you are asked to do. The facts will normally be followed by some such request as 'Discuss'; 'Advise Ann'; or 'Advise Ken of his liability to Lee'. Do not ignore this: questions of standpoint and objective are as important to the student as the practitioner; so, in dealing with problems always remember who you are advising and what you are trying to do. For example, it may be that the problem concerning Ken and Lee also involves a third party, Mary. But if you have not been asked about Mary's rights or liabilities, it would be a serious error to discuss them. If 'Discuss' is used then you have a freer rein.

Problem questions are usually constructed on a number of levels. Chiefly, this enables teachers to differentiate more clearly between the various qualities of answer. Most will therefore have one or two major issues, plus a number of less obvious legal points, or 'twists' to the facts which, for example, could distinguish the events from an earlier case which you might cite as a precedent. Particularly in examinations, it can be difficult to sort out the factual material and assess its legal implications in the time available. There is no instant solution to this. The answer lies in having a good working knowledge of the relevant law (this helps you to identify those facts which will have legal significance) and in adopting a systematic approach to the question.

By 'systematic' we mean that you must learn to use the question to help construct an answer. Let us explain. Most problems involve a sequence of events, so that x happens, followed by y, then z. Often x, y, and z have separate legal consequences, so by following the facts as laid down you can explore the consequences of each event, as it 'happens'. This should help ensure that you do not miss elements of the question completely. However, you may also need to rearrange the discussion.

For instance, imagine you are studying the law of wills (often called the law of succession) and the question states that, 'Ms Lee was an elderly lady who rewrote her will on her deathbed to leave everything to her solicitor. Her previous will left all her estate to two of her children (Ann and Bob) in equal measure but omitted any reference to her third child, Christopher. Ann and Bob wish to challenge the latest will and Christopher wishes to challenge both wills. Discuss.' Probably the best way to deal with this is to concentrate on the final will first and test its validity (it may not be valid because the solicitor exercised undue influence or even fraud or perhaps it was not witnessed properly). If that will stands, then no further discussion would be necessary in reality. However, the examiner would expect you then to analyse the position where that 'final' will is invalid, because Christopher was left out of the first will (this is an example of an 'unspoken' question in the problem, seen in the specific reference to Christopher). You would introduce this with a sentence which begins: 'Assuming, however, that the final will is invalid…' and then go on to discuss the possibilities. So, if the final will is invalid we need to examine whether the law allows the first will to be revived in these circumstances and, if it can be revived, whether it can validly exclude Christopher.

You would need to examine how he might challenge the will. You then need to explain the consequences of that first will being either valid or invalid. Here, you have worked chronologically, but in reverse.

Sometimes, of course, one fact becomes relevant only when linked with something else which appears later in the question. So long as you make the right links, and do not lose sight of them, the same technique can apply. Again, you may find using 'mind maps' helps you to keep track of facts and the legal issues they raise. Above all else, developing a good problem-solving technique takes practice; do not miss out because of a lack of it. On most law courses that practice is offered in seminars, tutorials, or workshops which 'test out' different answers to legal problems.

One key weakness identified by lecturers all over the world seems to be that of 'applying' the law to the facts, so here is an exercise in that as regards the use of case law (you will find similar exercises on answering legal questions on precedent at **Exercise 12** in **Chapter 7** and concerning the interpretation of statutes at **Exercise 18** in **Chapter 9**). **As we have not fully discussed the operation and importance of statutes or case law, we will take some shortcuts here, but you may find it useful to return to this exercise when you have read Chapters 6 and 7**. Our example here concerns the law on age discrimination.

EXERCISE 5 An age of discrimination

Outline of the law: Employers can no longer dismiss an employee 'for retirement' at age 65 or any other age unless they can demonstrate why this is not 'unfair' (as statutorily defined) and why this would not be age discrimination.

 QUESTION

Keith is 57 and is employed by a company which specialises in removing asbestos from old buildings. He is told by his employer that he will be forced to retire in six months' time when he reaches 58 as this is the company's 'normal retirement age'. He does not wish to retire and so challenges this as amounting to discrimination and unfair dismissal. He points out that his colleague, Xena, who works in the finance department is the same age as Keith and she is not being 'retired'. The company claims that because of the strenuous nature of the work it has a general policy of retiring workers in Keith's job at 58 for health reasons.

 ANSWER

First you need to marshal your information (as noted earlier). This will mean acquiring information on: (a) the relevant legislation (if there is any); and (b) case law on 'retirement'. You find that the legislation is mainly contained in the Equality Act 2010 and follows the outline described previously but that there is quite a lot of UK and EU case law on the meaning of 'retirement'. You must now read that case law in depth. One thing you notice from the case law is that an employer can force someone to retire at a particular age— called an 'employer-justified retirement age' (EJRA)—but it must not be discriminatory and the justification must clearly apply to the particular employee affected. This is how you might apply that information (we have not used real case names or section numbers):

The Equality Act 2010 prevents employers dismissing employees on the grounds of 'retirement' (see section x) but allows for a company to have an EJRA (see section y). However, the case of

continued

EXERCISE 5 *continued*

A v *B* set out the conditions for establishing an EJRA. One key aspect of that case was that the EJRA must not be discriminatory and that it had to be clear that the EJRA applied directly to the affected employee (here, Keith). The case of *C* v *D* also emphasised that this must be clear from the contract: that something did not constitute an EJRA just because that was what normally happened—there must be a contractual requirement to retire at that age.

[**Comment: this is good at establishing the basic ground on which to build the application. It is not *application* itself because we have not related our findings to the question yet; we have not solved Keith's problem—now we need to do that**].

Here is how you could apply your research:

In our problem Keith is 58 at the point of 'retirement'. Any dismissal for retirement reasons will be unfair unless there is an effective 'employer-justified retirement age' (EJRA) at the company which could apply to him (see Case *A* v *B*). The company's general policy might be an EJRA if it can clearly be shown to apply to Keith, but the case of *C* v *D* requires us to find a clear contractual term to this effect and the case of *E* v *F*, a German case in the Court of Justice of the European Union, tells us that there must be some 'social policy' ground for the retirement age. The evidence we have from Keith (which may be disputed) is that the contract does not allow for this. If Keith is correct (*note here that if the question does not tell you about a key point the examiner expects you take account of both possibilities*), there can be no EJRA and the dismissal is unfair. (*This applies your finding on the facts to the law you have discovered so that you can reach a conclusion as to consequence.*) Only if the 'company policy' can be interpreted as a contractual term which applies directly to Keith will the company have an effective EJRA to enforce against him. We know that *C* v *D* established that 'company policies' will generally not be regarded as binding contractual terms, so (*application of that case to the facts*) it seems unlikely that the policy will bind Keith. Further, even if they have a policy which is deemed a term of the contract but they do not enforce it against, say, female secretaries, then this will mean the EJRA is discriminatory and not effective. The company may, however, overcome the claim of discrimination if they can show justification (here, related to the so-called health reasons—which should fall within the reasoning of the Court of Justice in *E* v *F*). (*These last points show a lawyer's caution in accepting that we may possibly lose the argument on whether a policy is a contractual term, but we have a reserve argument on discrimination. The evidence in Keith's favour is given in the question—the reference to Xena. On the whole examiners do not put in facts without a reason so this should always be a clue for you. This is an example of a 'hidden fact' or 'twist' inasmuch as the question does not ask you about discrimination explicitly but hints at it through the reference to Xena. This is not unfair: very often you have to extract this sort of thing from real clients in practice as they do not know the significance of the facts themselves.*)

Note that what we have not done here is to make general statements about how older people should be treated, nor have we tried to say whether we think such treatment 'fair' or 'unfair' except in the statutory sense. We have taken the key points in the question and *applied* those to the statute and case law. **In other words, we have tested the facts as given against the law we researched in the same way as if responding to a real client.** It is vital, when dealing with problem questions to actually address the problem raised. However banal or obvious this seems, the major reason that law students do badly when answering problem questions (other than lack of knowledge) is their failure to attempt to solve the client's problem.

4.3 How to Present Your Answer

There are a number of models and strategies available. Though some law teachers take the view that these can be too formulaic, we think they are a useful tool in developing competence and confidence in answering problem questions. One of the most widely used is **'IRAC'**. This requires you to break your answer down into four elements:

- Introduce the **Issues**: show that you have correctly identified that the problem raises the issues (say) of the *mens rea* in homicide and defences to murder, or of what steps can constitute consideration in contract.
- Discuss the **Rules**: this enables you to show that you know the law. Don't use it as an opportunity just to write everything you know about murder, or negligence. Keep it focused to the issues, but don't stray into the detailed analysis of fact at this stage. Imagine, for instance, that the problem posed is this: *'Tired of being kept awake at night by the howling of the local fox population, Alex takes his shotgun, goes into the garden, and fires at some foxes. He kills two but with the third shot he misses a fox as it passes by a house, the shot goes through an open window into the house, and kills Bob. Alex is charged with murder. Discuss.'*

  The question clearly relates to the problem area of the lines to be drawn between murder (with intent or recklessness) and manslaughter. For these purposes we will concentrate on intent and recklessness. Your research reveals that *Blackstone's Criminal Practice 2015* [at A2.6] says that recklessness is 'essentially concerned with unjustified risk-taking' and that 'the precise meaning of the term "recklessness" has been the subject of great controversy…'. The text then shows that there are many ways intention and recklessness can overlap. Now, if all you do is to copy and paste section A2.6 there is little to reward. You need to explore the cases and the classifications given by *Blackstone's*, but keeping in mind A's case, not just a general description:

- **Apply** the rules to the facts in this scenario. Make sure here that you state the legal implications of all the material facts, and identify any issues of doubt. Cross-refer to authorities (statute, precedent, or maybe even academic authority) wherever possible— most of these you will have already discussed in the **Rules** part of your answer. What does your research tell you about Alex's case? When he fired at the fox (as it passed a house) what category of intent or recklessness (if any) did he fit into according to any legal authorities you have explored?
- **Conclude** by summarising your analysis. This is an opportunity to make clear that you have appreciated your instructions. If the question says 'advise Diana', then phrase your conclusion as legal advice to Diana—make it clear (so far as the information given to you allows) whether, on these facts, you think Diana is liable. If you cannot come to a definite conclusion, clearly state why and identify what information you would need to complete your advice.

4.4 Planning Your Answers

Whatever you are writing, take note of two fundamental principles. First, there is one vital ingredient in any writing—will power. Unfortunately, essays do not write themselves, and most universities enforce strict deadlines. The hardest part of any piece of writing is actually to sit down at your desk and begin. It is much easier to go and make the tenth cup of coffee that evening, or decide that cleaning the fridge *now* is imperative. Such delaying tactics can reflect a whole variety of difficulties—from a lack of confidence to total boredom with the subject matter, though normal human inertia is probably the most common cause. We cannot pretend to have a magic cure, but offer the following advice:

- Find a period in which you can work reasonably undisturbed. Time to think and plan is normally vital to producing good written work, particularly as careful planning can remove much of the apprehension that surrounds the writing process.

- The hardest parts to write are often the introduction and/or the conclusion, so leave these until last. Draft the various points of your argument first and then come back to the finishing touches. Probably the worst thing you can do is to try to finalise your opening sentence before anything else has been written.

- Pace yourself. Many of us justify leaving things to the last minute on the basis that we 'work better under pressure'. That is nearly always a myth. Perhaps some of us *only* work under pressure; but it is rarely the best that we can do. Instead it is usually hurried and full of half-developed ideas that sound fine at 2.00 a.m., but are much less convincing in the cold light of day.

The second piece of general advice is: never miss an opportunity to check your work before submitting it. Many minor errors can be found this way. We all make these mistakes. They can be humorous at times (e.g. one student who meant to write 'The jury is the last bastion of freedom left in the English legal system', but wrote 'The jury is the last bastard of freedom...') or the shop sign in Exeter which read 'Buy your wedding gown get a Bridesmaid half price', but frequent occurrences demonstrate carelessness. Re-reading also gives you an opportunity to review your own writing critically, and make sure that it makes sense. A student who begins an essay on the cost of litigation with the sentence 'Litigation is expensive, particularly if the defendant contests the case' will probably be given the benefit of the doubt; but repeat that sort of error too often in one piece of work and the marker will inevitably question your understanding of the subject.

4.4.1 Spelling and Punctuation

Do these things matter? The short answer is yes—lawyers deal with words and the presentation of information. Universities are more tolerant of mistakes than practitioners, especially if there is a question of dyslexia. Clients, on the whole, are not tolerant of anything which does not serve their purpose. A badly written essay will annoy but probably will not be penalised (certainly under examination conditions); a badly written letter or claim will annoy judges and clients alike.

This is not a text on spelling, grammar, syntax, etc. However, we would advise that you do all you can to avoid or correct mistakes and to try to be observant. If you see that in some cases a word is spelt, say, as 'principle' but in others it appears as 'principal', or you see 'discrete' and 'discreet', or 'prescribe' and 'proscribe', or 'uninterested' and 'disinterested', or 'substantive' and 'substantial', and do not know the differences, do not dodge the issue: find out why they are different. Arm yourself with a good dictionary, a good legal dictionary, and any other help you can find—and do not always trust your computer's 'spell-checker' to save the day.

By way of consolation, even experienced lawyers can make some interesting mistakes (and we recognise we may have been guilty of such errors in this text too). Here is a Practice Direction from 1965: 'The Lord Chancellor and the Lords of Appeal in Ordinary have agreed that from the beginning of next term Queen's Counsel appearing before the Appellate Committee of the House of Lords will only wear full-bottomed wigs when their Lordships are sitting in the Chamber either for the hearing of appeals or for delivering judgments.' The idea of barristers appearing *only* in full-bottomed wigs needs no further comment.

An extreme example of how punctuation can turn apparent nonsense into sense is the sentence: '*Where James had had had Julian had had had had had had had my approval*'. This can be made to make sense with the careful placement of punctuation. Imagine James had written an essay which included the sentence, 'The lawyer had permission from the court but had failed to make use of it' but Julian had more accurately written, 'The lawyer had had permission from the court but had failed to make use of it'. The teacher prefers Julian's use of the pluperfect tense in his sentence ('had had') and comments on the essays thus: '*Where James had had, "had", Julian had had "had had"; "had had" had my approval*'. This conundrum has been around for some time: see for example, *A New Miscellany-at-Law* by R.E. Megarry (2005: 203). In the real legal world it has not been unknown for the fate of millions of pounds to rest on the placing of a comma in a sentence.

4.5 Referencing Your Work

4.5.1 The Significance of Referencing

Referencing is an important skill, particularly if you are undertaking coursework or completing a project. Referencing matters for two main reasons:

- Without showing that you have legal authority to make a point all you are doing is giving your opinion and, as we noted previously, that does not carry any weight.
- Referencing is really a matter of integrity. It demonstrates that you have credited someone else's thoughts or words. In practical terms it also means that you cannot be accused of plagiarism. Many students think that by showing where they obtained an idea they will lose marks for lack of originality. The opposite is true: all tutors welcome originality but will also give credit for sound research and clear authority. **So, citing your sources is a sign of strength, not weakness.** Effective referencing should: (a) be clear and accurate enough for your reader to identify precisely the sources you have used and your care and accuracy in using them; (b) enable you to show accurately the breadth and depth of your research, and hence to obtain the credit you deserve for that effort. The originality can come into play when you bring all your sources together and then come up with a good argument.

4.5.2 How Should You Reference Your Work?

There are a number of approaches, and you may find that your law school (or even a particular tutor) has a preferred style. The following options are more or less standard, and in the absence of more specific guidance, should be considered.

Footnotes/endnotes

These perform the same function. Footnotes appear at the bottom of the page on which the reference is referred to, endnotes are collated at the end of the document. All good word-processing packages have automatic footnote/endnote facilities which make the creation of notes relatively easy. If you are using footnotes/endnotes, you should provide a full bibliographic reference to your sources:

- Any list of **books** should identify author(s), title, edition, place of publication and publisher, date of publication, thus: Holland, J.A. and Webb, J.S., *Learning Legal Rules*, 9th edition (Oxford: Oxford University Press, 2016).

- **Articles** should cite the author(s), title, and journal reference. The title of the journal may either be cited in full or, if there is one, by using a recognised abbreviation (see the list of citations provided), thus: Webb, J., 'Being a Lawyer/Being a Human Being' (2002) *Legal Ethics* 130 or Webb, J., 'Being a Lawyer/Being a Human Being' (2002) LE 130.

- **Cases**, except where the case name appears in the text, should include the full case name and its citation using the accepted form of reference for that series of reports (see also the list provided), thus: *R v Simpson* [2003] EWCA Crim 1499. This example only has the 'neutral citation' but other cases might have a law report reference too. If so, both should be used: for example, *Actavis UK Ltd v Merck & Co Inc* [2008] EWCA Civ 444; [2009] 1 All ER 196. Of course, if the case dates from before the creation of the 'neutral citation' in 2001 it will only have a law report reference. It is acceptable for the note to give the year and citation for that reference only where the case name appears in the text. Be aware: wherever you are quoting or paraphrasing a particular passage of a book, case, article, or statute, you **must** reference it. Your reference should include the specific page number of the resource to which you refer.

Harvard referencing

This is much less used in legal scholarship than it is in the social sciences, but you may come across this style in interdisciplinary or socio-legal materials and courses, so it is helpful to be aware of how it works. It is also a means of referencing without resorting to footnotes (this is why we used a modified form of Harvard referencing in *Learning Legal Rules*). The system works like this:

- Works are cited in the text by author and year only (with page references if appropriate), thus: 'a number of writers (e.g. Flood, 1996; Martiny, 1999) argue that the international law firms are extremely sensitive to "choice-of-law" problems that may arise when conflicts occur in their clients transnational business transactions'; or you could say 'Flood (1996: 170) argues that...' (where 170 is the relevant page number).

- The references in the text are then cross-referable to your bibliography where they should appear thus: Flood, J. (1996) 'Megalawyering in the Global Order: The Cultural, Social and Economic Transformation of Global Legal Practice', *International Journal of the Legal Profession*, 3: 169. [Note: here '3' is the volume number and '169' is the first page; note also that standard journal abbreviations are not used with the Harvard method.]

- The format for citing books is similar, thus: Downes, D. and Rock, P. (2003) *Understanding Deviance*, 4th edition (Oxford: Oxford University Press).

- Cases and statutes must be cited in the text when you are using Harvard. It is acceptable to use the standard system of case citation, however.
- Current UK Law Report and journal citations were dealt with in **Chapter 3**.

4.6 How Are Law Essays Marked?

We have already seen that any answer to a legal question must contain authorities (generally cases or legislation but also the published views of other academics and practitioners). Marks are always given for the use of authorities, as long as they show something relevant. However, a list of cases alone is not enough—there must be some comment/application.

4.6.1 Marking Standards

There is an ongoing debate across education about how to define exactly what constitutes a first-class mark or a bare pass. Each university (and subject area) adopts similar guidelines, but there are variations. **You need to check with your own university's regulations to see how each category is defined.** As a basic guidance only we would suggest that the lines are drawn in the following way (these are adapted from a variety of sources, often referred to as 'benchmarking standards' issued by various 'quality assurance' bodies, e.g. those of the Quality Assurance Agency for Higher Education, found at http://www.qaa.ac.uk/assuring-standards-and-quality). For instance, the QAA states at 4.15 of the UK Quality Code for Higher Education Part A: Setting and Maintaining Academic Standards (at http://www.qaa.ac.uk/en/Publications/Documents/qualifications-frameworks.pdf):

> Bachelor's degrees with honours are awarded to students who have demonstrated:
> - a systematic understanding of key aspects of their field of study, including acquisition of coherent and detailed knowledge, at least some of which is at, or informed by, the forefront of defined aspects of a discipline
> - an ability to deploy accurately established techniques of analysis and enquiry within a discipline
> - conceptual understanding that enables the student: to devise and sustain arguments, and/or to solve problems, using ideas and techniques, some of which are at the forefront of a discipline; to describe and comment upon particular aspects of current research, or equivalent advanced scholarship, in the discipline
> - an appreciation of the uncertainty, ambiguity and limits of knowledge
> - the ability to manage their own learning, and to make use of scholarly reviews and primary sources (for example, refereed research articles and/or original materials appropriate to the discipline).

First class (70%+)

This will be an answer which builds upon a full, extremely accurate, and well-structured exposition of the subject area. Where appropriate the answer will contain sophisticated criticism or originality. There should be a clear and rigorous analysis of source materials and authorities, and a sustained, detailed consideration of alternative arguments. Within the relevant word limit or time constraint the student will therefore demonstrate an ability to be concise without losing detail. First-class answers are not perfect answers but they are ones that are exceptionally good for undergraduate level and most guidelines tend to focus on a student excelling in at least one and probably several of the following criteria:

- comprehensiveness and accuracy;
- analysis and critical evaluation;
- clarity of argument and expression;
- integration and use of a wide range of materials;
- evidence of wider reading; and
- insight into the theoretical issues.

Excellence in one or more of these areas should be in addition to the qualities expected of an upper second class answer.

Upper second class (60–69%)

This will be a critical and perceptive piece of work with an extensive and authoritative deployment of source materials. There will be a sustained development of the theme or analysis of the problem and conclusions will be reached by confident manipulation and synthesis of materials and authorities. One is looking for a mature and developed style of writing with a precise attention to detail and physical presentation. This class of answer covers a wide band of students. Some will be only marginally better than a lower second answer; some will only just fall short of a first-class mark. These are highly competent answers and would typically contain the following qualities:

- be accurate as regards all key areas;
- be reasonably comprehensive;
- be well-ordered and structured;
- show evidence of some wider reading;
- contain a sound grasp of basic principle;
- demonstrate a good understanding of relevant details;
- be succinct and cogently presented; and
- display evidence of some insight.

The upper second-class answer should have addressed all the key issues. The work should be well ordered, major and minor issues spotted, and legal argument accurately and comprehensively addressed. An accurate conclusion must summarise the work undertaken.

Lower second (50–59%)

This will be an accurate and ordered exposition of the subject area with proper use of source materials, both primary and secondary, containing a logical development of the theme with conclusions which show a clear understanding of the topic. Consistent and correct use of authorities and sound physical presentation should be present. An acceptable level of competence is required. Quality indications of such requirements are that the answer:

- is generally accurate;
- provides an adequate attempt to locate the subject within the dissertation field;
- is clearly presented;

- shows some but little development of the arguments; and

- contains some errors/omissions.

A lower second-class answer may be an answer which is good in parts but there is insufficient attention to detail or one which displays only average analytical ability.

Third class (40–49%)

One would expect an adequate exposition of the subject area with either insufficient or partially inaccurate use of authorities. This answer is likely to contain an ill-defined structure and with poor or no development of the theme, containing little or no criticism. The answer will not always be lucid and there will be inattention to detail. A third-class answer is one which demonstrates some knowledge or understanding but may be weak in any or more of the following areas:

- is descriptive only;

- omits an attempt to answer the problem/hypothesis;

- misses discussion of key points/issues;

- contains serious inaccuracies;

- covers material sparsely; and

- makes assertions which are unsupported by evidence.

A fail clearly does not even make it to the bottom of the third-class category. Apart from lack of knowledge, many students fail because they fall foul of some of the points made in the following section.

4.6.2 Common Errors

Here we list some of the things to be avoided in a piece of written work. This should be read in conjunction with all we have already noted:

- **Poor structure:** By this we mean answers which jump all over the place, dealing with one point and moving onto another only to return to the first later. Structure is very important in legal argument, so think about this carefully (use headings, etc. if this will help).

- **Questions you do not want the reader to ask when they have read a sentence, paragraph, etc. which you have written:**

   So what is the point or conclusion you are making?

   Why did you say that?

   On what legal authority is that argument based?

   What else is there (e.g. case law or statutes)?

- **'Wolf in sheep's clothing' phrases. These are phrases you might use which look like your friend—but they are not:**

   Therefore...

   Thus...

   It follows...

As can be seen…

Surely…

It is obvious that…

This seems unfair…

Clearly…

Why are these phrases dangerous? In themselves they are not, but usually there is little or no substance to justify them and they often demonstrate a personal view, rather than a legal argument. For instance, say you read the following passage:

> The law of negligence demands that there must be a direct link between the accident and the injury or damage suffered. We have seen that Adam and Berni were involved in an accident in which Berni says Adam failed to slow down approaching the junction and that Berni has suffered a broken leg from the collision. Therefore (or 'Thus', or 'Clearly', or 'Surely', etc.) Adam is liable to compensate Berni for all her injury.

There is a superficial air of logic about this, until you analyse it. What does the 'therefore' relate to? The first sentence is a general proposition (generally correct as it turns out). But after that all we really know is that Adam and Berni had a collision. We do not know whose fault it is (presumably this is being disputed). And even assuming Adam was negligent (and there are a number of other factors to consider before making that judgement), we do not know if Berni contributed to the accident in some way, so that Adam would not be liable to pay for *all* her injuries.

Here is another example:

> We know from the facts that Maud shot Simon at close range and that he died of his wounds. Surely she is therefore guilty of murder.

The one word 'Surely' betrays such a lack of knowledge in terms of both dealing with evidence and the law on homicide that this sentence is quite frightening. Even a non-lawyer would be able to see that Maud may not have meant to fire the gun or she may have fired it in self-defence. Once you have studied criminal law, you will also see that there may be other technical reasons why she is not liable for murder. So, the use of the word 'surely' is very dangerous: it pretends that there cannot possibly be any other answer and, in doing so, reveals an inability to think (never mind to think like a lawyer).

Essay openings to be avoided

'X is clearly liable'—*Really? So why was the question asked? Do not start with a conclusion.*

Saying everything about the area of law when most is irrelevant—*The classic 'shotgun' approach. This fails to answer the question posed. Merely describing the law (however accurately) does not bring with it many marks.*

Saying nothing; simply listing cases with some joining text. *The 'I've learned all this so I must pass' approach. As this shows no analysis or application (but may show a good memory), it will fail or be a borderline pass at best.* Here is an example of this bad practice: 'The law on nuisance was summed up in Case A and will apply here. Thus the landowner may be liable to others (see cases B, C and D along the same lines)'.

Incorrect use of cases

'X will be liable for his offer: see *Carlill* v *Carbolic Smoke Ball Company.*' *So, exactly why should we see Carlill? Does it cover X's case as well? This cannot be given credit as there is no reasoning present. Cases are authorities, to be used to demonstrate an argument, not pieces of jewellery to be worn ostentatiously.*

'The case of *Carlill* will apply here.' *But I'm not going to tell you how. This is a key point in our description of applying the law: merely noting or listing something is not application. What is needed instead is something like: 'In Carlill the specific terms set out in the advertisement (mainly the promise that money had been deposited at the local bank) turned an invitation to treat into an offer. The specific terms in our case are similar in that the company has offered a "guarantee" for all its work…'*

'*Carlill* clearly established that advertisements can amount to offers.' *Well, it did in part, but this does not explain the reasoning why an advertisement may sometimes constitute an offer (and there are cases which demonstrate when an advertisement will not amount to an offer too, so this is an incomplete summary).*

'As *Donoghue* v *Stevenson* does not apply on these facts, there can be no negligence.' *This tells us nothing: the dodge phrase is 'on these facts' and this really amounts to telling the reader to do the analysis themselves.*

All these points are simple examples. They are real: we have come across them in many essays across many universities. You need to avoid them because they will damage all your good work. Instead, we would advise you to follow the simple approaches we have advocated.

4.6.3 Plagiarism

One of the most damning accusations in academic circles, classed as a form of cheating by many, is that the essay plagiarises other people's work. Plagiarism is defined in subtly different ways and your own university may have specific guidance on it. Essentially, the definition is a simple one: if you pass off someone else's work or someone else's idea as your own, then you have committed plagiarism. It is a form of literary theft and is taken very seriously in universities.

The music industry is littered with examples of plagiarism, most often unconscious plagiarism but nevertheless ones that cost the plagiarising author a share of royalties. John Lennon, George Harrison, Oasis, Led Zeppelin, Vanilla Ice, Coldplay, amongst many others, have fallen foul of plagiarism and, as we write, Robin Thicke and Pharrell Williams are battling it out with Marvin Gaye's estate over the origin of the song 'Blurred Lines'.

With music the difference between being 'influenced' by another artist and copying can be difficult to draw and chord patterns, for instance, do not have unlimited variations. The position is different where you can cite the source in an essay. Here, plagiarism can be avoided very easily and the plea of 'unconscious plagiarism', or 'I didn't mean it' is not so persuasive.

By way of contrast, in the art world 'plagiarism' basically means forging and many works of art exist which never saw the paintbrush of Rembrandt, Monet, Van Gogh, for example, but make claims to have done so. And this is at the heart of what we are discussing here: a work presented as being painted by J.M.W. Turner which is not actually by Turner is a fraud and an essay by you which you never really wrote is also a fraud, though admittedly not many forgers 'accidentally' create a Rembrandt whereas some students do, to be fair, 'accidentally' plagiarise.

Nor should you think that plagiarism is limited to 'borrowing' the work or ideas of established authors. Relying on or even copying the work of fellow students is also plagiarism, as we shall note below.

Examples of plagiarism

- You come across an idea that you wish to use, though you are not going to use a direct quote. Let us say that the idea you have discovered is that in order to understand contract law properly you need to place it in its historical context—originally concerning a set of laws about market dealings which underwent severe reform in the late nineteenth century in favour of consumers. You obtained this idea from two old textbooks. By all means present the idea **but give credit**, e.g. by saying 'Down and Burek both suggested that the real origins and explanations of modern contract law lie in analysing nineteenth-century reforms. They note that before judges such as Bowen LJ shaped the law of contract the idea of "consumer" rights barely existed in legal terms.'

- If Down or Burek actually said these words then the words themselves need to be credited, e.g. 'As Down said "The real origins and explanations of modern contract law…"' and then give the page, etc. using the systems we described earlier. This is not difficult and does avoid having a note (or worse) in your essay pointing out the plagiarism.

As one of the authors to this text wrote on a student essay once: 'I agree with this statement—but I would, as I wrote it and you haven't bothered to credit that fact.' One error of this kind is annoying; many errors may lead to a plagiarism hearing and penalties being imposed.

The same applies to quoting a judge in a case. Indeed, forget plagiarism for the moment: if you are in court and you claim to be citing a judge in a case, you will have to have very specific references available, otherwise you will feel the wrath of the court. Again, this is straightforward—credit the judge, put the extract in quotation marks and show where it is from, e.g. '… As Foster J. said in *Morning Star Co-Operative Society Ltd* v *Express Newspapers Ltd* [1979] FSR 113, at 117 when answering the question whether the title "Morning Star" might lead someone to buy that paper thinking it was the "Daily Star"': '"if one puts the two papers side by side I for myself would find that the two papers are so different in every way that only a moron in a hurry would be misled."'

Avoiding plagiarism

It makes no sense to rely on the 'moron in a hurry' defence. However, there are tactics you can use to avoid being accused of plagiarism:

- Keep a note of any quotation or idea you have come across and, when you write your essay, give credit to the originator of that thought. You will not lose marks; you will most likely gain marks. As we have already seen, the use of authorities in law is a key aspect of both legal academia and practice, so citing accurately those authorities is not going to do you down. If you cannot find the quote again because you did not reference it properly then leave it out. Further, giving credit can be achieved in different ways. One obvious method is to put quotation marks around the section you are using and then give the name of the author and the source (universities use different styles for this so check on what is expected from you). Another method is to paraphrase an author but say something along the lines of: 'As Dickens says, we should regard this as the Law of Torts not the Law of Tort because there has never been a coherent development of this area (see *The Strange Case of Christmas Past* (2015) SPQR, 13)'. Again, you will need an accurate reference. It is not enough just to add a book or article title to your bibliography—the reference needs to be more specific and more closely tied to the text:

- It should also be noted here that merely stringing together quotes from authors or accurately citing their ideas without any original input or comment provided by you is bad academic practice and unlikely to win awards. You may have avoided a charge of plagiarism but you have not created anything along the way.

- As seen in the examples above regarding contract law, plagiarism is not just about transcribing another person's words. Even if you paraphrase someone else's work (however expertly) you need to credit them with the original thought.

- Make use of the guidance provided by your university; not just as regards the rules (whether 10% 'duplication' counts as plagiarism or not, for instance) but also the advice given online or in handbooks.

- Make use of online checkers. There is a long list of such programs and your university may well suggest some to use.

- Do not read fellow-students' work, even 'for inspiration' and, if you work together with a colleague then make sure the final product is yours and does not contain structures and approaches you may both have found or discussed.

- Do not lend out your work. One risk in doing this is that the other student copies your work and you both end up facing a charge of collusion. It is no defence to say your work was stolen when you facilitated this.

- Do not buy material from websites etc. Presenting someone else's work as your own is plagiarism or outright cheating.

- Do not use material you have written before and used in another essay (this applies particularly if you are unfortunate enough to be resitting a subject). Copying from yourself—however strange it appears—counts as self-plagiarism. Our best example here combines these last two points: one student was found to have copied from an essay traced to an online 'help' site, this coming to light when another student presented the same essay. Further investigation showed that the first student had actually written the essay and sold it to the site the year before. Both students were penalised—and you may question how much the essay was worth in the first place, given the source.

- Remember that to be found guilty of plagiarism you do not have to have intended to steal another's work. The authors have sat on many panels dealing with cheating and plagiarism charges. As with our famous songwriters, in many cases the actions were unintentional and born of bad research practice. You may just escape punishment if your error is a minor breach (sometimes referred to as bad academic practice) but tolerances are low and all the stories about time pressure, last-minute illnesses, being ignorant as to the meaning of plagiarism, or the dog dying have all been tried before. It does not matter if your plea is genuine in these circumstances; you face a jaundiced audience.

 ## CONCLUSION

As we said at the start of this chapter, this is a very brief guide on 'writing' styles. The books mentioned in the References section are much more detailed and their sole purpose is to help students in the art of studying (rather than the art of 'thinking like a lawyer', which is our purpose). In one form or another, every text makes the same basic points we have made:

- Your aim is to convey *information*. The previous chapters of this text demonstrate how to find that information and understand it.
- You need to construct an *argument* based on the information you have acquired. The remaining chapters in this text demonstrate how to do this using the skills that all lawyers have at their fingertips.
- You must *apply* that information and the arguments to the essay title or the problem posed.

Legal authority is everything. Your opinion has no weight unless you can tie it in to some established case, statute, or legal text. This does not mean you cannot be original, but you must show how you derive your argument, your originality, from legal sources. The exceptional students will be able to take these sources and develop them into something special, but legal thinking is most often centred on a 'building blocks' technique of applying and distinguishing authorities (on which we have more to say in the next few chapters). To ensure that you do this convincingly you need to do the following:

- Structure your answer carefully. The easier you make the task of reading, the more you carry the reader with you. Plan your essay and decide whether you need to adopt a chronological approach or one which addresses each legal point or each person's case separately. Use headings; use sub-headings. In fact, use any device which makes your answer clear. Practising lawyers do this in court with what are termed 'skeleton arguments' and many judges now do this in their judgments (this was not always the case). Follow their example.
- Cite your authorities, both because this lends weight to your argument and also because it avoids any problems of plagiarism. The pupil master to one of the authors (some time in the past) once advised on legal ethics: 'if you are an honest person and the act you are considering feels wrong in any way, then it is wrong'. The same applies to literary theft: if the ideas are not your own or the words are not your own, then you have stolen them unless you acknowledge the source.

CHAPTER REFERENCES

*Bengoetxea, J. (1993), *The Legal Reasoning of the European Court of Justice* (Oxford: Clarendon Press).

Bryson, B. (2002), *Troublesome Words* (3rd edn, London: Penguin).

*Buzan, T. (2002), *How to Mind Map: The Ultimate Thinking Tool That Will Change Your Life* (London: Thorsons).

Finch, E. and Fafinski, S. (2015), *Legal Skills* (5th edn, Oxford: Oxford University Press).

Foster S. (2012), *How to Write Better Law Essays: Tools and Techniques for Success in Exams and Assignments* (3rd edn, London: Pearson).

*Gordon, J.D. (1991), 'How Not to Succeed in Law School', 100 *Yale Law Journal*, 1689.

Gowers, Sir Ernest (2015), *Plain Words* (Originally *Complete Plain Words*, now revised and updated by Gowers, R.) (London: Penguin).

Greetham, B. (2008), *How to Write Better Essays* (*Palgrave Study Skills*) (2nd edn, Basingstoke: Palgrave MacMillan).

Higgins, E. and Tatham, L. (2010), *Successful Legal Writing* (2nd edn, London: Sweet & Maxwell).

Levin, P. (2009), *Write Great Essays!* (2nd edn, Maidenhead: Open University Press).

Mcvea, H. and Cumper, P. (2006), *Exam Skills for Law Students* (2nd edn, Oxford: Oxford University Press).

*Maughan, C. and Webb, J. (2005), *Lawyering Skills and the Legal Process* (2nd edn, Oxford: Oxford University Press).

*Megarry, R.E. (2005), '*A New Miscellany-at-Law*' (Oxford: Hart Publishing).

Strong, S. (2014), *How to Write Better Law Essays & Exams* (4th edn, Oxford: Oxford University Press).

Trask, R.L. (2002), *Mind the Gaffe: The Penguin Guide to Common Errors in English* (London: Penguin).

Truss, L. (2009), *Eats, Shoots and Leaves* (London: Fourth Estate Limited).

Warburton, N. (2007), *The Basics of Essay Writing* (London: Routledge).

*Watson-Brown, A. (2009), 'Defining "Plain English" as an Aid to Legal Drafting', 30 *Statute Law Review*, 85.

Webley, L. (2009), *Legal Writing* (3rd edn, Abingdon: Routledge).

5

Law, Fact, and Language

In any legal argument that gets to court someone wins and someone loses. So why are people prepared to go to court when statistically they may only have a 50 per cent chance of success? There may be many more or less rational reasons, but usually a litigant will go to court only if advised that he or she has an arguable case. So what is it about legal disputes that means that *both* parties can be sufficiently certain of the 'truth' of their claim and the legal merits of their case to go to court, even though only one of them can win? Surely their lawyers read the same law?

The answer to this conundrum lies in the difference between the law in books and the law in practice. In practice, legal disputes are often affected by a range of variables that are not wholly predictable. In this chapter we shall explore some of these variables through two key factors. These tell us much about how legal disputes are actually *constructed* in court. The elements we consider are the relationship between:

(a) law and fact; and

(b) law and language.

We shall close the chapter by attempting to pull those two strands together in a discussion of how these elements combine to give the judges a high degree of flexibility in deciding cases.

In exploring these issues, it is important to bear in mind that the range of problems discussed probably does not affect all cases, and certainly does not affect them to the same degree. The greatest difficulties arise in those cases which are conventionally described as 'hard cases', that is, cases for which there is no clearly recognised or accepted legal solution.

5.1 Law and Fact

Law does not operate in a vacuum. Obviously, legal disputes only arise out of factual situations—e.g. a boundary dispute between neighbours or an assault by one person on another. This means that such disputes will always involve a mixture of law and fact—e.g. to prove in negligence that X has acted in breach of his or her duty of care, requires us to establish as a matter of *law* that there is a duty of care governing X, and that on the *facts* X has broken that duty.

We can define 'questions of fact' as all questions which attempt to prove what happened. They are established by various types of evidence, e.g. oral witness statements, forensic evidence, etc. 'Questions of law' arise in connexion with legal principles that may be argued in a case (e.g. whether borrowing an article may, in some circumstances, fall within the legal concept we call 'theft'), together with any procedural matters (e.g. the jurisdiction of a particular court). We can explore the practical importance of this a little more deeply.

5.1.1 Using the Law–Fact Distinction

Our experience with both undergraduate and postgraduate students shows that it can be very difficult to grasp the implications of the law–fact distinction.

The difference between questions of law and of fact is used in three ways, which we deal with in the following sections.

To define the function of judge and jury

In many courts it is lay people who act as assessors of fact (notably as a jury in some criminal trials, and in tribunals), while judges deal with the legal problems. One needs to be sure which issue is decided by which person(s).

However, in many criminal and virtually all civil cases, the function of the jury as **tribunal of fact** (as it is called) has been taken over by judges. They will be responsible for ruling on both law and fact in the case before them. Nevertheless they are legally obliged to keep those functions separate within their own minds. This may seem an odd requirement, and in reality it sometimes requires the kind of mental gymnastics that even experienced judges can find difficult to maintain! However, it does emphasise that the determination of the issues of fact is separate from the ultimate issues of law before the court.

To establish rights of appeal

This applies particularly to the higher courts, where appeals on issues of fact are commonly outside the jurisdiction of the appellate court.

To establish the boundaries of precedent

As we shall see in **Chapter 7**, only a decision on a point of law is capable of creating a binding precedent for use in later cases.

5.1.2 The Limits of the Law–Fact Distinction

Although it is easy enough to provide an abstract definition of fact and law, they can be difficult concepts to apply on a case-by-case basis. Given its significance, the difficulty we have in distinguishing between law and fact may seem rather surprising. We argue that, at its root, it is difficult because English lawyers have traditionally treated the question 'what is fact rather than law?' as context specific. In other words, different approaches have been applied in different situations. This may enhance the flexibility of the courts' response to that question, but it can make it difficult for anyone actually learning the law. As a guide, but nothing more, we suggest that the following broad principles need to be considered.

Normally, the question is resolved by the substantive law

The statutory or common law rules governing a particular issue may well make explicit that a certain matter is a question of fact, rather than law, or *vice versa*. Again, the issue is complicated by a lack of consistency. Thus, for example, for many purposes the issue of 'reasonableness' is treated as a matter of fact—as in the uses of the 'reasonable man test' in both civil and criminal law (see, e.g., *Qualcast (Wolverhampton) Ltd* v *Haynes* [1959] AC 743; [1959] 2 All ER 38). Conversely, on a criminal charge of malicious prosecution, the question whether the accused had 'reasonable cause' to bring the prosecution is a question of law for the judge.

Similarly, further complexity can be caused by the courts' recognition that many issues may raise mixed questions of fact and law. For example, in cases of defamation it is necessary for a claimant to establish that the words used by the defendant had a defamatory meaning, and that they were defamatory to the claimant. The issue of defamatory meaning is a question of law, while the requirement of actual defamation of the claimant is one of fact. Again, there are no general guidelines to recognising where an issue raises such mixed questions—it is purely a matter where we have to be guided by the substantive law.

Special principles govern questions of interpretation of words

The meaning of words can be a question of fact or law. It is now well established that the *ordinary* meaning of words is a matter of fact. In *Brutus* v *Cozens* [1973] AC 854; [1972] 2 All ER 1297, the House of Lords had to decide whether an accused who had disrupted a tennis match at Wimbledon as a protest against the presence of a South African player at the tournament had been properly convicted of using 'insulting behaviour' likely to occasion a breach of the peace, contrary to the Public Order Act 1936, s. 5 (now repealed). Their Lordships noted that the Act did not define the word 'insulting', nor was there anything to suggest that the word was to be given any special or technical meaning. Therefore, they held that 'insulting' was to be given its ordinary meaning (which they did not attempt to explain), and that the question whether behaviour was insulting was a question of fact to be determined by the magistrates.

One final point, which may be causing you some confusion, needs to be considered. In establishing this principle of interpretation, the courts have arguably extended the concept of 'fact' in law beyond its most obvious usage, which reflects the normal, but rather narrow idea of facts as observable events which may be proved by evidence from an eyewitness or an ear witness, to a wider notion of facts as including any statement that is verifiable according to some objective or agreed standard. Thus the principle in *Brutus* v *Cozens* in fact illustrates the doctrine known as **judicial notice**, which allows the court to take as given certain established facts (here, the ordinary meaning of words) that are of such common knowledge that to require evidence to prove them would be absurd. Similarly, a court may, unless an Act expressly provides otherwise, take judicial notice of all Acts of Parliament—Interpretation Act 1978, s. 3 and sch. 2(2).

The principle that the ordinary meaning of words is a matter of fact will often have the effect of excluding debates about statutory meaning from the process of appeal, or, in public law matters, the process of judicial review. This must be contrasted with those situations where the courts will, as a matter of *law*, find some *implied meaning* within the words of a statute or other document. Thus, in a famous American case, *Riggs* v *Palmer* (1889) 115 NY 506, the question was whether the beneficiary under a will was entitled to take his bequest, despite the fact that he had murdered the testator. The local wills legislation was silent on the issue, but the Ohio Supreme Court disqualified the beneficiary by applying the long-established principle that a wrongdoer should not benefit by his own wrong. This, the Court said, should be implied into the legislation. (A similar principle has been established in English law: see *Re Sigsworth* (1935), discussed in **Chapter 9**.)

So, given these principles, the next logical question is, how do we actually establish the facts in a case?

5.1.3 Proving the Facts

The first job of the court must be to establish the existence of the facts alleged within a given case. That does not mean that all the possible issues of fact will actually be considered. A feature of the adversarial process is that the legal contest is managed by the two sides involved. (We have already seen in **Chapter 1** how the Woolf reforms have limited some aspects of adversariality, but those changes do not impact on the argument presented here.) It is therefore common practice for the parties to sort out in advance the scope of their dispute. This applies as much to questions of fact as it does to questions of law, so that it is not uncommon for certain facts to be agreed or admitted before a case comes to trial. For this reason we conventionally talk of **material facts** as a way of denoting those facts which remain at issue and which will subsequently form the basis of the judge's decision. Assessing the materiality of facts is chiefly dependent upon the legal issues involved in each case. A knowledge of substantive law is always required, because the substantive law will tell us what facts the parties are required to establish to win their case. What appears to be material to a client is often immaterial to the lawyer, and *vice versa*. This does not always help the lawyer–client relationship!

Let's now try to illustrate the issue of materiality by way of a simple exercise.

EXERCISE 6 'On your bike', or the case of the missing bicycle

Andrea has a bright-red bicycle which she rides to school every day and leaves unsecured in the bike shed. One afternoon, after classes have ended at 4 p.m., she discovers that her bicycle is missing. She reports this fact to the head teacher. By 4.30 p.m. the bike has mysteriously been found outside Andrea's home. Ben tells Andrea that he saw her friend Caroline riding a red bike at about 4.15 p.m.

Which of these facts would you consider important in assessing whether Caroline had attempted to steal the bicycle?

We suggest two are of obvious importance:

(a) that the bike has been taken from Andrea, apparently without her knowledge; and

(b) Caroline was seen riding a red bike at a time consistent with the theft.

Others might, of course, be relevant in assessing the veracity of Andrea or Ben as witnesses, though that is a slightly different issue.

Are these sufficient to support the conclusion that Caroline is a thief?

Certainly not, though that is a possibility, there is still relatively little to connect Caroline to the theft. If Caroline was unable to explain Ben's evidence, then our hypothesis that Caroline is the thief would be strengthened. If she merely denied the allegation, we would be little further forward. There is at present insufficient evidence to say 'beyond reasonable doubt' that Caroline took the bike.

continued

EXERCISE 6 *continued*

There are a number of other explanations, some more plausible than others, that need to be explored, e.g.:

(a) Andrea had forgotten that she had not gone to school by bike that day.

(b) Caroline has a red bike of her own, and was seen riding that.

(c) Ben had mistakenly identified Caroline.

(d) Ben had taken the bike, and blamed Caroline to hide his own guilt, and so on …

The facts we have are therefore far from conclusive (see further the section on the burden of proof, later in the chapter).

This example enables us to expand upon some of the points made so far. It highlights that the facts in any given case are unlikely to be of equal importance, and that their significance will often depend on their interrelationship with other facts in the case. Assessing what facts are material will depend in part on our ability to create an over-all picture of events. For example, the statement that Andrea rides her bike to school every day does not appear to be particularly relevant to the legal issues—unless our inquiries lead us to discover that force of habit had caused her to forget that today her mother had driven her to school. Do not forget that experience and knowledge of the law will also play a part in establishing what facts are relevant and material. Thus, in the bicycle case discussed above, once we know that the legal definition of theft requires that the thief has an intention to deprive the owner of that property perma-nently, Caroline's intentions regarding the future of the bike (assuming she took it) acquire a whole new significance—did she mean to keep it, or was she just borrowing it? This also illustrates an important point about the relationship between law and facts, which is that their dependence works *both ways*. We need a good knowledge of the facts to create a viable legal argument, but at the same time, we need knowledge of the law to sort out the legally relevant facts from the mass of information that will surround a case. We shall return to the relationship between law and fact later in **Chapter 12**.

The process whereby the material facts are established is referred to as one of **proof.** There exists within any legal system a variety of procedural rules governing what facts may be proved. Such rules vary from system to system in their restric-tiveness. English rules of proof are widely regarded as among the more restrictive, though the rules regarding proof in civil cases tend to be less strict than in criminal procedure. Put briefly, the basic evidentiary requirements for proof of a fact are that it is *relevant and admissible*, and that the evidence is sufficiently strong to satisfy the *burden of proof.* We shall consider these points separately.

Relevance and admissibility

A fact will be **relevant** if it enables the court to reach a conclusion on any of the issues before it. In practice facts are often like the pieces of a jigsaw, where you cannot make out the picture until it is nearly complete; so it may be difficult for the court to see where the proof of a single fact is leading. This means that counsel may legitimately be asked to justify why a particular fact should be admitted.

Admissibility is a technical rule. It provides the courts with a means of excluding evidence that is relevant, but for some reason is inherently so unreliable that the court should refuse to be swayed by it. The best example of this is probably the rule in criminal evidence excluding a concocted confession under the Police and Criminal Evidence Act 1984, s. 76. Admissibility in English law is complicated by the fact that it operates by means of a mass of exclusionary rules and exceptions thereto.

Questions of relevance and admissibility will depend, in part, upon the standpoint and objectives of the person using the information. To put it simply: what facts are important may well depend upon whether you are acting for a claimant or defendant; in either case you will seek to emphasise those facts which support your case, and play down, discredit, or even seek to exclude those which support your opponent. In that respect facts do not represent an objective truth, but sometimes an accurate, or sometimes a crude, estimate of the most convincing version of events.

The burden and standard of proof

The emphasis in law on notions of proof and probability is also a way of acknowledging that facts are not as concrete as they may seem. All cases, whether criminal or civil, are decided according to the **burden of proof**. This too is a complex subject, and too intricate for full discussion here, though some basic points can be made. The burden of proof places the responsibility for establishing a particular fact on its proponent, i.e. the person claiming the fact to be true, so that if A claims that B injured her by his negligent driving, it is up to A to make out a case. The requirement of proof means that facts must be established to the satisfaction of the court, but this does not mean absolute certainty. It will be relatively unusual for facts in a case to be *conclusive*.

The term **conclusive** is one which needs to be used with great caution. Technically, evidence is conclusive only where, by virtue of a rule of law, it cannot be contradicted—a widely cited example is the rule of law treating a child under the age of 10 as incapable of committing a crime. This technical meaning is thus different from the popular sense of the term, where it is used to describe evidence that effectively clinches the case. In reality, what is popularly called 'conclusive' is no more than evidence which carries a very high degree of probability. Lord Guthrie (among others) has made the obvious point that, '[o]utside the region of mathematics, proof is never anything more than probability' (*Nobel's Explosives Co.* v *British Dominions General Insurance Co.* 1918 1 SLT 205, at 206). Consequently, to ensure certainty and consistency in law, we specify not just the burden but also a **standard** of proof, which is a way of asking the tribunal of fact to consider whether the evidence presented on a particular allegation of fact is strong enough for the proponent to satisfy the tribunal on that point. In civil cases we generally require proof 'on a balance of probabilities', i.e. proof that the version alleged is simply more probable than not. In criminal cases a 'higher standard' is required, of 'proof beyond reasonable doubt'; it is sometimes said that this means that the trier of fact must be 'certain, so that they are sure'. What these abstract concepts come to mean in individual cases remains somewhat uncertain. The use of terms such as 'proof beyond reasonable doubt' may often work to disguise the extent to which conclusions about the facts of a case are subjective. Put simply, it is not easy to draw the boundaries between doubts which are reasonable and those which are not.

For example, criminal cases in particular may turn on questions of identification. Witness A may say that the person she saw looked like the accused X, whereas witness B may have given a different description. Identification is a question of fact, but do not let the terminology fool you; in establishing whether X is the guilty person, the court will be working in part from a whole range of conscious and unconscious perceptions regarding the person of the accused and the veracity of the witnesses, only some of which are reducible to rules of law, in an attempt to establish 'the facts'. Let us now consider how problems of establishing the facts may have disturbed the verdict in a real case.

5.1.4 The Case of William Wallace

At the time our story begins, in 1931, William Wallace was a 52-year-old insurance collector living in Anfield, Liverpool, with his wife Julia. They had been married for about seventeen years. They were known as a quiet, rather formal couple, with relatively few social acquaintances. Wallace was an unremarkable man, except in respect of his beliefs. He was a follower of Stoicism, a virtually dead philosophy based upon the *Meditations* of the Roman general, Marcus Aurelius; as Wallace wrote in his diary: 'For forty years I have drilled myself in iron control and prided myself on never displaying an emotion outwardly in public.'

Wallace was a regular chess player at a club in the city. On the evening of Monday, 19 January 1931, the captain of the club took a telephone message for Wallace from 'R. M. Qualtrough', leaving an address and a request for Wallace to visit at 7.30 the following evening. When Wallace arrived at the club half an hour later, he said that he had not heard of Qualtrough, but took a note of the address, assuming the call was in connexion with his insurance business.

The following evening, Wallace left home sometime between 6.30 and 6.50 p.m., caught a tram at 7.06 to his supposed destination, where he spent over half an hour looking for Qualtrough's address. It did not exist. He caught the tram home, where he was seen by his neighbours at 8.45, trying to enter the house. He explained that, unusually, both back and front door were locked, and he could get no reply from Julia. On trying the back door again, it opened. Inside was Julia's body; she had been beaten to death with an iron bar. The front bedroom of the house had been ransacked and £4 removed from the cash box in which Wallace kept the monies he collected (though this was subsequently discovered inexplicably stuffed into a vase in the upstairs of the house).

An immediate search of lodging houses, the railway, cafes, and clubs in the area revealed no one who might be the murderer. Furthermore, the fact that there was no evidence of a forced entry to the house, or of a struggle between killer and victim, suggested either that Julia was taken wholly by surprise or that she knew her murderer. The police felt that they were left with two possible suspects.

The first was Gordon Parry, a former colleague of Wallace's, who had a record of petty theft and a reputation as a womaniser. Rightly or wrongly, this was sufficient to make him an initial suspect. He knew Julia; the layout of the Wallace's house; and that normally, on a Tuesday night, the cash box would have contained over £100—the sum of Wallace's weekly collection. He might also have held a grudge against Wallace, who had caught Parry helping himself to insurance money that he was supposed to be collecting. However, Parry had an alibi. His girlfriend had told the police that they had been together the whole evening. He was dropped from the police enquiries.

The second suspect was Wallace himself. The police had by now heard rumours that the relationship between the Wallaces was far from happy, though this Wallace strenuously denied. There remained no clear motive for the killing. However, Wallace also seemed abnormally calm; he was observed, while being questioned by the police on the night of the killing, casually leaning over Julia's body to flick cigarette ash into an ashtray. This behaviour almost certainly aroused some suspicions. Did the police have a cold, calculating killer in their midst?

But didn't Wallace, like Parry, have an alibi? In a sense he did. Several witnesses, including a police officer, had spoken with Wallace in his search for Mr Qualtrough. However, there was no reliable assessment of the time of Julia's death. One pathologist put it at about 6 p.m.; another at 8 p.m. It was not inconceivable that he had killed his wife before leaving for his appointment with the fictitious Qualtrough. Indeed, Qualtrough could have been a creation of Wallace's own plans. The telephone call to the chess club which created the whole alibi had been traced to a telephone box only some 400 yards from the Wallaces' house. Even so, how could the police deal with the fact that no blood was found on Wallace after such a ferocious killing? They surmised that he had worn only a macintosh, found partially burned under the dead woman's body, to commit the killing. As traces of blood were found in the bathroom, this seemed to suggest that whoever had killed Julia had stopped in the house long enough to try to wash the blood off.

On 2 February Wallace was charged with his wife's murder. He was committed for trial before the Liverpool assize in April 1931. At the trial, the Crown pressed its case in a manner that was later described as 'oppressive'. Counsel claimed that Wallace had planned the entire thing, to the extent of faking his own alibi; witnesses were called attacking Wallace's demeanour; to all this he listened, impassively. The defence countered by emphasising the circumstantial nature of the evidence; the limited time Wallace would have had to commit the crime, clean himself up, and leave for his appointment; and the fact that the macintosh could as easily have been burned by the gas fire in the room as by some deliberate act of the killer—this view, it was argued, was supported by the fact that Julia's skirt had been partially burned by coming into contact with the fire, presumably as she fell. On the fourth day of the trial, the jury retired to consider its verdict.

Obviously it is impossible to recreate accurately the atmosphere and arguments of a capital trial in a few short lines, but from the outline here, what would you expect that verdict to be? Innocent or guilty?

For Wallace, the answer came quickly. After retiring for an hour, the jury returned a verdict of guilty. He was sentenced to death. The day after his trial he was told that he was due to be hanged on 12 May. His lawyers immediately entered an appeal against his conviction. His appeal was heard on 18 and 19 May (sentence having been postponed) by the Court of Criminal Appeal. After what must have been a mercifully short judgment for Wallace (who was present at his appeal), the Court handed down its decision— see *R* v *Wallace* (1932) 23 Cr App Rep 32. The conviction was quashed on the basis that it was unsupported by the evidence. He was free to go.

So, how was it that the trial court had convicted Wallace? The Court of Criminal Appeal (*per* Lord Hewart CJ, at 35) made it clear that no fault lay with the judge; the problem was evidential. This was a case of considerable difficulty and doubt, where much of the evidence was consistent with both innocence and guilt. In the end, the jury had (in the eyes of the appeal court) simply got it wrong.

The conviction was thrown out on the basis that the prosecution had not satisfied the burden of proof. They had failed to exclude the possibility that someone else had committed the murder. The reasons behind Wallace's conviction by the jury are difficult to ascribe, and of course, we shall never know the real answer, but it is submitted that there are a number of likely possibilities. Taken together these may help account for what was, with hindsight, a perverse verdict.

First, the jury itself lost sight of the differences between fact and speculation. A court is not concerned, as Lord Hewart said in *Wallace*, 'with suspicion, however grave, or with theories, however ingenious'. The prosecution case was full of ingenious theorising—for example the assertion that Wallace had worn the coat found under Julia's body to commit the murder and then sought to burn it—but few of these hypotheses could finally be substantiated.

Secondly, contemporary accounts indicate that there was a powerfully *presented*, aggressive, case by the prosecution. This, ironically, was probably aided by Wallace's own stoicism. His air of detachment in the courtroom probably did little to gain him sympathy, and may have helped foster the image of a cold and calculating killer. The defence also alleged that the police had been unduly obstructive to the preparation of their case (though this view was not supported by the Court of Criminal Appeal, more recent research suggests that it may have had greater foundation than was then realised, or acknowledged—see Wilkes (1984)). Taken together these might have served to distort the perceived strength of the prosecution case. The significance of questions of presentation and style will be further considered under the heading 'law and language' (in the next section).

Thirdly, there is also evidence that the defence miscalculated badly in the presentation of its case by failing to apply to the judge to have the prosecution case rejected for a lack of evidence. This point illustrates rather graphically how much can depend on the forensic skills of the lawyer rather than upon either the actual facts or law in a case. A great deal, perhaps too much, in the adversarial process can depend upon tactics and techniques of argument.

5.2 Law and Language

The legal process is intrinsically bound up with language. The popular image of law is one that emphasises the oral element of legal tradition, that is, the process of argumentation before a court. Even the reality, which for most practising lawyers is rather more prosaic than television would have us believe, is still a world in which legal documents fill up much of the day. Words thus dominate the legal landscape; this is hardly surprising, because without language there could be no law. As Bernhard Grossfeld argues: 'Law certainly uses language, but language is the stronger' (1990: 99). In the context of legal methods and techniques, there are two issues that need to be addressed; one essentially theoretical, the other more practical. These are the relationship between language and power, and the problem of the flexibility of language.

5.2.1 Law, Language, and Power

It is widely recognised that there is a substantial gap between legal and 'everyday' language. In some respects, that gap is narrowing as lawyers are being encouraged to use more naturalistic language (e.g. the changes in terminology introduced by the Woolf reforms, discussed in **Chapter 1**), but the continued relevance of old statutes and precedents means that what are really archaic forms of language are still in legal use, though it has to be said that lawyers are not wholly innocent in the perpetuation of this gap. The law has always tended to be a conservative institution, and the traditional usage of legal jargon has often been presented as part of the attraction or mystique of law. Some terms still in use, such as *autrefois convict* or *habeas corpus*, reflect law's origins in the language of the medieval aristocracy or the church; others illustrate specialist usage of quite ordinary words—e.g. the meaning given to the term 'consideration' in contract law. This specialist language has to be learned. There is no escape.

However, the existence of a distinct 'legal language' has wider social effects than just making the law student's life rather difficult. Here we shall discuss two important examples of those wider effects:

Law as camouflage

The extent to which law relies upon its own language is a very basic indication of the closed nature of legal argument. The term 'mystification' is used as a description of the way in which the language of the law defines who can participate in legal argument. The need to develop the 'special' skills of a lawyer has the effect of excluding non-lawyers from entering into legal discourse, with, it is argued, consequent limits upon the ability of citizens to gain access to justice. The special use of certain forms of language also serves to disguise rather than enhance our understanding of the legal system. This reflects what Grossfeld describes as 'law as camouflage' (1990: 47). He gives a simple example of this from the United States' Constitution which, until amended after the American Civil War, contained rights to slave ownership. Despite this, the term slavery was constantly avoided in the legal terminology; instead slavery was always called the 'particular institution'.

In practice, the process of disguise may often be far more sophisticated. In the early common law, for example, we talk of the way in which actions could be based on 'legal fictions'—fictional pleadings which did not reflect the true dispute but were used to overcome technicalities and give a suitor access to the courts. A more modern analogy would be the way in which proof of marriage breakdown, particularly 'unreasonable behaviour', will be (to some extent) artificially constructed in divorce proceedings. Here it is employed to put an end to a marriage which, in reality, both parties wish to escape from, but without the restriction of separating and waiting for two years to obtain a divorce by consent. The use of the term 'unreasonable behaviour' thus camouflages the true workings of one aspect of the law of divorce.

This facet of language creates difficulties not only for the lay person, but also for lawyers outside the system. Getting past the camouflage is one of the major problems lawyers face in reaching an accurate understanding of a foreign legal system. Hence legal language is an important symbol of the power of law itself both to define, deliberately or otherwise, who may exercise legal rights, and to disguise the uses of law by those within the system from those outside. We would suggest that there are also other, more immediate ways in which use of language involves a significant exercise of power. This also enables us to posit formally the links between law, fact, and language in the title of this chapter.

Facts, power, and the legal process

We have already shown that facts are not plucked out of the air, ready-made. They need to be described—a process which, of course, requires language. Hanson (1959) makes the fundamental point that language and fact are dependent upon each other. This leads us to the conclusion that the way in which facts are described, not surprisingly, governs our perception of the nature of those facts. Linguistic differences thus can be said to affect the 'reality' created. Consider the example of the Inuit language which contains many different words to describe types of snowfall. We could imagine a situation where a witness is asked to describe the weather conditions at a particular time. The picture of the facts painted by an English-speaking witness saying 'it was snowing hard' would then be very different from the presumably more graphic image created by an Inuit witness speaking his or her own language.

In the legal environment, the ability of a witness to communicate what she or he has seen will be of great importance, because it is that act of communication which creates the facts of the case. Of course, not all witnesses share the same degree of linguistic competence, least of all in a pressured, artificial setting such as a court. Stories are often presented in a broken, fragmentary way; narrative patterns can become distorted by lawyers' attempts to discredit testimony. Witnesses can become confused and uncertain.

Variations in presentation can have a dramatic effect on the court's perception of witnesses' credibility, and from there of the court's structuring of the facts. In a study in the early 1980s, O'Barr and his colleagues (1982) analysed the way in which different language styles emerged in court. They identified in particular a difference between 'powerful' and 'powerless' speech. Powerless speech, they found, was typified by the use of more qualified statements; deferential speech styles, hesitation, and other factors which did not affect the nature of the facts contained in testimony, but changed its presentation. In one experiment in particular, the researchers recorded the same information on tape, changing only the language style and the gender of the speaker. The witnesses giving information in a powerful style were rated by subjects as significantly more convincing, trustworthy, and competent than those whose linguistic style was 'powerless'. Subjects also tended to rate women speakers generally as being less powerful than men—even on the basis of identical material. Clearly, therefore, the medium can be as significant as the message itself.

5.2.2 The Flexibility of Language

The English language has over the last two or three hundred years become virtually the first global language. It is spoken in some form by, some estimates suggest, nearly one billion people around the world. Influenced by many different cultures, it has become one of the richest and most complex languages in the world. The current *Oxford English Dictionary* lists some 500,000 words in recognised use (though many may be highly obscure). This represents probably the most extensive vocabulary of any modern language. Buried somewhere within its midst are the many terms that constitute what might be called 'legal English'; but lawyers do not operate exclusively in a linguistically closed environment. Legal discourse must involve large numbers of 'ordinary' English words as well. Given the apparently huge range to choose from, one would have thought that a high degree of precision should be attainable. Unfortunately, this is not always the case.

It is said that legal rules suffer from a problem of indeterminacy, meaning that it is often difficult to predict the scope of those rules. Neither the judges nor Parliament will necessarily provide you with exhaustive explanations of what they mean to say, and much of the indeterminacy of laws is traceable to the flexibility of legal language. Some of that indeterminacy can be avoided by precision—the *correct* use of language (so far as is possible) is vital to the work of a lawyer. At times it is easy to be overly cynical on this matter: to say that lawyers are simply playing with language. But, trite though it sounds, words are all that a lawyer has at his or her disposal. Though whether changes to legal forms of language could reduce the scope for ambiguity, or whether our problems are inherent in the generally flexible and imprecise nature of language, remains a hotly debated question.

Problems in establishing meaning affect two stages of the legal process. Meaning must be considered at the point of drafting any legal document, and also subsequently at the stage of interpreting that document. The essence of the problem is that the law has tended to assume that meaning can be safely ascertained only from the document itself. In many situations we have little alternative. If a court is interpreting the contents of a will, for example, it may have little choice in the matter. The document may have been drafted twenty or thirty years ago; the person whose wishes it contains (called the testator) will be dead, and the memories of others involved at the time (if they can be found) may be unreliable. In practice, in such situations, the courts may resort to oral evidence or other documentary evidence that could shed light on the testator's intentions, but that tends to be a last resort. As we shall explain in **Chapter 9**, special rules govern statutes as opposed to other documents, but the starting point is essentially the same.

There is, however, an element of artificiality in this approach. The belief that we can establish the meaning of a document purely from the words used seems to assume that we can overcome two discrete problems: first, the difficulty of ascribing meaning to individual words; and, secondly, the problems created by the need to interpret more complex syntactic structures.

The meaning of words

To understand the problems of meaning we need, once again, to think about the relationship between legal and everyday language. We have already said that legal discourse involves the use of both specialist and general language. It has been suggested that the relationship can be described diagrammatically, as represented by **Figure 5.1**.

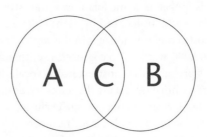

Figure 5.1 The interrelation of language: general–legal (source: Knapp (1991: 10))

These two circles represent three linguistic subsets. Group A represents words used only in the general language; group B contains words used in legal language only, and group C represents words which are common to both legal and general English. On this basis, group (B C) represents the sum of the legal language. These sets and subsets are open; their boundaries will change over time. New words will be developed to reflect technological and other changes in society. Words may actually move across the dividing line between the general and the legal language (as an example of the latter, Knapp cites the phrase 'corrective measures'—a general expression which had acquired a specific legal meaning in some of the former socialist states). We shall see in **Chapter 9**, in the context of statutory interpretation, that major difficulties can arise in ascribing a meaning to the words used in an Act of Parliament or in delegated legislation. We shall also see how the courts have developed principles of interpretation in an attempt to deal with this. Without anticipating too much of that discussion, it can be said that primarily the courts start from the assumption that words should be given their ordinary, everyday meaning unless the context suggests a special or technical meaning is intended. It is an approach that has wider applications than just statutory interpretation. Courts are regularly engaged in thinking about the meaning of words in interpreting contracts and other written documents, and in applying rules of common law to specific cases. In such situations, lawyers face three major problems in respect of the meaning of words. These are considered in the following paragraphs.

(a) Dealing with *semantic ambiguity*: to say that words should be given their ordinary common-sense meaning is not always as simple as it sounds. Many words have more than one meaning, and it can be difficult to resolve which of a number of shades of meaning is intended in a particular legal document.

This problem may be especially acute in respect of words in subsets A and C, just described. A feature of terms used only in legal language (subset B) is their tendency to be used in a manner that is unequivocal. By and large, legal language can convey very precise meanings—at least to other skilled users of legal language.

By contrast, where words exist in both legal and general usage (i.e. words in Knapp's subset C), there may be quite distinct ordinary meanings; that is, an ordinary everyday meaning and an ordinary legal meaning—such as the term 'consideration', for example. In some instances such a range of meanings may be a cause of confusion. It may be difficult to determine which of the meanings is intended. Though the problem of meaning often can be resolved by looking at the linguistic context (for example, if a written contract contains the phrase '… in consideration whereof Jane Smith pays Alan Brown £200', it is pretty obvious that the legal meaning of consideration is the one intended), there are times when such a simple resolution is not possible. With words in subset A (the general language) the difficulties can be profound. The richness of our language means that many words have a multiplicity of meanings which are in general usage, or a range of meanings, some of which are general, others technical. The general language also lacks the common interpretative community which gives (much) legal English its precision. So, how do we resolve problems of interpreting the general language?

It may be argued that a lot of these problems can be resolved if we can accept that most ambiguous words have a central meaning that would be widely accepted as the most ordinary meaning of the word. To take a commonly used example, few of us would argue that a car or truck is not a 'vehicle' but what about a bicycle? Or a kiddies' push chair? Similarly we would likely agree with the Court of Appeal that attempting to call a jet-ski a ship is patently absurd—see *R* v *Goodwin* [2005] EWCA Crim 3184. However, to do that we seem to be accepting two ideas: (i) that a particular word does have a distinguishable core or standard meaning, and this itself may be highly debatable in some specific cases, and (ii) that the core meaning of a term is, in Schauer's phrase, 'language-determined' (2008: 1111). Both of these assumptions are, to a degree, problematic. Consider the following as an illustration of where the real problem lies:

> Let us suppose that in leafing through the statutes, we come upon the following enactment: 'It shall be a misdemeanour, punishable by a fine of five dollars, to sleep in any railway station.' … Suppose I am a judge, and that two men are brought before me for violating this statute. The first is a passenger who was waiting at 3 a.m. for a delayed train. When he was arrested he was sitting upright in an orderly fashion, but was heard by the arresting officer to be gently snoring. The second is a man who had brought a blanket and pillow to the station and had obviously settled himself down for the night. He was arrested, however, before he had a chance to go to sleep. (Fuller, 1958: 664)

The word 'sleep' in this example is clearly ambiguous (we might say). It can denote both the actual state of being asleep, and the action of spending the night in some place in order to sleep. Which is the core meaning? The point is of course that, in the abstract, it doesn't have one. The word sleep itself is of comparatively little assistance to us in such cases, and it will frequently be necessary to look to the context—linguistic and/or social—in which the language is used in order to construct some kind of settled meaning for the word being used. Often, it will be sufficient to consider other parts of the same document, which may make it clear, either expressly or by implication, what meaning is intended.

In Professor Fuller's example, it would not be too difficult to argue that such legislation would really be aimed at sleeping in the second sense we have identified. The Act would thus catch homeless people and others entering the railway station with the intention of using it as a shelter for the night, without making genuine passengers who 'nod off' waiting for a train guilty of an offence. But, just as we have created an argument in support of the second meaning, could not another lawyer create an argument supporting the first? It is quite possible for lawyers to construct contradictory but equally viable arguments as to why one or other meaning or inference should be applied. In cases of true ambiguity, it is almost impossible to say that there is a particular right answer. Fortunately, such instances are comparatively rare, and where they do arise the problem is not that the word itself is fundamentally ambiguous, but rather its application. This ultimately is Fuller's point: that we cannot understand the meaning of a rule in isolation from its use. This directs us to a further phenomenon that H.L.A. Hart (1994) referred to as the 'open texture' of legal rules. To talk of terms as 'open textured' is to recognise that every word, every sentence, has the *potential for vagueness* when confronted by the unplanned or unexpected (Schauer, 2008: 1126–7). The unexpected renders uncertain that which previously seemed clear, as our 'no sleeping in the railway station' rule demonstrates. More realistically, we can see this happening all the time in the relationship between law and science, where technological and medical progress often leaves legal regulation struggling to catch up. As Schauer puts it, the problem is often not that our language fails us, but our law does; we are not caught out by the open texture of language so much as the open texture of law.

(b) Attempting to explain meaning: where problems with interpretation of a word arise, it is easy to assume that such problems can be resolved by simply explaining that word in different terms. In fact, that process is not always easy, and may create a new and unexpected set of difficulties.

One way of trying to define a word is to use a **synonym** for it. Synonyms are not ambiguous in themselves, but they often arise out of attempts to avoid ambiguity. A synonym is one word which has the same meaning as another. Sometimes it is tempting to use a synonym in the hope that it will carry a clearer sense of what is intended than the original word. Thus, in *Brutus* v *Cozens* [1973] AC 854; [1972] 2 All ER 1297, counsel sought to define 'insult' by reference to its dictionary definition and by the substitution (*per* Lord Kilbrandon, at 1304) of terms such as 'insolence' or 'affront'.

In using synonyms two difficulties can arise. First, given the flexibility of language, it can be dangerous to assume synonymous meanings exist, particularly if one is dealing with technical legal concepts. Take the term 'fraud' for example; this is widely used in both civil and criminal law. The ordinary meaning connotes, according to the *Shorter Oxford English Dictionary*: 'Criminal deception; the using of false representations to obtain an unjust advantage …'. Thus, in ordinary usage fraud could be considered synonymous with deception. In law the terms are not synonymous, however. Mr Justice Buckley distinguished fraud and deception in the case of *Re London and Globe Finance Corporation Ltd* [1903] 1 Ch 728, at 733:

> to deceive is by falsehood to induce a state of mind; to defraud is by deceit to induce a course of action.

So, a person may be deceived without being defrauded in the eyes of the law. Secondly, even if the word is a good synonym for the one which it replaces, it will rarely advance our understanding—as Lord Kilbrandon pointed out in respect of our earlier examples from *Brutus* v *Cozens*, such words are all equally 'as much, or as little, in need of interpretation'. In short, synonyms are not really of great value as aids to understanding.

If synonyms are unhelpful, should we seek to explain concepts by the use of some alternative formulation? This may be a superficially attractive way for us to deal with uncertainty of meaning, particularly where ordinary words carry within them complex notions of probability or desirability. But it is an approach that carries a real risk of increasing misunderstanding, as research has shown. Consider now the meanings of the set of words in our next exercise.

EXERCISE 7 The uncertainty of uncertainty

The following ten words/expressions are all used as verbal measures expressing some degree of uncertainty. They are not ordered in any deliberate ranking:

Probable

Quite Certain

Unlikely

Hoped

Possible

Not unreasonable that

continued

EXERCISE 7 *continued*

Expected

Doubtful

Not certain

Likely

Now place these in rank order from 1 to 10, starting with the term that is MOST UNcertain and descending to the LEAST UNcertain. If you can, do this as a group exercise, so that each of you compiles his or her own list WITHOUT DISCUSSION; then compare your list with those of other members of the group. What do you find?

There is not, of course, a set of right answers to this task. Do not be surprised if you find considerable disagreement. When this same exercise was attempted by a group of forty executives on general management courses at a business school, it was found that there was a high level of overlapping between ranks, and hence considerable inconsistency between respondents. Thus, for example, the term 'expected' was on average placed the second most uncertain term in the list; its position for individual respondents nevertheless ranged from first to sixth. 'Unlikely' came bottom of the average rankings, but its range of ranks varied from third to tenth! In fact, the variation was such that only three out of the forty respondents produced identical lists (Moore and Thomas, 1988: 127–8).

In case you are wondering, **Exercise 7** does have important implications for legal decision-making. If, in a legal environment, we attempt to define a word or phrase by using some alternative formulation, there is no guarantee that our audience will give our words the same meaning as we intended. This has, in fact, been borne out by research into jury trials (LSE Jury Project, 1973), where 'jurors' have been asked to respond to what lawyers perceive to be equivalent ways of expressing the burden of proof. Needless to say, the subjects of the research did not always agree that the alternatives were equivalent at all!

(c) Interlingual ambiguity: as law becomes an increasingly international and therefore interlingual phenomenon, it is to be expected that a new crop of linguistic problems will arise. These difficulties tend to take a number of forms, but share a common basis in our (in)capacity to translate legal concepts from one jurisdiction to another. We shall focus on two specific issues here: interlingual synonymy and homonymy.

We have already considered problems of synonymy within a legal language. Between different languages, problems of synonymy arise where terms that appear to be synonymous in fact are not. In the most extreme cases, terms may have direct linguistic equivalents in another language, but in fact mean very different things. Knapp (1991: 14) uses the example of the term *lichnaya sobstvennost* in Soviet law. This could be translated literally into English as 'personal property', but the English and Soviet legal notions of personal property are, as Knapp puts it, 'mutually incomparable'. Our translation would therefore be highly misleading. A rather less extreme, but not less difficult, problem arises where there is only a partial overlap of meaning. For example, English law uses the term 'easement' to describe certain rights that one person may acquire over another's land—such as a right of way. French law recognises the similar concept of *servitude*—but although there is some common ground between the concepts that these terms denote, they are not identical. Easement would not provide a precise translation of the term *servitude* and *vice versa*.

A similar problem arises with legal homonyms (a homonym is a term which is either phonetically or in written form more or less identical to a word in another language). Again, these may convey very different ideas through the same term. Knapp (1991: 15) uses the example of the term 'magistrate' and its homonyms. In English, 'magistrate' refers to a very particular kind of judge, sitting in the magistrates' court. In French, *magistrat* refers more generally to the professional judiciary, and as Weston (1991: 109–10) shows, the term is extremely difficult to translate accurately into English, though at least the English and French terms do have judging in common! By contrast, the Czech term *magistrát* has nothing to do with the judiciary. It refers to a city administration—a kind of city council. Of course, just to increase the confusion, what is a misleading homonym for some comparisons is not necessarily so for others—the French *magistrats* and Italian *magistrati* are similar institutions.

Although this all sounds very academic, such interlingual problems are of practical significance. In multilingual legal communities such as the European Union, problems of translation and of linguistic and conceptual equivalence arise at the stages of drafting and interpreting legislation (see respectively **Chapters 8** and **11** of this book where the EU legal context is developed more fully). These difficulties can occur both at national and supranational levels. Interlingualism may also need to be addressed in domestic courts when dealing with matters established by international treaty, or when applying conflicts of law rules—e.g. in dealing with international trade matters or with the recognition of foreign divorces.

Interpreting syntax

In law, a second level of difficulty emerges out of syntax, by which is meant the grammatical use of words. Lawyers do not just have to work out the meaning of individual words; words are, of course the constituent parts of more complex linguistic structures, such as phrases and sentences, and in reality these can create separate problems from those which arise in the interpretation of a single word. The point we are making here is a specific one, which recognises that even when we are interpreting a single word in a statute, we are reading it in its grammatical and linguistic context. Here what we are focusing on are those situations where it is the grammatical context that is the problem, not the word itself. The primary difficulty is **syntactic ambiguity**. This phrase is used to describe the alternative constructions that are created by the use of qualifying phrases and dependent clauses within a sentence or paragraph. Bryan Niblett (1980: 10–11) explores this problem by drawing a comparison between the syntax of a legal proposition and that of a computer program. Both constructs can suffer from what computer programmers call the 'dangling else' ambiguity. Niblett presents us with the following expression to illustrate this:

if (condition 1) then if (condition 2) then
(statement 1) else (statement 2)

If we consider this expression, it does not take long to work out how the ambiguity arises. If conditions 1 and 2 are satisfied, there is no problem, since statement 1 obviously applies; but what if neither condition is satisfied, or only condition 1? When does statement 2 come into play? The ambiguity is there because we do not know from this expression to which *then* the *else* is an alternative. The ambiguity thus does not depend upon the words used but upon the way the expression is structured. Syntactic ambiguity is a particular problem of statute or delegated legislation. In practice, such instances of ambiguity have to be resolved by the courts choosing one of a number of competing interpretations, or sometimes by Parliament amending the ambiguous construction.

This can be seen from another of Niblett's examples, taken this time from a real statute, namely, the Guard Dogs Act 1975. Section 1(1) of the Act provides:

> A person shall not use or permit the use of a guard dog at any premises unless a person ('the handler') who is capable of controlling the dog is present on the premises and the dog is under the control of the handler at all times while it is being so used *except while it is secured so that it is not at liberty to go freely about the premises.* (emphasis added)

The phrase in italics in that section is a classic example of the 'dangling else'. Does it qualify the whole of the foregoing section, or does it just qualify the requirement that 'the dog is under the control of the handler at all times …'? Just by looking at the words themselves, either answer is acceptable. The Divisional Court in *Hobson* v *Gledhill* [1978] 1 WLR 215; [1978] 1 All ER 945 was faced with exactly that conundrum. The accused used three Alsatian dogs to guard his premises. There was no handler present on the premises, but the dogs were secured and could not move freely about the property. If our first interpretation was correct, then no offence had been committed; the dogs were secured, so no handler was required. But if the second construction was correct, the accused would be guilty of an offence under the Act. Even if the dogs were secured, it was necessary to have a handler on the premises. The Court decided the case by taking the first interpretation, a process which it justified by reference to a principle of statutory interpretation, which we shall consider in the next section.

Syntactic problems also sometimes arise where courts have to determine the effect of the connecting words used between phrases and concepts. We can call such connexions 'conjunctive' or 'disjunctive'. The most common and most important of these connectors are 'and' and 'or', and it is surprising just how many problems these everyday words can cause. 'And' is a conjunctive connector: it joins propositions together. Thus the phrase 'if condition *a* and condition *b*, then outcome *c*', tells us that both *a* and *b* have to be satisfied for outcome *c* to arise. By contrast, the 'or' connector is obviously disjunctive—it separates rather than combines propositional statements. Thus: 'if condition *a* or condition *b*, then outcome *c*' tells us that outcome *c* will be adopted if either *a* or *b* is met. So far, so obvious, you may think. But (yes, of course there is a 'but'—this is law, after all!) the use of the conjunctive and disjunctive can create all kinds of interpretation problems.

Sometimes it is not clear from the drafting or from the context whether all conditions in a section or regulation are intended to be mandatory, even if they are joined by 'and'—see the Working Time Regulations 1998, Reg. 2 for a recent example of an area where lawyers are having this kind of debate. 'Or' likewise can be problematic, not least because it can create a variant of the dangling-else problem we have already considered. An example of this is the case of *Cockerill* v *William Cory & Son Ltd* [1959] 2 QB 194. Here the plaintiff's husband had died after falling through an open hatchway on a ship. The Docks Regulations 1934, Reg. 45 provided that 'no person shall … remove … any fencing, gangway, gear, ladder, hatchcovering … or other thing whatsoever required by these regulations to be provided …'. The question arose in court whether 'required by these regulations' governed everything that went before those words, or governed only any 'other thing whatsoever'. If the latter interpretation was correct, then the listed things—including hatchcoverings—were excluded from the regulations and the plaintiff's case would fail. At first instance, based on an *obiter* comment from the Court of Appeal, McNair J. had adopted this second interpretation. Fortunately for the plaintiff, the Court of Appeal disagreed and adopted the opposite interpretation, based on an *eiusdem generis* reading (see **Chapter 9**) of the regulation.

Because of these sorts of syntactic ambiguities, courts have sometimes had to engage in semantic gymnastics to make sense of a provision, and there are examples of courts declaring that, in a particular context, 'and' has been used disjunctively (e.g. *Associated Artists* v *Inland Revenue Commissioners* [1956] 2 All ER 583) or that 'or' actually means 'and'—e.g. *Federal Steam Navigation Co. Ltd* v *Department of Trade and Industry* [1974] 1 WLR 505. This is not a uniquely English problem. Indeed in the USA it has been argued that the laxity in the legislative use of conjunctive and disjunctive terms is such that the courts should treat them as virtually interchangeable—*Ledwith* v *Bankers Life Insurance Co.* 156 Neb 107 (1952).

Now, let us look more specifically at a couple of problems that can arise with conjunctive and disjunctive propositions, and how we can use basic logic to help us untangle the ambiguities (we will talk at greater length about the importance of logic in **Chapter 12**).

We can begin again by considering our basic disjunctive conditional statement: 'if condition *a* or condition *b*, then outcome *c*'. The first question is, what if **both** condition *a* **and** condition *b* are met? Will outcome *c* follow? On the face of it, you might think there is no problem; couldn't the court just choose which condition it decided was operative? Well that might be true, but it is not necessarily so. This is where formal logic comes in. Logically, 'or' can operate as either an *exclusive* or *non-exclusive* disjunction (see, e.g. Fisher, 2004: 176). So, if the 'or' is exclusive, then only one of those conditions can apply— it is rather like a waiter telling you that you can have chips or boiled potatoes; the statement conveys the assumption that you can have only one kind of potato, not both.

If the 'or' is non-exclusive, however, it takes on the meaning '*a* or *b*, **or possibly both**'. Thus, strange though this may sound, 'or' can logically have a kind of implicit conjunctive function. Indeed, this is what we commonly intend by 'or' in a conditional statement such as ours: if both *a* and *b* are met, we tend to assume the condition will apply. In Latin this distinction is clear from the word used—the exclusive or is '*aut*' and the non-exclusive is '*vel*'. Unfortunately, in English we lose that linguistic distinction, so we have to work it out from the context. Thus, in law, the court may need to look at the wider syntactic setting, or if that is not sufficient, at the legislative intent, to assess which kind of 'or' is being used.

The second problem we will consider arises where the conjunctive and disjunctive are used in the same conditional statement. Thus, we might have the following conditional statement:

'if condition *a* and condition *b* or condition *c*, then outcome *d*'.

Put like this, the problem becomes readily apparent: the statement is ambiguous because it is not clear at what point the disjunctive conditional c takes effect. In other words, together, the conjunctive and disjunctive create another problem akin to the dangling else. This provision could mean:

- outcome *d* will apply only if EITHER conditions *a* AND *b* are satisfied OR condition *c* is satisfied;

or it could mean:

- outcome *d* will apply if and only if condition *a* is satisfied together with one of condition *b* OR *c*.

We can actually see the ambiguity even more clearly if we use the standard notation of formal logic (logicians use certain symbols to overcome the uncertainty of language and make logical relationships more transparent—see, e.g., the Appendix in Fisher, 2004). Thus, in formal logic these statements are represented respectively as:

$$(a \mathbin{\&} b) \mathbin{v} c$$

and

$$a \mathbin{\&} (b \mathbin{v} c)$$

where

   & = and

   v = vel – the non-exclusive 'or' (we will assume vel applies for the reasons already discussed), and

   ( ) indicate a non-ambiguous logical relation between propositions.

We are not suggesting the courts actually use formal logic in this way, but it is an effective way to make such syntactic differences more obvious. For the courts, such problems may ultimately be resolved by logic, by looking at other semantic features of the legislation, or by reference to legislative intent. It would, of course, be more satisfactory if drafters consistently used clear and unambiguous ways of listing provisions that avoided such ambiguity in the first place, but sometimes that is easier said than done.

More complex forms of ambiguity may arise, particularly within lengthy legal documents, where there is a contradiction between provisions. This is not, strictly speaking, a problem of syntax, just inconsistent drafting. However, it will raise difficult questions about which of the two conflicting provisions should prevail.

5.3 Fact, Language, and the Judicial Construction of Cases

In the next four chapters of this book we shall be looking at the rules or principles that have been developed, chiefly by the courts, to assist in the interpretation and use of existing statutory and common law authorities. The purpose of this chapter has been to get you to consider the background against which such principles operate. This is not simply a question of setting the scene. Many of those principles exist precisely because of the linguistic difficulties we have discussed in this chapter, and are there to provide guidance to the courts in overcoming such difficulties.

At the same time, however, it would be wrong to assume that such principles create a highly structured body of rules which can dictate with a high degree of certainty how issues, and hence legal cases, will be resolved. Cases are ultimately constructed in the courtroom. In *Hobson*, for example, the Court was able to justify its decision by reference to a principle of statutory interpretation, which requires ambiguity in a statute imposing criminal liability to be construed in favour of the accused. However, as we shall see in later chapters, the majority of these principles are not hard-and-fast rules of law which the judge can apply only one way. Such principles provide a framework. They are part of what circumscribes and defines the boundaries of 'acceptable' legal argument. Nevertheless, they are mostly broad and leave much to the wisdom of the particular judge in each case. This means that judges have a considerable degree of discretion in choosing the principles they apply, and hence the meanings they give to statutes and other legal documents.

Similarly, though true semantic ambiguity can be a major problem, flexibility in assigning meaning to words provides another source for the exercise of discretion. This has both positive and negative effects on the development of English law. On the one hand, problems of precision in definition may be such that judges and draftsmen become reluctant to define a word at all, or else avoid the issue by taking the 'ordinary meaning' approach of cases such as *Brutus* v *Cozens*. On the other hand, the lack of a precise definition may be equally indicative of a positive decision not to impose what might be an unduly restrictive definition on a particular concept. Whether this is desirable is ultimately a political rather than legal question, but it does have a legal cost in that a lack of formalised definitions can sometimes allow the law to develop without the internal coherence and consistency that we might expect. So what, ultimately, dictates how a judge's discretion is applied?

Of course, there is not a straightforward answer to that question! To understand what is going on here, and at the same time to help explain the dilemma with which we opened this chapter, we need to touch on the nature of legal argumentation, a subject we will return to in greater detail in **Chapter 12**.

5.3.1 Interpretation and Justification in Legal Argument

Legal argumentation is a particular kind of activity that exists only in language and in the specific process of communication in legal settings. Putting it at its simplest, we can say that legal argument requires actions of both interpretation and justification.

Legal argument is posited first on interpretation. By this we don't just mean statutory interpretation—though that will be part of it. Interpretation provides meaning to a whole range of legal texts—statutes, law reports, the formal statements of case which are the basis for bringing a court action, and so on (one can include oral testimony here as well, as it is commonly reduced to writing as part of the preparation for a trial). The range of possible interpretations of such documents is itself defined by the norms and practices of legal interpretation—another way of putting this would be to think of legal interpretation as the product of the specific 'interpretative community' of the law. Interpretation is the first step in legal argument because interpretation defines what is being argued about, both as regards the rules in a case and the facts to which they apply. It is the means of establishing a basic consensus of understanding out of which we can define the issues about which there is dissensus, and thus a need for argument.

Next, legal argument requires some kind of grounding in reasons which provide a *justification* for the position being taken. Again, in relatively simple terms, legal justification can adopt broadly one of two forms (see Summers, 1978). First, it can be *consequential*, that is, it focuses on the goal, outcome, or consequences of legal action. Consequential reasoning thus seeks to justify a decision through a balancing of the different interests affected in a case. This can be seen, for example, in judicial references to public policy. Thus a court may refuse a claim for compensation because to allow it would risk swamping the courts with similar claims, or because to do so would impose an unacceptable burden on actual and potential defendants. Secondly, it can involve what Summers calls '*rightness reasons*'. In other words, the justification can be found by reference to objective and sometimes, perhaps, universal rights or principles (e.g. 'torture is wrong') which are said to apply in this case.

The role of the lawyers and the judge, therefore, is:

(1) to construct an interpretation out of a set of contingent facts; some of this interpretation will be agreed or assumed; other elements will be the subject of argument, with a decision on the 'true' facts to be made by the tribunal of fact;

(2) to provide justification for an outcome which is permitted on normative grounds; and

(3) which provides a compelling story that integrates the facts with the law in a manner that is both normatively and 'narratively coherent' (Jackson, 1988), i.e. in which there is a good 'fit' between the facts and the legal outcome.

If we focus now on the role of the judge within this system we can begin to see how discretion arises, and how we are justified in talking about the judicial construction of cases.

5.3.2 Discretion, 'Judicial Style', and the Construction of Cases

The idea that there are acceptable forms of legal argument both constrains and creates the scope for judicial discretion, since it gives the judge some, sometimes considerable, freedom of interpretation and freedom of justification. The critical question may thus be how far is the judge prepared to push his or her freedom within or even beyond the boundaries of what is acceptable? This, we suggest, in large part comes down to a question of what we may call the 'judicial style' of the judge. This question of judicial style will be significant in determining how a judge handles a case, including the way in which he or she uses precedent—see Llewellyn (1960)—or principles of statutory interpretation (a point to which we shall return in **Chapter 9**). We can illustrate the operation of judicial style, first, by reference to two decisions on the law of negligence.

In negligence, it is necessary for the plaintiff to show that the injuries suffered are 'reasonably foreseeable' if the claim is to succeed.

In *Bradford* v *Robinson Rentals Ltd* [1967] 1 WLR 337; [1967] 1 All ER 267, the High Court had to deal with an unusual claim. In this case, the plaintiff was claiming in respect of frostbite suffered as a result of driving his employer's unheated van during an exceptionally harsh winter. On these facts, the plaintiff succeeded in his claim; the employer was negligent in allowing the plaintiff out in such a vehicle and the plaintiff's injuries were a reasonably foreseeable consequence of that action, despite the fact that the precise kind of injury suffered was uncommon in England.

In *Tremain* v *Pike* [1969] 1 WLR 1556; [1969] 3 All ER 1303, the plaintiff, a farm worker, contracted a rare disease called Weil's disease which is caused by the sufferer being infected by an organism found in rats' urine. His claim was that his employer had been negligent by allowing the rat population on the farm to grow to such an extent as to place his health at risk. The Court did not deny that such behaviour was negligent, but it refused the plaintiff's claim on the basis that the *type* of injury was not foreseeable. What was foreseeable was a more obvious kind of 'rat injury' such as a bite. In effect, the Court held that you cannot foresee a rare disease.

Is the latter decision inconsistent with the former? If the approach in *Bradford* had been followed in *Tremain* there would certainly be grounds for suggesting that contracting Weil's disease is no less foreseeable than contracting frostbite. But the Court in *Tremain* was not bound by *Bradford*; the judge consequently had greater freedom of justification in applying the reasonable foresight test than he might otherwise have done. The difference thus lies not in the actual tests used, but in the attitude to the test displayed by the two courts. In the second case, the judge took a very restrictive (and consequentialist) view, requiring that the precise *type* of injury should be reasonably foreseeable. In *Bradford*, the judicial view was more relaxed. It was foreseeable that some kind of injury would follow from being thus exposed to the extreme cold, and that was taken to be sufficient. It was not necessary that the precise nature of the injury should be foreseen.

Judicial style may also affect the way in which facts are used. We have already confronted the idea that facts in law are not a wholly objective truth. They are in part constructed within the courtroom and may be affected by a whole variety of highly subjective factors; for example, the presentation by counsel, the language, and appearance of witnesses, or the ability of the jury (or judge?) to comprehend the issues. We have also noted that the judge is, in many cases, the arbiter of fact. We suggest that questions of judicial style might thus also influence the reception and interpretation of those facts.

In two studies, by Jackson (1988) and Twining (1990), the judgment of Lord Denning in *Miller* v *Jackson* [1977] QB 966; [1977] 3 All ER 338 has been considered. Although the two authors adopt different standpoints, they have both used *Miller* critically, as an example of how judges may manipulate a case through the statement of facts. We have used an extract from that judgment as the basis for the final exercise in this chapter.

EXERCISE 8 It's just not cricket!

Consider the following passage taken from Lord Denning's judgment in *Miller* v *Jackson* (pp. 340–1):

> In summer time village cricket is the delight of everyone. Nearly every village has its own cricket field where the young men play and the old men watch. In the village of Lintz in County Durham they have their own ground, where they have played these last 70 years … The village team play there on Saturdays and Sundays. They belong to a league, competing with the neighbouring villages. On other evenings after work they practise while the light lasts. Yet now after these 70 years a judge of the High Court has ordered that they must not play there any more. He has issued an injunction to stop them. He has done it at the instance of a newcomer who is no lover of cricket. This newcomer built, or has had built for him, a house on the edge of the cricket ground which four years ago was a field where cattle grazed. The animals did not mind the cricket. But now this adjoining field has been turned into a housing estate. The newcomer bought one of the houses on the edge of the cricket ground. No doubt the open space was a selling point. Now he complains that, when a batsman hits a six, the ball has been known to land in his garden or on or near his house. His wife has got so upset about it that they always go out at weekends. They do not go into the garden when cricket is being played. They say that this is intolerable … And the judge, much against his will, has felt that he must order the cricket to be stopped; with the consequences, I suppose, that the Lintz Cricket Club will disappear. The cricket ground will be turned to some other use. I expect for more houses or a factory. The young men will turn to other things instead of cricket. The whole village will be much the poorer. And all this because of a newcomer who has just bought a house there next to the cricket ground.

continued

EXERCISE 8 *continued*

 QUESTIONS

From this statement can you:

(a) Predict Lord Denning's decision on the law: did he find in favour of the cricket club, or of the Millers?

(b) Distinguish fact from supposition within that case?

 ANSWERS

The answer to (a) will probably come as little surprise. Lord Denning found in favour of the cricket club. He held that there was no actionable nuisance by the club, and discharged the injunction. His Lordship was not, in the end, wholly successful in carrying the rest of the Court of Appeal with him. The other two judges found that there was an actionable nuisance; however, only one of them felt that it was such that an injunction (a discretionary remedy) should be granted, so that Lord Denning was in a majority in favour of dismissing the injunction granted by the High Court.

Is it not rather odd that we can guess the final decision from what is supposed to be a statement of facts? Yes—if one assumes that the facts are supposed to be a fairly objective part of the process. Lord Denning's comments illustrate, as Twining notes, the way in which facts can be formulated so as to advance a particular argument, albeit that, here, Lord Denning's formulation is far more explicitly biased than one would normally expect from a judge. Jackson argues that his technique is strongly rhetorical. Through its choice of language and a range of rhetorical techniques, it builds an image of a rural community bound together by its love of cricket; it is an idyll that is threatened by an outsider who can destroy that traditional way of life. The effect is to create a narrative framework 'laden with disapproval' (1988: 96).

In respect of (b), the construction of a narrative built upon both fact and supposition is another aspect of Lord Denning's attempt to carry us along to his conclusion. He thus creates a picture of socially undesirable consequences that might flow from the continued injunction: the replacement of the cricket ground with houses or a factory; the fear that young men will turn 'to other things' which, though remaining unspoken, are clearly undesirable. These are, of course suppositions, without evidence; they should not impinge on the case, and yet they do.

 CONCLUSION

In saying that language is open textured and that judicial style is an important determinant of cases, we are not suggesting that judges have, in effect, a free rein to decide cases as they think fit. As we have said at various points in this chapter, judges (and lawyers) operate within a linguistic community and culture which creates limits on what is acceptable practice. The existence of objective rules and principles, applied within a setting which expects decisions to display at least some normative and narrative coherence, means that in most cases there will be one story and one outcome that is more 'correct' than another. Indeed, one reason why Lord Denning's judgment in *Miller* v *Jackson* has been so extensively criticised is precisely because he stepped beyond the boundaries of acceptable judicial argumentation, and challenged the perception, perhaps even the ethical expectation, we have that a judge will maintain his or her air of neutrality.

While the framework of rules and principles within which judges operate does impose some constraints on them, clearly it may not always be sufficient. Does this matter? Should the judges be made more constrained, more accountable for their decisions? Before you dismiss this question as irrelevant to legal method, consider the role of the guiding principles of precedent and interpretation that make up much of this book. To what extent are these self-imposed, and therefore capable of revision from within the judiciary itself? As Llewellyn (1960: 53) pointed out: a sense of legal tradition may guide lawyers, but it is the lawyers who may reshape and mould it for the future. Who should decide whether the lawyers are right to do so?

 ## CHAPTER REFERENCES

FISHER, A. (2004), *The Logic of Real Arguments* (2nd edn, Cambridge: Cambridge University Press).

FULLER, L. (1958), 'Positivism and Fidelity to Law—A Reply to Professor Hart', 71 *Harvard Law Review*, 630.

GROSSFELD, B. (1990), *The Strength and Weakness of Comparative Law* (trans. T. Weir) (Oxford: Clarendon Press).

HANSON, N. (1959), *Patterns of Discovery: An Inquiry into the Conceptual Foundations of Science* (Cambridge: Cambridge University Press).

HART, H.L.A. (1994), *The Concept of Law* (2nd edn, Oxford: Clarendon Press).

JACKSON, B. (1988), *Law, Fact and Narrative Coherence* (Roby: Deborah Charles Publishing).

*KNAPP, V. (1991), 'Some Problems of Legal Language', 4 *Ratio Juris*, 1.

LLEWELLYN, K. (1960), *The Common Law Tradition* (Boston, Mass.: Little Brown).

LSE JURY PROJECT (1973), 'Juries and the Rules of Evidence', *Criminal Law Review*, 208.

MOORE, P.G. and THOMAS, H. (1988), *The Anatomy of Decisions* (2nd edn, London: Penguin Books).

NIBLETT, B. (1980), 'Computer Science and Law: An Introductory Discussion', in B. Niblett (ed.), *Computer Science and Law: An Advanced Course* (Cambridge: Cambridge University Press).

O'BARR, W., *et al.* (1982), *Linguistic Evidence: Language, Power and Strategy in the Courtroom* (New York: Academic Press).

SCHAUER, F. (2008), 'A Critical Guide to Vehicles in the Park' 83 *New York University Law Review*, 1109.

SUMMERS, R. (1978), 'Two Types of Substantive Reasons: The Core of a Theory of Common Law Justification', 63 *Cornell Law Review*, 707.

TWINING, W. (1990), *Rethinking Evidence: Exploratory Essays* (Oxford: Basil Blackwell).

WESTON, M. (1991), *An English Reader's Guide to the French Legal System* (New York/Oxford: Berg).

WILKES, R. (1984), *Wallace: The Final Verdict* (London: Grafton).

6

The Doctrine of Judicial Precedent

6.1 Introduction

In this chapter we begin to examine how we use case law to solve legal problems. In the study and practice of law we seek to analyse legal principles; and the 'principles' in English law are derived from pure case law or from case law dealing with statutes.

6.1.1 What is Case Law?

So, what exactly do we mean by 'case law'? In earlier chapters we discussed the idea of cases (see, for instance, sections **1.7.4**, **1.8**, and **2.4**) and we examined procedure and law reporting. In this and the next chapter we will discuss case law in much greater depth. Although this is not a book on the English legal system we will begin with an explanation of some basic points on what 'cases' are and how they come about.

Criminal law cases, of course, come about because the police make an arrest and charge the accused, the legal arguments of the case being taken up by the Crown Prosecution Service (CPS). Indeed, the CPS may well have been involved at the 'charging' stage, advising on the strength of the evidence, etc. The CPS then brings the prosecution on behalf of the Crown. The charge must be clearly defined. Lay people often talk of a person being 'charged with theft' (or rape, or murder, etc.), but the CPS has to frame the charge according to strict rules and with reference to established and recognised common law or statutory crimes. This will lead to what is termed the 'indictment', which will first set out the charge (e.g. 'Arson contrary to section 1(2) and (3) of the Criminal Damage Act 1971'). There will then appear the 'Particulars of the offence'—the basic facts—such as 'Claude Nero on October 3rd 2015 did without lawful excuse damage by fire a caravan, having a value of £17,000, belonging to Vyacheslav Molotov intending to damage such vehicle by fire and intending by such damage to endanger the life of Vyacheslav Molotov'). These will be given to the jury at the start of the trial.

Before the matter comes to trial (in front of magistrates for lesser offences or, in the Crown Court, before a judge and jury) there will be other preliminary matters to deal with and perhaps even detailed legal arguments about admissibility of evidence. Many of these cases are reported in the local and national press, but they are only really interesting to a lawyer if and when they go on appeal, for it is at that point that the key legal arguments start to bite.

Civil cases are obviously different. Here, the usual position is that one individual or company is suing another for some form of compensation arising from a loss. But suing for what? A litigant cannot just 'sue' someone: they have to sue them for some identifiable legal reason. They must have what is called a 'cause of action'. This means that the set of facts must show something which the law recognises as giving rise to potential liability. If you are injured in a car accident, for instance, you do not just 'sue' the other driver, you must sue for and show 'negligence'; if someone does not do what they promised to do you may have a claim (a cause of action) for breach of contract. If someone floods your land, you may have claims in negligence, breach of contract, or nuisance (to name but a few).

The point of this is that when you fill out your claim form you must identify what it is you are suing for—otherwise neither the court nor the defendant can respond. Indeed, the importance of establishing the cause of action lies even earlier than this: if you write to a potential defendant in advance of bringing a claim (which you have to do in many instances under what are known as 'Protocols') you must spell out why you think they are liable. You must also specify the damages (or compensation) you are seeking. Be careful here: the cause of action identifies what legal right you are claiming has been breached, the damages you are seeking is your **remedy** for that breach. Unless you establish your cause of action and meet all the requirements to be found there you cannot receive any damages.

So, from the moment a client walks into the office and starts to tell her story, a lawyer has to be thinking:

(i)   What legal principles are involved (what is the cause of action here)?

(ii) What is the relevant law regarding these principles (where can the up-to-date authorities be found)?

(iii) What evidence will we need to prove or defend the case? and

(iv) Which court do I have to apply to?

In fact, this is a very similar thought process to that in a criminal law case—just substitute the word 'charge' for 'cause of action'.

Concentrating on civil cases: let us assume all attempts to settle the case fail. As with the criminal justice system there are procedures to go through before trial (these form part of what is generally called the 'case management' system). These will include things such as disclosing and exchanging relevant documents, obtaining experts' reports, and agreeing how long the case will take. These are often dealt with before a judge in what is referred to as a 'Directions hearing'. Here, the parties agree or are told what 'directions' the judge is giving on the management of the case. Assume these have happened but the case is going to trial—perhaps in a county court (in Bristol, London, Leeds, etc.—wherever is appropriate). The case is for a relatively small amount and is heard by a District Judge.

As we have noted previously, our system is an 'adversarial' one: when it comes to trial each side presents and argues their case according to rules of evidence and procedure, but before the trial each party must know what the other party's evidence will be. The idea that one side can 'surprise' the other with new evidence on the day of the trial is not part of our system. Further, during the trial judges may intervene and ask pertinent questions (especially if one side is not represented by a lawyer) but they are anxious to avoid 'stepping into the arena': it is not a judge's job to argue the case for either litigant.

The judge sees all the documents, sees any witnesses being examined and cross-examined, hears arguments on the law, and makes a decision. One party loses (there is no system of 'drawing'). In most cases they will have to pay some form of damages and also the costs of litigation for both sides (e.g. any court fees or lawyers' costs). And, as an aside, at no time in an English court does a judge ever use a gavel, no matter what contrary image TV and films portray.

The losing party wishes to appeal. In nearly all instances they can only do so on points of law. They will need permission from a court to do so (it is not an automatic right) and they must lodge the appeal within a prescribed time. Let us assume they get permission but lose again. The same mechanism operates. Now let us say they have arrived in the Court of Appeal. This is the stage where most decisions will be reported in the law reports (it can happen lower down in the hierarchy but, aside from specialist courts such as the Employment Appeal Tribunal, this is not common). All the arguments are about the legal principles involved. The facts are taken as proved by that stage. The same is true of criminal cases: the lower courts deal with both law and fact, but by the time a case reaches the Court of Appeal (Criminal Division) the issues tend to be purely legal ones.

So now, when we talk later in the chapter about precedents, *ratio decidendi*, and other matters, we are usually talking about cases heard in the Court of Appeal or the Supreme Court. What we are concerned with is not who won or lost but the legal principles that can be extracted from the case. As a law student, this is the setting you are most concerned with (if you become a practitioner you will of course have had to deal with questions of fact, evidence, and procedure, as well as the law, in the lower courts).

This is a very sketchy view of case-law procedure, but it serves our purpose—we now know that:

- there must be a cause of action (or a charge/indictment in criminal cases);
- that analysing this involves matching the facts to legal principles;
- that the facts must be proved in court (balance of probabilities in civil actions, beyond all reasonable doubt in criminal cases);
- that it is generally arguments about the legal principles that form the basis of appeals; and
- that it is the legal analysis in these appeals which forms the basis of 'law reports' and therefore precedents.

'Case law' is the term we use to describe the collection of all the legal principles emanating from all the reported cases on a given topic. The case law on the law of negligence, for example, consists of thousands of individual cases, all building one on another, year after year, exploring different aspects of the law and seeing whether the principles of law apply or do not apply (or need changing) to different sets of facts. Each case 'tests out' the relevant principle in the light of new facts.

Indeed, it is often said to be a strength of English law that it is built upon the concrete examples of case law rather than hypothetical models. This contrast with the European approach, which does depend upon 'models' (called 'Codes'), will be drawn and expanded upon later. As regards the common law fixation with a case-by-case development of the law, it is worth noting the observations of Lord MacMillan that, unlike the civil law lawyer, the Englishman:

has found that life is unconformable to any fixed theory and that principles always fail because they never seem to fit the case in hand, and so prefers to leave theory and principle alone. (1937: 81)

We shall explore the significance of this statement over the next two chapters. One difficulty with this case-by-case development is that it does leave us with a slight 'Goldilocks problem' in that when there are very few cases on a topic we cannot be sure how far the precedent will be applied or changed and when there are hundreds of cases we have trouble sorting through all the detailed applications to get to the general principle—rarely are things 'just right'.

6.1.2 What is Precedent?

The doctrine of judicial precedent is concerned with the importance of case law in our system. It is about achieving consistency. It is really the lawyer's term for legal experience. We all tend to repeat things we have done before: law is essentially no different. Nor should it be if we want some degree of certainty in our law. If one case has decided a point of law then it is logical that that solution will be looked at in the future. Even small children recognise the need for consistency and certainty in how they are dealt with and how they deal with others. The American judge, Oliver Wendell Holmes Jr., once said that: 'The life of the Law has not been logic; it has been experience'. Miles Kington put it rather more cynically in *Punch*: judicial precedent means: 'A trick which has been tried before, successfully'.

But if judicial precedent is simply legal jargon for experience, why does it deserve our attention? Why can we say that, during your training in law and afterwards, you will have to possess a clear understanding of the intricacies of judicial precedent? The answer lies in the fact that the term 'experience' only begins to describe the situation.

First, even when a layperson uses the term 'precedent' there is an implication that what was done before should be done again—that a starting point in trying to solve a problem is to see what examples exist where this (or similar) problems have been tackled before. The example—the precedent—is at least a good guide and probably will be followed. This achieves consistency, if nothing else. As was said by the Court of Appeal in *Howard de Walden Estates Ltd* v *Aggio and others; Earl Cadogan and Cadogan Estates Ltd* v *26 Cadogan Square Ltd* [2007] EWCA Civ 499; [2007] All ER (D) 408 (May): 'This principle serves the interests of legal certainty. The need of litigants and their advisers to know where they stand is not served if a lower court is free to create a conflict of authority by declining to follow the relevant decision of a higher court.'

The corollary is that people making decisions are often afraid to do something in case 'it creates a precedent'. As MacCormick stated:

> To understand case-law ... is to understand how it is that *particular* decisions by particular judges concerning particular parties to particular cases can be used in the construction of *general* rules applying to the actions and transactions of persons at large. (1987: 155)

In other words, combining the remarks of Lord MacMillan and MacCormick, the principles of English law are derived from observing the development of a line of particular cases on a particular topic. This is a key factor in English law. Because English lawyers are so avidly fixed on case law, principles do not develop unless claimants bring cases. Academics and practitioners may speculate on the development of legal principles, but it takes real-life cases to settle them. And the judges in each case, to a greater or lesser extent, draw upon the principles established in those earlier cases in reaching their decision. It should be noted, however, that there are also weaknesses in this system and we will return to these later.

As we have already noted on the development of case law in negligence, this is a piecemeal, case-by-case progression. In 1950 the head of the judiciary in Scotland, Lord Cooper, put it this way: 'The civilian [i.e. lawyers using the Civil Law system] naturally reasons from principles to instances, the common lawyer from instances to principles' (Cooper: 1950). Lord Wright had already put it even more graphically in 1938 when he described how the common law judges 'proceed from case to case, like the ancient Mediterranean mariners, hugging the coast from point to point, and avoiding the dangers of the open sea …'. Lawyers like security. Richard Buxton (2009: 60) also notes that: 'The purpose of any case is to decide the issue between the parties, and not to reform the law'. There are many intriguing academic aspects in the study of law but this quote emphasises that the purpose of law is to solve problems and disputes.

Slavish adherence to precedent has also been described whimsically as one which 'follows the trail of the calf'. The metaphor goes: many hundreds of years ago a calf wandered home and cut a path through the wood. The calf wandered all over the place but the trail it made was clear. Other animals followed this indirect path because it was easier to do so. Eventually there was a road, but one which did not necessarily go in a straight line. However, everyone subsequently followed that route. There are a number of sources for this idea, e.g. a 1905 poem by Sam Walter Foss called the 'Calf-Path'. It was quoted by Professor Max Radin (a nineteenth-century American jurist) in 'The Trail of the Calf' (1946: 137, 150) but the author goes on to show that the adherence to precedent is not as passive as this analogy leads us to believe: the path is not always followed slavishly but is in fact subject to modifications by its followers. Nevertheless, it is a fun way to visualise the somewhat meandering development of case law.

As an example of this more active and thoughtful case-by-case development of precedent imagine a case in, say, 1930, which decided that any person selling parrots was under an implied contractual duty to ensure that the parrot could talk. A layperson reading about this case might think it interesting, especially if he has just bought an unwanted dumb parrot. A lawyer, however, immediately starts to think of the ramifications of the case: what is its wider significance? How does it stand with other cases? What level of court made the decision? Thus, to the lawyer, the case presents further questions:

(a) Would this principle still apply if the pet shop owner clearly told the customer that the parrot could not talk?

(b) Does the same principle apply to similar birds such as budgerigars?

(c) Should the principle apply to any bird (e.g. that they twitter pleasantly even if they are not 'talkers')?

(d) Wider still, is there a general principle to be found in the case which might mean that a similar duty (say as to standards of health) might apply to the sale of all animals?

Thus, as MacCormick indicates, the particular case concerning parrots may consequently be seen as giving birth to a more general principle on the duties owed by pet shop owners to their customers, e.g. that they owed a duty always to deal in good faith. It is not beyond speculation that the same principle might one day then be applied to sellers of other types of goods such as televisions (not even in common use in 1930) or cars. Eventually a textbook writer will sum up the case law in one general statement on the duties owed by vendors of goods. Looking back at the history of the cases, we might find that the principle concerning one case about a mute parrot is now applied to all cases on defective merchandise.

The case of *Whittall v Kirby* [1947] KB 194 serves as a good, simple example to illustrate the development, from one case to another, of a legal principle, and we shall return to this throughout the next two chapters to demonstrate different aspects of judicial precedent.

In 1946 Henry Kirby was convicted of driving his lorry while intoxicated. This meant he would lose his licence unless, under the Road Traffic Act 1930, there was a 'special reason' not to disqualify him. The magistrates decided that, as he had no previous convictions, drove the lorry for a living, and had been given a substantial fine, these constituted special reasons not to disqualify him. On appeal by way of case stated (a special provision dealing with legal points alone) it was held that none of these reasons was a 'special reason': to be a 'special reason' that reason, it was said, had to be special to the facts of the offence, not to the offender. Being a lorry driver was only something special to the offender and so not enough to avoid disqualification. Something else would be needed to avoid disqualification. At this point, in 1947, however, would we know whether the same principle applied to, say, a taxi driver or to a commercial traveller? We only have one concrete example: a lorry driver. At its most obvious level the case can only concern lorry drivers. However, it is at this point that the specific words used by the judge in his judgment provide some guidance for later judges. Here, Lord Goddard stated: 'That a man is a professional driver cannot, as it seems to me, by any possibility be called a special reason.' This rather indicates that the case will be authority on the wider class of professional drivers, not just lorry drivers. But in 1947 lawyers did not know what this might mean; it would take further cases to establish this. Therefore, we will return to this example later to demonstrate the workings of case law and how this decision 'panned out' in future cases.

One interesting development as regards creating a form of 'restatement' of the law came in *R v Hunter* [2015] EWCA Crim 631; [2015] 2 Cr. App. R. 9 where the Court of Appeal effectively issued a diktat, stating [103]: 'We have deliberately conducted a very thorough review of the case law so that it will be unnecessary in future for other courts to do the same. Reliance on this judgment, *Vye* and *Aziz* should suffice.'

6.2 The Idea of Binding Precedent (*Stare Decisis*)

We now need to add one further ingredient. It is this: an important and distinctive element of English law is that the reasoning and decisions found in preceding cases are not simply considered with respect or as a good guide, but can be **binding** on later courts. This is known as the principle of *stare rationibus decidendis*; usually referred to as *stare decisis*. It translates simply as 'Let the decision stand'. *Stare rationibus decidendis* is the more accurate statement because, as we shall see, it is the reasoning (*rationibus*) that is the vital binding element in judicial precedent. However, nobody actually refers to it this way.

What *stare decisis* means in practice is that when a court makes a decision in a case then any courts which are of equal or lower status to that court **must** follow that previous decision if the case before them is similar to that earlier case. So, once one court has decided a matter other inferior courts are bound to follow that decision, whether they agree with it or not.

You must be careful here: the 'decision' of a case can mean a number of different things. At its simplest, the 'decision' is that X won and Y lost. Thus X and Y are (subject to any appeal) bound by that decision; this is referred to as *res judicata* (a matter which has been adjudicated upon). But when we use the word 'decision' in the context of legal analysis we are referring to something much wider. We are referring to the *whole* reasoning process that went into deciding that X won—we are referring to *why* X won and we shall explore how we set about this later. For instance, in *Whittall* v *Kirby* (see section **6.1.2**) the decision was not merely that a lorry driver convicted of being drunk in charge could be disqualified but that he was disqualified because the idea of a 'special reason' under the statute had to be special to the offence and not the offender.

So, you must be aware right at the start that legal reasoning is not simply a process of matching one case against another; it is not merely a question of drawing direct analogies. Finding analogous cases is a good starting point but there will always be differences in the facts of the two cases, if nothing else. Equally, the status and therefore the importance of the decision depends upon which court made it. We shall look at the court structure and which court is bound to follow the decision of another court in section **6.4**.

Before that, however, we need to be clear on what we mean by 'similarities' and 'differences' between cases. It is very easy to fall into the trap of comparing cases on their facts without, as we noted above, looking at the *reasoning* used in reaching that decision. For instance, just because the facts of two cases are apparently similar does not mean they should be decided in the same way. You would not, for instance, say that if a tabby cat called Henry miaows like a banshee, then every other tabby cat called Henry will do so too.

We can translate this into something more realistic and legally orientated.

EXERCISE 9 Zebras on the North Circular

Let us say that in *case (1)* a man driving a Ford Mondeo runs over an old lady who was lawfully using a zebra crossing. The man is held to be liable in negligence.

Let us say that in *case (2)* a woman driving a BMW runs over an old man who was crossing the road. Should she be found liable, too, or do you need to ask some further questions? If there are other questions, what might they be?

We do not present a formalised answer to this, because we wish to explore the ramifications of the issues it raises, but you may check your ideas against the comments which follow in the text. We have seen in earlier exercises that a proper assessment and analysis of factual detail is essential to the application of rules. You might wish to know, for instance, what were the weather conditions in each case, were either of the drivers speeding, was the old man crossing the road at a safe point?

All these matters will come out in the evidence given by the parties. The judge will decide, on the strength of the evidence, which version of the 'truth' he or she believes. The judge will then apply the law (i.e. the existing judicial precedents) to the facts of this case to decide whether, on the facts as found, the defendant is liable to pay damages to the claimant. The more similar the facts of this new case are to existing precedents, the easier it is for the judge to decide that the law which is found in those precedents applies to the new case; the more the new facts differ from existing precedents (or raise completely novel points), the more difficult it will be to find a match. As you will see much later in this book (in **Chapter 12**) there are various reasoning techniques a judge may employ (reasoning by induction, deduction, analogy, or even through policy considerations) but the basic idea is that he or she has to choose whether the new case should be decided in the same way as the older cases. This leads us to ask: what similarities or differences in the facts might be significant here? Are the cases, for instance:

(a) sufficiently similar that the decision of *case (1)* should be applied in *case (2)*?; or

(b) sufficiently different that the decision of *case (1)* should not be applied (never mind be considered binding) in *case (2)*?; or

(c) are the factual differences of minimal significance so that *case (1)* is likely to be applied to *case (2)*?; or

(d) are the facts different, but the principle underlying the decisions in the cases similar? This can be a difficult one. Here you need to be sure what was the **principle** that was established in the first case: does the reasoning—the '*why?*'—in the first case apply to the second even though the facts differ? In some instances this may even involve using one case in, say, shipping law, to answer a question about the liability of a fairground company to a local authority in the law of contract (as was the point in a real case dealt with by one of the authors). The factual settings are miles apart but the contractual principle involved might be common ground. In this particular example, for instance, involving such widely different facts, the legal *principle* in question was whether a contract could exist when there were three parties involved and, if so, between which parties (the fairground, the local council, and a booking agent on the one hand and a yacht club and two race contestants in the shipping law case).

In the next chapter we shall explore in more depth how we assess the '*why?*' in a case. For the moment, imagine that when you read the report of *case (1)* you found that the case went all the way to the Supreme Court who pronounced that whenever a driver injures a pedestrian, irrespective of how careless the pedestrian was, the driver is to be held to be at fault. This would mean that, whatever the differences in fact between *case (1)* and *case (2)*—which in our example involved a woman driving a BMW running over an old man who was crossing the road—it looks as if the driver in *case (2)* will be liable because the **general** principle established in *case (1)* would apply.

On the other hand, perhaps the principle found in the Supreme Court's decision in *case (1)* was simply that drivers will always be held to blame if pedestrians are injured while using a zebra crossing. If that is the principle established in *case (1)* then the presence or absence of a zebra crossing is of utmost importance and it is arguable that the decision in *case (1)* should not apply to the facts of *case (2)* as *case (2)* did not involve a zebra crossing.

6.3 Establishing the Principle in a Case

As can be seen from this discussion, the doctrine of judicial precedent is not simply a mechanical process of matching similarities and differences as in some weird game of 'Snap'. It is not merely a science of comparisons for it embodies the art of interpretation; the art of propounding the **principle** to be derived from each case. It also involves the lifeblood of a lawyer: argument. We will deal with this aspect of precedent in depth in the next chapter. However, by way of introduction we can look at one case from the nineteenth century (the one which appears in the box: *Household Fire Insurance* v *Grant*) and see how it was treated as a precedent when cases, which at first sight seemed quite similar to it, came before later courts.

 Household Fire Insurance Co. v Grant (1879) 4 Ex D 216

Grant made an application in writing to the company for shares. A deposit was paid, the remainder to be paid within 12 months. The company allotted shares to Grant and posted the allotment to him. The letter never arrived. The company later went into liquidation and the liquidator sought the balance of Grant's application which was still outstanding. Grant maintained he had no contract with the company because his offer had not been accepted. No contract would mean no liability to pay. The company maintained that the offer had been accepted when their letter of acceptance had been posted even though it never arrived.

In case you have not studied contract law yet (or are not going to), we should explain that a contract is formed when there is an offer which is accepted, without the addition of new terms, by the other party. A person making an offer is termed the *offeror* (in the earlier example that would be Grant); the person receiving the offer is the *offeree* (Household Fire Insurance). The general rule is that acceptance has to be communicated by the offeree. There is no contract simply because, in his or her own mind, the offeree is willing to accept. However, a major problem arises when the parties are not face to face. If they communicate by post, for instance, when does the acceptance take place? Should it be when the letter of acceptance is posted by the offeree, or only when it arrives with the offeror?

By the end of the nineteenth century there existed a number of authorities on what is now termed the 'postal rules' of acceptance in contract. These stretched back to *Adams* v *Lindsell* (1818) 1 B & A 681, but the key case under scrutiny was to be the House of Lords case of *Dunlop* v *Higgins* (1848) 1 HLC 381; 9 ER 805. In this case Dunlop wrote to Higgins offering to sell some iron, reply to be by return of post. The offer was accepted by Higgins in a letter but bad weather delayed the post. In the meantime there had been an increase in the price of iron. It was in Dunlop's interest to argue that no contract had been concluded with Higgins because then Dunlop would still own the iron and be able to sell it to other customers at the new (higher) price. So, Dunlop informed Higgins that the reply had not been made by return of post and so was invalid. The House of Lords decided otherwise: a contract existed when the letter of acceptance was posted.

What was the reasoning behind the decision? In *Household Fire Insurance* v *Grant* all three judges in the Court of Appeal analysed whether *Dunlop* v *Higgins* applied to the case before them. Lord Justice Thesiger said that the decision in *Dunlop* v *Higgins* rested 'upon a principle which embraces and governs the present case'. To say that the acceptance takes place when the letter is posted and arrives late (as with *Dunlop v Higgins*) but not if it never arrives (as with *Household Fire*) would be illogical. The principle was, therefore, that once the letter of acceptance was posted the parties were bound. Of course, the offeree would have to convince a court on the facts that this had happened; but that point of evidence was irrelevant to the legal principle.

When Bagallay LJ looked at *Dunlop v Higgins* he concluded (at 227–8):

> I think that the principle established by that case is limited in its application to cases in which by reason of general usage, or of the relations between the parties … or of the terms in which the offer is made, the acceptance of such offer by a letter through the post is expressly or impliedly authorised.

Thus the principle in *Dunlop v Higgins* was seen by Bagallay LJ as being more limited than Thesiger LJ's approach—it would not apply in all cases where the post was used; but on the facts Bagallay LJ decided that the present case still fell within the rule because the offer had stated that reply should be by return of post.

Lord Justice Bramwell dissented. He thought there was *no contract* because the letter never arrived. He argued that *Dunlop v Higgins* had been completely misinterpreted: at best it was authority for the rule that acceptance takes place on posting only where the letter arrives (albeit late and within a reasonable time).

So the same authority was used by two Lords Justices to find for the company but they had quite different interpretations of what *Dunlop v Higgins* really decided. Of course the same case was also used by Bramwell LJ to argue a completely different conclusion—showing at least that simply knowing about the existence of a case is not enough; you must be able to argue its relevance or irrelevance to the case in hand. This means that you must read cases in depth. If you choose not to, then you run the risk of being caught out by your opponent in a legal argument. To adapt slightly a quote from Mark Twain: the person who does not read cases has no advantage over the person who cannot read them.

In this chapter we shall concentrate on the position where the facts are sufficiently similar that the cases are 'alike'. How will the doctrine of *stare decisis* affect our analysis? In answering this question it becomes important that we should look at the mechanical side of precedent. The courts stand in a defined hierarchy: which courts are **bound** to follow the decisions of which other courts? This is not usually perceived as the most exciting part of legal studies, but understanding the workings of *stare decisis* depends upon having a sound grasp of the court structure. In turn, an efficient system of precedent depends upon dependable law reporting. You should familiarise yourself with the court structure and know how to use a law library. You will find these matters explained earlier in this book, detailed in any text on the English legal system, and nearly every law course now includes extensive instruction on how to use a law library (both hard copy and legal databases).

6.4 The Mechanics of *Stare Decisis*

The system of precedent itself involves a fair degree of detail, but the basic principle to keep in mind is that the precedents created by superior courts bind lower courts and, generally, courts of equal status. We considered the basic court structure in **Chapter 1** (at **1.7.3** and **Figures 1.1** and **1.2**). You are advised to refer to **Figures 1.1** and **1.2** to see the relationship of the courts discussed hereafter. It is also interesting to note that this idea of **binding** precedent was not always present in our law and, in reality, was only clearly established as late as 1898. Prior to that, as Lundmark notes (2003: 161), 'case decisions in their totality were [seen] as a reflection of the law' rather than individual precedents.

One other idea you need to bear in mind is that not all precedents are binding. For if some precedents are binding, there must be others which are not. These we call **persuasive precedents**. **Persuasive** precedents arise out of a number of contexts:

(a) Decisions of *lower courts* such as the County Court and tribunals cannot bind. They may be persuasive.

(b) Decisions of the High Court at first instance (i.e. the trial stage) are persuasive authority for later cases in the High Court (but are binding on lower courts such as county courts).

(c) Decisions of the Judicial Committee of the Privy Council.

(d) Decisions of the Scottish and Northern Irish courts.

(e) Decisions of other courts within the common law world: see, e.g. the use of the Australian case of *Sutherland Shire Council v Heyman* (1985) 60 ALR 1 in *Murphy v Brentwood DC* (1990), detailed later.

6.4.1 The Supreme Court (formerly the House of Lords)

The decisions of the Supreme Court/House of Lords bind all lower courts. For some 100 years the Law Lords also considered themselves bound by their previous decisions (though, oddly, the Judicial Committee of the Privy Council, consisting of the same people but hearing the final appeals of the British Empire, strictly speaking did not). This changed with the *Practice Statement (Judicial Precedent)* [1966] 1 WLR 1234 where the House of Lords said that though the doctrine of being bound had many commendable points: 'too rigid adherence to precedent may lead to injustice in a particular case and also unduly restrict the proper development of the law'. The Supreme Court has not re-issued the Practice Statement but, in *Austin v Southwark London Borough Council* [2010] UKSC 28, [2010] 3 WLR 144, at para 25, Lord Hope DP (with whom all other members of the Court agreed) stated that this 'has as much effect in [the Supreme Court] as it did before [in the House of Lords]'. This view has been incorporated into Practice Direction 4 of the Supreme Court, which details how to make an application to the Supreme Court. Thus the Lords decided that they could depart from their own previous decisions; but would do so only in rare circumstances (there is a technical distinction between *departing from* a decision and *overruling* it, but the terms are used interchangeably even by the House of Lords itself). Remember that the Supreme Court/House of Lords is the highest court in the land (save, in a quite different way, on interpretations of European Union law). Its pronouncements (only about 100 a year) need to be seen to create an air of certainty in business dealings, in criminal law, in land law, and so on. Changing its mind may do 'justice' to a particular case, but at the cost of certainty. The level of reluctance can be seen in Lord Hoffmann's words in *Horton v Sadler* [2006] UKHL 27, [2007] 1 AC 307 (at [40]):

But the fact that the House as now constituted would have decided *Walkley* differently is not a suf-ficient reason for departing from a decision which has stood for nearly 30 years and which the House has followed on two subsequent occasions. If the House in its judicial capacity has erred, it is usually better to leave it to Parliament to change the law prospectively than for the House to undo its mistake with retrospective effect.

Again, the reluctance to disturb legal positions which have been adopted widely by practitioners on the basis of previous House of Lords/Supreme Court decisions can be seen in the words of Lord Hope in *Austin v Mayor and Burgesses of the London Borough of Southwark* [2010] UKSC 28 at [31]: 'There are very good reasons for accepting that the law as declared in *Thompson* [1987] 1 WLR 1425, however unsatisfactory it can now be seen to be, should not be disturbed.' This view is often repeated, as in *Haile v London Borough of Waltham Forest* [2015] UKSC 34 at [73] where Lord Reed JSC said: 'First, we should be very slow before departing from an earlier decision of this court or the House of Lords.'

However, despite this, the Law Lords have changed (and the Supreme Court will change) their minds. As Lord Hoffmann continued in *Horton*: '[T]he situation which has been created by *Walkley* falls squarely within Lord Reid's description in *R v National Insurance Commissioner, ex parte Hudson* [1972] AC 944, 966 of a case in which it would be right for the House to depart from a previous decision.' There, Lord Reid had said: 'It is notorious that where an existing decision is disapproved but cannot be overruled courts tend to distinguish it on inadequate grounds. ... On balance it seems to me that overruling such a decision will promote and not impair the certainty of the law.'

The same was seen in *A v Hoare* [2008] UKHL 6; [2008] 1 AC 844 where their Lordships chose to overturn one of their decisions which was barely fifteen years old (*Stubbings v Webb* [1993] AC 498). The reason for this was that *Stubbings* was found to have placed too much weight on authorities external to the statute in question and so was simply wrongly decided (we cover which authorities can be used in **Chapter 9**). In general terms, it would seem to need a fundamental change in circumstances or evidence that adherence to a previous decision will result in unforeseen serious injustice to generate such departures.

A further example comes where decisions of the Court of Justice of the European Union or the European Court of Human Rights contradict earlier House of Lords' or Supreme Court decisions. The primacy of these courts in their respective jurisdictions means that the Supreme Court must consider departing from its own precedents: see, for instance, *Smith and another v Ministry of Defence (JUSTICE and another intervening); Ellis and another v Same (Same intervening); Allbutt and others v Same (Same intervening)* [2013] UKSC 41, [2013] 3 WLR 69.

So, such occasions are rare, but here are a few more cases which show this in action (see also the now ageing but still excellent analysis of this topic in Harris, 2002).

British Railways Board v Herrington [1972] AC 877; [1972] 1 All ER 749

The Lords faced a number of nineteenth-century and early twentieth-century decisions wherein they had held that there was only a limited duty of care in negligence owed to children who trespassed onto property. This duty was that the occupier should not act recklessly with regard to children whom he knew to be there; and public policy dictated that there was no duty at all to keep out such children or to make the premises safe for them. Since then changes in perceptions of public policy and the development of the law of negligence had altered the approach to the whole topic of responsibility for negligent actions. Thus their Lordships felt able to ignore the earlier decisions and impose on British Railways a duty of care in keeping railway line fences repaired.

Miliangos v *George Frank (Textiles) Ltd* [1976] AC 443; [1975] 3 All ER 801

The House of Lords had previously decided that all awards of damages in an English court had to be made in sterling. In this case, however, because of changes in international trade and the status of sterling they felt the time had come not to adhere to their previous decisions.

R v *Shivpuri* [1987] AC 1; [1986] 2 All ER 334

The case concerned the law as to criminal attempts. A decision of the House of Lords one year earlier (*Anderton* v *Ryan* [1985] AC 560; [1985] 2 All ER 355) had received great criticism. In *R* v *Shivpuri* the House of Lords changed its mind on whether it was possible to attempt to do the impossible. This is a rare example of the House of Lords overturning its own decisions **simply because it felt the earlier decision was wrong**. Usually the Lords look for wider policy considerations (cf. our earlier discussion).

Indeed, in *Food Corp. of India* v *Antclizo Shipping Co.* [1988] 1 WLR 603, [1988] 2 All ER 513, Lord Goff (on behalf of the court) stated that their Lordships would not depart from a previous House of Lords' decision unless:

(a) it felt free to depart from *both* the reasoning and decision of the earlier case; *and*

(b) such a review would affect the resolution of the actual case before them and not be of mere academic interest.

This decision, however, has not had the impact first anticipated and has not been referred to on many occasions. But the *Antclizo* case does allow us to say one further thing, to which we shall return. That is, when a case first appears, stating a principle of law, one can never really be sure of the impact the case will have. At the instant it appears, when there are no other cases which have attempted to apply it, one can only speculate as to its impact.

This is the difficulty that faces practitioners every time a new case appears—what is the legal principle of the case and how far-reaching will it be? We noted with *Whittall* v *Kirby* (in section **6.1.2**), for instance, that in 1947 we did not know for sure whether the reasoning as to what constituted a 'special reason' applied to all professional drivers or just lorry drivers. One thing is clear: there is no single principle by which the Supreme Court/House of Lords sets about overturning its own precedents. In *Murphy* v *Brentwood District Council* [1990] 3 WLR 414; [1990] 2 All ER 908, for instance, their Lordships were again prepared to overturn one of their previous decisions (*Anns* v *Merton London Borough Council* [1978] AC 728; [1977] 2 All ER 492) and there were various reasons given by their Lordships for why they were prepared to do this. Lord Mackay, the (then) Lord Chancellor, felt that the earlier case was taken as a preliminary issue of law so that the facts had not been considered in detail (i.e. the point had not been argued fully so the authority was weak). The case may have worked in theory but did not relate to real facts. On the other hand, Lord Keith looked at *Sutherland Shire Council* v *Heyman* (1985), an Australian case which had rejected *Anns*, and some US cases which had analysed the older cases on which *Anns* itself was based and proved these earlier authorities to be faulty. Thus, said Lord Keith, departure from *Anns* could be justified on the ground that the case was 'unsatisfactory'. Lord Oliver also noted academic criticism of the decision in *Anns*.

There is no obvious pattern to be found and nor can there be in reality. In the end the House of Lords/Supreme Court has had to, and will continue to have to, try to balance questions of certainty, flexibility, legal, commercial, and social developments and the influence of European and international law. These concepts are often in direct conflict. It is hardly surprising, therefore, that no model emerges as to when the Supreme Court will change direction.

Thus, *Arthur J.S. Hall & Co. (a firm)* v *Simons* [2002] 1 AC 615 saw the House of Lords, by majority, depart from their own decision of *Rondel* v *Worsley* [1969] 1 AC 191 and remove the immunity from being sued previously enjoyed by advocates (for alleged negligence in the conduct of civil proceedings). This was done on the basis that the public policy reasons for the immunity being granted no longer stood up to scrutiny in today's society. On the other hand, in *R* v *Kansal (Yash Pal) (No. 2)* [2001] UKHL 62; [2002] 2 AC 69 (again with dissenting voices) the House criticised their own previous decision in *R* v *Lambert (Steven)* [2001] UKHL 37—on the application of the Human Rights Act 1998 to matters arising before that Act came into force—but did not overrule *Lambert*.

The problem is no different when considering criminal law cases as opposed to civil matters: the function of the Supreme Court is to lay down clear and just principles in both areas. There is, however, another problem which lies hidden in all this: it travels under the name of 'prospective overruling'.

6.4.2 Retrospective and Prospective Overruling

As we have already seen, courts make findings on disputed questions of fact, identify and apply the relevant law to the facts agreed by the parties or found by the court, and award appropriate remedies. But when a court is faced with a decision on what the law means (whether on 'pure' case law or the interpretation of statutes) it might depart from or overrule a previous decision. When it does this the court can adopt one of three different approaches:

(i) *Approach 1:* say that the law is [x] and, if that differs from what everyone thought the law was, then hard luck—it was always [x] but we did not know it until now. Here, any decision which changes the law from what it was previously thought to be operates *retrospectively* as well as *prospectively*. It is retrospective in that the parties to the case are caught by the ruling and so are all those who have, say, created leases or contracts on the basis of what was thought to be the law. Despite their best endeavours, it now turns out they were wrong. You can imagine that this can produce very unfortunate results. *Approach 1* is also prospective in that this is the 'new law' so all future cases will be decided this way. In the case of *In Re Spectrum Plus Ltd (In Liquidation)* [2005] UKHL 41; [2005] 3 WLR 58 Lord Nicholls explained the position this way:

[7] The ruling will have a retrospective effect so far as the parties to the particular dispute are concerned ... Further, because of the doctrine of precedent the same would be true of everyone else whose case thereafter came before a court. Their rights and obligations would be decided according to the law as enunciated by [the court] in that case even though the relevant events occurred before that decision was given.

[8] People generally conduct their affairs on the basis of what they understand the law to be. This 'retrospective' effect of a change in the law of this nature can have disruptive and seemingly unfair consequences.

The *retrospective* effect of precedents has been made abundantly clear in the House of Lords case of *Kleinwort Ltd* v *Lincoln City Council* [1999] AC 349; [1998] 4 All ER 513.

In this case, the House of Lords overruled long-established Court of Appeal author-ities and abolished the rule that money paid under a mistake of law could not be recov-ered. Their Lordships were agreed that the idea of retrospective effect means that once the law has been changed it applies not only to the case in hand but to all subsequent cases coming before the courts even though the events in question occurred before the previous authority was overruled. What they were not in agreement over was how this applied to the actual case on whether a mistake of law arose *at the time of the contract* when the law was later changed; on this they were divided 3:2 in favour of saying there was a mistake of law:

(ii) *Approach 2:* say that the law is [x] but, because everyone has organised their affairs until now on the basis that the law was [y], the new view of the law only affects events occurring **after** the decision. So, using our previous examples, only contracts or leases formed *after* the date of the judgment would be affected by the 'new' law, [x]. Contracts and leases, etc. formed *before* the judgment would continue to fall under the 'old' law, [y]. This is the 'purest' form of *prospective* overruling. It was popular in the US courts for a while. Most statutes work on this basis. The law is said to 'change' only from that decision in the case onwards. Prospective overruling (sometimes described as 'non-retroactive overruling') is therefore a judicial tool fashioned to mitigate the adverse consequences of making major changes in the law. This is what Lord Nicholls had to say:

[9] In its simplest form prospective overruling … has the effect that the court ruling has an exclusively prospective effect. The ruling applies only to transactions or happenings occurring after the date of the court decision. All transactions entered into, or events occurring, before that date continue to be governed by the law as it was conceived to be before the court gave its ruling.

(iii) *Approach 3 (mixtures):* it is possible to come up with other variations on this theme. For instance, the decision might be held to be prospective as regards everyone not involved in the case but retrospective in its effect as between the parties to the case in which the ruling is given. Or the ruling may be prospective as regards everyone not involved in the case but retrospective as between the parties in the case in which the ruling was given *and also* as between the parties in any other cases already pending before the courts on the same issue. Lord Nicholls also noted at [11] that:

In 2005 Advocate General Jacobs suggested an even more radical form of prospective overruling. He suggested that the retrospective and prospective effect of a ruling of the European Court of Justice might be subject to a temporal limitation that the ruling should not take effect until a future date, namely, when the State had had a reasonable opportunity to introduce new legislation: *Banca Popolare di Cremona* v *Agenzia Entrate Uffficio Cremona* (Case C–475/03) (unreported) 17 March 2005, paras. 72–88.

What does this mean in practice? Imagine that you have just completed some complicated contractual negotiations, basing your law on a case from 1990. One morning you read that the Supreme Court has 'changed' the law of contract: it is no longer what you (and everyone else) thought it was. Under this new interpretation the deal you have just concluded is worthless. Now, you know that this means if you are negotiating a contract *today* you must take into account the 'new law'. But does the ruling affect the contract you concluded last week? If the Supreme Court ruling is *retrospective* then the answer is 'yes'. If it is only *prospective* then your contract is safe (it will be interpreted under the 'old' law) but any new contracts would have to be drafted with the recent decision in mind. The idea of prospective overruling therefore looks attractive but it hides a real problem: we could have different laws applying to the same types of contract—the only differences being when they were dated.

You may have guessed from the earlier quotes that the House of Lords' decision in *In Re Spectrum Plus* reviewed the law regarding retrospective and prospective overruling—and Lord Nicholl's crystal-clear speech is worth reading for its explanation of case law. In the end, Lord Nicholls showed some enthusiasm for allowing prospective overruling (but only in exceptional circumstances) and Lords Hope and Walker agreed with Lord Nicholls; Lords Steyn, Scott, and Brown accepted that one should never say never about such matters, but were not in favour of using prospective overruling—Lords Steyn and Scott expressly stating that they would not allow prospective overruling in relation to statutory interpretation, only 'pure' case law.

On this basis, retrospective overruling is still the norm—so, in our contract example, you would be advised to try to negotiate new terms.

6.4.3 The Court of Appeal

The importance of this court, both because of its place in the hierarchy and because of its heavy workload, means that you need to be aware of how it deals with precedent. Most of the important cases you will deal with in your studies were reached by this court or its nineteenth-century predecessors such as the Court of Exchequer Chamber.

There are two important questions concerning the Court of Appeal and the notion of *stare decisis*. They are: (i) to what extent is the Court of Appeal bound to follow the decisions of the House of Lords/Supreme Court; and (ii) to what extent is it bound to follow its own decisions?

To what Extent is the Court of Appeal Bound to Follow Decisions of the House of Lords/Supreme Court?

Strictly speaking, the answer is always. But there have been campaigns in the Court of Appeal to overcome the principle. The principal crusader was Lord Denning MR. His retirement signalled a halt to the conflict.

The *per incuriam* campaign

In his major attack Lord Denning advocated that if a House of Lords' decision had been made *per incuriam* it need not be followed. A *per incuriam* decision is one where a court failed to take into account all the relevant and vital statutes or case authorities and that this had a major effect on the decision. The analogy might be made with the writing of a scientific paper. Let us say a famous scientist produces a theory, and that a few years later it is discovered that his research was faulty: he had not read two of the leading papers.

Would you say there are grounds for arguing that the theory should be open to scrutiny or even doubt?

The *per incuriam* rule is a well-established technical rule; but you must be careful here. Saying that a decision was made *per incuriam* does not simply mean the earlier court got things wrong. It only means there was a significant oversight. As we shall see later in this chapter, not only must there have been a failure to take account of relevant authorities, that fault must also have been such a major defect that it seriously affected the reasoning in the case and would have affected the outcome. So, with the example of the scientist, if it is now discovered that if he had researched thoroughly and read the two leading papers this would still have had no effect on his theory, the fault is a technical one of methodology and does not affect the conclusions drawn.

Lord Denning MR tried this form of reasoning in *Broome v Cassell* [1971] 2 QB 354; [1971] 2 All ER 187, convincing the other members of the Court of Appeal that an earlier House of Lords' decision (*Rookes v Barnard* [1964] AC 1129; [1964] 1 All ER 367) was a decision made *per incuriam* because it had failed to consider even earlier House of Lords' authorities.

> However, when *Broome v Cassell* went to the House of Lords, the Law Lords rebuked Lord Denning for adopting such a rule because they believed he had plainly looked for an excuse not to adhere to *stare decisis*. Lord Hailsham, the (then) Lord Chancellor, said: 'In the hierarchical system of courts which exists in this country, it is necessary for each lower tier, including the Court of Appeal, to accept loyally the decisions of the higher tiers': [1972] AC 1027, at 1054.

The 'lapsed rule' campaign

Let us say that the House of Lords reached a decision some years ago based upon a particular rule or set of facts, e.g. that damages in English courts can be given only in sterling because of the stability of the currency and established forms of procedure. Now let us say that the reason for the rule has disappeared: the forms have changed and sterling has lost its stability. Should the precedent created by the House of Lords be followed even though the whole basis of this precedent has disappeared?

This was the question considered by the Court of Appeal, led by Lord Denning, in *Schorsch Meier GmbH v Hennin* [1975] QB 416; [1975] 1 All ER 152. Like so many things in law, a Latin maxim describes the rule Lord Denning wished to use: *cessante ratione legis, cessat ipsa lex* (with the reason for the rule ceasing, the law itself no longer exists). On this occasion the Court of Appeal was split. Lord Denning and Foster J. agreed that a 1961 decision of the House of Lords (*Re United Railways of Havana and Regla Warehouses Ltd* [1961] AC 1007; [1960] 2 All ER 332) had run its course. In fact, the rule that damages should be awarded only in sterling seems to have existed for over 300 years. Lord Justice Lawton, however, did not recognise that the Court of Appeal had such power and found himself bound to follow the House of Lords.

This case did not go on appeal to the House of Lords. However, as we shall see later, the House of Lords soon had opportunity to comment on this issue in a case named *Miliangos v George Frank (Textiles) Ltd* [1977] QB 489; [1976] 3 All ER 599; and once again disapproved Lord Denning's attempts to vary the notion of *stare decisis*. With a touch of irony, though, their Lordships did overrule their own previous decisions on the same grounds proposed by Lord Denning, i.e. the 'lapsed rule' idea.

Thus one is forced to say that Lord Denning's campaigns failed. It is for the Supreme Court to change its mind, not for the Court of Appeal to decide the issue for it. On the positive side, this helps to create certainty. Equally, such strict adherence to *stare decisis* may increase costs (because of the need for further appeals), as well as appearing to invite the veneration of rules whatever the logic or perceived justice. This is an age-old problem in law: balancing the need for certainty with the desire for the law to be flexible.

To what Extent is the Court of Appeal Bound by its Own Previous Decisions?

This is the key area as regards questions of *stare decisis*. The basic rule is that it is bound. This was decided in *Young* v *Bristol Aeroplane Co. Ltd* [1944] KB 718, though three exceptions were given by Lord Greene MR on behalf of the court. This is the case you will see cited time and again on this topic. The exceptions to *stare decisis* given in this case are considered in the following sections.

The first exception: the Court of Appeal can choose between its own conflicting decisions

Such conflict should not arise in an ideal world, but it does, and Lord Greene MR did not explore *which* of the conflicting decisions should be followed. Academic and judicial debate over the years tended to indicate that a later Court of Appeal faced with this problem would probably be free to decide which authority it should follow, with the result that the one not chosen is overruled (for a full debate, see Cross (1991: 144)). If a general rule has emerged, it has been that the latest case would probably be followed in preference to the earlier decision.

The situation can occur for a number of reasons; the most usual ones are:

- because the Court of Appeal does not hear one case at a time (there may be two or three hearings going on at the same time in different courtrooms in the Strand, before different members of the court). Further, each case may be heard on a number of days spread over a period of months. These cases may involve similar legal principles and the various courts may reach different conclusions which later appear contradictory. When the Court of Appeal decided *Young* there were only six Lords Justices. Now there are up to twelve courts sitting at any time with over forty members of the Court (plus others who are entitled to sit), which means there is a greater possibility of conflicting judgments;

- it is also possible that some earlier cases may not have been reported;

- equally, one court may look at the previous decisions and consider them distinguishable for one reason or another while another may think they are not distinguishable and should be followed (which highlights the point we have made before on this being a matter of interpretation rather than pure science).

It was this last reason that gave rise to the problem in *Starmark Enterprises Ltd* v *CPL Distribution Ltd* [2001] EWCA Civ 1252; [2002] 4 All ER 264. The case concerned a rent review clause in a lease of property. Two earlier Court of Appeal decisions (which we shall simply call decisions 1 and 2) had followed on from, considered, and applied an even earlier decision of the House of Lords. Unfortunately, the two Court of Appeal cases appeared to be in conflict. In *Starmark* the landlord argued that decision 2 (the latest) was unsupportable and decision 1 should be preferred; alternatively, that decision 2 was distinguishable on the facts from the present case. It should therefore be ignored and, again, decision 1 should be followed. The tenant argued that there was no conflict between decisions 1 and 2 and decision 2 was entirely consistent with the original House of Lords' approach; equally, the facts in the present case and decision 2 were indistinguishable and so decision 2 plainly had to be followed.

Lord Justice Kay decided that decisions 1 and 2 **did** conflict and that he preferred the views expressed in decision 1 (which was also the minority judgment in decision 2) and was bound to follow the reasoning in decision 1. Lady Justice Arden held that decisions 1 and 2 involved the same principle and could not be reconciled; it was not possible to distinguish them. But Her Ladyship agreed with Kay LJ and held that decision 2 was faulty and should not be followed. The final judge, Peter Gibson LJ, stated at [97]:

> Where the ratio of an earlier decision of this court is directly applicable to the circumstances of a case before this court but that decision has been wrongly distinguished in a later decision of this court, in principle it must be open to this court to apply the ratio of the earlier decision and to decline to follow the later decision. In my judgment the majority of this court in [decision 2] wrongly distinguished [decision 1]. The ratio decidendi in [decision 1] … should in my judgment have been applied in [decision 2] and is decisive of this case.

Thus, in *Starmark*, the latest authority was not followed. Lord Justice Kay's remark (at [3]) perhaps sums up the frustration of encountering conflicting decisions, when he said: 'It is unfortunate that over 15 years after … [cases 1 and 2] … were decided, the legal effect of a common provision in a rent review clause is still unknown. This is the common law at its least impressive.' The Court followed the same approach in *Patel v Secretary of State for the Home Office* [2012] EWCA Civ 741 and decided to go with the decision it preferred when faced with what it termed 'irreconcilable differences' between two of its own previous judgments.

It is also worth noting that Lord Denning led another attack on what he clearly perceived to be the fetter of *stare decisis* in the case of *Davis* v *Johnson* [1979] AC 264; [1978] 1 All ER 1132 (HL); [1978] 2 WLR 182; [1978] 1 All ER 841 (CA). This was not an instance of cleverly adopting rules to excuse departure from precedents. Here, Lord Denning sought to apply the 1966 Practice Statement to the Court of Appeal as well as the House of Lords. The argument was that, if the Court of Appeal could simply depart from previous decisions when justice demanded (as the House of Lords can now do), this would save wasting time and costs of further appeals to the House of Lords. Once again, however, the attempt failed (not least because Lord Denning had conveniently forgotten that procedures already existed whereby a case could be allowed to 'bypass' the Court of Appeal for this very reason: see section **6.6**).

The second exception: if its own previous decision has been overruled expressly or impliedly by the Supreme Court/House of Lords, it need not be followed

Thus if the order of cases ran:

- Court of Appeal's decision (1954);
- House of Lords' decision (disapproving the Court of Appeal's reasoning) (2001);
- your case in the Court of Appeal (today)

then the Court of Appeal in your case **must** follow the House of Lords and not the first Court of Appeal decision.

But this does not answer the question which path should be chosen where the order of cases is:

- House of Lords' decision (1980);
- Court of Appeal's decision (2008)—which, for some reason, is contrary to the earlier House of Lords' decision;
- your case in the Court of Appeal (today).

Now the Court of Appeal is caught between two rules: one saying it is bound to follow its own previous decisions, the other that it is bound to follow the House of Lords.

This situation arose in *Miliangos* v *George Frank (Textiles) Ltd*. Only a year after the Court of Appeal (in the *Schorsch Meier* case) had ignored earlier House of Lords' authority and decided to award judgment in a currency other than sterling, the same issue came before the Court of Appeal again. Should it follow its decision in *Schorsch Meier* or follow the decision of the House of Lords which had been bypassed in *Schorsch Meier*? You may wish to speculate as to which answer, which strand of *stare decisis*, you think should be the most appropriate.

The Court of Appeal in *Miliangos* chose to follow its own previous decision and not the House of Lords. When the case went before the House of Lords their Lordships agreed that judgment could be given in a currency other than sterling, thereby overruling their own previous decision; but took the opportunity to criticise Lord Denning's approach in the *Schorsch Meier* case for ignoring the doctrine of *stare decisis*. However, to add to the confusion, whereas Lord Simon in the House of Lords agreed that the Court of Appeal in *Miliangos* should have followed its own precedent created in *Schorsch Meier*, Lord Cross felt that the Court of Appeal in *Miliangos* should have ignored its own pre-cedent in *Schorsch Meier* because that decision was in conflict with the earlier House of Lords' decision. So, the short answer is: nobody really knows.

As a side point, it is interesting to note that Lord Greene's statement in *Young* v *BAC* (that the Court of Appeal is bound by its own decisions) actually conflicts with some earlier Court of Appeal decisions which stated that the Court of Appeal was *not* bound by its own previous decisions. The sort of panic that this can send a student into should be avoided; Lord Greene's words reflected the history of the Court of Appeal since its creation and are generally taken as gospel today.

The third exception: the Court is not bound by its own decisions found to have been made *per incuriam*

We noted the *per incuriam* rule earlier. For some reason this rule appeals to students and it tends to be used on many occasions (usually incorrectly). It is worth repeating, therefore, that it does not simply mean that the Court made a mistake. The fact that the case being examined had weaknesses in argument, or in the judgment, does not make the decision *per incuriam*. Thus in *Morelle* v *Wakeling* [1955] 2 QB 379; [1955] 1 All ER 708, Lord Evershed MR limited the use of the *per incuriam* rule to cases where:

- there was ignorance of authority which would have been binding on the court; *and*
- that ignorance led to faulty reasoning.

The *and* is very important. To this the Court of Appeal has added that the rule can be applied only where, had the court reviewed these authorities, the court *would* (not just might) have reached a different decision. Thus in *Williams* v *Fawcett* [1986] QB 604; [1985] 1 All ER 787 and *Duke* v *Reliance Systems* [1987] ICR 491; [1987] 2 All ER 858 the Court of Appeal has shown itself ready to use the *per incuriam* rule regarding its own decisions, but with reservations.

In the case of *Rakhit* v *Carty* [1990] 2 WLR 1107; [1990] 2 All ER 202, the Court of Appeal was faced with the situation where a Court of Appeal decision (*decision 1*) was plainly *per incuriam* as it had missed some vital statutory provisions. *Decision 1* had been followed without question in another Court of Appeal case (*decision 2*). Could the present Court of Appeal still declare *decision 1* to be *per incuriam* and therefore *decision 2* of no binding effect? Lord Donaldson MR said (at 208):

> If, therefore, that court [*in decision 2*], having all the relevant authorities before it, had concluded that [*decision 1*] was rightly decided, I would have felt bound to follow it, leaving it to the House of Lords to rectify the error.

As this was not the case, the Court of Appeal in *Rakhit* v *Carty* declared *decision 1* to have been reached *per incuriam*, thereby invalidating both *decision 1* and *decision 2* as precedents.

The Court of Appeal confirmed all that has just been said above in *Peter Limb* v *Union Jack Removals Ltd and Honess* [1998] 1 WLR 1354; [1998] 2 All ER 513 (see section **6.7**).

In *Young* v *BAC* Lord Greene stated that a finding of *per incuriam* would only occur in the rarest of cases. This has been proved true: a search of the law reports reveals a great number of cases where a *per incuriam* argument has been tried but very few cases where it has proved successful. One case, however, interestingly combines two 'exception' heads: *Singh (India)* v *Secretary of State for the Home Department; R (on the application of Khalid)* v *Secretary of State for the Home Department* [2015] EWCA Civ 74. Here Underhill LJ found [at 41] that: 'If the outcome on issue (A) depended on making a choice between *Edgehill* and *Haleemudeen* I would follow *Edgehill*. Although formally the situation may fall within the first exception in *Young* v *Bristol Aeroplane Co Ltd* . . . in that we are confronted by two conflicting decisions of this court, the truth is that *Haleemudeen* was decided *per incuriam* because of the failure to draw the court's attention to the implementation provision; and in those circumstances I think that the better view is that we should treat ourselves as bound by *Edgehill*.'

6.5 Are there any other Exceptions to the Application of *Stare Decisis* to the Court of Appeal that have Emerged since 1944?

The short answer to this is: yes, but not many.

6.5.1 Criminal Matters

The Criminal Division of the Court is traditionally more relaxed on *stare decisis*, especially where an individual's liberty is at stake. This seems a little strange, given that the

House of Lords/Supreme Court has often espoused the view that, in order to promote certainty, it should rarely change its mind on criminal law matters (see, for instance, its reluctance to change its mind in *R v Shivpuri*). But then, in the hands of the Supreme Court rests the final appeal; which is the very issue that caused all the controversy discussed earlier.

The Court of Appeal addressed this issue again in *R v Parole Board, ex parte Wilson* [1992] 2 WLR 707; [1992] 2 All ER 576. The case concerned the right to see documents submitted to a parole board. The Court applied the principle that, where liberty is at stake and injustice might occur, *stare decisis* was not applicable. However, the Court of Appeal found the earlier precedents distinguishable in any case so that the comments on *stare decisis* were not strictly necessary. In *R v Simpson* [2003] EWCA Crim 1499; [2003] 3 All ER 531 the Court of Appeal affirmed this approach. There, Lord Woolf CJ stated that the power to depart from earlier decisions was not akin to the power of the House of Lords under the 1966 Practice Statement. He said:

> We appreciate that there may be a case for not interpreting the law contrary to a previous authority in a manner that would mean that an offender who otherwise would not have committed an offence would be held to have committed an offence. However, we do not understand why that should apply to a situation where a defendant, as here, wishes to rely upon a wrongly decided case to provide a technical defence. While justice for a defendant is extremely important, justice for the public at large is also important. So is the maintenance of confidence in the criminal justice system.

Thus, in dealing with criminal law matters the Court of Appeal generally adheres to *stare decisis* but also recognises that there have to be exceptions, given that a person's liberty is at stake. These exceptions arise, as *Halsbury's Laws* puts it: '(a) where the applicant is in prison and in the full court's opinion wrongly so; (b) where the court thinks that the law was misunderstood or misapplied; and (c) where the full court is carrying out its duty to lay down principles and guidelines in relation to sentencing …'.

This power is not exercised lightly, as illustrated in the conjoined cases of *R v Magro and others* [2010] EWCA Crim 1575; [2011] QB 398. A Court of Appeal decision the year before, *R v Clarke (Joseph)* (2009) *Times*, 1 July; [2009] 4 All ER 298; [2010] 1 WLR 223, had held that the Crown Court had no power to make a confiscation order against a defendant following conviction if he received an absolute or conditional discharge. This is what had happened to Magro and the others so their appeal centred on this issue. The Crown argued that the decision in *Clarke* was made *per incuriam* and was not binding.

The Court of Appeal held that, even if the decision in *Clarke* was wrong and even though the Court here would indeed have reached a different conclusion had it not been for the authority of *Clarke*, it was still binding. The exercise of discretion set out in *Simpson* did not establish that a five-judge constitution was entitled to disregard or deprive the only previous decision of the three-judge court of its authority on a distinct and clearly identified point of law, reached after full argument and close analysis of the relevant legislative provisions. Interestingly, when the case went to the Supreme Court (under the name of *R v Varma* [2012] UKSC 42), it was held that *Clarke* had been wrongly decided—but not on the basis of its being decided *per incuriam*.

Nevertheless, instances can be found of the Court of Appeal not following its previous decisions in criminal law matters. One such case is *R v Ahmad and another* [2012] EWCA Crim 391; [2012] 1 WLR 2335, which received approval in *R v Hunter (Nigel) and Others* [2015] EWCA Crim 631. A key reason for this departure from precedent in

Ahmad was that the earlier authority had been the subject of academic and practitioner criticism. The Court of Appeal agreed with the criticisms (though not the rather patronising tone used by some critics). And Bettinson (2011) has argued that the Court of Appeal, in *R* v *C* [2011] EWCA Crim 1872; [2012] 1 Cr App R (S) 89, may have extended the notion of *per incuriam* (at least in criminal law) to include departing from an earlier decision: 'not on account of a lack of consideration of *legal* authorities, but due to the fact that …' certain material and significant arguments had not been before the Court in its earlier decision. It is respectfully submitted that this 'inadequate advocacy' argument is the gateway to a quagmire.

6.5.2 Blocked Appeals

If, in exceptional cases, the Supreme Court cannot review a decision of the Court of Appeal then the Court of Appeal becomes the final point of appeal and can choose not to follow its own precedent: *Rickards* v *Rickards* [1989] 3 WLR 748; [1989] 3 All ER 193. The *Rickards* case involved very technical arguments concerning extensions of time in which to bring a case. Under those special rules the case could not go to the House of Lords: so such occasions are not common.

6.5.3 Decisions of a Two-judge Court of Appeal

The normal number for a panel in the Court of Appeal is three or five. In *Boys* v *Chaplin* [1968] 2 QB 1; [1968] 1 All ER 283 it was held that if the court consists of only two judges this will not bind a later full Court of Appeal. That is no longer the position. A two-judge Court of Appeal is now accorded the same powers of creating binding precedents as a full court: *Langley* v *North West Water Authority* [1991] 1 WLR 697; [1991] 3 All ER 610.

Historically, two-judge Court of Appeal panels dealt with what are called interim (previously called interlocutory) matters. An interim decision generally concerns pre-trial matters. For instance, if there is a dispute as to the procedure to be followed on, say, getting experts' reports then this will be an interim matter. Injunctions are another example of interim orders. Here, one party is seeking to prevent the other doing something before the full case can be heard. Examples are domestic violence cases, where the injunction may exclude one party from the family home temporarily, defamation cases (used to prevent publication as, once published, it cannot be withdrawn even if it was defamatory), confidentiality, and restraint of trade claims.

However, over the years two-judge panels have taken on what are called more 'substantive' cases. 'Substantive' means cases that deal with the full issues. As two-judge panels have become more common, cases have therefore arisen which were not interim matters but proved to be important substantive decisions (e.g. *National Westminster Bank* v *Morgan* [1983] 3 All ER 85, *Harris* v *Wyre Forest District Council* [1988] QB 835; [1988] 1 All ER 691, and *Interfoto Picture Library* v *Stiletto Visual Programmes Ltd* [1988] 2 WLR 615; [1988] 1 All ER 348). The *Interfoto* case, as we shall see, had the added complication of the judges agreeing on the decision but disagreeing on the reasoning.

It is rare for a two-member Court of Appeal to disagree on the decision. However, this did happen in *Farley* v *Skinner* (Court of Appeal, unreported November 1999). One judge allowed the appeal and the other dismissed it. Therefore there was no actual result. The parties sought a relisting of the appeal before a three-member panel as is permitted under the Supreme Court Act 1981, s. 54(5), which states that: 'Where (a) an appeal has been heard by a court consisting of an even number of judges; and (b) the members of the court are equally divided, the case shall, on the application of any part to the appeal, be reargued before and determined by an uneven number of judges not less than three … ∴'. The case was reheard accordingly (and expensively): see *Farley* v *Skinner* [2000] Lloyd's Rep. PN 516.

By way of contrast, in the Supreme Court, if you start with an odd number of judges, lose one on the way and then find the voting divided equally it seems that the old maxim *semper praesumitur pro negante* still applies. This means that the presumption is always in favour of the negative, which means that the appeal fails. A fascinating example of this arose in *Charter* v *Charter* (1874) LR 7 HL 364, where four of their Lordships were divided evenly as to the outcome and the remaining member died without leaving an opinion.

6.5.4 Decisions Made by Other Courts

The Court of Appeal may find itself in the position where decisions on a topic have been made by the House of Lords/Supreme Court, the Judicial Committee of the Privy Council, the Court of Justice of the European Union, or the European Court of Human Rights. If these decisions conflict with existing precedents of the Court of Appeal (or, indeed, with each other), what is the Court of Appeal to do?

Decisions of the House of Lords/Supreme Court and the Judicial Committee of the Privy Council

We saw earlier that where a Court of Appeal decision is followed by a House of Lords/Supreme Court judgment then any later Court of Appeal must follow the Lords/Supreme Court (see section **6.4.3**). And, as we noted earlier at section **1.7.3**, whereas the Judicial Committee of the Privy Council (JCPC) was once the final court of appeal for the courts of the British Empire, it now acts as the final court of appeal for a diminishing number of countries in the Commonwealth. The JCPC is therefore not part of our system and cannot create **binding** precedent, but, practically speaking, as the judges are made up from the Justices of the Supreme Court sitting in a different guise, any decision of the JCPC is treated as highly persuasive.

So what should the Court of Appeal do in the light of a JCPC decision which conflicts with an earlier Court of Appeal authority? This issue arose in *Doughty* v *Turner Manufacturing Co. Ltd* [1964] 1 QB 518; [1964] 1 All ER 98 and the Court of Appeal chose to follow a JCPC decision (that of *The Wagon Mound (No. 2)* [1967] 1 AC 617; [1966] 2 All ER 709) rather than its own precedent which had been set in *Re Polemis* [1921] 3 KB 560; [1921] All ER Rep 40.

In *HM Attorney General for Jersey* v *Holley* [2005] UKPC 23; [2005] 3 All ER 371 there was an appeal from the Court of Appeal of Jersey to the JCPC concerning the law on provocation as a (partial) defence to murder. Jersey law on this subject was the same as English law. In *R* v *Smith (Morgan James)* [2000] 4 All ER 289; [2001] 1 AC 146 the House of Lords had considered this defence in English law. Unfortunately, the decision in *Smith* was in direct conflict with the decision of the JCPC in *Luc Thiet Thuan* v *R* [1996] 2 All ER 1033; [1997] AC 131. Further, *Smith* was not easy to reconcile with some other House of Lords' decisions. In *Jersey* v *Holley* the JCPC formed a specifically enlarged Board of nine to resolve this conflict and clarify both English and Jersey law. The majority disapproved the House of Lords' decision in *Smith* and approved the previous JCPC decision in *Luc Thiet Thuan*. So, what should be considered the precedent in English law: *Smith* or *Jersey* v *Holley*? The answer came fairly soon in the case of *R* v *Faqir Mohammed* [2005] EWCA Crim 1880: the Court of Appeal followed the JCPC without any hesitation as it represented the latest, considered, and authoritative statement on the law and this view was confirmed by the Court of Appeal in *R* v *James*; *R* v *Karimi* [2006] EWCA Crim 14.

'Normality' was restored, however, in *Sinclair Investments (U.K.) Ltd* v *Versailles Trade Finance Ltd (in administrative receivership)* [2011] 3 WLR 1153, where the Court of Appeal considered *R* v *James*; *R* v *Karimi* and held that the Court of Appeal should not follow a Privy Council decision in preference to a decision of its own, unless, as the practitioners' text *Archbold* put it: 'there is domestic authority that shows that its own decision was *per incuriam* or at least of doubtful reliability … the course taken in *R* v *James*; *R* v *Karimi* was, however, justified as it was a foregone conclusion that, if the case had gone to the House of Lords, they would have followed the Privy Council decision.' So, despite the fact that the JCPC is not part of our system and cannot create **binding** precedent, its decisions are still highly persuasive (sometimes to the point of overcoming the strict rules of *stare decisis*).

Decisions of the Court of Justice of the European Union

As we shall see shortly (at section **6.8.3**) and again in **Chapter 11**, the Court of Justice (CJEU) is the only court that can make authoritative rulings on the meaning and interpretation of European legislation. Thus, all courts in the EU should follow the CJEU's decisions. It should be noted, however, that the CJEU only decides what the law means; it does not decide the cases themselves. In other words, once the CJEU has made an authoritative ruling on the *meaning* of the law the *application* of that interpretation to the facts of the particular case is the province of the national court. So, if there is a decision of the CJEU on the meaning of European law which the Supreme Court then applies, the Court of Appeal should, strictly, follow the Supreme Court on the factual analysis and the CJEU on the pure legal analysis.

The CJEU itself has frequently stated that EU law takes supremacy over the national laws of Member States. The issues usually arise in the context of conflicts between national legislation and EU law, but the principles must apply equally to questions of *stare decisis*. Certainly, where there is an existing precedent and a later decision of the CJEU in that area then, as the Employment Appeal Tribunal commented in *Sharp* v *Caledonia Group Services Ltd* [2005] All ER (D) 09 (Nov), insofar as there is a conflict between the later CJEU decision and earlier UK decisions, the CJEU decision should be followed. To this extent, therefore, *stare decisis* is disapplied.

Decisions of the European Court of Human Rights

What should lower courts (such as the Court of Appeal) do when a House of Lords/Supreme Court decision conflicts with one made by the European Court of Human Rights (ECtHR)? As you will see in **Chapter 10**, the ECtHR is not part of our system. Indeed, it is even less a part of our system than the CJEU. Decisions of the ECtHR must simply be 'taken into account' by our judges, but they do not create precedents (and the decisions are not enforceable in our courts).

The question of which decision to follow was considered in *Price* v *Leeds City Council* [2005] EWCA Civ 289; [2005] 1 WLR 1825. The case concerned the rights of gypsies to occupy land and whether attempts to remove them breached their rights under the European Convention on Human Rights, Art. 8 (Art. 8 concerns 'respect for private and family life'). The problem here was that a House of Lords' decision (*Harrow London Borough Council* v *Qazi* [2003] UKHL 43; [2004] AC 983) was incompatible with a subsequent decision of the ECtHR (*Connors* v *United Kingdom* (2005) 40 EHRR 9). Lord Phillips MR provided the solution on behalf of the Court at [33]:

> It seems to us that in these circumstances, the only permissible course is to follow the decision of the House of Lords but, to give permission, if sought and not successfully opposed, to appeal to the House of Lords, thereby and to that extent taking the decision in *Connors* into account. If in due course the House considers that we have not followed the appropriate course, it will no doubt make this plain.

That statement has been acknowledged as the rule in later cases.

6.5.5 International Obligations

The court must have regard to the principle that Parliament is presumed to legislate in conformity with the United Kingdom's international obligations and, therefore, as an off-shoot of the *per incuriam* rule, a failure to take into account such obligations may mean that the previous case is not binding: *Crown Prosecution Service, Secretary of State for the Home Department* v *Varsha Bhadresh Gohil, Bhadresh Babulal Gohil* [2012] EWCA Civ 1550.

6.5.6 Patents

In *Actavis UK Ltd* v *Merck & Co Inc* [2008] EWCA Civ 444; [2009] 1 All ER 196 the Court of Appeal came to the conclusion that, as regards the very technical and specialist area of patents law, the international and commercial aspects of decisions in this area called for flexibility. They said [at 107] that 'this court is free but not bound to depart from the *ratio decidendi* of its own earlier decision if it is satisfied that the [European Patents Office] Boards of Appeal have formed a settled view of European Patent law which is inconsistent with that earlier decision. Generally this court will follow such a settled view.'

6.6 Does Every Case have to be Heard by the Court of Appeal before it can Proceed to the Supreme Court?

Fortunately the answer is no. If the Court of Appeal is bound by the Supreme Court and itself then a system which demanded it to hear every case anyway would be ludicrous. Thus a civil case may be allowed to go on appeal from the High Court to the Supreme Court, bypassing the Court of Appeal. This is known as the 'leap-frogging' procedure. However, if the case began life in the county court then an appeal from that court lies to the Court of Appeal, not the High Court; thus the leap-frogging procedure would be irrelevant.

It is only fair to say that however much writers and judges try to explain the system on a rational basis there will always be some uncertainty and some cases that simply break the rules. For one thing we have yet to consider in depth how one case can be distinguished from another so that the precedent in question (and therefore the application of *stare decisis*) is sidestepped. For another, judges occasionally surprise everyone with an admission that they were wrong in an earlier case (see Lord Denning in *Dixon* v *BBC* [1979] QB 546; [1979] 2 All ER 112, discussing his earlier judgment on the same issue in *BBC* v *Ioannou* [1975] ICR 267; [1975] 2 All ER 999 or even Lord Greene MR in *Young* v *BAC*, at 730: 'I should perhaps add, speaking for myself individually, with regard to the observations in *Unsworth's case* mentioned in this judgment, that I have carefully considered my own observations there mentioned in *Perkins' case* and I have come to the conclusion that the criticism of them in *Unsworth's case* is justified, and that what I said was wrong').

This is reassuring when considered in the context of human frailty, but likely to set a practising lawyer's teeth on edge and is little consolation to the party in the overruled case who originally lost (and probably paid costs which cannot be recovered). Even more surprising, perhaps, was Lord Denning's admission in one case that his own reasoning in an earlier case (which he now wished to avoid) was not legally correct, but that he had reached that earlier decision to do justice—'It was not really [a case which fell within the definition of dismissal] ... but we had to stretch it a bit', he commented. The comment occurred in *Western Excavating* v *Sharp* [1978] ICR 221, 227; [1978] 1 All ER 713, 718 in relation to *Marriott* v *Oxford and District Co-operative Society Ltd (No. 2)* [1970] 1 QB 186; [1969] 3 All ER 1126.

It is also worth commenting at this stage (as we noted at section **6.4.2** on retrospective and prospective overruling), that when a decision of a higher court alters the law by overruling a line of established precedents, that decision does not merely affect the law from that moment on. The court setting the new precedent is stating the law as it *always has been*. Thus, commercial contracts concluded on the old law are in danger of being open to a different interpretation from that intended when they were formed; so too, property deals, licences, employment contracts, and so on. Therefore, one part of the work of lawyers is to review these earlier matters in the light of the new decision.

A question often posed by students is whether the aggrieved party in the case which has been overruled can now revive the case with the cry, 'There you are, I was right all along'. The answer is no. Parties to a case have to lodge an appeal within time limits. If these have expired it is unfortunately too late to do anything about it.

6.7 Precedent in the Higher Courts: Summary

In discussing the *per incuriam* rule earlier we noted the case of *Peter Limb*. That case also made some general comments on precedent and the Court of Appeal. Lord Justice Brooke stated that there were five main principles to be derived from the authorities:

(a) Where the court has considered a statute or a rule of law which has the force of a statute, the court's decision stands on the same footing as any other decision on a point of law (the reason for saying this is that there used to be a vague rule that precedents could not relate to decisions on statutory interpretation points).

(b) A decision of a two-judge Court of Appeal on a substantive appeal (as opposed to an application for leave) has the same authority as a decision of a three-judge or a five-judge Court of Appeal.

(c) The doctrine of *per incuriam* applies only where another division of the Court has reached a decision in ignorance or forgetfulness of a decision binding upon it or of an inconsistent statutory provision, and in either case it must be shown that if the court had had this material in mind it must have reached a contrary decision. In *Cave* v *Robinson Jarvis & Rolf* [2001] EWCA Civ 245; [2002] 1 WLR 581 the Court of Appeal expressed the view that the decision in question had to be 'manifestly wrong' before it would be declared *per incuriam*.

(d) The doctrine does not extend to a case where, if different arguments had been placed before the court or if different material had been placed before it, it *might* have reached a different conclusion.

(e) Any departure from a previous decision of the court is in principle undesirable. Even if the previous decision is manifestly wrong it will be necessary to take account of whether the decision purports to be one of general application and whether there is any other way of remedying the error, for example by encouraging an appeal to the Supreme Court.

Lastly, it is worth noting a trend over recent years for the Court of Appeal to bunch together issues arising in a number of cases, set aside a specialist panel to look at all the cases, hear a selection, and issue general guidelines on the area. This has mainly happened in connexion with procedural matters (*Peter Limb* was such a case). The most famous occurrence was in *Bannister* v *SGB plc* [1998] 1 WLR 1123; [1997] 4 All ER 129 (which was also the first Court of Appeal decision to be published on the Internet immediately after the decision was given, so that all 200-plus affected parties could know the outcome as soon as possible). And, interestingly, in *Greig Middleton & Co. Ltd* v *Denderowicz* [1998] 1 WLR 1164; [1997] 4 All ER 181 (which was on the same issue as *Bannister*) the Court of Appeal took the opportunity to add as annexes to the *Greig* judgment some reserved judgments in other related cases and to produce a revised judgment of *Bannister*, directing that it would be the revised version which should appear in the law reports.

6.8 Other Courts

6.8.1 Trial Courts

All courts which are lower in status than the Court of Appeal (such as the High Court, Crown Court, magistrates' court, county court, and the various tribunals) are bound by *stare decisis* in the normal way. It should be noted, however, that the important tribunals also have their own appellate tribunals (e.g. the Employment Appeal Tribunal for employment tribunals) which often incorporate their own variations on the rules of right to appeal and the binding nature of precedent within that system (e.g. neither the Employment Appeal Tribunal nor the Competition Appeal Tribunal bind themselves). Courts like the Crown Court are trial courts, dealing for the most part with fact and evidence rather than questions of high legal analysis. They do not, therefore, create precedent. There is, however, some attempt to follow the reasoning employed in courts of the same level, e.g. as between divisions of the High Court when these courts are sitting as 'courts of first instance', i.e. trial courts. In *Colchester Estates (Cardiff)* v *Carlton Industries plc* [1984] 3 WLR 693; [1984] 2 All ER 601 it was stated that the latest decision should be preferred provided it was reached after full consideration of the earlier decisions. An example of this in operation arose from a decision of Butler-Sloss J. (as she then was) in *Re Cherrington* [1984] 1 WLR 772; [1984] 2 All ER 285 which was not followed in a case on exactly the same point (*Re Sinclair* [1984] 3 All ER 362) because there had not been a full discussion of all the issues in *Re Cherrington*. However, one High Court decision cannot bind a later court: *R (Amin)* v *Secretary of State for the Home Department* [2009] EWHC 1085 (Admin).

6.8.2 Divisional Courts

For mainly historical reasons the High Court has a supervisory and limited appellate jurisdiction over the trial courts. Each division of the High Court—Queen's Bench, Family, and Chancery—has what is termed a 'Divisional Court'. Thus:

(a) The Divisional Court of the Chancery Division can hear appeals from a county court in bankruptcy cases.

(b) The Family Division may hear appeals on guardianship matters from either the magistrates' courts or county courts.

(c) The most common appellate function relates to the Queen's Bench Division. Say a party to a criminal case in a magistrates' court wishes to appeal on a question of law from the magistrates' decision. This can be done by asking the magistrates to **state their case**, i.e. to set out their legal reasoning. Strangely, for historical reasons, the issue goes before the Divisional Court of the Queen's Bench Division (which is a civil and not criminal court). This is known as an 'appeal by way of case stated'. A full rehearing (e.g. an appeal against the conviction relating to fact rather than law) of the case would go to the Crown Court. An appeal by way of case stated can also lie in limited circumstances, from the Crown Court to the High Court.

These Divisional Courts are bound by *stare decisis* in the usual way as regards decisions of higher courts. When it comes to Divisional Courts binding themselves, the rule is similar to that used in the Court of Appeal: on civil matters they are bound but not necessarily so on criminal issues: *R* v *Governor of Brockhill Prison* [1997] 1 All ER 439, 451. In all cases, however, there is a reluctance to depart from earlier decisions, as noted by Sir Brian Leveson P in *R (on the application of JC and another)* v *Central Criminal Court* [2014] EWHC 1041 (Admin) where it was said, citing earlier judgments: 'it would only be in rare cases that a divisional court will think it fit to depart from a decision of another divisional court exercising this jurisdiction'.

6.8.3 The Court of Justice of the European Union

Though **Chapter 11** deals extensively with the European influence and 'European legal method', specific reference to European Union institutions and legal method is needed here to explain the context in which our law now operates. As we said in **Chapter 1**, leaving the 'European dimension' until later in the book should not be seen as relegating the topic to some form of afterthought.

Throughout this book you will see that both the 'European' way of dealing with cases (the procedure) and the technique of analysing cases (the legal method) are quite different from our approach. This is because the system used by the Court of Justice was created by countries which rely on the civil (or Roman) law system, such as France and Germany. For various reasons our common law system used in England and Wales and Ireland (but not Scotland) developed separately from the civil law system used on the Continent.

It should be noted that another Member State—Cyprus—is a quasi-common law jurisdiction. It was under British administration from 1878 until 1960 and so heavily influenced by the common law. The common law's systems, traditions, and doctrines were retained expressly by the Constitution after independence, but the law itself is a mixture of common law and civil law traditions (with some religious law in disputes regarding families). Similarly, another EU Member State, Malta, gained independence from Britain in 1964, choosing a codified system but drawing on common law precedents.

The final court to note then (one of increasing importance) is the Court of Justice of the European Union (CJEU), formerly called the European Court of Justice (ECJ).

We have listed a little later a few general points on the Court of Justice which you should bear in mind when reading about the legal method used in English law. For a more detailed description of EU Law we recommend reference be made to Steiner and Woods (2014).

Most of the law you will deal with in your studies will be 'pure' English law; but the direct or indirect effects of European law continue to grow: a matter vividly anticipated in Lord Denning MR's famous statement in *HP Bulmer Ltd v Bollinger SA* [1974] Ch 401, 418; [1974] 2 All ER 1226, that 'when we come to matters with a European element, the Treaty is like an incoming tide … It cannot be held back.' Remember here, however, that we are dealing with the Court of Justice, not the way individual countries' legal systems work.

What is the jurisdiction of the CJEU?

The CJEU exists to ensure that in the interpretation and application of Treaty provisions EU law is observed. It is therefore the supreme authority on the interpretation and validity of EU law. However, unless the law in question was generated by the EU or is an area affected by EU law (and there are various ways this can occur), the CJEU has no jurisdiction. Many criminal law matters, for instance, are questions of domestic law and have nothing to do with the EU, though this is changing constantly with matters such as the European Arrest Warrant, financial crime, and money laundering. Indeed, EU criminal law is probably the fastest growing area of EU law at the moment.

As well as dealing with general agricultural matters, administrative law, company law, etc. the effects of EU law appear in everyday life (such as employment rights and consumer law), even when most people have no idea of their EU origins. Thus an increasing number of matters fall within the jurisdiction of the CJEU.

How does a case come before the CJEU?

Actions may be brought against individuals, Member States, or the institutions of the EU. We will concentrate in this book on the most common way in which a case will come before the Court of Justice—a reference to the Court for a *preliminary ruling* under Art. 267 of the Treaty on the Functioning of the European Union (TFEU).

Under Art. 267 TFEU, any country's domestic courts or tribunals can ask the Court of Justice for a ruling on the meaning of EU law; but it is that domestic court or tribunal which implements the decision by applying that interpretation to the facts.

It is for the domestic court to decide whether it wishes to refer a matter to the CJEU and there are various rules relating to this which we shall explore later. The domestic court is only asking for an authoritative interpretation of that particular part of EU law. It does this by posing questions in the abstract; it does not ask for the solution to the particular case before it. **Chapter 11** deals with the Court in depth (see particularly section **11.1.3**).

Does the CJEU use a system of judicial precedent?

A major distinction between how European lawyers (and courts) reason and the reasoning of common law lawyers is the use of *stare decisis*. European lawyers are, traditionally, merely persuaded by precedent. The same is true of the CJEU.

Obviously, as Stein has said, 'Every legal system has case law in the sense that the scope of the rules is illustrated by their application to a set of facts' (1984: 85), but this is not the same thing as holding to a doctrine of binding precedent. Further, any legal system seeks to avoid inconsistencies, but that does not mean that system inevitably has to adopt a strict doctrine of *stare decisis*. For whereas the common law relies on declaring law only when the occasion requires it (i.e. through litigants bringing cases), the civil law system relies heavily on Codes: written, logical, reasoned, and systematic statements of principles of law. As Lord MacMillan observed:

> From these principles the whole law [can] be deduced, and with the aid of these principles the law [can] be methodised and arranged. It is the conception of order, logic and reason in the regulation by law of human affairs. (1937: 79)

Cases, in simple terms, become examples of applications of the Code; hardly the stuff of which *stare decisis* is made.

The Codes vary in form and technicality of language. The language employed in the French Code is aimed more at the layman than is the case with the German Code, for instance. Now, the civil law lawyer bases his argument on the explicit or implicit statements in the written law (the Codes and academic writing), not overtly on the opinions given in earlier cases. Developing this point, reliance on the Codes and the principles stated therein drives the civil lawyer away from an obsessive interest in the facts of earlier cases. It is the issue that matters. The common law lawyer, on the other hand (as we shall explore in the next chapter), holds tightly to the concept of 'material facts' and the importance of individual cases.

Indeed, the predominance of issue over fact has to be the pattern of thought employed by the CJEU because the function of the Court is to *interpret* EU law. As the Court is required only to answer abstract questions from the national court and does not make decisions in a particular case, so the facts of a case (which are so important to the English law lawyer in distinguishing one case from another) take on less significance. This does not mean the facts are ignored, because it is almost impossible to answer a legal question without some reference to the context in which it has arisen. But it does mean that our system of *stare decisis* cannot apply to the CJEU. Further, the Court is the final court on these questions and the only thing that can alter such a decision (other than the Court changing its mind at a later date) is an alteration made to the Treaties themselves. As annual minor alterations to the Treaties are an impossibility—major or complete revisions for political reasons are the only likely source of alterations—the Court has to favour flexibility over certainty.

6.9 Impact of Human Rights Legislation

Under the Human Rights Act 1998 all common law rules and precedents that are incompatible with Convention rights are potentially open to challenge, especially if those precedents relate to the interpretation of statutory provisions. Further, the Act expressly requires the British courts to *take into account*, among other things, the judgments, decisions, and advisory opinions of the ECtHR, thereby adding another court to the list of things to be aware of in giving legal advice (though note the comments made at section **6.5.4** on the case of *Price* v *Leeds City Council* and the question of the precedent value of such decisions).

 CONCLUSION

Both the common law and the civil law traditions utilise the concept of precedent. No case has a meaning by itself; each case stands in a relationship to other cases. Like tracing one's ancestors, therefore, it is at least theoretically possible to go backwards in time, step by step, to see how a complicated principle emerged from perhaps a single case. It is not uncommon to find gross inconsistencies or jumps in logic, but for the most part the changes will be evolutionary rather than revolutionary. It is rare to make this journey in a practical or even academic setting, but it does beg the question: what came before the original case?

Sometimes the answer is that the seminal case derived its principle from a mixture of other cases on related (often barely related) principles: see, for instance *Rylands* v *Fletcher* (1868) LR 3 HL 330. On other occasions the principle may be derived from ancient Roman, Greek, or biblical laws. Occasionally the source may lie in a perception of fundamental rights and wrongs, such as laws prohibiting murder (crimes which are sometimes referred to as being *mala in se*, meaning 'bad in themselves' as opposed to specifically created laws on trading or parking, for instance, known as laws which are *mala prohibita* (bad because they are prohibited)). Often the answer lies in works written by eminent scholars centuries ago—their views on the law being accepted by judges in later cases and then set as legal doctrine by the mechanisms of judicial precedent. The fact that these initial cases or scholarly writings were illogical, have exceeded their 'best before' date, or have been misinterpreted does not mean that they can be easily upset.

Much of this reification of (sometimes) archaic principles is due to the fact that there is a world of difference between merely recognising the source and value of precedent and the concept of *stare decisis*. Courts in nearly all major legal systems have a system of precedent (even in Islamic law where the decisions are those of the judges acting as individuals under spiritual guidance). A notable historical exception was the Socialist bloc countries. Since the demise of the communist bloc most of the affected countries have adopted some form of civil law system.

However, the common law system (especially as practised in Britain) goes beyond the mere seeking of guidance by reference to a level of being constrained by deference: a previous decision may not only be helpful, it may be binding.

The great value of the doctrine of *stare decisis* is that it provides certainty. On the other hand, there are dangers: first, that in order to avoid the conclusions of *stare decisis* courts are sometimes forced to find hair-splitting distinctions between cases; secondly, the doctrine limits flexibility and can make unassailable some principles which should have been abandoned long ago. Equally, as Max Radin observed in 'The Trail of the Calf', noted earlier, '[T]he question has not really been whether precedent should be followed, but where and under what circumstances it was desirable to disregard it … .'. Thus, the research skills of a lawyer rest with finding the relevant authorities, the advocacy skills often rest with persuading a court not to follow a precedent.

A rare example of a long-established legal concept being overturned can be found in *R v R* [1991] 3 WLR 767; [1991] 4 All ER 481. In *R v R*, public policy, together with historical and social considerations, came under review. This case concerned 'marital rape' and posed the question whether a husband could be criminally liable for raping his wife if he had sexual intercourse with her without her consent. The idea that a man would not be guilty in these circumstances could be traced back to Sir Matthew Hale in his *History of the Pleas of the Crown* written in 1736. Texts and cases since that time had taken this proposition as an accurate expression of the law (which it probably was in 1736). In *R v R*, however, the House of Lords took the opportunity to restate the law concerning marital rape and declared that the husband could be guilty of rape in these circumstances. As Lord Keith said: 'The common law is … capable of evolving in the light of changing social, economic and cultural developments.'

You may, however, ask yourself one final simple question: why should we stand out from the rest of the legal world with our fixation that once a superior court has decided a matter an inferior court *must* follow it?

 ## CHAPTER REFERENCES

*ARCHBOLD, *Criminal Pleading Evidence & Practice*, 2013 edn.

BETTINSON, V. (2011), 'Has the Court of Appeal extended the per incuriam exception?', *Journal of Criminal Law*, 448.

BROWN, L.N. and KENNEDY, T. (2000), *Brown and Jacobs: The Court of Justice of the European Communities* (5th edn, London: Sweet & Maxwell).

*BUXTON, R. (2009) 'How the Common Law Gets Made: *Hedley Byrne* and other Cautionary Tales', 125 *Law Quarterly Review*, 60.

*COOPER, T.M. (1950), 'The Common and the Civil Law: A Scots View' 63 Harv LR, 468 at 471.

*CROSS, R. (1991), *Precedent in English Law* (4th edn, Oxford: Clarendon Press).

GILLESPIE, A.A. (2010), 'Precedent and the limits of Simpson' *Journal of Criminal Law*, 492.

HARRIS, B.V. (2002), 'Final Appellate Courts Overruling their Own "Wrong" Precedents: The Ongoing Search for a Principle', 118 *Law Quarterly Review*, 408.

HARRIS, J.W. (1990), 'Towards Principles of Overruling—When Should a Final Court of Appeal Second Guess?', *Oxford Journal of Legal Studies*, 135.

LUNDMARK, T. (2003), '"Soft" Stare Decisis: The Common Law Doctrine Retooled for Europe', in R. Schulze and U. Seif (eds), *Richterrect und Rechtsfortbildung in der Europäischen Rechtsgemeinschaft*, 27, at 161–8.

MACCORMICK, N. (1987), 'Why Cases have *Rationes* and What These Are', in L. Goldstein (ed.), *Precedent in Law* (Oxford: Clarendon Press).

MACMILLAN, Lord (1937), *Law and Other Things* (Cambridge: Cambridge University Press).

PATTENDEN, R. (1984), 'The Power of the Criminal Division of the Court of Appeal to Depart from its Own Precedents', *Criminal Law Review*, 592.

*RADIN, M. (1946), 'The Trail of the Calf', 32 *Cornell Law Quarterly*, 137.

RODGER, A. (Lord) (2005), 'A Time for Everything under the Law: Some Reflections on Retrospectivity', *121 Law Quarterly Review*, 57.

SCANLON, G. (2004), '*Stare Decisis* and the Court of Appeal: Judicial Confusion and Judicial Reform, 23 (JUL), 212.

STEIN, P. (1984), *Legal Institutions: The Development of Dispute Settlement* (London: Butterworths).

STEINER, J. (1995), *Enforcing EC Law* (London: Blackstone Press).

*STEINER, J. and WOODS, L. (2014) in L. Woods and P. Watson, *Steiner and Woods EU Law* (12th edn, Oxford: Oxford University Press). Editions 1–10 of this work were entitled *Textbook on EC Law*.

7

How Precedent Operates: *Ratio Decidendi* and *Obiter Dictum*

7.1 Introduction

The concept of *stare decisis* as outlined in the previous chapter provides us with only the ground rules of precedent. It tells us that one court must follow the decision of a superior court when dealing with similar cases. It describes the environment in which our system of precedent operates. What it cannot tell us is **when** two cases are sufficiently similar that the doctrine should be applied.

If the facts of cases were identical we would have no problem. But the facts change from case to case—sometimes in an obviously major way; other times in an apparently insignificant way. Clearly we are not looking only for **identical cases**. What we must be trying to prove is that two (or more) cases are sufficiently similar to illustrate the same *principle* so that the doctrine of precedent can be applied. A comparison of facts will obviously help us achieve this. But we must also, and more importantly, try to see if the *reasoning* in the earlier case can be applied to the new set of facts in our case. It is worth remembering that lawyers cite cases in order to give authority to their argument. The question raised by the practitioner or academic is therefore: what is the principle of law for which that case is authority, and how does it relate to the case in hand? Or, to put it the other way: is there a case which is authority for the point I wish to make? This is the way that a busy practitioner is more likely to pose the question.

In the previous chapter we presented an exercise on fact comparison:

- In *case (1)* a man driving a Ford Mondeo runs over an old lady who was lawfully using a zebra crossing. The man is held to be liable in negligence.

- In *case (2)* a woman driving a BMW runs over an old man who was crossing the road. Should she be found liable too? Does the principle in *case (1)* apply to *case (2)*?

We asked whether you might examine the facts more closely, or ask more questions, before deciding on the answer. Students new to legal studies (and others who should know better) tend to say that the woman in *case 2* is liable. If asked why this is so, the poor student tends to say: 'It's obvious'. Such students may have a shorter or less successful career in law than they anticipated. Slightly better students say: 'The woman is liable because *case (2)* is the same as *case (1)*'—but with no explanation. Still better students say: 'The woman may not be liable because the old lady in *case (1)* was on a zebra crossing, but that is not so in *case (2)* so the answer may be different.' The best student will ask himself/herself: '**Why** was the man liable in *case (1)*? Before I know that I cannot really say whether *case (2)* will follow *case (1)*.' For all we know there may be a law against driving Ford Mondeos.

You might think this is a trite statement of the obvious. Don't! These examples of analysis (on a variety of facts) have all surfaced in seminars and tutorials, in different universities and colleges, in different countries, spoken by LLB undergraduates, undergraduates in other degrees who study law, and even by postgraduates. Karl Llewellyn offered these words of advice (or admonition) in 1930 to American Law students:

> Now the first thing you are to do with [a case] is to read it. Does this sound commonplace? Does this amuse you? There is no reason why it should amuse you. You have already read past seventeen [legal] expressions of whose meaning you have no conception … The next thing is to get clear the actual decision, the judgment rendered … You can now turn to what you want peculiarly to know … what has the case decided, and what can you derive from it as to what will be decided later? (1960: 41).

Any law lecturer will echo these words, but it is easy to forget as an academic or practitioner just how daunting reading cases for the first time can be. From the student perspective things look a little different, but the point we are making is still the same. To show you that you are not alone in the minefield of case law, consider the words in the highlighted box next, written by Scott Turow (1988: 28)—better known for his legal thrillers—detailing his experiences as a law postgraduate student at Harvard. Anyone who has ever studied law will have sympathy with these words.

> OK. It was nine o'clock when I started reading. The case is four pages long and at 10:35 I finally finished. It was something like stirring concrete with my eyelashes. I had no idea what the words meant. I must have opened *Black's Law Dictionary* twenty-five times and I still can't understand many of the definitions.

The aim of this chapter, therefore, is to emphasise that legal analysis is not just a question of comparing facts or using a set of balancing scales to see if the facts weigh about the same. The game is more complicated, more stimulating, and much more enjoyable than that.

7.2 Development of Case Law

Take a look at the following exercise. It sets out the facts of two well-known cases together with the result in each case. Ask yourself *why* the second case should be decided in the same way as the first.

EXERCISE 10 Dead snails and exploding underpants

 Case 1: *Donoghue* v *Stevenson* [1932] AC 562

Bare facts: Mrs May Donoghue and a friend went into a cafe in Paisley. The friend ordered ice cream and ginger beer for both of them. Francis Minchella, the shopkeeper, poured out some of the ginger beer over the ice cream. Mrs Donoghue

continued

EXERCISE 10 *continued*

consumed some of the mixture. Her friend poured out the remainder of the ginger beer for Mrs Donoghue and a decomposed snail fell out of the bottle. The bottle was of dark opaque glass so that the contents could not have been detected.

What was the claim? The claim was against the manufacturer of the ginger beer (Stevenson) for negligently causing Mrs Donoghue to suffer gastro-enteritis and nervous shock; the negligence arising from the manufacture of the product. So we say that her **cause of action** (as explained at section **6.1.1**) was negligence and she was seeking **damages** (compensation) for her loss. As you will see in your contract law course, Mrs Donoghue could not claim against Mr Minchella because she had no contract with him (her friend had bought the ginger beer); and she had no claim in negligence against him either as there was no way he could have known the snail was in the bottle (made of opaque glass).

What was the decision? Mrs Donoghue succeeded in her claim; the House of Lords holding Stevenson liable by a majority of 3:2 (note how close such an important decision was). Lord Atkin, in the majority, said that a manufacturer of products will be liable for want of reasonable care if he sells those products in a form which shows they are meant to reach the ultimate consumer in the same form as when they were manufactured (with no reasonable possibility of intermediate examination) and if he knows that the absence of reasonable care will cause injury.

 Case 2: *Grant* v *Australian Knitting Mills* **[1936] AC 85 (Privy Council)**

Bare facts: Grant purchased two pairs of underpants from a retailer in Australia. He contracted severe dermatitis (mainly around the ankles—they were 'long johns') owing to an excess of sulphites in the garments which should have been removed by the manufacturing process. He was ill for a year.

What was the claim? He sued the retailer for breach of contract; and brought a negligence action against the Australian Knitting Mills. This demonstrates that more than one claim can arise from one set of events. However, Grant would not be able to get damages twice: if Grant was successful then one claim would be offset against the other.

What was the decision? Grant won the breach of contract action against the retailer and the claim for negligence against the manufacturer was also successful, following the principles laid down in *Donoghue* v *Stevenson*.

Q QUESTIONS

(a) Why do you think Grant was successful in his claim for negligence? Why should *Donoghue* v *Stevenson* apply to his case?

(b) What arguments would you have used if you had been representing the Australian Knitting Mills?

continued

EXERCISE 10 *continued*

 A ANSWERS

(a) 'Exploding underpants' and dead snails are not the same thing. If you have thought carefully about the cases you will have experienced some problems in assessing why *Donoghue* v *Stevenson* was applied in *Grant* v *Australian Knitting Mills*. But remember, both sides in *Grant* thought they had convincing reasons why they should win. Neither side could simply say 'dead snails equal (or do not equal) underpants'. The Privy Council assessed the principle of *Donoghue* v *Stevenson* by quoting Lord Atkin:

> A manufacturer of products, which he sells in such a form as to show that he intends them to reach the ultimate consumer in the form in which they left him with no reasonable possibility of intermediate examination, and with the knowledge that the absence of reasonable care in the preparation or putting up of the products will result in an injury to the consumer's life or property, owes a duty to the consumer to take that reasonable care.

The Privy Council stated that their understanding of *Donoghue* v *Stevenson* was that the principle in that case could be applied only where the defect is hidden and unknown to the consumer; in *Grant* the chemical in the underpants represented a latent (and therefore hidden) defect equivalent to the snail in the opaque bottle.

(b) The lawyers acting for the Australian Knitting Mills raised a number of arguments. Among these were: (i) *Donoghue* v *Stevenson* only applied, at its widest, to cases of food and drink—that when Lord Atkin referred to 'products' he could only refer to the product in the case; (ii) the decision was not unanimous, especially as regards the interpretation of earlier cases; (iii) there had been no possibility of anyone tampering with the bottle, but the underpants were loosely packed (it was not alleged there had been any tampering but the fact that this could have occurred was argued as being a distinctive difference between the cases); and (iv) that Grant should have washed the underpants before wearing them (which would have removed the danger).

All these arguments failed. The principle behind a case concerning a dead snail in an opaque ginger-beer bottle had been applied to a very different set of facts.

So, however we try to compare the facts of two or more cases we cannot answer the question whether the woman in our example of *case (2)* should be liable for her negligent driving without first understanding *why* the man was liable in *case (1)*. What were the issues on which the first case turned? Was it important that the old lady was using a pedestrian crossing? Was it important that she was an old lady? The fact that you discover two cases which are similar on their facts is not enough. Two cases may look similar but produce different results because of a different perception of the apparently similar facts or because of a vital distinction in the reasoning employed by the judges. In other words, cases may be *distinguished* as well as *applied* on the material facts or the reasoning employed.

And if we are asking *why* the court decided one way we must equally be aware that cases do not exist in isolation—there is a whole history behind the issues involved in a case. All these previous cases will have affected the language used by the judges and the decisions they reached. The way that a word was legally defined in, say, 1850 may have an enormous impact on the reasoning of a judge in 2014.

Thus when we talk of a judge being bound by a precedent we mean something more than matching the facts of cases—we say that a judge is bound to follow the *ratio decidendi* (the reason for deciding—usually referred to as the *ratio*) of the earlier higher authority. The judge only has to follow the *ratio*. It is not only the facts of the earlier case which are important, but also how the judge expressed the law in relation to those facts—how the judge justified the decision in law. For as long as you study law the *ratio* of any case will be vital to your investigations.

7.3 Trying to Define *Ratio Decidendi*

Difficulties still lie ahead. Various judges and academics have tried to define what we mean by *ratio decidendi*. It is a surprisingly difficult problem. One complication is that a judgment may last for two, ten, or fifty pages. Somewhere in there is an account of the facts as found, a discussion of legal principles, a comparison with earlier cases, and a decision on the facts as to who won. A judge may apparently formulate a *ratio* only to continue with his judgment and formulate the *ratio* again; this time with slightly different words, with slightly different emphasis. For instance, a judge might say: 'A person cannot be excused from drinking and driving merely because they are called upon by friends to drive them when otherwise they would have been stranded', only later to say, 'As I have indicated, being surprised by a turn of events is no excuse for drinking and driving, unless arising from a genuine emergency.' The second statement confirms the first but then goes wider by adding the proviso about 'genuine emergency': so which is the 'real' *ratio*? Well, as we shall see, one limiting factor is what actually happened in the case (was there an arguable emergency in the case or was the judge just speculating about what might be?).

Another example might be where the judge switches words around (which are not true synonyms). For instance, a judge might refer to a duty as arising unless it would be 'unreasonable' to impose it, but later say the duty arises unless it is 'impracticable' to impose it. These are not necessarily the same thing. This can prove galling. It happens. And nowhere will you find a sentence saying: 'Here comes the *ratio*'.

Yet another complication is that a judge in a later case may perceive the principle (the *ratio*) that is to be derived from the earlier case as something different from that which the original judge intended. If this strikes you as particularly odd, just consider the following everyday example: you always go to the local mall rather than the town centre because you think the shopping is better there. Your friend thinks you go there because the parking is easier. Maybe both are true, but there is a difference in perception and interpretation over a fairly simple decision. And even if you insist your reason is the quality of shopping, your friend may accept that but still think the parking point (although unsaid) can be inferred from your decision.

A question frequently posed by students at this stage is: 'So, how do I spot the *ratio*?' The question is a fair one. If there is an answer, it is the rather unsatisfactory one that, for both the practitioner and academic, this is a matter of skill and interpretation built on experience. After years of reading cases one instinctively formulates an opinion on what a case means (the basic theories of legal method having long been forgotten). The word we wish to stress here, though, is 'opinion'; and opinions can always be wrong or at least open to argument. Further, saying that experience aids one's understanding does not provide any help to someone new to the study of law. Thus, in the following text we have attempted to take a practical line by trying to find the most understandable and useful starting point for analysing the *ratio* of a case.

There are a number of excellent articles and books which take this academic debate to its limits: see, e.g., MacCormick (1987); Montrose (1957); Goodhart (1959). However, our experience is that at the outset of legal studies such in-depth analysis tends to produce confusion rather than comfort. We are in some agreement with Twining and Miers that the intricacies of the debate can (at least with regard to students beginning their legal studies) be a 'long and rather sterile' one. Nevertheless, as you encounter a greater range of cases and gain in confidence you may then wish to explore the problem of defining *ratio* in more depth.

There is no set single test for defining what is meant by *ratio* or for establishing the *ratio* of a particular case. As Cross stated: 'It is impossible to devise formulae for determining the *ratio decidendi* of a case'. But before you lose heart altogether, Cross also stated that 'this does not mean it is impossible to give a tolerably accurate description of what lawyers mean when they use the expression' (1991: 72) and we shall see that that is true.

At its simplest, *ratio decidendi* is the 'because' factor. We can say things such as: the owner of a scrap metal yard was responsible for the injuries occasioned by trespassing children when metal fell on them *because* he had not taken sufficient care to fence the dangerous site and to keep them out. Or we can say that the owner of a scrap metal yard was not liable for the same injuries *because* he took sufficient care to protect potential trespassers (especially children), or *because* the trespassers were adults. We might even say: the owner was responsible *because* previous authority had determined that scrap metal dealers owe a duty of absolute liability to child trespassers. In all instances we are trying to get to the bed of reasoning employed in reaching the decision.

Like so many things in law this problem of identification is not unique to legal studies. Think of the plot to a book or a film. The facts are clear, the storyline can be described, but if some people were asked to say what the film, etc. was *about* then opinions would vary. Some might see the film as nothing more than, say, an adventure film; others might see a social or political message in it; others might think the director was clearly paying tribute to an earlier famous director. Even if the writer or director was asked to spell out the meaning, the purpose, of the film (equivalent to reading the judgment of a case) the onlooker's reply could still be: 'You may have meant that, but you produced something different'. Thus, to the student who asks 'how do I spot the *ratio*?', Twining and Miers would respond:

> Talk of finding the *ratio decidendi* of a case obscures the fact that the process of interpreting cases is not like a hunt for buried treasure, but typically involves an element of choice from a range of possibilities. (2010: 306)

It is unwise, therefore, to presume that there is one and only one possible *ratio* to a case. As Jacob LJ said on behalf of the Court of Appeal in *Actavis UK Ltd v Merck & Co Inc*

[2008] EWCA Civ 444; [2009] 1 All ER 196 (mentioned in **Chapter 6** at section **6.5.6** in relation to *stare decisis*):

> [78] … As every law student will know it is not always easy to find what the *ratio* of a decision is, and it can be harder the more there are different judgments.
>
> [79] Moreover there are cases where there is simply no *ratio*. It is wrong to assume that every decision must have a *ratio* if only it can be found. A clear example of a no-*ratio* decision would be where three judges in the Court of Appeal each reached the same ultimate conclusion for different reasons …
>
> [80] As for an individual judgment, although we suppose every judge who writes his or her own decision tries to articulate a *ratio* it would be an article of faith and contrary to reality to say that every judge has succeeded or that a *ratio* (or *rationes*) can readily be distilled from every judgment.

Be assured, however, that there are many cases—usually older cases dealing with fundamental principles in a particular area—where lawyers have accepted a general formulation of the *ratio*. For instance, textbooks will normally say more or less the same thing about the nineteenth-century 'offer and acceptance' cases in contract law, but reading a case is an exercise in interpretation; an exercise in exploring the range of possibilities. This is why we stressed the word 'opinion' earlier. Consequently, there is nothing wrong in reading a case and thinking: 'That case is not really authority for the proposition stated in the textbook; or even that stated by a judge.' All you have to do then is prove you are right; but it is surprising how many times the cases cited in footnotes as authority for a legal proposition turn out to be nothing of the sort (e.g. the famous Contract Law principle drawn from the 1602 case of *Pinnel* (1601) 77 ER 237—that part payment of a debt is no payment at all—is based on an inadequate reading of the report so that it misses the fact that the case was actually decided on the basis of poor pleading of the defence and, had the case been presented better, the decision would have gone the other way).

Now, one of the classic ways of 'defining' what *ratio* means is to say that it is the material facts of the case, plus the decision made in relation to those facts. We will discuss what is meant by 'material facts' shortly. For the moment we will take the term as meaning those facts which were important in the judge's formulation of his decision; and so, the formulation of a rule which proceeds an inch beyond those material facts is suspect.

This approach was taken by Goodhart (1931: 25). It has been criticised mainly on the ground that Goodhart focused on the way in which the original judge formulated the *ratio* and that this fails to recognise sufficiently the role played by later judges in interpreting and applying the earlier case. We can agree with this criticism but it does not weaken the proposition that there is advantage to be gained in concentrating on what facts were material in a case, provided that one does not lose sight of the fact that a case does not stand in splendid isolation. How the case in question relates to other cases plays an important part in assessing its implications.

What the *ratio* of a case is *not* is a mere description of what happened. It is true that, at its simplest, finding the *ratio* of a case can be said to be like formulating a précis of the case—where one is trying to put into a few words or sentences an accurate summary of all that has been said (as you get when you read the headnote to a case). But in law we are looking for the *principle* that comes out of the case, not a mere description of the facts. We use the facts to illustrate that principle. If all one does is recount the facts it is a bit like trying to say that the *ratio* of Shakespeare's *Macbeth* is: nobleman gets told by a bunch of witches that he will be king and cannot be slain by man born of woman; he and his wife set about murdering everyone in their way; there's a lot of blood that will not wash off for some reason; Macbeth becomes king but is in turn killed by Macduff—who conveniently happens to have been 'from his mother's womb untimely ripped', (i.e. through a Caesarean section) and so not 'born of woman' for the purposes of the story. This outlines the plot but it does not tell you what the play is really about, e.g. how one action can lead inexorably to another or the role of ambition. So, what we need to do is look for the principle in a case that is brought out by the material facts. Think back to the case of *Whittall* v *Kirby* [1947] KB 194 to which we referred in **Chapter 6**. That was the case about the intoxicated lorry driver being disqualified from driving because what constituted a 'special reason' to avoid disqualification was said to have to be special to the offence not to the offender. First, the decision as to what was meant by 'special reason' in the statute was a key part of the reasoning or the principle (and therefore the *ratio*) in this case. Secondly, merely being a lorry driver with a previously clean licence was not enough to constitute a 'special reason'; so this is part of the *ratio* too—and that reasoning was explained by Lord Goddard LCJ stating that lorry drivers were not immune from disqualification merely because they were 'professional drivers'; that status did not amount to a special reason (so, this is also arguably part of the *ratio*). Thus, the principle to emerge from that case is that being a lorry driver (perhaps we might guess at extending this to being a 'a professional driver') who is a first-time offender does not amount to a special reason under the Act so as to avoid disqualification.

7.4 Perception and *Ratio*

The points raised in the last few paragraphs frequently cause students problems. It is not illogical when first studying law to believe that, if cases form the basis for legal propositions, you should be able to read a case and say what authority it stands for. After all, if you look at a maths equation you would expect to apply it time and time again in the same way. Why should the same not apply to legal cases?

First of all, maths equations are not always as certain and unchanging as we believe. For most of the time most mathematical equations will hold true; but in extreme circumstances they have to be modified. Thus Newton's general laws of gravity stood the test of time until some modifications had to be made following Einstein's work on relativity. The same is true for law. Many basic principles are well established and safe; what you learn now will probably still be true in fifty years' time. But law, in particular, has two key problems to deal with. First, as new cases arise in a particular area they have to be set against the established principle; and it may be that the principle has to be modified to accommodate these new cases. Think of it this way. Begin with a simple rule, then start asking questions along the '*What if?*' line of reasoning. This is illustrated in **Table 7.1**.

Table 7.1 How rules are created and modified

Rule: A vehicle must never cross double white lines in the middle of the road (the rule may be derived from an early case or might be a section in a statute—it does not matter for our purposes here).		
What if...?	*Decision*	*Possible later alterations/additions to the original rule*
Case 1: The road is blocked by a parked car?	The general rule should not apply strictly in such cases.	*Case 1* has modified the original rule, so that the rule now reads: You must never cross double white lines in the middle of the road **unless your right of way is blocked by a car** (*or another vehicle*).
Case 2: The left-hand side of the road is flooded?	The alteration to the general rule seen in *Case 1* should also apply here.	*Case 2* has modified the original rule (and added to the explanation in *Case 1*), so that the rule now reads: You must never cross double white lines in the middle of the road **unless your right of way is blocked by a car or passage is impossible because of an obstruction.**
Case 3: You are turning right into a driveway and this means you must cross the white lines?	This is no different from *Cases 1* and *2*—an exception to the general rule.	*Case 3* has modified the original rule (and applied the reasoning in *Cases 1* and *2*), so that the rule now reads: You must never cross double white lines in the middle of the road **unless ... or you are turning right into a driveway** (*and no other signs prevent you doing so?*).
Case 3 again:	**OR, if the decision was that you cannot cross the white line in such cases.**	Here *Case 3* has limited the modifications seen in *Cases 1* and *2*, so that the rule now reads: You must never cross double white lines in the middle of the road **even when you wish to turn right (into a driveway). This case is distinguishable from *Cases 1* and *2*.**
Case 4: A police officer directs you to do so?	The instructions from the officer override the general rule.	*Case 4* has again modified the original rule, so that it now reads: You must never cross double white lines in the middle of the road **unless directed by a police officer** (*and no other danger is obvious?*).
Case 5: The double white lines have been partially obliterated in some way?	Partial obliteration does not detract from the safety aspects of the general rule.	*Case 5* has applied the original rule but added a new role about knowledge being irrelevant, so that the new rule now reads: You must never cross double white lines in the middle of the road **even when they have been partially obliterated.**
Case 5 again:	**OR, if the decision was that partial obliteration means that it would be unfair to enforce the general rule.**	This version of *Case 5* has modified the original rule, so that it now reads: ... **unless they have been partially obliterated** (*and no other signs warn you of the presence of restrictions*).

This is a very simple example and most of the answers are obvious, but the same principle applies here as with the comparison of previously decided cases.

Secondly, lawyers have to use words to express the principles and concepts, and particular words do not always mean the same thing to different people. It is at this point that problems of *perception* arise.

We are used to problems of perception when they concern the senses. Optical illusions are probably the best example of different perceptions, though hearing (e.g. music) and taste (e.g. of foods) also show the range of subjective responses to standard data. Somehow with *words* we expect our interpretation to be both universally accepted and certain. Any level of experience tells us this is not so; but the sanctity we impart to words (especially our own utterances) seems to overcome our experience.

7.5 *Ratio* and Interpretation

Imagine that we have a case concerning the law on the protection of confidential information; we shall call it *Park Ltd* v *Moloney*. The issue is whether an employee, on leaving the company, can disclose his former employer's confidential information to another company. The case is heard in the Court of Appeal and the leading judgment is given by Tomlinson LJ. He rules that the employee is free to use the information. Tomlinson LJ states:

> During his employment an employee must not disclose any of his employer's confidential information to a third party. But once that employment has ended an employee should be free to use information which he has come by in the course of his employment unless that information amounts to a trade secret. The information in this particular case is confidential but not so confidential as to amount to a trade secret. Therefore the employee cannot be restrained from making use of it on termination of the contract of employment.

How might judges in later cases react to this ratio? Imagine we have a later case, *Harry George* v *Down Ltd*. Here are some examples of how judges in that case might express their different perceptions of Tomlinson LJ's *ratio* in *Park Ltd* v *Moloney*:

- *Judge 1:* 'In *Park* v *Moloney* Tomlinson LJ clearly established the principle that an ex-employee is bound to observe his former employer's secrets only in very limited circumstances. Unless Mr George's actions fit those exceptional circumstances, he will not be bound to keep his ex-employer's secrets once the contract of employment has come to an end.'

- *Judge 2:* 'In *Park* v *Moloney* Tomlinson LJ did not give ex-employees a free hand to disclose secrets on leaving employment. There are clear words of limitation in the phrase "trade secrets". All manner of things, in particular circumstances, may amount to a trade secret. We therefore need to explore what is meant by "trade secret".'

- *Judge 3:* 'When Tomlinson LJ stated that an employee "should be free to use information which he has come by in the course of his employment" he could not have meant this to apply where the employee has signed a contract specifically forbidding him from disclosing information once the contract has ended. The use of the word "should" clearly shows that there are limits to this freedom. In *Park Ltd* v *Moloney*, Mr Moloney had not signed such an agreement; here, Mr George had.' The cases are distinguishable.

- *Judge 4:* 'In *Park Ltd* v *Moloney* Tomlinson LJ clearly stated that an employee could use information which he has "come by in the course of his employment". The use of the words "come by" is interesting. I doubt whether his Lordship meant his judgment to include cases where the employee has not "come by" information by accident but has been specifically entrusted with the information by his employer, as is the case here.'

Although the *Park* v *Moloney* case and the comments are fictitious, they are based closely on real cases. They are simplified versions of how a judgment may be perceived by later judges, but they give you a taste of how a *ratio* is open to further interpretation.

7.6 Summary of Points Covered

Before looking at a short exercise on this idea of 'interpreting the *ratio*', we can summarise the points made so far:

(a) Many cases do not give rise to much argument as to what they mean, what the *ratio* was. Formulating a *ratio* can often be a simple and speedy exercise (especially if the textbooks give you a big clue). Indeed, sometimes you can use a sentence or paragraph from a judgment which sums up the case perfectly: it may not be labelled 'the *ratio*' but you can spot it quite easily. Or a later judge may have formulated a *ratio* for the earlier case which you can borrow (as with our fictitious example of *Park Ltd* v *Moloney*).

(b) Every case is, however, open to some reinterpretation. As we noted in **Chapter 6** (and will return to in **Chapter 9**), this may prove to be a particularly significant point if the earlier case law is seen to be in conflict with principles of human rights as set out in the Human Rights Act 1998.

(c) The earlier cases will have dealt with specific facts. Later cases will deal with different specific facts. Your job as a lawyer will be to show how these similarities or differences affect your case.

(d) The need to interpret the *ratio* of these earlier cases arises when you try to apply that case to the new set of facts in front of you. In a legal argument do not expect that your interpretation of the *ratio* will just be accepted.

(e) The judge's formulation of the *ratio* in any particular case is not always clear.

(f) Whether it is clear or not, later judges have the right to interpret these words, to add an emphasis which the earlier judge may not have intended, or which the earlier judge would have intended had he or she been faced with the new set of facts in question.

(g) Every time a case is decided in a particular area it may:

    (i) apply;
    (ii) confirm;
    (iii) extend;
    (iv) reinterpret;
    (v) distinguish;
    (vi) criticise;
    (vii) narrow;
    (viii) modify;

(ix) limit;

 (x) weaken;

(xi) obliterate; or

(xii) ignore

the principles established by the earlier cases.

Clearly, precedents do not simply develop in a 'straight line': they develop from encounters with different facts and different ways of viewing the facts.

EXERCISE 11 Things likely to do mischief

The case of *Rylands* v *Fletcher* (1868) LR 3 HL 330 is one of the more famous tort cases in English law. It was heavily criticised when it first appeared because many perceived the judges as having invented a legal principle not previously found in the case law (perhaps reflected in the fact that the form of liability derived from the case is simply known as the Tort of *Rylands* v *Fletcher*). Nevertheless the case stood the test of time until fairly recently.

In *Rylands* v *Fletcher*, the House of Lords had to consider whether Fletcher could recover damages against Rylands when a reservoir constructed by Rylands burst through some disused mine shafts on his land and flooded the mines of Fletcher, who was Rylands' neighbour. On the facts, Rylands had not been negligent in constructing the reservoir. In holding that Rylands was nevertheless liable for the damage caused, Lord Cairns cited the judgment of Blackburn J. in the court below:

> We think that the true rule of law is, that the person who, for his own purposes, brings on his land and collects and keeps there anything likely to do mischief if it escapes, must keep it in at his peril; and if he does not do so, is prima facie answerable for all the damage which is the natural consequence of its escape.

Q QUESTIONS

(a) Do you think that this expresses a clear legal proposition which you could apply to other cases?

(b) Earlier in Lord Cairns' speech he referred to the 'non-natural' use of land. Should this be read in to the statement given above?

(c) Do you foresee difficulties with the words used? What do you think was meant by 'for his own purposes', 'brings on', 'escape', 'likely to do mischief'?

(d) Do you think a later judge might say that the principle was expressed wider than was necessary to decide the actual case?

(e) Would later judges be justified in applying or not applying the words used to situations with very different facts? For instance, how would you use the principle where a visitor to a munitions factory is injured by the explosion of a shell which is being manufactured in the factory? (See *Read* v *J. Lyons & Co. Ltd* [1947] AC 156, [1946] 2 All ER 471.)

continued

EXERCISE 11 *continued*

COMMENT

The first and second questions help to illustrate that the *ratio* is not set in stone but is subject to interpretation. The fact that textbooks give you the *rationes* of many cases only means that this is the conclusion the author reached after doing the same exercise. Textbooks are not legal authority. As was once said in criticism of an employment tribunal: 'The tribunal therefore took the bold step of not following a decision of [the Employment Appeal Tribunal] … and did so upon the basis of what had been written … in *Harvey*, which, albeit a leading text, is a textbook and is not legal authority … however correct it may later be held to be.'

However, if lawyers have been proposing *rationes* for centuries, then it is not an impossible art to master. For instance, quite often (as in *Rylands* v *Fletcher* itself) a fairly clear idea of the *ratio* can be found in one sentence or paragraph. It is also part of a lawyer's skill to gather the *ratio* from reading the whole judgment (or judgments). This may test one's ability to deal with concepts and linguistics, but it is not an insurmountable task. Although it is sacrilegious to say this, when starting out studying law a good idea of what most people will regard as being the *ratio* of a case is contained in the headnote to the case. This is written by an experienced barrister and most practitioners would admit that, on many occasions, this is all they have read in a case. But this is a dangerous practice when used long term. It gives only one interpretation, does not actually quote what the judges said, and, in some famous cases, may actually be wrong—even the most experienced barristers muck it up sometimes.

The third question illustrates the point that, even if the *ratio* is easy to spot, words do not always have a clear, single meaning. The word 'escape' was a major issue in the case of *Read* v *Lyons*, noted in question (e).

One question we did not pose, which can be dealt with only by reading the case itself is: what earlier authorities were cited by the court? We noted in the introduction to this exercise that *Rylands* v *Fletcher* was criticised for 'inventing law'. Nevertheless, the judges still referred to a number of cases; cases which they said were analogous to this situation. Hence our previous comment that cases do not stand in splendid isolation.

The fourth and fifth questions lead us into a discussion on another vital aspect of reading a case—the question of what constitutes a *material fact*. This question exemplifies the idea that the *ratio* of a case strictly relates only to the actual facts of that case, but is often expressed in wider terms. The fifth question asks you to decide whether changing a material fact (here, that *Read* was on the premises and not outside so how could the explosive material be said to have 'escaped') might make such a difference that the original *ratio* should not be applied. But before analysing what is meant by the term *material fact* we will take the opportunity to note that not everything said by a judge when giving judgment can constitute a precedent. As Cross indicates (1991: 39), the *ratio* can only relate to pronouncements of law, not the facts of the case; and then only those pronouncements which the judge considers necessary for his decision are said to form part of the *ratio*.

7.7 Obiter Dictum

Anything else said in the case that does not relate to the material facts is called an *obiter dictum* (this means 'a thing said by the way'—the plural, 'things said by the way', is *obiter dicta*). *Obiter dicta* statements are not binding on a later judge. MacCormick describes *obiter dicta* as 'statements of opinion upon the law and its values and principles in their bearing on the instant decision, statements which in some way go beyond the point or points necessary to be settled in deciding the case' (1987: 156).

Obiter comments can arise in many ways—here are a few examples:

(a) where the judge makes a hypothetical pronouncement, e.g. 'If the facts had been different (in some respect) then my decision would have been …'; or

(b) the judge might say what he would have decided had he not been bound by *stare decisis*; or

(c) the pronouncement by the judge might be entirely relevant to the material facts, but his or her judgment was in the minority. A minority judgment has its own *ratio*, but that cannot form part of the *ratio* of the case, since that judge's view did not prevail;

(d) the judge may make a number of general comments on the topic of law under discussion. In *Donoghue* v *Stevenson*, for instance, Lord Atkin made a number of observations about liability for negligent acts. One observation was that one owed a duty of care not to injure one's 'neighbour'—a person so closely affected by one's acts that one must take reasonable care not to injure them. This is an *obiter* statement because it is not directly related to the facts; it proceeds far beyond that in its generality. To form part of the *ratio* the comment would have had to be narrower and closer to the actual facts: for example, relating to the duty owed by manufacturers to the ultimate customer.

In our running example of *Whittall* v *Kirby* Lord Goddard CJ inserted into the judgment, towards the end, a comment that: 'It is certainly difficult to visualize what could amount to a special reason in the case of driving under the influence of drink or drugs, though perhaps one might be found if the court was satisfied that a drug had been administered to a driver without his knowledge, as for instance where a driver had taken a dose of medicine which he believed to be an ordinary tonic but which in fact contained a powerful drug.' These two thoughts would occupy the courts for many years to come, despite being said *obiter dicta*.

Most *obiter dicta* were never intended by the judge to be anything else. However, as you will see (especially in **Exercise 12**), a later court may always decide that what was said by a judge in the prior case was unnecessary to the decision and therefore not part of the *ratio*. This 'reassessment' is one of the devices used to overcome the binding element of precedent discussed in **Chapter 6**.

A judge can decline to follow anything that is not the *ratio*. This is why the classification is important. However, do not cast aside *obiter* comments. For one thing, if the *ratio* of a case is an arguable point you should not be too hasty in relegating a comment to the status of *obiter dictum*; one man's *obiter* may be the next man's *ratio* to a case. For another, *obiter* comments can turn out to be much more influential than the actual *ratio*. Lord Atkins's 'neighbour principle' was not an irrelevancy: far from it. Rather, it was used by later judges to form the basis upon which the law of negligence was to develop. From a case about dead snails the 'neighbour principle' has been extended to consumer items, industrial accidents, road accidents, misstatements, and many other areas.

The same is true of the *obiter* comment in *Whittall* v *Kirby*. In *Newnham* v *Trigg* [1970] RTR 107 the comment that a special reason might exist where a person took 'medicine which he believed to be an ordinary tonic' was tested when Mr Trigg's wife gave him some medicine containing whisky. He knew it contained whisky but not how much and, after taking it, drove a friend home; that is when he was stopped by the police. Lord Goddard CJ's *obiter* comment in *Whittall* on what may be a 'special reason' was held to be sound but not applicable here because of Mr Trigg's knowledge. But there was another *obiter* comment here, this time from Lord Parker CJ: '[This case] is quite different, it seems to me, from the case which may arise and may amount to a special reason though I am not saying that it does, where a man thinking he is drinking, we will say ginger ale, has, unknown to him, strong drink put into it behind his back. Ignorance of the quality of the drink may amount to a special reason, but ignorance of the exact quantity that he is drinking cannot in my judgment do so.' This led to a long line of cases as to when a person who had had their drink 'spiked' could avoid disqualification. So, one *obiter* had built influentially on another *obiter* comment.

Throughout the remainder of this chapter we concentrate on the two important aspects of analysing *ratio decidendi*: 'how precedents develop' and the 'material facts' of cases. These two topics are intertwined and, in our experience, it would be ideal to consider them both simultaneously. Unfortunately, there is no simple way of doing this. Therefore, by way of explanation and introduction we will summarise the points to begin with:

(a) In the next section 'How Precedents Develop', we will seek to show that, from the starting point of a single case, a line of cases can arise with similar facts which can apply or modify the *ratio* found in the first case. This exercise is something like analysing the history of computers. Forty years ago it took a computer the size of a room a long time to produce fairly simple results. Working from the same principles as that early machine, computers became smaller and did the same job more quickly. The use of silicon chips changed the size again and brought about added refinements and advantages. The modern computer is the state of the art—but this will change yet again, so that each generation is, in many respects, quite unlike its ancestors—certainly its distant ancestors. However, the basic or underlying principles have generally remained the same. What we will stress is that in law it is the *reasoning* employed in a case that is passed on for examination to the next generation, even though the facts change with each case.

(b) In section **7.10** 'Material Facts' we will attempt to explain which parts of the previous cases are considered vital to the decision. In other words, if the facts of each case are inevitably different to some degree, which facts do we consider material (vital) enough to say: 'That case was decided in a particular way and this case is sufficiently similar to it that it too should be decided in the same way'?

7.8 How Precedents Develop

7.8.1 Comparing the Reasoning in Cases

Once a case has been decided, it falls to judges in later cases sitting in an inferior court to apply the case, or find reasons not to apply it. This much is demanded by the doctrine of *stare decisis*. Even if there is no binding element attached to the earlier decision, it will not simply be ignored (the persuasive nature of precedent should not be underestimated) as we have seen with developments flowing from *Whittall* v *Kirby*. The reality is that the later judge will (to a greater or lesser extent) formulate his own opinion as to the *ratio* of the earlier case. This may not be exactly the same as the opinion held by the judge in that earlier case. There may be a difference of emphasis. It may be a wider *ratio* than the first judge intended; it may be narrower. It is rather like the writing and singing of a song: even when the same words are being sung the interpretation of different artists may be quite striking—consider the various versions of 'My Way' (e.g. that of Frank Sinatra and that of the Sex Pistols' Sid Vicious).

A common mistake made by law students, however, is to ignore all this and, as we indicated earlier, to discover a similarity and take the analysis no further. A lawyer cannot rest like this. Various arguments might be presented regarding the similarities of cases, such as:

- 'This present case is on all fours with the previous case'; or
- 'The facts are dissimilar at first sight, but both cases illustrate the same principle'; or
- 'The present case is clearly distinguishable from the earlier case because one of the material facts of the earlier case is missing here'; or
- 'The present case is clearly distinguishable from the earlier case because there are additional material facts in this case which were not present in the earlier case'; or even
- 'When Lord Justice Bloggs formulated the principle in the earlier case he paid insufficient attention to fact A which he should have treated as material.'

This last point is illustrated well by the discussion of 'materiality' in *Frozen Value Ltd v Heron Foods Ltd* [2012] EWCA Civ 473; [2012] 3 All ER 1328 where members of the Court of Appeal disagreed on the binding status of a previous decision which had dealt with the same area of law but had not covered what was now seen to be a material fact in the light of the facts before the 2012 court. Jackson LJ did not regard the earlier case as binding, arguing that it had failed to deal with the issue; Lloyd LJ regarded the earlier case as binding because the present issue had not been relevant to the facts in the earlier case (had not been material) so the lack of comment on it was understandable—if the issue had not been material to the earlier case (or even argued in the case) it was not surprising that the Court had not dealt with it.

There are therefore many ways in which one can try to use apparently dissimilar cases to argue your case; or argue that apparently similar cases are of little or no use at all. Remember, when you are arguing your client's case you are trying to persuade the judge to apply the *rationes* which are helpful to you and disapply the rest. It is a matter of legal ethics that you have a duty as an advocate to bring to the court's attention all relevant authorities. Advocates are required to cite the authorities they wish to rely upon (usually in what are termed 'skeleton arguments'), together with the proposition of law which the authority demonstrates, and the specific parts of the judgment which demonstrate this. This extends to informing the court of cases which are against you as well, but that does not stop you arguing that the ones against you are worthless or distinguishable.

By way of illustration the simple timechart in **Figure 7.1** shows how a case might develop.

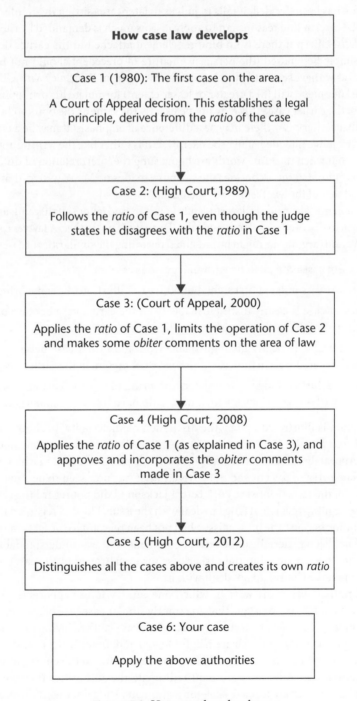

How case law develops

Case 1 (1980): The first case on the area.

A Court of Appeal decision. This establishes a legal principle, derived from the *ratio* of the case

Case 2: (High Court,1989)

Follows the *ratio* of Case 1, even though the judge states he disagrees with the *ratio* in Case 1

Case 3: (Court of Appeal, 2000)

Applies the *ratio* of Case 1, limits the operation of Case 2 and makes some *obiter* comments on the area of law

Case 4 (High Court, 2008)

Applies the *ratio* of Case 1 (as explained in Case 3), and approves and incorporates the *obiter* comments made in Case 3

Case 5 (High Court, 2012)

Distinguishes all the cases above and creates its own *ratio*

Case 6: Your case

Apply the above authorities

Figure 7.1 How case law develops

We can show this in action a little more specifically by returning to the example of the road accident first set out in **Chapter 6**. You may remember that the facts were: in *case (1)* a man driving a Ford Mondeo runs over an old lady who was lawfully using a zebra crossing. The man is held to be liable in negligence. In *Brenda's case—case (2)*—a woman driving a BMW runs over an old man who was crossing the road.

The question before the court is therefore: how does the decision in *case (1)* apply to the facts in *case (2)*? (We should state here that none of what follows is meant to be an accurate statement of the law—we have simplified many things to illustrate our general point.)

We shall start by assuming that *case (1)* took place in 2011 and the driver (we shall call him Alfred) argued that he was not liable because the old lady stepped onto the zebra crossing so late that he could not stop. The court did not accept that this was a legitimate excuse and Alfred was found liable in negligence to the old lady for the injury he caused her. Alfred's appeal to the Court of Appeal failed. By looking at the judgment of the trial judge and taking the comments of the Court of Appeal, we can put together the following **material facts**:

(a) The weather conditions were excellent.

(b) The old lady was on a zebra crossing.

(c) The fact that she stepped onto the crossing late did not, in law or on the facts, excuse Alfred from liability because:

   (i) Alfred was speeding;

   (ii) Alfred's attention was distracted as he was using his mobile phone at the time.

We might say that the *ratio* of this case is: where a person is not paying adequate attention and is speeding, they will be liable for their negligence if they injure a pedestrian who is using a zebra crossing, even where the pedestrian steps onto the crossing late, provided a careful driver (taking account of the weather conditions) could have still avoided causing injury.

The fact that Alfred is male, that the injured person is female or old, that the car was a Ford Mondeo, have not been held to be relevant as **material facts**. Indeed, the court seems not to have concentrated on the use of the mobile phone but taken a more general line about 'careful driving'. Now we have to apply this reasoning to *case (2)*—the woman (Brenda) driving a BMW, who hits an old man crossing a road. It is 2012. First, **Table 7.2** shows a simple comparison of (material) facts.

Table 7.2 Application of facts to Brenda's case

Material facts in Alfred's case	*Facts in Brenda's case*
Fact (a): use of a zebra crossing	Not present— this was a straight piece of open road
Fact (b): speeding	Brenda was also speeding
Fact (c): attention distracted by use of mobile phone	Similar— attention distracted by noisy child in the back seat
Fact (d): the old lady stepped onto the crossing late	Not present— the man is not at a zebra crossing
Fact (e): weather conditions good	Same

We shall assume that the court in *Brenda's case* decides that the absence of facts (a) and (d) does not affect the general principle to be found in *Alfred's case*. This means that the judge in Brenda's case believed that the fact the old lady in *Alfred's case* was injured whilst using a zebra crossing was not material to the *ratio* of *Alfred's case* when looked at in the light of the present case so that the same principle applies even where the injured person is crossing another part of the road. This is interesting: perhaps the textbooks written after *Alfred's case* thought that the protection given to the old lady only applied because she was using a zebra crossing—if so the texts will have to be rewritten. The judge will have fixed on the presence of facts (b), (c), and (e) in *Brenda's case* as the determining factors (even though they are not identical to *Alfred's case*).

The *ratio* of *Brenda's case* **might then be: where a person is not paying adequate attention and is speeding, they will be liable for their negligence if they injure a pedestrian who is crossing the road, provided a careful driver (taking account of the weather conditions), could have still avoided causing injury.**

Our perception of the legal principles relating to driving negligently has been widened, even if only slightly. Gone is the requirement for the presence of the zebra crossing and the related fact of the person stepping onto it late. Also gone now is the basis for any argument which tried to limit the *ratio* of *Alfred's case* to inattention caused by the use of mobile phones. If we were being very precise, we only know that using a mobile phone or having a noisy child in the back of the car do not amount to sufficient excuses to overcome the 'inattention' point. Perhaps other distractions might be excused. However, we are at least beginning to get a clearer picture of what is required for liability and what does not matter.

We can now introduce a final example. *Carol's case* involves a woman driving a VW Golf, who runs over a student crossing the road (this time on a bend). It is 2013. **Table 7.3** sets out the material facts for this scenario.

You can see that the facts have moved on a little from each of the first two cases. It is possible that this shift will mean that Carol is not liable. It is also possible that the judge may find that the differences are immaterial to the general principle so that she is liable.

Table 7.3 Application of facts to *Carol's case*

Material facts in Alfred's case	Material facts in Brenda's case	Material facts in Carol's case
Fact (a): use of a zebra crossing	Not present —this was a straight piece of open road	Not present —accident on the bend in a road
Fact (b): speeding	Brenda was also speeding	Carol was *not* speeding
Fact (c): attention distracted by use of mobile phone	Similar: Brenda was distracted by a noisy child in the back seat	Similar: Carol was distracted by seeing a dog, which was not on a lead and which was wandering around the roadside
Fact (d): the old lady stepped onto the crossing late	Not present	Not present
Fact (e): weather conditions good	Same	Different: it was raining

This is what judges do: they make decisions. In any decision there is a point where a judgment has to be made and this is not a purely mechanical exercise (one reason why it is so difficult to invent a computer-based 'expert system' for deciding cases). As the great lateral thinker Edward de Bono once commented, 'In the end all decisions are emotional' and much of behavioural economics centres on this concept too. If it helps: we have described this moment of decision to our students as the 'Marmite moment'—a point where logic comes to an end and a judge either loves or hates your argument (to those readers who have not encountered the joys of Marmite, it is a yeast extract used as a spread on toast, etc.—even its own advertising campaign plays on the fact that people are divided on the taste).

We shall say that Carol is also found to be liable. This means that the judge has confirmed that the principles of liability as originally set out in *Alfred's case* are:

(a) not limited to cases involving zebra crossings (though this probably came out of *Brenda's case* anyway);

(b) not limited to accidents occurring on straight roads (as had been the fact in *Brenda's case*);

(c) not limited to cases where the driver is speeding (which was the position with both *Alfred* and *Brenda* but not Carol);

(d) not limited to cases where the weather conditions were good (previously we would have been unsure but in *Carol's case* it was raining and the same principles were still applied); and

(e) not limited by the fact that Carol's attention was distracted by a genuine and understandable concern that a loose dog might run into the road. On this, we can now speculate that any excuse regarding lack of attention will be very limited in its scope.

The *ratio* for *Carol's case* might be: where a person is not paying adequate attention, even where there is an understandable reason for that lack of attention, they will be liable for their negligence if they injure a pedestrian who is crossing on the bend of a road, provided a careful driver could have still avoided causing injury.Table 7.4 compares the possible formulations of *ratio* in the three cases. How important are the minor differences?

Table 7.4 *Rationes* of the three cases

Alfred's case	Brenda's case	Carol's case
Where a person is not paying adequate attention and is speeding, they will be liable for their negligence if they injure a pedestrian who is using a zebra crossing, even where the pedestrian steps onto the crossing late, provided the driver (taking account of the weather conditions) could have still avoided causing injury.	Where a person is not paying adequate attention and is speeding, they will be liable for their negligence if they injure a pedestrian who is crossing the road, provided a careful driver (taking account of the weather conditions) could have still avoided causing injury.	Where a person is not paying adequate attention, even where there is an understandable reason for the lack of attention, they will be liable for their negligence if they injure a pedestrian who is crossing on the bend of a road, provided a careful driver could have still avoided causing injury.

This type of exercise is fine for examining decided cases—as you will do throughout your studies. But there is the practical 'prediction' aspect of law too. For instance, let us assume for a moment that you are a solicitor interviewing a client. The client, David, tells you that he injured a young man in a car accident. The man was crossing the road, at a junction, in a wheelchair. Can you say that the cases we have discussed will apply? Is the introduction of a new fact—that the injured person had been in a wheelchair—sufficiently different from the precedents that they may have no application?

One thing you would certainly have to do is to read the cases. We have simplified things. There are no statements here from judges as to *why* they reached these decisions. It might even be that there is an *obiter* comment in one of the cases where a judge said that had the injured person been in a wheelchair or similar device the decision would have been different. This *obiter* comment is not binding but it might be highly persuasive to a later judge; the judge in your case perhaps.

Distinguishing cases

When the material facts are found to be sufficiently similar, then the later court is bound to follow the decision of the earlier *superior* court (and possibly that of a court of equal status): it must apply the principle of law pronounced in the earlier case. The only other alternative is to **distinguish** the case. By this we mean that the lawyer or judge will seek to show a significant difference in the material facts or the reasoning employed in the two cases such that the court should not feel obliged to follow the earlier case. It is almost impossible to define coherently when courts will or will not feel inclined to distinguish a case. But do not be put off by this. The ability to argue differences in cases, to argue why a case should or should not apply, lies at the heart of the common law. This is what you are training to do. The fact that the judge finally disagrees with you may be annoying, but it's a fact of life. Sometimes your talents will be recognised even in the most hopeless of cases, as with Lord Donaldson's comment on David Pannick, QC in *Attorney-General v Barker* [1990] 3 All ER 257 at 261e: 'My abiding impression of this case is that I have confirmed my admiration for counsel … as an advocate in his ability to dress up the wholly unarguable as if it had a scintilla of a basis of reason.'

So, imagine you are David's lawyer in the driving case noted earlier. You wish to distinguish David's case from Alfred's, Brenda's, and Carol's. What arguments could you use? It will not be enough to show that the injured person was using a wheelchair. You will have to show that the injured person's use of the wheelchair in crossing the road at a dangerous point meant David was not at fault:

(i) You will need David not to have been speeding because, even though that was irrelevant in *Carol's case*, if he was speeding he will certainly be liable under the authority of *Alfred* and *Brenda*.

(ii) Even if he was not speeding you will need to show why *Carol's case* still does not apply. Maybe, when viewed more closely, you can show that Carol's speed was still close to the limit which, given that it was raining, affected the decision. Perhaps here the weather conditions were better and so the 'speeding' point is distinguishable. You would need to read the judgment in *Carol's case* carefully to see what was said by the judges and whether any comments were made *obiter* on this issue.

(iii) You will need David not to have been distracted (or, if he was, find a way of saying that the form of distraction was such that it went beyond what happened to Carol).

If you could show these things, you might be able to argue that the *principle* found in the earlier cases is not that a driver who injures a pedestrian is always liable but that he is only liable where he is clearly at fault— and these facts show he was not at fault.

Because of our system of precedent, distinguishing cases is central to case-law analysis. If, for instance, you feed the search term 'distinguish!' into Westlaw the system goes into overload and comes up with over 10,000 occurrences (the exclamation mark allows for different endings such as distinguish*ing*). Accepting that some are not directly relevant, this is still a huge number. Most distinctions are drawn in relation to a comparison of facts, though some relate to pure legal issues. An example of the first can be seen in *R v Pleydell (Michael Aaron)* [2005] EWCA Crim 1447 which distinguished another Court of Appeal judgment (*R v Woodward (Terence)* [1995] 1 WLR 375; [1995] 3 All ER 79). Both cases concerned causing death by dangerous driving. In *Woodward*, the fact that the driver had been seen with a glass of alcohol in his hands just before driving was held not to be admissible as proof that he had been over the limit while driving because there was no evidence of quantity consumed or effect (he had been injured in the crash and no samples had been taken). But this was **distinguished** in *Pleydell* where there was evidence that the driver had consumed cocaine before driving. Here the court drew the distinction with these words:

> [30] In short, in our judgment, the mere fact that he had taken a drug, very shortly before the incident, if such could be established by the prosecution, was potentially relevant … Quantification of the precise amount of cocaine consumed would not take matters any further.
>
> [31] In our judgment, therefore, the Crown were correct in asserting that the jury was entitled to view the consumption of the cocaine per se as relevant to the issue of driving dangerously, in contrast to perhaps modest consumption of alcohol.

There are, of course, many such examples. Sometimes the distinction is more technical and can cross different areas of law. In *Pacitti Jones (A Firm)* v *O'Brien* [2005] IRLR 888, for instance, the Employment Appeal Tribunal distinguished a House of Lords' decision (*Dodds v Walker* [1981] 1 WLR 1027; [1981] 2 All ER 609) when they held that the definition of a 'month' was different under an employment law statute than under a landlord and tenant statute.

This process is not unique to law. You distinguish things every day. At its simplest level, you distinguish physical objects—a television from a DVD recorder for example. Their size, shape, and functions tell you that these objects are different. At a more complicated level, human beings share over 95 per cent of their DNA with chimpanzees and about 60 per cent with bananas, but, on the whole, we can tell the difference. More inexplicably we all distinguish the faces of billions of people, despite the fact that they are built of the same, limited number of component parts. We would submit that, saying *exactly* why Deb and Jane are not the same person might, in the end, be more difficult than distinguishing between *Alfred's case* and *Carol's case* in our earlier examples.

What the 'negligent driving' exercise tells us is that the analysis of the *ratio* of a case involves a high degree of interpretation—of applying the *principle* in one case to the different facts in another. The principles that emerge from a case can thus often be seen only in retrospect. Looking back at *Alfred's case*, knowing that later cases have expanded upon such things as the position of the pedestrian on the road, we tend to generalise. Our account of the *ratio* of *Alfred's case* is much more general than it would have been immediately after *Alfred's case* was reported. When the decision in *Alfred's case* was given in 2011 you could not say with any certainty that the presence of the pedestrian crossing or the fact the driver was speeding would be irrelevant to liability. It might be that you now feel you could extract a wide principle from the three cases, e.g. that a driver who does not look where he or she is going, for any reason, is guilty of negligent driving. Perhaps this is accurate; but would you have been confident in saying this when *Alfred's case* was the only decided case?

It is like watching a game of chess where you have not been told all the rules. You might see a knight move and conclude that chess pieces move in an 'L' shape. Only in subsequent observations do you find that this principle applies to only one piece; and you may not have deduced yet that the knight has the ability to jump over other pieces. The real attributes of the knight—the first case—are seen only as things develop and by comparison with other events. This comparison was once used by the physicist Richard Feynman to describe the discovery of scientific principles; it applies equally here. And, as with Feynman's analogy, there is always the possibility that just when you think you understand everything about chess (or science, or legal principles) something totally unexpected happens, such as 'castling'.

For instance, assume that a new major case has just been reported. At this stage you cannot say with certainty how it will be used in the future. How will later judges apply it to different facts? Is the *ratio* going to be restricted to the particular facts of the case, or used in many other similar (but possibly only remotely similar) cases? In other words, how will judges in later cases use the precedent?

If we might borrow and adapt an example of this form of reasoning from Dworkin (1987: ch. 7) we can see that this twisting and turning of principles can apply outside the legal context too. Consider that Charles Dickens had never written *A Christmas Carol*. You have been commissioned to do so. In writing chapter 1, you have a completely free hand in deciding on the character of Scrooge and what will happen to him. Think of this as the first case in a line of precedents.

Now imagine that someone else is commissioned to write chapter 2. She takes your basic material, but places a different emphasis on it—maybe one you never intended. By the end of the novel (with even more authors having contributed) Scrooge, instead of seeing the error of his ways and being redeemed, is taught his lesson and still cast into hell. Your original idea has been changed out of all recognition, despite the fact that each chapter follows logically from the previous one.

7.8.2 Multiple and Inconclusive *Rationes*

It will not now come as a surprise that a case can be said to have different *rationes* in that there may be different interpretations of what is the proposition of law for which the case stands as authority. Equally, you need to be aware that: (i) even 'crystal-clear' judgments occasionally contain more than one *ratio*; and (ii) that in some cases no one can find the *ratio*.

Different formulations of a *ratio*

At section **7.3** we noted that a judge may reformulate the *ratio* by using different words later in his judgment. That certainly adds confusion but in many ways it is part of a normal thought process. Here, we have in mind a slightly different position—where a judge says: 'I find for X for the following reasons ... I would also say that there is another (unconnected) reason for which I find for X.' Which is the *ratio*? This occurred in the Court of Appeal case of *Turner* v *London Transport Executive* [1977] ICR 952. The traditional answer is that both statements are *ratio*. Later judges do not, however, follow a consistent line when dealing with such cases; they 'relegate' one of the statements to mere *obiter dictum*: see Lord Denning's comments on *Turner* in *Western Excavating* v *Sharp* [1978] ICR 221; [1978] 1 All ER 713 (also Court of Appeal).

This technique also even enables later judges in lower courts to reassess the *ratio* of an earlier case. Thus, in *Great Peace Shipping Ltd* v *Tsavliris Salvage (International) Ltd* [2002] EWCA Civ 1407; [2002] 4 All ER 689 Lord Phillips of Worth Matravers, MR in the Court of Appeal reassessed the words of Lord Atkin in the famous House of Lords contract law case of *Bell* v *Lever Bros* [1932] AC 161 and concluded that Lord Atkin had proposed two *rationes*, the first of which was based on very weak authority and so could be ignored in favour of the second *ratio*. Had he been alive at that time this would probably have been news to Lord Atkin.

No clear *ratio*

We also have in mind a number of confusing cases which the lawyer usually relates as being 'an authority for any proposition of law for which you care to use it'. This will arise where the judges are agreed as to the decision (X won) but present their reasons in quite different formulations. *Bell* v *Lever Bros* is one example.

Chaplin v *Boys* [1971] AC 356 has long been cited in this area as a case where their Lordships in the House of Lords agreed on the result but were faced with three possible grounds for reaching their decision; if one adds up the various opinions one discovers that each of the grounds was actually rejected by three of the five Law Lords. The High Court of Australia managed to do something similar in *Northern Sandblasting Pty Ltd* v *Harris* (1997) 188 CLR 313. Nicole Harris, a nine-year-old, had been electrocuted and reduced to a vegetative state when water pipes had become live owing to the negligence of an electrician. Because the case involved rented accommodation, the law on who was responsible had particular complications outside the scope of this text. In deciding to award substantial damages, two judges found for Nicole on what we shall call ground (a), but the other five judges rejected this reasoning; two found for Nicole on ground (b) but four of the remaining judges rejected this ground, the final judge not dealing with the issue.

Another case along the same lines is the contract law case of *Esso* v *Commissioners of Customs and Excise* [1976] 1 WLR 1; [1976] 1 All ER 117. The issue was quite simple. Esso had established a campaign whereby their garages were giving away free 'World Cup' coins (tokens bearing the faces of England's 1970 World Cup squad), with every four gallons of petrol. Customs and Excise claimed these coins were chargeable to purchase tax (the forerunner of VAT) because they were 'produced in quantity for general sale'. The customs officials placed a value on the coins and claimed £200,000.

The House of Lords held that Esso was not liable to purchase tax on the coins. But when one reads the judgments one finds that:

(a) Two Law Lords held that there was no intent to create legal relations as regards the coins: they were gifts (see Viscount Dilhorne and Lord Russell).

(b) Two Law Lords held that the advertisement on the garage forecourts was an offer which the customers accepted when they bought the petrol. However, the coins themselves were ancillary to the main contract and were transferred only when the motorist bought the petrol. Therefore the coins themselves were not produced for sale (Lord Simon and Lord Wilberforce).

(c) Lord Fraser dissented, finding that there was intent to form a contract and the coins were part of that contract.

This summary ignores the many *obiter* statements which add greater confusion.

These cases do not occur that often, but they do exist. They help to illustrate our over-riding point that cases are not merely objects that remain fixed and unaltered every time you look at them. Moreover, even if they could be considered as objects they would be more like audio systems than washing machines: the washing machine is a unit which does not change from purchase but the audio system can be altered substantially (new cables, speakers, etc.), and though it still performs its original purpose it does so with very different results—and may even accommodate a completely new component such as the introduction of an HDMI interface.

Different elements to be drawn from the case

Leaving aside any question of confusion, a case may be authority for more than one principle. *Carlill* is usually cited, for instance, as a case on when an advertisement may amount to an offer. However, there is also much said in the judgments on when a person has effectively accepted an offer and, since this point was pertinent to the decision in *Carlill* it may also be cited as a distinct authority, but this time on the law relating to acceptance.

7.9 Answering Legal Questions on Precedent

In **Exercise 12** we have drafted a problem on *ratio* and *stare decisis* based on both the information presented earlier and that in **Chapter 6**. Its aim is to reiterate some of the points made and to show you a general plan in answering legal questions. It also relates back to what we said in **Chapter 4** on writing essays and gives us an opportunity to note that in legal education, if not in practice, you will be asked to write essays relating to quotations as well as being asked to analyse problem situations.

EXERCISE 12 Precedent and the congenital idiot

 QUESTION

Lord Asquith once recounted a joke told to him regarding *ratio* and *obiter* that: 'The rule is quite simple, if you agree with the other bloke you say [the statement] is part of the *ratio*; if you don't you say it is *obiter dictum*, with the implication that he is a congenital idiot.'

Discuss.

continued

ANSWER

This question asks you to analyse how a judge uses or avoids precedent: what do the terms *ratio decidendi* and *obiter dictum* mean; and is a judge really bound by the doctrine of *stare decisis*? Thus this is a specific question which demands a **specific** answer—not merely general comments. This style of question is one which is commonly found throughout all areas of law: a quotation questioning or denying the logic of a fundamental rule. For instance, the question might be: 'The formation of a contract is not based on assessing the parties' true intentions but on what the law defines as their intentions according to their conduct set against established case law. Discuss.' Or: 'When people talk of the United Kingdom losing its sovereignty since joining the EU they fail to recognise that sovereignty is an economic fact, not a political aspiration. Discuss.' You are asked to perform four tasks, each of which is considered in turn in the following paragraphs:

(1) **IDENTIFY THE AREA CONCERNED**. In this case this hardly presents a problem because of the introductory words. But a quotation on theft, or misrepresentation in contract, may have hidden points.

(2) **LIMIT YOURSELF TO THE TOPIC IN QUESTION**. In the context of this chapter, this again is not difficult; but when such a question appears at the end of a course the task becomes more difficult. It is vital to see at what limited area the question is aimed. Not all the topics that fall within 'legal method' are relevant to the question posed here. Thus the **poor student** will tend to do one of two things:

   (a) Launch into a lengthy discussion of various or all aspects of precedent. This is known as the 'shotgun' approach: something has to hit the target. With a question on provocation in criminal law, for instance, nearly every defence under the sun will emerge at some time.

   (b) Spend too much time on introductory matters, such as describing the court structure in detail. This would not be the crux of the question. This might be even more obvious when one glances down the examination paper to discover a question asking for just this type of information. With a question on contract law, for instance, there may be a page introduction setting out as many aspects of contract formation as possible when the question is only concerned with one aspect of offer and acceptance.

The **good student** will therefore focus on the key issue lying behind the quotation, namely, how a judge in one case deals with the *ratio* of an earlier case with which he or she disagrees. One method whereby the earlier inconvenient judgment can be avoided is to 'distinguish' the earlier authority by finding differences in the material facts of the two cases (see section **7.10** on 'material facts'). Another method (and the one alluded to here) is to 'reclassify' what the earlier judge said as not really being part of the *ratio* of the earlier case and so not binding. We saw this at section **7.5** in the fictitious case of *Harry George* v *Down Ltd* where Judges (3) and (4) redefined what had been said in the earlier case of *Park* v *Moloney*.

continued

EXERCISE 12 *continued*

(3) **STRUCTURE THE ANSWER**. Do not leap into a discussion of the topic without planning the development of the essay. An examiner has difficulty following an answer that constantly repeats itself, restates points or arguments for no apparent reason, or makes sense from sentence to sentence but not from paragraph to paragraph. A safe bet is to begin with some (we stress *some*) introductory words.

For example:

You might then go on to explain the difference between *ratio decidendi* and *obiter dicta*:

> The doctrine of precedent is central to the development of common law. The doctrine of *stare decisis* provides the mechanism for the operation of judicial precedent. *Stare decisis* demands that where a decision has been made on a particular point of law then later inferior courts (or courts of equal status in many cases) must not be merely persuaded by the earlier decision, but are bound to follow it. In its strictest form, therefore, this approach promotes certainty. However, the doctrine does not mean that all judges are simply machines, applying fixed rules already laid down. If that were so then the two sides would probably not be arguing the point. The difficulty is that the doctrine demands that *like cases should be decided in the same way*. This always leaves room for deciding when two cases are sufficiently similar that the doctrine of *stare decisis* should be applied: i.e. cases can very often be distinguished on their facts and the key point of *stare decisis* rests in the analysis of the *ratio* and *obiter dicta* of the earlier case. It is the principle in the earlier case that must be followed, not merely the decision.

(4) **REFER TO THE QUESTION**. To obtain the best marks, you should try to relate your comments to the quotation. At various points in your answer review the relevance of parts of your answer to the quotation. Here is an example:

> We have said that the doctrine of *stare decisis* provides certainty. Thus we can say that the 'law' on a topic can be discovered, and *stare decisis*, in particular, narrows down the enquiry. But such an approach assumes that the principle of a case (its authority) is not open to interpretation itself. If, however, **as the question implies or at least suggests**, the judge has at some early stage decided which way the case should go then his task is one of showing how the authorities that he wishes to follow are very similar to the case before him; and how the other 'apparently' similar cases are based on entirely different facts. But even if one does not take such a cynical line, it is also true to say that the *ratio* of any case is not fixed and immutable. Different judges perceive cases as authority for differently stated principles.

(5) **REFER TO SOME CASES TO ILLUSTRATE YOUR ARGUMENTS**. Here you could use cases which distinguished other cases on seemingly minor points, for

continued

instance—or cases where a judge felt compelled to follow earlier cases even when he believed them to be wrong. You could choose cases from areas you have studied, e.g. contract law or criminal law. Legal method, remember, is about how law is analysed; it is not a separate subject in itself.

Cases are cited in a number of ways. We shall take this opportunity to look at these methods of citation. Here are five general examples of alternative methods. The case is on employment law and the legal definition of 'dismissal'. Do not worry about understanding the legal issues. The key point is that if an employee resigns he may still claim, in law, that he was dismissed. The aim of this provision is to prevent employers forcing an employee to resign without any remedy; it is referred to as 'constructive dismissal':

(a) In *Western Excavating* v *Sharp* an employee was short of money following disciplinary action by his employer. He asked for an advance of his pay but, in keeping with company regulations, this was refused. He resigned in order to obtain his holiday pay; and because he felt his employer was acting unreasonably. The question before the Court was: did a resignation because of 'unreasonable' conduct on the part of the employer fall within the legal definition of dismissal? The Court of Appeal held that a resignation could constitute a dismissal only where the employer had committed a serious breach of contract, not just because he may have been acting unreasonably. Hence there was no 'dismissal' here. [**NB: if you have time to do this for each case you cite in an examination you can write more quickly than any student we know!**]

[There is always a compromise to be drawn—even with coursework where there will be word limits—but the same is true in real cases where very often there are time limits to observe in making your submissions. So, the remaining examples make some form of compromise.]

(b) The principle was established in *Western Excavating* v *Sharp* that an employee can resign but still claim he was dismissed if the employer has seriously breached the contract. [NB: case names appear in italics in texts (underlined if handwritten). In essays it is always best to emphasise case names for clarity.]

(c) The Court of Appeal in *Western Excavating* v *Sharp* stressed that the employer must be in serious breach of contract, not just acting unreasonably, before an employee can resign and still claim he was dismissed.

(d) A resignation cannot be classed as a dismissal unless the employer has seriously breached the contract: *Western Excavating* v *Sharp*.

(e) In the 1970s there existed much judicial disagreement on when a resignation might constitute a dismissal. One camp argued that if the employer acted unreasonably this would constitute a constructive dismissal. Others pressed the point that what was required was a serious breach of contract on the employer's part. The issue was apparently settled in *Western Excavating* v *Sharp*, wherein the Court of Appeal pronounced in favour of the 'contract test'.

continued

EXERCISE 12 *continued*

(6) **CONCLUDE.** The reality of the quotation is probably that some judges feel they must adhere to precedent at all cost because this promotes certainty; while others take a more creative standpoint. In the end it is probably true to say that judges do both things: they adhere to precedent and also use or adapt precedent to justify their decisions. The statement merely confirms that, despite our strict views of *stare decisis*, there exists the role of choice in our judicial process. Judges, after all, try to achieve 'fairness'. And if judges did not modify the law from one year to the next then, as Lord Goff commented in *Kleinwort Ltd* v *Lincoln Council* [1999] AC 349: 'the common law would be the same now as it was in the reign of Henry II ... [but it] is a living system of law, reacting to new events and new ideas ...'. The idea that judges merely 'declare' what existed in the common law all along and do not actively make law was also finally put to rest (if anyone ever believed it) by Lord Browne-Wilkinson in the same case.

The statement also recognises the interpretative element in describing the *ratio* of a case. The finer points of distinguishing cases, or showing how one case relates to others, can lead to a justifiable disagreement as to what is the *ratio* of a case.

7.10 Material Facts

The facts of a case are revealed in the documents, statements, and evidence produced. All these are relevant to a case, but they are not all relevant to the *ratio* of the case. In our case of negligent driving, the legal reasoning is unlikely to hinge on whether the claimant was called Alfred, or what make of car he drove, or the colour of the car. Whether he was speeding is more **likely** to be material.

There is no set hierarchy of facts which will always be important or irrelevant. Change the issue before the court and different questions have to be posed. Alfred's name could be important where he is claiming that *he* is the 'Alfred' cited in a millionaire's will; so too his height, nickname, and age. The colour of the car might be the whole issue at stake in a breach of contract action where Alfred has ordered a red car and is presented with a yellow car which he refuses to accept, but most likely irrelevant in a road traffic accident.

7.10.1 Classifying Material Facts

Classifying which facts are 'material' and which are not is not an intuitive exercise; it is a skill developed through reading a lot of judgments. However, the first thing you always need to know is: what was the case about? What were the facts and what was the legal point being argued? In other words, what was the 'cause of action'? (see section **6.1.1** for the meaning of this term). Once you have established this then certain facts cannot be material because they cannot relate to the issues involved. The same applies to the 'Charge' in a criminal case.

Here are some examples:

(i) *Cause of action: negligence.* The key parts of this to prove are:
- the claimant was owed a duty of care by the defendant;
- the defendant breached that duty;
- there was an unbroken chain of events between breach and loss; and
- the type of loss suffered (e.g. the particular injury) was foreseeable.

So, the facts that will be 'material' are those which go to show these elements of the cause of action—which facts show 'breach' and which show 'type of loss'?

(ii) *Cause of action: private nuisance.* The claimant must show that the defendant:
- committed an act or omission;
- which interfered with, disturbed, or annoyed the claimant;
- in the exercise or enjoyment of his ownership or occupation of land or some right used or enjoyed in connexion with land.

(iii) *Cause of action: breach of contract.* The claimant must show:
- that there was a properly formed contract (i.e. that there was an offer which was accepted, there was intent to create legal relations and some consideration was exchanged);
- what the relevant terms were (express or implied) and that they were incorporated in the contract;
- breach by the defendant causing a type of loss which was within the contemplation of the parties when the contract was made.

Obviously not every case on each of these areas will be about all aspects of the cause of action. The cases will most likely focus on one legal issue. Strictly speaking, the only facts which can be 'material' are those relating to the parts of the case being argued about. So, any comments on other issues would not be 'material' and therefore not form part of the *ratio*. For instance, in a private nuisance action noted in (ii), the case might be about what is meant by 'the ownership or occupation of land or some right used or enjoyed in connexion with land'. Thus, the key feature of the case might be whether a person with a lease on a flat can bring an action for nuisance against a neighbour: is a lease covered by the law? It may have been accepted by the parties that, *if* a leaseholder had the right to claim, there was evidence of disturbance, etc. So, even if the judge details the problems with noise—which generated the claim—these comments are not 'material' to the decision of the rights of a leaseholder. In a breach of contract action, the argument might be about whether a term can be implied in the contract, so it will be the findings of fact on this issue that will be material.

7.10.2 Abstraction of Facts

The second thing you need to be aware of is that facts can be viewed as 'narrow' or 'general'. This depends upon the level of **abstraction** (or generalisation) with which one views the facts of a case; whether one takes only the literal facts as being relevant or one observes the facts as merely representing something wider. For instance: in **Figure 7.2**, how would you describe what you see?

Figure 7.2 Levels of abstraction

The different levels of 'abstraction' (ranging from the general to the more specific) include:

- A flower
- A white flower
- A Camellia
- A white Camellia
- A rose-form Camellia
- A white rose-form Camellia
- A (white) rose-form Camellia, April 2006
- A (white) rose-form Camellia in Bristol, April 2006.

So, to the question, 'How would you describe what you see?' all these answers are correct, but the level of detail is quite different. However, the relevance of this detail might not surface until you look back at the answer and try to apply it to a new question. That is when you face the problem whether the earlier case is authority for the law concerning (in our example) any flower or only Camellias or even only white rose-form Camellias.

In **Table 7.5** we show how this idea of abstraction of facts operates in a case-law context. The three columns, each representing a wider abstraction of facts, are based on the analysis by Stone (1959) of the case of *Donoghue* v *Stevenson*. We considered *Donoghue* v *Stevenson* in **Exercise 10** in deciding why two cases should be decided the same way. To repeat the facts in brief: Mrs Donoghue and a friend went into a cafe in Paisley. The friend ordered ice cream and ginger beer for both of them. The shopkeeper poured out some of the ginger beer over the ice cream. Mrs Donoghue consumed some of the mixture. Her friend poured out the remainder of the ginger beer for Mrs Donoghue and a decomposed snail fell out of the bottle. The bottle was of dark opaque glass so that the contents could not have been detected. Mrs Donoghue sued Stevenson (the manufacturer of the ginger beer) for negligently causing her injury. She succeeded.

Table 7.5 Abstraction of facts—based on *Donoghue* v *Stevenson* (source: Stone, 1959: 597)

Narrow facts	Wider facts	Widest interpretation of facts
1. The case is only about dead snails	The case is about the presence of any animal	The case is concerned with liability for any foreign body
2. The material point is only about the sale of liquids	The material point is that the bottle was opaque; the liquid is irrelevant	The case is about articles in containers, not necessarily bottles
3. The defendant must be a manufacturer of ginger beer	The defendant simply has to be a manufacturer of foodstuffs	Anyone dealing with an item for consumption is potentially liable
4. It is material that the plaintiff was a Scottish widow	It is material that the plaintiff was a woman	Any person may claim
5. A key point is that the snail was not visible	The snail was not discoverable without damaging the container	The defect must not be discoverable by anyone who could reasonably be expected to inspect the item

In the first column is a material fact that relates very closely to what happened. The next two columns go wider in their interpretation. Picture yourself as a judge and ask which level of generalisation you would adopt in a later case to see whether the decision in *Donoghue* v *Stevenson* should be applied. Our experience is that students are attracted to the 'widest interpretation of the facts' on points 1, 2, and 4; the 'wider facts' column tends to be preferred on points 3 and 5. You may feel differently.

The point of this experiment is that the wider you set your *abstraction* of the facts, the easier it is to apply one decision concerning a particular set of facts to another case concerning different facts. Conversely, a narrower abstraction will provide a more accurate description of what actually happened (and therefore the less challengeable the conclusion will be). However, this also means that you have limited the usefulness of the precedent when dealing with new cases because it is unlikely that the same facts will arise again.

Assessing whether facts are 'material' or not can therefore be a difficult exercise. There is no set formula because it depends upon how narrowly or widely you view each fact. The case of *Donoghue* v *Stevenson* is about dead snails, ginger beer, and a Scottish widow, but if that was all it stood for as an authority we would wait centuries before those facts resurfaced in a new case. Meanwhile, the slightest difference in facts would mean that when your client asked you for advice and she was an English widow, the drink was milk, and a dead mouse had emerged you would be starting your argument afresh. Clearly you would abstract from *Donoghue* v *Stevenson* a slightly wider set of material facts than this, but how wide?

In this light you might look again at *Grant* v *Australian Knitting Mills* in **Exercise 10** and consider whether the Court took a narrow or wide view of the material facts in *Donoghue*. You can follow this up by looking at a textbook on torts to discover what has happened to the principles enunciated in a simple 1932 case about dead snails. You will discover, surprisingly perhaps, that the law went through many twists and turns before the modern all-encompassing law of negligence appeared in about 1970 and that *Donoghue* v *Stevenson* did not receive immediate universal approval. For instance, in the leading textbook, *Salmond on Torts* (8th edn, 1934) it was said: 'We cannot do more than take Lord Atkin's general principle as a useful guide and it cannot be regarded as an authoritative proposition of law', and, in another leading text, *Pollock on Tort* (as late as 1951): 'It is inconceivable that all these doctrines have been overruled by the *ipse dixit* [meaning 'an unsupported statement'] of a single Lord of Appeal.' This is not rapturous approval.

One method we have tried as an exercise in discovering material facts, and which has proved successful with students, is to analyse the importance of facts by removing them one by one from the description of the case in hand and asking whether this would have made a difference to the decision. If the reasoning would have been altered and the decision would consequently have been different, it seems highly likely that something hinged on the now-missing fact. Hence the removed fact would appear to be 'material' and crucial to the formulation of the *ratio*.

7.10.3 Material Facts and the Question of 'What If [x] happened?'

We can attempt to put this into practice with one of the most famous cases in law: *Carlill* v *Carbolic Smoke Ball Co.* [1893] 1 QB 256. The defendants placed an advertisement in various newspapers relating to their product, 'The Carbolic Smoke Ball'. The advertisement claimed that by using the smoke ball properly the purchaser could avoid influenza, colds, and a whole variety of other complaints ranging from neuralgia to whooping cough. The claim was made that many thousands of these smoke balls had been sold and in no ascertained case was influenza contracted by those using the smoke ball. It was stated that a £100 reward would be paid to anyone who used the smoke ball properly and who still contracted these illnesses. The advertisement went on to say: '£1,000 is deposited with the Alliance Bank, Regent Street, showing our sincerity in the matter'. Mrs Carlill read the advertisement, bought one of the smoke balls, used it as directed, and caught influenza. She claimed the £100 'reward'.

The issue was whether the advertisement constituted an offer which could be accepted, or whether it was only an 'advertising puff'. If it was an offer, and had been validly accepted by Mrs Carlill's correct use of the smoke ball, there was a contract and she was entitled to the £100. One of the main arguments propounded by the defendant was that the vagueness of the document showed that no contract was ever intended.

Following the outbreak of the 'Russian Flu' pandemic in 1889 there were many other advertisements like this: *Dr Drake's Universal Pill*, for instance, claimed to cure, amongst many things, bad blood, underdevelopment, flat feet, smarting loins, and weakness of knees. Dr Williams' superbly-named *Pink Pills for Pale People* (a Canadian product) claimed to cure 'paralysis, anaemia and scrofula'. Medical science was not highly developed during this era and there were no key statutes dealing with quackery. Arguing a cause of action based on fraud would not have been seen as viable. Nor should one regard Mrs Carlill as some weak-minded, gullible individual. Many people bought these 'cures' and 'protections' in the hope of staving off illnesses, the causes of which were not understood.

When Mrs Carlill's claim came before the Court of Appeal she won her case. The question for us to address, then, is what should be the *ratio* of the case? For a true appreciation of this, of course, one would have to read the judgments. For the moment, however, we will take the case as described and ask: in formulating a *ratio* for *Carlill*, which facts would be material? Under the test proposed earlier we will eliminate or alter some of the facts. If this alters the reasoning and result of the case we can regard that affected fact as material:

- **If the advertisement had appeared in a shop window only, would that have made a difference to either the result or the *ratio*?** Unlikely. The case acknowledges that the offer was made to the 'world at large'. A smaller audience is hardly relevant. However, the use of a newspaper might carry with it more credibility than a shop window and so exhibit a greater degree of seriousness.

- **If Mrs Carlill had not used the smoke ball as directed, would that have made a difference?** This must be material because Mrs Carlill would otherwise not, in law, have accepted the terms of the offer. Hence, whatever the status of the advertisement, there could have been no contract.

- **If the sums of money had been £10 and £100, would that have made a difference?** The usual response to this is that the amount is generally immaterial. However, some would argue that the large amount (for 1893) indicated a serious intent on the part of the defendant and so is material. For instance, one of our past students once argued persuasively that the converse was true: that the sums of £100 and £1,000 set against the cost of the smoke ball (ten shillings—now 50p) showed that the tenor of the company's claim was so extravagant that it was only on the outer limit of being taken seriously. A smaller 'reward' might indicate sincerity more easily. (£100 would now be worth about £10,000 using a 'purchasing power' comparison.)

- **If the defendants had not deposited the £1,000, would that have made a difference?** Our experience in conducting this exercise is that this question causes a split in the student vote. Many feel that it is this element which lent intention to the defendants' claim. Others feel that the *promise* to deposit was the key point.

- **If the defendant had not promised that it had deposited a sum of money, would that have made a difference?** Most students draw the line here. The presence of the promise is seen as a vital factor in the case. The Carbolic Smoke Ball Company clearly felt that this is why it lost: shortly after the decision a new advertisement appeared, this time offering £200 reward but now minus both the testimonials and the promise of having deposited £1,000.

- **If Mrs Carlill had not known about the advertisement, but had bought the smoke ball anyway, would that have made a difference?** Here we enter the realms of the relevance of other case law. Other cases had tackled the problem as to whether one needs to know of an offer before performing an act in order to accept it legally. We put this question to reiterate that, though the analysis of material facts aids our understanding of the authority of a precedent, we must be aware that one case stands in relation to others, e.g. here *Williams v Carwardine* (1833) 5 C & P 566.

- **Mrs Carlill contracted influenza whilst using the smoke ball. What if she had not done so until some weeks after using it: would that have made a difference?** If you read the case you will find that Lindley and Bowen LJJ agreed on the outcome and on most aspects of the reasoning for the decision but, on closer scrutiny, you will find that they disagreed as to whether the claim made by the company was that the product would be effective only during its consumption or for a reasonable time afterwards. This did not matter on the facts as Mrs Carlill contracted influenza whilst taking the medicine—so they were disagreeing on an *obiter* point. But, if we take out the material fact of Mrs Carlill becoming ill whilst using the smoke ball and substitute that fact with one of her contracting the illness three weeks after finishing the course of medicine this disagreement might matter. The third judge, AL Smith LJ, did not engage in the debate. He said as regards this 'time' factor: 'It is not necessary to say which is the correct construction of this contract, for no question arises thereon.'

One final question, to show that legal analysis need not be merely an abstract exercise but relates to the society in which it operates.

- **Influenza in the nineteenth century was a more serious illness than it is generally perceived to be now (though some recent influenza scares have given us an insight into the panic levels that can be generated) and many people died in the epidemics, including one of Queen Victoria's grandchildren. So if the product claimed only to cure, say, bunions, do you think that that would have made a difference?** If you think there would have been a difference, is this because the question of seriousness and intent would have been affected? Or might it be that the judicial attitude would have been different for reasons really unconnected with legal technicalities, i.e. the social setting? Some years ago, one of our part-time degree students, a medical practitioner, once added a gloss to this: the smoke ball claimed to *prevent* an illness, whereas the 'bunion product' would be claiming to cure a condition. Thus, although concerned with a less serious topic, the bunion *cure* was less speculative and, as a *cure*, might be taken more seriously. Interestingly, while the advertisement in the *London Illustrated News* (the one we often see reprinted) claimed to 'positively cure' influenza, the advertisement in the *Pall Mall Gazette* (which Mrs Carlill read) did not make such a claim. It did not matter in the end, but had Mrs Carlill read the *London Illustrated News* her claim would have been even stronger.

We have been doing what many judges in later cases do when reviewing earlier authorities. Later judges must assess the extent to which the facts of the original case fit the case before them. In doing this they interpret the *ratio* of the earlier case by evaluating the importance of the facts: placing them in a narrow or wide setting. What we have not the space to do, however, is to consider whether the order in which one removes the facts might matter, or the effect of removing groupings of facts. You might wish to consider this with *Carlill*.

One interesting feature of *Carlill* is how the Carbolic Smoke Ball Company's lawyers assessed what they perceived as the material facts of the case. Just after the case, a new limited liability company was formed. The new company started producing the smoke ball, accompanied by its infamous aggressive advertising campaign. A new advertisement appeared, stating that, '£100 reward was recently offered by the Carbolic Smoke

Ball Company [and] many thousands of smoke balls were sold on these advertisements, but only three persons claimed the reward of £100, thus proving conclusively that this invaluable remedy will prevent and cure the above-mentioned diseases'. The company now offered a '£200 reward' should anyone use the smokeball and contract influenza etc. This time, however, no promise was made of £1,000 having been deposited in a bank, use of the smoke ball had to be supervised by the company at their premises, and a three-month time period for bringing a claim appeared in the small print. So, it is clear that the company's lawyers regarded the 'promise' element as the key material factor—and also guarded against any 'time' or 'usage' arguments as raised by Bowen and Lindley LJJ by imposing these new specific terms.

Mrs Carlill lived until 1942. She died aged 96, principally from old age but also from the effects of contracting influenza. It is not often commented upon that her husband was in fact a solicitor and probably the driving force behind this claim. The Carbolic Smoke Ball Company only lasted until 1896.

7.11　What Can Happen to a Case?

There are seven main possibilities:

(a) The case may be followed in its strictest form, or applied, in later cases. As we noted in **Chapter 6**, under the doctrine of *stare decisis* the earlier case may be followed even though the later judges disagree with it.

(b) Sometimes the later court may be superior in status to the earlier court. If it follows the reasoning of the inferior court it is said to have *approved* the earlier case. Obviously it may equally disapprove of or overrule the earlier case. Disapproval may diminish the status of the earlier case. In the case of overruling, the earlier case ceases to be an authority of any sort (unless an even more superior court reinstates it at a later date). *Overruling* is not that common, at least where the principle has been established for some time; but it does happen. In **Chapter 6**, for instance, we noted the case of *R v R* [1991] 3 WLR 767; [1991] 4 All ER 481 where the House of Lords overruled a long line of case law on marital rape; in *Pepper (Inspector of Taxes) v Hart* [1992] 3 WLR 1032; [1993] 1 All ER 42 the House of Lords did the same in connexion with the rules on statutory interpretation; in *Polkey v Dayton* [1987] AC 344; [1988] ICR 142 the House of Lords again overruled a decade's worth of Court of Appeal decisions on the question of determining fairness in an unfair dismissal.

(c) The term *overruling* tends to be applied when a court reviews previous precedents. However, if a court's decision is subject to an appeal the higher court obviously has to allow or dismiss the appeal. If the higher court reaches a different decision, it is said to *overturn* or *reverse* the decision of the lower court. The higher court might not overturn the actual result of the lower court (i.e. X still wins) but may reformulate the law or approve of only part of the decision in the lower court.

(d) When the facts are found to be dissimilar the later court is said to *distinguish* the earlier case. The art of distinguishing cases is a major weapon used by advocates, especially when confronted with problems of *stare decisis*. The attack is usually concentrated on showing a difference in the material facts of the two cases (see section **7.8.1**).

(e) The later case may decide that the decision in the earlier case was reached *per incu-riam*. As we noted in **Chapter 6**, this means that the earlier case missed some vital authority and that that omission would have made a difference to the decision.

(f) An Act of Parliament may change the law. Ironically, the example we have used in (b) since the first edition—the case of *Polkey* v *Dayton*—is a good illustration of this point too. In 2002, *Polkey* was limited in its effect by amendments made to the Employment Rights Act 1996 and the creation of a new section—s. 98A. The very case law *Polkey* had overturned was reinstated by this section. However, the Employment Act 2008 then removed s. 98A and thereby reinstated the analysis used in *Polkey*.

(g) The later case may state that the earlier case has no clear *ratio* and is therefore not binding. See on this *Esso* v *Commissioners of Customs and Excise*, detailed earlier.

EXERCISE 13 Tales from the grave

This exercise centres on the law of succession, in particular the requirement for a testator to sign a will in order for it to be valid. The purpose of the exercise is to examine the possible ways you might attack an earlier precedent to show why it should not be applied in your case. Although we have used a particular case, this is by way of illustration only. The techniques and questions raised here can be used in any exercise on criminal law, torts, contract, etc. where you are comparing cases.

The earlier precedent: In *Wood* v *Smith* [1992] 3 All ER 556 the testator made a will two days before he died which started, 'My will by Percy Winterborne ...'. He did not sign his name at the foot of the will and when the witnesses pointed this out to him he replied that he had signed it at the top (referring to the opening statement) and that it could be signed anywhere. The will was contested on the ground that it was not val-idly executed. The Court of Appeal held that this was indeed a valid signature for the purposes of the Wills Act 1837, s. 9 (as amended), so that the will was valid.

The relevant statute: Wills Act 1837, s. 9, states that no will shall be valid unless: '(a) it is in writing and signed by the testator ... (b) it appears that the testator intended by his signature to give effect to the will; and (c) the signature is made or acknowledged by the testator in the presence of two or more witnesses present at the same time ...'.

Your case: John Doe decided to make a will and purchased a 'will form' from a local shop. He started drafting it one day at work but was interrupted and did not complete the will until the following day. The first line of the will reads: 'John Doe—this is my last will and testament'. A witness pointed out to him that there was no signature on the will, but Doe said that this was all right since he had run out of space and pro-vided wills were written on 'will forms' there was no need to sign them. The will was properly witnessed.

 QUESTION

What devices (e.g. distinguishing the cases) could you use to argue that *Wood* v *Smith* does not apply to this case?

continued

EXERCISE 13 *continued*

 ANSWER

The best way to approach this exercise is to read *Wood* v *Smith* and all the cases it cites. You should concentrate on four things in particular:

(a) Which court are you in? This matters in relation to questions of *stare decisis*. Assume in this exercise that you are in the Court of Appeal.

(b) Exactly *why* did the Court of Appeal decide that the will was valid?

(c) What precise words did Scott LJ use to explain the decision?

(d) What differences in material facts can you find?

Whether or not you have had the opportunity to read the case, consider the following points in your argument.

Attack 1: Argue that the earlier case should not apply to the present one

(a) Is the case of *Doe* distinguishable on its facts from *Wood* v *Smith*?

(b) Is the case of *Doe* distinguishable as regards the issue of law raised in *Wood* v *Smith*?

Attack 2: If the case is not distinguishable, argue that *stare decisis* has no application

(c) Was there a clear *ratio* in *Wood* v *Smith*?

(d) Was the decision in *Wood* v *Smith* made *per incuriam*; or did it at least misinterpret the reasoning in earlier cases?

(e) When *Wood* v *Smith* had to decide matters that had not been raised in earlier cases, was the reasoning doubtful or unclear?

(f) Has *Wood* v *Smith* been doubted in other cases?

(g) Are there any decisions of the same level which conflict with *Wood* v *Smith*?

(h) Are there substantive conflicts in the reports of the case found in the All England Law Reports and the Weekly Law Reports?

(i) Were there any *obiter* statements which might help because they show that had the present facts arisen the Court would have decided differently?

Attack 3: Argue that the case should be bypassed on more general grounds

(j) Has *Wood* v *Smith* been criticised by academic writers?

(k) Were the words used by Scott LJ clear as to why the will was valid; and were those words limited to the special circumstances of *Wood* v *Smith*?

(l) Have social conditions changed so radically that the earlier case should be doubted in a modern setting? (Not particularly useful in relation to *Wood* v *Smith* itself.)

One can see much of this at work in the cases flowing from *Donoghue* v *Stevenson*. However, by way of giving a different example we shall turn to the postal rules of acceptance in the law of contract to illustrate the development of a *ratio*.

7.12 The Postal Rule Cases

In **Chapter 6** we took some of the 'postal rules' cases as examples of how judges use earlier authorities. We attempted to show that the doctrine of judicial precedent is not simply a mechanical process of matching similarities and differences; cases can appear to be similar at first glance, without necessarily proving to be so. As promised, we return to these cases to illustrate the development of a rule (see **Table 7.6**).

The format for this part of the chapter is to combine a description of the development of a simple rule with some exercise-type questions. You should be able to formulate opinions on the information provided; but, as always, you might devise better answers if you read the cases themselves.

As we explained in **Chapter 6**, a contract is formed when there is an offer which is accepted, without the addition of new terms, by the other party. The general rule is that acceptance has to be communicated. If the offeree communicates by post, when does the acceptance take place? When the letter of acceptance is posted, or only when it arrives with the offeror?

The first 'postal rule' case (some would argue, the first case on what we now term the rules of 'offer and acceptance') was *Adams v Lindsell* (1818) 1 B & A 681. Here an offer was made by post to sell some wool. The letter was sent on 2 September, reply to be by return of post. The letter was misaddressed and was not received until 5 September. It was accepted by post immediately. On 7 September the offeror had not received his reply by return of post and sold the wool elsewhere the day after. The letter of acceptance arrived on 9 September. Was there a contract established by these letters? If there was a contract, then the seller was in breach because he had sold the wool to another person.

Held: There was a contract at the moment the offeree posted the letter of acceptance.
Questions:

- *How would you present the* ratio *of this case?*
- *Which facts should be seen as material; and how wide a description would you give to them?*
- *Should it be a material fact, for instance, that the offeror misaddressed the offer letter, but that the letter of acceptance did eventually arrive?*

Table 7.6 Development of a rule—based on the postal rule (1)

Possible narrow ratio	*Possible wider ratio*
Where an offer to form a contract is sent by post but is late reaching its destination because the letter was misaddressed by the offeror, the acceptance will be valid from the moment of posting, provided the offeree complies with the relevant conditions of the offer and the acceptance eventually arrives.	If the offeror chooses to use the post as a means of communicating an offer, he must take the consequences. Thus, he will be bound by a postal acceptance from the moment the acceptance is posted.

Dunlop v *Higgins* (1848) 1 HLC 381; 9 ER 805 was the next case to deal with this problem (see **Table 7.7**), as we noted in **Chapter 6**. Dunlop wrote to Higgins offering to sell some iron; reply to be by return of post. The offer was accepted by Higgins in a letter but bad weather delayed the post. In the meantime there had been an increase in the price of iron. Dunlop maintained that because the reply had not been by return of post there was no contract—which would allow them to sell to other customers at the new price.

Held: The House of Lords decided that a contract existed when the letter of acceptance was posted.

Questions:

- *How would you present the* ratio *of this case?*
- *Which facts should be seen as material?*
- *Should it be a material fact that the parties were trading companies?*
- *How does this decision alter the original principle established in* Adams v Lindsell? *Is the 'postal rule' now (in 1848) wider or narrower? For instance, does it now matter that, in* Adams v Lindsell, *the offeror misaddressed the offer letter?*

Table 7.7 Development of a rule—based on the postal rule (2)

Possible narrow ratio	Possible wider ratio
Where an offer to form a contract is sent by post but the acceptance is late reaching its destination because of bad weather, the acceptance will be valid from the moment of posting, provided there is a trade usage to use the post and the letter of acceptance is properly addressed.	The use of the post is an exception to the rule that communication of acceptance must be effective. If the offeror chooses to use the post as the means of communicating an offer, he must take the consequences. Thus, he will be bound by a postal acceptance from the moment it is posted, provided the letter eventually arrives.

Effect on *Adams* v *Lindsell:* The narrow *ratio is* formulated differently and one would now (in 1848) need to ask whether the offeror's error in *Adams* v *Lindsell* is crucial to the point (see **Table 7.8**). The possible formulation of the wider *ratio* has not changed substantially. However, you will remember that in **Chapter 6** we saw that the judges in *Household Fire* v *Grant* (see immediately below) disagreed about the real meaning of *Dunlop* v *Higgins*.

In *Household Fire Insurance Co.* v *Grant* (1879) 4 Ex D 216 Grant made an application in writing to the company for shares. A deposit was paid, the remainder to be paid within twelve months. The company allotted shares to Grant and posted the allotment to him. The letter never arrived. The company later went into liquidation and the liquidator sought the balance of Grant's application which was still outstanding. Grant maintained he had no contract with the company because his offer had not been accepted. No contract would mean no liability to pay. The company maintained that the offer had been accepted when their letter of acceptance had been posted, even though it never arrived.

Held: Grant was liable to pay the outstanding amount on the shares. The letter of acceptance was valid on posting even though it never arrived.
Questions:

- *How would you present the* ratio *of this case?*
- *Which facts should be seen as material?*
- *Should it be a material fact that the letter of acceptance never arrived?*
- *How does this decision alter the original principle established in* Adams v Lindsell? *Is the 'postal rule' now (in 1879) wider or narrower?*

Table 7.8 Development of a rule—based on the postal rule (3)

Possible narrow ratio	*Possible wider ratio*
Where an offer to form a contract is sent by post the acceptance will be valid from the moment of posting even though it never arrives, provided the letter of acceptance is properly addressed and the parties expressly or impliedly agree to the use of the post as a means of communication.	If the offeror chooses to use the post as a means of communicating an offer, he must take the consequences. The non-arrival of the letter of acceptance does not alter the general rule.

Effect on *Adams v Lindsell*: The narrow *ratio* is formulated differently and one would now (in 1879) need to ask whether the late arrival of the letter of acceptance in *Adams v Lindsell* was crucial to the point.

In *Henthorn v Fraser* [1892] 2 Ch 27 (CA) Henthorn visited Fraser's offices. Henthorn was given an option to purchase a house (i.e. an offer). Fraser withdrew the offer by letter, but not before Henthorn had accepted by post. So the letters crossed in the post. All letters arrived at their destinations on time. (See **Table 7.9**.)

Held: The acceptance was valid when posted. The rule was not limited to trade usage but, in the words of Lord Herschell, extended to: 'Where the circumstances are such that [the use of the post] must have been within the contemplation of the parties'.
Questions:

- *How would you present the* ratio *of this case?*
- *Which facts should be seen as material?*
- *Should it be a material fact that Fraser was attempting to withdraw the offer by use of the post?*
- *How does this decision alter the original principle established in* Adams v Lindsell? *Is the 'postal rule' now (in 1892) wider or narrower? For instance, has the fact that the offer was not made by post made a difference?*

Table 7.9 Development of a rule—based on the postal rule (4)

Possible narrow ratio	*Possible wider* ratio
An acceptance which arrives at its destination will be valid from the moment of posting, provided the letter of acceptance is properly addressed and the parties expressly or impliedly agree to the use of the post as a means of communication. This applies even where the offer was made in person and not by post.	Where the circumstances allow for the use of the post as a means of communicating as acceptance the offeror must take the consequences. Where the parties live in different cities, there may be an indication that using the post is acceptable.

Effect on *Adams* v *Lindsell*: The narrow *ratio* is again formulated differently and one would now (in 1892) need to ask whether much of what actually happened in *Adams* v *Lindsell* is now regarded as crucial to the point.

Finally, for our purposes, we have the case of *Holwell Securities* v *Hughes* [1974] 1 WLR 155; [1974] 1 All ER 161. Here, an offer of an option to purchase property was sent by post. It stated: 'The option shall be exercisable by notice in writing to the vendor within six months.' Holwell accepted the offer, properly addressing the letter; but the letter never arrived (see **Table 7.10**).

Held: There was no contract. The acceptance was not valid on posting. The specific wording of the offer letter showed that the acceptance was only valid when delivered to the offeror. The postal rules were held not to apply in all cases where there is postal acceptance: '[They] probably do not operate if their application would produce manifest inconvenience and absurdity'. *Adams* v *Lindsell* was distinguished.

Questions:

- *How would you present the* ratio *of this case?*
- *Which facts should be seen as material?*
- *How does this decision alter the original principle established in* Adams v Lindsell? *Is the 'postal rule' now (in 1974) wider or narrower? For instance, can we now say that the postal rules can be excluded? If so, do we know which other forms of wording will be effective?*

Table 7.10 Development of a rule—based on the postal rule (5)

Possible narrow ratio	*Possible wider* ratio
Where an option (offer) is granted in writing and specifies that the acceptance must be 'by notice in writing to the vendor' an acceptance which is never delivered will not be valid from the moment of posting.	The language used in the offer may be such that the express terms override the postal rules. The postal rules are rules of convenience only.

We can now pose five questions to conclude this discussion:

(a) If you were writing a textbook on the law of contract, how would you present a general principle which would summarise these cases and describe the 'postal rules of acceptance'?

(b) Do you think the development of this area of law was affected by socio-economic matters such as the fact that in 1818 there was no real postal service?

(c) If the cases had occurred in a different sequence, do you think the rule might have been differently formulated?

(d) Should these rules, by analogy, be applied to other forms of communication, e.g. telex, fax, email, text messages, or messenger rider?

(e) *Adams* v *Lindsell* was the seminal case from which all the other cases cited are directly descended. Do you think the judges in *Adams* v *Lindsell* could have forecast how their judgment would be applied in those later cases? After all, much of what seemed to matter in 1818 has probably disappeared. So is the position analogous to Dr Jacob Bronowski's comment on the 'Ascent of Man': that the ancestors of human-kind two million years ago would not recognise us today as their own descendants?

7.13 The 'Uncertainty Principle' of Cases

Our final comment on the development of case law brings us to a theory in physics known as the 'Heisenberg Uncertainty Principle'. One of the themes we have tried to develop throughout this chapter is that later cases often change our perceptions of earlier cases. This often causes students problems, but, as we have said, discerning the *ratio* of a case is not like a hunt for buried treasure; it is one of interpretation and argument.

The problem is not unique to legal studies. The German physicist, Werner Heisenberg, argued in 1927 that as soon as you set about investigating an object you alter its state. If, for instance, you try to measure the temperature of a hot bath, then the introduction of the thermometer alters the temperature—however slightly (we accept the points made by physicists who have read this text and who have politely informed us that this is a bit of an oversimplification). The same is true with reading legal cases: the supposed *ratio* of an earlier case is open to reinterpretation by lawyers in later cases. Once the earlier case is looked at in the light of a new set of facts, the perception of the case may be altered. Further, the way you phrase your question as to the meaning of the earlier case has an impact—which facts you concentrate on; which judicial phrase you subject to scrutiny.

In *Adams* v *Lindsell*, for instance, there is a marked difference in asking: (a) is the case authority for the rule that acceptance does not always have to be communicated? and (b) is the case authority for the proposition that an offeror must always accept the risk for any mistakes he makes in *his* communication? The question posed as to the relevance of *Adams* v *Lindsell* will depend upon the facts of the case in front of you now and the issues thereby raised.

EXERCISE 14 Parking tickets and Jiffy bags

 1. Please read the facts of *Thornton* v *Shoe Lane Parking*. What is your formulation of the *ratio* of the case?

Question 2 follows the case description. It would be best if you could read the actual reports of the cases. Failing that, however, we provide a short summary of the issues raised.

continued

EXERCISE 14 *continued*

 Thornton v Shoe Lane Parking [1971] 2 QB 163; [1971] 1 All ER 686

The plaintiff drove into the entrance to the defendant's automatic car park. A notice outside stated: 'All cars parked at owner's risk.' He took a ticket from the machine, the automatic barrier lifted and he drove into the garage. He looked at the ticket to see the time printed on it. The plaintiff also noticed some printed words on the ticket which he did not read. When he went to collect the car an accident occurred in which he suffered personal injuries, partly through the negligence of the defendant garage.

The defendant admitted fault but relied on the ticket which contained the clause: '... *issued subject to the conditions of issue as displayed on the premises*'. These conditions were displayed on the back of the ticket; they were lengthy, and excluded liability on the part of the garage for loss or damage to customers' property, or personal injury, howsoever caused. These, said the defendant, were contractual clauses which bound the plaintiff.

Mocatta J. held the defendants liable. They appealed.

Lord Denning reviewed the relevant cases, some of which are noted here:

- *Parker* v *South Eastern Railway* (1877) 2 CPD 416. The plaintiff deposited a bag in a railway cloakroom. He was handed a ticket on which were the words 'see back'; on the back there were printed conditions excluding liability for loss or damage. The bag was lost. The Court of Appeal held that the key questions were:

    (a) Did the plaintiff read the clause?

    (b) Did the railway company do what was reasonably sufficient to give the plaintiff notice of the clause?

- *Olley* v *Marlborough Court Ltd* [1949] 1 KB 532; [1949] 1 All ER 127. It was held that a notice in a hotel bedroom which excluded liability for damage to guests' luggage was not valid, as the contract had been made in the lobby of the hotel so that notice of the clause came too late.

Lord Denning dismissed the appeal. He indicated that the 'ticket cases' such as *Parker* were based on the theory that the customer, on being handed the ticket, could refuse it and decline to enter the contract on those terms. However real that theory was, it could not apply to a ticket which was issued by an automatic machine: 'The customer pays his money and gets his ticket. He cannot get his money back. He may protest to the machine, even swear at it; but it will remain unmoved.'

Lord Denning applied the reasoning given in *Olley* v *Marlborough Court*. In *Thornton* the offer was contained in the notice at the entrance giving the charges for garaging and saying 'at owner's risk'. The acceptance took place when the customer put his money into the slot. The terms of the offer contained in the notice placed on or near the machine could be binding only if they were sufficiently brought to his notice *before* the contract was concluded. So, once the customer had accepted the offer, a contract was concluded on the terms known to exist which could not then be altered.

Parker v *South Eastern Railway* meant that, unless the customer knows that the ticket is issued subject to a clause to be found on the back of the ticket, or the company did what was reasonably sufficient to give him notice of it, the company cannot avoid liability by relying on the later exclusion clause.

continued

EXERCISE 14 *continued*

Counsel for the defendants admitted here that the defendants did not do what was reasonably sufficient to give the plaintiff notice of the exempting condition. Lord Denning held that the exclusion clause was:

> so wide and so destructive of rights that the court should not hold any man bound by it unless it is drawn to his attention in the most explicit way … In order to give sufficient notice, it would need to be printed in red ink with a red hand pointing to it, or something equally startling.

Lord Justice Megaw also dismissed the appeal. He declined to comment on when the contract was concluded. As regards the other points, His Lordship was in general agreement with Lord Denning MR. Under the three conditions noted in *Parker*, he concluded that the plaintiff in *Thornton* did not know of any printing on the ticket or, therefore, that there were any contractual conditions. As well as this, however, His Lordship laid stress on the fact that the conditions in this contract contained the sorts of restrictions that were unusual. Thus:

> at least where the particular condition relied on involves a sort of restriction that is not shown to be usual in that class of contract, a defendant must show that his intention to attach an unusual condition of that particular nature was fairly brought to the notice of the other party.

Lord Justice Megaw thus linked the type of clause in question (whether it was an unusual or usual clause in this type of contract) to the amount of effort needed on the defendant's part to bring the clause to the notice of the customer.

Sir Gordon Willmer agreed with both Lord Denning and Megaw LJ, saying: 'any attempt to introduce conditions after the irrevocable step has been taken of causing the machine to operate must be doomed to failure'.

2. **Read this second case—*Interfoto Picture Library Ltd v Stiletto Visual Programmes Ltd* [1988] 1 All ER 348; [1988] 2 WLR 615—and:**

   (a) decide whether the *ratio* of *Thornton* applies;

   (b) reach a decision on the *Interfoto* case;

   (c) formulate a *ratio* for your decision, either applying the *Thornton ratio* (in whole or part) or distinguishing *Thornton* on the facts.

> The defendant ordered certain photographic transparencies from the plaintiff. The photographs were consigned in a jiffy bag to the company messenger with the 'delivery note'. The defendant's manager ignored the note but, impressed by the contents of the bag, telephoned his acceptance.
>
> There were a number of conditions contained in the delivery note. Condition 2 set the daily charge for retaining the transparencies beyond the stipulated date of return. These charges were exorbitant, representing a figure ten times higher than that charged by other comparable agencies. The central issue was whether condition 2 was enforceable by the plaintiffs.

We provide no answer for this exercise except to indicate one or two salient points. The first is that the *Interfoto* case is interesting because it posed the question

continued

EXERCISE 14 *continued*

whether the logic used for a number of years and in a number of cases regarding one type of clause—one which *excluded* liability—could be applied to a 'similar' type of clause: one which sought to impose onerous terms on the other party. The second is that if you read the case in full you will see that there were only two judges in the Court of Appeal. It is as well that they agreed with each other as to the outcome of the case.

The final point is that the judges were not in full agreement as regards how the law should be expressed. The decision reached was the same: that condition 2 was not valid; but the reasoning employed by the judges differed greatly. Lord Justice Dillon took a conventional line of arguing from precedents. All the existing precedents concerned exclusion clauses and he drew a correlation between these 'exclusion' clauses and the 'onerous' clause contained in this contract. Lord Justice Bingham took a wider, more European, approach and looked to general notions of 'acting in good faith' to hold that the clause could not stand. This conceptual style of reasoning is very interesting; especially as there is no formula for defining 'good faith' in the English law of contract.

To see how academics reacted to this case at the time, we strongly recommend you to read the contrasting views seen in the following articles: Chandler and Holland (1988) 104 LQR, 359; McLean (1988) 47 CLJ, 172; MacDonald (1988) LMCLQ, 294.

To see how the case was employed in the next important case on this topic, see *Circle Freight International Ltd* v *Medeast Gulf Exports Ltd* [1988] 2 Lloyd's Rep 427. This case involved two businesses which had frequently dealt with each other on standard terms. These terms, which included an exclusion clause, had never been read by the party who suffered loss. Were these terms effectively incorporated into the contract?

 CONCLUSION

Discovering the *ratio* of a case and predicting how that *ratio* will be interpreted and applied in the future are some of the skills with which a lawyer must come to grips. There is no magic formula for acquiring these skills; they develop from practice. In turn, that practice must have some thought behind it. Reading a coaching text on your favourite sport will not, in itself, make you an Olympic athlete; and practising without analysing your play will get you only marginally further.

The key point we wish to make with this chapter is that there is nothing resembling a template that can be placed over a decision to highlight and reveal the *ratio* of the case. Whether it is a student, a practitioner, or a judge reading the case the exercise is still one of interpretation; and that form of exercise extends to persuasive precedents as well as binding ones.

Perhaps the most helpful thing we can offer is to address some of the most commonly raised questions we have had from students over the years. In **Table 7.11** we have listed these student questions in the left-hand column and provided some short answers opposite.

Table 7.11 Students' FAQs relative to the *ratio* of a case

Does each case have one defined *ratio*?	**No.** There is no 'fixed' *ratio* to a case, though there may be a generally accepted one (e.g. to be found in textbooks or in later cases). When you first start to study law, you will have to accept these texts as accurate, but, later, with experience, you will develop your own ability to question other lawyers' analysis.
Can a case stand for more than one legal principle?	**Yes.** A case may contain more than one *ratio*. This depends on what part of the case you are examining and why you are analysing it. The *Thornton* case above is a good example: there are statements about the incorporation of exclusion clauses and also statements as to when a contract is formed through the use of a ticket machine.
What does the *ratio* consist of?	In general terms the *ratio* of a case is made up of a legal principle based on: (i) existing case law prior to the case in hand; (ii) the material facts of the case; (iii) the decision in the case.
Materiality: do judges make this obvious?	**No.** Judges sometimes expressly state that they regard particular facts as 'material'. But, most often, you have to work this out by inference from the judgment.
Can later courts reassess the importance of the facts of the earlier case?	**Yes.** Facts may not appear to be 'material' until looked at later in comparison to a new case, i.e. even if a judge says that certain facts are material that does not determine the status of those facts forever. The status of those facts can (*sometimes*) be reassessed in later cases (see the 'negligent driving' example earlier; and the development of 'non-natural use' in *Rylands* v *Fletcher*).
Can later courts promote other facts (which the first judge seemed to rate as not a 'material' part of the decision) to the status of now being classed as 'material'?	**Yes.** Other facts which did not appear that important at first sight in the earlier case might be seen to be material when that case is later analysed. Again, we saw this with the driving example above. In fact, this reflects human nature—things that did not seem that important are viewed differently when new circumstances arise.
What is meant by 'abstraction of facts'?	Facts may be viewed as narrow or representative of something wider (see the 'Scottish widow' or 'dead snail' examples in *Donoghue* v *Stevenson*). **This is the basis of arguing that an earlier case should be 'applied' or 'distinguished'.**
Can you have different 'levels' of *ratio*?	**Yes.** In the same way that one fact may be taken as a literal example (ginger beer) or representational (drink) or more abstract (consumable item, or even any product), so too can the *ratio* of a case exist at different levels. A case concerning a lorry driver, for instance, may just be about lorry drivers' liabilities but it may also be about professional drivers or even any drivers. This is one of the key points to observe in the 'abstraction of fact'.

Who creates the 'legal principles'?	**Judges.** Cases do not exist in a legal vacuum. It is very unlikely that the case you are examining was the first of its kind. There will be a whole history of similar cases before it. These have to be looked at, as the legal principle involved in those cases will have helped to determine the 'materiality' of the facts in the case being examined. You need to know why facts were regarded as material and the extent to which *stare decisis* has influenced the judge's analysis in order to formulate a *ratio*.
Is it important *how* the judge expresses the legal principle?	**Vital:** the exact words used by a judge are at the core of ascertaining the *ratio* of a case. The judge may have thought the words used were clear, but all words are open to interpretation. This is why reading a summary in a textbook or on a database (or even the headnote to the case) is inadequate legal research.
What happens when you have more than one judgment in a case?	Each judge in a case may give a judgment (formerly called an 'opinion' in the House of Lords but this has changed to 'judgment' in the Supreme Court). Each judgment given will contain a *ratio*. The overall *ratio* of the case is derived from the *rationes* of the majority judgments. Thus, we have seen that there can be substantial argument as to what the *ratio* of a single judge's decision might be and this is made even more problematic when trying to formulate a 'general' *ratio* of the combined judgments. Differences in the individual *rationes* of judges (even those who agree on the overall result) often relate to different emphasis being placed on material facts or the use of particular words to describe the legal position (e.g. the *Interfoto* example above).

CHAPTER REFERENCES

BINGHAM, T. (2000), *The Business of Judging: Selected Essays and Speeches* (Oxford: Oxford University Press).

*CROSS, R. (1991), *Precedent in English Law* (4th edn, Oxford: Clarendon Press).

DWORKIN, R. (1987), *Law's Empire* (London: Fontana).

GOODHART, A. (1931), *Essays in Jurisprudence and the Common Law* (Cambridge: Cambridge University Press).

GOODHART, A. (1959), 'The *Ratio Decidendi* of a Case', 22 *Modern Law Review*, 117.

LLEWELLYN, K. (1960), *The Bramble Bush* (Chicago, Ill.: University of Chicago Press).

MACCORMICK, N. (1987), 'Why Cases have *Rationes* and What these Are', in L. Goldstein (ed.), *Precedent in Law* (Oxford: Clarendon Press).

MONTROSE, J. (1957), 'The *Ratio Decidendi* of a Case', 20 *Modern Law Review*, 587.

STONE, J. (1959), 'Ratio of the *Ratio Decidendi*', 22 *Modern Law Review*, 597.

TUROW, S. (1988), *One L: What They Really Teach You at Harvard Law School* (London: Sceptre).

TWINING, W. and MIERS, D. (1991), (1999), and (2010), *How to Do Things with Rules* (3rd, 4th, and 5th edns, London: Weidenfeld & Nicolson and later Cambridge: Cambridge University Press).

8

Making Sense of Statutes

8.1 Introduction

On the whole, statutes are not a fun read. Worse still, they are written in a style and format quite different from those of many other documents (though insurance documents and many credit card agreements are written in similarly dense styles). The language used is traditional (if not archaic) and often has a very flat-prose style and a dependence on complex phrasing and language (see Maughan and Webb, 2006). But, of course, an Act is not meant to be a piece of amusing literature; it is not designed to entertain but to declare the law on a particular topic.

The aim of this chapter, therefore, is to introduce you to the techniques and problems of analysing the **structure** of statutes. Making sense of statutes (or, at least, some statutes) can be a real problem for students, practitioners, and judges alike. However, legal method tutors from around the world have told us that, for some reason, students are having more trouble *reading* statutes than used to be the case.

So, before we look at how to interpret statutes in the next chapter, we need to begin by describing how statutes are set out, what tricks are employed, what particular catchphrases mean, and how to make sense of the opaque language often used. For an extremely good explanation of how we inherited the system we have today and also why, as one author puts it, 'The language of our legislation cannot be reduced to baby talk for consumption by the masses', see Hunt, 2002: 24.

In **Chapter 3** we dealt with the basics of what statutes look like, e.g. how sections are organised and the use of subsections, schedules, long titles, etc. (recapped in **Table 8.1**) and in **Chapter 9** we will explore the techniques used to *interpret* words in a statute. In this chapter we are concerned with finding the best way to read, understand, and analyse the structure used—in other words, how to work your way through what is often a very complex layout. The problem arises because there are always many different ways of explaining even the simplest idea and what is an acceptable arrangement of the material to one person is confusion to another.

We have ignored the pattern by which legislation is grouped into 'Parts', 'Chapters', 'Headings', and 'Marginal notes' in this summary and we will deal with European legislation in **Chapter 11**. Further, particularly with sections in an Act, there may be even more sub-divisions. Section 34 Theft Act 1968, for instance, breaks down to s. 34(2)(a)(i) while s. 2 Law of Property Act 1925 uses a slightly different layout, with the Roman numeral (v) coming before the lower case (a): s. 2(3)(v)(a). If further divisions are needed, draftsmen then conscript Greek letters.

Table 8.1 Recap on the basic structure of UK legislation

Title	Main division	Sub-division	Main sub-sub-division
Statute	Section e.g. s. 1	Subsection e.g. s. 1(1)	Paragraph e.g. s. 1(1)(a)
Schedule to a statute	Paragraph e.g. sch. 1, para 1	Sub-paragraph e.g. sch. 1, para 1(a)	(None)
Statutory Instrument*	Regulations (or Rules) e.g. reg. 1 (or r. 1)	Paragraphs e.g. reg. 1(1)	Sub-paragraphs e.g. reg. 1(1)(a)

* Statutory Instruments often appear with the title 'Order', as with The Public Bodies (Abolition of the Commission for Rural Communities) Order 2012 or 'Regulation', as with The Transfer of Undertakings (Protection of Employment) Regulations 2006. Both forms have the same type of citation (year and number) as in SI 2006/246.

8.2 Drafting Styles

Imagine you have been given the job of drafting a rule defining when a ball (in whatever sport) is 'in' play or 'out of' play. First, you need instructions from the rules committee as to what it wants: does it want a ball which is 'on the line' to be in play or out of play? (it varies with different sports, e.g. in football and tennis the line is in play but in golf the line itself is out of bounds). Let us assume here that the committee wants the line to be 'in play'. So, how could we put this into rule form?

The simplest method must be something like: 'A ball is always in play until it has completely crossed the line.' Rule 22 of the International Tennis Federation's Rules puts it like this: 'A ball falling on a line is regarded as falling in the Court bounded by that line.' FIFA's rules for football (law 9) talk of a ball being in play until it has 'wholly crossed the [line]' but add 'whether on the ground or in the air'. But this still only provides us with a very simple formulation; it does not cover exceptions and does not add definitions. So a draftsman has to consider how these extra elements will be woven into the document. Should he or she start with a general point and then add variations? Or maybe begin with definitions and then go on to the rule itself? Or deal with each individual aspect of the rule, bit by bit?

It is often quite easy to explain rules to someone orally because you can keep going back over points of confusion, or put things in slightly different ways. In a written document such devices are not available. So, a draftsman has to spell out the idea as fully as possible.

Table 8.2 provides an example of how two different draftsmen might use quite dissimilar methods of drafting to convey the same message using (very nearly) the same words but arranging them quite differently. We shall use the term 'playing field' here, though the rule could refer to a 'court' or 'pitch', etc.

Note that the first style uses phrases such as 'subject to ...' in s. 1 and both styles use 'for the purposes of ...', together with cross-references to later sections or schedules in the Act. This is not everyday speech. Both versions also attempt to state general points and then move onto the specific definitions, etc. The second version does this by avoiding using 'subject to ...' and similar phrases, but it still has to include cross-references and has also had to include an additional section. In the end, both these methods of explanation say the same thing and each of them uses techniques common in drafting statutes. You will encounter various forms of drafting throughout your studies and in practice and we therefore aim in this chapter to give you some clues as to how to recognise and utilise them.

Table 8.2 Contrasting drafting styles

First drafting style	Second drafting style
Section 1: Subject to sections 2 and 3 of this Act a ball is always in play until the whole of the ball has crossed the relevant line forming the border of the playing field	*Section 1:* A ball is always in play until the whole of the ball has crossed the relevant line forming the border of the playing field. ...
Section 2: For the purposes of section 1, and subject to section 3(1), the whole of the ball has crossed the relevant line only when it has cleared the outside boundary of the relevant line.	*Section 2:* For the purposes of section 1 'whole of the ball' shall mean the full circumference of the ball, as would be evident if viewed directly from above.
Section 3: For the purposes of this Act: (1) 'ball' shall mean only a ball which complies with the official measurements as authorised by [the governing body]; (2) 'line' shall mean only the official measurements of a line as authorised by [the governing body], these being set out in Schedule 1 to this Act. (3) any reference to the term 'whole of the ball' shall be construed as relating to the full circumference of the ball as would be evident if viewed directly from above. (4) a ball is: (a) in play unless and until it has been propelled by a player across any line of the playing area or it has been struck by a player and rebounds from the referee so as to cross the line; but (b) is out of play where the whole of the ball has crossed the line.	*Section 3:* A ball will remain in play unless and until: (a) it has been propelled by a player across any line of the playing area; or (b) it has been struck by a player and rebounds from the referee so as to cross the line. provided always that the whole of the ball, as defined in section 4, has not cleared the outside boundary of the relevant line.
	Section 4: For the purposes of this Act the words 'ball' and 'line' shall mean only balls and lines which comply with the official measurements as authorised by [the governing body], these being set out in Schedule 1 to this Act.

A good place to start with real drafting practices is with a fairly straightforward stat-ute, namely the Theft Act 1968. Section 1 is headed 'Basic Definition of Theft' and it reads as follows:

> (1) A person is guilty of theft if he dishonestly appropriates property belonging to another with the intention of permanently depriving the other of it; and "thief" and "steal" shall be construed accordingly.
>
> (2) It is immaterial whether the appropriation is made with a view to gain, or is made for the thief's own benefit.
>
> (3) The five following sections of this Act shall have effect as regards the interpretation and opera-tion of this section (and, except as otherwise provided by this Act, shall apply only for purposes of this section).

The language used is not particularly complicated, but there are a number of techni-calities and hidden depths. For instance, what is meant by 'dishonestly'? What does 'appropriation' mean? Where would you find the answers to these questions? In one sense these are matters of interpretation and therefore fall within the province of **Chapter 9**, but, in structural terms, the Theft Act 1968 is set out in a very helpful way, so that all the words in s. 1 are expanded upon in subsequent sections. Therefore, to understand s. 1, you need to cross-refer to the definitions in ss. 2–6.

For instance s. 3 says that 'appropriation' means:

> (1) Any assumption by a person of the rights of an owner amounts to an appropriation, and this includes, where he has come by the property (innocently or not) without stealing it, any later assump-tion of a right to it by keeping or dealing with it as owner …

Thus, this meaning of 'appropriation' has to be 'read into' the definition of theft in s. 1(1). Equally, s. 4 tells you what the word 'property' means in this context; So, for instance, we can see the effect of ss. 3 and 4 in *R v Greenberg* [1972] Crim LR 331. Here, a man was found not guilty of theft (under s. 1) when he filled his car with petrol and then decided to drive off without paying. He had appropriated the petrol honestly but become dishonest later in relation to his own 'property' because property rights, but not ownership, passed when he mixed the new petrol with that in his tank. Further, s. 5 deals with 'belonging to another', and s. 6 covers 'with the intention of permanently depriving the other of it'.

This is a common method of drafting statutes. Other, similar, methods employ detailed explanations within the section itself, or make use of specific definition sec-tions elsewhere in the Act, or provide more detail in the schedules. For example, in s. 8 of the Theft Act 1968, when the section uses the word 'steal', then, without anything else appearing in the statute to the contrary, that word takes on the meaning given to it in s. 1, even though there is no specific cross-reference. Section 8 states: 'A person is guilty of robbery if he steals, and immediately before or at the time of doing so, and in order to do so, he uses force on any person or puts or seeks to put any person in fear of being then and there subjected to force.'

We should also note that many draftsmen use words knowing that there is a body of case law which defines these words and upon which judges will rely, so no explanation is offered in the statute itself, e.g. where an Act uses the word 'offer' in a contractual setting the court will presume it bears the meaning derived from hundreds of years of case law (see the case of *Fisher* v *Bell* [1961] 1 QB 394; [1960] 3 All ER 731 as a good example—or the strange case of *R* v *Collins* [1973] QB 100; [1972] 2 All ER 1105, which centred on whether a man, naked except for his socks and perched on the sill of an open window was 'trespassing' for the purposes of committing burglary under the Theft Act 1968, s. 9 should any part of his anatomy cross the plane of the building).

One tends to be more sympathetic with the problems facing the draftsmen when one tries to draft a document oneself. It is worth spending a few minutes on the next exercise.

EXERCISE 15 The minimum speed limit

 QUESTION

In this exercise you are a parliamentary draftsman appointed to deal with the problems of slow-moving traffic. Assume that you have been instructed to draft legislation which will introduce a 'minimum speed limit' in country areas and on motorways. The purpose of this exercise is:

(a) to explore the style of wording you use—how many clauses you need; how concise the wording should be;

(b) to see how difficult it is to anticipate all the possible situations that may occur.

 ANSWER

There is of course no single right answer to this problem. Instead here are a few situations which we think your legislation should allow for. Glancing through them you may feel your drafting covers them, more or less. Our experience is that it is a sobering (or exasperating) exercise to get a friend to compare the situations with your piece of draftsmanship. The chances are that at one stage (at least) you will find yourself saying: 'Yes, but I meant it to cover that …' or 'Of course it covers that'. But does it?

Consider whether your legislation covers: stopping at junctions or traffic lights; stopping at hazards such as temporary roadworks; breakdowns; having to slow down because of moving hazards such as tractors; separate criteria for tractors and other agricultural vehicles (if so, how do you define an agricultural vehicle?). For that matter, how did you define 'vehicle'? Did you have the same speed limits for different roads, e.g. the B4106, the A4018, and the M5? Did weather conditions come into the definition, such as fog or bad visibility?

We will examine some of the problems of structure in more depth shortly. Before that, however, it is worth noting one or two points on why statutes are drafted this way.

8.3 The Problems of Drafting Statutes in English Law

Although for constitutional purposes primary legislation is created by Parliament, the actual drafting of statutes is the province of civil servants. Most of the work is done by the various government departments together with parliamentary draftsmen in the Office of Parliamentary Counsel (see http://www.cabinetoffice.gov.uk/content/office-parliamentary-counsel for further details and Regan (2013:32) for an account of the problems of drafting from the perspective of a parliamentary draftsman). There are only about fifty of these specialist draftsmen (plus support staff). Their job is to translate the political objectives behind a proposed Bill into the appropriate legal form, to assess its impact upon the existing law, and to make sure that changes to the existing law are effected properly. This is a demanding task. So, how do the draftsmen approach that task? In a major article published some years ago Francis Bennion (1978), another former Parliamentary Counsel, identified nine targets of the draftsman's work; these he describes as:

(a) **legal effectiveness:** the draftsman must take sometimes very generalised political policy and convert that into a legal form without losing sight of its intended aims. This is not always straightforward, particularly as one Bill may reflect a range of intentions, not all of which may be equally practicable.

(b) **procedural legitimacy:** the Bill must comply with the formal procedures for creating legislation laid down by both Houses of Parliament.

(c) **timeliness:** the draftsmen are constrained by the fact that they must work within the time constraints created by the parliamentary timetable. A government wishing to push through large quantities of reforming legislation will inevitably impose considerable pressure on the draftsmen. Time pressures may mean, as one Member of Parliament has put it, Bills entering Parliament as 'ill-formed, ugly or premature progeny': Rhys Williams (1987: 138).

(d) **certainty:** (see **section 8.3.1**)

(e) **comprehensibility:** (see **section 8.3.2**)

(f) **acceptability:** the language of legislation has to be 'acceptable'. By this Bennion means that it must obey the rules traditionally prescribed. Bennion himself once drew considerable criticism from within the House of Commons for using the phrase 'tried his best' rather than the more conventional 'used his best endeavours' and there is a long-running debate on whether the word 'shall' should be used in legislation.

(g) **brevity:** one should not necessarily assume that brevity and clarity go hand in hand. One of the lessons we have already learned from attempts to develop 'plain English' styles of legal document drafting is that it may take *more* words, not fewer, to increase the clarity of legislation. Brevity itself is not always the answer: a classic example from the Law of Succession is the case of *Thorn v Dickens* [1906] WN 54 where the will read 'All for Mother'. That appears reasonably clear but the will was contested successfully—'Mother' was the term used by the testator to refer to his wife, not his mother.

(h) **debatability:** legislation should ideally be framed in such a way that the general principles are debatable in Parliament. This requires counsel to consider carefully both the complexity and even the order of clauses.

(i) **legal compatibility:** the draftsman must finally work out how the proposals fit in with the existing law. This apparently simple statement disguises a number of difficulties. First, the draftsman needs to know what the existing law actually says. In that respect, the briefings from the instructing department are often an essential starting point, but any draftsman would then engage in research to determine not just what the law says but *how* it says it. As a general principle, a draftsman ought to attempt to use the same form of wording as appears in other legislation covering the same subject matter. Secondly, the draftsman should also indicate the manner in which and extent to which existing legislation is amended by the proposed Bill. This often requires further, sometimes difficult, research. Details of this will appear in the 'Repealing Schedule' to the Act.

Although we can describe points (a)–(i) as targets they are not all mutually compatible; as a result, drafting tends to be rather like negotiating a path through a maze of both political and technical legal constraints. All of these points are important but, for the purposes of this chapter, we will concentrate on 'certainty' and 'comprehensibility'. The ultimate aim of any draftsman is to produce as clear a version as possible of the law that Parliament wants. For sure, it is best to avoid clauses such as the one that appeared in an American statute: 'No one shall carry any dangerous weapon upon the public highway except for the purpose of killing a noxious animal or a policeman in the execution of his duty.' Chauvinistic smugness would be misplaced: there are English law equivalents. The most-cited example (possibly related to the ill-fated Tanganyika groundnuts scheme) is the supposed 1948 Statutory Instrument which read: 'In the Nuts (unground) (other than ground nuts) Order, the expression nuts shall have reference to such nuts, other than ground nuts, as would but for this amending Order not qualify as nuts (unground) (other than ground nuts) by reason of their being nuts (unground)'—we say 'supposed' because, sadly, this is probably an excellent and much-promulgated spoof; no such statutory instrument exists in the UK archives.

8.3.1 Certainty

Although it is desirable that a provision should normally only have one clear meaning it is an ideal that is often difficult to achieve for a number of reasons:

(a) As we sought to show in **Chapter 5** the English language itself is not always a very precise tool. In achieving certainty the draftsman has to bear in mind the ordinary or, if necessary, technical meaning of the term he wishes to use.

He must also be aware of the approach that the courts are likely to take when approaching questions of interpretation. Let us illustrate each of these points.

For instance, using a thesaurus, look up any word, e.g. *invention*. The range of synonyms is: contraption, design, device, discovery, gadget, fabrication, development, fantasy, fiction, illusion, creativity, ingenuity, innovation, inventiveness, originality.

But if you perform the same exercise with one of the words in the list, e.g. *fabrication*, then you get a further list: falsehood, fib, lie, prevarication, story, construction, manufacture, production.

A sentence in a statute that therefore reads:

An employee must surrender to his employer any invention made in the course of his employment

is unlikely to mean:

An employee must surrender to his employer any fantasy made in the course of his employment but it could mean:

> An employee must surrender to his employer any fabrication made in the course of his employment

or:

> An employee must surrender to his employer any design made in the course of his employment

A design and a fabrication are not, however, the same thing, even accepting that 'fabrication' does not mean 'lie' or 'fib' in this context. 'Design' and 'fabrication', for instance, would have a different meaning in the fashion industry from that in the computer industry when applied to any definition of 'invention'. Clearly, the context of the word in the statute and the problem before the court must affect the meaning and accuracy of the application of the word.

Anticipating the reaction of the courts is not always easy. The word, or wording, does not even have to be complicated to cause problems. The statute can be about a very simple topic, and yet lead to many odd cases. Consider, as an example, the Wills Act 1837, s. 9. This section originally stated that the signature to a will must appear at 'the foot or end' of the will. But did this mean the physical positioning at the end of a document, or that the signature was the last thing written on the will, i.e. that the signature could appear anywhere as long as, in terms of time, it came at the end of making the will? Signatures appeared everywhere on wills because people always manage to do strange things. Some judges were lenient as to the physical positioning of the signatures; others were not (we will concentrate on how you can get variations in interpretation in the next chapter). In 1852 the Act had to be amended to read that the signature should come:

> At or after, or following, or under, or beside, or opposite to the end of the will, that it shall be apparent on the face of the will that the Testator intended to give effect to the will.

This still produced problems and the wording to this section was changed again in 1982, by the Administration of Justice Act of that year. It became:

> No will shall be valid unless … it appears that the testator intended by his signature to give effect to the will …

This removed any reference to the position of the signature, so that should have resolved all the earlier problems. Nevertheless, the case of *Wood v Smith* [1993] Ch 90; [1992] 3 All ER 556, CA (which we touched on at **section 7.11** in **Exercise 13**) shows that, even with the amended wording, the judges can still manage to disagree about the effect of the section. In this case the deceased had signed his will at the top, then written out the various bequests, and finally had it signed by his witnesses. At first instance, the High Court held that it was not a valid will. It was the natural construction of the words of the Act that the maker should sign the will *after* making the various dispositions, not before. There has to be something in the nature of a disposition before a will exists and can be signed. The Court of Appeal took a rather different view of the issue. It decided that a signature did *not* have to be appended after the dispositive provisions of the will had been written, provided that the writing of the will and its signing by the testator constituted 'one operation' (a concept which is barely defined by the courts). So, on this point the High Court was overruled, since there was no doubt on the facts that the testator had completed his will as a single operation. In its final version *Wood v Smith* thus appears to have done what the legislation intended, and, for the majority of cases, the decision shifts the court's focus away from the position of the signature, and on to the issue of testamentary intent. The logic of *Wood v Smith* did not, however, save a will in the case of *Marley v Rawlings* [2012] EWCA Civ 61; [2012] 4 All ER 630, where husband and wife had each managed (under the supervision of a solicitor, no less) to sign each other's will.

(b) The desire for certainty frequently leads to undue verbosity, precisely because the draftsman is seeking to delineate meaning to such a high degree. That is why we find examples of such extremely dense prose as the Social Security Act 1975, s. 16(1):

> If a person is more than 5 years below pensionable age on the qualifying date in any period of interruption of employment then, subject to the following provisions of this section, in respect of every day of that period in respect of which he is entitled to an invalidity pension, he shall also be entitled to an invalidity allowance at the appropriate weekly rate specified in relation thereto in Schedule 4, Part I, paragraph 3; and 'the qualifying date' means the first day in that period (whether before the coming into force of this section or later) which is a day of incapacity for work or such earlier day as may be prescribed.

It is not exactly light reading. If we look at what makes it so difficult, we can see a number of factors. One is the cross-referencing to other technical issues, both implicit in the use of terms such as 'pensionable age' or 'relevant amount', which are defined elsewhere in the Act, and explicitly in the reference to sch. 4. A second is the actual length of the sentence, and the number of dependent clauses it contains. By the time we reach the end, there is a real risk that we will have forgotten what the subsection first set out to do (i.e. define entitlement to invalidity allowance). The third factor is the use of terms which would be redundant in ordinary usage, but are used to emphasise the interrelationship between different parts of an Act. Here there are two such examples: 'subject to the following provisions of this section'; and 'specified in relation thereto'. Students find such phrases very difficult to deal with and we will shortly discuss how to handle these problematic terms.

(c) Sometimes it may happen that a provision is left deliberately vague. As Bennion points out this may well happen where the framers of the Act are themselves uncertain of how to handle it. Cynically, one might say that the courts are simply burdened with the responsibility. The most common 'signs' for this can be seen in phrases imposing duties on people such as factory owners to maintain health and safety standards 'where reasonably practicable' or where matters of judgment are deliberately left to 'the court's discretion' (e.g. s. 2 Health and Safety at Work Etc Act 1974 uses the (undefined) term 'reasonably practicable' to describe an employer's duty to his employees—and it does so on six occasions). Indeed, sometimes words are deliberately left vague as a political measure to get a clause through Parliament without inducing opposition from certain MPs (e.g. those opposing changes to family law).

8.3.2 Comprehensibility

Despite what we have just said, draftsmen do aim for legislation that is understandable. However, in so doing they tend to have a specialist audience in mind, in that legislation is designed to be read first and foremost by lawyers. Ideally it should also be comprehensible to Members of Parliament, who may not share the same degree of expertise as a legal audience. How effectively it reaches the latter audience is certainly debatable (e.g. Rhys Williams, 1987: 140). What is beyond doubt is that legislation is not drafted for lay people to read and understand with ease.

Comprehension also implies some degree of clarity and logical structure. We have already illustrated how linguistic problems affect clarity. However, clarity can also be influenced by the overall structure of an Act, particularly in the way it is broken down into composite parts and sections. In our system, it used to be considered good practice that draftsmen should start with matters of general principle, before getting buried in consequential detail, though this principle was frequently overlooked. Sir William Dale, one of the sterner critics of English drafting, has cited a number of examples of poor arrangement in an article published some years ago. One of those Acts, the Unfair Contract Terms Act 1977 (UCTA), was briefly introduced in **Chapter 3**. (see Dale, 1981: 148–9). However, it has become more common practice (in line with many European jurisdictions) to set out all the definitions used in the Act at the start of the document before laying out any principles (see, for instance, s. 2 of the Consumer Rights Act 2015, which has the heading 'Key definitions'). Lawyers are divided on the efficacy of this approach.

Another example of a confusing structure can be seen in the Public Interest Disclosure Act 1998, which this time starts (s. 1) by inserting a range of sections into another Act, numbering them as s. 43A, s. 43B and so on, and then states:

- 43A. In this Act a 'protected disclosure' means a qualifying disclosure (as defined by section 43B) which is made by a worker in accordance with any of sections 43C to 43H.

It follows that up immediately with:

- 43B(1)—In this Part a 'qualifying disclosure' means any disclosure of information which, in the reasonable belief of the worker making the disclosure, tends to show one or more of the following ...

Five reasons follow in paras. (a)–(f). In s. 43B(2) the term 'relevant failures' appears. Only when we get to s. 43B(5) are we told:

- In this Part 'the relevant failure', in relation to a qualifying disclosure, means the matter falling within paragraphs (a) to (f) of subsection (1).

So, only now do we know that a 'protected disclosure' is a 'qualifying disclosure' which consists of a worker showing a 'relevant failure' by the organisation.

With all this in mind, therefore, it is worth looking at some examples of statutes to see how they are put together or, more importantly, what techniques you need to master in order to take them apart and apply them to factual situations (see also Stark, 2002, on approaches to drafting statutes).

8.4 Examples of Drafting Practices and How to Approach Them

Students new to the study of law can sometimes be put off delving into statutes simply because the words or structure used are confusing. To show that, like all legal method techniques, this is not really a black art to be mastered by only the few, we have selected a few statutes which show some of the different drafting techniques you will encounter in your studies. These examples are drawn from statutes which have caused our own students problems in the past. Our aim is simply to reveal the tricks used and how very often the most complicated-looking provision is really nothing of the sort. The subject-matter of each Act is irrelevant.

The most basic 'trick' of all sounds a little patronising, but it is still worth stating. *Each word counts: read the Act carefully, word by word, in the order it is set out.* One very common mistake students make when faced with an Act is to 'jump in' at the wrong point. For instance, a question asks you to determine whether there is a defence to a particular criminal charge; you see that section 8 is labelled 'exceptions', or even 'defences'. You cite section 8. This is not wrong in itself, but what has been missed per-haps is the definition of the offence in, say, s. 1, or some other exceptions in s. 2 (not so helpfully labelled). The offence (defined in s. 1) might have said that the defendant had to be 'negligent' or 'wilful' or 'malicious' or to 'have acted with knowledge' or even have other qualities such as being an adult or male, etc. These are constituent elements of the offence and therefore if the defendant has not been negligent, etc. there will have been no offence at all, so the exceptions will not even come into play.

This 'cascading' analysis is central to reading statutes. For instance, in s. 1 of the Criminal Damage Act 1971 we have an offence described thus:

> (2) A person who without lawful excuse destroys or damages any property, whether belonging to himself or another—
>   (a) intending to destroy or damage any property or being reckless as to whether any property would be destroyed or damaged; and
>   (b) intending by the destruction or damage to endanger the life of another or being reckless as to whether the life of another would be thereby endangered; shall be guilty of an offence.

There are key points here, not least what we mean by 'intending' or 'being reckless', but even before that we have the phrase 'without lawful excuse' and we do not know what that means. We can in fact discover what it means by turning to s. 5 of the Act, but that is not obvious on a first reading of s. 1.

All this is similar to reading a recipe. There is no point leaping in at instruction 7 (grill the steak) only to find that item 1 told you to marinade the steak for at least 24 hours.

We are still not yet concerned with how to *interpret* these (or any other) statutes; we are concerned only with how best to approach reading and understanding them. In par-ticular, we are looking at how to deal with phrases such as 'subject to section 2 …', or 'notwithstanding the duties laid out in section 2 …', or 'Save as permitted by section 2 …'.

The best way to set about this is for you to read the wording of the Act given in the left-hand column in **Tables 8.3–8.7** in **sections 8.4.1–8.4.5**, and see what sense you can make of it; then have a look in the right-hand column and you will see suggestions as to how to approach the statute.

8.4.1 The Knives Act 1997

We start with a reasonably simple section. This extract from the Knives Act 1997 illustrates the basic rules of structure noted earlier—a general opening statement describing the offence followed by more specific 'definitional' matters (see **Table 8.3**).

Table 8.3 Understanding how to read rules (1)

Wording of section	Commentary
Unlawful Marketing of Knives 1. (1) A person is guilty of an offence if he markets a knife in a way which— (a) indicates, or suggests, that it is suitable for combat; or (b) is otherwise likely to stimulate or encourage violent behaviour involving the use of the knife as a weapon.	Section 1(1) sets up the offence, which has two disjunctive elements—(a) or (b). The use of the word 'or' creates two very different ways of committing the offence. Note, however, that it is the 'marketing' of the knife that is illegal, not the mere possession. At this stage in your reading of the statute you should also have been wondering what words such as 'markets', 'suitable for combat', or 'stimulate' mean. At first sight the Act appears unhelpful in that it does not tell you if these words are going to be defined (but they are, just a few subsections later). So, in reading the section, establish what you think is the basic offence; you can fill in details later.
(2) 'Suitable for combat' and 'violent behaviour' are defined in section 10.	Subsection (2) gives us a cross-reference to further explanations in s. 10, where you will find a long list of definitions. Thus, in s. 10 'suitable for combat' means 'suitable for use as a weapon for inflicting injury on a person, or causing a person to fear injury'. This definition is thus 'read into' s. 1.
(3) For the purposes of this Act, an indication or suggestion that a knife is suitable for combat may, in particular, be given or made by a name or description— (a) applied to the knife; (b) on the knife or on any packaging in which it is contained; or (c) included in any advertisement which, expressly or by implication, relates to the knife.	Another definition subsection (which applies to the whole Act—sometimes definitions only apply to particular sections or parts of Acts). Here, subsection (3) defines the rather vague terms we first saw in s. 1(1)(a). However, the wording of subsection (3) does not help much as you will notice that it has the term 'in particular' hidden halfway along. This must mean that although points (a)-(c) are clear examples there may be others.
(4) For the purposes of this Act, a person markets a knife if— (a) he sells it or hires it; (b) he offers, or exposes, it for sale or hire; or (c) he has it in his possession for the purposes of sale or hire.	Finally we get the meaning of the word 'markets', so, again, this has to be read back into the original description of the offence. Note that 'possession' still has to relate to the sale or hire of the knife. This subsection does not create a separate offence in this Act of 'possession'.

This statute was introduced following a public outcry when a headmaster was stabbed by a pupil outside his school. Legislation already existed prohibiting the carrying of offensive weapons: what society demanded was more legislation on the *sale* of knives. To outlaw the sale of all types of knife was obviously impracticable, so some other approach was needed—outlawing the marketing of knives which could be used as a weapon—the phrase eventually chosen being 'combat knives'.

8.4.2 The Wild Mammals (Protection) Act 1996

This next example looks like a mess on first reading (see **Table 8.4**). To start with it begins with the puzzling phrase 'If, save as permitted by this Act ...' and then goes on to list a whole range of forbidden activities. But appearances can be deceptive: it is actually very straightforward. The phrase 'save as permitted ...' appears quite often in statutes. It means that the actions listed in s. 1 might still be lawful if made so elsewhere in the Act. You are not told where this 'saving' provision might be, so it could appear anywhere in the Act and even arise from the context rather than specific wording.

Table 8.4 Understanding how to read rules (2)

Wording of section	Commentary
1. Offences If, save as permitted by this Act, any person mutilates, kicks, beats, nails, or otherwise impales, stabs, burns, stones, crushes, drowns, drags, or asphyxiates any wild mammal with intent to inflict unnecessary suffering he shall be guilty of an offence. *[2. ... omitted here]* **3. Interpretation** In this Act 'wild mammal' means any mammal which is not a domestic or captive animal within the meaning of the Protection of Animals Act 1911 ...	A formidable list, but not that confusing when dealt with one at a time. Any other act of cruelty you can think of might still fall within this section if it is *like* the action listed. Note also the key point at the end that 'intent to inflict unnecessary suffering' is required. So, if someone impales or burns a wild mammal accidentally or for some good reason they will not have committed an offence under the Act. Section 3 gives definitions, but you need to refer to another Act to understand them. Such external source cross-referencing is very annoying but very common.

8.4.3 The Copyright, Etc. And Trade Marks (Offences and Enforcement) Act 2002

As with the Wild Mammals Act example, this section sets up a general rule but tells you, right at the start, that rule has to be read with exceptions. This time, instead of using the phrase 'save as permitted', it uses the more direct phrase 'subject to ... [a particular subsection]',—so at least you know where to look this time. The trick here is to ignore the 'subject to ...' part until you have worked out clearly what the general rule is. Students often make the mistake of trying to read the subsection referred to before establishing the general rule. That way lies madness.

This extract in **Table 8.5** deals with the situation where someone has breached another person's copyright and made illegal recordings of their material, e.g. pirated CDs. What should be done with those CDs?

Table 8.5 Understanding how to read rules (3)

Wording of section	Commentary
Section 4	*[subsecs. (1)–(7) omitted here]*
(8) **Subject to subsection** (9), where any illicit recordings are forfeited under this section they shall be destroyed in accordance with such directions as the court may give.	A straightforward subsection which presents a **general** rule that illicit recordings which have been forfeited by the court will then be destroyed. But the opening words demonstrate that, whatever is said here, may be overridden by subsection (9).
(9) On making an order under this section the court may direct that the illicit recordings to which the order relates shall (instead of being destroyed) be forfeited to the person having the performers' rights or recording rights in question or dealt with in such other way as the court considers appropriate.	Subsection (9) sets out the exceptions referred to by the phrase in subsection (8), 'subject to subsection (9)'. In this case, illicit recordings will be destroyed unless the court decides: (i) to allow them to be forfeited for the benefit of certain people involved in their creation or (ii) dealt with in another way. This latter point clearly allows the court a very wide discretion. So subsection (8) is the normal procedure, but it can be varied according to subsection (9).

8.4.4 The Churchwardens Measure Act 2001

There is nothing particularly complicated about this next, rarely-cited Act, but it is useful because it illustrates two things: (a) how a statute can set up an elaborate system and then provide exceptions; (b) the use of the word 'notwithstanding', which draftsmen love using (see **Table 8.6**).

Table 8.6 Understanding how to read rules (4)

Wording of section	Commentary
1 Number and qualifications of churchwardens	This subsection lists who may be churchwardens.
[subsecs. (1) and (2) omitted here]	Note the requirements are **cumulative** so if one condition is not met, the person cannot be a
(3) The churchwardens of every parish shall be chosen from persons who have been baptised and— (a) whose names are on the church electoral roll of the parish; (b) who are actual communicants; (c) who are 21 years of age or upwards; and (d) who are not disqualified under section 2 or 3 below.	churchwarden. The 'and' which occurs between subsections. (c) and (d) is meant to illustrate that the whole list is deemed to have 'ands' in it. Where an Act sets out alternatives (as in the Knives Act—see **Table 8.3**) it will usually have the word 'or' between each subsection but sometimes uses the device of just having the 'or' between the last two subsections.

Table 8.6 Continued

Wording of section	Commentary
(4) If it appears to the bishop, in the case of any particular person who is not qualified by virtue of paragraph (a), (b), or (c) of subsection (3), that there are exceptional circumstances which justify a departure from the requirements of those paragraphs the bishop may permit that person to hold the office of churchwarden notwithstanding that those requirements are not met. Any such permission shall apply only to the period of office next following.	Subsection (4) is an example where the word 'or' only appears once but applies to each paragraph. This subsection provides exceptions to subsection (3). There must be 'exceptional circumstances' (not defined) before this operates. The subsection allows a bishop to appoint a person as a churchwarden *even though* (in the Act the term used is 'notwithstanding the fact') that person does not meet the requirements of s. 3(a), (b), or (c). But what the bishop cannot do (and it is easy to miss this) is ignore the requirement set out in s. 1(3)(d) because only (a), (b), and (c) are mentioned here.

If you search for occurrences of the word 'notwithstanding' in LexisLibrary there are so many entries your search is automatically limited. The word 'notwithstanding' basically means 'despite', or 'in spite of', or 'even though' (the normal legal usages) as with a phrase such as: 'Notwithstanding the doctor's advice she went skiing anyway'. Less frequently it can mean 'although' or 'nevertheless'. It appears in sentences such as: 'Subsection (1) shall have effect **notwithstanding** any agreement to the contrary ...' (meaning: subsection (1) will apply even if the agreement says otherwise); and 'The acts and proceedings of any person appointed to be a member ... of a Service Authority and acting in that office shall, **notwithstanding** his disqualification or want of qualification, be as valid and effectual as if he had been qualified' (meaning: 'despite his disqualification'). It is quite common to see the phrase, in, say s. 5 of an Act: 'Notwithstanding the generality of s. 3 ...'—meaning that however wide the rule in s. 3 appears to be s. 5 varies it, qualifies it, or expands upon it. An example appears in the Merchant Shipping (Fire Protection: Large Ships) Regulations 1998, where reg. 68 para. 1 sets out the 'means of escape' which must be provided on a ship, such as doors and stairways, and reg. 68 para. 2 states: 'Notwithstanding the generality of paragraph (1), in every ship the following shall be complied with ...' and goes on to describe the size and shape of bulkheads. that have to conform to the rules. With this in mind, note how the word is used in the following Act.

8.4.5 The Trustee Act 1925

We end this list of examples with this beauty—a section which always causes students problems. The law is not that complicated; it is the density of the prose that is the problem—s. 36(1) is actually all one sentence (see **Table 8.7**). However, though this looks daunting, it can be broken down into simpler elements (whether you use a flowchart approach or other device is a matter of preference). The key is to get the general picture of it first; later you can fill in the specific requirements and/or exceptions. If you can master this, you are well on your way to handling the structure of statutes.

Table 8.7 Understanding how to read rules (5)

Wording of section	Commentary
36 Power of appointing new or additional trustees (1) Where a trustee, either original or substituted, and whether appointed by a court or otherwise, is dead, or remains out of the United Kingdom for more than twelve months, or desires to be discharged from all or any of the trusts or powers reposed in or conferred on him, or refuses or is unfit to act therein, or is incapable of acting therein, or is an infant, then, subject to the restrictions imposed by this Act on the number of trustees— (a) the person or persons nominated for the purpose of appointing new trustees by the instrument, if any, creating the trust; or (b) if there is no such person, or no such person able and willing to act, then the surviving or continuing trustees or trustee for the time being, or the personal representatives of the last surviving or continuing trustee; may, by writing, appoint one or more other persons (whether or not being the persons exercising the power) to be a trustee or trustees in the place of the trustee so deceased remaining out of the United Kingdom, desiring to be discharged, refusing, or being unfit or being incapable, or being an infant, as aforesaid.	**STEP 1:** The heading is usually a good indication of what the section is about (though, very occasionally, it can be misleading). So we know this section concerns the appointment of trustees. **STEP 2:** First, take the opening words of s. 36(1) '**Where a trustee …**'. The next few clauses merely make clear *which* trustees are covered, so ignore them for the moment. **STEP 3:** The second key phrase is: '**is dead (or other things have happened)**'. We are merely trying to find out what the general position is here, so do not get concerned yet about these. **STEP 4:** The next key word is '**then …**,' i.e. what is going to happen or be allowed? So, the gist so far is: '**Where a trustee is dead (or something else has happened) then …**' **STEP 5:** The phrase '**Subject to the restrictions …** ,' merely puts you on guard that the Act has other provisions covering the numbers of trustees which we will have to look at later. Ignore this for the moment. **STEP 6:** At first sight paras. (a) and (b) look like the 'then' noted in STEP 4, but in fact they merely describe who has the power to act when the trustee is dead, etc. So, ignore this too for the moment. Annoying though this may be, this style of drafting is quite common (and, to be fair, it is difficult to set up such a rule without doing something like this). You need to look to the final paragraph to see exactly what is going on. **The essence of the section so far is that when a trustee is dead (etc.) some people have the power to do certain things.** **STEP 7:** Finally we get to what these persons may do. We find that they may appoint others to be trustees in place of the trustee who died (etc.). The only other point you have to note is that the appointment must be made 'by writing'. Amazingly straightforward in the end!

Statutes of course do not exist merely to provide exercises in analysis. They have to be applied in practice; so, having done your work on the wording of the Trustee Act 1925, you can now put that to use with a client's problem.

For example, say your client is a trustee of a charity and tells you that one of the other trustees has died and he wants to appoint a replacement.

- You know that s. 36(1) is generally about this sort of situation. You can now look at the detail to see that the first requirement of the section is met (i.e. that an existing trustee has died).

- You would next have to ask: does such an appointment fall foul of the number of trustees allowed under the Act? You would therefore need to look elsewhere in the Act. It is unlikely to be a problem, as the new appointment is merely a replacement. If there will be too many trustees, then there may have been too many all along but, of course, it is possible that when the trustees were appointed four were allowed but since then the law has changed and now only three are permitted—so you do need to check your law on this.

- If all is well, then you would need to see if your client falls within paras. (a) or (b), i.e. does he/she have the right to make the appointment or do we need to get someone else to do it?

If all these requirements have been met, you would then advise that such an appointment has to be made in writing.

8.5 Amending Earlier Statutes

Another aspect of drafting practice you need to master arises when an Act (say, one passed in 2013) amends an earlier Act (say, one of 1990). The amendment may be wholesale: the earlier Act may be repealed and replaced by the later Act (or a whole string of Acts may be **consolidated** into the new Act). But, more commonly, the later Act will amend only parts of the earlier Act or Acts. It is quite common, therefore, for one Act to 'insert' new words or even new sections into an existing Act. There is nothing too puzzling about this and the new wording or section is simply referred to as if it had always been in the original Act; the real problem is that if you went and looked at the original Act you would not see the amendment (though you would in the electronic versions to be found on LexisLibrary and Westlaw). Laypersons representing themselves in court often make the mistake of relying on the original wording of the statute without realising there has been an amendment. Lawyers are presumed to know better.

8.5.1 Inserting and Substituting Words

Words or phrases in statutes may be amended by later Acts or Statutory Instruments. This is usually straightforward and databases such as Westlaw and LexisLibrary will contain the amended wording (usually with an accompanying note of where that amendment came from). To find the original wording (which is sometimes necessary when dealing with a claim which arose before the amendment) one needs to go to the relevant government website: http://www.legislation.gov.uk/ukpga.

Figure 8.1 shows how Westlaw pages deal with this. The text reflects the law in practice and the footnotes demonstrate the changes made to the original statute.

8.5.2 Inserting New Sections

The most usual method of inserting new sections is to put A or B, etc. after the old section number. We saw an example of this in **section 8.3.2** with the Public Interest

Figure 8.1 How databases deal with insertions and substitutions

Disclosure Act 1998 in which s. 1 inserted a range of sections into a 1996 Act, numbering them as s. 43A, s. 43B etc, so that the amended 1996 Act now reads: s. 43, s. 43A, s. 43B, s. 43C … s. 43M, then s. 44. The idea is that this saves having to renumber the whole Act. Here is an expanded example from the Theft Act 1968. Section 12 dealt with the taking of a vehicle without authority. Parliament later decided it needed to create a specific offence to cover the situation where a vehicle was taken without authority and then damage or injury resulted from that action—what is termed an 'aggravated' offence (here meaning 'intensified', 'heightened', or 'serious', not 'irritated' or 'provoked' as it is sometimes used). The Aggravated Vehicle-Taking Act 1992 came into being and, to more closely relate the basic offence with this 'add-on', s. 12A was placed in the Theft Act 1968 with appropriate cross-references to the original s. 12. The 1992 Act used these words to bring this about in s. 1:

New offence of aggravated vehicle-taking

(1) After section 12 of the [1968 c. 60.] Theft Act 1968 (taking conveyances without authority) there shall be inserted the following section—*[The new s. 12A was then set out, so the whole thing now reads:]*

12 Taking motor vehicle or other conveyance without authority

Subject to subsections (5) and (6) below, a person shall be guilty of an offence if, without having the consent of the owner or other lawful authority, he takes any conveyance for his own or another's use or, knowing that any conveyance has been taken without such authority, drives it or allows himself to be carried in or on it *[remainder omitted]*

12A Aggravated vehicle-taking

(1) Subject to subsection (3) below, a person is guilty of aggravated taking of a vehicle if—

(a) he commits an offence under section 12(1) above (in this section referred to as a "basic offence") in relation to a mechanically propelled vehicle; and

(b) it is proved that, at any time after the vehicle was unlawfully taken (whether by him or another) and before it was recovered, the vehicle was driven, or injury or damage was caused, in one or more of the circumstances set out in paragraphs (a) to (d) of subsection (2) below …

Amendments do not make a great deal of sense when read in isolation and 'textual amendments' (such as the instruction, 'in s. 54 insert after the word "building" the words "or land thereon"') are usually wholly meaningless out of context. The points we made earlier on 'inserting words' regarding databases and the original text apply equally to 'inserting sections'.

8.6 Other Points on Drafting

There is also an increasing problem in ensuring compatibility with EU law. The drafting complexities created by EU membership are twofold:

- First there is a general obligation on Member States to avoid legislating in contravention of EU law.
- Secondly, there is the further problem of implementing EU directives. Implementation involves expressly transposing a piece of EU legislation into the form of domestic law. Ideally, it should be achieved without misinterpreting the substance of the original legislative Act. The difference in styles between EU and UK or Irish legislation may make this problem more acute in Britain and the Republic of Ireland than elsewhere in the EU. The difference in style is a point to which we shall return in more detail later in this chapter. First, we should note one or two points on the different drafting style used on the Continent and therefore in EU legislation.

8.7 European Legislative Drafting

8.7.1 The Drafting Process

The English style of drafting can be directly contrasted with the techniques adopted in the civilian systems of continental Europe and, in EU law. Given that many areas of our law are now dominated by EU-derived legislation, this is a topic we cannot ignore.

You will recall that in **Chapter 1** we made the point that the great majority of civilian systems are built upon the principles of codified law. That emphasis on codification has, of course, had an impact on the whole legal process, not just on the drafting of legislation. For that reason, before we focus on the specifics of drafting technique, it is worth thinking about the general characteristics of codified as opposed to uncodified law. We shall focus on five key features.

Coherence

One of the problems with the common law, it is said, is that it lacks coherence. It is fragmentary and dispersed through a variety of sources, with negative consequences for both the clarity and certainty of the law. Restatement in a codified form potentially overcomes this problem, by bringing the law together within a single document or coherent set of documents. This view of course overstates the coherence of codified law, which also has to grow and adapt in the same way as the common law.

Comprehensiveness

To a greater or lesser extent, codes claim to be complete restatements of the area of law to which they apply. This is not always easy to achieve, and may require a degree of complexity that is ultimately undesirable—an extreme example of such was the *Allgemeines Landrecht* promulgated in Prussia in 1794 which ran to an unmanageable 17,000 articles. The extent to which codes are complete statements depends on a variety of factors: most notably the extent to which the code has been updated by subsequent codified and uncodified legislation. Codes are difficult to replace in their entirety (for one thing it is an extremely lengthy legislative process), and attempts to dismantle an established Code may be politically sensitive. For example, the revolutionary roots of the French Civil Code give it a 'sanctity' which would make its repeal an extremely emotive issue. Such problems encourage a policy of tinkering, by amending the 'outdated' parts by new legislation.

Knowledgeability

In theory, codification has been seen as a means of democratising law by making the form and wording of the law easier for non-lawyers to understand, thereby extending knowledge of the law to the ordinary citizen and curbing the power of the judiciary—the original French Civil Code, the *Code Napoléon*, is one example of codifying law passed with this aim in view. The extent to which the common law lacks knowledgeability is a longstanding criticism. Jeremy Bentham (1748–1832), one of the most influential English members of the codification movement, pointed to this in his famous statement that the common law was 'dog law': the pragmatic, case-by-case development of the common law meant that people were punished for their actions *ex post facto*, as you would beat a dog only after it had misbehaved. (For further discussion of Bentham and the movement for codification in nineteenth-century England, see Lobban, 1991.) However, a lack of knowledgeability is not a characteristic unique to the common law. As the range of human activities demanding regulation has expanded, knowledgeability has been the chief victim, and is one attribute that is not widely found in modern codified systems, other than as an idealised notion of how the law ought to be.

Clarity

Knowledgeability and clarity are obviously related concepts, since clarity of language and exposition can greatly influence the knowledgeability of the law. But clarity is also a relative concept; some codes may seek to achieve a very high degree of brevity and simplicity in their formulation, while others may settle for a more technical level of clarity. One aim of codification has always been the clarification of law by the removal of what Vandévelde (1967) calls (to paraphrase) obscurity, doubt, and ambiguity in the formulation of legal rules. Most common law draftsmen share those aims. It is possible to argue that, in many instances, both common and civil law systems have been tried and found wanting so far as clarity is concerned—see the discussion later in this chapter.

The absence of contradiction

The process of *redaction*—of converting uncodified law to a codified form—gives the lawmaker an opportunity to resolve contradictions which may be present in uncodified law—e.g. in conflicting customary or case law. On the positive side, it is thereby possible to create greater certainty, but it may involve the lawmaker in a more or less subjective choice of one formulation of a rule over another. This part of the codifying process will often prove controversial. Problems of this sort have arisen in the attempts to produce a Draft Criminal Code for England (see de Búrca and Gardner, 1990).

8.7.2 The Perceived Benefits of Codification

As the preceding discussion suggests, the benefits of codification are somewhat debatable. Before you make up your own mind, let us consider how these general principles (and problems) come to be reflected in the technicalities of continental drafting.

Once again, generalisation is a little difficult. Most European states have laws that are not fully codified; in Spain, for example, the Civil Code (*Código Civil*) is often of only subsidiary force in some of the regions where the *Fueros*, or local law, can still hold greater sway. Similarly, some states have a federal system or other form of subsidiary legislature capable of legislating in its own right—for example, the codification of the *Fueros* by some Spanish regional governments; or the legislative activities of the German *Länder*. The following comments are only really exemplary of the more 'conventional' systems of codified national laws.

The drafting process in many European countries is, in some senses, a less specialised activity than in England. The initial drafting is usually completed solely by lawyers within the relevant ministries, or else by external commissions set up both to review a problematic issue and propose a draft law upon it.

After the initial drafting, the proposal will be revised. In France this is the function of the *Conseil d'Etat*—a consultative as well as judicial body—which is empowered to propose detailed changes to the legislation, and, though the government is not obliged to follow that advice, it generally does so (see Ducamin, 1981). A similar system exists in Italy and in the Netherlands, while in Germany that function is performed by the Ministry of Justice. In all these countries it is only after this first revision by legal experts that further revision before Parliament takes place: a significant variation on the British pattern of legislating.

8.7.3 The Style of Drafting

In most codified systems much of the basic legal structure is now firmly established, and drafting styles broadly reflect the forms adopted by the eighteenth- or nineteenth-century authors of their codes. To a lawyer trained in any other tradition, British legislation comes as something of a shock; as a Bulgarian commentator has suggested:

> It is a challenging and arduous task to find one's way through the intricacies of English law when, as a translator, or professionally as a continental lawyer, one has to acquire a working knowledge of this uncommon law. (Dodova, 1989: 69)

In this section we shall therefore try to identify the key distinguishing features of civilian forms of drafting, then look at some of the specific drafting issues surrounding EU law. There is a distinct contrast between common law and civil styles, summed up graphically in the description of the common law style as 'fussy' (over-detailed) and the civil style as 'fuzzy' (lacking in detail): Campbell, 1996.

Structure

We have already said that one of the arguable failings of British drafting is its poor arrangement—for example, the lack of rational distinction between points of principle and of detail. By comparison, civilian law often shows a far greater concern to establish a rational overall structure. One of the clearest examples of this is the German Civil Code—*Bürgerliches Gesetzbuch* (BGB).

The BGB consists of five books and approaching 2,500 paragraphs. The five books reflect the main conceptual divisions of the German Civil Law, which tend to follow the classical 'institutional' divisions of the French Civil Code. Thus, Book One is the General Part; Book Two covers the law of obligations; Book Three, property; Book Four is on family law; and Book Five contains the law of succession. The provision of the General Part carries an explicit message about the purpose of those provisions. It denotes a high degree of conceptual abstraction, whereby the rules of Book One are of widespread application and are not tied to a specific institution.

This movement *from the general to the particular* is a common feature of codified laws and greatly aids interpretation by allowing us to establish general rules clearly before we look for exceptions. The structure of the BGB, for instance, can be contrasted with English law, where often general rules either do not exist, or lack a unified legislative source, or can appear illogically ordered within the Act (e.g. UCTA as discussed earlier).

Linguistic simplicity

Here, there is perhaps much greater practical variation in style between continental systems. The Swiss Civil Code of 1907 and the original Napoleonic Code of France are frequently cited as good examples of legislative simplicity, whereby principles are expressed in clear, naturalistic language. This ideal is not always sought, let alone achieved, even within a codified system. The BGB, for example, is noted for its technical language, though it still maintains a high degree of clarity for all that, and some of the later French Codes are similarly of greater complexity than the *Code Napoléon*—perhaps not least because they are dealing with modern legal phenomena such as social security rights, which are not as amenable as some areas of law to (relatively) simple exposition.

Brevity

Connected with our second point, we can often see in civilian legislation an attempt to keep legal statements brief and to the point. British proponents of the 'European approach' to drafting (e.g. Dale, 1981) often cite this as a key difference between British and continental styles.

Dale provides a graphic example by a comparison of various national copyright laws. He concludes:

> All these copyright laws give effect to common international obligations, and … are much the same in substance. The United Kingdom Act is twice as long as the German, more than three times as long as the French, and five times as long as the Swedish. (1981: 145)

British lawyers argue that a lack of definition actually creates uncertainty. As we have seen, certainty has always been the great virtue claimed by the British for their legislation. But if it is so certain, why do our courts spend so many hours arguing over questions of construction? In part, this is down to dealing with shades of meaning and, to that extent, exactly the same problems arise in Europe. However, one can argue that the British make a further rod for their own backs by attempting to produce lengthy and 'exhaustive' definitions, both of specific words and of situations in which the Act is to apply. As Sir William Dale has long argued, however, definition does not make for certainty; his own position (which we support) is to agree with the Italian jurist Calamandrei that, 'The statutes cannot foresee all the cases that reality, much richer than the most fervid imagination, brings before the judge' (1981: 159). In other words definition can often cause, as much as alleviate, uncertainty by creating doubt whether certain fact situations are covered.

Approachability is also a matter of the form into which those words are put. The verbosity of British statutes is a throwback to the style of drafting which existed prior to the 1860s. Then sections were very densely written, with minimal punctuation (resulting in sentences that could run to many lines), and virtually no attempt to separate criteria within sections. Compared with this the highly technical structure of modern British statutes provides far more clarity, but the form of language is not wholly dissimilar.

Before we jump to the conclusion that civilian drafting styles are superior, we should remember that civilian lawyers today are facing many of the same legislative problems and criticisms as their British counterparts. As Jean-Eric Schoettl, a member of the French *Conseil d'Etat* explains:

> In France the situation is far from being satisfactory … the main reasons for this are well known. The first is the rapidity with which changes take place under the pressure of events, or under the imperious pressure of political will. We can be very hasty in the way we prepare provisions. They are superimposed one on another without clearly fitting with previous law. The chief draftsman at the Ministry of the Interior, M. Latournerie, calls this 'panic' legislation.
>
> The second reason is the fact that legal language is no longer reserved for a small circle of people brought up in the same nursery. All branches of human activity are involved. Technical government departments, independent administrative authorities, local authorities, trade unions, employers—all these people take a part in drafting, and they have not necessarily had the same intellectual preparations. They come to law in different ways, and they have very different concerns. The result of this is what M. Latournerie calls 'legal babel'—the law is expressed in a multitude of dialects.
> (Dale, 1986: 36)

Plus ça change, plus c'est la même chose?

8.8 The Style of EU Legislation

Not surprisingly, the structure of EU legislation more closely reflects civil as opposed to common law style. For example the important Equal Opportunities Directive 2006/54/EC states in Art. 4:

> For the same work or for work to which equal value is attributed, direct and indirect discrimination on grounds of sex with regard to all aspects and conditions of remuneration shall be eliminated.
>
> In particular, where a job classification system is used for determining pay, it must be based on the same criteria for men and women and so drawn up as to exclude any discrimination on grounds of sex.

Again, it is apparent that the Article concentrates heavily upon general principle, though this Directive has more detail than the one it replaced (the Equal Pay Directive 75/117).

This general lack of technical detail is not a consistent feature of all EU legislation; some directives and regulations can be highly detailed and technical *where the subject matter so requires*—for example, Directive 82/501 on health and safety at work, which laid down a fairly complex notification scheme for certain hazardous industries. But even there the layout and language of the provisions are less dense than in much British legislation.

It is interesting that there is no equivalent of the Parliamentary Counsel in the EU. Instead, the actual drafting (of, say, European directives) is normally undertaken by staff within the European Commission—one of the key law-making institutions of the EU. This is normally followed by a detailed consultation period involving committees of experts appointed from within the Member States, and the Legal Service of the Commission, which must ultimately approve the draft before it goes before the Commission itself. Once approved, the proposal is set before the Council of Ministers (the other body with direct law-making power); it may sometimes be placed simultaneously before the European Parliament. From there, the process becomes extremely complex, with procedures depending upon the nature of the legislation and the criteria laid down for its revision and implementation. In most cases, consultation with Parliament is required before the Council can adopt the proposal, though this is not always necessary; in other cases the Parliament has power to propose amendments to legislation, though the Council retains the last word. Only when legislation has finally been adopted by the Council is it signed by the President and thus capable of having the force of law. So, that is straightforward.

There are two further, special, dimensions to EU law which make questions of drafting/interpretation rather interesting.

8.8.1 Languages in the EU

Language (or languages) can be a problem. EU legislation has to be translated from the language in which it was originally drafted (which may be any of the Member States' languages, depending upon the preference of the team engaged in drafting) into the official EU languages (twenty-four at the time of writing—though commonly only the 'Procedural Languages' of French, German, and English are used in the Commission). This can create an element of doubt. Can we be sure that translation effectively carries the legislative intent of an act across the linguistic divide? There are specific legal terms in French, for instance, which have no equivalent in other languages.

This is not solely a problem within the EU, but afflicts any state where legislation is enacted in more than one language. Canada provides a good comparative example, where, since 1982, all legislation has been enacted in both English and French. McEvoy (1986) illustrates the problem by reference to s. 8 of the Canadian Charter of Rights and Freedoms, which reads:

> Everyone has the right to be secure against unreasonable search or seizure.
>
> Chacun a droit à la protection contre les fouilles, les perquisitions ou les saisies abusives.

One assumes that the legislature intended these to be equivalent provisions. Certainly, both cover seizures ('*les saisies*' in French) and searches, though the French is actually more precise than the English as '*les fouilles*' and '*les perquisitions*' clearly cover searches of both persons and property. The difficulty arises in the apparent equation of 'unreasonable' and '*abusive*'. *Abusive* in French denotes something which is excessive or unauthorised. As McEvoy argues, therefore, 'it is not a true cognate' (1986: 158) of the English 'unreasonable'; though there is clearly an area in which the terms overlap (something which is excessive is surely unreasonable), the fit is not exact: is something unreasonable necessarily unauthorised? This may seem to be a (semantic) storm in a teacup, and may be a lesser problem in countries where the lawyers are less inclined towards literalism than the common law-orientated Canadians. Even so, as McEvoy shows, there is a case for saying that courts dealing with bilingual enactments should not just *assume* linguistic equivalence.

In the EU, this seems to have been acknowledged. There are many cases where the Court's attention has been drawn to linguistic differences as part of the interpretative process; see, e.g., Case C–372/88 *Milk Marketing Board* v *Cricket St Thomas Estate* [1990] ECR I–1345; [1990] 2 CMLR 800 (a comparison of French and German versions of the Treaty with the English version). Sometimes the nuances may be so fine as to make no practical difference in the context; though occasionally the Court of Justice has found conflicting versions, and been forced to adopt a version which seems to accord either with the majority of the texts, or with the presumed legislative intent. For example, in Case 13/61 *de Geus* v *Bosch* [1962] ECR 45, the Court was faced with a provision in the Treaty of Rome where all four authentic texts conveyed a different meaning. Advocate General Lagrange submitted that the Court was free to decide the issue according to the spirit of the text. Certainly no single language is treated as having primacy in interpretation.

We shall leave the last word here to Jeremy Gardner and the European Court of Auditors' publication (2013:4):

> Over the years, the European institutions have developed a vocabulary that differs from that of any recognised form of English. It includes words that do not exist or are relatively unknown to native English speakers outside the EU institutions and often even to standard spellcheckers/grammar checkers ('planification', 'to precise' or 'telematics' for example) … .

We are reminded of a 'No Parking' sign in Sardinia: 'Those who will be otherwise surprised will be subject to penalty'.

8.8.2 Directives

A further problem in EU law arises out of the use of directives. We mentioned in **Chapter 1** that a directive becomes fully effective in a Member State only once implemented by domestic law. In the United Kingdom and Ireland implementation requires a major transition of style. There is as yet little evidence that the Westminster draftsmen are adopting different stylistic techniques in respect of EU-based as opposed to 'home-grown' legislation. This means that we still have the problem of how effectively a broadly drafted directive can be converted into the form and language of a British Act or statutory instrument. The position is not helped by the UK government occasionally going into a 'sulk' when it feels it has had a directive foist upon it—and simply transposing the text of the directive into UK legislation without any real regard to what specific terms might mean in that English translation. We will return to this in **Chapter 11**.

 CONCLUSION

Perfecting any legislation is a very difficult task. The balancing of clarity, generality, conciseness, precision, and the avoidance of excess verbiage to achieve a satisfactory statute requires a great deal of skill. Further, certain words are, as we saw in **Chapter 5**, probably beyond universally applicable definition—words such as 'reasonable' or 'practicable'.

Which of the British and European styles is ultimately the more effective? In some cases that is possibly debatable, but it would be a hardened Anglophile who would support the case of British drafting without hesitation.

In terms of structure, the way in which a British Act is put together can, at best, aid interpretation by clarifying the relative degree of dependency that sections, subsections, and paragraphs have on each other. Sometimes, however, the structure imposed by the British draftsman can seemingly obscure that very same relationship. Much depends upon the quality of the drafting which, as we have seen, may be affected by a number of variables.

In terms of the detailed language used, there seems to be much in British legislation that is redundant, or redolent of a formalised language that is largely unrecognisable to the majority of the community. The greater emphasis on detail and definition in British legislation certainly does not make legislation any more litigation proof. One suspects that what it does do is to shift the level of judicial debate from a consideration of the purpose and effect of legislation to a dispute over semantic detail. The reasons for this can be briefly explained.

Once a question of interpretation arises, continental judges are normally given substantial discretionary powers. For example, Art. 1 of the Swiss Civil Code entitles the judge, in the absence of clear statutory authority, to decide an issue 'in accordance with the rule he would establish as legislator'. In this sense, civilian systems imply a partnership between Parliament and court, whereby the latter is there (to paraphrase Lord Denning) 'to fill the gaps and iron out the creases' left by the former. It is often expressed as a power to interpret legislation according to its objectives, or the intention of its authors. This power may be explicit in the legislation itself, or in the jurisprudence of the court—see, e.g., para. 133 of the BGB; also the decision of the Court of Justice in Case 22/70 *European Commission* v *Council of the European Community* [1971] ECR 263.

In the UK judges also seek to implement the will of Parliament. But unlike the codified approach seen on the Continent, British judges have not (at least until recently) shown much inclination to claim extensive powers to look at the general purpose of the Act. For the most part they will therefore adhere to the plain meaning of the words, so far as that proves possible. The way in which they go about these tasks forms the subject of the next chapter.

CHAPTER REFERENCES

*BENNION, F. (1978), 'Statute Law Obscurity and the Drafting Parameters', 5 *British Journal of Law and Society*, 235.

CAMPBELL, L. (1996), 'Drafting Styles: Fuzzy or Fussy?', 3 *Murdoch University Electronic Journal of Law*, No. 2.

DALE, W. (1977), *Legislative Drafting—A New Approach* (London: Butterworths).

DALE, W. (1981), 'Statutory Reform: The Draftsman and The Judge', *International and Comparative Law Quarterly*, 141.

DALE, W. (ed.) (1986), *British and French Statutory Drafting* (London: Institute of Advanced Legal Studies).

DE BÚRCA, G. and GARDNER, S. (1990), 'The Codification of the Criminal Law', 10 *Oxford Journal of Legal Studies*, 559.

*DODOVA, L. (1989), 'A Translator Looks at English Law', *Statute Law Review*, 69.

DRIEDGER, E. (1976), *The Composition of Legislation* (2nd edn, Ottawa: Department of Justice).

DUCAMIN, B. (1981), 'The Role of the *Conseil d'Etat* in Drafting Legislation', 30 *International and Comparative Law Quarterly*, 882.

EDITORIAL (2014), 'In Honour of the Moribund "Shall"', 35(2) *Statute Law Review, v-vi*.

GARDNER, J. (2013), Misused English Words and Expressions in EU Publications (European Court of Auditors), available at http://www.eca.europa.eu/en/Pages/OtherPublications.aspx.

HANSARD SOCIETY (1992), *Making the Law* (London: Hansard Society).

HODGES, C. (1998), 'Development Risks: Unanswered Questions', 61 *Modern Law Review*, 560.

HUNT, B. (2002), 'Plain Language in Legislative Drafting: Is it Really the Answer?', *Statute Law Review*, 24.

HUTTON, N. (1979), 'Legislative Drafting in the United Kingdom', *The Parliamentarian*, no. 253, 100.

LAWS, S. (2011), 'Giving Effect to Policy in Legislation: How to Avoid Missing the Point', 32 *Statute Law Review*, 1.

LOBBAN, M. (1991), *The Common Law and English Jurisprudence*, 1760–1850 (Oxford: Clarendon Press).

MCEVOY, J. (1986), 'The Charter as a Bilingual Instrument', 64 *Canadian Bar Review*, 155.

MAUGHAN, C. and WEBB, J. (2006), *Lawyering Skills and the Legal Process* (London: Butterworths).

REGAN, P. (2013), 'Enacting Legislation—a Civil Servant's Perspective', 34(1) *Statute Law Review*, 32-8.

*RENTON COMMITTEE (1975), *The Preparation of Legislation*, Cmnd. 6053 (London: HMSO).

RHYS WILLIAMS, B. (1987), 'Legislation and Parliament', *Statute Law Review*, 38.

SMITH, J. (1980), 'Legislative Drafting: English and Continental', *Statute Law Review*, 14.

STARK, J. (2002), 'Learning from Samuel Johnson about Drafting Statutes', 23 *Statute Law Review*, 227.

VANDERLINDEN, J. (1967), *Le Concept de Code en Europe Occidentale de XIIIe au XIXe Siècle* (Brussels: Editions de l'Institut de Sociologie, Université Libre de Bruxelles).

9

Interpreting Statutes

9.1 Introduction

Most people are willing to believe that case law can present problems because facts are never precisely repeated; at the same time most people also believe that statutes are precise and accurate so that anyone can 'look up' the law in a statute. For the most part the implementation of statutory provisions will indeed be a routine matter, but this is not universally true. Once words appear in a statute they are open to all manner of argument and interpretation. Those arguments may be about the meaning of the language used in the statute (a sort of translation exercise), or about the application of the language to the facts (application exercise), or about both.

By a 'translation exercise' we mean instances where the court has to decide what a particular word or phrase means. These can be technical terms or plain, simple words. The court might be called upon to determine what specialised words like 'copyright', 'dismissal', or 'dishonesty' mean; equally the problem may centre on an apparently straightforward word such as 'vehicle' or 'animal'—or any other word you can think of. One thing you should bear in mind, though: the courts do not try to act like a dictionary editor; they are not trying to define a word for its own sake. Instead, they are trying to find the meaning of the word in the *context of the statute*. All that is said in this chapter concerns ascertaining meaning in context. So you will see that we often have to investigate a wide range of sources in order to discover the meaning of a word or phrase. For instance, consider the meaning of the apparently simple word 'parent'. This may refer to a natural parent, a step-parent, to parents where the child was conceived through IVF or through a sperm donor, to adoptive parents, to foster parents, to people deemed to stand in the position of parents (the Latin phrase being *in loco parentis*, as might apply to teachers or child-carers) and so on—the meaning often turning on the context and the purpose of the statute.

We must also take account of punctuation and grammar. Words can change meaning with different punctuation. For example, note the significance of the hyphen in the term 'pickled-herring salesman'—with the hyphen, this is a salesman selling pickled herrings; without it we have a salesman of herrings who is pickled (taken from Lynne Truss's excellent book *Eats, Shoots & Leaves: The Zero Tolerance Approach to Punctuation*). Heathrow airport once had a sign which read: 'No passenger carrying vehicles beyond this point'. Good health advice—and avoids breaching the rules on hand luggage.

The same problems arise, of course, in ordinary life with insurance policies, contracts, and even the rules of games. We saw this in **Chapter 8** as regards the structure of statutes, and the same applies here when interpreting the words used. Take a look, for instance, at the rules of Monopoly. Under the heading *Landing on 'Chance'* or *'Community Chest'* the rules state: 'A player takes the top card from the pack indi-cated and after following the instructions thereon, returns the card face down to the bottom of the pack.' Let's say you land on 'Chance'. You know (because you have been concentrating) that the only card still to come is a property repairs card; a fact which will cause you severe problems. Do you have to take the card? What arguments could you use not to? Do you have to show the card to anyone? Would the type of argument be the same as when you argued (but presumably lost) that you did not have to take the card at all?

When you look at any document the meaning attached to words is often influenced both by the fact that you wish your interpretation to be accepted and also by your general approach to life. What we mean by this last point is that some people are by nature apt to take words at their literal meaning—'it says X so it should mean X' (or, the Monopoly rules say 'take the card' so you must take the card)—while others naturally find themselves looking for the purpose behind the words—'what are these words try-ing to do?' (or what is the point in having cards marked 'Chance' if they leave you no choice whether to take them or not; surely there is a difference between 'Chance' and 'Community Chest'?).

Statutes are designed in the same way as the rules of a game or the rules of a commit-tee. They seek to tell you what you can do, what you cannot do, and perhaps how you are meant to do it. Equally, as we have seen in the previous chapter, they need to be drafted very carefully. Written words are not like conversation: there is no inflexion, no stress, no sense of irony; no opportunity to ask 'what do you mean?' The lifeblood of everyday speech is missing. The reader therefore has to give life to the words by interpreting what they mean and how they are meant to apply to particular situations. This is what is meant by statutory interpretation. The problem is: how do you do this? What rules do you use? When do you know you have found the *correct* meaning?

9.2 The So-called Rules of Interpretation

If you look in textbooks and cases written over the last five centuries, especially those on land law or the law of succession or the law of contract, you will see that lawyers have classified the basic means of reading documents under four headings:

- *the literal rule* (take only the plain, literal meaning of the words used because those are the words the draftsman chose to employ);

- *the golden rule* (take the whole of the statute together, placing the word or section in its context and giving the words their ordinary meaning unless this produces an absurd-ity or inconsistency—in which case the judge must try to give the words some other contextual meaning);

- *the purposive rule* (try to ascertain what the draftsman intended by the words by examining the general purpose of the section and the social, economic, or political context); and

- *the mischief rule* (which directs you to look to the previous common law and the his-tory of the Act (or other document) to see what was wrong with the law, what was the mischief, that the draftsman sought to remedy).

These are rather crude labels for describing a complex mechanism, i.e. making sense of what someone else has written. The labels are still in common use, but they are dangerous. For a start, they use the word 'rule', and this gives the impression that if you follow a particular pattern you will not go wrong. They also have an aura of scientific authenticity about them when the reality is (as Lord Templeman said in the original Foreword to this book) that interpreting any document is more of an art than a science. Indeed, in the case of *Re M (A Minor) (Care Order: Threshold Conditions)* [1994] 2 FCR 871, Lord Templeman himself had to deal with an argument about a child's welfare under the Children Act 1989. The argument was about who should take care of the child and the complication was that the statute set out rules where the child 'is suffering ... or ... is likely to suffer significant harm'. The child had been in such danger but, at the time of the trial the circumstances had changed, so the case centred on the meaning of the phrase '*is* suffering'. Was this limited to one moment or did it have to have a continuing element? Lord Templeman had this to say about interpreting the statute: 'My Lords, this appeal is an illustration of the tyranny of language and the importance of ascertaining and giving effect to the intentions of Parliament by construing a statute in accordance with the spirit rather than the letter of the Act.' The Act was created to protect children and Lord Templeman regarded the arguments on the use of the present tense in the statute as a distraction from that aim. One might see this as a 'purposive' approach, but in reality this is an example of judicial practicality and a desire to see justice done. It is certainly more about art than science.

Generations of lawyers have had problems applying these 'rules'. It is almost impossible to resist believing that if you know what the 'rules' mean you can apply them universally in understanding a section, a statute, or any document. One of the great writers on statutory interpretation, Rupert Cross, experienced this problem as a student; and when he became a lecturer at Oxford he found that his students shared his dilemma (Cross, 1995: Preface):

> Each and every pupil told me there were three rules—the literal rule, the golden rule and the mischief rule, and that the courts invoke whichever of them is believed to do justice in the particular case. I had, and still have, my doubts, but what was most disconcerting was the fact that whatever question I put to pupils or examinees elicited the same reply. Even if the question was, What is meant by 'the intention of parliament'? or What are the principal extrinsic aids to interpretation? back came the answer as of yore: 'There are three rules of interpretation—the literal rule ...'

The equivalent in legal practice (witnessed by one of the authors in the Court of Appeal) is:

[Counsel] 'I urge the Court to adopt a literal interpretation.'

[Judge's response] 'I have no idea what that means. Which one? I can see three possible literal meanings.'

In the text which follows we will explain these 'rules' in some more depth and will give some examples of their operation. The fact that we have chosen to do this seems almost hypocritical, given what we have just said. But we do so only because no matter what is written by commentators on statutory interpretation, lawyers and judges persist in using these terms because they are well-understood shorthand labels. But let us be blunt about this: they are, in fact, about as much use as the label on a product lambasted in *Which? Magazine*: the product was peanuts and the label contained the warning, 'This product may contain nuts'. In our own lectures we spend less than fifteen minutes noting these 'rules'. In effect, they boil down to our common childhood experiences of trying to justify our actions to our mothers. So, when your mum says 'Do not go to the shops on your own', how do you analyse her intention?

- The literal approach means you simply do not go to the shops on your own. You can go elsewhere on your own, or be accompanied by someone to the shops, but you take the words at their exact and limited meaning.

- The purposive approach means what your mum meant you should do or not do (i.e. 'Do not wander too far away from home—the shops being the limit and not a specific destination—unless I am with you'). This is therefore wider than the literal approach and limits you much more. Equally, you cannot be quite sure of those limits.

- The mischief rule means that the limitation relates to the behaviour or problem your mum was trying to correct (just beyond the shops lies a dangerous road on which a number of children have been injured). The action she is seeking to prevent you undertaking is about this danger element.

So, when, as a young child, you and a friend were discovered exploring beyond the shops and crossed the dangerous road you probably chose as your defence a literal approach ('I didn't actually go to the shops—and I wasn't alone'), but your mother will most likely have overruled you with a purposive approach or mischief rule interpretation to which your ill-judged childhood response was likely to be: 'If you meant that you should have said it'. Parents rely quite heavily on these approaches, even when using the interrogatory: 'What did I tell you not to do'?

9.2.1 Why Do We Still Refer to the 'Rules'?

In continuing to refer to these 'rules' we have, along with other writers, been accused of perpetuating an outdated approach to interpretation (Cross, 1995: 198). But, surprisingly, coming from such a distinguished text, this criticism misses the point we have made since the first edition of this book: no lawyer believes that by merely saying 'we should adopt a literal (or purposive) approach' one has *interpreted* the statute or constructed an argument. The terms are 'legal shorthand' for a complex analytical process—nothing more. However, as the terms appear in judgments and also in textbooks on contract, torts, etc. you need to be aware of their usage. Put another way: merely because a map or satnav has recognised or even recommended routes on it does not mean you have to follow them slavishly; but being ignorant of these routes is negligent, and trying to cut loose across country where there are no roads is unlikely to get you to your destination. The labels, the 'rules', are useful as map signs (especially when you are just starting your legal studies) but they do not tell you *how* to navigate, let alone how to drive.

The one *caveat* we would make at this point is that the 'purposive' approach is not a licence for invention or a substitute for that time-honoured phrase issued by students and unsuccessful litigants alike, 'But it's not fair'. Both your client and you (or any other combination) may well feel that the wording of a piece of legislation, or its interpretation, is 'unfair'. However, this is not an argument in itself, and no lawyer can afford to depart from the wording of a statute merely because it does not suit his or her client's case or his or her own sense of justice. Each interpretation offered has to have reasoning behind it and must actually bear some relevance to the words as they appear. And remember: what is fair or unfair is a question of opinion, not fact, and may be governed by other rules. This can apply even to things such as sports. In a tennis match, a player can win the match 0–6, 0–6, 6–4, 6–4, 6–4 because it is the number of sets which count; but if you tally the games, the winner only won eighteen games while the loser won twenty-four.

Perhaps the main difficulty with these 'rules' lies in the fact that, in order to see them in operation, one invariably looks at the reasoning given by the judge. Thus, you come across judicial utterances such as, 'If we apply the literal rule to these words we can see that ... '. However, to analyse the 'rules' by looking at which one a particular judge chose to apply in any given case is a bit like looking at the results of a horse race and then pretending the outcome was clear all along, because it now seems so obvious. Looking at a judgment, or at a results sheet, means that you are looking at a **conclusion**; what you still need to know is why the conclusion was reached or why that particular horse won. The problem with reading statements like the one just mentioned is that an impression is gained that there was a *correct* analysis and that if only you looked for it more carefully you could have found it. Instead, you need to think of these 'rules' as *approaches* to interpretation, as tools of argument.

Very often, one lawyer will try to argue a literal interpretation ('the words say this and nothing more'), while the other seeks to use a more purposive approach ('the words may say this but they cannot be taken so literally when you look at the purpose behind the section'). But there are many instances of a literal v. literal argument or a purposive v. purposive one. The essence of statutory interpretation is the construction of arguments which favour your client's case. The judgment reflects whether you were successful; and this depends on a whole host of things such as how well you and your opponent presented your arguments, whether the judge was by nature more inclined to accept one approach, the context in which the words appear, and whether there were any precedents that helped or hindered you.

9.2.2 How Do We Use these 'Rules' in Legal Argument?

General textbooks cannot spend much time on approaches to statutory interpretation and so present these 'rules' as though they are fixed and adhered to in an unchanging logical form. Such generalisatons are attractive because they look simple but they are misleading. Here, we certainly agree with Cross. The reality is much less certain, because these 'rules' are really nothing more than techniques of reading a document, and may be used singularly or in any combination. There is nothing wrong, for instance, in an argument which runs:

1. 'The plain meaning of these words show that my client's actions conformed with the requirements of the section [*a literal approach to the wording*].

2. Further, if we look at the purpose behind this section we find that it was designed to remedy the very problem for which my client seeks redress [*a purposive argument*].

3. And indeed, if we look at why this Act came about the history of this area shows that the Act was necessary to overcome the problems with previous cases in this field' [*use of the mischief rule*]'.

In *Oliver Ashworth (Holdings) Ltd* v *Ballard (Kent) Ltd* [1999] 2 All ER 791, Laws LJ explained the reality of these 'rules' (at 805): '[I]t is now misleading—and perhaps it always was—to seek to draw a rigid distinction between literal and purposive approaches … frequently there will be no opposition between the two, and then no difficulty arises. Where there is a potential clash, the conventional English approach has been to give at least very great and often decisive weight to the literal meaning of the enacting words. This is a tradition which I think is weakening … .'

So do not get too worried about these rules for now. You must know what they are seeking to do, but only as a tool for the way you argue your case; and so that you can make some guess at how the judge might decide the issue. Instead of thinking about statutory interpretation as just another legal topic—like homicide, theft, or offer and acceptance—you should think about the ideas outlined shortly and try to make use of them, either in academic discussion or in practice, across the whole range of legal subjects.

But we must emphasise again that these are not fixed rules of law; for the most part they are examples of the use of language generally. Cross, for instance, refers to cases which decided such awe-inspiring questions as 'Is a bicycle a "carriage"? Is a goldfish an "article"?' and concludes:

> Conundrums of this sort are part of the daily bread of judges and practitioners. In solving them the courts usually pay due regard to the context, but, in many instances, the answer must … be treated as a matter of common sense. (1995: 75)

Being aware of the 'rules' of statutory interpretation is important, therefore, because:

(a) Judges are not robots; their personality affects the way they will approach a problem of interpretation. Judges do not follow a 'critical path' analysis, progressing from one rule of interpretation to another in a logical fashion. If they did, we would have far more 'expert systems' available where people could just answer a series of questions generated by a computer and obtain an answer at the end. At some point a judge reaches what we called (in **Chapter 7** when looking at case law) the 'Marmite Moment'—the stage at which all argument has been made and he or she has to favour one or the other. You need to be aware, therefore, what range of analytical options are open to a judge in reaching that point.

(b) When arguing your case, or analysing the advantages and disadvantages of pursuing that case, you need to know the framework in which you are operating. It is often said that a bad workman always blames his tools; a workman who does not even know which tools exist deserves all he gets.

(c) It helps if you can combine (a) and (b), but that means you need to know how the judge is likely to react to the approach you have chosen. An argument based on the grand purpose of a statute delivered to a judge who believes firmly in a literal interpretation of words will fall on stony ground. You will discover from reading cases which senior judges favour which approach. This may not help on your first appearance in court before an unknown junior judge—which is why point (b) is important.

9.3 Examples of the 'Rules' in Action

These traditional 'rules' may be explained as follows.

9.3.1 The Literal Rule

The 'literal rule' is founded on the assumption that the words chosen by Parliament in the Act clearly show its intentions in passing that Act. The rule demands that one looks at what was said, not at what it *might* mean; that one is concerned with linguistics rather than considerations of the purpose of the Act or the wider context in which the statute was enacted. To do otherwise, as was said in *Duport Steel* v *Sirs* [1980] 1 WLR 142; [1980] 1 All ER 529, 541, might mean that the court is not interpreting the Act but really making law. There, Lord Diplock said:

> Where the meaning of the statutory words is plain and unambiguous it is not for the judges to invent fancied ambiguities as an excuse for failing to give effect to its plain meaning because they consider the consequences of doing so would be inexpedient, or even unjust or immoral.

Presented in this way the rule is seen as a safe bet—judges simply apply what is there. Safe bet or not, it is not a true reflection of reality. If the words were that clear, nobody would have brought the case in the first place. The literalist is prepared for this challenge. What the literalist would be looking for is the *primary* or most *obvious* meaning of the word, not any *general* or *secondary* meaning. And he will usually do this by looking at the way the word or sentence fits into the rest of the section or even the Act as a whole (see Summers and Marshall, 1992: 213). But, as Slocum comments, 'Courts generally do not, however, have good answers to the question of what makes a given meaning the ordinary one, as opposed to an inappropriately broad or narrow or technical meaning' (2012: 39).

The literal rule at its most extreme echoes the approach of a fundamentalist: consideration of the word or phrase as written is sacrosanct. The rule does not demand that the word be viewed in isolation from the rest of the sentence or section, but demands steadfastly that the investigation as to meaning does not stray beyond this point.

Thus the literal rule does not call upon a judge to consider the consequences of the interpretation. Sometimes this can still lead to what appear to be pretty odd results. The literal rule does not always generate a feeling that justice has been done even though it may be linguistically precise. Nor does it bear mathematical precision. As Willis stated:

> it is quite possible for all the members of the court to agree that the meaning of a section is so plain that it cannot be controlled by the context and yet to disagree as to what the plain meaning is. (1938:2)

Many examples can be given of judges relying upon the literal rule. But if we listed 100 cases all we would see is 100 different examples of the rule being used. The examples would not necessarily tell us how to interpret the next case. However, here are three examples that might help to give a flavour of literal interpretation in action.

In *R* v *Harris* (1836) 7 C & P 446 a statute made it an offence to 'stab, cut or wound' another person. Harris bit off her friend's nose in a fight—and then the policeman's finger. Was she guilty under the statute? The answer was no. The words in the statute pointed towards the use of a *weapon*. Teeth (even false?) are not a weapon. This conclusion was given further force by the fact that elsewhere in the section were references to the use of weapons, such as the word 'shooting'. You may think she should be guilty of something, but she was not guilty **as charged**.

It is also well worth reading the strange case of *R v Munks* [1964] 1 QB 304; [1963] 3 All ER 757 on the meaning of the word 'engine' in the Offences Against the Person Act 1861, s. 31. Here, the question was whether the action of Munks in wiring up a metal-framed doorway so as to electrocute his wife amounted to constructing an 'engine'. The judgment deals with literal interpretations and also a rule of grammar we shall return to (*eiusdem generis*). The judgment in *Munks* essentially limited the meaning of 'engine' to a 'mechanical contrivance' but this has been re-examined in *R v Cockburn* [2008] EWCA Crim 316; [2008] QB 882. It is also worth noting that *Cockburn* is an interesting example of the courts using all three of these so-called 'rules' in reaching their judgment as the discussion also deals with the purpose behind the 1861 Act and the 'legal mischief' which brought it into being. This is a good example of how 'applying the rules' is not some form of box-ticking exercise.

In *Fisher v Bell* [1961] 1 QB 394; [1960] 3 All ER 731, an Act of 1959 made it an offence to 'sell or hire or offer for sale or hire' certain offensive weapons such as flick-knives. Bell placed a flick-knife in his Bristol shop window with a price tag on it. Was he guilty of the offence? Again the answer was no. As you will see in the law of contract, placing an item on display is not the same thing as 'offering it for sale'. If the statute had used the phrase 'expose for sale', the answer would, on this analysis, have been different.

EXERCISE 16 Are we still on strike?

Take a look at the following case summary. We pose a few questions at the end of the account.

 Stock v Frank Jones (Tipton) Ltd [1978] 1 WLR 231; [1978] 1 All ER 948

This concerned the dismissal of employees who were on strike. Under the Trade Union and Labour Relations Act 1974 an employee who was dismissed for striking could not claim unfair dismissal unless 'one or more of the employees, who also took part in that [strike], were not dismissed for taking part'. So all employees taking part in the strike had to be treated the same way. If one employee, e.g. the shop steward, was victimised by being the only person dismissed, he could claim that the dismissal was unfair (which would be decided on the facts). In this case the employees were on strike and, following fairly normal industrial relations tactics, the employer threatened them with dismissal if they did not return to work. Some did return. The employer dismissed those who did not return and they claimed unfair dismissal.

 QUESTIONS

Using the literal rule, what do you think the words 'employees who took part in that [strike]' mean? Do they mean:

(i)   all the employees who originally took part in the [strike]? or

(ii) those employees who were still taking part in the [strike] when some of the others had returned to work following the threat?

What are the consequences of choosing each option?

continued

EXERCISE 16 *continued*

 A ANSWERS

Under the law which applied at the time of the case the House of Lords decided that 'employees who took part in the [strike]' could only refer to those employees who were participating in the strike **when the strike began**. Thus, when some employees returned and were not dismissed they still counted in the number of those who 'took part in the [strike]'. The employees who had been dismissed had therefore been 'victimised' and could claim unfair dismissal.

If the House of Lords had taken the second and less literal option, then, provided all those who stayed out on strike had been dismissed (which had happened), the employer would have been protected against any claim for unfair dismissal. After this case employers argued that this made nonsense of industrial relations for if the employer threatened to dismiss anyone not returning to work and one person out of a thousand did return the employer would either have to dismiss no one or dismiss everyone, including the one who returned! As a consequence the legislation was changed soon afterwards and it has changed considerably on many occasions since.

It is often said that the literal rule will not be used when it would lead to inconsistency or absurdity. This must not be taken too widely. Many people would disagree with the decisions in these cases; this is not the same thing as saying that relying on a literal approach produced an absurd result. So, when will judges deem the literal rule inappropriate?

9.3.2 The Golden (and Purposive) Rules

The golden rule can be best described as an *adaptation* of the literal rule. It tells you to read the word in the context of the statute as a whole. We use this form of interpretation every day when reading signs such as 'Stop Children'; hardly an instruction to act like Herod! The context aids the interpretation. The classic exposition of the rule is to be found in *River Wear Commissioners* v *Adamson* (1876–77) 2 App Cas 743, at 764–5, *per* Lord Blackburn:

> I believe that it is not disputed that what Lord Wensleydale used to call the golden rule is right, viz, that we are to take the whole statute together and construe it all together, giving the words their ordinary signification unless when so applied they produce an inconsistency, or an absurdity or inconvenience so great as to convince the court that the intention could not have been to use them in their ordinary signification and to justify the court in putting on them some other signification which, though less proper, is one which the court thinks the words will bear.

Sadly, his Lordship did not offer us much assistance on **how** the interpretation is to proceed once we have discovered the absurdity. We can overcome this by arguing that the only logical way to deal with an absurd interpretation is to correct it by assessing what Parliament was trying to do. But how is this to be ascertained? In its strictest form the golden rule still required the judge to focus only on the text of the Act and therefore the internal context of the word or phrase in question. Slowly but surely other (external) aids were brought to bear in trying to give meanings to words. This led to a more purposive approach.

The golden rule is a bridge between literalism and purposiveness. Whereas literalism focuses only on the words themselves, the golden rule developed this by making more use of context: the widest context is the setting which brought the Act into being (its purpose). One word of warning here: the term 'purposive' is not used consistently by the judges, as we shall see later.

In *Stock* v *Frank Jones (Tipton) Ltd* [1978] ICR 347; [1978] 1 All ER 948 Lord Simon advocated departure from the literal rule only when:

(a) there is a clear and gross anomaly;

(b) Parliament could not have envisaged the anomaly and would not have accepted its presence;

(c) the anomaly can be obviated without detriment to the legislative intent; and

(d) the language of the statute allows for such modification.

This is in keeping with the tenor of statements made by judges in the nineteenth century, particularly Lord Wensleydale in *Grey* v *Pearson* (1857) 6 HL Cas 61, which linked the idea of absurdity with the situation where a literal meaning would prove repugnant or inconsistent with the rest of the section or Act (the *internal* context). The emphasis is laid on establishing that the literal meaning is nonsense when the rest of the statute is considered; it clearly does not mean that an absurdity can be said to arise merely because a literal meaning might offend one's sense of justice.

Viewed this way the golden rule can be seen as an accessory to, or shadow of, the literal rule. It does not exist independently of the literal rule but comes into play only as a back-up when the literal rule has failed; usually focusing on the range of secondary meanings of the word or phrase in question. The literal rule will be departed from mainly where there is confusion *within* the Act—that a clear interpretation is not possible because of surrounding words and sections. It is interesting to note, however, that many of the cases which developed the golden rule were in fact cases on the interpretation of another type of document: testators' wills. And even a cursory study of the interpretation of wills in the law of succession reveals that there has always been a major conflict of judicial attitude here: do you follow only what the testator wrote, or do you look for other evidence of his intentions? The law of succession has had the same problems as seen in statutory interpretation. It has not produced a satisfactory answer. Even Lord Wensleydale, the sometime father of the golden rule, was known to adopt a strong literal approach when interpreting wills (see, for instance *Abbott* v *Middleton* (1858) 7 HLC 68).

It is respectfully submitted that Lord Simon's guidelines are still useful, although they leave us with the one major problem with the golden rule: how do we know when something is an anomaly, an ambiguity, or absurd? This is a question most frequently avoided by commentators and even recourse to dictionaries does not solve the problem. The Oxford English Dictionary, for instance, says of 'absurdity' that it is: 'the quality or state of being extremely unreasonable, illogical, or inappropriate … '; and on the meaning of 'absurd': 'against or without reason or propriety; incongruous, unreasonable, illogical'. This does not in reality help too much. Cross, however, does make a number of helpful points on this problem (1995: 81–92).

First, says Cross, the primary meaning cannot be abandoned, 'simply because it produces a result which [the judge] believes is contrary to the purpose of the Act. No judge can decline to apply a statutory provision because it seems to him to lead to absurd results.' That is always worth remembering. It is not the function of a judge to create law; judges are creative in the law's interpretation and application, but they cannot just make things up or disregard a law they do not like.

Equally, however, judicial treatment of the topic does not lend itself to simply saying judges are concerned only with the *internal* context of the words. Cross is forced to conclude that judicial applications of the rule tend to show that 'absurdity' 'does mean something wider than irreconcilability with the rest of the instrument' (1995: 89). In other words, some judges at least will go beyond merely examining the words of the section, etc. and probe into the purpose of the Act. Discovering whether something is absurd when matched against the purpose of the Act may involve examining the wider legal, and even social, setting of the Act. That is to say, judges, to a greater or lesser extent, will look to the *external context* of the statute.

Indeed, it is fair to say that the *purposive approach* has become the dominant judicial interpretation technique. Judges may not ignore the words written in statutes, but they are now more inclined to adopt a purposive interpretation whenever possible. This is partly due to the effects of EU legislation which, as we will see, works on the basis that a purposive interpretation will be given to the wording. It may also be related to the questionable standard of drafting seen in modern statutes.

HRA

Again there are many cases which illustrate the rule, but that is all they do—*illustrate*. As a lawyer you are concerned with using the rule to argue—it is of little value citing a case which simply proves that the courts do occasionally use the rule if the case cited has nothing to do with your argument. So an essay which involves interpreting a statute on tax law, say, which tells the reader that the court could use a purposive approach and then simply cites *River Wear Commissioners* as an example of when the courts used this approach has taken the argument nowhere.

Here, however, are two famous examples of the golden rule in operation: *R v Allen* (1872) LR 1 CCR 367: Allen, who was already married, married a woman called Harriet Crouch. The statute in question said: 'whosoever being married shall marry any other person during the lifetime of his spouse' shall commit bigamy. Now, Harriet was in fact closely related to Allen so this apparently bigamous marriage was actually void. Thus Allen argued that he had not married Harriet (because at law this was impossible) and so had not committed bigamy. He argued that the second marriage had to be a legal marriage before bigamy could be committed. But this would of course produce an absurdity because logically no bigamous marriage is lawful by its own definition; so, if Allen's argument was accepted, the judges would have had to pretend that the section was meaningless. Therefore they took a more purposive approach and read the words in the section 'shall marry' as meaning 'going through the ceremony'.

Re Sigsworth [1935] Ch 89; [1934] All ER Rep 113: Mrs Sigsworth was found dead. An inquest found that she had been murdered by her son, who was also found dead.

Mrs Sigsworth's will left everything to her son. However, old rules of public policy dictated that the son (and therefore his estate) could not inherit in these circumstances.

Therefore Mrs Sigsworth died intestate. But, under the Administration of Estates Act 1925, s. 46, the person entitled on intestacy was her son and, through him, his estate. The money had gone round in a circle; and the statute dealing with intestacy said nothing about murderers being barred from inheriting.

The Court held that the statute could not have been intended to allow murderers to inherit, despite being silent on the point. The old rule which applied to inheriting under a will was applied to intestacy on the grounds that cases such as *Sigsworth* would be 'obnoxious' to that old principle and must be read as being subject to it.

EXERCISE 17 Not all there; or, present and correct?

Please read the following case summary. We pose only one question at the end of the account.

Under the Statute of Frauds 1677 it was a requirement that a will had to be signed by the testator 'in the presence' of witnesses.

In *Casson v Dade* (1781) 28 ER 1010 Miss Honora Jenkins went to her attorney's office to execute her will. She signed the will but then felt faint and was taken outside to sit in her carriage with her maid. The witnesses to the will remained in the office and gave their signatures to the will. The maid gave evidence that at the moment the witnesses were signing the carriage horses reared up, causing the carriage to move into a line of sight with the office window. The maid stated that, had Miss Jenkins looked through the window she would have seen the witnesses sign.

 QUESTION

Was the will validly witnessed?

 ANSWER

The Court held that the will had been properly witnessed. Miss Jenkins was 'in the presence' of the witnesses even though she was not physically present in the same room. The fact that she was in the line of sight of the witnesses and could have seen them sign had she looked was enough. For, as had been said in the 1687 case of *Shires v Glascock* 21 ER 1134, to demand otherwise would mean that 'if a man should but turn his back, or look off, it would vitiate the will'. In modern parlance, it would be absurd to hold otherwise!

9.3.3 The Mischief Rule

Akin to the purposive rule is a much older aid to interpretation called the mischief rule, or the rule in *Heydon's Case* (1584) 3 Co Rep 7a, 7b.

Like both the golden rule and the purposive rule, the mischief rule stresses the need to interpret an enactment in such a way as to give effect to its objectives: in this case, what problem was the Act meant to overcome? However, the mischief rule is, formally, of narrower application, in that the approach is located purely in the context of an identifiable common law status quo which existed prior to the Act. Thus the courts are required to consider four things:

1. What was the common law before the Act?
2. What was the 'defect or mischief' for which the common law did not provide?
3. What remedy did Parliament intend to provide?
4. What was the true reason for that remedy?

Great care must be taken when relying upon this rule in argument: first, when *Heydon's Case* was determined the mischief could in fact be discovered within the Act itself because the reason for the Act's existence was always stated in the **preamble**. Thus a judge did not have to go beyond the bounds of the Act to discover the mischief it sought to remedy. The *internal* context was sufficient. A classic example of the use of preambles comes in the **Charitable Uses Act 1601** which states:

> WHEREAS Lands, Tenements, Rents, Annuities … have been heretofore given, limited, appointed and assigned, as well by the Queen's most excellent Majesty, and her most noble Progenitors, as by sundry other well disposed Persons; some for Relief of aged, impotent and poor People, some for Maintenance of sick and maimed Soldiers … which Lands, Tenements, Rents, Annuities … nevertheless have not been employed according to the charitable Intent of the givers and Founders thereof by reasons of Frauds, Breaches of Trust, and Negligence in those that should pay, deliver and employ the same: For Redress and Remedy whereof Be it enacted …

Lord Diplock recognised this in *Black-Clawson International Ltd* v *Papierwerke Waldhof-Aschaffenburg Aktiengesellschaft* [1975] AC 591; [1975] 1 All ER 810 when he said:

> So, when it was laid down, the 'mischief rule' did not require the court to travel beyond the actual words of the statute itself to identify the 'mischief and defect for which the Common Law did not provide' … the mischief rule must be used with caution to justify any reference to extraneous documents for this purpose.

The point concerning 'extraneous documents' is significant. As we will see shortly, judges have not, traditionally, been allowed to look at any and every source in order to discover the mischief. Recently this approach has altered.

Secondly, 'mischief' itself can be difficult to define. All Acts came about for **some** reason, be it social, economic, political, or because of some technical legal defect. This last reason is a reasonably safe basis upon which to attach the tag 'mischief'. One can easily find out what the law was before the Act came into effect; and thereby see the apparent changes the Act sought to make in the law. The other means of identifying the mischief are fraught with danger because they clearly involve making value judgements.

Thirdly, as was noted by Lord Bingham in *R* v *Secretary of State, ex parte Spath Holme* [2001] 1 All ER 195 (HL), an Act may have more than one mischief and the interrelationship between these may affect the question of interpretation. Two good examples of the mischief rule in operation are the cases of *Gorris* v *Scott* (1874) LR 9 Ex 125, and *Smith* v *Hughes* [1960] 1 WLR 830; [1960] 2 All ER 859. In *Gorris* v *Scott*, Scott contracted to transport some sheep by sea. The sheep were swept overboard because they had not been fenced in. Orders in Council made under the Contagious Diseases (Animals) Act 1869 required that the sheep should have been put in pens. Gorris thus claimed that Scott was in breach of the Act. The Court of Exchequer held that the purpose of the Act (which was clear from the preamble) was to prevent the spread of diseases among sheep or cattle en route to Britain; not to give a right to claimants like Gorris.

In *Smith* v *Hughes*, the Street Offences Act 1959, s. 1 stated: 'It shall be an offence for a common prostitute to loiter or solicit in a street or public place for the purposes of prostitution.' Prostitutes began trying to attract customers by signalling to the men from balconies or from windows. The report notes that the prostitutes would indicate the price by raising three fingers—and that on one occasion they received a counter-offer of two raised fingers! The Divisional Court of the Queen's Bench Division (on an appeal by way of case stated) decided that the mischief of the Act was to 'clean up the streets'. The words of s. 1 did not indicate **who** had to be in the street; and so an offence had been committed under the section.

It is probably fair to say that, today, the distinction between the mischief and golden rules is, in the minds of some judges, so fine as to be virtually non-existent. It could even be argued that both rules have become subsumed within a general purposive approach. An example of such thinking can be seen in Lord Diplock's approach to the Abortion Act 1967 in *Royal College of Nursing* v *DHSS* [1981] AC 800; [1981] 1 All ER 545. His Lordship began by defining his method for discovering the purpose of the Act:

> one starts by considering what was the state of the law relating to abortion before the passing of the Act, what was the mischief that required amendment, and in what respect was the existing law unclear.

He continued his analysis by looking at the whole context of the abortion problem—its social and economic aspects, as well as its legal history. He then concluded that:

> the wording and structure of the section are far from elegant, but the policy of the Act, it seems to me, is clear. There are two aspects to it: the first is to broaden the grounds upon which abortions may be lawfully obtained; the second is to ensure that the abortion is carried out with all proper skill and in hygienic conditions.

Be careful, however, not to assume that, in discovering the 'purpose' of an Act the judges are dealing with some sort of absolute, clearly definable, objective. Be prepared for contrary argument. Discovering the purpose of a rule is often an act of creative interpretation by the judge. Purposes and reasons for legislating are at least as indeterminate as the rules themselves.

9.4 Secondary Aids to Construction

The three 'canons of construction' so far considered are sometimes called **primary** aids to interpretation. It is now necessary to consider a set of **secondary rules** that can be employed within the framework of the primary aids to facilitate interpretation. These relate either to the use that can be made of parts of the statute itself, or to external (*extrinsic*) materials. Many of the rules noted later in the chapter are simply rules of grammar which are not unique to legal terminology. For instance, to borrow part of the exercise we have set at the end of this chapter, consider the following list: *cats, dogs, horses, cattle, sheep, pigs, and snakes or insects common to the British Isles.* Is it only snakes and insects that have to be common to the British Isles?

9.4.1 The Title of the Act

It is very tempting to point to the long or short title in order to show the purpose of the Act. It should be stressed that the long title is rarely used for this purpose and the short title is practically irrelevant. A classic example of this is the case of *R v Galvin* [1987] QB 862; [1987] 2 All ER 851. Galvin acquired 'restricted' Ministry of Defence documents. When Galvin was charged under the Official Secrets Act 1911 he argued that the documents had ceased to be secret and had never actually been 'official'—which, he said, is what the title of the Act demanded. Nevertheless he was found guilty because the section referred only to 'documents' and the title, being merely a label, had to give way to the words actually used in the section. The conviction, however, was quashed on other grounds.

On the use of the long title, see *Vacher v London Society of Compositors* [1913] AC 107. Here, the House of Lords referred to the long title of the Act but only to supplement and explain the meaning of the words in the section, not to contradict them. Note also that special rules will apply to the use of the Schedules that often appear at the end of an Act: see *Buchanan & Co. Ltd v Babco Forwarding & Shipping Ltd* [1978] AC 141; [1977] 3 All ER 1048.

9.4.2 Inclusory Words and Lists

A word which often arises in a statute is 'include': thus you find a section which might read:

> For the purposes of this Act references to sending include delivering, causing to be sent or delivered, transferring and posting.

The question would then be whether the word 'include' meant all the subsequent terms were included **and everything else was excluded** or that the subsequent terms were examples only, so that other terms might also be included. For instance, should 'distributing' or 'handing out' be included? In *R v Sheppard and another* [2010] EWCA Crim 65; [2010] 1 WLR 2779 the Court of Appeal had to consider whether racially inflammatory material published on the web fell within the ambit of s. 29 of the Public Order Act 1986 in the phrase: '"written material" includes any sign or other visible representation', or whether the term was limited to things such as 'signs'. It held that the phrase extended to the web, i.e. that 'includes' here did not close off the list.

Again, think of an everyday example: if you say that the Football Association Premiership includes Manchester United, Liverpool, and Arsenal, does this mean that there is no other team in the league? On the other hand, if you say that the Grand Slam tournaments in golf include the US Masters, the (British) Open, the US Open, and the US PGA, there are in fact no others, so this list has 'included' everything.

This problem was considered in *Coltman* v *Bibby Tankers* [1988] AC 276; [1987] 3 All ER 1068. In this case a ship sank off the coast of Japan with the loss of all hands. The administrators of the estate of one of the engineers sued the ship's owners under the Employer's Liability (Defective Equipment) Act 1969, alleging that the owners had provided defective equipment inasmuch as the ship was unseaworthy. The House of Lords therefore had to decide whether the words in s. 1(1) of the Act—'equipment provided by his employer for the purposes of the employer's business'—as explained in s. 1(3)—'equipment *includes* any plant and machinery, vehicle, aircraft, and clothing'—covered a ship. What was the effect of the italicised word 'includes'? The House of Lords solved the problem by looking at other sections in the Act which listed things. These other lists were very specific when not introduced by the word 'include'. This tended to indicate that when the word 'include' did occur it was merely stating examples, so that items not stated in the list might still fall within the definition of 'equipment' in the Act. So, although a ship was not mentioned in the Act specifically it was nevertheless 'included' in the definition of equipment. Lord Oliver stated:

> [I]t is quite clear ... that the word 'includes' in subsection (3) cannot be construed as 'means and includes' so as to confine that which is embraced in the word 'equipment' to the exemplars there specified. Granted that there may be circumstances in which an inclusive definition of this sort can have a restrictive effect, that cannot, in my judgment, possibly apply in the case of this statute. Here, where the draftsman intends a restricted meaning, he makes it quite clear. One has only to contrast the definitions of 'business,' 'equipment' and 'personal injury,' all of which are by reference to what is included, with those of 'employee' and 'fault,' where the Act makes it clear that there is to be a single exclusive meaning for the purposes of the Act. Subsection (3) cannot, therefore, be used to cut down the meaning of the word 'equipment' as it is used in subsection (1). It must have been inserted in the statute either for the purpose of enlarging the word by including in it articles which would not otherwise fall within it in its ordinary signification or it must have been inserted for clarification and the avoidance of doubt.

Thus the mere fact that a list is introduced by the word 'includes' does not automatically mean that the list is open ended. Much more needs to be considered. Indeed, we strongly recommend that you read this case, as it encompasses many of the techniques of statutory interpretation discussed in this chapter—including a reference to the long title of the Act which is introduced without excuse or explanation (showing how judges—if not students—can bend the rules when they so wish).

Legal maxims (there are more to come and many we do not cover) used to be the lifeblood of any lawyer; today they are looked on with some disdain, especially as they are often contained in Latin phrases. But this loses sight of the history by which they came about (we are not the first generation of lawyers to struggle making sense of a document) and the fact that they are still useful grammatical tools. As long as we do not regard ourselves as slaves to these maxims, they can still help a great deal (see also Graham, 2001). Nevertheless, we know from bitter experience that students do not like dealing with these maxims (not least because of the problems of pronunciation).

9.4.3 *Expressio Unius est Exclusio Alterius*

Closely connected to the problem of what is meant by 'include' is the position where a simple list of words appears. Can other words be added to the list? As always there is a Latin maxim to cover this: *expressio unius est exclusio alterius* (the expression of one thing is the exclusion of another). Using this maxim one can argue that if the legislature produces a list of items, then it is logical that all other items were specifically excluded. Why else would the legislators have provided a list? Thus one might use this rule to decide whether a faith healer fell within 'clairvoyant, fortune teller, or diviner'. This maxim might have applied in *Coltman* had it not been for the presence of the word 'include'. Similarly, where words like 'such as' or 'etc.' appears in the list the maxim does not work. One should take care with this maxim, however. It is not seen as a particularly strong presumption and is frequently overridden by examining the context of the words. Hence, Lord Bingham's statement in *R (on the application of Smith) R (on the application of West)* v *Parole Board* [2005] UKHL 1; [2005] 1 WLR 350 [29] that 'the maxim *expressio unius exclusio alterius* can seldom, if ever, be enough to exclude the common law rules of natural justice'.

9.4.4 *Eiusdem Generis*

What should happen when an Act employs a generic but non-exhaustive list? For example, an Act may state that a licence is required to keep 'dogs, cats, budgerigars and **other animals**'. Would you consider that a cow could be included on that basis? Obviously it is difficult to say without more information about the context in which those words appear. We can, however, identify a specific legal method of dealing with such a problem by saying that where general words follow a list of specific words then the general words must be read according to the *genus* (i.e. type or group) of the preceding specific words. It is the legal equivalent of explaining what one means by 'et cetera'. Thus, we must discover the *genus* which our named categories have in common and then interpret the general words ('other animals') so that they do not conflict with the specific words ('dogs' etc.). This is called the *eiusdem generis* rule.

Although this is a very useful rule of grammar, that is all it is; one still has to persuade the court that the *genus* of the preceding words is what you say it is. A good example of the arguments that may surround this rule arose in *Massey v Boulden* [2002] EWCA Civ 1634; [2003] 1 WLR 1792 where the Court of Appeal had to decide whether a person had the right to drive a vehicle along a track which ran across a village green, owned by another person, in order to gain access to his home. The owner of the village green submitted that the use of the track contravened the Road Traffic Act 1988, s. 34(1)(a) which states that a person commits an offence if 'without lawful authority [they drive] a mechanically propelled vehicle—(a) on to or upon any common land, moorland or land of any other description, not being land forming part of a road ... '. The Court held that it was quite difficult to identify what the *genus* might be here but a village green would certainly fall within its scope (other types of land might be more difficult to decide upon). The use of the track therefore contravened s. 34.

In our example concerning the phrase 'or other animals' we could therefore argue, depending upon context, that 'other animals' could refer to any commonly domesticated animal, or to **any** commonly domesticated animal normally **kept as a pet**. Either interpretation might be feasible, which is why it is important to remember that such rules are secondary aids—and therefore used only within the context of our understanding of the provision as a whole.

See, for examples of this rule in operation:

(a) *Powell* v *Kempton Park Racecourse* [1899] AC 143 on whether Tattersall's Ring (a place where horses are sold at a racecourse) fell within 'other place' in the phrase 'house, office, room or other place'—it did not (but only on a majority decision and involving detailed interpretational arguments on both the 'literal meaning' and the 'purpose' behind the legislation); and

(b) *R* v *Staniforth, R* v *Jordan* [1976] 3 WLR 887; [1976] 3 All ER 775 on whether pornographic material could fall outside the definition of obscene material under the Obscene Publications Act 1959 as being 'in the interests of science, literature, art or learning, or of other objects of general concern'. The argument was that the obscene material had psychotherapeutic value, so falling within the definition. That argument failed in the House of Lords.

9.4.5 *Noscitur a Sociis*

Linked with the *eiusdem generis* approach is the maxim *noscitur a sociis*—a word is known by its associates. The meaning of a word is affected by the surrounding words and should be interpreted accordingly. This rule is similar to the *eiusdem generis* rule and students often confuse the two. The *noscitur* rule is in fact of wider application than *eiusdem generis*.

The *eiusdem generis* rule is more limited because it comes into effect only when dealing with general words at the end of a list. Thus if we take the Wills Act 1837, s. 20 as an example, one of the ways of revoking a will is by 'burning, tearing, or otherwise destroying'. The *eiusdem generis* rule tells us that 'or otherwise destroying' is to be read in the light of burning and tearing; the cases showing us that this requires an act of physical violence rather than, say, amending the text or crossing things out.

The *noscitur a sociis* rule would not be used in this example merely because the *eiusdem generis* rule performs the same sort of task as regards general words at the end of lists. However, one would turn to the *noscitur a sociis* rule if the section read: 'burning, tearing, mutilating, or defacing' as there are no general words at the end of the list. In reality, though, you perform nearly the same analysis by asking 'what type of burning or defacing is included in this section?' So, one could ask: what if the will had been partially destroyed by fire? How should you read the word 'burning'? Does the burning have to be complete before the will is revoked, or is partial burning enough? From the surrounding words, especially 'mutilating' and 'defacing', it seems that this action does not have to be complete—that burning could be read as including partial burning.

Another good illustration comes from *Tektrol Ltd* v *International Insurance Co. of Hanover Ltd and another* [2005] EWCA Civ 845. Tektrol carried on business in the provision of computer-related energy-saving devices. A 'source code' played a crucial part in the business. By a very unusual series of unrelated incidents involving both a computer virus and a burglary, Tektrol lost all of its copies of that code and sought to recover money through its insurance policy. The case hinged on what was meant by 'loss' in the insurance policy. Sir Martin Nourse concluded:

> [27] 'Loss' is a word whose meaning varies widely with the context in which it is used. If a man said to you: 'I have lost my wife', you would understand him to mean one thing outside the maze at Hampton Court and another outside an undertakers in the high street.
>
> [28] Here we have to decide what ... is meant by 'other ... loss ... of information on computer systems or other records programmes or software.' Judging those words as they stand, I would find it difficult to say that they comprehended a loss of information caused by the loss of a computer in which the information was stored. That would not seem to be a loss of information on computer systems etc. The computer could be lost but the information retained.
>
> [29] If, however, 'loss' is read in its context, its meaning becomes plain. The expression [in the policy] 'other erasure loss distortion or corruption of information' demonstrates that the loss contemplated is loss by means of electronic interference; **noscitur a sociis**. It is not just the effect of the other three words, but the order in which the four appear. 'Loss' follows 'erasure'. While erasure can be expected to result in loss, a careful draftsman would not necessarily assume that it was the only way in which information might be lost. Then follow 'distortion or corruption', which seem to refer to interference causing something less than erasure or loss and between which, as Buxton LJ has observed, it is difficult to suggest a clear distinction. I agree with him that all four are overlapping words used by the draftsman to ensure that he had not omitted any case in which the information on the computer systems etc. was interfered with by electronic means.

In the latest case to debate the use of the rule (*McDonald (deceased) (Represented by Mrs Edna McDonald) v National Grid Electricity Transmission plc* [2014] UKSC 53, [2015] AC 1128) the Supreme Court had to decide whether regulations on the use of asbestos covered the death of a former worker. One part of the case hinged on whether his work, which involved mixing asbestos with water, amounted to 'mixing' within the statute because the surrounding words seemed to limit the word 'mixing' to a more technical meaning used in the industry. Two Supreme Court Justices held that the *noscitur a sociis* rule applied: the word was in the company of other technical words and so limited by them. However, three went the other way to say that the term 'mixing' in the Regulations should be read in a wider context and so should not be given a restricted, technical meaning, but should include the work in question—mixing asbestos powder.

Such a divergence of opinion by the most senior judges in this case demonstrates quite vividly that all these are merely rules of grammar. A judge does not have to apply these rules if he or she believes the wording of the Act does not justify their use.

9.4.6 *Ignorantia Legis non Excusat*

Perhaps the most famous maxim of all: ignorance of the law is no defence (though this is in fact derived from Roman law and was a maxim created when laws were fewer and more widely published, though not necessarily simpler). A 'Charlie Brown' cartoon once included this maxim. In the cartoon, Charlie Brown states the maxim and a puzzled Snoopy responds with: 'But what if you never know what's going on?'

9.4.7 Other Statutes

Provided statutes are *in pari materia* a word in one Act can be given the same meaning it had in an earlier Act. *In pari materia* means concerning the same matter. This interpretive technique should be used cautiously: as has been noted on a number of occasions, *par* or *pari* means 'equal' not just 'similar'. Thus the way the word 'horse' was interpreted in an Act concerning breeding rights could not be used readily to interpret the same word in an Act pertaining to the definition of a dangerous animal.

As a good example of the use of *in pari materia*, see *R v Wheatley* [1979] 1 WLR 144; [1979] 1 All ER 954 on whether 'explosive substance' in the Explosive Substances Act 1883, s. 4, included a pyrotechnic device. The 1883 Act gave no definition, but the Explosives Act 1875 dealt with the same subject matter and encompassed pyrotechnic devices in the term 'explosive'. Note also *British Amusement Catering Trades Association* v *Westminster City Council* [1988] 2 WLR 485; [1988] 1 All ER 740, in which, in order to decide whether video games in an amusement arcade fell within the meaning of 'exhibition of moving pictures' in the Cinematograph Act 1982, the Court considered every occurrence of this phrase within the long line of Cinematograph Acts dating from 1909 and the Cinemas Act 1985. The device can even be seen in operation across common law geographical boundaries, e.g. in *Wing Joo Long Ginseng Hong (Singapore) Co Pte Ltd* v *Qinghai Xinyuan Foreign Trade Co Ltd* [2009] SGCA 9; [2009] FSR 13 the Court of Appeal of Singapore found that the Trade Marks Act 1992, s. 39(1) (Singapore) was *in pari materia* with ss. 46 and 47 of the UK Trade Marks Act 1994.

The principle does not involve a hindsight factor: the meaning of words used in later Acts cannot be used as authority for establishing the meaning of the same words or phrases in earlier Acts: see *R (On the application of George)* v *Secretary of State for the Home Department* [2014] UKSC 28, [2014] 1 WLR 1831.

Linked with the idea of *in pari materia* interpretation is what is sometimes referred to as the 'Barras principle'. It is taken from the speech of Viscount Buckmaster in *Barras* v *Aberdeen Steam Trawling and Fishing Co. Ltd* [1933] All ER Rep 402, 411: 'It has long been a well established principle to be applied in the consideration of Acts of Parliament that where a word of doubtful meaning has received a clear judicial interpretation, the subsequent statute which incorporates the same word or the same phrase in a similar context, must be construed so that the word or phrase is interpreted according to the meaning that has previously been assigned to it.' One would have to say, however, that this is not really a principle of interpretation, more a useful starting point or presumption. It should be used with great caution (as was stated by the other Law Lords in *Barras* itself and again *per* Lords Scarman, Roskill, and Templeman in *R v Chard* [1984] AC 279; [1983] 3 All ER 637) but was applied most recently by the Supreme Court in *R (on the application of CN)* v *Lewisham London Borough Council; R (on the application of ZH)* v *Newham London Borough Council (Secretary of State for Communities and Local Government, interested party)* [2014] UKSC 62; [2014] 3 WLR 1548, the court finding that the word 'dwelling' should have the same meaning in the Housing Act 1996 as had been given by the court in relation to the same word in the Protection from Eviction Act 1977.

9.4.8 The Interpretation Act 1978

You should be aware of the existence of this Act, but it is not as helpful as it first sounds. The Act simply states that certain words will have a standard meaning unless specifically changed.

Thus 'month' means a calendar month and not 30 days; 'he' is read as including 'she'; singular words include the plural, 'oath' and 'affidavit' include affirmation and declaration, and 'swear' includes affirm and declare; 'distance' is measured in a straight line on a horizontal plane; 'British Islands' means the United Kingdom, the Channel Islands, and the Isle of Man; 'Land' includes buildings and other structures, land covered with water, and any estate, interest, easement, servitude, or right in or over land, and so on. It also contains statements on how legislation should be read, such as s. 20A: 'Where an Act passed after the commencement of this section refers to a EU instrument that has been amended, extended or applied by another such instrument, the reference, unless the contrary intention appears, is a reference to that instrument as so amended, extended or applied.'

9.4.9 Punctuation and marginal notes

The modern view is that punctuation can be used as an aid to interpretation. Traditionally, however, this was not true of headings and marginal notes in a statute. That approach changed following *R v Montilla* [2004] UKHL 50; [2004] 1 WLR 3141.

Marginal (or side) notes are just what they sound like. Prior to 2001, when a Bill was going through Parliament each clause of the Bill had a note (drafted by Parliamentary Counsel) in the margin explaining the function of the clause for ease of reference. In 2001 these notes were moved so that they now appear in bold type as headings to each clause (later to become section) in the version of the statute which is published by the Stationery Office. Parliamentary Counsel very occasionally, on the advice of the Bill's drafter, alter marginal notes and headings which, because of amendments or for some other reason, have become inaccurate, but for the most part they stay the same even if the clause/section is redrafted. The question then is whether headings and marginal/sidenotes, although generally unamendable, can be considered in construing a provision in an Act of Parliament.

The resistance to making use of these notes has always been justified on the grounds that they can sometimes be misleading. An example of this can be seen in the Animals Act 1971 where s. 3 reads: '*Where a dog causes damage by killing or injuring livestock, any person who is a keeper of the dog is liable for the damage …*' and s. 11 adds, '*In this Act "damage" includes the death of or injury to any person*' but the marginal note to s. 3 states: '*Liability for injury done by dogs to livestock*'—which is not quite the same thing.

Nevertheless, in *R v Montilla* the House of Lords decided that they could be used: 'the headings and sidenotes are as much part of the contextual scene as these materials, and there is no logical reason why they should be treated differently' (at [36]). Interestingly, the Irish Supreme Court has held to the traditional approach (see *Fitzgibbon v Law Society of Ireland* [2014] IESC 48).

Montilla does not mean that all such sidenotes, etc. are determinant of the meaning of the section. They are aids only. As Arden LJ put it this way in *Murphy v Wyatt* [2011] EWCA Civ 408 at [75]: '[W]hile **marginal notes** to a statute do not have great weight in the interpretation of a statute they have some weight' (see also Horn (2011) on the use of headings and drafting techniques). Further, where statutes have been amended by later Acts it may well be the case that the accompanying notes (unamended) become misleading. Such was noted in *R (on the application of Smith) v Parole Board; R (on the application of West) v Parole Board* [2005] UKHL 1; [2005] 1 All ER 755. Here, the sidenote to the Criminal Justice Act 1991, s. 39 referred to both long-term and life prisoners. This was an accurate description of the contents of the 1991 Act when it was enacted. However, as a result of a complex series of repeals, s. 39 no longer dealt with life prisoners. The sidenote therefore had to be ignored and their Lordships suggested that similar misunderstandings could be avoided by draftsmen and Parliament in the future if a section whose substance has been so changed as to make the sidenote an unreliable guide to its contents were to be repealed and replaced by an entirely new section, with its own appropriate sidenote.

9.4.10 Explanatory Notes

Explanatory notes have been appended to statutory instruments for some time and began to accompany Acts in 1999. As with marginal notes these explanatory notes are attached to Bills and draft statutory instruments as they go through Parliament. They seek to offer a simplified guide to the legislation. As well as appearing in printed form you can also find them on the Internet (at www.legislation.gov.uk/). The opening part contains a 'health warning', such as appears in the Child Benefit Act 2005:

> These explanatory notes relate to the Child Benefit Act, which received Royal Assent on 24th March 2005. They have been prepared by the Inland Revenue in order to assist the reader in understanding the Act. They do not form part of the Act and have not been endorsed by Parliament.

One would presume from this that they cannot be used to interpret the Act itself. Not so. That these notes could be used as a means of identifying the mischief behind a *statutory instrument* was established in *Pickstone v Freemans plc* [1989] AC 66; [1988] 2 All ER 803, at least in a European setting. More recently they have been applied to statutes.

This is how it came about. In *Coventry and Solihull Waste Disposal Co. Ltd v Russell (Valuation Officer)* [1999] 1 WLR 2093; [2000] 1 All ER 97 it was said that an explanatory note may be referred to as an aid to construction where the statutory instrument to which it is attached is ambiguous. And in *R (on the application of Westminster City Council) v National Asylum Support Service* [2002] UKHL 38, [2002] 1 WLR 2956 Lord Steyn commented specifically on explanatory notes—this time in relation to a statute (the Immigration and Asylum Act 1999). He did not rely on the notes to the Act but sought to clarify their status (his comments were therefore *obiter*). He observed that: *obiter*

> [5] The question is whether in aid of the interpretation of a statute the court may take into account the explanatory notes and, if so, to what extent. The starting point is that language in all legal texts conveys meaning according to the circumstances in which it was used. It follows that the context must always be identified and considered before the process of construction or during it. It is therefore wrong to say that the court may only resort to evidence of the contextual scene when an ambiguity has arisen … Insofar as the explanatory notes cast light on the objective setting or contextual scene of the statute, and the mischief at which it is aimed, such materials are therefore

always admissible aids to construction. They may be admitted for what logical value they have. Used for this purpose explanatory notes will sometimes be more informative and valuable than reports of the Law Commission or advisory committees, government Green or White Papers, and the like ...

[6] If exceptionally there is found in explanatory notes a clear assurance by the executive to Parliament about the meaning of a clause, or the circumstances in which a power will or will not be used, that assurance may in principle be admitted against the executive in proceedings in which the executive places a contrary contention before a court ... What is impermissible is to treat the wishes and desires of the government about the scope of the statutory language as reflecting the will of Parliament. The aims of the government in respect of the meaning of clauses as revealed in explanatory notes cannot be attributed to Parliament. The object is to see what is the intention expressed by the words enacted.

A short time later came *Regina (Confederation of Passenger Transport UK)* v *Humber Bridge Board and Another* [2003] EWCA Civ 842; [2004] QB 310. This case also concerned a statutory instrument, but, here, one in which there was no ambiguity *per se*: instead there was a clear drafting error. The error was that, in setting the level of tolls to be paid for crossing the Humber Bridge no provision had been made for tolls on buses carrying sixteen passengers or more ('large buses'). Previous statutory instruments on the tolls had included large buses. The history of these previous relevant statutory instruments and the explanatory notes to the statutory instrument made it obvious that large buses should have been included.

The Court of Appeal therefore had to consider whether, when construing a statutory instrument, it was permissible to add, omit, or substitute words in order to correct an obvious drafting error. It was held that, having regard to the historical context of the Orders, it was inconceivable that the bridge company or the Secretary of State had intended to exclude large buses from the classes of vehicle expected to pay tolls. The Court of Appeal held that, provided that the court was sure:

(a) of the intended purpose of the provision in question;

(b) that the draftsman had failed to give effect to that purpose by inadvertence; and

(c) of the substance of the provision that would otherwise have been made,

then reference to material extraneous to the statutory instrument could be made as an aid to its construction where the instrument was ambiguous, obscure, or led to absurdity and the material made the intention of the instrument clear.

Again, in *R* v *Montilla* it was noted that it had become common practice for their Lordships to ask to be shown the explanatory notes when issues were raised about the meaning of words used in an enactment. Their Lordships cited themselves with approval (which is handy if somewhat circular) in *R (on the application of S)* v *Chief Constable of South Yorkshire* [2004] UKHL 39; [2004] 4 All ER 193 (*per* Lord Steyn at [4]: 'they may potentially contain much more immediate and valuable material than other aids regularly used by the courts, such as Law Commission reports, government committee reports, Green Papers, and so forth'). So, whatever the 'health warning' in the notes themselves, it seems that they can be used to interpret provisions in an Act: see, for instance *R (on the application of the Public and Commercial Services Union)* v *Minister for the Civil Service* [2010] EWHC 1027 (Admin); [2011] 3 All ER 54 which distinguished 'notes on clauses' distributed to MPs privately to explain the nature of a

Bill from 'Explanatory Notes'. The privately distributed notes were excluded as an aid to interpretation in direct contrast to the explanatory notes which were simply accepted as a normal part of statutory interpretation techniques.

Despite this, some judges are still wary of relying on explanatory notes or other such material and the full extent to which they can be used is tied up with the debate on another House of Lords' decision (*Pepper v Hart*) which we will discuss shortly at section 9.5, so we shall leave this for the moment. One interesting aside here comes from Underhill LJ in *Jessemey v Rowstock Ltd and another* [2014] EWCA Civ 185; [2014] 3 All ER 409 with the line [at 36]: 'this explanation cannot be reconciled with para 353 of the explanatory notes (*at least if these were produced by the draftsman of the section, rather than by someone else trying to reconstruct his thinking*)'. The high-lighted section rather begs the question as to the strength of a note depending on proof of authorship.

9.4.11 Dictionaries

Dictionaries can be used by judges where a word has no specific legal meaning. One must be careful here, however, as words can change meaning by dint of time, usage, and context.

One example of a court using dictionaries to interpret sections arose in *Flack v Baldry* [1988] 1 WLR 393; [1988] 1 All ER 412. The case concerned the legality of possessing a 'stun gun' which could administer an electric shock of 46,000 volts. Did this offend against the Firearms Act 1968 as a 'weapon designed for the **discharge** of any noxious liquid, gas, or other thing'? The Court found that 'discharge' had a dictionary mean-ing of 'emit' rather than 'physical ejection', so that the stun gun was caught by the Act. Dictionaries also came to hand in *R (on the application of Robinson) v Torridge DC* [2006] EWHC 877 (Admin); [2007] 1 WLR 871 in deciding a bridge could 'choke' a river under the Public Health Act 1936, s. 259 (see Munday, 2008 for a discussion on this slightly weird problem of interpretation).

One has to tread carefully here, though. Different dictionaries often give different slants to the meaning of words. For instance, in one exercise we give to our students a key question arises whether a person has committed an act of 'violence' when he has been found guilty of causing criminal damage to a snack bar. Depending upon which dictionary is used you tend to get definitions which will stress either that 'violence' relates only to causing injury to people, or that it includes damage to property as well as injury to people. Finding the one dictionary that most favours your interpretation is sometimes referred to as 'dictionary shopping'.

9.4.12 *Travaux Préparatoires*

This translates literally as 'preparatory works'. In the English context it refers to the consideration of public materials by the courts in order to discern the purpose of the legislation. A common example is the reports or working papers (though not the rec-ommendations) of law reform bodies such as the Law Commission or Criminal Law Revision Committee. The question as to whether White Papers may be referred to in aid of interpretation has been inconclusively mooted by the Court of Appeal in *Thomas v Chief Adjudication Officer and Secretary of State for Social Security* [1990] IRLR

436; [1990] 3 CMLR 611; but for earlier contrary authority see *Katikiro of Buganda* v *Attorney-General* [1961] 1 WLR 119.

In the European context, the willingness to consider *travaux préparatoires* has traditionally been greater. EU case law, for instance, thus includes references to the use of legislative proposals as published in the *Official Journal* and parliamentary debates in Member States, though never to the deliberations of the Council or Commission. Similarly, in the Commonwealth, the (English) exclusionary rules have gradually been relaxed across most jurisdictions since the early 1980s: see Zander (2004) for examples.

9.5 The Use of Hansard

In contrast to what we have just said about the use of *travaux préparatoires* in European courts, the English courts had already until recently taken a restrictive view of the range of documents which may be so used. For instance, all parliamentary debates in the House of Commons and House of Lords are recorded in a text called Hansard. Traditionally, Hansard could not be referred to explicitly by a court in order to gauge Parliament's intention (although some judges have admitted over the years to looking at the debates anyway). In the international context, such as dealing with the interpretation of international treaties, the English courts had already taken a more relaxed attitude: see *Fothergill* v *Monarch Airlines* [1981] AC 251; [1980] 2 All ER 696. And, in the European context, as more and more legislation has owed its origins to the (then) European Community the House of Lords began to use Hansard on several occasions and moved more towards harmonisation with European methods of interpretation in the use of *travaux préparatoires*: see *Pickstone* v *Freemans* [1988] 3 WLR 265; [1988] 2 All ER 803; *Litster* v *Forth Dry Dock* [1990] AC 546; [1989] 1 All ER 1134; and *R* v *Secretary of State for Transport, ex parte Factortame Ltd* [1990] 2 AC 85; [1989] 2 All ER 692.

9.5.1 *Pepper* v *Hart*

In 1992 the House of Lords delivered a blockbuster in the case of *Pepper (Inspector of Taxes)* v *Hart* [1992] 3 WLR 1032; [1993] 1 All ER 42. By a six to one majority (Lord Mackay LC dissenting) the House of Lords decided to allow reference to be made to Hansard in limited circumstances. Reference to parliamentary materials would be allowed where:

(a) legislation is ambiguous or obscure, or leads to an absurdity;

(b) the material relied upon consists of one or more statements by a minister or other promoter of the Bill, together if necessary with such other parliamentary material as is necessary to understand such statements and their effect;

(c) the statements relied upon are clear.

In this case, the effect of permitting reference to Hansard was that the literal meaning of the statute in question was not followed (and it is probably fair to say that justice was therefore done).

Some comments by their Lordships are worth noting here. Lord Bridge stated (at 1039H, WLR) that:

> It should, in my opinion, only be in rare cases where the very issue of interpretation which the courts are called on to resolve has been addressed in Parliamentary debate and where the promoter of the legislation has made a clear statement directed to that very issue, that reference to Hansard should be permitted.

Lord Oliver commented (1042H, WLR):

> It can apply only where the expression of the legislative intention is genuinely ambiguous or obscure or where a literal or prima facie construction leads to a manifest absurdity ...

Lord Mackay (dissenting) observed:

> I believe that practically every question of *statutory* construction that comes before the courts will involve an argument ... [on (a) to confirm the meaning of a provision as conveyed by the text, its object and purpose; (b) to determine a meaning where the provision is ambiguous or obscure; or (c) to determine the meaning where the ordinary meaning is manifestly absurd or unreasonable] ... It follows that the parties' legal advisors will require to study Hansard in practically every such case to see whether or not there is any help to be gained from it. I believe this is an objection of real substance. It is a practical objection not one of principle ... (1037G, WLR)
>   Such an approach appears to me to involve the possibility at least of an immense increase in the cost of litigation in which statutory construction is involved. (1038B, WLR)

Lord Bridge further commented on the issue of additional costs (1039H, WLR):

> Provided the relaxation of the previous exclusionary rule is so limited, I find it difficult to suppose that the additional cost of litigation or any other ground of objection can justify the court continuing to wear blinkers which, in such a case as this, conceal the vital clue to the intended meaning of an enactment ... [W]here Hansard does provide the answer, it should be so clear to both parties that they will avoid the cost of litigation.

9.5.2 The Rise and 'Fall' of *Pepper* v *Hart*

Despite Lord Bridge's reassurances, *Pepper* v *Hart* initially cut major inroads into the traditional methods of statutory interpretation. In the six months immediately following the decision the House of Lords itself had made express use of Hansard in no fewer than three important cases: *Chief Adjudication Officer* v *Foster* [1992] 2 WLR 292; [1993] 1 All ER 705, *Stubbings* v *Webb* [1993] 2 WLR 120; [1993] 1 All ER 322, and *R* v *Warwickshire County Council, ex parte Johnson* [1993] 2 WLR 1; [1993] 1 All ER 1022.

In contrast to this, however, reservations or scepticism concerning this new-found research source began to emerge. Thus in *Sheppard* v *Commissioners of Inland Revenue*, [1993] STC 240, Aldous J. expressed concern regarding the problem of determining what is an 'ambiguity' for the purposes of reference to Hansard (on which, see section **9.5.4**) and on the level of clarity required in a Minister's statement specifically on the issue in question. Indeed in *Melluish (Inspector of Taxes)* v *BMI (No. 3)* [1996] AC 454, the House of Lords itself expressed reservations on the over-use of *Pepper* v *Hart* (e.g. *per* Lord Browne-Wilkinson, who had been one of the Law Lords in *Pepper* v *Hart* itself, that the statement by the appropriate minister must be 'directed to the very point in question in the litigation', effectively creating a fourth condition).

However, before that, the full potential of *Pepper* v *Hart* was realised in *Thomas Witter Ltd* v *TBP Industries Ltd* [1996] 2 All ER 573. This case neatly illustrates the true width of the problem: the potential ambiguity of *any* statutory provision and the fragility of our existing understanding of established areas of the law. This case involved examining the Misrepresentation Act 1967, s. 2(2). Jacob J. considered this subsection to be ambiguously drafted and, relying on the support of *Pepper* v *Hart*, decided to examine the relevant extracts from Hansard. His Lordship concluded that these extracts were sufficient to establish that the accepted meaning of the subsection was incorrect. This of course meant that the previous understanding of the great majority of academic writers (endorsed by judicial *obiter* comments) and practitioners since the inception of the Act was erroneous.

Such a reassessment of an area of law has occurred before, on many occasions and in many different ways—the flexibility of case law depends upon such changes. Nevertheless, it is worrying (especially for practitioners advising clients) if *all* long-established principles built up using the pre-*Pepper* v *Hart* methods of interpretation are potentially open to re-examination, especially given the quality of the actual debate cited, taking place at 3.30 am in a near-empty chamber). For contemporary comment on this case, see Chandler and Holland (1995: 503).

More recently, however, case law has shown that the practice of referring to debates which, at the date when they took place, would not have been admissible as evidence in court of Parliament's intention (i.e. debates prior to 1992), may no longer be permissible: see *McDonnell* v *Congregation of Christian Brothers Trustees* [2003] UKHL 63; [2004] 1 AC 1101.

After all this initial confusion and enthusiasm things began to calm down. A trawl through the cases shows an increasing reluctance to rely on extracts from Hansard unless the guidelines noted earlier have been shown to justify the search.

It is not surprising, therefore, to find more and more decisions where the courts were reluctant to allow references to Hansard without a fair bit of persuasion. A good example of this can be seen in the comments of Silber J. in *Zafar* v *Director of Public Prosecutions* [2004] EWHC 2468 (Admin); [2004] All ER (D) 06 (Nov.). The case involved the law relating to drink-driving and the accuracy of intoximeters when the driver being tested was suffering from heartburn and stomach reflux. The argument centred on the meaning of the word 'breath' in the Road Traffic Act 1988, s. 5 and the Road Traffic Offenders Act 1988, s. 15(2). When invited to refer to statements made by Baroness Blatch as recorded in Hansard, Silber J. concluded:

[20] In my view, the appellant cannot rely on the statements of Baroness Blatch as an aid to construing the sections with which the Case Stated is concerned because first the word 'breath' in section 5 of the RTA is not ambiguous, second the statement of Baroness Blatch was not made in relation to section 5, which is the section under review and third, her statement was made not by the promoter of section 5 but as the promoter of an amendment, which was made eight years later.

The case clearly demonstrated that, merely because a particular interpretation is arguable or may lead to a perceived injustice against your client, it does not mean that the word or section is ambiguous or absurd so as to trigger a reference to Hansard. The court must be persuaded that such a reference is justified. One way to do this is to show internal inconsistencies within the Act, or to demonstrate the logical consequences of following only one line of interpretation, or to show that case law on this area has already been divided on the topic, as was the case in *Mirvahedy* v *Henley* [2001] EWCA 1749; [2002] QB 769.

Equally, it should be stressed that the mere discovery of a ministerial statement does not mean anything in itself. Not only must that statement be clear but (as was illustrated in *Hone* v *Going Places Leisure Travel Ltd* [2001] EWCA Civ 947 and many cases since) one must also have regard to the context in which the statement was made: in this case it was apparent that, looking at the full text of the speech, the minister had not been purporting to construe the relevant legislation at all. One might regard this decision as effectively imposing an additional requirement for the citation of Hansard. Indeed, to many, it would be a fifth requirement for, as we noted previously, even in 1996 Lord Browne-Wilkinson (who set out the original 'rules') had confined references to parliamentary statements directed *to the specific statutory provision under consideration* or to the problem raised by the litigation (see *Melluish (Inspector of Taxes)* v *BMI (No. 3)* [1996] AC 454; [1995] 4 ALL ER 453).

The Irish approach, given that they use the same methods of interpretation, to this question is again interesting. There, s. 5(1) of the Interpretation Act 2005, entitled 'Construing ambiguous or obscure provisions, etc' provides similar rules to *Pepper* v *Hart* for referencing other material where there is ambiguity. It states that, 'the provision shall be given a construction that reflects the plain intention of the Oireachtas [the National Parliament] … where that intention can be ascertained from the Act as a whole'. Thus, investigation as to Parliament's intention is restricted to the Act itself.

There are real obstacles to making use of Hansard reports. However, one method used to persuade a court to look at Hansard is to ask the judge to take the point *de bene esse*.

9.5.3 The *De Bene Esse* Approach

This means 'For what it's worth'. A judge may take a point *de bene esse*, which means he or she will allow it to be argued for the present (i.e. conditionally or provisionally) but to make no ruling on whether, once things have been more fully argued, it will be accepted. In other words, to overcome the rather circular arguments that can arise over whether there is an absurdity and what Parliament really meant to do, judges sometimes allow the lawyer to refer them to Hansard but, in doing so, they do not accept that what is said in Hansard determines the point. The court is said to 'admit' the evidence contained in Hansard without deciding on the weight to be attached to it. Effectively the judge looks at the Hansard reference without deciding whether it is permissible to do so on the basis that he or she will decide that point later. It is a bit of a cheat—rather like looking at the answers to a crossword 'just to check' you are on the right lines. An example can be seen in the Court of Appeal decision of *R* v *Deegan* [1998] 2 Cr App Rep 121. The case concerned the Criminal Justice Act 1998, s. 139. Deegan had been found in possession of a folding pocket-knife which was capable of being locked into an open position. Section 139 made it an offence to have in a public place 'any article which has a blade or is sharply pointed except a folding pocket-knife'. Previous case law had held that a knife which locked open was not a *folding* pocket-knife for the s. 139 exemption. It was argued that a reference to Hansard under the *Pepper* v *Hart* rule would reveal statements showing that the type of knife being carried by Deegan was intended to be excluded from the section. The Court looked at these extracts *de bene esse*. After expressing the view that this was not an easy case, Waller LJ stated:

> Although in one sense the statements made in Parliament were clear, in that they undoubtedly thought they were excluding from this section not just pocket-knives that fitted the previous case law's interpretation of 'folding', but some which 'locked' when the blades were open, we think that in the sense required by *Pepper* v *Hart*, they were not clear. They were not clear because 'locking pocket-knives' is itself an ambiguous phrase. If in answer to that point it were said that the court could attempt to define the phrase by for example saying that it should only include 'locking pocket-knives' that were manually locked and manually unlocked ... that would be asking the court to go beyond its proper function. It would no longer be interpreting the intention of Parliament, it would be writing the legislation it thought was reasonable. In those circumstances we do not think that the conditions of *Pepper* v *Hart* are fulfilled ...

The *de bene esse* approach was evident again (though not specifically referred to) in *R* v *Hinks* [2000] 4 All ER 833 (a case dealing with the meaning of 'appropriates' in the Theft Act 1968, s. 1). Lord Steyn quoted a famous statement by Lord Reid in the *Black-Clawson* case (see section **9.3.3**) that: 'We often say that we are looking for the intention of Parliament, but that is not quite accurate. We are seeking the meaning of the words which Parliament used. We are seeking not what Parliament meant but the true meaning of what they said.' Lord Steyn used this as the basis for his refusal to allow counsel to submit (supposedly under the rule in *Pepper* v *Hart*) a memorandum written by the drafter of the Theft Act to the Larceny Sub-Committee of the Criminal Law Revision Committee, explaining what he had thought he had meant by the term 'appropriates'. At the time this was perhaps not too surprising, as it really was pushing the boundaries to argue that such a memorandum fell within the *Pepper* v *Hart* guidelines. However (illustrating the divergence of approaches in this area) within three years of *Hinks* the Court of Appeal, in *R* v *Humber Bridge Board* (noted earlier), had admitted both explanatory notes and even a 'decision letter' from the relevant Secretary of State in the interpretation of a statutory instrument (a 'decision letter' is a ministerial response to a matter arising from a formal inquiry; these letters are not statements made in Parliament and have no connexion with legislation). That documents such as 'decision letters' might be referred to therefore cast doubt on the exclusion of the memorandum in *Hinks*.

9.5.4 What is meant by 'ambiguity'?

The triggers set out by Lord Browne-Wilkinson in *Pepper* v *Hart* for the use of Hansard require there to be an ambiguity, obscurity, or absurdity evident in the legislation. In *R* v *Secretary of State, ex parte Spath Holme* [2001] 2 AC 349; [2001] 1 All ER 195 the House of Lords confirmed the importance of these 'trigger events'.

On the facts their Lordships held that, as the words in question were not ambiguous, reference to Hansard was not permissible. However, the key area of disagreement in this case ironically concerned what was meant by 'an ambiguity'. Their Lordships were clear that if the words in the statute were ambiguous then Hansard could obviously now be referred to. This does not mean that just because a word may be difficult to define precisely it is ambiguous. In *Cooke* v *MGN Limited* [2014] EWHC 2831; [2015] 2 All ER 622, for instance, the High Court refused a *Pepper* v *Hart* reference on the term 'serious harm' in a defamation case on the basis that 'serious' was an ordinary word in common usage.

However, what if the words themselves were clear but there was some 'ambiguity' as to what the words were *meant to do*: what was the policy or purpose behind the statute? Could this type of ambiguity justify a reference to Hansard?

The issue in *Spath Holme* was whether a minister could issue an order capping rent increases for certain types of tenants. The words were clear as to the minister's powers; the argument was as to when he could exercise those powers. The history of the relevant statutes showed that such a power was first introduced because of massive problems of inflation in the 1970s, but updating and consolidating legislation had since been added, when no such inflation existed. All the Acts were silent as to whether the policy or purpose was limited to introducing capping only where there were problems of inflation or on wider grounds, but there were some statements to be found in Hansard. So, the ministerial power was clear, but was it limited to interfering only when there was high inflation, or could it be invoked for other reasons?

Lords Bingham, Hope, and Hutton felt that *Pepper* v *Hart* was never designed to allow reference to Hansard in order to ascertain what the Executive (the Government) had in mind as their policy. Their Lordships felt that this was extending the decision in *Pepper* v *Hart* well beyond its limits, and one which usurped the power of Parliament and the courts. However, Lords Bingham and Hope thought there might be rare instances where this would be permissible. As Lord Bingham stated: 'Only if a minister were, improbably, to give a categorical assurance to Parliament that a power would not be used in a given situation, such that Parliament could be taken to have legislated on that basis, does it seem to me that a Parliamentary statement on the scope of a power would be properly admissible' (at 212a). However, Lords Nicholls and Cooke took the opposite line and felt that *Pepper* v *Hart* 'ambiguities' *could* extend to matters of policy: 'The purpose for which a statutory power is conferred is just as much a question of interpretation of the statutory provision as is the meaning of a particular word or phrase' (*per* Lord Nicholls at 218b). Though Lord Cooke also noted that 'Government statements, however they are made and however explicit they may be, cannot control the meaning of an Act of Parliament ... it is for the court ... to decide how much importance, or weight, if any, should be attached to a government statement' (at 218h).

9.5.5 The Practice Direction

To help deal with the real and practical difficulties of referring to Hansard material, there is a practice statement relating to the use of Hansard: *Supreme Court Practice Direction* (Hansard: *Citation*) [1995] 1 WLR 192 (repeated in later consolidating Practice Directions covering the Court of Appeal (Civil Division at [1999] 1 WLR 1059, and Criminal Proceedings at [2002] 1 WLR 2870). This demands, for instance, that anyone wishing to rely on Hansard must serve copies of the extract on the court and other parties, together with a brief summary of argument, not less than five working days before the hearing.

9.5.6 Views on *Pepper* v *Hart*

There is extensive division in the legal world as to the efficacy of *Pepper* v *Hart*. Indeed, there is some division between the authors of this book. There are certainly undoubted advantages in making use of all relevant materials to interpret a statute, and the cases to date have often allowed perceived justice to win over technicalities. The rule was being eroded prior to 1992 anyway, in practice if not in law. Equally, Lord Mackay's words as to the extra level of research and costs involved in litigation should not be disposed of lightly. Possibly more pertinent to this book is the fact that practitioners, academics, and law students will now have to come to terms with a new source of material in their research. Even with modern databases, such research can prove difficult and electronic access relates only to recent years; for any other research one has to overcome the appalling indexing for Hansard. Moreover, reports on the Committee stage are held in only a handful of libraries across the country—and yet this is where many important amendments are recorded. All this is in addition to the fact that when you start you can never be sure you will find anything at all—a point which your paying client will only be too happy to appreciate and pay for.

On a wider scale, however, one of the objections to *Pepper* v *Hart* might be that it encourages (perhaps even obliges) the courts to adopt an assumption of ministerial infallibility when describing the meaning or purpose of statutory language.

9.5.7 Current trends regarding *Pepper* v *Hart*

After the initial 'settling-in' period it became obvious that all was not well within the judiciary as regards the operation of *Pepper* v *Hart*. Some judges took a very strict approach to the use of Hansard; some made use of the *de bene esse* approach (though usually concluded that the reference had either been of no help or simply confirmed the decision they would have come to anyway—see, for example, *R (Jackson)* v *Attorney-General* [2005] EWHC (Admin) 94). Others were minded to allow reference even where the rules for reference laid out in *Pepper* v *Hart* were not adhered to (but then neither did their Lordships do so in *Pepper* v *Hart* itself).

By the late 1990s and the early part of this century the divisions of opinion on *Pepper* v *Hart* (even within the House of Lords) were becoming very obvious. In 1997 Lord Hoffmann and Lightman J. expressed their views, extra-judicially (meaning, not in a case but in a lecture or article), that there were problems with *Pepper* v *Hart*. Lord Millett, in another lecture, referred to the case as 'a regrettable decision'. Then, in 2000, a powerful attack on the use of Hansard was launched by Lord Steyn in his Oxford Hart Lecture and published shortly afterwards in the *Oxford Journal of Legal Studies* (see Steyn, 2001)— the reference to 'Hart' is coincidental and relates to one of our great jurists. We would strongly recommend that you read this article. Although another extra-judicial statement, this lecture was viewed as sounding warning bells that *Pepper* v *Hart* should only be used in limited cases; or even its death knell.

From that moment on the cases show what has been called a 'retreat from *Pepper* v *Hart*'. Even one of the early uses of *Pepper* v *Hart* by the House of Lords (in *Stubbings* v *Webb*) has been overturned by another House of Lords' case for placing too much weight on non-statutory material (see *A* v *Hoare* [2008] UKHL 6; [2008] 1 AC 844).

Yet, in the midst of this 'retreat', as we have seen, there were cases such as *R v Humber Bridge Board* permitting references to explanatory notes (the reference to which does not require an ambiguity in the Act) and *R (on the application of Amicus-MSF Section) v Secretary of State for Trade and Industry* [2004] EWHC (Admin) 860 admitting a letter from the General of the General Synod and the Archbishops' Council to the Parliamentary Joint Committee on statutory instruments. So, while references to Hansard were falling into disuse, other non-statutory material was being admitted. Lord Steyn defended such toing and froing in *R (Westminster City Council) v National Asylum Support Service* [2002] UKHL 38; [2002] 1 WLR 2956 on the basis that references to explanatory notes did not evoke the same sort of constitutional arguments witnessed in Hansard references. However, that dodges the unequal resources argument and the possible deliberate influencing of statutory interpretation by ministers and their civil servants, using extra-legislative material to aid their cause.

Equally, as noted in a fascinating article by Professor Vogenauer (designed as a reply to Lord Steyn's lecture) the Court of Appeal throughout this time has not shown the same level of antagonism to *Pepper v Hart* as had been witnessed in the House of Lords— which is ironic given that they started the whole thing. On a key point, for instance, the House of Lords have demonstrated time and again that references to Hansard are generally inadmissible except to bind Parliament to ministerial assurances given on the limitations of the legislation (what is sometimes called the 'estoppel' argument, meaning that the government should be stopped or prevented from relying on statements which support their own later preferred interpretation).

At the same time the Court of Appeal has tended to disregard this view and perceive *Pepper v Hart* references in a much more welcoming light on a much wider range of issues (see Vogenauer, 2005). Most recently, for instance, Underhill LJ allowed reference to explanatory notes in *Innes v Information Commissioner and Another* [2014] EWCA 1086, [2015] 2 All ER 560. The question was whether, under the Freedom of Information Act 2000 an applicant was entitled to choose the type of electronic format by which to receive the information requested (e.g. Excel or Pdf) or was stuck with whatever the provider gave him. Underhill LJ allowed a Ministerial statement in Hansard to overrule his own initial interpretation. His Lordship commented [at 36]:

> [T]his seems to me one of the rare cases in which the *Pepper v Hart* criteria are satisfied: the Minister did in the passage which I have quoted make a clear statement directed to the very question of whether an Applicant is entitled to request information in hard copy or electronic form.

Such disagreements, however, do not help practitioners or students and even here the Court of Appeal (*obiter*) has at times shown antagonism to *Pepper v Hart* as regards its use in interpreting penal statutes (see *Massey v Boulden* [2002] EWCA Civ 1634; [2003] 1 WLR 1792). The doubts on using Hansard references in criminal cases were expressed forcefully by Lord Phillips of Worth Matravers CJ again in *Thet v Director of Public Prosecutions* [2007] 1 WLR 2002 where he stated, at p. 227 para. 15:

> I would, however, question the use of *Pepper v Hart* [1993] AC 593 in the context of a criminal prosecution … If a criminal statute is ambiguous, I would question whether it is appropriate by the use of *Pepper v Hart* to extend the ambit of the statute so as to impose criminal liability upon a defendant

where, in the absence of the Parliamentary material, the court would not do so. It seems to me at least arguable that if a criminal statute is ambiguous, the defendant should have the benefit of the ambiguity.

Obiter observations from Lord Phillips in *R v Tabnak* [2007] EWCA Crim 380; [2007] 1 WLR 1317 then indicated that *Pepper v Hart* could be invoked by a *defendant* in a criminal case, though, interestingly, in *R v JTB* [2009] UKHL 20; [2009] 2 WLR 1088 the same judge made use of Hansard (and the other Law Lords agreed) but this time in favour of the prosecution. The case was a criminal case where the defendant was tried on counts of causing or inciting a child under thirteen to engage in sexual activity. He had been twelve years old at the time of the alleged offences. At one time there was a rebuttable presumption that a child aged ten to fourteen was *doli incapax* (incapable of committing an offence). However, the Crime and Disorder Act 1998, s. 34 stated: 'The rebuttable presumption of criminal law that a child aged 10 or over is incapable of committing an offence is hereby abolished'. The technical argument was whether only the presumption had been abolished or the whole defence. To decide this, Lord Phillips used a number of aids described earlier but also turned to entries in Hansard, stating at [35]:

I further consider that this is one of the rare cases where it is both legitimate and helpful to consider ministerial statements in Parliament under the principle in *Pepper v Hart* [1993] AC 593. Furthermore, the proposed amendment was moved on the premise that the clause, as drafted, would abolish not merely the presumption but the defence of doli incapax.

On this analysis, the boy was not able to make use of the defence—so here is a case where a *Pepper v Hart* reference was used in a criminal case as against the defendant. All their Lordships referred to this as a 'rare event' but it demonstrates that there is no hard-and-fast rule here.

Vogenauer's article surveyed all the *Pepper v Hart* decisions from 1992 to 2005. He concluded (before launching his own counter-attack) that: 'On the whole, the scope of *Pepper v Hart* has been reduced to such an extent that the ruling has almost become meaningless'. However, it is worth noting the words of the editor of *Statute Law Review* here as regards both *Pepper v Hart* and the use of other materials in a 2014 setting:

[L]aw students have always been taught to identify the range of materials to which the courts will have regard in determining the mischief or context of legislation. Nowadays it would be more tempting to give students a list of materials to which the courts will not have regard; except that since *Pepper v. Hart* it is not at all clear that there would be any items on the list.

Year on year the courts appear to expand both the range of materials to which they are happy to have regard in making decisions about interpretation and application and also the extent of the reliance that they are prepared to place on those materials. (2014: v)

One example the editor cites is that of *Cooke v MGN Ltd*, noted above regarding *Pepper v Hart* references, where the learned judge commented:

I consider that it is proper to refer to the Ministerial foreword to the draft Bill, to the Joint Committee's report on the draft Bill, and to the explanatory notes to the Act, to identify the mischief at which it was aimed. I also consider that the parliamentary history, and in particular any respect in which the Act differs from the original draft Bill, may be highly illuminating. It is also proper to refer to statements made by the promoters of the Bill (that is to say the sponsoring minister in each House or the proposer of any successful amendment) in order to resolve a genuine ambiguity in the Act.

9.5.8 *Pepper* v *Hart* and Human Rights Cases

The Human Rights Act 1998 (see section **9.8** and the full discussion in the next chapter), has also arguably added to the pressure on courts to look to Hansard in the process of assessing whether legislation is compatible with the UK's obligations under the European Convention on Human Rights. It has become increasingly common for evidence from government departments in such cases to contain lengthy memoranda detailing the legislative history and debate about the statutory provision under examination. This practice has, however, also attracted a certain amount of criticism from the judiciary, most notably in *Wilson* v *First County Trust* [2003] UKHL 40, where Lord Nicholls observed:

66. I expect that occasions when resort to Hansard is necessary as part of the statutory 'compatibility' exercise will seldom arise. The present case is not such an occasion. Should such an occasion arise the courts must be careful not to treat the ministerial or other statement as indicative of the objective intention of Parliament. Nor should the courts give a ministerial statement, whether made inside or outside Parliament, determinative weight. It should not be supposed that members necessarily agreed with the minister's reasoning or his conclusions.

67. Beyond this use of Hansard as a source of background information, the content of parliamentary debates has no direct relevance to the issues the court is called upon to decide in compatibility cases and, hence, these debates are not a proper matter for investigation or consideration by the courts ...

So, even in the context of human rights legislation, *Wilson* did not really change the pattern of the 'retreat' from *Pepper* v *Hart*. At the moment, therefore, we can only say that any reliance on references to Hansard, in the context of human rights or wider, is fraught with difficulties.

9.5.9 Summary of *Pepper* v *Hart*

Pepper v *Hart* represented a major shift in interpretive techniques (as well as stirring up a whole range of constitutional issues). After initially being received by many with enthusiasm, it now looks more like last-year's Christmas toy. But, just as the Supreme Court has dropped the toy, its junior sibling, the Court of Appeal, appears to have taken to it quite fondly. The current rules appear to be:

- The starting point now seems to be to regard Hansard as generally inadmissible. Consequently, even the sleight-of-hand *de bene esse* arguments have generally fallen from favour.
- If it is admissible, the three triggers originally identified in *Pepper* v *Hart* itself must be present. On the meaning of 'ambiguity' see *R* v *Secretary of State, ex parte Spath Holme* and *Mirvahedy* v *Henley*.

- If it is admissible it seems that it is confined to cases which turn on the meaning of words in the legislation, not on questions of the policy behind the Act (see *Hone* v *Going Places Leisure, Spath Holme* and *Melluish*).

- An exception to this is seen in *Spath Holme* where references can be used as *against the Government* to show how a minister gave a categorical assurance on the use of discretionary powers—what is sometimes termed the 'estoppel' argument (*estoppel* being a Norman-French word meaning that where a person acts on your words or conduct there are limitations on how much you can then change your position if this adversely affects the other person).

- The High Court and Court of Appeal have adopted a more liberal attitude to references to Hansard. There is therefore some conflict between the Supreme Court and the lower courts.

- Even the Court of Appeal has intimated that Hansard cannot be used in certain situations (see the *obiter* comments in *Massey* v *Boulden* as regards use in penal statutes).

- The use of material such as explanatory notes and headings does not fall under the same set of limitations (*R* v *Montilla*).

- If there is authority on a point which was reached at a time when Hansard was not admissible, this should not be departed from (*McDonnell*). Contrast this to the case of *Thomas Witter* (dealt with at section **9.5.2**).

9.6 From Rules to Reality

The question posed by all students at some stage is: in what order will the rules be applied? The analysis of statutory interpretation found in many textbooks begs the same question. Most of them fail to answer it. The reality is that not only is there no answer; it is the wrong question to ask.

The right question is: how do judges choose to explain the construction they have placed on the statute? Posed this way the question recognises, as Willis put it, that there is not 'one great sun of a *principle*, "the plain meaning rule", around which revolves in planetary order a series of minor rules of construction. ... Any one of these approaches may be selected by your court' (1938: 1). There is no rule that says a judge must look at the literal meaning of words first. The fact that many judges do this is simply the recognition that most English judges do not want to be seen to be *creating* law, and a logical starting point in reading any document is to see what has actually been written. By examining the literal meaning of the words judges appear to take a logical and safe line. However, if they wish then to rely on a more purposive argument they will do so by finding absurdity or inconsistency; they have at least guarded against some criticism.

9.6.1 Styles of Interpretation

We would suggest that interpretation is a question of *style*, not rules. By emphasising the *style* of judging we would draw a parallel with Llewellyn's analysis of how judges use case law. In 1960 Llewellyn drew attention to two different approaches used by judges; he termed these 'grand' and 'formal'. The 'grand' style reflects a judicial willingness to base a decision on public policy and to take a creative or flexible approach to precedent. Conversely, the 'formal' style demands rigid adherence to traditional doctrine and the denial of a creative judicial function.

So too, we submit, is this the case with statutory interpretation. Judges who employ the 'grand' style place substantial emphasis on the external context of the statute. They place less weight on the dictionary meaning of words, preferring to seek out the sense of the provision in question. One who adopts the 'formal' style, however, is more concerned with the form the statute takes, the internal context, and the perceived hierarchy of the rules.

The formalist will, therefore, frequently seek to find a safe embarkation point in a literal approach. This does not prevent the formalist then making use of the golden and mischief rules; but this method of 'follow the pathways' analysis provides appropriate justification for departing from a strictly literal interpretation. Such 'formalism' can be seen extensively in the House of Lords' decision in *Duport Steel v Sirs* (cited earlier).

On the other hand, the 'grand' style will encompass those judges who will tend to move much more easily to reliance on the external context for interpretation. Such can be seen in *Royal College of Nursing* v *DHSS*; but equally its ranks will also be filled by judges prepared to go beyond this point to using a 'teleological' approach. A teleological approach is a rather grandiose name for an interpretation which is based on the purpose or object of the text confronting the judge. It goes beyond the inquiry as to the external context of the Act; examining instead the broader social, economic, perhaps political reasons behind the Act. It thereby attempts to give the fullest effect to the grand design of the law. It is, in the end, not really different from a purposive approach; it is more an extreme method of discovering that purpose and surfaces more in the analytical styles of European judges than in English law.

The hallmark of the 'grand' style is often that the approach is extremely credible from a common-sense viewpoint: the authority for such (often) sweeping statements is less clear.

9.6.2 Example of the Use of Different Styles

In support of the foregoing analysis any examples are inevitably somewhat selective. However, we suggest that a good illustration of these styles in action is a case we first mentioned in **Chapter 6** concerning *stare decisis*: *Davis* v *Johnson* [1979] AC 264; [1978] 1 All ER 841 (CA) and 1132 (HL).

Jennifer Davis and Nehemiah Johnson were joint tenants of a council flat. Davis was subjected to extreme violence by Johnson and eventually fled the flat with her infant child. She applied to the county court, under the Domestic Violence and Matrimonial Proceedings Act 1976 (DVA), s. 1, for an injunction restraining Johnson from assaulting or molesting her or the child and ordering him to vacate the flat and not return. At first the injunction was granted and then withdrawn. We are concerned with the case in the Court of Appeal and the House of Lords. The case illustrates the points we have been making because, even when the various judges were agreed as to the outcome, their approaches to the question of interpretation differed extensively.

The case is dealt with in texts mainly as regards the issue of *stare decisis* raised by the Court of Appeal's judgment. We will not dwell on that aspect of the case in this analysis. However, the case is a fine example of the areas of judicial precedent and statutory interpretation overlapping; and this is an aspect of statutory interpretation that is worth noting. As with judicial precedent, cases concerning statutory interpretation do not exist in isolation. When a court is considering the meaning of a statute it will frequently have to interpret it in the light of previously decided cases.

no jurl statutory interpretation

Returning to *Davis* v *Johnson*: in the Court of Appeal Lord Denning MR, Sir George Baker P., and Shaw LJ found in favour of Ms Davis and the injunction was granted. Lords Justices Goff and Cumming-Bruce dissented. The House of Lords unanimously dismissed Johnson's further appeal. These are three points we need to examine here:

(a) What was the question of interpretation?

(b) How did the judges in the Court of Appeal set about the question of interpreting the statute? and

(c) How did the House of Lords interpret the statute?

We shall now consider each of these.

What was the question of interpretation?

The DVA, s. 1 stated:

> (1) Without prejudice to the jurisdiction of the High Court, on an application by a party to a marriage a county court shall have jurisdiction to grant an injunction containing … [(a) and (b) are irrelevant here] … (c) a provision excluding the other party from the matrimonial home …
>
> (2) Subsection (1) above shall apply to a man and a woman who are living with each other in the same household as husband and wife as it applies to the parties to a marriage and any reference to the matrimonial home shall be construed accordingly.

So, did this section apply to the case in hand? It was argued that s. 1 was procedural in its effect; it had not changed the existing law on property rights and could not have been meant to do away with these rights. In other words, if the man had property rights in the home (e.g. as a joint tenant, as was the case here) he could not be excluded from the property.

The *stare decisis* point (see **Chapter 6**) was that there were two binding Court of Appeal decisions where similar applicants to Davis had failed: *B* v *B* [1978] Fam 26; [1978] 1 All ER 821, and *Cantliff* v *Jenkins* [1978] 2 WLR 177n; [1978] 1 All ER 836.

How did the judges in the Court of Appeal set about the question of interpreting the statute?

Lord Denning began by recounting the history of the Act—an Act designed to protect 'battered wives'. He then commented that 'No one, I would have thought, could possibly dispute that those plain words [s. 1 above] by themselves cover this very case.' One sees here a reliance on the literal reading of the section (though without full explanation) and hence the 'formal' style in operation.

In reviewing the two earlier Court of Appeal decisions, Lord Denning set about proving they had inadequately interpreted the section. If *B* v *B* was right, he argued, the only woman who could obtain an injunction would be one who owned the property solely. Thus, he said, 'In order to give s. 1 any effect at all, the court must be allowed to override the property rights of the man' (849b). Even when faced with House of Lords authority which appeared to give preference to the protection of property rights, Lord Denning reacted: 'Social justice requires that personal rights should, in a proper case, be given priority over rights of property … I prefer to go by the principles underlying the legislative enactments rather than the out-dated notions of the past' (849e–f). This is a purposive approach in the 'grand' style. The term 'social justice' looks like a logical and analytical argument, but in fact it has appeared from nowhere. Try to look up 'social justice' as a legal term of art: you will have difficulty.

Lord Denning then returned to the history of the Act and investigated Reports of Select Committees and statements made in Parliament. This was more than simple reliance on the 'mischief rule' and again demonstrates a 'grand' style purposive approach.

Sir George Baker P. began by discerning the 'mischief' on which the DVA centred by reference to legal history and the long title of the Act. There is nothing apparently unconventional in this. On the whole this is still a 'formal' approach; though it moves away from the strict canons of interpretation by its premature use of the long title. That mischief was the protection of family partners (married or unmarried) from violence. His analysis continued on a 'formal' basis: he rejected the idea that only a woman who was a sole owner could bring such an action. This interpretation he justified on the grounds that any other interpretation would deprive the Act of any practical meaning or purpose. Although Sir George Baker P. talks of 'purpose', the style of the judgment is still 'formal'. He had to make the point as to 'purpose' in order to overcome the decision in *B* v *B*. What he is actually saying is that:

(a) a literal reading of s. 1 produces this solution; it gives the woman a right to have the violent male excluded; it does not even mention a limit to be placed on this; and

(b) it was the earlier cases which had gone beyond this literal reading by importing into the wording the sanctity of property rights and, in doing so, had not implemented the purpose of the Act. He is therefore arguing that it is the use of a 'formal' style which produces the real purpose and not the 'grand' style.

Lord Justice Shaw first considered that the meaning of the section was plain: nothing in the wording took account of the 'other party's' property rights so it could not have intended this to be relevant. He reviewed the arguments to the contrary, and, though attracted by them, concluded that the 'section would be utterly stultified' if nobody but a sole owner could gain the injunction. The general theme of the section was to subordinate property rights to the need to protect the victim of violence. Lord Justice Shaw's decision thus has a strong 'formalist' feel about it, though there are odd hints of a wider approach such as: 'The construction of a statute dealing with a morbid aspect of society must, it seems to me, be pursued in the practical context of the evil sought to be remedied rather than with analytical detachment' (876a).

Lord Justice Goff (dissenting) dwelled on the *stare decisis* aspect and felt bound by the earlier decisions although he expressly did not agree with them. However, he made some comment on the interpretation of the section. He reiterated the point that a woman should not have to be sole owner of the home in order to make the application, for this would deprive the section of all effect. Lord Justice Goff continued in a classic 'formalist' vein by analysing the relationship of s. 1 to other parts of the Act. He concluded that, if he were free of binding precedent, he would adopt a 'liberal approach' and grant the injunction because:

> the strict construction … virtually strikes the power of eviction in s. 1(1)(c) … since where the (woman) is sole owner of the property she does not need it … yet where she is not sole owner and so the Act is needed to protect her from just the same evil, it is held inapplicable. (874: d)

His Lordship was prepared to make reference to the mischief of the Act, but only by discovering that mischief on the accepted (limited) grounds. The meaning of Parliament, he said, must still be found in the words used in the Act.

Lord Justice Cumming-Bruce (also dissenting) agreed with the decision in *B v B* and, for the most part, with Goff LJ; but concentrated his reasoning on points of precedent. The tenor of his judgment is in the 'formal' style. This is particularly noticeable in his references to the mischief rule and his consequent disapproval of using debates in Parliament to assess the purpose behind the Act on which he says (at 885): *agree with rules use*

> The task of this court is to decide what the words of the Act mean. The subject should be able, as in the past, to read the words of an Act and decide its meaning without hunting through Hansard to see whether the Act has a different meaning from that which is to be collected by application of the subtle principles of construction that this court has worked out over the last three centuries.

How did the House of Lords interpret the statute?

The House of Lords unanimously dismissed Johnson's appeal but the Law Lords were not of one mind in their reasoning.

Lord Diplock stated a preference for a narrow 'formal' approach to the interpretation of s. 1, to which he added adverse comment on the practice of looking at reports on parliamentary debate to discern the meaning of a statute. This latter point was treated in the same way by the other Law Lords.

Viscount Dilhorne stated (at 1145) that the 'language is clear and unambiguous and Parliament's intention apparent'. To differentiate between married and non-married women would 'frustrate the intention of Parliament'. At first sight this appears to be a 'formal' style; but it is difficult to see from where Viscount Dilhorne derives his conclusions apart from the line (at 1145): 'Subsection (1) is not concerned with property rights.'

Lord Kilbrandon took a literal approach to the section; expressly agreeing with Lord Salmon and Lord Scarman.

Lord Salmon adopted a 'formal' style, moving from a literal reading ('It has been said that its [s. 1] meaning is as plain as a pikestaff. I agree') to a more purposive stance based on an examination of the legal history of the Act and the mischief it

Procedure

sought to remedy. This also illustrates our point that judges can use any of the so-called 'rules of interpretation' as they feel it necessary to do so in order to explain their conclusions.

Finally, Lord Scarman also looked to the mischief the Act was designed to remedy. Out of this Lord Scarman identified the purpose of the Act and had no difficulty extending this purpose to allow an unmarried woman with no property rights to be, nevertheless, granted the injunction. His Lordship's speech lies between the 'formal' and 'grand' styles. Lord Scarman concentrates on the mischief. There are wide statements of purpose (at 1156): 'I would expect Parliament, when dealing with the mischief of domestic violence, to legislate in such a way that property rights would not be allowed to undermine or diminish the protection being afforded.'

All this illustrates the point that the logic of decision-making (and the method of reaching those decisions) does not follow one particular, predictable, line. For instance, if one just adds up the decisions of all the judges (merely who won and who lost) in this case as well as *B v B* and *Cantliff v Jenkins* one finds seven Lords Justices on one side and the Master of the Rolls, the President of the Family Division, and two Lords Justices, together with five Law Lords on the other. And, as we have shown, this simple arithmetic does not reveal the diversity of approach. Even where the judges are in agreement as to the outcome, the route they followed in getting there is not always shared by others. And one judge does not always maintain a consistent style. You may recall that Lord Denning, in *Davis v Johnson*, relies on a literal reading of the section at one stage, only to turn to the purpose of the Act later. He was not alone in doing this and you, as an advocate, should be prepared, in the same way, to advance arguments along different fronts.

9.6.3 Criticisms of the Styles of Interpretation

Two final points need to be made here. First, it is very tempting to criticise those who adopt the 'grand' or purposive style as inventing reasons to fit decisions they have already reached. But on closer examination, when a judge adopts a more 'formal' style it is still often difficult to understand exactly where *the purpose* to which he refers came from, as we can see with the treatment of the phrase 'living with each other'. The 'formal' style, ranging from literalism through to a more purposive approach, is not automatically entitled to be termed logical.

Secondly, if you approach the problems of interpretation by only asking 'which rule will be used?', you will miss the point. To adapt the chess analogy we used in **Chapter 7**: knowing that your opponent *can* 'castle' does not tell you that he *will* 'castle'. There is no set moment when your opponent will 'castle'—if at all. And if you are playing chess and do not know what 'castling' is, and when it may be used, you are at a serious disadvantage. Thus the rules describe the limits of what *may* happen; and they tell you what will *not* happen. Your opponent cannot move his pawn as if it were a knight, for instance. Equally there are limitations placed, by convention and common sense, on even the most purposive of judges. The rules may tell you *what* will happen in terms of basic structure; they cannot tell you *how* the game will progress. Each player has his own style.

We agree, therefore, with Twining and Miers that 'We do not believe that there is one right answer in hard cases or that problems of interpretation can be solved primarily by rules' (1991: 376) and with Zander that 'The rules and principles of interpretation therefore do nothing to solve problems. They suggest arguments that can be advanced and then justify conclusions often reached on other grounds' (2004: 184). It is not unfair for a student new to legal studies to ask which rule will be used; it is unfair, however, for us to pretend there is a 'right' answer.

However, most of your academic life will be spent presenting an argument for one side (the same will be true if you go on to practise law). Your problem does not therefore lie in which approach you should use to *determine* a case: that will not be your function. Instead, your problem lies in determining which approach to adopt so that your argument is at its most convincing. Consequently, if you can master the types of reasoning available to you described previously and learn to judge when one style is more applicable than another then you will have done all you can in presenting your argument professionally. The fact then that there is no single correct way to read a statute becomes a less daunting prospect.

9.7 Interpretation and the European Union

The influence of the European Union and the civil law's more 'purposive' approach to interpretation has begun to produce changes in judicial technique, even as regards legislation unconnected with the EU.

We have seen throughout this book that the civil law tradition is different from ours as regards case law. Here we must recognise that European legislation is structured in a manner that is also very different from English Acts of Parliament. The former follows the *civilian* tradition in emphasising simplicity of drafting and a high degree of abstraction, which is quite different from the exhaustive approach adopted by common law draftsmen. This means that a wide-ranging purposive approach (a teleological approach) is even more central to the interpretive process in the context of EU legislation. Here, questions of broad economic or social aims are regularly considered by the courts, in a way that could be attacked in the English courts as a 'naked usurpation of the legislative function'.

This difference in approach has increasingly been recognised by the English judges when considering EU legislation, or even when considering English legislation that has been passed to fulfil an obligation under EU law. Indeed the House of Lords completely (and openly) ditched the literal approach in *Litster* v *Forth Dry Dock* [1990] AC 546; [1989] 1 All ER 1134, where the statute in question was derived from a Directive of the (then) European Community. Instead of the literal approach the Lords adopted a very wide purposive approach in line with European judges.

There have been inconsistencies of approach: the decision in *Litster* can be compared with that of a differently constituted House of Lords in *Duke* v *GEC Reliance (formerly Reliance Systems)* [1988] AC 618; [1988] 1 All ER 626, which took a far more traditional (i.e. narrow) approach to a related problem of interpretation. And few

English judges have followed the line taken by Lord Denning in *Bulmer* v *Bollinger* [1974] Ch 401; [1974] 2 All ER 1226, to argue that the English courts should generally adopt a broad purposive approach, akin to the European style, in *all* cases.

We have left describing the methods utilised by European judges and lawyers to interpret legislation until **Chapter 11**.

9.8 Interpretation and the Human Rights Act 1998

In the next chapter we will deal with the topic of human rights at some length. For the moment we can note the following:

- The HRA 1998 selectively incorporates elements of the European Convention on Human Rights by giving them a special legal status as 'Convention rights' under s. 1 of the Act.

- The HRA 1998 requires judges to interpret legislation, so far as possible, consistently with Convention rights, and where consistency cannot be achieved, to declare such laws incompatible with Convention rights.

Thus, there is the potential that courts may be presented with arguments which require the judges to embark upon a radical rethink of all legislation that comes before them, whenever that legislation was enacted. However, it should also be noted that the case of *Price* v *Leeds City Council* [2005] EWCA Civ 289; [2005] 1 WLR 1825 determined that where there is a conflict between (what are now) Supreme Court decisions and those of the European Court of Human Rights, precedent demands that the Supreme Court be followed.

9.9 Interpreting Secondary Legislation

When looking at the rules of statutory interpretation, it is easy to forget that much legislation is not created by statute but by statutory instrument or by-law. You will recall that we considered the growth, and importance, of this whole area of 'secondary legislation' in **Chapter 1**. We now need to consider the principles of interpretation that apply to secondary, or delegated, legislation.

As a starting point, we can say that generally the same rules do apply; which is a relief. The courts will look at the words used in a regulation, and interpret them according to their immediate linguistic context, only straying beyond this point in cases where the judge finds some absurdity or ambiguity demanding a more purposive approach. However, within this framework there are a number of substantive differences which reflect the fact that delegated legislation is, ultimately, a different creature from primary legislation.

This is because delegated legislation does not stand alone, in the way that an Act of Parliament does; it forms part of a legislative 'package' which includes the parent Act, and possibly other sets of regulations, which may affect our assessment of meaning. It is also because the courts are less constrained by problems of sovereignty when dealing with secondary as opposed to primary legislation.

These various differences can be explored in relation to two issues: the way in which we define the context of secondary legislation; and the way in which the courts handle questions of validity.

9.9.1 Defining the Context

As we have said, delegated legislation is to be read within a potentially wider context than statute law. The meaning of a particular provision is to be ascertained from the whole body of regulations of which it forms part, the parent Act and the common law. Exceptionally, the environment within which the regulations operate may also be considered as part of the context. The part played by each of these will be considered.

The regulations

The principle here is the same as that applied to statute. Just as you would not take one section of an Act out of context, so you should not consider a regulation outside its instrument. This may be particularly important if a reading of the parent Act offers alternative interpretations.

The parent Act

This is of central importance in defining meaning. This is emphasised by the fact that the Interpretation Act 1978, s. 11 requires words used in secondary legislation to be read as having the same meaning as in the parent Act, unless a contrary intention appears. That is fine, of course, so long as the meaning in the empowering legislation is clear! If it is not the court has to work it out for itself, from possibly a variety of competing explanations. Where there are doubts about the meaning of a word used within the parent Act, then it seems permissible for the court to look at both the parent Act and the regulations in assessing meaning: see *Nurse* v *Morganite Crucible Ltd* [1989] AC 692; [1989] 1 All ER 113.

The common law

This can also be of significance. The courts will be reluctant to interpret any delegated legislation in such a way that it conflicts with an established and fundamental principle of common law. For example, in *R* v *Secretary of State for the Home Department ex parte Anderson* [1984] QB 778; [1984] 1 All ER 920, the Court had to assess the validity of order 5A(34) made by the Secretary of State under powers contained within the Prison Rules 1964, which were themselves made under the authority of the Prison Act 1952, s. 47(1). The order sought to prevent prisoners from obtaining visits from their legal advisers regarding complaints about their treatment in prison. Section 47(1) was silent in respect of such rights of access, so the Court resorted to the common law. As a result it held that the fundamental right of access to the courts was wide enough to include a prisoner's right of access to legal advice. Parliament could not be deemed to have legislated against that right purely by implication, so order 5A(34) was held invalid. The courts' powers to declare secondary legislation invalid is a point to which we shall return.

9.9.2 The Principle of Validity

We noted in **Chapter 1** that the courts have the power to declare secondary legislation invalid where it involves an exercise of power exceeding that granted by Parliament. The decision to invalidate is thus dependent upon a question of interpreting, first, the scope of the powers contained within the delegated legislation and, secondly, the scope of the grant within the parent Act. In dealing with these situations, the courts have developed a number of principles.

First, in some specific instances, they have ruled that delegated legislation may only do certain things if there is express authorisation within the parent statute. There are two particularly significant situations where this applies:

(a) The courts apply a presumption against retrospectivity to prevent instruments affecting events which precede their introduction. The presumption may be used to require not only that the possibility of retrospective effect is specifically alluded to within the instrument, but that it was also within the ambit of the original grant of power by Parliament—see, e.g., *Marshall's Township Syndicate Ltd* v *Johannesburg Consolidated Investment Co. Ltd* [1920] AC 420, *Webb* v *Ipswich Borough Council* (1989) 21 HLR 325.

(b) Parliament will not be presumed to have authorised the amendment of primary legislation by secondary legislation without clear authority within the parent Act. Thus, in the case of *McKiernan* v *Secretary of State, Guardian*, 28 October 1989, the Court of Appeal refused to imply that social security regulations modified an otherwise mandatory condition laid down under the parent Act in the absence of express authority. Even where such powers have been granted, the courts have tended to construe them narrowly.

Secondly, the courts have, as we suggested at the beginning of this section, shown a marked reluctance to allow secondary legislation to be invalidated purely because of problems of ambiguity or uncertainty—*Percy* v *Hall* [1996] 4 All ER 523. The courts have used the maxim *ut res magis valeat quam pereat* ('it is better for a thing to have effect than to be void') to justify whichever of competing interpretations would be a valid exercise of power. This principle has become widely used in common law jurisdictions to avoid treating delegated legislation as *ultra vires*. Strictly speaking, it should not be adopted in cases where the meaning of the regulation is clear from the face of the document, or where its application would require a virtual rewriting of the legislation. In that respect it is no more than a manifestation of the rules against ambiguity.

Thirdly, in cases where delegated legislation is only partially invalid, the courts recognise that they have a power of 'severance'. Severance is a process whereby invalid portions of a document may be separated from those which are valid, leaving those valid parts still standing. As such, it can be seen as a derivative of the principle of validity. The mechanics of 'severance' are extremely complex and we do not recommend that you consider them in any greater detail at this stage in your studies.

9.10 Illustration of How to Analyse a Case on Statutory Interpretation

The following case illustrates a number of these points on statutory interpretation. After the headnote etc., the judgment is noted in the left-hand column, with notes on legal method aspects appearing in the right-hand column. The case contains many of the aspects discussed throughout this book and highlighted earlier in the chapter—the notable exceptions, because of the specific issues and the date the case was heard, being that of any EU law or human rights references.

Director of Public Prosecutions* v *Bull [1994] 3 WLR 1196
[QUEEN'S BENCH DIVISION]
1994 March 28: Mann LJ and Laws J
May 5

CATCHWORDS

Crime—Sexual offences—Soliciting—Man charged as common prostitute—Whether 'common prostitute' applying exclusively to women—Street Offences Act 1959 (c. 57), ss. 1(1), 2(1)

HEADNOTE

The term 'common prostitute' in section 1(1) of the Street Offences Act 1959 applies exclusively to female prostitutes. Where, therefore, a stipendiary magistrate accepted a submission of no case to answer to a charge that a male respondent, being a common prostitute, loitered in a street or public place for the purpose of prostitution, contrary to section 1(1) of the Act of 1959, and the prosecution appealed:
Held, dismissing the appeal, that the submission of no case to answer had been rightly accepted (post, p. 1201C–D, G).

CITATIONS

The following cases are referred to in the judgment of Mann LJ:

Fothergill v *Monarch Airlines Ltd* [1981] AC 251; [1980] 3 WLR 209; [1980] 2 All ER 696, HL(E)
Pepper v *Hart* [1993] AC 593; [1992] 3 WLR 1032; [1993] 1 All ER 42, HL(E)
R v *De Munck* [1918] 1 KB 635, CCA
R v *McFarlane* [1994] QB 419; [1994] 2 WLR 494; [1994] 2 All ER 283, CA
Wicks v *Firth* [1983] 2 AC 214; [1983] 2 WLR 34; [1983] 1 All ER 151, HL(E)

The following additional cases were cited in argument:

Dale v *Smith* [1967] 1 WLR 700; [1967] 2 All ER 1133, DC
R v *Ford (Graham)* [1977] 1 WLR 1083; [1978] 1 All ER 1129, CA
R v *Gray* (1981) 74 Cr App R 324, CA
R v *Kirkup* [1993] 1 WLR 774; [1993] 2 All ER 802, CA
R v *Webb* [1964] 1 QB 357; 3 WLR 638; [1963] 3 All ER 177, CCA

FACTS

Case Stated by the Wells Street Metropolitan Stipendiary Magistrate.
(Statement of facts as appears in the report omitted. Facts are stated in the judgment below.)

COUNSEL

Jeremy Carter-Manning QC and John McGuinness for the applicant.
Adrian Fulford for the respondent.
Cur. adv. vult.

JUDGMENT	COMMENTS ON THE TEXT

5th May

Mann LJ read the following judgment: There is before the court an appeal by way of case stated. The appellant is the Director of Public Prosecutions and the respondent is Andrew John Bull. The case has been stated by Mr Ian Michael Baker, metropolitan stipendiary magistrate for the Inner London commission area, in respect of his adjudication as a magistrates' court sitting at Wells Street Magistrates' Court, London, W1, on 27 April 1993.

§ *History of the case*

§ *A stipendiary magistrate is now called a District Judge (Criminal) or District Judge (Magistrates' Court)*

On that day Mr Baker had before him a charge against the respondent to the effect that on 4 December 1992 he, being a common prostitute, did loiter in a street or public place for the purpose of prostitution contrary to section 1(1) of the Street Offences Act 1959. At the conclusion of the prosecution case counsel for the respondent submitted that there was no case to answer on the basis that section 1(1) applies only to female prostitutes. This submission was upheld by the magistrate, who has now posed this question for the opinion of the court:

§ *Outline of facts and arguments*

Whether I was correct in construing section 1(1) of the Street Offences Act 1959 so as to limit it to the activities of female prostitutes and to exclude from its scope the activities of male prostitutes.

§ *Phrasing of the Case Stated by the magistrate for consideration in the High Court*

The magistrate made certain findings of fact to which I think it unnecessary to refer. Suffice to say that he remarks in paragraph 7 of the case stated that had the submission not been accepted he would have held that there was a case to answer. So far as is material, the long title to the Act of 1959 is:

An Act to make, as respects England and Wales, further provision against loitering or soliciting in public places for the purpose of prostitution ...

§ *Indeterminate reference made to long title*

The further provision is to be found in sections 1 and 2. The material subsections of section 1 are subsections (1) (2) (as substituted by the Criminal Justice Act 1982, section 71) and (3):

§ *Key aspects of section 1 highlighted*

(1) It shall be an offence for a common prostitute to loiter or solicit in a street or public place for the purpose of prostitution.

§ *Wording of the Act (as later amended)*

(2) A person guilty of an offence under this section shall be liable on summary conviction to a fine of an amount not exceeding level 2 on the standard scale ... or, for an offence committed after a previous conviction, to a fine of an amount not exceeding level 3 on that scale.

(3) A constable may arrest without warrant anyone he finds in a street or public place and suspects, with reasonable cause, to be committing an offence under this section.

The material subsection of section 2 is subsection (1), which provides:

§ *Reference to a related section in the Act*

Where a woman is cautioned by a constable, in respect of her conduct in a street or public place, that if she persists in such conduct it may result in her being charged with an offence under section 1 of this Act, she may not later than 14 clear days afterwards apply to a magistrates' court for an order directing that there is to be no entry made in respect of that caution in any record maintained by the police of those so cautioned and that any such entry already made is to be expunged; and the court shall make the order unless satisfied that on the occasion when she was cautioned she was loitering or soliciting in a street or public place for the purpose of prostitution.

The other legislative provision which is material is the earlier section 32 of the Sexual Offences Act 1956, which provides: 'It is an offence for a man persistently to solicit or importune in a public place for immoral purposes.'

§ *Reference to a related Statute (of three years earlier)*

As Mr Jeremy Carter-Manning for the appellant pointed out, there are differences between the components of an offence under section 32 of the Act of 1956 and those of an offence under section 1(1) of the Act of 1959. Thus (i) section 32 requires actual soliciting *or importuning*; section 1(1) requires either actual soliciting *or loitering* (ii) section 32 requires *persistence*;

Section 1(1) does not, and (iii) section 32 requires *an immoral purpose*; section 1(1) requires a *prostitutional purpose*.

§ *Key differences in the working of the two Acts observed*

The submission for the appellant was that section 1(1) of the Act of 1959 is unambiguous and is not gender specific. Our attention was drawn to the following factors which were relied upon:

§ *Reference to the arguments put to the court.*

(i) The phrase in section 1(1) 'a common prostitute' was linguistically capable of including a male person.

§ *Linguistic argument*

The *Oxford English Dictionary*, 2nd edn (1989), includes within the possibilities for 'prostitute,' 'a man who undertakes male homosexual acts for payment'.

§ *Use of dictionary*

(ii) Lord Taylor of Gosforth CJ has recently said in *R v McFarlane* [1994] QB 419 424D that 'both the dictionary definitions and the cases show that the crucial feature in defining prostitution is the making of an offer of sexual service for reward'. I do not regard this factor as of significance. Lord Taylor CJ was speaking in a case which concerned a woman who had been clipping.

§ *Case quoted but distinguished ('clipping' means offering sexual services for reward, being paid in advance, but never intending to provide the service)*

(iii) Section 1(2) and 1(3) of the Act of 1959 refer respectively to 'a person' and 'anyone'.

(iv) In contrast section 2(1) refers specifically to 'a woman'. The reason for this is conjectured by Mr Carter-Manning to be that until the Sexual Offences Act 1967 homosexual acts between men were criminal offences and thus cautioning was inappropriate.

§ Wording of related section and subsections analysed

§ Historical analysis

(v) Since 1967 male prostitution has been in certain circumstances not unlawful and accordingly in the new environment it is open to the court to interpret section 1(1) of the Act of 1959 as being applicable to prostitutes who are male 'even if this was not the original intent of the provision'. This in my opinion is a bold submission.

§ Response to Counsel's invitation to read present law and social attitudes into the Act

It was based upon observations by Lord Bridge of Harwich in *Wicks* v *Firth* [1983] 2 AC 214, 230C–E, but Lord Bridge was dealing with a situation where an enactment has been re-enacted in a new context.

§ Use of earlier case rejected on the ground it is distinguishable

(vi) Where Parliament intends to deal with gender specific prostitution it uses specifically the word 'woman', 'girl', or 'her' as in sections 22, 28, 29, 30 and 31 of the Sexual Offences Act 1956. See also section 5 of the Sexual Offences Act 1967 as regards a 'woman' living on male prostitution.

§ Analysis of terms in other Acts in pari materia

It is to be observed, for completeness, that Mr Carter-Manning recognised he could obtain no assistance from the gender provisions of section 6 of the Interpretation Act 1978 because the provision that words importing the feminine gender, as does ordinarily the phrase 'common prostitute', include the masculine is inapplicable to enactments such as the Act of 1959 (see Part I of Schedule 2 to the Act of 1978). Mr Adrian Fulford, who appeared for the respondent, submitted that the phrase 'common prostitute' was for many years before 1959, and is now, regarded as a term of art which had the meaning formulated by Darling J when delivering the judgment of the Court of Criminal Appeal in *R* v *De Munck* [1918] 1 KB 635. He said, at pp. 637–638: 'The court is of opinion that the term "common prostitute" in the statute is not limited so as to mean only one who permits acts of lewdness with all and sundry, or with such as hire her, when such acts are in the nature of ordinary sexual connection. We are of opinion that prostitution is proved if it be shown that a woman offers her body commonly for lewdness for payment in return.'

§ Application of section 6 Interpretation Act 1978—which states that 'In any Act, unless the contrary intention appears,—(b) words importing the feminine gender include the masculine'— rejected because later parts of the 1978 Act state that these words do not apply here

§ Reference to case law to show what might have been the draftsman's presumptions in using the terms and comment on an earlier related Act

The statute referred to was section 2(2) of the Criminal Law Amendment Act 1885 (48 & 49 Vict. c. 69) which however was gender specific for it spoke of 'women or girls'. Although the decision was in that context, I believe there to be great force in Mr Fulford's submission that 'common authority prostitute' is ordinarily regarded as signifying a woman. The statute was

§ Statutory history of the area

referring to a common law concept. Mr Fulford drew our attention to the only text-book which appears to deal with the problem, Rook and Ward, *Sexual Offences* (1990), where at para. 8.12 the authors state: 'The better view is that the offence under section 1(1) may be committed as principal only by a woman.'

§ *Reference to an academic text*

However, Mr Fulford's main submission was that the court should avail itself of the report which led to the Act of 1959 and of the parliamentary debate upon the Bill for the Act *Pepper* v *Hart* [1993] AC 593.

The availability of a report which led to an Act as an aid to interpretation is discussed in Bennion, Statutory Interpretation, 2nd edn (1992), p. 450. He cites *Fothergill* v *Monarch Airlines Ltd* [1981] AC 251, 281, where Lord Diplock said:

§ *Reference to* Pepper v Hart

§ *Reference to a practitioners' text*

> Where the Act has been preceded by a report of some official commission or committee that has been laid before Parliament and the legislation is introduced in consequence of that report, the report itself may be looked at by the court for the limited purpose of identifying the 'mischief' that the Act was intended to remedy, and for such assistance as is derivable from this knowledge in giving the right purposive construction to the Act.

§ *Discussion of the method of identifying the mischief*

Section 1(1) of the Act was a result of a recommendation in paragraph 256 of the Report of the Departmental Committee on Homosexual Offences and Prostitution (1957) (Cmnd. 247) ('the Wolfenden committee'). The relevant chapters of the report are Chapters VIII and IX and a perusal of them leaves me in no doubt that the committee was concerned only with the female prostitute. Thus, and for example:

§ *Analysis of mischief as recounted by the report of the investigating committee*

223. It would have taken us beyond our terms of reference to investigate in detail the prevalence of prostitution or the reasons which lead women to adopt this manner of life

261. ... The problem of the prostitute is, in terms of numbers, far greater than that of the male importuner and, for that matter, far more of a public nuisance. In any event, we think it would be too easy to evade the formula by a game of 'general post' in which an individual prostitute would not loiter in a particular place though the number of prostitutes in that place at a given time might be constant.

262. Our second difficulty related to the criteria which would enable the police to infer that a person was loitering 'for the purposes of prostitution'. We have in mind the possibility that any woman might, from ignorance or in discretion, put herself in a position in which she might be said to be loitering, and by conduct which was quite innocent give rise to a suspicion in the mind of an observant policeman that she was loitering for the purposes of prostitution.

It is plain that the 'mischief' that the Act was intended to remedy was a mischief created by women. The assistance which I derive from the report confirms my strong impression that, notwithstanding the use of 'a person' and 'anyone' in subsections (2) and (3), section 1(1) of the Act of 1959 is confined to women. The term 'common prostitute' is ordinarily regarded as applying to a woman and, importantly, it seems improbable that Parliament intended to create a new male offence which was but subtly different from the extant section 32 of the Sexual Offences Act 1956.

§ *Conclusion on the mischief and a return to the analysis of the wording in the Act*

Accordingly I would dismiss this appeal and answer the magistrate's question in the affirmative. I add this. I have not sought to avail myself of the doctrine in the parliamentary debates it would become plain that section 1(1) of the Act of 1959 was intended to be applicable only to women. Had I concluded as a matter of interpretation that section 1(1) applied to male prostitutes, then a curious situation would have arisen. The judicially ascertained expressed intention of Parliament would have been at variance with what the court had been told was the actual intention of the promoters. The ensuing problems may have to be addressed if concessions of the type made here are repeated on another occasion.

§ *Decision*

§ *Further comments on the rejection of use of* Pepper v Hart

§ *Obiter comment on the use of* Pepper v Hart
§ *Recognition of the duty of counsel to cite all matters for and against him*

Laws J: I agree.

§ *Other judgment in the case*

ORDER Costs out of central funds.

§ *Appeal dismissed.*
§ *Someone has to pay the costs and an order always has to be made (though not always reported)*

 CONCLUSION

By way of conclusion we would like to suggest a rough guide on how you might approach the problem of interpreting a statute and then end with a short exercise on answering problems in this area.

Checklist for reading a statute

Table 9.1 contains a checklist of research points you need to consider when reading a statute. The left-hand column sets out the general headings you should bear in mind, and the right-hand column explains these in more detail.

1. Read the section(s) carefully.	This may include:
	(1) noting any technical legal terms. For example, words such as 'property'; 'possession'; 'dismissal'; 'recklessness' all have technical legal meanings. In particular, check whether the word is covered by the Interpretation Act 1978;
	(2) noting any other technical terms relating to specialist areas, or trades or industry. The Act (e.g. a Finance Act) may well have been drafted with these in mind;
	(3) checking dictionaries;
	(4) referring to any related sections in the Act;
	(5) checking the schedules to the Act;
	(6) checking for interpretations in the section and/or later interpretation sections;
	(7) checking related statutes which are *in pari materia* with this Act.
2. Research academic texts which will provide general guidance on the meaning of the section and point you to other authorities.	(1) textbooks;
	(2) articles and case notes in legal journals;
	(3) monographs;
	(4) practitioners' texts;
	(5) the Internet (with great care).
3. Understand the mischief of the Act.	(1) refer to any annotations, e.g. in 'Current Statutes Annotated';
	(2) check for any Law Commission Reports;
	(3) look at social, economic or political background;
	(4) check whether you have found the mischief or whether there are multiple mischiefs;
	(5) check Hansard under the rules in *Pepper* v *Hart*;
	(6) check the long title of the act: *Vacher* v *London Society of Compositors*.
4. Check for any European derivation.	Does the Act in question derive from a Treaty, Regulation, or Directive? If so, refer to **Chapter 11** for the implications.
5. Research existing or related case law.	(1) Are you sure your legal research has unearthed all the authorities? • English case law? • Possibly decisions of the Judicial Committee of the Privy Council? • Relevant cases in foreign jurisdictions? • European case law at the Court of Justice or as applied in the UK?
	(2) How will you present the *ratio* of each case?
	(3) How will you deal with *obiter dicta*?
	(4) You must decide how you are going to argue the relevance of helpful cases and distinguish unhelpful authority.
6. Are there any Human Rights Act 1998 implications?	(1) Direct reference to human rights on basis that any case will be taken against a public authority?
	(2) Possible 'horizontal' use of Human Rights Act 1998?
7. Be aware of any technical rules of grammar.	For example, the *eiusdem generis* rule.

8. Be aware of judicial trends in methods of interpretation.	Are judges now more purposive in their approach? How will this affect your argument?
9. Be aware from which perspective you are viewing the problem and adopt the appropriate style of argument.	Are you acting as an advocate? Are you arguing the general possibilities? Answering an examination problem is quite different from acting as an advocate in a moot, for example. Even in real-life advocacy or the provision of legal advice, you must decide how to pitch your case in terms of emphasis on literal or purposive approaches.
10. Decide how to marshal your authorities to substantiate your approach.	For example, what degree of emphasis will you put on each case or other relevant material? Good arguments emphasise the key points, not every single point.

Exercise on application

EXERCISE 18 Perilous poodles and rabid fish

This very short exercise explores the basic methods of interpreting statutes.

PROBLEM

It is to be assumed that, as a result of a recent outbreak of rabies (and following a consequent Law Commission recommendation) the **Rabies and Dangerous Animals Act 2015** has been passed. It states:

Section 1: It is an offence to leave animals unattended in any hotel, public house, restaurant, or other public place.

Section 2: The keeping of any animal, other than a domesticated one, without an appropriate licence, is an offence. The form and cost of such a licence will be determined by orders issued from time to time by the Minister. A domesticated animal is one so defined by sch. 9 of this Act.

Section 3: Private dwelling houses are exempted from the provisions of this Act.

Schedule 9: For the purposes of this Act a 'domesticated animal' includes cats, dogs, horses, cattle, sheep, pigs, and snakes or insects common to the British Isles.

Using the rules of statutory interpretation that have been developed, present arguments **as if you were counsel for the defence** in the following cases.

(1) *R v Alfred*

Alfred left his poodle in the changing rooms at his local tennis club while he played tennis. He is charged with contravening s. 1 of the Act.

(2) *R v Bert*

Bert keeps piranha fish in a pond in his front garden. The garden is unfenced. He is charged with not having the appropriate licence under s. 2.

continued

EXERCISE 18 *continued*

Points to note in this exercise:

1. Alfred

Start any problem of this nature by breaking down the constituent elements of the section(s) involved. What is required for conviction here?

- there must be an animal (not a problem here);
- that animal must be left unattended; and
- in any hotel, public house, restaurant, or other public place.

However simplistic this may seem, it really is not (especially if the section is more complicated). As we noted earlier, you will find in seminars that many of your colleagues, when asked to analyse a problem like this, 'jump in' all over the place commenting on different aspects of the offence (or saying 'this is nonsense'). Structure matters and wins hands down over a disorganised argument. Here, remember, if the Crown fails to prove any one of the constituent elements of the offence, there can be no conviction.

Next, make sure there are no other parts of the Act which have to be taken into account, e.g. a definitions section. Here, the only one that could be of relevance to Alfred is section 3.

Next, marshal your authorities (case law, statutes *in pari materia*, explanatory notes to this Act, any possible *Pepper* v *Hart* references, etc.). Let us say, for instance, that you find a reference in Hansard to a speech made by the Home Secretary which might help your case. When can you use this? If you can use it, is it precise enough to help your argument?

From this we can say that the defence may rest on three grounds:

(a) The Act refers to 'hotel, public house, restaurant, or other public place'. Does a tennis club, therefore, come within that last, general, category? The phrase 'or other public place' could be read *eiusdem generis* to restrict the general words to the genus of the preceding specific words. What is the genus of the preceding words? The prosecution will argue that these words show that the tenor of the section is to prevent animals being left in a place to which the public have general access. The defence could argue that the words indicate a place restricted to food and drink establishments. Further, if the tennis club is private (or has a limited membership) there might be a defence here. The express exclusion of private dwellings under section 3 could also be cited in support of this interpretation (since we are entitled to look at the effect of the **whole** Act).

This is a weak point but could be used by ignoring the problematic word 'dwelling' and concentrating on the privacy element.

(b) In the alternative, the defence could argue that this phrase is not sufficiently specific to create a genus, and that therefore, since a literal interpretation of such general words is virtually meaningless, the court should inquire into the purpose of the Act. A formal style of discovering 'purpose' would be to analyse the Act mainly by referring to the internal context. The short title of the Act is the Rabies and Dangerous Animals Act. This cannot itself be used, unlike the long title, as an aid to construction: *R* v *Galvin*. However, it does suggest that the Act is particularly concerned with the threat

continued

EXERCISE 18 *continued*

of dangerous animals (note the exclusion of domesticated animals by s. 2 and sch. 9). This argument could be used to deny the application of the section to pet dogs, and the long title of the Act (if it has one) could be cited in support (if it offers that support—the question is silent on this). See *Vacher* v *London Society of Compositors*, where it was stressed that the long title could be used as a minor aid to construction, provided it did not contradict the express language of the Act.

Seeking the purpose in the 'grand' style one can move away from the Act itself to matters such as social conditions. Similarly, the Law Commission's report could also be used in support, if that was the case (*Black-Clawson*), and even Hansard might prove useful on this point if the court will admit it. Perhaps the Home Secretary answered a question on the scope of the Act by saying: 'The Act is designed to ensure people's safety, but we cannot seriously banish dogs from all public places. We have sought to balance personal freedoms and public safety by prohibiting dogs from being left unattended in public areas where people are being entertained.' Is this useful or not?

(c) Finally, one could argue that 'unattended' does not mean the animal always has to be in the owner's presence (or that 'presence' simply means 'in the line of sight' as in *Casson* v *Dade*).

2. Bert

Use the same structure as with Alfred. Here, the relevant section is section 2. What is required for conviction here?

- an animal must be involved (will a fish be included?);
- the Act does not apply to domesticated ones; and
- there must be no appropriate licence.

Again, make sure there are no other parts of the Act which have to be taken into account e.g. a definitions section. Here, there are two: s. 3 (exempting private dwelling houses) and sch. 9 (defining domesticated animals).

The first point to note is that you may have to do some research on what is an 'animal' (see various dictionaries, biology books, etc.). It comes as a surprise to many that fish are animals and so will require a licence unless sch. 9 exempts them.

The defence is threefold:

(a) The most obvious line of attack is the purposive argument that, although fish may be animals, they are incapable (to the best of the authors' knowledge) of carrying rabies. The prosecution may well point out that the Act is concerned with both rabid *and* dangerous animals; a dangerous fish falls within the provisions of the Act. However, the purpose of the Act, as exemplified perhaps in the long title (not provided here) and gained through an examination of the social setting for the Act, would probably demonstrate that the two ideas were connected.

(b) The offence created by s. 2 is absolute, save for the exclusion of domesticated animals in sch. 9. Though a literal approach apparently catches Bert he might be able to utilise s. 3. One must argue an extended meaning to 'private dwelling houses'. Land is usually included in such terms.

continued

EXERCISE 18 *continued*

Bert could try to argue that as the fish are kept in his garden they should be excluded under section 3. This could be argued on the basis that the purpose of the Act is only to protect the public in places to which they normally have resort. As such, there is an argument that an individual's garden is as much his private property as his house, and that any wider meaning could create absurd results. One might try to find other statutes which have defined the term in an acceptable way for the defence. Finding one *in pari materia* might be more difficult. One such possible example might be the Dangerous Dogs Act 1991. And, indeed, the very question whether a garden path constituted a 'public place' under section 10 of the Act arose in *Fellowes v DPP, The Times* 1 February 1993. Fellowes was convicted of having a dog which was dangerously out of control in a public place contrary to the Dangerous Dogs Act 1991 s. 3(1), after his dog bit a paper boy who was delivering a newspaper to the house. The Queen's Bench Division Divisional Court held that this was not a public place because of the purpose of the Act and that people entered the private premises only as visitors, not as general members of the public. Again, the same court has decided that a dangerous dog in a private car in a public car park had to be muzzled because, although a car is not in and of itself a public place, when the car is in a public place everything inside the car is deemed to be in a public place for the purposes of the Act (*Bates v DPP, The Times*, 8 March 1993; (1993) 157 JP 1004). So, if the mischief in our fictitious Act is perceived as relating to 'danger', the unfenced pond is still a problem in our argument.

However, a different slant was put on this in *R v Roberts (Leroy Lloyd)* [2003] EWCA Crim 2753; [2004] 1 WLR 181 where the accused had a 'lock knife' in his own (very narrow) front garden. This was held not to have occurred in a 'public place' for the purposes of the Criminal Justice Act 1988, s. 139(7). The Court decided it was inappropriate to construe the phrase 'public place' in s. 139(7) as embracing land adjacent to areas where the public had access, so long as the harm against which the Act was designed to provide protection could not be inflicted from that place.

(c)   The categories of animals referred to in sch. 9 are wide; wider, perhaps, than a literal reading of the word 'domesticated' would lead us to expect; although it is presented as an inclusive definition. The case of *Cottman v Bibby Tankers* [1988] AC 276 considered the dual meaning that can be given to 'inclusive' definitions. The list might be either exemplary or exhaustive. It is notable that fish are excluded, and so if the definition is exhaustive, the prosecution might seek to argue the principle *expressio unius est exclusio alterius*. This would be difficult to counter, and the defence's only response, it is submitted, might be to argue that the definition is exemplary; that 'domesticated' here is sufficiently wide to include all animals that are in fact kept as 'pets'. Whether piranhas are on that basis common to the British Isles might nonetheless be a difficult point to argue!

CHAPTER REFERENCES

ARDEN, M. (2008), 'The Changing Judicial Role: Human Rights, Community Law and the Intention of Parliament', 67 *Cambridge Law Journal*, 487.

*CHANDLER, A. and HOLLAND, J. (1995), 'Pepper v Hart: Unearthing the Meaning of Rescission', *Journal of Business Law*, 503.

*Cross, R. (1995), *Cross: Statutory Interpretation* (3rd edn by Bell, J. and Engle, G., London: Butterworths).

Feldman, D. (1992), 'Commencement, Transition and Retrospective Legislation', 108 *Law Quarterly Review*, 212.

Graham, R.N. (2001), 'In Defence of Maxims', 22 *Statute Law Review*, 45.

Graham, R.N. (2009), 'What Judges Want: Judicial Self-interest and Statutory Interpretation', 30(1) *Statute Law Review*, 38.

*Horn, N. (2011), 'Legislative Section Headings: Drafting Techniques, Plain Language, and Redundancy', 32 *Statute Law Review*, 186.

Krishnaprasad, K.V, 'Pepper v. Hart: Its Continuing Implications in the United Kingdom and in India', 32(3) *Statute Law Review*, 227.

Llewellyn, K. (1960), *The Common Law Tradition* (Boston, Mass.: Little Brown).

Manchester, C. and Salter, D. (2011), *The Dynamics of Precedent and Statutory Interpretation* (4th edn, London: Sweet & Maxwell).

*Munday, R. (2008), 'The Bridge that Choked a Watercourse or Repetitive Dictionary Disorder', 29(1) *Statute Law Review*, 26.

*Slocum, B.G. (2012), 'Linguistics and 'Ordinary Meaning' Determinations', 33 *Statute Law Review*, 39–83.

Smith, J.C. (1995), 'The Criminal Appeals Act 1995: (1) Appeals Against Conviction', *Criminal Law Review*, 920.

Steyn, J. (2001), '*Pepper v Hart*: A Re-examination', 21 *Oxford Journal of Legal Studies*, 59.

Sullivan, R. (2001), 'Some Implications of Plain Language Drafting', 22 *Statute Law Review*, 175.

*Summers, R. and Marshall, G. (1992), 'The Argument from Ordinary Meaning in Statutory Interpretation', 43 *Northern Ireland Legal Quarterly*, 213.

*Twining, W. and Miers, D. (1991), *How To Do Things with Rules* (3rd edn, London: Weidenfeld & Nicolson and 5th edn, Cambridge: Cambridge University Press).

Vogenauer, S. (2005), 'A Retreat from *Pepper v Hart*? A Reply to Lord Steyn', 25 *Oxford Journal of Legal Studies*, 629–74.

*Willis, J. (1938), 'Statute Interpretation in a Nutshell', XVI *Canadian Bar Review*, 1.

Yihan, G. (2008), 'A Comparative Account of Statutory Interpretation in Singapore', 29 *Statute Law Review*, 195.

*Zander, M. (2004), *The Law-Making Process* (6th edn, Cambridge: Cambridge University Press).

10

'Bringing Rights Home': Legal Method and the Convention Rights

10.1 Introduction

In **Chapter 1** we introduced the idea that English law has increasingly become subject to two powerful pan-European legal forces. The most significant to date has, of course, been the influence of European Union law. However, since 2000, we have had another 'incoming tide' to deal with following the limited incorporation of the European Convention on Human Rights (ECHR) by the Human Rights Act (HRA) 1998, and by the legislation governing devolution in Scotland and Wales.

In outline, the HRA 1998 is designed to work in one of two ways. First, it makes it unlawful for a **public authority** to act in a way that is incompatible with the human rights set out in the HRA (called *Convention rights*). Where it is alleged that a public authority has breached a person's Convention rights, the claimant has a distinct cause of action against that public authority for breach of those rights. The term 'public authority' has not been defined in the Act but will obviously include bodies such as central government departments, the courts, and local councils.

Secondly, and in the alternative a person may *indirectly* rely on the rights contained in the HRA in actions against people who are not public authorities, but only to 'back up' existing legal rights, i.e. they cannot sue for a breach of human rights *per se* but can sue for, say, breach of contract and then ask the court to interpret or apply the law so as to comply with the rights set out in the HRA. This is because the courts fall within the definition of a 'public authority' in the HRA, consequently any decision they reach must itself comply with Convention rights.

In coming to a decision where there is a human rights issue under the HRA:

1. All courts must apply common law precedent so as to comply with Convention rights.

2. All courts and tribunals must interpret *all* relevant legislation, so far as it is possible to do so within the rules of statutory interpretation, to comply with Convention rights.

3. In interpreting the scope of the Convention rights, all courts and tribunals must take into account the jurisprudence of the Convention, which means all the decisions of the European Court of Human Rights (abbreviated to ECtHR), whenever a Convention right arises (HRA 1998, s. 2). However, UK courts are not **bound** to apply the decisions of the ECtHR.

4. The higher courts may declare primary legislation incompatible with Convention rights (HRA 1998, s. 3—though they cannot disapply it), so that Parliament may choose to use a special fast-track procedure for amending it (see the reference to 'remedial orders' in **Chapter 1**, and section **10.3.2**).

5. Courts also have limited powers to disapply subordinate legislation which is found to contravene Convention rights.

A person may still take a case to the ECtHR at Strasbourg, but only after having exhausted all domestic remedies. If the Court rules in their favour, the government is required, by Art. 46 of the ECHR, to give effect to the Court's ruling. As a matter of international law this is, as Lord Sumption has observed, an absolute obligation: *R (Chester) v Secretary of State for Justice; McGeoch v Lord President of the Council* [2013] UKSC 63; it does not, however, seem to impose any equivalent obligation on the UK courts to follow that ECtHR decision—see further section **10.6**.

In the remainder of this chapter we shall expand on these summary points by outlining the scope of the ECHR, explaining the process of incorporation of the ECHR through the HRA, and by exploring the impact of the HRA on legal method.

10.2 The European Convention on Human Rights

10.2.1 What is the ECHR?

The ECHR is an international treaty which was signed in Rome on 4 November 1950, and came into force on 3 September 1953. It sets out basic civil and political rights. The ECHR was the first major convention to be created under the auspices of a body called the Council of Europe. Although a number of other treaties have followed, the ECHR remains probably the most significant.

The Council itself was established by treaty in 1949, largely as a reaction to the failures of democracy and ethics that accompanied the rise of fascism in inter-war Europe. It exists as a political association of European states committed to advancing European unity, social and economic progress, and human rights. Although, historically speaking, it shares certain common roots with the EU, it is institutionally and politically quite separate. There has, of course, been significant overlap in membership of the Council of Europe and the EEC/EU, though the Council has always tended to be the larger body. There were ten original members of the Council (as compared with the EEC's six), namely the Benelux states together with Denmark, France, Italy, Ireland, Norway, Sweden, and the United Kingdom; the Council today has forty-seven members, with most of the former Eastern bloc states having joined since 1989.

States signing up to the Convention have been allowed to enter reservations to or derogations from particular provisions of the ECHR. A *reservation* is a statement made by a signatory, at the time of signing, that it recognises and reserves a position in which its laws are (to some specified extent) inconsistent with the Convention. A *derogation*, on the other hand, is a statement whereby a state notifies the Council that it is suspending certain rights under the Convention 'in time of war or other public emergency threatening the life of the nation' (ECHR, Art. 15). This is a fairly elastic concept, though there are certain Convention rights from which it is not possible to derogate (under

Arts. 2, 3, 4, and 7). The power of derogation was carried over into the HRA 1998 by s. 14 of that Act.

10.2.2 The Scope of the ECHR

The ECHR is concerned with the identification and protection of what are often called 'fundamental' human rights and freedoms. These are prescribed in quite broad terms in the various substantive sections or 'Articles' of the Convention. The main substantive rights are set out in **Figure 10.1**.

Art. 2	Right to life
Art. 3	Prohibition of torture, inhuman or degrading treatment or punishment
Art. 4	Prohibition of slavery or forced labour
Art. 5	Right to liberty and security of person
Art. 6	Right to a fair trial
Art. 7	Prohibition of punishment without law
Art. 8	Right to respect for privacy and family life
Art. 9	Right to freedom of thought, conscience and religion
Art. 10	Right to freedom of expression
Art. 11	Right to freedom of assembly and association
Art. 12	Right to marry and establish a family
Art. 14	Prohibition of discrimination with respect to rights under the ECHR

Figure 10.1 Rights and freedoms under the ECHR

There are also eleven Protocols which constitute additions to the Convention since it was originally drafted. Some of these Protocols are substantive, such as the Sixth Protocol which committed the signatories to the Convention to abolition of the death penalty, whereas others are procedural, such as the Eleventh Protocol, discussed later. Rights under the ECHR are expressed either as 'absolute' or 'qualified' rights. Where rights, such as the right to life or freedom from torture, are absolute, this means that they cannot be restricted or derogated by signatory states. Where rights are qualified, there is scope to balance different rights and interests, and some restrictions can be justified. The basis for legitimate constraint is expressed in terms within the relevant articles of the Convention. Thus, for example, freedom of expression may be curtailed provided it is in a manner 'prescribed by law' and 'necessary in a democratic society' in the interests of national security, or for the protection of health or morals, or to prevent disclosure of confidential information. However, the extent of constraint in specific cases must then be determined by reference to the principle of *proportionality*. Proportionality is an extremely important general principle of human rights law, and is also significant in the jurisprudence of the CJEU (see further **Chapter 11**). It provides what has been described as:

a common analytical framework ... [which] influences (some would say controls) how courts reason to conclusions in many of the great moral and political controversies confronting political communities. (Hustcroft *et al.*, 2014:2)

Different formulations of the proportionality test are used in different contexts (the precise detail goes beyond the concerns of this chapter), but, broadly, it can be said that proportionality always requires that the body seeking to limit a right must demonstrate that a reasonable relationship or 'balance' exists between the (legitimate) policy objective to be achieved and the means used to achieve it. If the means used are disproportionate, then the restriction or interference will be struck down. Thus, for example, in *Campbell* v *United Kingdom* (1992) 15 EHRR 137, the Court determined that opening and reading all correspondence between prisoners and their solicitors was a disproportionate interference in the prisoners' rights. By contrast it would be reasonable for the prison service to open letters without reading them, to see if they contained illicit enclosures.

10.2.3 Enforcement

The Convention created its own enforcement procedures, separate from any measures taken by individual contracting states. Under Convention procedures, complaints about breaches of the ECHR may be brought by a signatory state or, in some circumstances, by an individual petitioner.

An action can be brought only against the state allegedly in breach. Any state that is a signatory to the ECHR can potentially be sued for alleged breaches. Protocol 11, which came into force in 1998, made recognising the right of individual petition compulsory for signatory states. However, there is generally no possibility of one individual suing another before the ECtHR.

A party must have exhausted all domestic remedies before petitioning the ECtHR. Admissibility is determined in a preliminary hearing, with court data suggesting that about 85 per cent of cases fall at this hurdle. If the case does proceed, it will normally be heard by a chamber of seven judges. The Court also has the power to sit in a Grand Chamber of seventeen judges where a case raises a particularly important question of interpretation of Convention rights.

10.3 Incorporation under the Human Rights Act 1998

The purpose of the HRA 1998 was, as we have said, to achieve the partial incorporation of the Convention into English law. The method chosen for incorporation involves a fairly typical piece of British pragmatism. One of the great arguments against incorporation has been the damage that it could cause to parliamentary sovereignty by increasing the powers of unelected judges—both by ceding authority directly to the ECtHR, and by giving greater constitutional power to the British judiciary. The HRA 1998, its supporters claim, has maintained a balance between enabling judicial protection of human rights and protecting the sovereignty of Parliament (though this continues to be contested by the Act's opponents). At the heart of this attempted balancing act are three features of the 1998 Act:

1. The Act has not simply declared the ECHR to be part of English law, it has, rather, selectively given elements of the Convention a special legal status as '**Convention**

rights' under HRA, s. 1. Strictly speaking, this is not the same as incorporation of those rights in a constitutional sense. As Dwyer (2005: 362) points out, the HRA:

> maintains the dualist distinction between the United Kingdom's obligations in international law and the provisions of domestic law. The United Kingdom's international obligations are not directly applicable in domestic law.

2. Secondly, the HRA 1998 has given domestic judges two significant legal powers. One of these is the duty to interpret legislation, so far as possible, consistently with Convention rights, and the other, where consistency cannot be achieved, is to declare such laws incompatible with Convention rights.

3. The third point flows from this: any action to deal with incompatibility of primary legislation rests with Parliament, not the courts. Breach of Convention rights cannot, unlike fundamental breaches of EU Law, post-*Factortame*, empower the courts to disapply an Act of Parliament.

In the remainder of this section we will look at the substantive elements of the HRA 1998 in a little more detail, before moving on to consider the impact of the devolution Acts, and then the significance of all of this for legal method.

10.3.1 The Convention Rights in English Law

The HRA has been instrumental in creating a stronger human rights dimension to English law over the last decade. Thus, for example, the HRA:

- is playing an important, but gradualist role in marking out the boundaries of a modern privacy law in the United Kingdom (see, e.g., *Douglas v Hello! Ltd (No 1)* [2001] QB 967; [2001] 2 All ER 289; *Wainwright v Home Office* [2003] UKHL 53; *Campbell v MGN* [2004] UKHL 22);

- has played a substantial part in clarifying rights relating to personal identity, same-sex relationships, and, more generally, the enjoyment of family life (e.g. *Bellinger v Bellinger* [2003] UKHL 21; *Ghaidan v Godin-Mendoza* [2004] UKHL 30); *R (Mellor) v Secretary of State for the Home Department* [2001] EWCA Civ 472; *R (Baiai) v Secretary of State for the Home Department* [2008] UKHL 53);

- has influenced modern legal debate about fundamental moral and medico-legal issues such as the right to life (*In re A (Children) (Conjoined Twins: Surgical Separation)* [2000] EWCA Civ 254; [2001] Fam 147) and assisted dying (*R v DPP ex parte Pretty* [2001] UKHL 61; *R (Nicklinson) v Ministry of Justice* [2014] UKSC 38);

- has been instrumental in defining the scope of executive and legislative powers in respect of detention, e.g. of suspected terrorists (*A v Secretary of State for the Home Department* [2004] UKHL 56); as regards prisoner's rights during their incarceration (e.g. *Black v Secretary of State for Justice* [2009] UKHL 1), or the rights of those detained under the Mental Health Act 1983 (*R (H) v North and East London Regional Mental Health Review Tribunal* [2001] EWCA Civ 415), and the detention of persons pending deportation from the UK (*R (Saadi) v Secretary of State for the Home Department* [2002] UKHL 41); and

- has also enabled the House of Lords to rule unequivocally against the admissibility before a British court of evidence obtained by torture (*A* v *Secretary of State for the Home Department* [2005] UKHL 71).

So, how has it achieved these things?

First, as we have seen, the HRA gives the Convention rights a statutory basis in English law. Unlike the European Communities Act 1972, which simply incorporated EEC and subsequently EU law wholesale into English law, the HRA 1998 has selectively identified ECHR Arts. 2–12 and 14, together with the First Protocol, Arts. 1–3 and Sixth Protocol, Arts. 1 and 2 (see HRA 1998, sch. 1). This in fact encompasses all of the major substantive rights under the ECHR, subject to the existing derogations and reservations entered by the UK government (HRA 1998, s. 1(2)).

Secondly, HRA, s. 6 imposes a duty on all public authorities to act compatibly with the Convention rights. This is important because it places a proactive duty on public bodies to take human rights issues into consideration in all their activities.

Thirdly, the Act also provides a cause of action where a public authority has acted in breach of Convention rights. In these circumstances, HRA, s. 7(1)(a) enables a person harmed by that breach to bring proceedings against that authority. Sections 6 and 7 together are thus the key provisions which make the Convention rights actionable and give them their 'bite' under English law.

But there are also significant practical limits on the HRA's scope. First, claims can only be brought by someone who is a victim for the purposes of the Act. There is no particular magic to the word 'victim' in this context, it simply means a person (or group) whose Convention rights have allegedly been infringed, though this does prevent the Act being used by non-victims to bring 'public interest' or 'test' cases purely as a matter of principle—see, e.g., *Taylor* v *Lancashire County Council* [2005] EWCA Civ 284.

Secondly, claims can be brought only against a 'public authority' (HRA 1998, s. 6(1)). As a consequence, this creates a distinction akin to that in EU law between horizontal and vertical effect. The HRA 1998 has vertical effect, so that an individual can sue the state or a 'state-like' body, but it does not have horizontal effect, which would have allowed direct enforcement of rights between individuals.

'Public authority', however, is not defined in the Act, and its meaning has been the subject of litigation. Although there is an obvious core of organisations that fall into the public description, such as central government departments, local authorities, regulatory bodies (such as the Financial Services Authority, or the Solicitors Regulation Authority), the police, and the courts too, there will be others whose status as public or private bodies is debatable. The HRA 1998 tries to deal with this by recognising that the public–private distinction is not so much about status or ownership of the organisation, but rather about its functions if a body is publicly funded; exercising statutory powers; taking the place of central government or local authorities, or providing a public service, then it is more likely to be regarded as public. The Act thus recognises that 'hybrid bodies' (either 'private' organisations to whom the state has contracted out public functions, e.g. privatised utilities and professional bodies, or, conversely, essentially public bodies with some private functions) may be sufficiently public to come within the HRA definition for those functions.

Thirdly, as we have noted already in the chapter, we also need to be aware of the role played by the test of proportionality in UK human rights cases. Proportionality raises important questions regarding the intensity of judicial review, and the extent of 'judicial deference' to Parliament and, more particularly, the executive (see, e.g., Leigh, 2007; Poole, 2008). Whether the emphasis on proportionality in the HRA requires courts to engage in the more searching review undertaken by the ECtHR, or the traditional domestic ('*Wednesbury* reasonableness') approach to judicial review has divided both judges and commentators. Decisions in the House of Lords and Supreme Court have tended to swing back and forth like the proverbial pendulum, between acknowledging the need for an 'intense' review of government action (see, e.g., *per* Lord Steyn in *R* v *Secretary of State for the Home Department, ex parte Daly* [2001] UKHL 21, at [25]–[28] and *per* Lord Bingham in *A and others* v *Secretary of State for the Home Department* [2005] UKHL 56), and due respect (or 'deference') for executive decision-making (see *Huang* v *Secretary of State for the Home Department* [2007] UKHL 11, at [16]). These tensions emerged again in the markedly different views of Lords Sumption and Kerr in *R (Carlile)* v *Secretary of State for the Home Department* [2014] UKSC 60. We will take a moment to look at this case in some depth, not just because of what it says about the intensity of review in HRA cases, but also because it highlights important differences in judicial approach more generally, particularly in understanding how judges apply constitutional legislation that is potentially 'game-changing', such as the HRA.

In *Carlile* a group of British Parliamentarians had sought to invite Maryam Rajavi, a dissident Iranian politician resident in Paris, to speak at a meeting hosted by the House of Lords. As a consequence of her links with Iranian opposition groups, including *Mujahedin-e-Khalq*, which had at one time been a proscribed organisation, Rajavi had been made the subject of an exclusion order from the United Kingdom in 1997. Her Parliamentary sponsors now sought to have that exclusion lifted. The Home Office refused, citing advice from the Foreign Office that lifting the ban would cause significant diplomatic damage to the UK's relationship with Iran, and place British people and property in the region at risk. Lord Carlile with other members of the Lords brought judicial review proceedings arguing that the exclusion was disproportionate and an infringement of Article 10.

The Supreme Court, in its judgment, decided that the Court of Appeal had been wrong to apply the domestic standard of judicial review, but it also upheld the exclusion by a majority of 4:1. The individual judgments display a range of reasoning. Lord Sumption took the strongest stance against interfering with the Home Secretary's decision. While he accepted, with the remainder of the Court, that the HRA meant that there were no executive decisions that were immune from review, a degree of judicial 'deference' (though he disliked the term) was required—see paras. [19]–[47]. He justified this on two grounds, the first being 'constitutional' and the second, to adopt Professor Mark Elliott's (2014) term, 'institutional'.

Constitutionally, Lord Sumption argued that the HRA had only modified, not abrogated the traditional distribution of power between the courts and the organs of government. Consequently some degree of deference is constitutionally appropriate because '[h]owever intense or exacting the standard of review in [HRA] cases, … it stops short of transferring the effective decision-making power to the courts.' Institutionally, too, his Lordship argued that the fact of a court's constitutional competence to undertake a review should not blind it to the potential limits of its factual competence. In other words, a court should be wary of substituting its views of a matter for those of the constitutional decision-maker, particularly if that meant overriding the 'best qualified evidence before us' (here the Foreign Office risk assessment).

The remaining three judges in the majority (Lord Neuberger, Lady Hale, and Lord Clark) placed less emphasis than Lord Sumption on the role of deference, but broadly shared his institutional concerns, even though both Lady Hale and Lord Clark had reservations about the strength of the Home Secretary's objections. Lord Kerr, by contrast took the view that the court was both competent and constitutionally required to make an assessment, and that it would be an error to attach special weight to the Home Secretary's views—see paras. [150]–[162]. To that extent, he was clearly much less concerned about restricting judicial oversight on 'institutional' grounds.

These divisions in the Supreme Court in *Carlile* are not simply about technical interpretations of the scope of review under the HRA. They are more fundamental than that, reflecting the way in which differences in judicial approach (or 'style' as we have called it) often reflect fundamental differences in a judge's perceptions of the limits of their role. As Mark Elliott (2014) concludes:

> The text of the HRA simply does not speak to the questions about the judicial role with which the Supreme Court had to wrestle in *Carlile*. It is inevitable, therefore, that even if judges choose to characterise their views in terms of their understandings of what the HRA requires, what they are really doing is projecting onto that relatively blank canvas their own preconceived notions of the proper limits of the judicial function.

If there is a pattern, it is thus quite hard to discern. There is some indication that the courts are more likely to be robust in respect of unqualified rights (Leigh, 2007: 185–8). Courts have also tended to be less deferential, in general, where the issues fall squarely within their competence and experience, as in Art. 5 and Art. 6 'due process' cases (see also *per* Lord Walker in *R (ProLife Alliance) v BBC* [2003] UKHL 23)—though even this is arguable, especially once one brings allegations of terrorism into the mix, where the courts have adopted a more cautious approach, see Poole (2008).

To finish this section by stating the obvious, you should also be aware that the issue of proportionality needs to be taken into account in assessing the proper scope of secondary legislation, not just primary legislation. For example, see *R (British American Tobacco and others) v Secretary of State for Health* [2004] EWHC 2493 (Admin) where the Tobacco Advertising and Promotion (Point of Sale) Regulations 2004, which imposed new constraints on tobacco advertising, were held to be a proportionate regulatory response. The considerable health risks and economic costs to society caused by smoking meant, in the view of the court, that the Secretary of State was entitled to exercise considerable discretion in drawing the line between the competing interests of protecting free speech and protecting public health. Following the guidelines proposed by Lord Walker in the *ProLife Alliance* case, as a general principle, it is likely that less 'deference' will be shown towards powers expressed in secondary than primary legislation.

10.3.2 The Declaration of Incompatibility

The powers under HRA, ss. 3 and 4 to declare legislation incompatible with a Convention right were based by the draftsman on similar powers contained in the New Zealand Bill of Rights Act 1990, s. 6, requiring the courts to interpret legislation consistently with the rights and obligations of the International Covenant on Civil and Political Rights. The UK approach, however, goes further. It imposes a stronger duty to achieve a consistent interpretation under s. 3, *and*, unlike the New Zealand legislation, where no consistent interpretation is possible, it gives the domestic courts a clear *statutory* power to declare the legislation incompatible (s. 4).

A 'declaration of incompatibility' under s. 4 is simply a statement that the legislation is not 'Convention compliant', and it serves to put the government on notice of that fact. The only courts with the power to make a declaration of incompatibility are, in England and Wales, the High Court, the Court of Appeal, the Supreme Court, the Judicial Committee of the Privy Council, and the Courts Martial Appeal Court. In Scotland, the power can be exercised by the Court of Session and the High Court of Justiciary, in addition, of course, to the Supreme Court.

A declaration does not in any way affect the validity of the Act in question. It remains law unless and until Parliament deals with the incompatibility. Thus, the court must still apply the legislation as it stands and the positions of the parties to the actual case are unchanged by the declaration.

It is important to note that the courts have the *power* to make a declaration; it is not a *duty*, or certainly not in all cases. In particular, where the question of consistency falls within the UK's margin of appreciation (discussed later in this chapter), the courts may determine not to issue a declaration, on the basis either that Parliament is better placed to assess where the line falls, or that Parliament should at least be given an opportunity to consider the issue first: see *R (Nicklinson)* v *Ministry of Justice* [2014] UKSC 38.

There is no legal duty on the government to repeal or amend incompatible legislation, nor upon Parliament to accept the remedial measures the minister may propose, though the political or moral pressure to do so could be considerable. As a consequence the ECtHR has been reluctant to regard the declaration procedure as an 'effective remedy' under the ECHR: see *Hobbs* v *UK* (2002) (Application No. 63684/00, 18 June 2002). However, in the context of evidence that the UK government had acted to change the law in fifteen of the eighteen declarations that had become final since the passing of the HRA, the Grand Chamber of the Court in *Burden* v *UK* [2008] 2 FLR 787, expressed the view that future evidence of an established ministerial practice of giving effect to declarations could be sufficient to persuade the Court that the procedure is effective.

As Greer (1999: 15–16) points out, practically speaking, the declaration process is somewhat unsatisfactory as it must create uncertainty about how public authorities will deal with incompatible but not (yet) amended legislation. To try and minimise these practical problems, there is a 'fast-track' procedure under HRA 1998, s. 10 whereby ministers can amend non-compliant legislation by 'remedial order'—provided the minister concerned finds 'compelling reasons' (undefined by the Act) for doing so. Moreover, 'fast track' is itself a relative term, and it is perfectly legitimate for the minister to await the exhaustion of the normal appeals process before taking any action. This can add significant delays to the process and, possibly in some cases, hardship to litigants. The Parliamentary Joint Committee on Human Rights recommended in 2008 that a clear timetable for implementation should be established, with a normal expectation that action to address an incompatibility should be completed within six months of the declaration. This recommendation was, however, rejected by the government (Ministry of Justice, 2009).

10.3.3 Incompatibility of Delegated Legislation

The powers under s. 4 do not extend to secondary legislation. So, how do we deal with potentially incompatible secondary legislation?

The first issue is always whether the delegated legislation can be interpreted compatibly with Convention rights—the duty to achieve a consistent interpretation under HRA, s. 3 expressly extends to delegated or subordinate legislation. If consistency can be achieved, then that is the end of the problem—see **Figure 10.2**.

If a compatible reading cannot be achieved, we need to identify clearly where the potential incompatibility lies. If the real cause of incompatibility is the parent Act, then it is the Act that should be challenged, not the subordinate legislation. In this situation the subordinate legislation must remain in force unless and until the parent Act is repealed or amended, since, even if the parent Act is incompatible, it is still the law until that time. Both the courts and the minister or council (etc.) who made the rules can, in these circumstances, rely on the 'defence' that they are giving effect to laws necessarily made under primary legislation. If, on the other hand, the incompatibility lies within the secondary legislation itself, then, in the unlikely case that it cannot be reinterpreted to be Convention compliant, it may be struck down by the normal process of judicial review. In effect, the secondary legislation would be declared *ultra vires* its parent Act, because the Act did not require its powers to be used in a way that is incompatible with the Convention.

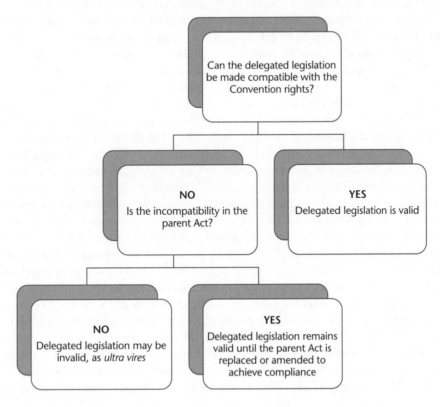

Figure 10.2 Addressing the compatibility of secondary legislation

Few declarations of incompatibility have been made: by March 2015 the total had reached only twenty-nine, twenty of which had become final (Joint Committee on Human Rights, 2015: 17). The Committee also noted that the rate at which declarations were being made had substantially reduced, with only three during the 2010–15 Parliament.

10.3.4 Making a Claim

We noted earlier that claims can only be brought by persons who are 'victims' under the Convention, and normally only against a 'public authority'. It follows from the latter point that private individuals cannot be sued directly for breaching Convention rights: that is, the HRA has no 'horizontal effect'. But this does not necessarily mean that individuals cannot ever claim compensation for breaches of their Convention rights by other individuals. There are two possibilities that can be considered.

First, an individual may, in any proceedings, cite a Convention right to aid their argument on other grounds. In other words, a claimant may bring a claim, e.g. for breach of contract, or negligence, or defamation, and include in that claim an argument that a particular application or interpretation of defamation (or whatever cause of action is involved) would breach their human rights. This is possible because, as we have seen, HRA, s. 6(3) includes courts and tribunals within the category of 'public authority', thereby requiring the court to take account of the relevant Convention rights when reaching its decision. Thus, in *Wainwright v Home Office* [2003] UKHL 53, the House of Lords recognised that courts could not use s. 6 to create a new tort of privacy. The most they could do, consistent with their s. 6 duties, was to develop existing torts consistently with the privacy requirements of ECHR, Art. 8.

Secondly, there is a significant body of authority within the case law of the ECtHR that places an obligation on the state to protect its citizens from the infringement of their rights by others. For example, in *X and Y v The Netherlands*, Series A, No. 91 (1985), the Court held that, where an alleged sex offender escaped prosecution because under Dutch law the apparent victim (who had a mental disability) was not competent to initiate the prosecution, this was a breach of the victim's rights under Art. 8. In other words, the Court may be prepared to give the Convention a kind of *indirect* horizontal effect by making the state liable for ensuring that private rights between individuals are consistent with the ECHR and protected accordingly. So far as we are aware, the UK courts have not yet had to take such an approach under the HRA, but the point is clearly an arguable one.

Claims under the Act can be brought in any proceedings (HRA 1998, s. 7(1)(b)), and so will encompass first-instance hearings before a court or tribunal, appeals, and judicial review in the Administrative Court. Claims against the courts themselves, however, can be brought only by means of judicial review, appeal, or any other procedure specifically created for that purpose by rules of court.

10.4 Incorporation under the Devolution Acts

As we noted in the introduction to this chapter, Convention rights are also built into the legislation which created the Welsh Assembly and the Scottish Parliament. So, let us now consider what this involves, and its implications.

Devolution of legislative powers to the National Assembly for Wales and Scottish Parliament was achieved primarily through Acts of the UK Parliament: the Government of Wales Acts 1998 and 2006, and the Scotland Act 1998. An important feature of the legislation is that both bodies are statutorily obliged to legislate in accordance with Convention rights as defined by the HRA 1998.

Consequently, primary legislation which breaches Convention rights falls outside those bodies' legislative competence, and is thus invalid (Scotland Act 1988, s. 29(1) and (2)(d); Government of Wales Act 2006, s. 94(3) and (6)(c)). This seems to envisage severance of the invalid parts, where possible, rather than the automatic striking down of the whole Act or Assembly Measure.

Any secondary legislation purported to be made by the Scottish government or the Welsh Assembly government which is not compatible with Convention rights is statutorily defined as *ultra vires* and therefore invalid—see Scotland Act 1998, s. 54(2) and Government of Wales Act 2006, s. 81(1).

The right of an individual to bring an action, is, as with the HRA 1998 itself, explicitly limited by the devolution Acts to individuals who are 'victims' within the meaning of ECHR, Art. 34.

10.5 The Consequences for Legal Method (1): Statutory Interpretation

To understand the impact of the HRA 1998 on our legal methods, it is essential first to remember the distinctive basis on which incorporation is to be achieved. The 1998 Act, you will recall, has *not* made the ECHR, with the attendant jurisprudence of the Court, 'lock, stock and barrel' part of English law. This leaves British judges relatively free to arrive at their own version of Convention rights, guided, but not bound, by the approach and meanings adopted by the ECtHR. We will now consider the implications of this, first, for methods of interpretation and second, for precedent.

10.5.1 Interpreting UK Legislation

The primary role of the national courts under the HRA 1998 is an interpretative one; they must interpret UK legislation in the light of the Convention rights, and this in turn means that they must interpret the scope and meaning of the Convention rights themselves. How will they go about these processes?

The key provision in the HRA 1998, for our purposes, is s. 3(1). As we have already noted, this imposes a statutory duty on all courts and tribunals to interpret primary and subordinate legislation in a manner consistent with the Convention rights. This duty extends to all legislation, including Acts and regulations passed before the HRA came into force. It follows also that, where there is an issue of compliance, the courts are no longer bound by pre-HRA precedent on the meaning of any particular statutory language—see *per* Lord Hope in *R v Lambert* [2001] UKHL 37; [2001] 3 All ER 577 at [81].

The duty under the HRA is precise: it expressly requires the courts to achieve compatibility only *in so far as it is possible to do so*. Not surprisingly, the choice of this form of words has been crucial to the way the courts have approached their interpretative task, and has been the subject of substantial academic and judicial debate. We now need to look at the arguments that have framed that debate.

Section 3 and the art of the possible

The core argument about s. 3 turns on the fact that there are essentially two ways of determining the effect of the phrase 'in so far as it is possible', one is to read it restrictively, the other is to read it expansively. These options were being debated in the academic literature even as the HRA came into force. The case for a restrictive approach was advanced by Marshall (1998), who suggested that s. 3(1) obliges the courts to find consistency only where that is achievable within the bounds of recognised principles of statutory interpretation. In other words, the courts should not artificially strain the meaning of statutory language to make it fit the Convention. This is also, arguably, consistent with the strong emphasis on parliamentary sovereignty implicit in the whole structuring of the Act, and particularly the procedures for a declaration of incompatibility.

Alternatively, it is possible to argue that the intention of s. 3 is to impose a stronger duty on the courts, akin, as Hunt (1999: 97–8) suggests, to the *Marleasing* obligation in EC law, which, by virtue of similar language to that of HRA 1998, s. 3(1), has been taken to oblige courts to achieve consistency except where that is manifestly *impossible* on the language of the legislation (see further: Case C–106/89 *Marleasing SA v La Comercial Internacional de Alimentación SA* [1990] ECR I-4135, explored in **Chapter 11**). This position too had its supporters in the early days of the Act (see, e.g., Ewing, 1999: 87; Bennion, 2000), who saw it is a logical consequence of incorporating human rights standards into UK law. Moreover, it was consistent with the view of the Lord Chancellor in debate on the Human Rights Bill that the courts should apply the declaration of incompatibility only where it is *impossible* to construe legislation consistently with Convention rights (Hansard HL Debates, vol. 583, col. 535, 18 November 1997). The difficulty this argument faces lies in the very ambiguity of words such as 'so far as possible'. Not only does this make a *Pepper* v *Hart* reference to the Lord Chancellor's views more difficult (though compare the extra-judicial comments of Lord Steyn, 2001), it begs the possibility that the language of HRA 1998, s. 3(1) may as readily be used to support as to deny the 'Marshall interpretation'.

This same conflict has been reflected in much of the case law on s. 3. As Lord Nicholls admitted in *Ghaidan* v *Godin-Mendoza* [2004] UKHL 30, at [27]:

> What is not clear is the test to be applied in separating the sheep from the goats. What is the standard, or the criterion, by which 'possibility' is to be judged? A comprehensive answer to this question is proving elusive. The courts, including [the House of Lords], are still cautiously feeling their way forward as experience in the application of section 3 gradually accumulates.

The high watermark of expansive interpretation so far has been the case of *R* v *A* [2001] UKHL 25; [2001] 2 AC 45; it also highlights the tensions that have existed between different judicial styles. The accused in this case had been charged with rape and wished at his trial to bring evidence of previous consensual sexual relations with the complainant as part of his defence. This, he argued, he was precluded from doing by the Youth Justice and Criminal Evidence Act 1999, s. 41(1) and (3), which had introduced a new 'rape shield defence' into English law, prohibiting a defendant from bringing evidence or asking questions about any prior sexual behaviour of the complainant without the leave of the court. This change in the law reflected longstanding concerns that questions about sexual history were too often used by defendants unfairly to undermine the evidence of alleged rape victims in court. On the other hand, there were also concerns that s. 41 had in fact gone too far in protecting the victim, to the extent that it now undermined the rights of the accused (see, e.g., Birch, 2000), because it did not distinguish the legally relevant (the complainant's sexual history with the accused) from the unduly prejudicial (sexual history with others).

The House of Lords accepted that s. 41 had gone too far, and had denied the defendant his due process rights under ECHR, Art. 6. In what is clearly the leading judgment Lord Steyn takes us through a number of steps. These are instructive in terms of approach.

First, his Lordship undertakes an extensive review of the content and legislative history leading up to the passing of s. 41. He then explores the scope of s. 41 itself, drawing extensively on both academic commentary and the Canadian 'rape shield' laws that were influential in shaping s. 41, while also considering proposals from the New South Wales and New Zealand Law Commissions. On this basis he concludes that s. 41 is too widely drafted and makes an 'excessive inroad into the right to a fair trial' (para. 36). His third step is to explore the interpretive options open to the complainant in the light of HRA, s. 3(1), *if* 'ordinary methods of purposive and contextual interpretation' (para. 39) fail. Using these options, his Lordship rejects a number of ways of restricting the breadth of s. 41 as impossible under both ordinary rules and HRA, s. 3(1). Finally, his Lordship focuses on two of the statutory exceptions built into s. 41. These give a judge discretion to admit evidence of a complainant's sexual history where:

- behaviour is relevant to the issue of consent and the relevant behaviour either took place at or about the same time as the event out of which the complaint came: s. 41(3)(b); or
- it was so strikingly similar to the behaviour of the complainant at or about the time complained of, that it ought to be admitted: s. 41(3)(c).

Having ruled out any possibility of using subsection (3)(b) in this case (because too much time had elapsed between any previous sexual activity and the event complained of), the Court focused on s. 41(3)(c). Lord Steyn argued that, although the subsection was not sufficient under ordinary methods of statutory interpretation to cure the problem, it was possible, by using HRA, s. 3(1) 'to subordinate the niceties of language' (para. 45) to interpret the provision to take account of 'modern considerations of relevance judged by logical and common-sense criteria of time and circumstances' (ibid.). Consequently, the House of Lords argued that the test of admissibility under s. 41(3)(c) in such cases becomes whether, 'due regard always being paid to the importance of seeking to protect the complainant from indignity and humiliating questions ... the evidence ... is nevertheless so relevant to the issues of consent that to exclude it would endanger the fairness of the trial under article 6 of the convention' (para. 46).

Now, whatever the House of Lords may call it, this involves a quite breathtaking disregard of statutory language—to the extent that one of their Lordships, Lord Hope, was clearly uncomfortable with what was being done. A narrow statutory exception, concerned only to admit what in the jargon we call 'similar fact' evidence, has consequently been rewritten as a much more generalised test of relevance.

Lord Steyn's approach to s. 3 in this case thus takes the 'strong consistency' approach to something of an extreme. Compatibility is to be achieved, even if the resulting interpretation is 'linguistically strained'—as it was (to say the least) in *R* v *A*. Only if there is an express restriction on Convention rights 'stated in terms' (i.e. made explicit on the face of the Act) should a declaration of compatibility be considered under s. 4.

By contrast, Lord Hope's position, taken in both *R* v *A* and in *R* v *Lambert* [2001] UKHL 37 is much closer to what we have called the 'Marshall interpretation'. Legislation cannot be made compatible with the ECHR if it contains provisions which, either expressly *or by necessary implication*, contradict Convention rights. The phrase in italics thus seems to run counter to Lord Steyn's expansive view. Case law since *R* v *A* can perhaps be read as indicating some attempt to consolidate practice and clarify common principles and approaches. Both Lords Steyn and Hope subsequently made statements which suggested that their positions were in fact closer than this initial juxtaposition would indicate. Lord Hope's later opinion in *Lambert* indicated that he accepted that it would sometimes be necessary to 'read in' words to legislation, whereas Lord Steyn in another later case—*R (Anderson)* v *Secretary of State for the Home Department* [2002] UKHL 46 [2003] 1 AC 837—stated that s. 3(1) would not be available 'where the suggested interpretation is contrary to express statutory words or is by implication necessarily contradicted by the statute' [at 59]. The fact that, in *Lambert*, Lord Steyn cited with approval Lord Nicholls' view in *Re S* [2002] UKHL 37, para. [40], that his (i.e. Lord Steyn's) 'observations in *R* v *A* should *not* [our emphasis] be read as meaning that a clear limitation on Convention rights in terms is the only circumstance in which an interpretation incompatible with Convention rights may arise', is suggestive of some attempt at retrenchment by Lord Steyn. Lord Nicholl's interpretation seems to us to have been a generous one to say the least, but it was one way to narrow the gap that was threatening to develop in the jurisprudence on s. 3.

Some commentators have taken this as indicative of a general retrenchment by the House of Lords. Danny Nicol (2004) thus argues that their Lordships' approach in *Re S*, *ex parte Anderson*, and *Bellinger* v *Bellinger* [2003] UKHL 21; [2003] 2 WLR 1174 indicates a move towards a more restricted use of s. 3 and a correspondingly greater willingness to issue a declaration of incompatibility under s. 4. However, others are less certain. Aileen Kavanagh (2004a), by contrast, sees evidence of judicial sensitivity to the context of each case rather than a clear trend. She points to the fact that the s. 4 declaration was a relatively 'easy' option for the courts in those cases. In *Anderson* and *Bellinger* in particular, there was already a strong indication that Parliament would change the law. This was not the case in *R* v *A*, which involved legislation that was already supposed to be HRA compliant.

Certainly it is our view that judicial practice today is still geared very much to treating the declaration of incompatibility as a remedy of last resort. This view is consistent with the House of Lords' approach in the leading case of *Ghaidan* v *Godin-Mendoza* [2004] UKHL 30, which concerned rights of succession to a statutory tenancy under the Rent Act 1977. The respondent had lived in a stable homosexual relationship with the deceased tenant. But the Rent Act only gave a right of succession to a person living with the original tenant 'as his or her wife or husband'—and, in any strict or proper sense of the terms, this could not therefore encompass same-sex partnerships. The respondent alleged that this violated his right under ECHR, Art. 14. The House of Lords agreed (Lord Millet dissenting) and construed the 1977 Act to allow succession, regardless of gender, provided the parties had been living together in a stable relationship.

The majority in *Ghaidan* agreed that any non-compliant literal meaning of a provision must readily give way, except where, in Lord Nicholls' words, such an interpretation would conflict with a 'fundamental feature' of the legislation. Moreover Lord Steyn (at [45]), strongly supported by Lord Rodger, once again explicitly rejected a narrow construction of s. 3(1):

> First, it applies even if there is no ambiguity in the language in the sense of it being capable of bearing two *possible* meanings. The word 'possible' in section 3(1) is used in a different and much stronger sense. Secondly, section 3(1) imposes a stronger and more radical obligation than to adopt a purposive interpretation in the light of the ECHR. Thirdly the draftsman of the Act had before him the model of the New Zealand Bill of Rights Act which imposes a requirement that the interpretation to be adopted must be reasonable. Parliament specifically rejected the legislative model of requiring a reasonable interpretation.

Subsequently, the superior courts have delivered a range of statements stressing the extent to which s. 3 itself imposes a 'strong interpretative duty on the courts, so that a declaration of incompatibility should be treated as exceptional': see, e.g., *Sheldrake v DPP* [2004] UKHL 43; [2005] 1 AC 264, para 28; *R v Waya* [2012] UKSC 51; [2012] 3 WLR 1188, para. 14. A number of cases have explicitly drawn, or at least accepted in argument, a comparison with the *Marleasing* approach in the way that Hunt (1999) has suggested—see, e.g., *Johnson v Medical Defence Union* [2007] EWCA Civ 262; *Vodafone 2 v Revenue and Customs Commissioners* [2009] EWCA Civ 446.

None of these cases, however, entirely resolve the uncertainties we have been discussing. Despite the direction of travel, we are not necessarily much closer to Lord Nicholl's elusive 'test'. And perhaps that is because the search for such a test is ultimately unrealistic. Aileen Kavanagh (2007: 132) thus makes the point that:

> Such an answer is elusive … because of the necessarily evaluative nature of the task which judges have to undertake when applying s. 3 by balancing two sets of values which pull in different directions.

In other words, we are back to the old truism that it really does depend on the circumstances of the case.

That in turn still leaves us with some uncertainty about just how far, practically, a court should be prepared to go to achieve consistency. What emerges from the case law is a range of techniques that the courts are prepared to use, and a few that they are not.

First, a court may *read down* the words of the Act to give them a narrower than usual scope and thereby make the offending provision Convention compliant.

Secondly, a court can *read in* Convention rights by implying words into a statute that are not there on a literal reading—*Ghaidan* is a good example of this; *R v A* perhaps the most extreme example so far.

Thirdly, there is some suggestion that, as Lord Hope expressed it in *Lambert* (at [81]), the courts can engage in a process of *translation*, that is, a process in which incompatible words are to be changed and read as if they were compatible. Both 'reading in' and 'translation' represent potentially radical departures from the tradition of literal interpretation.

There are also some things that the courts are reluctant to do. As we have noted already, the courts will not use s. 3 to interpret legislation compatibly if such a construction:

- clearly conflicts with the express words—see *Anderson*, and the comments of Lord Steyn earlier in the chapter;
- conflicts with a foundational aim or function of the statute—see *Re S*, earlier;
- requires reading in a substantially new provision (e.g. a whole new section) or the substantial redesign of a statutory scheme: *R (MH) v Secretary of State for the Health Department* [2004] EWCA Civ 1609; *R (Wright) v Secretary of State for Health* [2009] UKHL 3.

You need to be aware that, on the whole, the problem cannot be quantified in simple terms, such as 'it is OK to read in a few words, but not a whole subsection'. Section 3 cases are difficult precisely because it is hard to say *in general* where the dividing line between interpreting and legislating *should* be drawn. The courts, in their pragmatic fashion tend to treat s. 3 problems as largely contextual decisions which may be influenced by a number of general interpretive principles (see Kavanagh, 2004b), but which ultimately have to be decided on a case-by-case basis. While it would certainly be inconsistent with the spirit of the ECHR and the purpose of HRA, s. 3 to focus narrowly on literalist, linguistic approaches to interpretation, the current rather pragmatic emphasis on tele-ological interpretation does also carry with it some risks. In particular, we suggest, there must be a point where the proper, parliamentary redrafting of fundamentally non-com-patible legislation is desirable. This would at least maintain some relative transparency and certainty in the meaning of statute law, and help sustain the distinction between legislative and judicial functions. It would also allow Parliament rather than the judges to determine the merits of what may be important changes to social policy.

The process of interpretation under section 3

Whatever uncertainties we may face in determining when s. 3 will be used, there is an increasingly clear reasoning process by which the question of construction is decided. We summarise these various steps in **Figure 10.3**.

The critical first step is that we must identify precisely which statutory provision con-travenes the Convention (see *per* Lord Nicholls in *Re S*, at [41]). It is not enough simply to raise a general allegation of incompatibility against the statute as a whole.

If the court then decides there is a breach of Convention rights, it is not necessary to go straight to s. 3. If the problem can be resolved by reference to normal principles of construction, then the court should do so. If, and only if, this is not possible then the court must consider s. 3. In so doing, you should be aware that the court's approach will differ somewhat, depending on whether the Act in question was passed before or after the HRA. Where it was passed before the HRA, legislative intent is unlikely to be a decisive factor in any question of construction (unless, unusually, Convention compli-ance was identified as an issue at the time). Moreover any pre-HRA authorities on statu-tory meaning will not be binding on the court—*per* Lord Hope in *Lambert*, at [81]. In the case of post-HRA legislation, both legislative intent—as in *R v A*, discussed earlier, and relevant precedents do need to be taken into account, though any assertion that Parliament intended to legislate contrary to the HRA is likely to require very clear sup-porting evidence.

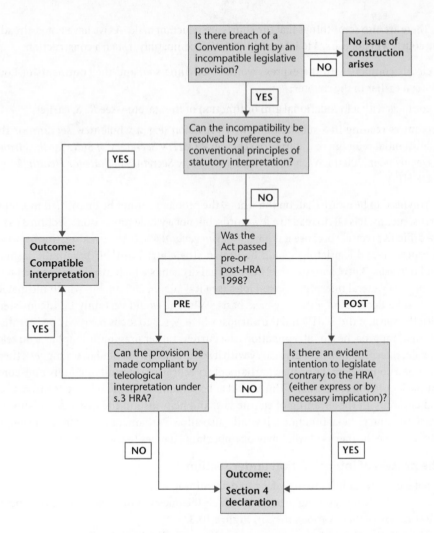

Figure 10.3 Steps to construction under HRA, s. 3

Legislative intent, Hansard, and the HRA

One final point, before we leave the discussion of s. 3, concerns the role of Hansard and other documentary sources that may provide evidence of legislative intent or legislative scope to the courts. As we saw in **Chapter 9**, following *Pepper* v *Hart*, under certain strict conditions it has become acceptable for the courts to refer to Hansard, the record of proceedings in Parliament. There was a concern that the HRA might add to the pressure on courts to look to Hansard, particularly in assessing whether legislation is compatible with the Convention. In fact, as with *Pepper v Hart*, more generally the courts have tended to discourage extensive reliance on legislative history. As Lord Nicholls observed in *Wilson* v *First County Trust* [2003] UKHL 40:

> 66. I expect that occasions when resort to Hansard is necessary as part of the statutory 'compatibility' exercise will seldom arise. The present case is not such an occasion. Should such an occasion arise

the courts must be careful not to treat the ministerial or other statement as indicative of the objective intention of Parliament. Nor should the courts give a ministerial statement, whether made inside or outside Parliament, determinative weight. It should not be supposed that members necessarily agreed with the minister's reasoning or his conclusions.

67. Beyond this use of Hansard as a source of background information, the content of parliamentary debates has no direct relevance to the issues the court is called upon to decide in compatibility cases and, hence, these debates are not a proper matter for investigation or consideration by the courts …

Similarly, the courts have also been reluctant to permit Hansard to be used in interpreting the HRA itself. Thus, the House of Lords in both *Aston Cantlow Parochial Church Council v Wallbank* [2003] UKHL 37; [2004] 1 AC 546 and *YL v Birmingham City Council* [2007] UKHL 27 declined to use Hansard to assist in understanding the scope of 'public authority' under HRA s. 6.

10.5.2 Interpreting the Convention Rights

The second point we need to explore is the courts' approach to interpreting the Convention rights themselves. There is of course already a substantial 'bank' of interpretive material in the jurisprudence of the ECtHR. However, one consequence of the 'free-standing' model of incorporation is that the English courts are not obliged to follow the interpretations laid down by the Court, though they are expected to have some regard to the decisions of that body (see the next section for more detail on this). Accordingly, it is conceivable that the English courts could develop a distinctive human rights jurisprudence which deviates significantly from the approach of the Court, provided that it does not fall below the threshold standards set by the ECtHR. This is because the HRA 1998 does not oust the jurisdiction of the ECtHR (though it does make the journey to Strasbourg rather longer). Claimants who fail to establish a breach of Convention rights before the UK courts are still entitled to appeal to Strasbourg for redress. If they win, under the ECHR, Art. 46 the UK government is obliged to apply the decision of the ECtHR (unless it has entered a derogation), thereby overriding the inconsistent approach of the domestic courts. A relatively recent and controversial example of this was the *Abu Qatada* case: see *Othman* v *United Kingdom* App. No. 8139/09, 17 January 2012. The Law Lords had considered that it would not be a violation of the Convention to deport the radical Islamic cleric Abu Qatada (Omar Othman) to Jordan, where he had been convicted in his absence of serious terrorist offences. However, the Strasbourg court held that Abu Qatada's deportation would be a 'flagrant' breach of Art. 6 on account of what was seen as a real risk that the Jordanian court would use evidence that had been obtained by the torture of third persons at the applicant's retrial. The ECtHR had never before found that deporting or extraditing a person would be a violation in those circumstances, and its decision 'sent political shockwaves through the UK establishment' (Dickson, 2012: 373). As a result, the United Kingdom and Jordan had to enter into a treaty agreeing that evidence of torture would not be used before Qatada could be deported. (He was subsequently acquitted in Jordan from involvement in two bomb plots, and released from prison in September 2014.)

Cases like this indicate that too much independence on the part of the British courts could be counter-productive if it simply generated more appeals to Strasbourg than the present system. At the same time, this does not mean that the English and European courts should necessarily proceed in absolute tandem. The ECtHR itself recognises that scope may exist for local variation in the application of the Convention and, regardless of whether a state has incorporated the Convention or not, allows a 'margin of appreciation'. This rather technical doctrine means that, in assessing compliance, the Court will in some respects defer to the appreciation of a problem by the national authorities, including the courts, thereby giving them some element of discretion. The extent of the margin of appreciation will depend on the nature of the rights involved. Where 'a particularly important facet of an individual's existence or identity is at stake' (*Dickson v United Kingdom* [2007] 41 EHRR 21; [2007] ECHR 44362/04 at 78) that margin will be reduced accordingly.

The operation of a margin of appreciation also helps explain why there is an obligation on national courts only to take the ECtHR's jurisprudence into account. The limit to this obligation means that domestic courts are permitted to take local conditions and local needs into consideration in applying the Convention. However, this framing of the obligation also means that the margin of appreciation is actually a 'two-way street'. While it prevents the ECtHR from applying the Convention too strictly across different national legal systems, it also prevents national courts from ignoring the Court's jurisprudence entirely. That would not be to take it into account.

Related to this is the question of what interpretative principles the domestic courts will bring to their analysis of Convention rights. We have already pointed out that the Convention rights are not necessarily capable of the kind of precise and detailed exposition that characterises a lot of domestic legislation. While the Convention may specify that we have a right to life and a right to privacy, the potential boundaries of these rights are difficult to define in the abstract, or in the detail often expected of legislation; similarly, problems will arise in defining the boundaries between competing rights. For example, is the practice of abortion to be protected because it constitutes an integral part of the woman's right to a private life, or challenged as a violation of the foetus's right to life itself? At what point may one right supersede the other? Resolving such problems requires not just analysis of the text, but a sensitivity to the 'spirit' of the Convention and to the social and ethical issues that such problems raise. Arguments about human rights often do not lend themselves to the narrower brands of legal literalism. In theory this should not be an insurmountable problem. British judges today are, given the EU context, far more familiar with broader, principles-based drafting and purposive styles of interpretation than they were thirty years ago, and generally more prepared for the kind of judicial activism that the ECHR demands. But the EU law analogy gives rise to a further question: should British judges consciously adopt the style of analysis used by the ECtHR? This is in some respects distinctive, reflecting both the special character of the ECHR and the general principles of interpretation developed under the Vienna Convention on the Law of Treaties (1969). The interpretive style of the Court is thereby characterised by three key elements: the 'textuality principle'; a 'teleological' approach to interpretation; and a capacity to supplement the express terms of the Convention by the recognition of 'implied terms'.

The **textuality principle** describes the Court's starting point, which, in common with all widely accepted traditions of interpretation, demands respect for the text of the Convention. As the Vienna Convention, Art. 31(1) puts it: 'A treaty shall be interpreted in good faith in accordance with the ordinary meaning to be given to the terms of the treaty in their context and in the light of its object and purpose.' It is an approach,

therefore, which avoids the extremes of literalism by accepting that the ordinary meaning is in large part determined by the context—both textual and social. This is reinforced
by an expectation that the Court will look at the meaning of words or provisions within
the context of the Convention as a whole. This has created some interesting problems,
because the Court has sometimes found areas of overlap between different provisions of
the ECHR, rather than, say, assuming that the express inclusion of one right in one part
of the Convention precludes its implicit inclusion in another article. For example, in
Rasmussen, Series A, No. 87, a question arose as to Danish paternity law. Denmark had
ratified the Convention but not the Seventh Protocol, which, in Art. 5, expressly defined
the rights of parents with regard to their children, and the Danish government therefore
sought to argue that the case was not justiciable. The Court rejected this argument by
finding that, despite the omission of the Seventh Protocol, the case could also be considered under ECHR, Art. 8. In theory at least this could raise interesting questions in
the British context, given that the Protocols not ratified by Britain are excluded from the
Convention rights within the HRA 1998.

The idea of a **teleological approach** is primarily a very European way of describing
purposiveness (cf. our discussion of European Community methods in **Chapter 11**).
The ECtHR has adopted a fairly cautious approach in this regard, seeking to tread a fine
line between possibly excessive interference with the domestic jurisdiction and powers
of individual states, and the need to give full effect to the aims and objectives of the
Convention in securing individual rights and freedoms. Consequently, the Court has
established a number of basic guidelines. For example:

(a) Where an article limits or qualifies an individual right, such limits are normally to
be interpreted narrowly.

(b) The Convention should be read as a 'living instrument', that is, by reference to current values and conditions, not those that existed when the Convention was adopted
in the 1950s.

(c) Closely related to this, following the Vienna Convention, Art. 31(3)(b) the interpreter
is entitled to take account of the subsequent practice of the state in the application
of the treaty. The precise scope and meaning of subsequent practice is, however, a
contested and somewhat thorny issue, beyond the scope of our present concerns.

(d) In addition the Court has recourse to a number of *general principles*, notably, the
'margin of appreciation' (discussed previously) and the principles of proportionality (see section **10.3.2**) and legal certainty (self-explanatory!), which it will use to
determine the limits of state liability and individual rights. This approach is again
one with which British judges have become more familiar through EC law, and, as
we have seen, increasingly have had to engage with under the HRA. This may be
particularly difficult when it forces judges further into the political arena than they
might wish when interpreting the Act (cf. Lord Lester, 1998).

The signs are, for the most part, that the English judiciary are adapting effectively,
though some might say rather conservatively, to both the Strasbourg jurisprudence
and approach. Signs are too that they are starting to find their way towards a more
distinctive UK jurisprudence, though there has been little evidence so far of the HRA
free-standing model being used as a justification to depart dramatically from the
ECtHR line.

10.6 The Consequences for Legal Method (2): Precedent

In looking at the impact of Convention rights and the HRA 1998 on precedent there are essentially two questions: what is the likely impact of the 1998 Act on the doctrine of precedent, and what is the status of decisions of the ECtHR under the HRA 1998?

As regards the first of these points, all common law rules and precedents that are incompatible with Convention rights are potentially open to challenge. This principle, we suggest, extends *expressly* to those precedents which are interpretations of statutory provisions, since, if inconsistent with Convention rights, they will be caught explicitly by HRA 1998, s. 3, and *implicitly* to all common law rules *per se*. This argument is based on the fact that all courts and tribunals are, as we have seen, themselves 'public authorities' under the Act. As such they are obliged to achieve consistency with the Convention in respect of the substantive and procedural rules they have made. The correctness of this view appears to be supported by Lord Hope in *R v Lambert* [2001] UKHL 37; [2001] 3 All ER 577, at [114], where he expressly took the view that both a court's duty to construe legislation consistently with the Convention under s. 3(1), and to decide cases on common law principles were 'acts' within the meaning of HRA, s. 6(1). The interesting technical question is how the courts face that particular challenge.

There is clearly some expectation with regard to previous (inconsistent) interpretations of legislation caught by s. 3 that all courts/tribunals will be required to disregard such precedents, though this is implicit in s. 3 rather than expressly spelled out in the Act (but see Home Office, 1997, para. 2.8, where the point is made explicit), nor is any such principle expressly established in respect of common law rules more generally. In this latter context, since all courts and tribunals are caught by the duties contained in HRA 1998 s. 6, there is clearly some basis for saying that the duty to override inconsistent precedents *in general* lies with all courts and tribunals, regardless of the status or authority of the precedent involved. The Court of Appeal's decision in *D v East Berkshire NHS Trust* [2004] QB 558 offers some limited authority consistent with this view. Here the Court of Appeal held, contrary to normal principles of *stare decisis* that the House of Lords' decision in *X (Minors) v Bedfordshire County Council* [1995] 2 AC 633 could not survive the introduction of the HRA 1998, because the HRA undermined the policy considerations that had shaped the House of Lords' reasoning in that case. This decision was affirmed on appeal to the House of Lords—see [2005] UKHL 23, and subsequently in *Kay v London Borough of Lambeth; Leeds City Council v Price* [2006] UKHL 10. However, in *Kay*, their Lordships also affirmed the priority of the common law principles of precedent, and stressed that the circumstances in *D v East Berkshire* should be regarded as wholly exceptional. Consequently, we must assume for the present that courts should follow established precedent, even if there is a conflict with Convention rights, except in the most extreme circumstances. In effect, it means that the Supreme Court becomes virtually the sole arbiter of whether or not domestic precedents are compliant, or should be overruled as non-compliant with Convention rights.

As regards the status of decisions of the ECtHR, HRA 1998, s. 2(1) expressly requires the British courts to *take into account*, among other things, the judgments, decisions, and advisory opinions of the Court and opinions and decisions of the (now defunct) European Commission. This was interpreted by the Court of Appeal in *Barclays Bank plc* v *Ellis* [2000] All ER (D) 1164 to mean that lawyers had to bring to the court's attention *all* the relevant case law of the ECtHR. Mere reference to the Convention, it was said, did not help the court and was not sufficient.

However, this is an obligation only to consider; there is no express statutory duty to **follow** the established European case law on the ECHR. This is consistent with the free-standing model adopted by the United Kingdom, and different from the UK's obligations as regards decisions of the CJEU under the European Communities Act, s. 2. That said, certainly for the first decade of the HRA, the courts tended to treat themselves as ordinarily obliged to adopt a consistent interpretation. In *R (Alconbury) v Environment Secretary* [2011] UKHL 23, for example, the majority of the Law Lords undoubtedly treated the Strasbourg jurisprudence as *prima facie* binding, even if only for pragmatic reasons. In Lord Slynn's words:

> [i]n the absence of some special circumstances it seems to me that the [UK] court should follow any clear and constant jurisprudence of the European Court of Human Rights. If it does not do so there is at least a possibility that the case will go to that court, which is likely in the ordinary case to follow its own constant jurisprudence. (para. 26)

This approach came to be reflected (no pun intended) even more strongly by the superior courts following the leading case of *R (Ullah)* v *Special Adjudicator* [2004] UKHL 26. This decision came to epitomise the development of the so-called 'mirror principle', by which the UK courts sought not just to apply the established Strasbourg jurisprudence, but to anticipate the way in which ECtHR would apply it to the case in hand. This was as, commentators have observed, a remarkably narrow, common law-influenced, approach to take. It only began to be disrupted at the end of the last decade as senior judges began to take a more circumspect, if not actually critical, look at ECtHR decision-making (see, e.g., Bates, 2015: 60).

Lord Neuberger's decision in *Manchester City Council v Pinnock* [2010] UKSC 45; [2011] 2 AC 104, is considered a marker for this sea-change in approach. Lord Neuberger thus reminded the UK courts that their duty was to 'take account' of Strasbourg jurisprudence, which might mean following a clear and constant line of decisions, but only provided their:

> 48 ... effect is not inconsistent with some fundamental substantive or procedural aspect of our law, and whose reasoning does not appear to overlook or misunderstand some argument or point of principle

As Bates (2015: 61–2) has observed, no court has yet had to cross this 'constitutional redline' constructed by *Pinnock*, but the decision can nonetheless be seen as part of a 'new equilibrium' between the UK courts and Strasbourg, the other side of which is the ECtHR's openness to a more dialogical approach with national courts, a move that was strongly signalled in the wording of the Council of Europe's 2012 Brighton Declaration on the future working of the Court.

Our discussion of s. 2(1) so far leaves unresolved one other issue: what should an English court do when confronted by the post-HRA precedent of a superior English court, which is inconsistent with a *later* decision of the ECtHR? This rather mind-bending question arose for the Court of Appeal in *Leeds City Council v Price* [2005] EWCA Civ 289. Here the Court was faced with the House of Lords' decision in *Harrow LBC* v *Qazi* [2004] 1 AC 983. This was a decision that was made, obviously, after the passing of the HRA, and was one in which the Lords had taken into account the relevant ECtHR jurisprudence. Unfortunately it was also obvious that *Qazi* was 'unquestionably' incompatible with the later decision of the ECtHR in *Connors* v *United Kingdom* (2004) 40 EHRR 189. What do you think the Court of Appeal should have done? Well, what the Court actually did was to follow *Qazi* and distinguish its own earlier decision in *D* v *East Berkshire NHS Trust* (discussed earlier), despite the conflict with the *Connors* decision. This was a decision made with some reluctance. Clearly, the judges felt caught between the proverbial rock and the hard place. The *Price* case was appealed to the House of Lords—see *Kay* v *London Borough of Lambeth*; *Leeds City Council* v *Price* [2006] UKHL 10, where, as we have seen, the Court of Appeal's decision was affirmed. Thus, it seems that a court faced by a conflict between a binding domestic precedent, and a contrary ECtHR decision must *normally* follow the domestic precedent. This was justified (*per* Lord Bingham at paras. [43]–[44]) on the need to preserve legal certainty, even in the Convention context, and by reference to the margin of appreciation granted by the Convention to national authorities, including the courts. However, the House of Lords did leave a loophole by allowing that in very exceptional circumstances departure from an otherwise binding precedent could be justified.

By an interesting twist, the consistency of the substantive decision in *Kay* with the ECHR was subsequently brought into question by the decision of the Strasbourg Court in *McCann* v *United Kingdom*, (2008) 47 EHRR 40 [2008] ECHR 19009/04. As a result the standing of the *Kay* decision itself fell to be considered again by the House of Lords in *Doherty* v *Birmingham City Council* [2008] UKHL 57. In *Doherty*, their Lordships declined to overturn the majority view in *Kay*, arguing that *Kay*, as a recent precedent, could only be overturned by a hearing before a panel of nine Law Lords (which it was not, as the problem of inconsistency was not foreseen at the time the case was listed), and that, in any event, inconsistencies with *McCann* could be dealt with by 'modifying' the majority view to take account of *McCann*.

Taken together these decisions indicate (a) the strong reluctance of the courts to set aside notions of *stare decisis*, and (b) their willingness to use their obligations under s. 6 to justify creatively reinterpreting their own precedents (as *Qazi* was in *Kay*, and then *Kay* itself was in *Doherty*), rather than overruling them. While some may see this as a complicated way of making UK law Convention-compliant, it nevertheless fits with an idea that we discussed earlier. That is, as Lord Bingham asserted in *Kay*, that the principle of a margin of appreciation allows national courts some freedom of action, not just as regards the extent of substantive compliance with ECtHR jurisprudence, but particularly in the choice of methods whereby compliance is achieved.

The search for consistency, as we have seen, also arguably leaves the UK law on human rights in a rather unsatisfactory position. It both limits the opportunity to develop a more distinctive UK jurisprudence, and also leaves the superior UK courts, and particularly the Supreme Court, in the position of playing 'catch-up' with Strasbourg. To some extent this may be inevitable. Our courts should not necessarily be expected successfully to anticipate the Strasbourg jurisprudence, particularly when, as in response to cases like *Al-Skeini* [2008] 1 AC 153 (see *Al-Skeini* v *United Kingdom* (2011) 53 EHRR 18) and *Abu Qatada*, the ECtHR decides to extend its own jurisprudence. Nonetheless, an approach that seems predominantly focused on hitting the required minimum standard will almost certainly see a continuing, if relatively small number of applicants beating a path to Strasbourg (see Dickson, 2012).

10.7 Legal Research and Argumentation

The HRA 1998 raises a number of important practical and conceptual issues around legal research and argumentation.

First, it has created an obligation on all British lawyers (rather than just the human rights specialists) to become familiar with new sources of law. This is not a small task. There is not just the matter of developing a familiarity with the Convention itself (one probably needs to understand the Convention as a whole, not just the Convention rights enacted in the HRA 1998, for the reasons of interpretation already considered), there is also the slight matter of over fifty years of case law. Reading decisions of the ECtHR is also a somewhat distinctive process. The judgments are drafted as something of a compromise between the common law and civil law styles we saw in **Chapter 3**. Until 1968, decisions of the Court adopted very much the continental style still used in modified form by the CJEU, with numbered paragraphs giving the Court's reasoning followed by a short judgment. This has been abandoned for a more flowing, narrative, style of analysis, with reference to its own earlier authorities as required (as we have briefly seen, the Court does abide by its own system of precedent, albeit not with the full rigour of the English model of *stare decisis*). Like the British courts, the Court requires decisions to be made by at least a majority rather than expecting unanimity. Judges may also, therefore, in common law fashion, offer separate opinions. This is clearly different from the collegial approach of the CJEU. In practice, it is relatively rare for judges of the Court to deliver separate opinions (though for a recent example, see *Sher* v *United Kingdom* [2015] ECHR 5201/11 (20 October 2015). Judges appear to have been very cautious in their use, and aware of the risk of undermining the authority of the Court by extensive divisions of opinion. Consequently, when the power has been used it is generally to deliver a dissent from the majority view, rather than a concurring judgment giving some distinctive reasoning. Joint dissenting opinions may also be delivered.

At a deeper level, as Hunt (1999) points out, the HRA 1998 more than ever forces lawyers to confront matters of morality and fundamental values, and this itself has implications for the form and content of legal argumentation. The traditional 'positivistic' conception of law has tended to keep law and morality separate. This is not to say that law is routinely assumed to have no moral content or foundation, but it does mean that legal and moral principles and reasoning have generally been treated as distinct species, with the courts being primarily concerned with the enforcement of law, not morals. By blurring that distinction the 1998 Act sometimes obliges lawyers, including the judges, to take account of a wider range of resources and forms of argument. This may involve both a wider academic literature, including the ethical and philosophical, not just the legal. As Lord Steyn has recognised, instead of trawling through endless *dicta* on *Wednesbury* unreasonableness, 'it may be more helpful to dip into Isaiah Berlin' (cited in Hunt, 1999: 99). Comparative material, particularly from other common law jurisdictions that have adopted a culture of positive rights, such as Canada, South Africa,

New Zealand, and the USA, is also relevant. Indeed, much of the HRA case law cited in this chapter illustrates the extent to which such materials are considered.

10.8 The Future of the Human Rights Act

'Bringing rights home' has been given a new twist by a growing debate over whether the HRA should be repealed and replaced by a 'British Bill of Rights'. The future of the Act has become a political hot potato, with the last (Coalition) government establishing an independent Commission to 'investigate the creation of a UK Bill of Rights that incorporates and builds on all our obligations under the European Convention' (Commission on a Bill of Rights, 2012). Though the Commission was split in its conclusions, the majority favoured a move, in principle, to a British Bill of Rights, and the Conservative Party subsequently went into the 2015 General Election with a manifesto commitment to scrap the Act.

At the time of writing, following the election of a majority Conservative government, planning is under way to bring in the necessary legislation to replace the HRA, though there are still uncertainties as to if and when this will happen. This final section of the chapter therefore explores the general issues and challenges of repealing and replacing the HRA, and some of its implications for legal method.

This is an important and both politically and legally divisive debate. Repeal of the HRA can be seen as consistent with a growing maturity and sense of the United Kingdom as a rights-based rather than liberties-based democracy. Proponents of the move see it as more consistent with British traditions of parliamentary sovereignty, though this is often coupled with concerns that the HRA is open to abuse by certain undesirable or undeserving litigants. Amongst the most politically contentious issues have been voting rights for prisoners, the Art. 6 rights of suspected terrorists, and the rights or otherwise of the state to deport foreign national prisoners at the end of their sentence (see, e.g., Horne & Miller, 2015).

A new Bill of Rights is thus seen as an opportunity to break the link with the ECtHR so as to allow a more distinctively 'British' culture of rights to develop (see, e.g., Commission on a Bill of Rights, 2012). It would also be an opportunity to address some of the technical problems we, and others, have identified with the HRA in its current form.

On the other side, many supporters of the HRA see the attacks on the Act as largely politically motivated and based on a mistaken conception of Strasbourg 'interference' in the domestic legal process, fuelled in part by media antagonisms. The recent Report of the Joint Committee on Human Rights (2015) thus highlighted negative reporting by the *Daily Mail*, *The Daily Telegraph*, and the *Sun* between 2012 and 2014, claiming that the United Kingdom lost a sizeable majority of cases before the ECtHR. As the Committee observed (2015: para. 2.2):

> In fact, the proportion of cases which the UK loses in the European Court of Human Rights is not 75% or 60%, as these press stories claimed, but closer to 1%. The newspaper stories did not take into account the large number of applications against the UK which are rejected by the Court as inadmissible.

In a debate with the potential to be shaped by 'lies, damned lies and statistics', we will attempt to offer a reasonably dispassionate view of the main constitutional and technical issues arising.

Assuming a British Bill of Rights is passed, how different will it be? At this stage it is quite hard to say, but, ultimately no Bill of Rights can move too far from the ECHR and similar international instruments such as the International Covenant without consequences. If the United Kingdom failed to meet these international benchmarks its international reputation and democratic legitimacy would undoubtedly suffer. This was reflected in the terms of reference of the Independent Commission, which precluded any question of the UK withdrawing from the ECHR as such.

Repealing the HRA will also face challenges in relation to devolved powers across the UK. Human rights are partially devolved in Scotland, Wales, and Northern Ireland. The Scottish Parliament has, for example, set up its own Scottish Human Rights Commission. While the scope for unilateral repeal is debated, most legal experts seem to agree that repeal of the HRA by the Westminster Parliament would likely violate the so-called 'Sewell Convention', under which the Westminster government does not normally seek to legislate on devolved matters in Scotland without the Scottish Parliament's consent. While this is a conventional principle, not a rule of law, given the Scottish government's declared opposition to repeal, unilateral action would likely provoke some order of constitutional crisis with Scotland. Similar understandings exist with the devolved legislatures in Wales and Northern Ireland.

The Conservative manifesto suggests that the Government's primary aims are to 'break the formal link' between the British courts and the ECtHR and (thereby?) limit what it described as 'mission creep' in its interpretation, which facilitates the bringing of 'spurious' claims.

We do not yet have a blueprint of how that could be achieved. As we have seen, the Strasbourg jurisprudence currently is not binding, but does potentially serve as some constraint on interpretation. 'Breaking the link' might therefore liberate a more conservative judicial interpretation, but that is very much in the gift of the judiciary, and ultimately, we argue, of the ECtHR and the Council of Europe. This is because a Bill of Rights will have to confront at least three significant challenges.

First, and most crucially, while Parliament can remove the general obligation in HRA, s.2 to take Strasbourg jurisprudence generally into account, any attempt entirely to disconnect the UK from its obligation to abide by ECtHR rulings to which it is a party will put the UK in breach of its international obligations. There is no easy or obvious fix to this. One suggestion, that the UK establish a special parliamentary procedure to consider whether to comply with European Court rulings does not actually resolve the problem: selective non-compliance is still (as a matter of international law) a breach of Art. 46 of the ECHR, and a policy that could, ultimately, see the UK expelled from the Council of Europe.

Secondly, it follows that, if decoupling the UK legislation from the general jurisprudence of the ECtHR does not give the UK interpretative *carte blanche*, it raises the prospect of an increased number of UK applicants having to turn ultimately to the ECtHR itself for a remedy—if they have the expertise and resources. In other words, the Bill of Rights may see a return to the pre-HRA two-track system of domestic litigation, followed by applications before the ECtHR. Extending the path to Strasbourg may well have disincentive effects, and therefore reduce the likelihood of direct rulings by the ECtHR on the scope of any Bill of Rights protections, but that is different from a formal decoupling.

Thirdly, quite simply, it will not be that easy to draft a set of rights that are both ECHR compliant and structured to give the UK courts greater freedom of interpretation than under the existing HRA. As we have seen, the Convention allows states a margin of appreciation, but that isn't magically going to get bigger just because the UK Parliament has replaced the HRA with a Bill of Rights.

Viewed objectively, the political and technical challenges are thus significant. Moreover, the Government still has work to do convincing some of its own backbenchers that repeal really is the right course of action. Indeed, the challenges are such that the Government has expressed its own reluctance to be 'wedded to a timetable' (*The Financial Times*, 31 May 2015), leading to speculation that it may be as late as 2017 before a draft Bill is proposed.

 ## CONCLUSION

There is no doubt that the HRA has had a significant impact in moving the United Kingdom from a system historically built around a loosely defined set of civil liberties, to a far more pro-active, rights-based model. The move to a Bill of Rights might set new limits, but it is unlikely to reverse that underlying seismic shift in legal culture.

In the fourth edition of this book we suggested that the HRA 1998 was likely to have some impact on what we have previously called 'judicial style'. At the very least, we suggested that it would curb some of the more pragmatic and unprincipled (in the sense of being without an underlying 'deep' rationale) decision-making that has frequently substituted for a more sophisticated discourse of rights in the English courts. As our discussion of proportionality in *Carlile*, and of the impact of HRA, s. 3 shows, such effects are now quite deeply embedded in English legal method and reasoning, though perhaps still not as deeply as we suspected in 1999. In short, with some exceptions, we take the view that the courts, and particularly the House of Lords and Supreme Court, have approached this revolution in a relatively conservative and careful fashion. Indeed, some might say in too conservative a fashion, though that is not the perception that one would tend to get from the pages of the *Daily Mail*.

One of the problems of legislation like the HRA is that it does seem to bring the courts much more obviously into the political arena. As Lord Irvine, the Lord Chancellor who introduced the HRA, made clear at the time, the intention of the HRA was 'to provide as much protection as possible for the rights of individuals against the misuse of power by the state' (Hansard HL Debates vol. 583, col. 808, 24 November 1997). In seeking to achieve that somewhat controversial objective, it is not surprising that the Act and the courts have attracted political criticism from both left and right.

Fifteen years after it came into force, the big questions for the future are how much longer the HRA will survive in its present form, and, if it does not, what implications that will have, both for human rights and legal method. Whatever happens, it is unlikely that the courts will simply be able to forget the accumulated experience and precedents built up over the last decade.

EXERCISE 19 Concept check

The following is simply a short comprehension exercise designed to assist you to become more comfortable with concepts used in this chapter. After reading the chapter, try to complete the following without referring back; then check your answers. Repeat the process of reading, answering, and checking until you are satisfied that you *understand* the material. Alternatively you can do this as a group task by swapping answers and checking each other's. If you find you have different answers, consider why? Sometimes this may bring out important differences in understanding.

What do the following concepts mean? Try to define them in your own words:

free-standing model of incorporation	margin of appreciation
declaration of incompatibility	textuality
right of individual petition	victim
principle of proportionality	Convention rights
legislative competence	implied terms

CHAPTER REFERENCES

BATES, E. (2015), 'The UK and Strasbourg: A Strained Relationship—The Long View', in K.S. Ziegler, E. Wicks, and L. Hodson (eds), *The UK and European Human Rights—A Strained Relationship?* (Oxford: Hart).

BENNION, F. (2000), 'What Interpretation is "Possible" under Section 3(1) of the Human Rights Act 1989?', *Public Law*, 77.

BIRCH, D. (2000), 'A Better Deal for Vulnerable Witnesses?', *Criminal Law Review*, 223.

Commission on a Bill of Rights (2012), *A UK Bill of Rights?—The Choice Before Us*, available at http://www.justice.gov.uk/about/cbr.

DICKSON, B. (2012), 'The Record of the House of Lords in Strasbourg' 128 *Law Quarterly Review*, 354.

DWYER, D. (2005), 'Rights Brought Home', 121 *Law Quarterly Review*, 359.

ELLIOTT, M. (2014). Human Rights, Proportionality and the Judicial Function: *R (Carlile) v Home Secretary* in the Supreme Court, *Public Law for Everyone* [blog], 13 November 2014. Available at http://publiclawforeveryone.com/2014/11/13/human-rights-proportionality-and-the-judicial-function-r-carlile-v-home-secretary-in-the-supreme-court/.

EWING, K.D. (1999), 'The Human Rights Act and Parliamentary Democracy', 62 *Modern Law Review*, 79.

*GREER, S. (1999), 'A Guide to the Human Rights Act 1998', 24 *European Law Review*, 2.

HOME OFFICE (1997), *Rights Brought Home: The Human Rights Bill*, Cm. 3782 (London: The Stationery Office).

*HORNE, A. and MILLER, V. (2015), *A British Bill of Rights?* House of Commons Library, Briefing Paper No. 7193 (19 May 2015). Available at http://researchbriefings.parliament.uk/ResearchBriefing/Summary/CBP-7193.

HUNT, M. (1999), 'The Human Rights Act and Legal Culture: The Judiciary and the Legal Profession', 26 *Journal of Law & Society*, 86.

HUSCROFT, G., MILLER, B.W, and WEBBER, G. (eds) (2014), *Proportionality and the Rule of Law: Rights, Justification, Reasoning* (Cambridge: Cambridge University Press).

JOINT COMMITTEE ON HUMAN RIGHTS (2015), *Human Rights Judgments: Seventh Report of the Session 2014–15* (London: The Stationery Office).

KAVANAGH, A. (2004a), 'Statutory Interpretation and Human Rights after *Anderson*: A More Contextual Approach', *Public Law*, 537.

*KAVANAGH, A. (2004b), 'The Elusive Divide between Interpretation and Legislation under the Human Rights Act 1998', 24 *Oxford Journal of Legal Studies*, 259.

KAVANAGH, A. (2007), 'Choosing Between Sections 3 and 4 of the Human Rights Act 1998: Judicial Reasoning after *Ghaidan v Mendoza*', in H. FENWICK, G. PHILLIPSON, and R. MASTERMAN (eds), *Judicial Reasoning under the UK Human Rights Act* (Cambridge: Cambridge University Press).

LEIGH, I. (2007), 'The Standard of Judicial Review after the Human Rights Act', in Fenwick et al. (eds), *Judicial Reasoning under the UK Human Rights Act* (Cambridge: Cambridge University Press).

LESTER, LORD, of HERNE HILL (1998), 'The Impact of the Human Rights Act on Public Law', in J. BEATSON, C. FORSYTH, and I. HARE (eds), *Constitutional Reform in the United Kingdom: Principles and Practice* (Oxford: Hart Publishing).

*MARSHALL, G. (1998), 'Interpreting Interpretation in the Human Rights Bill', *Public Law*, 167.

MINISTRY OF JUSTICE (2009), *Responding to Human Rights Judgments: Government Response to the Joint Committee on Human Rights' Thirty-first Report of Session 2007–08*, Cm. 7524 (London: The Stationery Office).

MINISTRY OF JUSTICE (2012), *Responding to Human Rights Judgments: Report to the Joint Committee on Human Rights on the Government's Response to Human Rights Judgments 2011–12*, Cm. 8432 (London: The Stationery Office).

Nicol, D. (2004), 'Statutory Interpretation and Human Rights after *Anderson*', *Public Law*, 273.

POOLE, T. (2008), 'Courts and Conditions of Uncertainty in "Times of Crisis"', *Public Law*, 234.

11

European Legal Method

The United Kingdom (UK) joined what is now called the European Union in 1973 (though parts of Great Britain such as Jersey and the Isle of Man are not members of the EU). Membership has meant that the English legal system has been radically affected by what is now called 'EU law', (but has been known as 'EEC law', 'EC law', and 'Community law' over the years). As we have noted before, and shall explore in this chapter, EU law takes precedence over all national laws, including legislation. Not only does this mean that some of the law affecting us is created by institutions of the European Union rather than by our national Parliament and courts, it also involves us in a different way of thinking. We have touched upon these matters throughout the book but, as the role of EU law tends to run parallel with English law rather than fit clearly into the hierarchy, we felt that too much detail on EU law in the earlier chapters might lead to confusion.

There is no doubt that students find the topic of 'EU Law' difficult so this chapter seeks to explain the basic structure and relevance of EU institutions, legislation, and case law and how these affect the methods of legal analysis we employ. As EU Law is now covered extensively in all law courses we will not go into detailed explanations of EU Law here. Instead, the chapter will be organised as follows:

- section **11.1** details the **sources** of EU law;
- section **11.2** sets out the **institutions** of the EU and their increasingly important role in our law-making;
- section **11.3** examines the main **analytical techniques** employed by European lawyers; and
- section **11.4** describes the **legal method** employed in the Court of Justice of the European Union and the effect of EU law on the **drafting and interpretation** of UK legislation.

Before going any further we should note some general myths about the EU and EU law which need to be dispelled. The myths most commonly encountered are:

- that the Court of Justice is a 'court of appeal';
- that EU law is imposed upon us;
- that the UK does not implement EU legislation effectively;
- that the European Parliament makes EU Law;
- that EU law is 'the same' in every Member State;
- that the Court of Justice and the European Court of Human Rights are the same court.

11.1 The Sources of European Union Law

EU law is made up from the originating and amending Treaties of the EU (what might be seen as the EU's foundations), the 'Acts' of the various EU institutions (sometimes referred to as secondary sources, e.g. 'Directives'), and the judgments of the Court of Justice of the European Union.

11.1.1 Origins and Treaties

The EU began life as the 'European Economic Community' (the EEC) in 1957 under the Treaty of Rome, signed by France, Germany, Italy, Belgium, Luxembourg, and the Netherlands.

The UK sought to join the EEC in the 1960s but its applications were blocked by France (particularly its President, General de Gaulle). After de Gaulle's death in 1970 the UK joined the EEC in 1973, alongside Ireland and Denmark.

International treaties are not automatically part of our law: they require an Act to be passed before they are incorporated. So, to allow for the UK to become a member of the (then) EEC and for the integration of EEC law to take effect, the UK Parliament passed the European Communities Act in 1972. This Act incorporated the Treaty provisions (including future ones) into our law as from 1 January 1973. Section 2(1) of the Act states:

> All such rights, powers, liabilities, obligations and restrictions from time to time created or arising by or under the Treaties, and all such remedies and procedures from time to time provided for by or under the Treaties, as in accordance with the Treaties are without further enactment to be given legal effect ...

The last few words are important: many matters contained in the various Treaties automatically become part of our law and so the Treaties are a primary source of law—there is no corresponding UK Act of Parliament incorporating those laws into our system. However, there are limits: the 1972 Act also makes it clear that certain matters cannot automatically become part of our law without a specific Act being passed in the UK, such as provisions which impose taxation and the creation of new criminal offences. That provides a safeguard for politically-sensitive areas, but, as we noted in **Chapter 6** EU criminal law is probably the fastest-growing area of EU law and this will ultimately have a major effect on both substantive and procedural law in domestic criminal justice systems.

Various treaties have since been signed dealing with specific developments. The Lisbon Treaty (2007) is the latest in a long line of treaties which try to deal both with the expansion in the number of Member States and the need to introduce improvements to regulate the EU. There are now two main consolidating treaties: the Treaty on the Functioning of the European Union (TFEU) and the Treaty on European Union 1992 (TEU). These form the backbone of the EU legislative framework.

The Treaty of Nice (2001) also proclaimed the Charter of Fundamental Rights of the European Union. This is based on the rights established in the European Convention for Human Rights (which we dealt with in the previous chapter) but goes wider in setting out the civil, political, economic, and social rights of European citizens. It does not have the force of law in the UK and, in reality, is a restatement of existing rights. The consolidated versions of TFEU, TEU, and the Charter of Fundamental Rights can be found in the EU's major publication, the Official Journal, at http://eur-lex.europa.eu/legal-content/EN/ALL/?uri=OJ:C:2010:083:TOC.

When you come to study EU law as a distinct subject you will need to be aware of the implications of these developments, but details, such as how EU law treats the free movement of persons or goods, or the powers of the President of the European Council, are outside the scope of this book.

Treaties are therefore mainly political, quasi-constitutional documents but they do contain laws which are of general application across the EU relating to matters such as equality, trade, and free movement. Each Treaty is subdivided into *Articles*, which are the equivalent of our *sections* in UK legislation.

The EU website contains details of the history, membership, laws, and Treaties: see http://europa.eu. There are twenty-eight Member States at the time of writing this text. The UK is set to have a referendum on its continuing membership, to be held before the end of 2017.

11.1.2 The Acts of the Institutions

Treaties do not appear that often and so clearly someone has to have the power to make law within the EU on a year-by-year basis. That power falls to two bodies, termed the *Council of the European Union* and the *Commission* (see later in the chapter). The pieces of legislation produced by these bodies are published in the *Official Journal* of the EU and are termed:

(a) Regulations;

(b) Directives; and

(c) Decisions.

Regulations and Directives are sometimes referred to as 'secondary' sources of legislation. However, we prefer to adopt the view taken some time ago by Brown and Kennedy (2000) that the Acts of the institutions are too fundamental and broad to be relegated to a 'secondary' tag. You need to be aware what the difference is between these forms of legislation:

• A *Regulation* has a general application across the EU. Like the Treaties themselves, a Regulation applies to all Member States and individuals, and is binding without further action on the part of the Member States. In one sense they are 'mini treaties'. This means that once a Treaty or Regulation has been signed by all Member States (and any operational date has passed) the articles become law across all Member States—no Act of Parliament is needed to introduce the new law. This is called 'direct application' and we shall return to it later in the chapter. It causes the UK no constitutional law problem but has created difficulties for some Member States.

- A *Directive* does not have 'direct application' so each Member State must bring in its own legislation to implement the Directive. A Directive is binding on Member States only as to the **result** to be achieved. TFEU, Art. 288 puts it this way: 'A Directive shall be binding, as to the result to be achieved, upon each Member State to which it is addressed, but shall leave to the national authorities the choice of form and methods.'

Thus, one of the myths noted previously (that EU law is the same in all Member States) can be struck off here—the implementation of a Directive in, say, Finland and Ireland may be quite different in detail even though the overall result must be the same:

- All this enables the EU as an entity to establish a legal principle while allowing individual Member States room to incorporate that principle within their own national legislation in the best way they see fit. As we will see shortly, this idea can lead to problems when the wording of the Directive and the national legislation do not correspond.

- The general principle is that a Directive has no effect in law until it is implemented by the state and Member States are invariably given a time limit for implementation— usually three years from enactment. There are special rules and procedures dealing with the situation where a Member State fails to implement the Directive after the time limit has passed or implements the Directive in a faulty way. Equally, the CJEU has had to deal with some actions by Member States who, prior to the implementation date, changed their laws in such a way as to make the anticipated Directive much less effective (e.g. Germany in the case of C–144/04 *Mangold* v *Helm* [2006] IRLR 143). We will deal with these problems later.

- A *Decision* is not something of judicial origin, though it sounds as if it should be. Instead it is a binding 'order' issued by an institution of the EU and addressed to an individual or state. These frequently arise in competition law cases, with the Commission determining the legality of agreements.

To these three binding legal provisions we can also add *recommendations* and *opinions* which will be of persuasive authority (they do not impact on 'legal method' as such and are technical matters best left until you study EU law later in your course).

11.1.3 The Court of Justice of the European Union

The Court is the supreme authority on the law relating to the EU. **It deals only with the interpretation and validity of EU-generated law**. The court is usually referred to as the CJEU but until 2009 itwas referred to in the UK as the European Court of Justice (ECJ). We will generally refer to the CJEU but, when we are speaking historically we will use the abbreviations 'ECJ'.

The CJEU is modelled on European systems, and most of its procedure and legal method bears little relationship to the common law world. The composition of the Court was noted earlier in **Chapter 3** and TFEU Section 5 deals with the jurisdiction of the Court. It states: 'The Court of Justice shall ensure that in the interpretation and application of (the Treaties) the law is observed.' The EU's own website says this: 'The Court of Justice interprets EU law to make sure it is applied in the same way in all EU countries. It also settles legal disputes between EU governments and EU institutions. Individuals, companies, or organisations can also bring cases before the Court if they feel their rights have been infringed by an EU institution.' Thus, the job of the Court is to make sure that EU law is interpreted and applied in the same way in all EU countries, thereby ensuring that the law is equal for everyone. It ensures, for example, that national courts do not give different rulings on the same issue. This does not affect the fact that a Directive might be implemented differently in Member States: the CJEU is concerned with whether the Directive has been implemented properly and the fact that, say, Italy has 'added' to a Directive by giving consumers in Italy even better rights than found elsewhere in the EU, for instance (but still complying with the requirements of that Directive), is not the concern of the CJEU.

The Court is located in Luxembourg and has one judge from each member country. The various Treaties give it a wide jurisdiction. Here are a few examples:

(a) it exercises judicial control over the institutions of the EU such as the Commission;

(b) it exercises powers of judicial review on the validity of EU legislation such as Regulations and Directives—in other words it can annul EU legislation;

(c) it hears cases brought by Member States or EU institutions against other Member States regarding violations of the Treaties;

(d) it decides whether international agreements entered into by the EU are compatible with the provisions of the Treaties; and

(e) it receives *preliminary references* and provides *preliminary rulings* under Art. 267 TFEU concerning the interpretation of EU legislation when asked to do so by a court of a Member State.

The CJEU actually consists of a number of courts: the Court of Justice itself, 'The General Court', and the 'EU Civil Service Tribunal' (which, as the name implies, covers disputes between the EU and its officials and other servants). These latter two courts are specialist courts: the main task of the General Court (previously called the 'Court of First Instance') is to hear and determine at first instance what are called 'direct actions' brought by individuals and the Member States. The General Court was introduced to lessen the burden on the CJEU. The list of 'direct actions' is defined fairly narrowly as:

• *actions for annulment* (against acts of the EU institutions);

• *actions for failure to act* (against inaction by the EU institutions);

• *actions for damages* (for the reparation of damage caused by unlawful conduct on the part of a EU institution);

• *actions based on an arbitration clause* (disputes concerning contracts in public or private law entered into by the EU, containing such a clause); and

• *appeals from the EU Civil Service Tribunal.*

The Treaty of Nice also addressed how the CJEU will be affected by the expansion in Member States: sharing tasks between the CJEU and the General Court more effectively and allowing for the creation of specialist Chambers according to particular areas of law. However, we are concerned with the Court of Justice itself and so, in this text, unless specifically mentioned, the term 'CJEU' will refer to the Court of Justice and not the other courts.

The CJEU can hear cases brought by one party against another but its main function arises in what are called *'preliminary references'* (noted at (e) earlier). As this is just one chapter of a book concerned with legal method, and we cannot hope to do more than to show the impact and influence of EU law on our system, we will concentrate most of our attention in this chapter on *'Preliminary References'*. We will explain shortly what these are and how they work. For the moment we can say that a preliminary reference is a question sent by a domestic court (e.g. the Court of Appeal) to the CJEU asking for an authoritative interpretation of the meaning of EU legislation.

11.2 The Institutions

There are six major institutions of the European Union. The first four listed next are the law-making bodies:

- The European Council (composed of the leaders of the governments/Heads of State of the Member States). When the government leaders are not involved, as explained shortly, this is simply referred to as 'The Council';
- The European Commission (which is the driving force and executive body);
- The Court of Justice (the court which ensures compliance with EU law);
- The European Parliament (the body elected by the peoples of the Member States);
- The European Central Bank; and
- The Court of Auditors (not actually a court but a body which oversees the sound and lawful management of the EU budget).

All institutions are equal, at least on a formal basis. In this book we shall not deal with the Court of Auditors, the EU Civil Service Tribunal, the European Central Bank, or some of the other institutions such as the Economic and Social Committee.

11.2.1 The European Council

Article 15 TEU and Arts. 235–6 TFEU state that the Council will ensure that the objectives set out in the Treaties are attained. The Council is based in Brussels and is a political body which has the final say on nearly all legislative matters. It is a key point of the EU that the parliaments of the Member States do not create EU legislation; nor is EU legislation subject to the approval/rejection of the national parliaments. The responsibility of the national parliaments is merely to implement the Regulations, Directives, and Decisions of the EU.

The Council is effectively the sovereign body of the EU. However, national power is not given up so easily: the Council is not an autonomous organisation of the EU, distinct from the national governments. It is made up of one ministerial representative appointed by each Member State. The representative sent by each state varies according to the issue at hand; economic matters will draw the Chancellors, other matters will require the appropriate minister, e.g. for agriculture or education. At the highest level the Heads of State will meet up to four times a year—indeed they are required to meet twice a year. When this occurs the Council is referred to as the European Council, or more informally as a 'summit'.

The Council is a policy or strategy body: it does not generate the legislation itself. That function, as we shall see, rests with the Commission. The importance of the Council, however, is that it decides whether proposals from the Commission shall take effect. The Council has as its head a President. This person is not the President of the EU as a whole—as most media commentators seem to believe—just the Council. The 'presidency' of the EU itself is more like the Chair of a committee and is taken by government leaders on a six-month rotational basis.

The Council itself is not a fixed body, it is not in permanent session, and the ministerial representatives change frequently in 'reshuffles'. In order to work effectively, therefore, there exists the full-time Committee of Permanent Representatives (COREPER), as well as a system of Management Committees. COREPER comprises state representatives of ambassadorial rank, and their function is to examine the Commission's proposals and sift through them to decide on the level of controversy they may generate when they come before the Council. Those issues which receive unanimous approval from COREPER are put on one list for the Council to 'rubber-stamp'. The Council can then dwell on discussing, or disagreeing on, the more contentious issues.

Voting on issues is a complicated business in the EU. Some matters require a unanimous vote in the Council and in some cases of vital national interest one state may insist on a unanimous vote even though the Treaty does not demand this, i.e. the state may exercise a veto. Other issues can be carried by a simple majority or by a qualified majority. The phrase 'qualified majority' relates to the fact that voting takes place on a weighting system so that the larger states (e.g. UK, Germany, Italy, and France) have more votes than the smaller ones such as Luxembourg or Malta.

The 'qualified majority' mechanism means that any action must have the support of at least 55 per cent of the EU Member States (comprising at least fifteen Member States) and at least 65 per cent of the population of the EU. A blocking minority must include at least four Member States.

11.2.2 The Commission

The Commission is based in Brussels and is the driving force in the legislative process. It meets at least once a week. The head of the Commission is elected by the Commissioners and is (again) called the President. Like the Council, the Commission consists of nationals drawn from each Member State—one member per state. This time, however, although nominated by their respective government, they are not representatives, and are supposed to act independently of their national governments. Each Commissioner is allocated a special task. The Commission plays a vital role in the legislative process of the EU. It has three responsibilities:

(a) to act as an initiator of legislation;

(b) to safeguard the objectives of the Treaty; and

(c) to act as the EU's executive.

Initiator

The Council may have the final say on nearly all matters of legislation, but it is the Commission which formulates and proposes that legislation. The right for citizens of the EU, under certain conditions, to propose legislation to the Commission was created by Regulation (EU) No 211/2011 (the Citizens' Initiative Regulation).

Watchdog

The Commission has the power to investigate and take proceedings in the Court of Justice against Member States infringing EU law. The term 'state' here includes the legislature, the executive, and the judiciary. The Commission will first issue an opinion on the failure by the state. Only if the state does not comply with the opinion will action be taken. However, even if the action proves successful no punitive measures will be levied by the Court of Justice, though it is rare for a state not to comply at this stage.

One such far-reaching action occurred in one of the *Factortame* cases. The issues underlying the *Factortame* cases are complex (for fuller details of the background, see Gravells (1989: 569–73)). At the centre of a lot of legal activity was a challenge to the legality of the UK's Merchant Shipping Act 1988, s. 14 by a number of Spanish nationals affected by the changes. It was alleged that s. 14 effectively prevented other EC nationals from registering fishing boats as British vessels (and hence entitled to greater fishing rights in British territorial waters) unless those vessels were at least 75 per cent British owned, and British managed. This, the Spanish fishermen argued, constituted unlawful discrimination against other EC nationals under the EEC Treaty, Art. 7.

The challenge to the legality of the Act was mounted first in the English courts, where the case went as far as the House of Lords, which then made a preliminary reference to the ECJ under what is now Art. 267 TFEU (see *R v Secretary of State for Transport, ex parte Factortame* [1989] 2 WLR 997). In the meantime, the European Commission itself began proceedings against the UK. In May 1989, the Commission issued an opinion, to the effect that the Act was inconsistent with EU law and used its power to grant interim relief, ordering the British government to suspend the operation of s. 14; see Case 246/89R *European Commission* v *United Kingdom* [1989] ECR 3125. In the eight cases which ensued, the main point of concern became: if the Act contravened EU law, should the affected parties be compensated by the UK government? The ECJ would eventually rule that compensation was due to a party where a Member State had failed to implement EU law properly: see the *Factortame* litigation (joined with another case, Case C–46/93 *Brasserie du Pêcheur SA* v *Federal Republic of Germany* [1996] 1 CMLR 889) and the case of *Francovich* [1991] ECR I–5357; [1993] 2 CMLR 66. That a Member State could be liable to pay compensation for its failings has since become a key aspect of EU law.

The Commission itself can also take action against individuals in relation to breaches of EU competition law.

Executive

The Commission is largely subject to the political control of the Council. However, the detail of legislation is the work of the Commission, and certain matters such as competition law and the rules on agriculture are decided by the Commission.

11.2.3 The Parliament

This body sits in Strasbourg, though many of its activities are carried out in Luxembourg (its administration) and Brussels (its committees). It was originally called the Assembly and its members were drawn from national parliaments. It was not a directly elected democratic body until 1979. Consequently it never was a legislative body in the way we would understand the term 'Parliament'. Rather it had the function of supervising and advising. This has changed in recent years, with the Lisbon Treaty increasing both its supervisory and law-making powers.

The Parliament can accept, amend, or reject legislation proposed by the Council. It cannot instigate legislation, though it may make recommendations to the Committee to be put before the Council.

Further, the Commission must report to the Parliament, and this includes answering questions. Ultimately, the Parliament may dismiss the Commission collectively or force individual members of the Commission to resign. Indeed, Parliament did effectively force a mass resignation following the corruption scandal of 1998–9 (although all but one of its members were back in post within months). The Council likewise reports to the Parliament on a formal basis, though the Parliament exercises no control over the Council. Finally, the Parliament can bring an action in the Court of Justice against the Council or Commission for failure to act.

It may not be a surprise to learn that the head of the Parliament is called the President.

11.2.4 The Court of Justice of the European Union

The Court of Justice sits in Luxembourg and actually pre-dates the creation of the EEC (now the EU). Unhelpfully, the UK's European Communities Act 1972 refers to it as the 'European Court' (and consequently some media coverage confuses this court with the European Court of Human Rights, which is also often referred to as the 'European Court').

The CJEU presently consists of twenty-eight judges—one for each Member State—and two sets of characters which have no equivalent in our system: the Advocates General and the Judge-Rapporteur. The role of an Advocate General is to act as filtering system in a case, assisting the Court by delivering independent opinions on cases for the judges to consider. There are nine Advocates General (five being nominated by the larger Member States). A Judge-Rapporteur (drawn from the panel of judges hearing the case) is responsible for the general management of the proceedings and the writing-up of the decision.

The Court may sit as a full court of twenty-eight judges in very exceptional circumstances, or as a Grand Chamber of fifteen judges (when a Member State or EU institution is involved and so requests, or in a complex case) or in chambers of three or five judges. There are eight of these chambers at present. As more countries join the EU so the number of judges will increase.

The Court deals with EU law only; it is not some supreme European court of appeal. Instead, it is a 'court of reference'. By this we mean that, although it can hear cases brought by Member States or EU institutions against other Member States regarding violations of the Treaties (and in this sense it can be a 'trial court'), its main function lies in relation to *preliminary references*. This jurisdiction is defined in Art. 267 TFEU and appears a strange beast to the English Law practitioner or law student.

What is a preliminary reference?

It is a basic premise of EU law that it is the duty of each court in Member States, not just the CJEU, to apply EU law and that EU law takes precedence over national law. However, where an authoritative interpretation of EU law is needed, that can be supplied only by the Court of Justice. Whatever the CJEU says is the *meaning* of an EU Directive, for instance, is binding on all courts in all Member States.

In most instances the national courts can interpret EU legislation quite happily themselves, but where that is not possible then any country's domestic courts or tribunals can ask the CJEU for a ruling—for clarification on the meaning of a piece of EU legislation. The domestic court will do this under Art. 267 TFEU. The question posed is called a *preliminary reference*; the answer given is called a *Preliminary Ruling*, and that judgment by the CJEU is definitive; no domestic court (in any country, not just the one which made the reference) can ignore it. So, a preliminary ruling in response to a preliminary reference posed by a Belgian court will apply to courts in the UK, Spain, Sweden, etc.

How does a preliminary reference come before the CJEU?

Only the domestic court hearing the case can decide whether to make a reference or not—the parties to the case will be consulted but have no rights in the matter. Thus, once a court or tribunal is faced with a problem involving the application of EU law it may ask the CJEU for an authoritative interpretation of a Treaty article or, for instance, an EU Directive. It does this by posing questions in the abstract; it does not ask for the solution to the particular case.

The CJEU has issued Practice Directions on the conduct of cases in preliminary hearings (see Protocol (No 3) to the Statute of the Court of Justice of the European Union, and OJ L31, 31.1.2014 for the latest version), which allow for expedited procedures in simpler cases or ones which raise no new issues, and in the UK there is a specific direction on how cases should be referred to the CJEU: see Part 68 of the Civil Procedure Rules and Practice Direction 68, and Rule 75.3 of the Criminal Procedure Rules. It is the responsibility of the court, not the parties, to settle the terms of the reference. That reference will identify the parties, summarise the nature of the proceedings, give the relevant facts, make reference to the rules of domestic law, and summarise the contentions of the parties. The reference will then identify the EU provisions at issue and formulate the question(s) to which an answer is requested—we give an example of this shortly—with an eye on the fact that these will have to be translated into the various EU languages.

A key point to emphasise is that the CJEU does not decide the result of the cases itself, i.e. it makes no findings of fact, nor does it apply the law to the facts: it makes rulings on interpretation, not decisions on who wins or loses the case. **On most issues, therefore, the CJEU is a court of reference, not a court of appeal**. It assists the domestic court in making its decision by giving authoritative rulings on the interpretation of the EU-derived legislation. When you hear news bulletins etc. speaking of the CJEU *hearing an appeal* from a UK court, these reports are simply incorrect—and reflect many of the misconceptions popularly held about the EU generally.

This role of the ECJ drew specific comment from Laddie J. in *Arsenal Football Club plc v Reed (No. 2)* [2002] EWHC 2695 (Ch); [2003] 1 All ER 137. The case concerned the alleged misuse of Arsenal FC's trade marks by Reed and was referred to the ECJ regarding the meaning of a Trade Marks Directive. In giving their judgment the ECJ drew specific conclusions of fact. When the trial resumed back in the UK, Laddie J. pointed out in no uncertain terms that the ECJ had exceeded its jurisdiction and the domestic court was not bound by its conclusion (although later again the Court of Appeal disagreed with Laddie J.'s interpretation on whether the ECJ had actually overstepped the mark).

How does the case proceed at the CJEU?

The question has been formulated and the case is now lodged with the Court of Justice—and joins the backlog! A reference to the Court of Justice is, in this procedure, just a step in the action being heard by the domestic court; it is not an appeal because the case in the domestic court has simply been adjourned pending the opinion of the Court of Justice. Thus, although we call it a 'preliminary ruling' this is a little misleading: the reference to the Court of Justice is made **during** the case before the domestic court, not before the case has started. It is preliminary to a decision being made by the domestic court, not preliminary to the proceedings themselves.

In **Chapter 3** we looked at the structure of a CJEU judgment and identified the various personnel involved in determining the case. Assuming the matter is not expedited as being simple or not being novel, the basic pattern by which a case reaches that stage can be outlined as follows:

1. The domestic court decides to make the reference.

2. The court, with the aid of the parties, sets about formulating the relevant question(s) and establishing a statement of facts and law which will accompany the reference as noted earlier. We note below some examples of the form these questions take.

3. The reference is translated by the CJEU into the working languages of the EU and published. Written submissions may be made within two months by interested parties, including Member States' governments.

4. The case is assigned to a specific Judge-Rapporteur and an Advocate General, if thought necessary.

5. The Judge-Rapporteur produces an initial report and advises on the forum (e.g. to be heard in a chamber or in plenary) and whether further inquiries of fact or law are necessary. He or she summarises the legal background to the case and the

observations of the parties submitted in the first, written phase of the procedure. In the light of the conclusions of the Advocate General appointed to the case, the Judge-Rapporteur draws up a draft ruling which is submitted to the other members of the Court.

6. The parties prepare for the hearing, provided the court thinks this is necessary.

7. The oral hearing takes place. Any interested party may make a submission.

8. The Advocate General gives an opinion on the case (the Judge-Rapporteur may also provide an opinion, especially if disagreeing with the Advocate General).

9. The Court discusses the case and goes into deliberation.

10. The Court produces a judgment in whichever of the official languages the case was heard. This is then translated. No dissenting opinion is delivered.

This procedure can take well over a year to complete, before the case is then taken up again at the domestic court. However, there is an accelerated procedure for cases of 'exceptional urgency'. The normal procedure is illustrated in **Figure 11.1**.

Once the case comes before the CJEU we see a difference in approach from the common law system. As we noted earlier in the book, English law still bears some relation to its roots in 'trial by battle'. The champion is now replaced by the solicitor

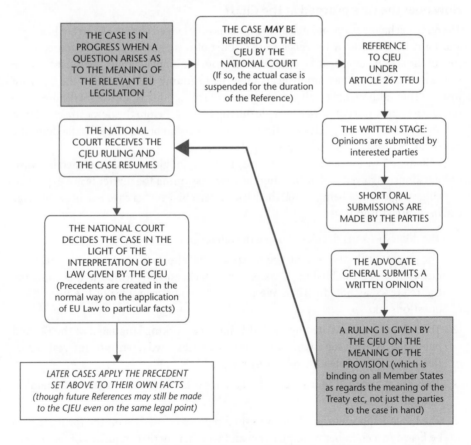

Figure 11.1 Preliminary rulings in the CJEU

or barrister, the swords replaced by words; but the basic plot is the same. Our system concentrates on the adversarial approach and depends greatly on oral argument. The continental approach depends far more on an inquisitorial procedure and written argument (though note that our own courts are increasingly demanding written submissions in advance of oral argument—called 'skeleton arguments'). Indeed, if the case is concerned with a *preliminary reference* there are, strictly speaking, no parties involved—the domestic court has sought an opinion, not a fight.

All documents are sent by the Court of Justice's Registry to the parties in the domestic court, the Member States, the Commission, and (possibly) the Council. All these parties have a right to make submissions on the case. For instance, in a case concerning part-time workers in Germany (Case 171/88 *Rinner-Kühn* v *FWW Spezial-Gebäudereinigung GmbH and Co. KG* [1989] ECR 2743; [1989] IRLR 493) a number of Member States (recognising that the case was of great importance) made submissions to the Court even though they were not directly involved. The next major difference lies in the presence of the Advocate General. The Advocate General, as already noted, acts as an adviser to the Court, sifting through the law on behalf of the Court and producing a reasoned opinion in each case. The Court is then free to follow that opinion or derogate from it in any way it thinks fit. Sometimes the Court will simply adopt the Advocate-General's opinion wholesale.

Remember, the Court of Justice is concerned only with ruling on the abstract question of law, not with deciding the case. There is thus no appeal from a judgment of the Court of Justice on a Preliminary Reference (though there are various mechanisms whereby the Court can review its own decision). Further, as we shall note again in relation to legal method later, there is only one judgment given by the Court; no dissenting voices are heard. That judgment is relatively short and sometimes without detailed reasons. One can find the presentation of reasoning which resembles that of the English judge in the opinion delivered by (accepted or not by the Court) the Advocate General.

When will a case go to the Court of Justice?

We said earlier that it is for the domestic court to decide whether it wishes to refer a matter to the Court of Justice. Article 267 TFEU states that where a question of interpretation of the Treaties:

> is raised before any court or tribunal of the Member State, that court or tribunal may, if it considers that a decision on the question is necessary to enable it to give judgment, request the Court of Justice to give a ruling thereon.
>
> Where any such question is raised in a case pending before a court or tribunal of a Member State, against whose decisions there is no judicial remedy under domestic law, that court or tribunal shall bring the matter before the Court of Justice.

It has to be said that any perusal of the Reports (CMLR or ECR) reveals some of the most boring questions and issues ever encountered in legal texts (usually concerned with import duties, VAT, and regulations concerning agricultural matters). The range of topics that can be covered is nevertheless very extensive and getting wider by the day. There are glimmers, therefore, of real-life questions. Many of these centre on employment issues such as discrimination and equal pay. Some take on more expansive parameters, such as the case of Case C–415/93 *Union Royale Belge des Sociétés de Football*

Association (ASBL) v *Bosman* [1995] ECR I-4921; [1996] 1 CMLR 645, for instance, which set the soccer world alight when it declared that certain transfer fees were in breach of Community Law, *viz* the Treaty of Rome, Art. 48.

On most EU law matters, any court or tribunal may refer a case to the CJEU; the court does not require permission from any higher court (though Part 68 Civil Procedure Rules, for instance, states that lower courts such as the County Court will not *normally* make a reference). It is clear, however, that national rules of precedent have no effect on a court's power to refer a matter to the CJEU, except that only the final appeal court (usually that will mean the Supreme Court in the UK) may make a reference to the CJEU as regards certain matters relating to the maintenance of law and order or internal security. Linked with this is the idea (which has always been present in EU law) that, if a court is dealing with any question of EU law and that court is the final appeal court, it *must* refer the point to the CJEU. Thus the Supreme Court should be bound to refer all cases to the CJEU which involve a problem of EU law, and so should the highest courts in all Member States—as to why they do not, see below. Further, there are rare instances where a case reaches a court from which there is no further appeal and that court is not the Supreme Court. If this happens then that final court of appeal, for that case, must refer the matter to the Court of Justice. There is no clear CJEU ruling on what happens when a litigant effectively reaches the end of the road, e.g. on being refused leave to appeal. If, for example, the Court of Appeal rules on a point concerning EU law and then refuses one of the litigants leave to appeal to the Supreme Court, has that Court of Appeal, for all practical purposes, become the final court in the process? In theory it is not the final court as the Supreme Court stands above it; but the litigant has been refused leave to go there. Thus, is the Court of Appeal now bound to refer any question on the EU law to the CJEU?

The Supreme Court and other final appeal courts do not, however, refer all relevant cases to the CJEU anyway. The key part of Art. 267 TFEU which requires explanation, as applied to both the discretionary reference relating to all courts and the mandatory reference, is the word 'necessary'.

What does 'necessary' mean?

Article 267 TFEU states that the domestic court need make a reference only where it considers that such a reference is necessary to enable it to give judgment. If the same question was decided upon by the CJEU last week, for instance, then making a reference would seem pointless.

A major point to establish, then, is that the decision to refer lies with the domestic court alone. This was decided early in the CJEU's life in Case 6/64 *Costa* v *ENEL* [1964] ECR 585. The decision to refer or not to refer cannot be restricted by any domestic system of precedent, nor does it matter whether the parties request such a reference to be made.

In Case 283/81 *CILFIT Srl* v *Ministero della Sanità* [1982] ECR 3415; [1983] 1 CMLR 472 the ECJ ruled that a reference is **not necessary** if:

(a) the question of EU law is irrelevant; or

(b) the provision has already been interpreted by the Court of Justice; or

(c) the correct application is obvious.

Steiner and Woods (2014) draw the parallel with this formulation and the French administrative law doctrine of *acte clair*, in which there can be no question of needing to interpret a provision if the meaning is clear. As Steiner and Woods point out, this is a deceptively simple idea, because what is clear to one person is not necessarily clear to another, as we saw in the chapters on statutory interpretation. Indeed this was illustrated in *R v Henn (No. 1)* [1978] 1 WLR 1031; [1978] 3 All ER 1190, where the Court of Appeal did not ask for a preliminary ruling on the ground of *acte clair*; the House of Lords did not find the matter so obvious and pursued a reference (*DPP v Henn and Darby* [1980] 2 CMLR 229). Equally, as we noted before, the CJEU is not bound by *stare decisis* and so is free to change its mind on a matter. This means that you are never entirely sure whether the key ruling by the CJEU on a point might be overturned by the CJEU on another day if the matter was referred to the court.

The question was addressed again in *Joseph Filipe Ferreira da Silva e Brito* v *Estado português* C-160/14 where the CJEU decided that in cases where the topic being debated was:

> characterised both by the fact that there are conflicting decisions of lower courts or tribunals regarding the interpretation of the concept … and by the fact that that concept frequently gives rise to difficulties of interpretation in the various Member States, the third paragraph of Article 267 TFEU (i.e. the question of 'necessity') must be construed as meaning that a court or tribunal against whose decisions there is no judicial remedy under national law is obliged to make a reference to the Court for a preliminary ruling concerning the interpretation of that concept (para. 45)

This meant that on the difficult subject of what is meant by a 'transfer of a business' the Spanish Supreme Court should have made a reference to the CJEU.

Taken to an extreme the notion of *acte clair* could spell disaster for the Court of Justice because there is no mechanism to force a domestic court to make a reference. But with one or two exceptional bursts of chauvinism from national courts (usually French) the spirit of cooperation and collaboration has prevailed.

A reference is made in the form of a question. The CJEU is keen to convert any question which seeks an answer on how to *apply* the law into a more abstract question on what the Treaty or other provision *means* or whether the provision is valid. As we have said: it is not there to decide the case itself. There is no set formula for putting these questions. The following is an extract taken from a House of Lords' Reference to the ECJ in *R v Secretary of State for Employment, ex parte Seymour-Smith and Perez* [1997] ICR 371 (it reads remarkably like a set of examination questions):

1. Does an award of compensation for breach of the right not to be unfairly dismissed under national legislation such as the Employment Protection (Consolidation) Act 1978 constitute 'pay' within the meaning of Art. 119 of the EC Treaty?

2. If the answer to question 1 is 'yes', do the conditions determining whether a worker has the right not to be unfairly dismissed fall within the scope of Art. 119 or that of Directive 76/207?

3. What is the legal test for establishing whether a measure adopted by a Member State has such a degree of disparate effect as between men and women as to amount to indirect discrimination for the purposes of Art. 119 of the EC Treaty unless shown to be based upon objectively justified factors other than sex?

Here is another example, this time from the Court of Appeal in *Société des produits Nestlé SA* v *Mars UK Ltd* (Case C–353/03):

> May the distinctive character of a mark referred to in Article 3(3) of Directive 89/104 and Article 7(3) of Regulation No 40/94 be acquired following or in consequence of the use of that mark as part of or in conjunction with another mark?

What this referred to is a little more approachable. Nestlé wanted to register the term, 'Have a break' as a trade mark. They argued that the term had acquired a distinctive character as a result of its use in advertisements in the slogan, 'Have a break … Have a KIT KAT'—the term being therefore linked to the chocolate bar 'KIT KAT' which was already a registered trade mark. The rival confectioner, Mars Ltd, opposed this. The argument centred on the meaning of the Directives noted earlier which sought to approximate the laws of the Member States relating to trade marks.

11.3 Analytical Techniques Employed by European Lawyers

In the foregoing text we have attempted to give a very brief description of the workings of the EU institutions. We will return to this topic shortly when we examine the specific legal method employed by the CJEU. To understand better the CJEU's techniques of legal analysis, however, we should first explain briefly how it is that European lawyers approach legal problems in a quite different way from common law lawyers.

Traditionally the English lawyer has a distrust of theory and principle and places his faith in pragmatism. The development of the common law has been the work of practitioners, not philosophers.

The civil law tradition, on the other hand, is different: here case law is seen as an application of deduction from established and more abstract principles. An attempt is made to rationalise and arrange fundamental principles by way of legislation, known as a Code. From these principles contained in the Codes the whole law can, it is hoped, be deduced. French judges, for instance, are expressly forbidden to create general and regulatory principles; they must decide the case before them only and their decisions relate to the text of the Code. It is the Code, therefore, that is ultimately authoritative, not the case law; though this does not mean at all that case decisions are irrelevant to the civil lawyer. Civil, or codified law, is widespread in the EU; indeed, like the common law, its influence extends beyond European boundaries.

11.3.1 A Comparison of Concepts

It is interesting, for instance, to compare the different treatment rendered to one concept—that of 'good faith'—in English, French, and German law. We will confine our very brief remarks to the general law of contract and not examine the various EU Directives now concerned with 'good faith' dealings. The aim is to sketch the different approaches, not to analyse contract law.

Most people instinctively know what 'acting in good/bad faith' is. It should be said, however, that no legal system has ever constructed a succinct legal definition of the term. This is why we chose it.

The notion of 'good faith' centres on principles of fair dealing. Traditionally, in English law, the search for a theory of 'good faith' offers little reward. It is, however, possible to unearth the odd clue and the occasional judicial or statutory reference to the requirement to act in 'good faith'. This is especially true of those cases or statutes owing their origin to mercantile law; but then the development of mercantile law owes a heavy debt to Continental influences. Allusions to elements of 'good faith' such as 'honesty', 'fair dealing', and 'reasonableness' can therefore emerge through the cases; but there is no overriding principle to be applied.

Consequently, the term sometimes emerges as an endorsement of other ideas, but it rarely stands on its own as justifying a decision. If a British judge wishes to rely on such an indefinable notion as 'good faith' he will often wrap it up, disguise it, with references to more orthodox, technical, conventional terminology such as terms being *implied* into a contract. Bowen LJ utilised the concept this way on a number of occasions in the late nineteenth century in shaping the law of contract. One of the authors of this text once described this process as: 'judges trying to pummel equitable notions such as good faith into a contractual setting like a Victorian belle being prised into her whale-bone corset'.

Sometimes, however, judges can surprise us and 'find' principles of good faith. Such was the case with Bingham LJ's judgment in *Interfoto Picture Library Ltd* v *Stiletto Visual Programmes Ltd* [1988] 1 All ER 348; [1988] 2 WLR 615 to which we referred in **Chapter 7**.

The French regard their contract law as part of a theory of Obligations. This last word demonstrates quite a difference of approach. Accordingly, in France we find express reference to the concept of 'good faith' in the *Code civil*. Contracts must be performed in good faith: *Code civil* (1804) article 1134(3). Thus, as regards **pre-contractual dealings** (such as negotiations), Nicholas (1992) stated that, 'the wider context is more favourable in French law to the importation of ideas of good faith or fair dealing (*loyauté*)' and 'there is a greater disposition to seeing silence (as to a fact which determined the other party's consent) as reprehensible'. However, Nicholas also noted that when it comes to analysing whether the **performance** of the contract has been fair, 'The French courts have made very little express use of Article 1134 ... It may be that, like the English courts, they are reluctant to set loose such a wide-ranging principle'.

The German approach to the same problem also proves interesting. The *Bürgerliches Gesetzbuch* (BGB, which is the German Civil Code relating to private law) contains references to the principle of good faith and the apparently innocuous s. 242 which states: 'The debtor is obliged to effect performance in such a manner as good faith requires, regard being paid to general practice.' This section regulates the manner in which contracts are performed. Horn, Kötz, and Leser (1982: 135) described this so:

> Unimpressive though it looks, s. 242 BGB is one of the most astonishing phenomena in the Code ... a statutory enactment of a general requirement of good faith, a 'principle of legal ethics', which dominates the entire legal system.

Finally, to complete this brief comparative survey, it is worth noting the approach adopted in the United States. Here we see the common law system in action. Yet we also find that the vague concept of 'good faith' is embraced in the case law through reference to the Uniform Commercial Code (UCC). Now this is not a *code* in the pure civil law sense. It is more like the original English Sale of Goods Act 1893, whereby the case law has been pulled together into a more systematic general restatement. The UCC is law in most jurisdictions in the USA by virtue of local (rather than federal) enactment.

In the UCC we find a number of provisions (called Articles) which gives us a general definition of good faith. Article 1§201 states that good faith means honesty in fact and the observance of reasonable commercial standards of fair dealing and Article 1§304 imposes a general obligation of good faith performance and enforcement. These provisions have given rise to varied judicial and academic debate; not least as to whether there is a requirement for objective good faith to be found ('reasonableness', 'fair dealing') or only a subjective test—what has been referred to as the 'pure heart and empty head test'. Here we see that the common law (here operating in the US) still cannot rid itself of its fixation with the need to define terms through the cases. It is unable to cope easily with pure conceptual thinking.

It may be, therefore, that the conventional contrast between the two traditions— experience and pragmatism on the one hand, concept and doctrine on the other—is not always as clear-cut as it seems. Nevertheless, although we may often reach the same conclusions, common law and civil law lawyers think differently and the key point here is that most EU laws are drafted and interpreted using the civil law approach. Szladits and Germain (1985: ix) described the problems thus:

> Because of a different training, of a different 'legal method', there is an unavoidable inclination on the part of Common Law lawyers to evaluate the importance of code provisions, of decisions of a higher court or of writings and comments in the light of his own background knowledge. He may attach undue importance to some decisions 'as precedents', and underrate the value of treatises or commentaries … He may also underrate the importance of cases and attach too exclusive force to code provisions. The continental lawyer, in contrast, will usually find himself at a loss among the innumerable precedents which are binding, but yet can be distinguished out of existence … and will vainly look for precise concepts among the legal synonyms, loosely phrased decisions and unsystematic textbooks …

11.3.2 The Use of Precedent in European Legal Method

We have already seen in **Chapter 6** that a major distinction between how civil lawyers (and courts) reason and the reasoning of common law lawyers is the use of *stare decisis*. As the quotation from Szladits and Germain indicates, however, it is wrong to say that case law is unimportant to the civil law lawyer. Reference to case law and precedent clearly exists in the civil law tradition. David and Brierley (1985: 133) point out that statements which flatly exclude cases as a source of law in the civil system:

> are somewhat ridiculous when used in countries such as France or Germany, where cases have been of primary importance in the evolution of some branches of law.

Indeed, in Germany there is a healthy debate as to whether the German Constitutional Court actually operates a system of *stare decisis* (by practice if not by name).

Cases are a source of law, in that a line of cases demonstrates a consistent pattern of thought. But whereas the common law judge draws openly on case law for his analysis, the civil law lawyer often hides behind the veil of 'interpretation' of legislation. The cases provide guidance on legal rules, but the rules do not carry with them any sense of obligation. Civil law judges are not compelled to analyse earlier cases or justify departure from them, but decisions, for instance, of the French supreme courts such as the *Cour de cassation* are in reality likely to be followed by lower courts.

11.3.3 Legal Method in the Court of Justice

The Court of Justice was created by civil law lawyers. It therefore bears the hallmarks of the points noted above. Two detailed and excellent examinations of European Legal Method, both as regards the tools used by the CJEU itself and the reactions of domestic courts, have been produced by Neergaard, Nielsen, and Roseberry (eds) (2011) and Neergaard and Nielsen (eds) (2013) with contributions from writers across the EU. The 2011 text demonstrates the development by the CJEU of legal method techniques and specific devices across the decades and demonstrates that it is not just the UK which has struggled to accommodate the expansion of EU law concepts and practices in its legal system.

The key 'legal method' questions which arise are:

(a) whether the Court of Justice really regards every question as being open to re-examination;

(b) in investigating how our domestic courts should approach the status of preliminary rulings;

(c) what is the future role of precedent in our courts; and

(d) finally, how should we examine and make use of other sources of law used by civil lawyers to analyse legal problems.

The first point, therefore, is: does the Court of Justice really regard every question as being open to re-examination? As we noted in **Chapters 6** and 7, the absence of any *ratio decidendi* in a CJEU decision rather destroys the essence of precedent as we know it (certainly, any idea of *stare decisis*). And, as we have also noted, the judgments are given as a collegiate decision, i.e. only one decision is delivered.

The CJEU does, nevertheless, allude to earlier judgments and prefers to follow those decisions but it is quite free to change its mind, develop principles, and create conflicting precedents as between Chambers. Part of this may be due to the fact that the Court sees its role as 'filling the gaps' in EU legislation. It is therefore openly creative and plays an active part in the law-making of the EU.

The Advocate General in a case will more frequently cite earlier cases; and the Advocate-General's opinion will be of persuasive authority in later cases, even where the Court did not follow it (you may notice, as a piece of absolute trivia, that there is no hyphen in 'Advocate General' except when referring to the possessive case).

The answer, therefore, to the question posed is that *every* question is open to re-examination; nothing precludes a domestic court, for instance, from seeking a further ruling on exactly the same point discussed in an earlier case (see Case 28/62

Da Costa en Schaake [1963] ECR 31 and Case 26/62 *NV Algemene Transport-en Expeditie Orderneming Van Gend en Loos* v *Inspecteur der Invoerrechten en Accijnzen, Veulo (10852T) (Tariefcommissie (NL))* [1963] ECR 1). The notion of *acte clair* is not *stare decisis* in another form.

In practice, of course, there is a strong tendency to try to establish and maintain a coherent, or settled, jurisprudence, which does require some reference to precedent. Indeed there seems to be some evidence to suggest that direct reference to case law is a growing judicial practice—for example, in Case C–229/89 *European Commission* v *Belgium* [1991] ECR I-2205; [1991] IRLR 393, the Court went to some lengths to justify its decision by reference to the earlier cases of Case 30/85 *Teuling* [1987] ECR 2497, which had decided a closely analogous point of law, and Case C–171/88 *Rinner-Kühn* v *FWW Spezial Gebäudereinigung GmbH and Co. KG* [1989] ECR 2743; [1989] IRLR 493. However, this still does not mean that the Court regards itself as strictly bound by its own earlier decisions.

11.3.4 The effect on common law legal method

How should our courts approach the status of preliminary rulings?

Two points arise here: first, if the CJEU is simply interpreting EU law, is any decision retroactive? That is to say, is the interpretation to be applied from the date of judgment onwards (as with our system), or does it also have effect from the date the provision originally came into force, which might be some years earlier? Secondly, how binding is a decision of the CJEU?

- **On the first point:** in general, the ruling will take effect from the date the legislation was brought into force—a retroactive approach. The Court is declaring what already existed. The Court may however choose not to do this (only the Court can decide this) on grounds of, say, the need for legal certainty. It did this in relation to equal pay rulings in Case 43/75 *Defrenne* v *SA Belge de Navigation Aérienne (SABENA) (No. 2)* [1976] ECR 455 and regarding equal pay and pension rights in Case C–262/88 *Barber* v *Guardian Royal Exchange Assurance Group* [1990] ECR I-1889; [1991] 1 QB 344; [1990] 2 All ER 660. Had its decision to equalise pensions for men and women been 'backdated' this would have caused economic chaos. This idea of retroactive decisions has always been a controversial matter. So much so that, because of the ruling in *Barber* v *Guardian Royal Exchange* a Protocol to the *Maastricht Treaty* created a broad principle of non-retroactivity in relation to pension rights.

- **On the second point:** given that a domestic court can always ask the Court of Justice for a ruling (even on matters previously decided) the Court of Justice's decisions are not binding as such. They are binding, however, inasmuch as the domestic court must either apply them or seek a new ruling; it cannot simply ignore the Court of Justice. This point was made by the ECJ, for instance, in *Amministratzione delle Finanze dello Stato* v *Simmenthal SpA (No. 2)* (Case 106/77) [1978] ECR 629) and, in the UK, is reinforced by European Communities Act 1972, s. 3(1) which states: 'For the purposes of all legal proceedings any question as to the meaning or effect of any of the Treaties, or as to the validity, meaning or effect of any [EU] instrument, shall be treated as a question of law (and, if not referred to the European Court, be for determination as such in accordance with the principles laid down by and any relevant decision of the European Court).'

There is no hierarchical system as *between* the various courts in Member States. What is decided in the *domestic* courts of Germany or France has no binding effect (though it may have a persuasive one) on our courts. As the Court of Justice is the only authority which can interpret provisions anyway, this should cause no problems. What should also be noted, however, is that if a question is posed to the CJEU on EU law by, say, Spain, the ruling given will, in most cases, apply as much to any other EU country as to Spain. The CJEU gives judgment on the interpretation of EU law, so it is irrelevant which country asks the question.

What will this mean for the future role of precedent in our courts?

First, much of our law still has no relationship with EU law. To this end the line of precedents on what constitutes an 'offer' or an 'invitation to treat' will continue to carry the same significance as fifty or more years ago. But where EU law is concerned, it is clear that the higher courts in our system can no longer bind the lower courts on the meaning of EU legislation; only the CJEU can make authoritative rulings. The Court of Appeal, for instance, is not bound by a decision of the Supreme Court on the *interpretation* of EU law. It may, however, be bound by a decision of the Supreme Court on the *application* of EU law to particular facts. Equally, UK legislation should not conflict with EU law (though there is still some debate as to the extent to which any legislation not ultimately derived from EU sources can be ignored).

All this is unlikely to bring about the abandonment of *stare decisis* and all its intricacies. Thus we now effectively have two systems of precedent:

- On questions of the meaning and interpretation of EU law, the authoritative body is the CJEU. Once the CJEU has pronounced on the meaning of EU legislation that must be followed throughout the EU.

- The CJEU does not seek to decide the case in hand. It sends its judgment back to the relevant court in the Member State and that court applies the interpretation to the facts before it. Thus, that domestic court creates the precedent regarding the *application* of the CJEU's interpretation.

11.4 The Effect of EU Law on the Drafting and Interpretation of UK Legislation

There are two key areas here:

- How is EU legislation enforced?
- What *style* of statutory interpretation is employed?

11.4.1 How is EU Legislation Enforced?

The main classification of EU legislation into 'Treaties', 'Regulations', and 'Directives' carries with it important concepts which determine how these various rules are actually implemented within the EU by the Member States. You need to understand these concepts in order to see how EU law is applied. Those concepts are:

- direct applicability;
- direct effect; and
- indirect effect.

Direct applicability

Because Treaty obligations and Regulations of the EU are designed to have overriding and universal application across Member States we have noted previously that they are given special status, termed *direct applicability*. This means that these rules *automatically* become part of the law of each domestic legal system without the need (in most cases) for confirmation of their legitimacy by formal enactment in the legislatures of the Member States. Thus you will not find these rules in any UK statute book; you must research the treaty or regulation itself. The idea of *direct applicability* is really aimed at the Member States; it tells them that they are not required to do anything more to implement the relevant rule.

The importance of this concept of *direct applicability* is that each Member State is bound by the rules contained in these Treaties and Regulations. *Direct applicability* is therefore reserved for rules which need to have immediate and EU-wide-binding enforceability. Matters such as equal pay and the free movement of workers, for instance, appear in Treaty articles. On the other hand, Common Agricultural Policy matters will generally surface in the form of regulations. These laws are all directly applicable.

Directives, on the other hand, do not have direct applicability because they lay down a **result** to be achieved rather than fixed and universal rules. A Directive is like an instruction which reads, 'When driving from home to work you may not use the motorway system': you (or the Member State if this were a legal direction) are then left to determine which roads (other than motorways) you may use. So, each driver/Member State can then dictate (within the given confines) what are the permissible routes, such as, 'you can only use A-roads', or 'you cannot use roads with a speed limit of 60 mph or more', etc. Each country might produce different systems, but they would all be legitimate within the Directive if they followed the general 'non-motorway' rule. It would not be legitimate, for, say, Ireland to allow motorway driving to go to work if the journey was more than a certain distance. What might still happen, however, is that at some point a reference might be made to the CJEU as to the exact meaning of 'motorway' (with all its translations) in this Directive.

We noted earlier that Directives have no effect at all on the laws of a Member State until that state's legislature incorporates the goals set out in the Directive into its own law. In the UK this means that Parliament must have legislated on the matter. Each Member State is given a time limit to achieve this (often two or three years from the date of the Directive). Thus, the process for implementation is as set out in **Figure 11.2**.

Directives therefore seek only to harmonise the laws of Member States, to make them approximately the same while still taking into account the economic, political, social, and legal differences that exist in each state. Directives **cannot** have direct

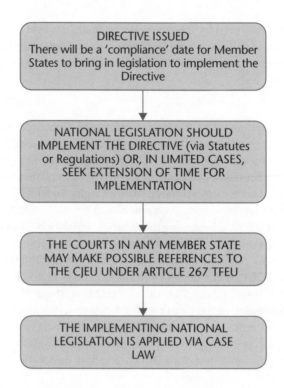

Figure 11.2 The procedure for implementing Directives

applicability because they are too general and vague in what it is they are trying to achieve. If we were to draw an analogy with the laws of Association Football: the rules on the size of playing area set out maximum and minimum measurements only (the length must be between 100 and 130 yards, for instance). This allows for the varying size of stadia, and can be likened to the way Directives are often framed. Thus, as long as the football club does not infringe the maximum or minimum size, its ground measurements do not have to be identical to those of any other club.

In the end, though, the fact that Member States are bound to obey directly applicable rules only really tells us about their obligations as between themselves and as between them and the European Union. We are still left with the problem of how EU legislation can be enforced by individuals and companies within the EU. After all, the domestic courts of Member States are under a duty to interpret and apply EU law (Treaties, Regulations, and Directives alike) to any relevant matters arising in the domestic courts. They are also bound to interpret domestic laws to maintain consistency with EU law. Thus there has to be a system whereby EU legislation can be relied upon by citizens of the EU in suing the state or, possibly, companies and individuals. This is achieved by courts across the EU using two devices—giving *direct effect* and *indirect effect* to EU legislation.

It is unfortunate that the terms 'direct applicability', 'direct effect', 'indirect effect', and even 'Directive' all sound so similar. They are often used, erroneously, as interchangeable terms—even by the courts occasionally. However, these are terms of major significance and one needs to be clear about the distinction and the interrelationship. We need, therefore, to examine what is meant by *direct* and *indirect* effect. We shall consider *direct effect* first.

Direct effect

The basic idea underlying direct effect is straightforward. *Direct effect* means that someone may cite a Directive as law without having to cite any domestic legislation which was meant to implement that Directive. It may seem strange that this is not done all the time. But remember that a Directive is designed to be implemented by the Member States rather than stand as domestic law in its own right. So what we are dealing with here is the situation (an increasingly common one) where a Directive is used as the governing source of law, thus bypassing the domestic legislation. The principle of *direct effect* was not established by the Treaty of Rome. Instead, in a famous and controversial judgment (Case 26/62 *NV Algemene Transport-en Expeditie Orderneming Van Gend en Loos* v *Inspecteur der Invoerrechten en Accijnzen, Veulo (10852T) (Tariefcommissie (NL))* [1963] ECR 1; [1963] CMLR 224) the ECJ said that where EU legislation creates **'clear and unconditional' obligations** on Member States, these were capable of creating individual rights enforceable in domestic courts. All forms of EU legislation are *capable* of having direct effect, provided they meet certain conditions. There are normally four overlapping conditions for a Directive to have direct effect, and these are set out in **Table 11.1**.

A useful example of a provision in a Directive **not** having direct effect can be seen in *East Riding of Yorkshire Council* v *Gibson* [2000] 3 CMLR 329 (CA). This case concerned the Working Time Directive 93/104 which, among other things, set a minimum annual leave entitlement for workers. Article 7 of the Directive stated the right as being:

(1) Member States shall take the measures necessary to ensure that every worker is entitled to paid annual leave of at least four weeks in accordance with the conditions for entitlement to, and granting of, such leave laid down by national legislation and/or practice.
(2) The minimum period of paid annual leave may not be replaced by allowance in lieu, except where the employment relationship is terminated.

The Court of Appeal held that this Article could not have direct effect because it was not sufficiently precise on a range of details. It did not, for instance, give a precise definition of 'working time'—upon which the whole entitlement to leave depends—nor the criteria to be used to assess entitlement during the first year, or a part year, of employment, nor what was to happen where there is more than one employer or the worker works part time or works on a commission basis. So, although the basic right was clear (four weeks' annual leave entitlement), how one calculated this in any given situation was not clear enough to allow for direct effect. This meant that the legislation passed in each Member State designed to implement the Directive was the sole determinant of rights and obligations.

However, to illustrate how flexible EU law can be as regards setting precedents (as noted earlier), the 1988 version of the Working Time Directive (Directive 2003/88), with slightly different wording, has been held to have direct effect.

Table 11.1 Conditions for direct effect

(a) *The provision of EU law must be clear and unambiguous.*	The approach of the CJEU to this issue is highly flexible; e.g. in the joined cases of Cases C–6/90, C–9/90 *Francovich and Bonifaci* v *Italy* [1992] IRLR 84 the Court recognised that the provisions of Directive 80/987/EEC, guaranteeing compensation to individuals for loss of employment through the insolvency of their employer, gave Member States a wide element of discretion (and so were not unambiguous). Nevertheless, the ECJ felt that it could discern a sufficient 'minimum guarantee' to make the provision precise enough to be capable of direct effect. In Case C–91/92 *Faccini Dori* v *Recreb srl* [1995] ECR I-3325; [1995] All ER (EC) 1, the ECJ returned to this concept and indicated that the provisions of a Directive can be sufficiently precise if they enable a domestic court to determine upon whom, and for whose benefit, the obligations are imposed, i.e. is it possible to determine minimum rights from the provision in question?
(b) *The provision must be unconditional.*	For example, it must not be subject to conditions requiring implementation by Member States, or giving Member States substantive discretion in respect of the period for implementation. However, as was noted in the case of *Maribel Dominguez* v *Centre informatique du Centre Ouest Atlantique* C-282/2010, [2012] IRLR 321: 'Even though [a Directive Article] leaves the Member States a degree of latitude when they adopt the conditions … [of the Directive] … that does not alter the precise and unconditional nature of the obligation laid down in that article.'
(c) *The provision must be capable of taking effect without further action by the EU or a Member State.*	For example, the EU legislation should not be dependent upon further clarifying regulations being passed in each Member State. Again, this test is of crucial significance in respect of both treaty obligations and Directives which are initially expressed to be conditional but become unconditional with the passing of time and thereby become directly effective.
(d) *The provision must be capable of creating rights for individuals.*	The provision in question must go beyond merely imposing obligations on Member States, e.g. in their relationship with other Member States or the EU as an entity. The provision must be drafted in such a way that an individual gains some enforceable right to sue the state or another individual.

The operation of the principle of direct effect has spawned an extensive body of case law, before both the CJEU and domestic courts. This has added greatly to the complexity of the principle, but the central idea is quite simple: a person in any Member State can refer to the wording of the Directive *as law*, no matter what the domestic statute says, **provided** the Directive is clear enough in its aims to be so enforceable. At this stage in your studies, judging exactly when a Directive meets these conditions is not something you should worry about.

The next thing you do have to worry about, however, is the question: can all Directives which have direct effect be relied upon by anyone suing another person or being prosecuted by the state?

The answer to this question is, 'No', because there is a further complication. A distinction is made between Directives having *vertical direct effect* and *horizontal direct effect*:

- **'Vertical effect'**. The word 'vertical' refers to the relationship between the parties. Something is a *vertical* action where an individual (including a 'legal person' such as a company) is suing or being sued by the state (or, in criminal law, the individual is being prosecuted by the state). If a Directive has vertical direct effect it means that an individual may rely on the specific words set out in a treaty, Directive (etc.) in any action against an organ of the state (see *Van Gend en Loos*) or against some other body having special powers to provide public services under the control of the state. Such bodies include, for example, a privatised industry under a statutory duty to provide a public utility—see Case C–188/89 *Foster v British Gas* [1990] ECR I-3313; [1991] 1 QB 405; [1990] 3 All ER 897 (ECJ); [1991] 2 AC 306; [1991] 2 All ER 705 (HL). The Court of Appeal has indicated that the definition of a 'public body' for these purposes should be a broad one: *National Union of Teachers v Governing Body of St Mary's Church of England (Aided) Junior School* [1997] 3 CMLR 630.

There was a time when most EU criminal law measures fell under what were termed 'Framework Directives'. These did not have direct effect but, post-Lisbon, Framework Directives are no more and criminal law Directives can have direct effect if the relevant conditions noted earlier are fulfilled.

- **'Horizontal effect'**. The word 'horizontal' again refers to the relationship between the parties. This time, a case can be described as a *horizontal* action where an individual is suing someone of equivalent legal standing—another person or a company, for instance—unlike vertical actions where the state exists in a superior (and therefore vertical) relationship with the individual.

What distinctions are drawn between these two types of action in terms of relying on directly effective Directives? Table 11.2 maps these out.

All that we have already said regarding vertical and horizontal direct effect has been concentrated on Directives. We should note here that treaty provisions are directly applicable and may also have direct effect (provided they are certain, unconditional, etc.).

Note: where treaty provisions have direct effect they will have *both* vertical and horizontal direct effect. For instance, you will find Directives which deal with discrimination and equal pay matters. However, the basic idea of 'equal pay' actually appears in Art. 157 of the Treaty on the Functioning of the European Union. So, when an air stewardess brought an equal pay claim against her employer (using the wording of the forerunner of TFEU) in Case 43/75 *Defrenne v SA Belge de Navigation Aérienne (SABENA) (No. 2)* [1976] ECR 455 the ECJ held that, because the article in question was part of a treaty and because it was clear and unconditional, it could be relied upon in this 'horizontal' action between employee and employer.

Table 11.2 Key points on vertical and horizontal direct effect

Vertical direct effect	Horizontal direct effect
It is now well accepted by the CJEU that Directives may have a vertical direct effect, for to deny a vertical direct effect (i.e. an individual against an organ of the state) would thus enable a Member State to rely upon its own non-implementation of EU law to avoid liability.	Whether Directives can have a horizontal effect has been hotly debated for many years and we will return to this in discussing the legal method employed in the CJEU. For the moment, we should say that Directives do not have horizontal direct effect.

Indirect effect

Case 14/83 *Von Colson* v *Land Nordrhein-Westfalen* [1984] ECR 1891 is credited with creating a further principle, termed *indirect effect*. Indirect effect sidesteps some of the problems created by the vertical/horizontal direct effect distinction and allows for some very creative judicial reasoning.

If a Directive does not have horizontal direct effect, it may be effective *indirectly* by means of domestic courts adopting an appropriately purposive form of interpretation for related domestic legislation. In other words, courts can read into the wording of the domestic legislation the *purpose* declared in the Directive. A court may thus give the citizen a right under domestic law where there would otherwise be none because the EU Directive lacks direct effect. The relationship between direct and indirect effect is a problematic feature of European jurisprudence. In many ways, the idea of *indirect effect* is more important than direct effect as it means that, irrespective of who is suing whom, the courts can try to implement the spirit of the Directive in a wider range of cases.

It does not matter, for the purposes of *indirect effect* whether there is a vertical or horizontal relationship between the parties as the court will try to do whatever lies within its powers to ensure that the Directive in question is fully effective and will have regard to the whole body of national law in doing so.

Indirect effect enables a court to 'read in' to the statute the wording and even the aims of the original Directive. It is called indirect effect for this reason, since it gives an individual a right of action through national law, but based *indirectly* on the Directive. This takes us full circle because we are now back in the field of *how* the courts interpret statutes as seen earlier.

We have to say that the position has become more and more convoluted. The guidelines issued by the ECJ in *Von Colson* were less than clear and at one time it was argued that the concept of indirect effect did nothing more than create a rule for dealing with ambiguities in domestic implementing legislation. In Case C–106/89 *Marleasing SA* v *La Commercial Internacional de Alimentación SA* [1990] ECR I-4135; [1992] 1 CMLR 305 the ECJ clarified this position to some extent by reaffirming the views expressed in *Marshall* and by noting that it is **domestic law** (not just legislation) which must comply with EU legislation, whether the Directive has been implemented, implemented improperly, or not implemented at all, once the time limit for implementation has passed.

In coming to this conclusion, the ECJ greatly extended the importance of indirect effect. Docksey and Fitzpatrick (1991: 113) went so far at the time as to suggest that indirect effect would become the normal mechanism whereby individuals could enforce rights contained in Directives, though this view has not altogether proved to be the case.

An easily understandable example can be seen in *Webb* v *EMO Air Cargo (UK) Ltd* [1990] ICR 442 (EAT); [1992] ICR 445; [1992] 2 All ER 43 (CA); [1993] 1 CMLR 259 (HL), which posed the question whether the dismissal of an employee on grounds of pregnancy constituted sex discrimination when the dismissed employee had been engaged specifically to cover for another employee's absence. The Employment Appeal Tribunal and the Court of Appeal thought not. They said that a claim fell under the Sex Discrimination Act 1975 only where a pregnant woman was treated less favourably by her employer than a hypothetical man would be in 'comparable' circumstances; for example, where he is suffering from an illness of similar severity and duration. Ms Webb had argued that the dismissal was discriminatory, based on the fact that a man can never be in the same position as a pregnant woman.

There was authority supporting Ms Webb's argument, derived from the Equal Treatment Directive EC/76/207, to be found in Case 177/88 *Dekker* v *Stichting Vormingscentrum voor Jong Volwassen Plus* [1990] ECR I-3941; [1991] IRLR 27. Ms Webb's counsel argued that the Directive as interpreted in *Dekker* (although not having direct horizontal effect) should be applied, using the *Marleasing* principles of indirect effect. The House of Lords in *Webb* indicated that, in its view, there was no discrimination here on a 'proper construction' of the 1975 Act. But their Lordships also stated that (*per* Lord Keith [1993] 1 CMLR 259, at 270):

> [I]t is for a United Kingdom court to construe domestic legislation so as to accord with the interpretation of the Directive as laid down by the European Court, if that can be done without distorting the meaning of the domestic legislation … This is so whether the domestic legislation came after or, as in this case, preceded the Directive …

Their Lordships found that the *Dekker* case was not direct authority on the facts in *Webb* (and so implicitly not 'binding' upon them), and sought a preliminary ruling from the ECJ on the meaning of the Directive.

The ECJ in Case C–32/93 *Webb* v *EMO Air Cargo (UK) Ltd* [1994] ECR I-3567; [1994] ICR 770 ruled that under Council Directive 76/207/EEC, Arts. 2(1) and 5(1), 'dismissal of an employee who is recruited for an unlimited term with a view, initially, to replacing another employee during the latter's maternity leave and who cannot do so because, shortly after her recruitment, she is herself found to be pregnant' is precluded. In other words, there does not have to be a 'male comparator'; dismissal of a pregnant employee for that reason is discrimination. In turn the case came back to the House of Lords (*Webb* v *EMO Air Cargo (UK) Ltd (No. 2)* [1995] ICR 1021) where their Lordships held that the Sex Discrimination Act 1975 must be interpreted in a manner consistent with the ruling by the ECJ.

Thus the specific wording of the Sex Discrimination Act 1975 was subsumed within the broad principles enunciated by the ECJ so that this decision certainly complies with the idea of indirect effect.

Another down-to-earth example may help. In the Irish case of *Smith* v *Meade* [2009] IEHC 99 a passenger was injured while being driven in the back of a van. He was not in a seat and the insurance policy did not cover passengers who were not seated. The relevant Directive had not been implemented by Ireland; had it been the passenger would have been covered by the insurance. The insurance company was not an emanation of the state so direct effect was inapplicable. Nevertheless, the Irish High Court ruled that, using the principles of indirect effect, the clause in the insurance contract excluding the passenger from compensation was to be regarded as void.

The concept of *indirect effect* still continues to be the subject of much argument, especially as regards the extent to which domestic courts may disapply national legislation in order to seek compliance with EU law. As regards civil liability the ECJ/CJEU has demonstrated that it is prepared to see EU law dominant, and use the principle of indirect effect to achieve this, even when this means exposing individuals to liabilities which were not there under national law (see *Pfeiffer*, joined Cases C–397/01 to C–403/01, [2004] ECR I-8835).

In C–144/04 *Mangold* v *Helm* [2006] IRLR 143 the ECJ extended the concept of EU law dominating domestic legislation by determining that the prevention of age discrimination was a 'general principle' of EU law so that domestic legislation could be overridden and horizontal direct effect could apply in such instances. However, these 'general principles' and 'fundamental rights' have no single accepted definition, so exactly which principles and rights are so sacrosanct as to be 'general' is not entirely clear (some attempts have been made, such as with the case of *Kadi* v *European Union Council* (Joined Cases C–402/05, C–415/05), [2008] ECR I-6351). In their chapter on the judicial method of English courts utilised in EU law cases, contained in Neergaard, Nielsen, and Roseberry (2011), Hervey and Sheldon note that this emerging doctrine of the primacy of 'general principles' of EU law is the latest challenge for English courts on legal method. It is an approach, illustrated by another case, *Kücükdeveci* v *Swedex Gmbh & Co* (C-555/07) [2010] 2 CMLR which, say the authors, 'blurs the boundaries between direct and indirect effect' (Neergaard *et al.*, 2011: 372) by taking a Directive which did not have direct effect and stating that domestic legislation should nevertheless be disapplied (this was another case on age discrimination being held to be a 'general principle' of EU law). Steiner and Woods (2014: 126) have also sounded warning bells on this form of incidental indirect effect.

The Court of Appeal has so far taken a robust approach to the dominance of EU law over national law: *Revenue and Customs Commissioners* v *IDT Card Services Ireland Ltd* [2006] EWCA Civ 29; [2006] STC 1252. That may be changing. However, the CJEU is much more reluctant to do anything which may impose on an individual criminal liability which was not present under national legislation (see Case C–168/95 *Arcaro* [1996] ECR I-4705; [1997] 1 CMLR 179).

Summary

- The idea of *direct applicability* is that the EU can instigate major and overriding legislation without having to rely on each Member State to implement it through its own parliamentary systems. Apart from matters such as Treaty obligations, this is not a common method of legislating. Member States, of course, have the right to vote on and sometimes even to veto such treaties and regulations. Some states allow for referenda on new treaties and, in such cases, the voting population may get to have a say on adoption or rejection (as happened with the Treaty of Lisbon in France, Holland, and Ireland—twice). In some cases, such as the Czech Republic—again with the Lisbon Treaty as an example—these matters may be regarded as constitutional issues.

- The idea of *direct effect* is to provide a mechanism whereby individuals can rely on the wording of EU legislation even when the Member State has implemented EU legislation (usually a Directive) incorrectly or not at all. For any EU legislation to have *direct effect* it must satisfy additional conditions of certainty and the time limit for implementation must have passed.

- Treaty obligations generally have *direct applicability*. In some cases this will mean that they also have *direct effect*, provided that they are certain and create rights for individuals (though even specific Treaty obligations may be couched in terms of desirability rather than detailed rules).

- Regulations also generally have *direct applicability*. In most cases this will mean that they also have *direct effect*, again provided that they are certain and create rights for individuals.

- Directives are not *directly applicable* and will have direct effect only in limited situations: 'They do not impose obligations as between private individuals' (Hervey and Sheldon in Neergaard *et al.* 2011: 371). The present position is that, even in these limited cases, they may have only *vertical direct effect*.

- The exact status of *indirect effect* cannot be stated with any clarity; it should be seen more as a tool of interpretation available to judges than as a fixed method of analysis. It can be used whether the Directive has direct effect or not.

- The key element in the relationship between national and EU law is that EU law trumps any national laws where there is conflict. Usually, the courts will try to interpret the national law so as to make it comply with EU law. Sometimes this will involve 'reading in' to the statute some key words derived from the Directive (as happened in *Litster* v *Forth Dry Dock & Engineering Co. Ltd* [1990] 1 AC 546; [1989] 2 CMLR 194). Occasionally even this will not be possible, in which case the national law must be disapplied. This (complicated) position was summed up nicely by Lord Walker in *Fleming (t/a Bodycraft)* v *HM Revenue & Customs*; *Condé Nast* v *HMRC* [2008] UKHL 2 [24]; [2008] 1 CMLR 48, where he says:

> It is a fundamental principle of the law of the European Union (EU), recognised in s. 2(1) of the European Communities Act 1972, that if national legislation infringes directly enforceable Community rights, the national court is obliged to disapply the offending provision. The provision is not made void but it must be treated as being … without prejudice to the directly enforceable EU rights of nationals of any member state of the EEC. …
>
> Disapplication is called for only if there is an inconsistency between national law and EU law in the way we have already described. In an attempt to avoid an inconsistency the national court will, if at all possible, interpret the national legislation so as to make it conform to the superior order of EU law and will make extensive use of the concept of *indirect effect* to do so: *Pickstone v Freemans Plc* [1989] AC 66; [1988] 3 CMLR 221; *Litster v Forth Dry Dock & Engineering Co Ltd* [1990] 1 AC 546; [1989] 2 CMLR 194. Sometimes, however, a conforming construction is not possible, and disapplication cannot be avoided.

In *Robertson* v *Swift* [2014] UKSC 50; [2014] 4 All ER 869 the Supreme Court cited the Court of Appeal decision in *Vodafone 2* v *Commissioners for Her Majesty's Revenue and Customs* [2009] EWCA Civ 446, [2010] Ch 77, to summarise the obligations on the English courts to construe domestic legislation consistently with Community law obligations as being:

(a) that the court is not constrained by conventional rules of construction;

(b) ambiguity in the legislative language is not a requirement;

(c) this is not simply an exercise in semantics or linguistics;

(d) courts are permitted to depart from the strict and literal application of the words which the legislature has elected to use;

(e) the implication of words necessary to comply with Community law obligations is permitted; and

(f) the precise form of the words to be implied does not matter.

Their Lordships added that: 'It is important to note that, in order to observe the imperative that this guidance contains, the court must not only keep faith with the wording of the Directive but must have closely in mind its purpose.'

Practical problem areas

In reality, the case law reveals that there are three main areas where the problem of *direct and indirect effect* will arise, and they all relate to Directives:

(a) where the Member State implements the Directive but there is a conflict between the relevant statute and the wording of the Directive;

(b) where the Member State fails to implement the Directive at all;

(c) where the general laws of the Member State (e.g. precedents not based on statutes) seem to be in conflict with the Directive.

If a Directive is not implemented or is not implemented properly, there is the question of whether a UK citizen can nevertheless enforce the rights given under the Directive. We saw earlier that if the Directive satisfies the conditions of certainty and has vertical direct effect, then the answer is generally 'Yes'; but if an individual wishes to rely on the Directive in suing another individual he/she must argue that the Directive has horizontal effect. This is more problematic. To give Directives horizontal direct effect, it is argued, equates them with Regulations—so what would be the distinction?

In one of the leading equal treatment cases, Case 152/84 *Marshall v Southampton and South West Hampshire AHA (Teaching)* [1986] ECR 723, [1986] 1 CMLR 688, [1986] 2 All ER 584 the ECJ denied the possibility of giving horizontal effect to Directives. Both the ECJ and the Advocate General agreed that the relevant Directive could be relied upon only in actions against the state (i.e. having vertical effect). On the facts, Ms Marshall succeeded in her claim, as it was conceded that her employer (the health authority) was an emanation of the state. If, on the other hand, she had been employed by, say, BUPA, the Directive would not have had direct effect because the relationship would have been 'horizontal'. This analysis was affirmed by the ECJ in *Faccini Dori v Recreb*. Here, the ECJ decided that there could be no such thing as horizontal direct effect as regards Directives—and again in Case C–192/94 *El Corte Inglés SA v Blázquez Rivero* [1996] ECR I–1281; [1996] 2 CMLR 507.

Like most things involving EU law, that was not to be the final word. A series of cases in 1996 cast some doubt on this, e.g. Case C–194/94 *CIA Security International SA* v *Signalson SA* [1996] ECR I-2201; [1996] 2 CMLR 372, Case C–441/93 *Pafitis and others* v *TKE and others* [1996] ECR I-1347; [1996] 2 CMLR 551, Case C–129/94 *Ruiz Bernáldez* [1996] ECR I-1829; [1996] 2 CMLR 889, and Case C–168/95 *Arcaro* [1996] ECR I-4705; [1997] 1 CMLR 179. However, we are in some agreement with the editor of the *European Law Review* that these cases do not destroy the principle of the ineffectiveness of horizontal direct effect; indeed, *Arcaro* illustrates and confirms the point that a Member State which fails to comply with EU law cannot use that failure against an individual. *Arcaro* concerned criminal proceedings relating to pollution. Had the state been allowed to pursue an action against the individual based on Directives (i.e. a vertical action, but 'top down') when there was doubt whether the Italian criminal legislation conflicted with EU Directives, this would have allowed Italy to benefit from its own failure to implement the Directive.

Indeed, more recent cases, focusing on both EU law and human rights law, have affirmed the *Faccini Dori* view of the inapplicability of horizontal direct effect: see *Ghaidan* v *Godin-Mendoza* [2004] UKHL 30; [2004] 2 AC 557 on similar problems in applying human rights' legislation plus *HMRC* v *IDT Card Services Ireland Ltd* [2006] EWCA Civ 29; [2006] STC 1252, *HMRC* v *EB Central Services Ltd* [2008] EWCA Civ 486; [2008] STC 2209, and C–282/10 *Dominguez* v *Centre Informatique du Centre Ouest Atlantique* [2012] IRLR 321 on EU law specifically.

11.4.2 State Liability: the *Francovich* Principle

The final stage in this saga is to note the joined Cases C–6/90 and C–9/90 *Francovich and Bonifaci* v *Italy* [1991] ECR I-5357; [1992] IRLR 84, where the ECJ held that, under certain conditions, a Member State is liable to make good damage to individuals if loss is suffered because the state failed to implement an EU Directive.

In Case C–46/93 *Brasserie du Pêcheur SA* v *Federal Republic of Germany* and Case C–48/93 *R* v *Secretary of State for Transport, ex parte Factortame Ltd and Others* (both reported at [1996] ECR I-1029; [1996] 1 CMLR 889) the ECJ considered this area again. These two cases concerned, respectively, damages suffered by a French company based in Alsace, which had lost a substantial sum of money owing to German import laws regarding beer (held to be in breach of EU legislation), and our old friends, the Spanish fishermen.

The ECJ identified three main conditions governing state liability:

(a) The EU legislation must have been intended to confer rights on individuals. The interpretation of this in the UK is that there must be an intention to create rights, not just a harmonisation of the law that incidentally creates such a right: *Three Rivers District Council* v *Bank of England* [1996] 3 All ER 558.

(b) The breach by the Member State must be 'sufficiently serious'. 'Sufficiently serious' breaches occur, according to the ECJ in Case C–127/95 *Norbrook Laboratories* v *Ministry of Agriculture* [1998] ECR I-1531, 'where a Member State, in the exercise of its legislative powers, has manifestly and gravely disregarded the limits on its powers'.

(c) There must be established a causal link between the breach and the damage suffered.

11.4.3 Direct and Indirect Effect: A Working Example

Imagine that a new Council Directive has appeared—the Fairness in Life Assurance Contracts Directive. This seeks to impose a duty on insurance companies to identify and explain clearly all 'surrender value' clauses in their policies. You wish to stop payments on your life assurance and receive the surrender value of the policy. You are told by the company that the wording of their surrender value clause means that they do not have to pay anything. You claim that the company's clause does not comply with the Directive. Can you make use of the Directive?

To answer this you will need to take account of the information set out in **Table 11.3**:

Table 11.3 Direct and indirect effect: a worked-through example

(a) Has the time passed when the Directive was meant to be implemented?	If not the Directive is, strictly, irrelevant.
(b) Assuming that the time period for implementation has passed, has the UK implemented the Directive?	(i) **If it has done so,** then the primary source for establishing your rights will be the UK legislation and the Directive will be relevant only as an aid to interpretation (indirect effect).
	(ii) **If it has done so but there is a conflict** between the relevant UK legislation and the wording of the Directive (e.g. difference in wording or gaps in the UK Act), the wording of the Directive itself can be used if the Directive is certain enough to have direct effect (but this will only apply to cases of *vertical effect*, i.e. actions against the state).
	(iii) **If the UK has failed to implement the Directive** at all, the position is the same as in (ii) above. But, since our fictional case is a claim against a company the claim is a horizontal one: effectively individual v individual.
	(iv) As vertical direct effect is not relevant, and horizontal direct effect is not possible, the courts may invoke the principle of *indirect effect*.
(c) In any case, if the government is at fault for not having implemented the Directive at all (or, more arguably, having implemented it incorrectly), the government may be liable to individuals, companies, etc. under the *Francovich* principle.	**This applies whether the Directive does or does not have direct effect.** The Commission may also take action but this is irrelevant to your particular claim.

We have sought to sum up this position in diagrammatic form (see **Figures 11.3** and **11.4**). We do not pretend that this level of uncertainty and complexity is justified.

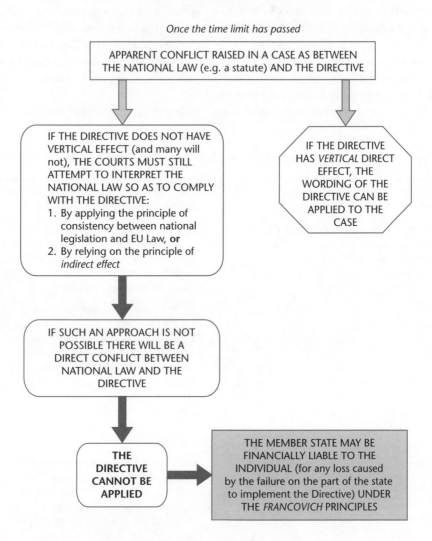

Figure 11.3 Directive improperly implemented

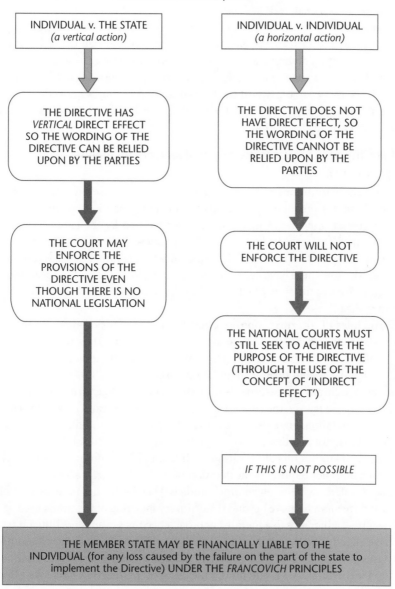

Once the time limit has passed

INDIVIDUAL v. THE STATE
(a vertical action)

INDIVIDUAL v. INDIVIDUAL
(a horizontal action)

THE DIRECTIVE HAS *VERTICAL* DIRECT EFFECT SO THE WORDING OF THE DIRECTIVE CAN BE RELIED UPON BY THE PARTIES

THE DIRECTIVE DOES NOT HAVE DIRECT EFFECT, SO THE WORDING OF THE DIRECTIVE CANNOT BE RELIED UPON BY THE PARTIES

THE COURT MAY ENFORCE THE PROVISIONS OF THE DIRECTIVE EVEN THOUGH THERE IS NO NATIONAL LEGISLATION

THE COURT WILL NOT ENFORCE THE DIRECTIVE

THE NATIONAL COURTS MUST STILL SEEK TO ACHIEVE THE PURPOSE OF THE DIRECTIVE (THROUGH THE USE OF THE CONCEPT OF 'INDIRECT EFFECT')

IF THIS IS NOT POSSIBLE

THE MEMBER STATE MAY BE FINANCIALLY LIABLE TO THE INDIVIDUAL (for any loss caused by the failure on the part of the state to implement the Directive) UNDER THE *FRANCOVICH* PRINCIPLES

Figure 11.4 Directive not implemented at all

11.4.4 The Style of Statutory Interpretation Employed

Historically, the civil law approach to statutory interpretation has been far more 'purposive' than that employed by the common law tradition. Civil law legislation, and therefore that of the EU also, is structured in a manner that is very different from British Acts of Parliament. The *civilian* tradition emphasises simplicity of drafting and a high degree of abstraction; UK statutes emphasise detail and comprehensiveness. What we saw in **Chapter 9**, however, is that the common law approach is changing inexorably, whether it is concerned with legislation derived from European sources or more 'home-grown' material.

This was foreseen by the decision of the House of Lords in *Webb* v *EMO Air Cargo (UK) Ltd* [1993] 1 WLR 49. Lord Keith, in particular, recognised the fact that English courts must interpret domestic legislation in accordance with EU law as far as possible, provided that this can be achieved without distorting the meaning of the domestic legislation. Thus, it does not matter if the legislation in question is derived directly from European sources, and it does not matter whether the domestic legislation was adopted before or after any EU legislation.

What are the other sources used by civil lawyers to analyse legal problems?

Common to both traditions are sources such as legislation, case law, and custom. As we noted in **Chapter 9**, preparatory materials leading to legislation (*travaux préparatoires*) are given greater importance in statutory interpretation by the civil system (though their use by the CJEU is variable). Again in **Chapter 9** we noted the different approaches used by civil law lawyers and the CJEU, in contrast to common law lawyers, in interpreting legislation. These have been referred to as the 'toolbox for European Judges' by Hesselink in Neergaard *et al.* (2011: 185). We shall now explore these in greater detail under three headings.

(a) **Principles of interpretation**. In considering questions of interpretation Brown and Kennedy (2000) detail the options available to the Court. They describe these as the literal, historical, contextual, comparative, and teleological methods. We shall briefly consider each of these in turn. It should be stressed that the CJEU is not bound to use only one approach; any one case may legitimately reflect a whole variety of judicial styles.

Like the English lawyer, the civilian lawyers, too, recognise and make use of different styles of interpretation. First, there is the **literal** approach: it should come as no surprise that every court, not just English courts, turns first to the words of the text. But this is not the English law 'literal rule' in disguise. It is simply a common-sense embarkation point which does not require the declaration of 'ambiguity' before it can be discarded. For a major difference between common and civil law judges lies in the degree of willingness and freedom to move beyond the ordinary meaning of the words used.

In the CJEU, adherence to a literalist approach becomes even more difficult because, as we have already noted, texts have to be translated from one language to another: see, for instance Case C–372/88 *Milk Marketing Board* v *Cricket St Thomas Estate* [1990] ECR I-1345; [1990] 2 CMLR 800 on the meaning of 'pasteurised milk'. As Miers and Page noted, however, there may also be a positive side to these linguistic differences: it may also be that 'the scope for doubt as to the meaning in one language may often be closed down by the language of the others' (1990: 184).

Having at least noted the wording of the text, European judges have four methods at their disposal. The **historical** approach is described by David and Brierley as one 'clarifying present texts in the light of previous circumstances and taking into account the legislator's intention' (1985: 125). This has been achieved by turning to all manner of source documentation in the form of *travaux préparatoires*. Brown argues that the English mischief rule bears resemblance to this approach, though concentrating on a more limited and 'objective' assessment of legislative intent, as we saw in **Chapter 9**. There is an irony here. While English lawyers are moving (slowly) towards admitting more in the way of *travaux préparatoires*, European lawyers, and, as noted by Hesselink in Neergaard *et al.* (2011: 202), especially the CJEU, have placed less reliance on such material.

The **contextual** approach, like the literal approach, concentrates upon the meaning of the words, except that it does not confine itself to investigating only the wording of *that* Act, but rather considers the whole legislative context. By this we mean that the Court must consider the 'framework of EU law'—the interrelationship of all aspects of EU law: see Cases 90–91/63 *European Commission* v *Luxembourg and Belgium* [1964] ECR 625; Case 6/64 *Costa* v *ENEL* [1964] ECR 585. This is perhaps one of the most important techniques used by the CJEU.

By **comparative** we mean that the judges of the CJEU are, by their very background, bound to draw upon their own experience as lawyers within the Member States. This means that inevitably the Court will seek to evaluate and maybe utilise solutions provided by the legal systems from which the judges are drawn, e.g. the adoption of the French Administrative law doctrine of *acte clair* to define when an Art. 267 TFEU reference is 'necessary': see Cases 28–30/62 *Da Costa en Schaake NV* [1963] ECR 31; *French Republic* v *Deroche, Cornet et Soc Promatex-France* [1967] CMLR 351. The term 'comparative' should not be taken as a euphemism for 'compromise'. The aim is to extract the appropriate principle, not to create some sort of mishmash.

The last, but probably the most important, approach we need to consider is the **teleological** method (also known as the *schematic* approach). This may be defined as a broad 'purposive' approach which requires courts to place the legislation within the entire setting and spirit of EU law: see Case 106/77 *Amministrazione delle Finanze dello Stato* v *Simmenthal SpA* [1978] ECR 629.

The teleological approach is widely used by the CJEU, and increasingly employed by national courts in interpreting EU law. Thus, in *Murphy* v *An Bord Telecom Eireann* [1988] 2 CMLR 753, the Irish High Court held that where there was a right to 'equal pay for equal work' in accordance with what was then Art. 141 (now Art. 157 TFEU), this must automatically include a right to equal pay for work of *greater* value. The Irish legislation stated only that equal pay was to be given for work 'equal in value'; and this had to be interpreted in keeping with the spirit of the then Art. 139. As Keane J. said, 'the literal construction … must give way in the present case to the teleological construction'.

Hervey and Sheldon in Neergaard *et al.* (2011) explore this approach; they use the term, 'the strong version of the EU compliance mischief rule'—meaning a willingness which has developed over the last few decades for UK courts to dig deep into the mischief behind the EU legislation and, where possible, force through an interpretation which remedies that mischief, even where that means 'writing in' words to the UK legislation (as in *Litster* v *Forth Dry Dock*).

(b) Doctrine. Legal writings (referred to as *doctrine*) hold a different place in the civil system from that in the common law tradition. The status and influence of such writings are greater on the Continent than here. As we have seen, if one is seeking influence and authority as a writer on English law the general advice is to be ancient and dead. The continental academic lawyer is not required to make the same sacrifice.

(c) General principles. Finally, when all else fails—whether it is the analysis of a Code or the application of precedent—there is the ultimate fallback of 'general principles'. We noted these earlier as regards the case of *Kücükdeveci*. Some countries draw upon these unwritten rules because their Code allows them to do so, e.g. Spain and Italy. Others, such as France, discover them in the spirit and tradition of the law; often more assumed than debated. As Szladits and Germain pointed out (1985: 44), it is in the systematising of these general principles that the role of *doctrine* can have its greatest effect. The common law too knows of 'general principles', though for the most part authority is still sought. Ultimately the common law lawyer will fall back on the notion that there exists an amorphous mass of laws termed 'the common law' from which the rules can be derived, or will refer to 'Equitable principles'.

As we have seen, the CJEU has developed its own sense of 'general principles' in the protection of fundamental human rights such as those found in the European Convention of Human Rights and Fundamental Freedoms. Thus we can discover principles of proportionality, equality, certainty, natural justice, and due process in the rulings of the CJEU.

CONCLUSION

There is a perceived difference between how the UK (and Irish) lawyer and the continental lawyer approach their tasks. Much of the difference may, in the final analysis, be more to do with form than fundamentals. However, the difference is perceptible, and the reality is that it is the UK and Irish lawyers who will have to change, more than their continental counterparts. Our system of precedent has been described as a system whereby 'we never clean our slates', or, more candidly, as an 'ungodly jumble'. It depends upon an immense network of narrow rules. It avoids working from general principles. It has only relatively recently begun, to embrace purposiveness in interpretation. It rests on the sanctity of case law and the practical testing and re-testing of ideas, rather than pure theory.

The contrast with civil law is obvious; perhaps the battle-lines are drawn. We may have to reassess the (perhaps apocryphal) headline in *The Times* last century: 'Fog in the Channel—Europe Isolated'.

CHAPTER REFERENCES

*BENGOETXEA, J. (1993), *The Legal Reasoning of the European Court of Justice* (Oxford: Clarendon Press).

BROWN, L. and KENNEDY, T. (2000), *Brown and Jacobs: The Court of Justice of the European Communities* (5th edn, London: Sweet & Maxwell).

COHN, E. (1968), *Manual of German Law* (2 vols) (London: British Institute of International and Comparative Law).

CRAIG, P. (1997), 'Direct Effect, Indirect Effect and the Construction of National Legislation', 22 *European Law Review*, 519.

CRAIG, P. (2009), 'The Legal Effect of Directives: Policy, Rules and Exceptions', 34 *European Law Review*, 349.

Craig, P. and DE BÚRCA, G. (2015), *EU Law: Text, Cases and Materials* (6th edn, Oxford: Oxford University Press).

*DAVID, R. and BRIERLEY, J. (1985), *Major Legal Systems in the World Today* (3rd edn, London: Stevens).

*DE BÚRCA, G. (1992), 'Giving Effect to European Community Directives', 55 *Modern Law Review*, 215.

DOCKSEY, C. and FITZPATRICK, B. (1991), 'The Duty of National Courts to Interpret Provisions of National Law in Accordance with Community Law', 20 *Industrial Law Journal*, 113.

FOSTER, N. (2015), *Foster on EU Law* (5th edn, Oxford: Oxford University Press).

GALMOT, Y. and BONICHOT, J.C. (1988), 'La Cour de Justice des Communautés Européennes et la transposition des Directives en droit national', 4 *Revue français de Droit administratif*, 1.

GRAVELLS, N. (1989), 'Disapplying an Act of Parliament Pending a Preliminary Ruling: Constitutional Enormity or Community Law Right?', *Public Law*, 568.

HARRIS, D. and TALLON, D. (1989), *Contract Law Today: Anglo-French Comparisons* (Oxford: Clarendon Press).

HARRISON, K. (1992), 'Pregnancy in the Court of Appeal', 142 *New Law Journal*, 462.

*HORN, N., KÖTZ, H., and LESER, H. (1982), *German Private and Commercial Law: An Introduction* (Oxford: Clarendon Press).

KENNEDY, T. (1998), *Learning European Law* (London: Sweet & Maxwell).

LANGRISH, S. (1998), 'The Treaty of Amsterdam: Selected Highlights', 23 *European Law Review*, 3.

LASOK, D. and BRIDGE, J.W. (1994), *Law and Institutions of the European Communities* (6th edn, London: Butterworths).

MARKESINIS, B.S. (1994), 'A Matter of Style', 110 *Law Quarterly Review*, 607.

*MIERS, D. and PAGE, A. (1990), *Legislation* (2nd edn, London: Sweet & Maxwell).

NEERGAARD, U. and NIELSEN, R (eds) (2013), *European Legal Method: Towards a New Legal Realism* (Copenhagen: DJØF Publishing).

*NEERGAARD, U., NIELSEN, R., and ROSEBERRY, L. (eds) (2011), *European Legal Method – Paradoxes and Revitalisation* (Copenhagen: DJØ F Publishing).

NICHOLAS, B. (1992), *French Law of Contract* (2nd edn, London: Butterworths).

*SAWYER, K. (2007), 'The Principle of "Interpretation Conforme": How Far Can or Should National Courts Go When Interpreting National Legislation Consistently with European Community Law?', 28 *Statute Law Review*, 165.

*SNYDER, F. (1993), 'The Effectiveness of European Community Law: Institutions, Processes, Tools and Techniques', 56 *Modern Law Review*, 19.

*STEINER, J. (1993), 'From Direct Effect to *Francovich*: Shifting Means of Enforcement of Community Law', 18 *European Law Review*, 3.

STEINER, J. (1995), *Enforcing EC Law* (London: Blackstone Press).

*STEINER, J. and WOODS, L. by WOODS, L. and WATSON, P. (2014), *EU Law* (12th edn, Oxford: Oxford University Press). Some previous editions of this work were entitled *Textbook on EC Law*.

SZLADITS, C. and GERMAIN, C. (1985), *Guide to Foreign Legal Materials: French* (2nd edn, New York: Oceana Publishing).

SZYSZCZAK, E. and CYGAN, A. (2008), *Understanding EU Law* (2nd edn, London: Sweet & Maxwell).

WEATHERILL, S. (2014), *Cases & Materials on EU Law* (11th edn, Oxford: Oxford University Press).

12

Exploiting Legal Reasoning

In this chapter, we will consider explicitly the theories underpinning legal reasoning, and the way reasoning techniques are employed in legal contexts. In so doing we will examine, first, the logical foundations of legal reasoning, and then explore the extent to which legal reasoning requires us to consider factors beyond those imposed by the strict necessity of logic (e.g. social values and political roles).

Law is often described as a system of 'practical reasoning'. We can see what this means when we think about what 'doing law' involves. Thus, a judge has to give judgment, lawyers have to advise their clients, legislators have to predict the impact of their laws. The key link between all these activities is that they are built upon some kind of reasoning process. The answers found by judges, lawyers, and legislators are not simply based upon some pre-existing knowledge of the law. Although the ability to find and use the various kinds of legal material is important, it is not enough, because your sources may not actually provide you with an answer. To be sure, there are some legal questions which can be resolved simply by searching for the answer in a book. If you wish to know what is the maximum compensation payable for, say, an unfair dismissal, you can find the answer in statute and statutory instrument, or in a textbook. But determining whether Jane Smith is likely to win her case, and what level of compensation she is likely to obtain cannot simply be looked up in a book. There is an important element of creativity, of working out an answer according to a whole range of supposedly rational criteria. Here and in the following section, we are concerned with how lawyers must go beyond the legal texts, to *construct* their own answers to discrete legal problems. It is this that constitutes what we have already called the process of *legal argumentation* (see **Chapter 5**).

Let's start by thinking about thinking itself. This is perhaps not something we are too used to doing, even in an educational setting. Obviously 'learning' is about acquiring new information—but don't forget that we have to be able to *use* that knowledge. Studying maths provides a good example. Mathematical skills reflect an ability to apply the appropriate formulae (knowledge) to a particular problem, e.g. calculating the sine of angle x in a triangle where the length of the sides are known. You might well know that the formula for that calculation is represented as:

$$\text{Sine x} = \frac{opposite}{\text{Hypotenuse}}$$

But that is not the end. You need to use that knowledge to produce a *specific* answer. That answer will of course vary according to the data you use. Similarly when structuring legal arguments we are working from a source of knowledge about law, and using that to construct an answer to a specific legal problem. It is the process of getting from knowledge to answer that involves our skills of practical reasoning. The aim of this chapter is to deepen our understanding of what this process involves.

12.1 Logic and Legal Reasoning

Legal argument is first based upon fundamental reasoning skills that are common to most disciplines. By 'reasoning', we mean, in essence, the process of deciding on a given course of action. It is important to distinguish 'reasoning' from the colloquial idea of 'having a reason'. Because we are quite relaxed about our use of language, it is easy, but wrong, to think of reasoning as simply a matter of cause and effect. It is not; reasoning reflects the ability to arrive at a rational, calculated decision.

Let us try to illustrate what we mean. If A hits B because B called him names, he has a reason. A is angry with B and has decided to hit him. Of course, since this is an emotional response, one could say it lacks rationality in the conventional 'thought out' sense that we use the term, since A's anger has probably got in the way of the reasoning process. Would A have been so quick to hit B had he thought about it and realised that later B would come looking for him, with his brother, the champion boxer, seeking revenge? This emphasis upon rationality means that we are essentially grounding legal decisions in the mental process we call *logic*. This point is hardly new. Leith and Hoey (1998: 279), for example, trace the contact between law and logic back through history to the Ancient Greeks, though, as their work shows, interest in the relationship has been given a modern boost by attempts to create computer models of legal decision-making. The link between law and logic has been frequently acknowledged by the judiciary, and notably by Lord Devlin in *Hedley Byrne* v *Heller & Partners* [1964] AC 465, at 516, where he said:

> The common law is tolerant of much illogicality, especially on the surface; but no system of law can be workable if it has not got logic at the root of it.

This is not to suggest that law is unusual; in much day-to-day life we are using basic logic without really knowing it. If I go out in the morning with only enough money for my bus fare back home, I have a simple choice: either I spend that money while out and walk home, or save it for the return bus ride. I know that I cannot do both. The conclusion that I have to choose is founded on a common-sense form of logic. Logic thus provides a commonplace basis for decision-making, by helping us plan our actions in a way that 'makes sense'. At this level, it is hardly surprising that logic is equally significant in helping us to make sense of legal argumentation; however, it is only fair to point out two things: first that the image of logic represented in this chapter is an extremely simplified one. Logic is a complex subject of academic concern in its own right, and, as Leith and Hoey point out, the view that most individuals have of logic as clear and precise is erroneous; logicians are as prone to arguing about the merits of different theories and systems of logic as academics of other disciplines! Secondly, logic will only take us so far. It may only get us to a point where we can say there are a number of feasible choices, at which point policy or other considerations may need to take over.

12.1.1 The Nature of Reasoning

Let us begin by formalising our notion of reasoning a little more clearly. We know that it reflects a particular kind of decision-making process, which, so far, we have described simply as 'rational'. By this, we mean that it is a structured form of discourse which involves passing from one proposition already known or assumed to be true, to another distinct from the first, but following from it. The classic example of the logical reasoning process is the 'syllogism', a verbal structure which draws a true conclusion from a major and minor premise, each of which is verifiable in its own right, thus:

All men are mortal

Socrates is a man

Therefore Socrates is mortal

In this case the logic is impeccable. We know as a matter of fact that men are mortal; we also know that Socrates is a man. The conclusion of Socrates' mortality is therefore inescapable.

Now, in fact, this represents only one kind of logical reasoning. In logic conventionally we make a distinction between two different processes, called **inductive** and **deductive** reasoning. Robert M. Pirsig uses the example of locating a fault in a motor cycle to illustrate these logical modes in the process of scientific method. If the analogy seems rather out of place, persevere, because it is as applicable to lawyers as it is to scientists:

> Two kinds of logic are used, inductive and deductive. Inductive inferences start with observations of the machine and arrive at general conclusions. For example, if the cycle goes over a bump and the engine misfires, and then goes over another bump and the engine misfires … and then goes over a long smooth stretch of road and there is no misfiring, and then goes over a fourth bump and the engine misfires again, one can logically conclude that the misfiring is caused by the bumps. That is induction: reasoning from particular experiences to general truths.
>
> Deductive inferences do the reverse. They start with general knowledge and predict a specific observation. For example, if from reading the hierarchy of facts about the machine, the mechanic knows the horn of the cycle is powered exclusively by electricity from the battery, then he can logically infer that if the battery is dead the horn will not work. That is deduction. (1974: 107)

There is an important distinction between these modes of reasoning. The form of deductive reasoning is such that, so long as the major and minor premises are correctly constructed, the conclusion has to be true. Thus the syllogism we have just considered is a representation of the form of deductive reasoning. Inductive reasoning does not provide us with the same degree of certainty. We can reach an answer inductively on the basis of an assumption that our particular experience is of general application. In some cases, such as Pirsig's, for example, our assumption is likely to be pretty accurate, and obviously the more information we have supporting our hypothesis, the more likely it is to stand up in the future. But, in terms of formal logic, we cannot say that our conclusion is conclusive. There is always the possibility that some other conclusion exists.

For example, Patrick Shaw (1981) tells of an experiment conducted in Birmingham some years ago. Drivers in the city were urged to use only dipped headlights at night.

During the experiment, it was shown that the number of road accidents had fallen sharply. The local papers immediately declared the experiment to have been a major success. However, it was subsequently found that there had been fewer vehicles on the road than usual during the experiment, so the press had not really got it right. There may have been some correlation between the dipped headlights and the reduction in accidents, but the connexion was not as great as had been assumed. The relative inconclusiveness of inductive reasoning is a point to which we shall return shortly.

Lawyers use both inductive and deductive reasoning, and legal decision-making will usually involve *both* those modes, used in conjunction with each other to produce a reasoned conclusion. It is, however, helpful to distinguish between a number of processes. First, in reasoning about legal rules, as we have seen, we conventionally distinguish between two distinct contexts: the interpreting of statutes and the use of precedent through case law. Secondly, lawyers are also involved in reasoning about facts (what we shall call, following Alexy (1989), **empirical reasoning**). We will consider each of these in turn.

12.1.2 Reasoning and Precedent

Using precedent involves both deductive and inductive reasoning, but of these the inductive element is the most important.

Inductive reasoning in law can, in its simplest terms be described as follows:

> In case x, factors A, B and C existed. Judgment was given for the claimant.
>
> In case y, factors A, B and C existed. Judgment was given for the claimant.
>
> In case z, factors A, B and C exist. Judgment should, therefore, be given for the claimant.

It is thus a process of reasoning by example. It is a technique that we have all used. A child may well reason that it is safe to climb a tree in a friend's garden, because that friend has just done so without falling. That child has reasoned, inductively from the example of his or her friend.

Edward Levi (1949: 2) developed this idea into what he called a 'three step process' of legal reasoning:

- *Step one* is where a judge sees a relevant factual similarity between an earlier case, or cases, and the present one.
- In *step two*, the judge identifies the rule of law on which the previous case(s) rested.
- Finally (*step three*) he or she applies that rule to the present case.

It is this final stage only, of applying the rule, that is deductive. As MacCormick (1978: 197) puts it, 'deduction comes in only after the interesting part of the argument, settling the ruling in law, has been carried through.' One of the clearest judicial examples to this effect comes from Lord Hailsham in *DPP* v *Morgan* [1976] AC 464, at 516. The case concerned the question whether an honest but unreasonable belief that the victim consented to sexual intercourse could negate the necessary intent on a charge of rape. His Lordship identified the following legal propositions as being correct: *If* ... the prohibited act in rape is non-consensual sexual intercourse *and* the guilty state of mind is an intention to commit' the prohibited act, *then*, he argued, an honest but mistaken belief as to consent must result in an acquittal (our emphasis, to highlight the deductive element of the argument). In effect, all he is saying is that the accused lacked the necessary intent,

---

Induction or analogy: Is there a difference?

Some writers (e.g. Golding, 1984) seek to distinguish 'true' induction from a related process—which they believe is the one used by lawyers—called reasoning by analogy, whereas others (e.g. Levi, 1949; Brewer, 1996; Farrar, 1997) seem to treat inductive reasoning and reasoning by analogy as synonymous. To be sure, there is much that these writers agree on. Inductive reasoning/reasoning by analogy clearly involves a process of pattern-matching from previous examples. As Levi notes, finding cases with appropriate similarities is a critical first stage in the process. Where the theoretical dispute emerges is with respect to what follows this stage: having found the cases, how does the judge create his analogy? Thus, Brewer argues that the judge discovers (or constructs) a *general* rule that explains the examples—strictly an inductive process, while Golding favours the idea of an 'instance classification without generalisation', i.e. a genuine analogical process of reasoning by inference from *the specific to the specific*.

  Philosophically, Golding undoubtedly has a point; analogy is a species of induction, but it is a subset that tends to be inferentially weaker. At the same time, we suggest that it is probably sensible to take the view that *both* the processes we have just described operate in common law systems—both reasoning by analogy from a specific set of facts and reasoning inductively from a set of cases, the latter arising where precedent has effectively hardened into an established common law principle.

Figure 12.1 Induction or reasoning by analogy?

but the strength of the argument lies, in his Lordship's view, in the fact that to convict would result in a logical absurdity. Up to this point in the reasoning, however, judges use an inductive process, often also called **reasoning by analogy** (though note, as a side issue, that there is a technical dispute between legal theorists about the nature of what is going on in this process and what we should call it—see **Figure 12.1**).

  In practice, of course, the process of reasoning from cases is not quite as straightforward as the first example we gave. More often, it involves weighing up and balancing a whole variety of differences and similarities. It will be unusual for the analogy to be so clear, and what is more likely is that only a few of the common factors (for example, **A** and **B**, but not **C**) will be present in the later case, so the judge must weigh up the relative importance of **C** in deciding whether to apply the analogy. We have already given you an example of that kind of technique in **Chapter 7**. This reflects the fact that inductive/analogical reasoning cannot be conclusive. Inductive/analogical reasoning is not about *proof* (unlike deductive reasoning); it is purely about *justification*. A case analogy justifies a later decision, it does not make it, logically, the only possible outcome. To use our earlier example, the child will not know conclusively that the climb will be safe. His or her friend may be lighter, stronger, or taller, all of which might make a difference to the outcome of the climb. It will be up to the child to weigh up the risks and decide whether the example is good enough to follow.

  Equally, it follows that the inductive stages inevitably involve a degree of discretion. Levi's first step gives the judge freedom of action in deciding what similarities—and differences as well—are relevant. In step two, the judge again has some freedom in deciding what rules of law are discoverable from the earlier cases (this is part of what in **Chapter 5** we called the judge's freedom of justification). A judge is obliged to follow a precedent only once satisfied that *the precedent fits*. By this we mean that the judge must have first accepted that the facts are, in material respects, sufficiently similar, and that the legal principle established in the earlier case(s) should apply.

This also gives us a clue to the main means we have for countering an argument based on analogy or inductive reasoning, namely demonstrating that the analogy is not a good fit. In law, this is what we do when we seek to *distinguish* a case, e.g. by saying the similarities are insufficient or insufficiently important, or by proposing another, better, analogy. Of course, this is not the same as proving the analogy demonstrably and finally false; indeed, inductive reasoning cannot readily be refuted in that way.

12.1.3 Reasoning and Statutory Interpretation

Using Pirsig's analogy from section **12.1.1**, consider the following question:

EXERCISE 20 Zen and the art of legal reasoning?

Statute requires that whosoever takes property belonging to another, with the intention of permanently depriving the other of it, shall be guilty of an offence.

X deliberately takes Y's bicycle and sells it to Z.

Has X committed the offence?

This is, of course, a simple example—but in reaching the logical conclusion that X is guilty, were you using inductive or deductive reasoning?

The process you used is in fact deductive. Our starting point is a general rule, laid down in a statute, which we are then applying to a specific instance. We could convert this into a syllogism, thus:

(a) An individual who takes another's property with the intention permanently to deprive that other of it, shall be guilty of an offence.

(b) The accused X has committed the prohibited act.

(c) Therefore X is guilty of the offence.

A general way of looking at this would be to say that the legal syllogism involves the following elements:

(a) a rule of general application (*the major premise*);

(b) the particular fact(s) (*the minor premise(s)*);

(c) a legal outcome (*the conclusion*).

On the face of it, therefore, statutory interpretation seems to be chiefly a deductive process. However this is something of an oversimplification. 'Pure' deductive reasoning can be used only when applying clear rules to specific fact situations (MacCormick, 1978). Statutory interpretation, however, will often involve a significant element of inductive reasoning or analogy, notably where:

- the meaning of words used may be derived from analogous statutory provisions;
- there are doubts about the scope of a statutory rule which have to be resolved on the basis of competing precedents.

Consequently it is a mistake to think of case law and statute as involving wholly separate reasoning processes. As our second point highlights, it is not unusual for cases which turn on a question of statutory interpretation to require the court to look at competing arguments about statutory meaning which have existing authority derived from case law. For example, in *R v Shivpuri* [1987] AC 1; [1986] 2 All ER 334, a case we have already considered, the essential problem was one of interpreting the scope of the Criminal Attempts Act 1981, s. 1. However, the House of Lords could not treat that simply as a question of interpreting the Act; it was required, by the rules of precedent, to consider the meaning given to the Act by an earlier House of Lords' decision in the case of *Anderton v Ryan* [1985] AC 560; [1985] 2 All ER 355, and had to justify their decision accordingly.

Where a decision is based on deduction, how can it be challenged? As we have already noted, the difference between induction and deduction is primarily the difference between providing justification for and proof of an outcome. Consequently, where a decision is deductively correct, it cannot, logically, be gainsaid. It follows that the means of challenging deductive reasoning are limited. Nevertheless, they exist.

Denying the premise

If you can show the major (statement of the rule) or minor premise (statement of fact) is false, you can defeat the argument. For example:

All cows eat grass

Cows are mammals

Therefore all mammals eat grass

In fact this syllogism is totally wrong. All we have are two independent statements: cows are mammals and they eat grass. Not only do the initial premises not establish a basis for saying that all mammals eat grass (there is no evidence here about the eating habits of other mammals, nor is there anything which predicates a sufficient similarity between cows and other mammals), the minor premise is flawed. If you think about it, it is really a rule (major premise) masquerading as a fact. Unsurprisingly, then, the conclusion as a matter of logic just does not follow.

By changing one or other of the premises to its 'correct' form we change the pathway through the problem, and hence the conclusion. So we could say:

All cows eat grass

Buttercup is a cow

Therefore Buttercup eats grass

What this actually means in law is that you will attempt to challenge those elements of the reasoning that are more likely to have been arrived at inductively in the first place—the formulation of the rule, or the statement of fact.

Question the validity of the logic

Even where the major and minor premises are verifiable, they may not lead to the conclusion alleged; for example, consider the following syllogism:

All MPs are elected

The Mayor of London is elected

Therefore the Mayor of London is an MP

The fallacy in the reasoning here can be exposed by reducing the syllogism to its basic logical structure. If we take the Buttercup syllogism as an example of one that works, it takes the form:

All As = B

if C = A

Then C = B

By contrast, the Mayor of London syllogism reduces to the form:

All As = B

if C = B

then C = A

and the fault in the reasoning becomes obvious. Judges are not likely to make this kind of mistake. Law students sometimes do. You have been warned!

12.1.4 Reasoning in Civil Law Systems

Does the civilian tradition reflect a significantly different approach to legal reasoning, and are there lessons we can learn from that?

Michel Villey makes the point that:

> Even today English law is the closest to the casuistic art of the classical Roman jurists. The law for the [English student] … is above all a matter of science; or rather of case law; because the law is to be induced from nature, and by the study of each case. (1975: 700)

So, do we assume from this that the role of induction, and hence of analogy, is of far less significance in continental European legal systems? Unfortunately (once again) it is not that simple. Legal theorists recognise that, in civilian systems too, legal reasoning takes on a hybrid form which is neither wholly deductive nor inductive. There are, however, two distinctive features of civilian systems which suggest some substantive differences from the common law lawyer's logic.

First, the codes are often said to provide an axiomatic basis for legal rules. By this we mean that they constitute often complete, self-contained principles of law. Secondly, as we have seen, precedent plays a lesser role in civil law systems, because of the interpretive traditions connected with codified law. Taken together these might indicate that deduction plays a larger role in civil law systems. However, the axiomatic basis of many of the codes only *reduces* (but does not obliterate) the need for the judges to reason from analogy.

The use of reasoning from analogy can certainly be traced back to the techniques used in Roman law and passed down to us through the civilian tradition in the work of the mediaeval scholars we collectively term the 'Glossators' and (later) the 'Commentators'. For them the distinction between *comprehensio legis* (the process of interpreting legislation) and *extensio legis* (the procedures for supplementing legislation) was already well understood. Within this tradition, two distinct analogical processes have been recognised (see, e.g., Zaccaria, 1991: 49–56; Esser, 1972).

First there is the notion of the *analogia legis*—the use of a single, statutory analogy (*Gesetzesanalogie* in German) to fill a gap in the legislation identified by a new or unforeseen situation. This operates by the court saying, in effect, 'the principle in Article 123 governs not only case A but also case B'. Cees Maris (1991: 71) offers an example from Dutch Criminal Law which, interestingly, resonates in English law as well.

Under the Dutch Penal Code of 1881, the offence of theft required, *inter alia*, that the accused 'take away' property belonging to another. In 1920, a Dutch dentist was convicted of theft for 'milking' his electricity meter, i.e. extracting electricity by bypassing the meter. He argued that, as electricity was an intangible, it could not be 'taken away' since that term (in its Dutch linguistic context) referred only to tangible property. Unfortunately for the dentist, the Dutch Supreme Court disagreed; it felt that extracting electricity was sufficiently similar to a taking away of tangible property to be caught by the Code.

An interesting comparison can be made with England, where a similar problem has arisen both under the old Larceny Acts and under the Theft Act 1968 that replaced them. In *Low* v *Blease* [1975] Crim LR 513, the Divisional Court held that electricity was not 'appropriated' (the Theft Act alternative to 'taking away' used in the Larceny Act 1916) by switching on the current, nor, the Court said, could electricity constitute 'property' within the Theft Act, s. 4. It may be that the Divisional Court was unduly influenced by the fact that a separate offence of abstracting electricity had been created by the Theft Act 1968, s. 13, as a way of dealing with milking the meter and similar situations (see *Boggeln* v *Williams* [1978] Crim LR 242), but its literalism was in stark contrast to the willingness of the Dutch court to reason, creatively, by analogy. As the commentary to *Low* v *Blease* points out, the decision does leave us with the rather bizarre situation where a 'trespasser who warms himself by lighting the gas fire is guilty of burglary while the trespasser who prefers the electric fire is not' ([1975] Crim LR 513). Clearly there are analogies and analogies.

Secondly, there is the *analogia juris*, which describes what German jurisprudence would call a legal analogy (*Rechtsanalogie*) as opposed to statutory analogy. This is where the judge reasons from outside the specific case or rule, usually by arguing that it is illustrative of a wider principle of law which can be applied to the new situation. Thus, for example, it is commonly accepted in the jurisprudence of many civil systems that judges may need to take an approach to resolving cases based on a sense of 'justice' (in Germany, again, one finds direct reference to this as the *Rechtsgefühl*) rather than on statutory rules. In French private law, for example, the judges have developed a theory of abuse of rights (*l'abus des droits*). This is sometimes used, *inter alia*, in contractual disputes to impose obligations on the contracting parties in much the same way as the English courts have used the notion of 'implied terms'.

Today, the use of certain general principles has become so formalised that, in some cases, the courts no longer rely on the process of analogy for justification. Rather, these fundamental general principles have effectively hardened into a source of law in their own right. Indeed, in some countries, the right of recourse to general principles has become enshrined in the codified law: see, e.g., Spanish Civil Code, Art. 6. Such general principles, including the principles of proportionality or reasonableness, meaning that state intervention must be restricted only to that which is necessary to achieve the aim of a particular law, operate in a number of domestic legal systems as well as in EU and European Human Rights law (as we saw in **Chapters 10** and **11**). Ultimately, therefore, we suggest that much of the supposed divergence between civil and common law techniques involves drawing a distinction without a measurable difference. If anything, the comparison of civil and common law traditions reinforces the view that, when it comes to legal reasoning, we may call the tools by different names, we may sometimes use them in different ways, but ultimately they all come out of the same toolbox.

12.1.5 Empirical Reasoning

Solving legal problems, we know, is not simply a question of reading the law. Legal arguments are not constructed in a vacuum, but arise out of real, human, situations. Legal rules are expressed only in very general terms. The application of a rule to a particular case is dependent ultimately on the court or tribunal deciding that the facts of that case fit the rule. This conceals what are in reality, as Ivainer (1988) notes, two distinct processes: the proving of alleged facts (see **Chapter 5**); and the subsequent interpretation of those same facts. The latter involves a reasoning process. It is up to the lawyers to construct a legal argument to the effect that the facts are x, y, and z, and that on those facts the rules should be applied in such-and-such a way. It is this aspect of the law–fact relationship that we shall concentrate upon for the remainder of this section, as the actual implications of finding that x is fact rather than law is best left to courses on the law of evidence, or on the particular area of substantive law concerned.

At the heart of empirical reasoning is an interpretive, process which seeks to draw a conclusion from the known facts in each case. This emphasis on interpretation is valuable in that it highlights again the extent to which the use of facts in the legal system involves a creative process, which we shall now examine.

From the perspective of the trial lawyer, as opposed to the judge, there are two discrete reasoning techniques that are central to the process of fact analysis. At the early stages of a case, the body of evidence relating to the case is likely to be incomplete; the first task of the lawyer is thus to establish what is sometimes called 'a theory of the case' (see Anderson and Twining, 1991; Maughan and Webb, 2005: ch. 10)—i.e. a plausible explanation of what may have happened and its legal consequences, which can then be used to assist further information-gathering. Developing a theory of the case itself involves two elements: the creation of both legal and factual theories. By *legal theory* we mean simply the creation of arguments for one or more potential causes of action, i.e. a claim for breach of contract, negligence, etc. Although a legal theory is triggered by the factual information you have available, it also underpins the process of fact analysis. A lawyer's legal theory is critical in determining how he or she organises and explains the facts of the case. As Paul Wangerin explains:

> Surprisingly, few lawyers and students seem to realize that creating a statement of facts must follow, rather than precede, creating the legal arguments. This chronology must be observed because the statement of facts plays two crucial roles for the advocate. The second role necessitates this order of preparation … [T]he statement of facts' first role is to generate psychological sympathy for the represented client. This role has nothing to do with the merits of any legal position … The statement of facts' second role is to prepare the reader for the legal arguments to follow. This is its key role, which explains why the legal theory must always be planned first. (1986: 435–6)

Creating a *factual theory* involves what is termed **abductive** reasoning. Anderson and Twining define this as 'a creative process of using known data to generate hypotheses to be tested by further investigation' (1991: 443). It is thus a style of reasoning that is essentially based on *inference*—on using your existing knowledge to infer potential facts and explanations. For example, assume that Lisa approaches you for advice. She tells you that her brother, Bart, was recently killed when his car ploughed through a motorway barrier and overturned. The road was quite wet when the accident happened, but no other car was involved in the accident. She cannot tell you whether there are any witness statements relating to the accident. She is convinced that there must be some explanation, other than Bart's own negligence. The accident occurred soon after he left home; he was not overtired, and he was an experienced and careful driver.

You know that, if you are to help your client, you need to establish that someone (other than Bart) was negligent or the vehicle was defective. So you would start by thinking about a legal theory of the case based either on negligence or, possibly, product liability. What factual theories might you develop? If no other car was involved, you might infer that you should rule out the negligence of another driver. So, alternatively, there is the possibility of a mechanical defect. You could hypothesise along the following lines— was the steering faulty; did a tyre burst, and, if so, was the burst due to a manufacturing defect or some other cause? And so on. Equally, you would have to consider the possibility of driver error: despite his sister's protestations, could Bart have fallen asleep at the wheel, for instance? To get an idea of abductive reasoning in action, see if you can construct a theory suggesting that there was negligence by another driver. (We pause here while you write.)

There are a number of possibilities. Perhaps a vehicle pulled into the lane too close to the front of Bart's car, causing him to brake hard and lose control on the wet road. Perhaps a vehicle in front temporarily lost control, because the driver fell asleep, or lost concentration, causing Bart to take avoiding action from which he was unable to recover, given the conditions. In both situations it is quite conceivable that the car causing the accident was not then caught up in it.

The key point to remember is that these are no more than hypotheses based on limited information. This means that, though akin to the inductive form of reasoning, the results of abductive reasoning are far more tentative, and would not be sufficient to persuade a court in your favour. To take the earlier example, it is pretty obvious that you would not get very far alleging that the accident was due to a burst tyre without evidence from a police accident report that a tyre had indeed burst, and expert evidence supporting your theory that the burst was due to defective manufacture. However, you must recognise that abductive reasoning techniques are necessary to establish the possibility that such an argument exists, before you can think about obtaining the evidence to change the possibility into a specific, supportable, theory of the case.

Once you have the evidence to establish a supportable theory, the reasoning process moves on to a second stage. Now your empirical reasoning falls firmly within the inductive sphere. Shakespeare, as usual, offers a suitably gory illustration (from *Henry VI*):

Who finds the heifer dead and bleeding fresh,

And sees fast bye a butcher with an axe;

But will suspect twas he that made the slaughter?

Inductively, the conclusion that it was the butcher who did it is acceptable. It is not of course, in formal logic, the only possible answer, but it is *probable*. In any given case of induction the probability will vary by degrees from the slight to the overwhelming—as we have seen already, the law sets its own standards of probability in fact-finding. Deductive reasoning, because it requires that the formal conclusion is absolute, not merely probable, plays little part in empirical reasoning, because the facts are seldom conclusive. The process, therefore, is essentially one of mustering the information that you have, and using it to draw logical inferences regarding the guilt/innocence/liability of a particular person.

In seeking to resolve factual problems there are a number of useful techniques, though in the end much of this boils down to careful application of common sense.

First, think dialectically: essentially all this means is that you need to think through alternative explanations. Do not be afraid to challenge your own assumptions. It is not advisable to develop your own theory of why or how something happened, and ignore other possibilities. This applies as much to the student answering a problem question (where there will often be gaps in the facts waiting for you to construct alternative solutions) as it does to the practitioner preparing a case.

Secondly, be systematic. It is usually important to have an accurate picture of the nature and course of events in order to create a structure within which you can develop your argument.

Thirdly, and following from the preceding points, proceed step by step in presenting the facts of a case. Proof is best built up in small stages. Making major quantum leaps from fact to conclusion may help in developing an initial strategy, but it is unlikely to build a convincing case. This too doubles as sound advice in dealing with problem questions as a student.

12.2 The Limits of Logic

In looking at the limits of logic, we shall again divide the issues into their two constituent areas of legal rules and facts.

12.2.1 Reasoning about Legal Rules

Under this heading there are two points to make. First, it follows from what we have already said that the form of logic in legal reasoning is qualitatively different in legal as opposed to scientific method. Secondly, the courts are willing to impose practical or policy-based limits on the extent to which they will apply logic. Let us consider each point in turn.

Earlier we suggested that reasoning is about discovering the truth. In law, we are not concerned with truth (or facts, if you prefer) in a scientific, i.e. verifiable, sense. The statement 'water is wet' is verifiable—no one would question the empirical truth of that (discounting the possibility that we are just brains in vats or neural cogs in some kind of massive *Matrix*-like video game). Also in scientific method, logic enables prediction, so that it is possible to say that if conditions A and B are satisfied, then C will follow as a matter of necessity. In law, we are dealing with rules which are—to use the technical jargon—**normative statements**. This means that they are based essentially upon a value judgement made by Parliament or a judge that a particular consequence *should* or *ought to* follow certain behaviour. The normative nature of law does not mean that we

are stepping outside the realm of induction, but it does introduce the qualitative difference between legal and scientific method that was intimated. This was explained by the
American jurist Karl Llewellyn (1960):

> in law your logical system refuses to remain on the level of description, of arranging existing observa-
> tion. Backed by the fact and doctrine of precedent, your logical system shifts *its content* to the level of
> Ought (this does not affect the logic). Its remarks change in tone and substance. Now they run: *'If I am
> a correct description of the accepted doctrine*, the future cases *a* and *b are* to have the outcome *x*—they
> *should* have that outcome, and if the judge is on the job he will see to it that they do' ... No longer are
> these initial data statements *merely* of how courts have held on given facts. They have—thanks to the
> addition of precedent—become each one a statement simultaneously of how a court *has* held, and
> in addition how future courts *ought* to hold.

Let's look more closely at this statement in respect of two issues: first, the problem of
defining accepted doctrine, and, secondly, the question of the relationship between prediction and what we shall call 'public policy'.

Defining legal doctrine

Llewellyn's 'if' in the foregoing extract is crucial. As we have already seen from Levi's
three-step process, the existence of competing analogies means that the arguments in
law are not necessarily just about the logical deductions in step three, but about the
premises upon which deduction is to be based. The difficult questions for law tend to
be located at the point of defining 'accepted doctrine', and it is there that pure logic
is often of little help. We can illustrate this by looking at two contrasting decisions of
the Employment Appeal Tribunal (EAT) in the cases of *Kidd v DRG (UK) Ltd* [1985]
ICR 405 and *Clarke v Eley (IMI) Kynoch Ltd* [1983] ICR 165. Both cases arose on very
similar facts whereby the applicants had alleged that redundancy schemes operated by
their respective employers were contrary to the Sex Discrimination Act 1975 in that, by
selecting part-time workers for redundancy first, they indirectly discriminated against
women, and married women in particular, who were disproportionately dependent
upon part-time employment. The legal basis of the women's claim, and the defence
raised by the employers in each case, were also closely comparable. In *Clarke*, the EAT
had found in favour of the women applicants, but in *Kidd* a differently constituted tribunal came to the opposite decision. How could this be? Had a strict analogy been applied,
then *Kidd* should have followed *Clarke*. In departing from the latter, Waite J., giving the
decision of the EAT in *Kidd*, recognised that their decision left the concept of indirect
discrimination 'exposed to criticism by the orderly minded as lacking form or precision'
(at 417). Clearly this did not unduly worry the tribunal; in fact, just the reverse, since
they justified the refusal to apply *Clarke* on the ground that they wished to preserve flexibility in this area of law by avoiding drawing general principles from specific cases. In
other words, the tribunal was really *rejecting* the need to define a precise legal doctrine
in the first place!

Prediction and public policy

Llewellyn's reference to outcomes means that we are preserving the element of prediction based upon logical deduction, but the legal context changes the nature of that prediction from one of fact to one of value, or, if you prefer, from 'is' to 'ought'. This change
is vital. We can see that there is a major qualitative difference between 'is' and 'ought'

statements. A parent's comment that a naughty child *is* going to be smacked obviously has a very different meaning from an onlooker's observation that the child *ought* to be smacked.

Precedents in law are very much the second kind of statement. They show that there may be an answer which logic predicts should apply, but what if that runs contrary to the system of values held by the judge deciding a case which is analogous to the precedent? Is he bound to follow it? The answer is plainly no. The judicial ability to distinguish what are perceived to be 'awkward' precedents can often provide a judge who is sufficiently determined not to apply precedent strictly with the means of so doing. Similarly, in statutory interpretation, the element of choice between literal and purposive approaches also reduces predictability. In short, differences within accepted legal methods can justify different results. The point is well made in more abstract terms by the French legal theorist, Jean-Louis Bergel (2001: 136):

> For this search for the legal solutions to factual situations, jurists use processes which come more from approximations than strict reasoning, principally analogy and induction. They cannot, equally, totally leave aside the various moral, social and human considerations from which the solution of the problem being considered could escape from only at the cost of being inadmissible or impractical. Reasoning which is formally correct can lead to unjust or absurd consequences, of such a kind that one cannot blindly accept the result. It has been said that 'the basis of legal reasoning consists not in finding the exact solution, that is to say the solution which is found to be in perfect harmony with the content of the premises'; the basis of this reasoning 'consists in arriving at a useful, practical, just and equitable result'. The jurist should reason, then, in a kind of reverse way, in considering the conclusion more than the premises. 'Legal wisdom' should consist in tempering the rigidity of logic.

The role of theoretical logic is thus limited by the fact that it may take the judge only as far as identifying a number of rational options. From there, the values that the legal system is seen to serve will play a significant part. This is often explicitly recognised in the legal process by reference to such terms as 'public policy' or 'public interest'. The idea of public policy has always played some part in the legal process. Many of the more recent innovative developments in the law have come about precisely because the judges have stopped to ask 'what is the best policy for the law to adopt'? Examples of this kind of reasoning have influenced developments in both the common law and the application of statute law. Thus, Lord Atkin's 'neighbour principle', developed in *Donoghue* v *Stevenson* [1932] AC 562, was clearly actuated by his Lordship's belief that a generally applicable test for negligence was desirable. The case could have been resolved without the 'neighbour principle', as established criteria already existed which could have included the issue of manufacturer's liability raised by the facts of that case. Moreover, *Donoghue* v *Stevenson* would not have become a landmark case if other judges had chosen to interpret it restrictively rather than expansively (freedom of justification again!).

Similarly, questions of value cannot be excluded from the process of statutory interpretation. We cannot just sit down and logically analyse an Act of Parliament without taking any account of a whole variety of variables, including not least judicial attitudes to that legislation. In particular, any judicial claim to be adopting a broadly purposive approach to statutory interpretation is likely to disclose some element of policy analysis—as in the abortion law case of *Royal College of Nursing* v *DHSS* [1981] AC 800; [1981] 1 All ER 545. Historically, the extent to which judges depend upon policy arguments has not been openly acknowledged, for fear that the judges would be seen as adopting a 'political' law-making role as opposed to a 'legal' interpretive role (see Frank, 1947). Theoretical accounts of what judges do commonly frame this in terms of a division between legal formalism and judicial activism.

Formalism is characterised by the practices of those judges who adhere more closely to some version of a 'declaratory theory' of judging, whereby the judicial role is simply to discern from existing legal principles what the law is. It can also be described in terms of a practice of 'judicial deference' to legislative authority, or, particularly in common law jurisdictions where the highest courts have a power of constitutional review of legislation (such as the USA and Australia), 'judicial restraint'.

Conversely, judicial activism may be said to encompass two different strands (see Devlin, 1981). First, it may involve a legitimate judicial commitment to ensuring that law keeps pace with the changing social consensus. Secondly it may be used as a synonym for what Lord Devlin referred to as 'judicial creativity' or 'judicial dynamism', an illegitimate process of judicial law-making that is 'ahead of the curve' of public opinion.

Debates about the nature and proper extent of activism, and the balance between judicial deference and judicial activism, continue to abound (cf. Sumption, 2011; Sedley, 2012), and in some respects can generate more heat than light. As one would expect, the issue is particularly critical with regard to the scope of action enjoyed by final appellate courts, such as the UK and US Supreme Courts (see, e.g., Paterson, 2013; Dickson, 2015), as well as courts such as the CJEU (Dawson *et al.*, 2013), since these tend to be most engaged with questions about the proper scope of judicial law-making. If we are really to understand the legal reasoning process in action we need to acknowledge the existence of this debate about the nature and role of legal argumentation.

Public policy and the politics of the judiciary

The point is, as Bergel (2001) and others have argued, that pure logic does not necessarily give the desired answer. It may be, therefore, of limited value either in determining a specific case or more generally in predicting future decisions. To return to our original simile, the observer's prediction that the child ought to be smacked will be a pretty poor predictor if the parent is actually opposed to corporal punishment. Legal arguments and decisions are inevitably influenced by the values of the actors within the legal process, and there is thus no guarantee that what is formally logical will necessarily be 'right'.

In recognising this gap between logic and 'good law' (whatever that may be), we must recognise that the limits of logic carry a definite cost. That is, that the introduction of policy or of notions of 'justice' creates greater uncertainty in legal reasoning. We might argue that it is worth the cost, because, as Lord Devlin recognised, it enables the judges, and hence the law, to be responsive to changes in (say) social or economic conditions, or to cases which are taken to be exceptional. In responding to such changes, the judges are inevitably acting with a degree of what we might broadly call subjectivity. Such decisions may also turn to an extent on what we have previously called 'judicial style' (**Chapter 5**). As Lord Dyson MR (2013: 11) has noted:

some judges are more conservative than others. Some are cautious and prefer to paddle in the warm and safe shallows of clear precedent. Others are more adventurous and are prepared to give it a go in the more treacherous waters of the open sea.

At the higher appellate level the impact of different legal styles is likely to be reduced by a mix of formal and cultural norms. The fact that judges in the appellate courts sit *en banc* of itself serves to limit the effect of individual differences. 'Backroom' meetings to discuss cases and the sharing of draft opinions, for example, can also operate in part to build collegiality and consensual decision-making, and reduce individual differences (cf. Paterson, 2013). Moreover, there is, overall, a high degree of institutional and cultural respect for the norms of judging and the perceived integrity of the legal reasoning process (see Duxbury, 2008; Paterson, 2013), which means that even instinctive judicial activists have to operate within certain bounds, if they are not to undermine their own legitimacy within the court.

Nor does this recognition of institutional or role conservatism necessarily mean that decisions are politically biased in an overtly party political sense, though the social and class homogeneity of the English judiciary has meant that judges may tend to speak with the voice of the 'Establishment' (see Griffith, 1997). As one senior judge admitted many years ago:

> Impartiality is rather difficult to obtain in any system. I am not speaking of conscious impartiality, but the habits you are trained in, the people with whom you mix, lead to your having a certain class of ideas of such a nature that, when you have to deal with other ideas, you do not give as sound and accurate judgments as you would wish. (Scrutton LJ, 1923: 8)

Given that the judges' work does bring them into the policy arena time and again, the question 'how much power do we want judges to have over the policy process?' is of real practical and constitutional importance. The core concern behind the deference/activism debate is thus essentially a public law debate about the *legitimacy and limits* of judicial action, recognising that courts exist as public institutions with limited authority over the governmental process.

In looking at the arguments, we can take for granted that a basic notion of judicial deference, not to a particular government or minister but to the larger constitutional separation of powers, is a constitutional fundamental. The problem, insofar as there is one, lies therefore with excessive dynamism (to use Devlin's term). This not only blurs the separation of powers, but has threefold consequences. First, it may be unfair on the parties, and particularly the loser, in litigation because it can retroactively undermine legitimate understanding of what the law was, and of how a case would be decided. Secondly, (it follows) it would tend to conflict with the underlying need for certainty and predictability in the law, which, for example, principles of precedent and statutory interpretation are intended to protect. To that extent it may even be said to undermine the rule of law (Bingham, 2010). Thirdly, some take these arguments even further by suggesting that, at a deeper level, activism thereby threatens what can be characterised as the 'integrity' of the law itself: that is, the need for a case to fit within the wider legal fabric, and demonstrate its continuity and coherence with law's past and its traditions.

On the other hand, this does not necessarily mean that judicial deference is an unqualified good, or that all judicial creativity necessarily take judges across the line from law into politics. The English legal and political systems together place a considerable onus on the courts to keep *government* (not the legislature) accountable for the legality of its decisions. That too is fundamental to the rule of law, and perhaps increasingly so in an age when public power is widely delegated to quasi-public and private entities. Where courts are dealing with broad and often flexible standards, they must turn to questions of purpose and legislative intent in applying the law, and, in that process, a degree of activism may not just be almost inevitable, but the only way to oblige bodies exercising public power to provide a clear rationale for their decisions. Given the courts' fundamental role in maintaining the rule of law, we might want to consider that, if judicial deference is the answer, it needs to be of a limited and authoritative, not a quiet and submissive kind. Moreover, some care needs to be taken to ensure due deference does not turn into a mere fetish of legal tradition (see Kirby, 2006).

The studies of the House of Lords and UK Supreme Court referenced in this chapter in fact indicate that the court's approach has consistently been cautious, to the point of being conservative. To that extent deference has, in practice, largely trumped activism. That of itself, as we have suggested, may not be a bad thing. What may be less helpful to those engaged with both the practice and the theory of the courts is the extent to which such a position has emerged only pragmatically over time, with little cogent attempt to consider the general limits of deference/activism, in the context of the courts' enlarged constitutional role - most notably in the wake of the European law and human rights developments discussed in **Chapters 10** and **11**. A similar point was made by Jonathan Sumption (2011: 22) shortly before his elevation to the Supreme Court, when he said:

> The reticence of English judges about the constitutional implications of their decisions has had unfortunate consequences. It has meant that English public law has not developed a coherent or principled basis for distinguishing between those questions which are properly a matter for decision by politicians answerable to Parliament and the electorate, and those which are properly for decision by the courts.

Lord Sumption's concern in this lecture was to question what he saw as the creeping activism of the courts. Perhaps somewhat ironically, as a growing body of academic work shows, the claim of creeping activism is empirically doubtful (at least as regards the House of Lords and Supreme Court). We should perhaps be equally sceptical whether the theoretical case for greater deference is any more proven. But Lord Sumption's call for greater openness and conceptual debate could in itself be welcome, if it brings greater clarity both to the process of legal reasoning and to the proper constitutional relationship between the courts, the legislature, and the executive.

12.2.2 Reasoning about Facts

In empirical reasoning, the quality of our decisions on the facts of a case will be dependent upon the quality of the fact-finding process, and it is this relationship which probably constitutes the greatest limit on the role of logic in empirical reasoning. We have already considered, in **Chapter 5**, some of the problems of fact finding. Here, we intend to develop some of those issues in a more abstract and theoretical fashion.

Most cases that come before a court concern a dispute over the facts. *R v Wallace*, discussed in **Chapter 5**, is a prime example. The difficulties referred to by the Court of Criminal Appeal in that case did not concern tricky questions of law, but arose in trying to sort out what actually happened.

The first limitation we explore concerns the way in which lawyers perceive facts. In the classic type of problems set by law teachers, that issue normally does not arise. You will be given a set of 'facts' and asked to advise on the law. Though such exercises have practical value in developing problem-solving skills, they inevitably bypass this rather fundamental issue.

Formal definitions of 'fact' in the abstract are, as we have shown, thin on the ground; though there are plenty of cases where the judges have to decide whether a particular issue is one of fact or law. This reflects the common-sense approach to facts, which says (to put it a little crudely): 'we all know what a fact is, don't we? Facts are things we know to be true. They just exist. So what's the problem?' We argue that this level of certainty itself is a problem. Our sense of what is fact is largely based upon observation (what we perceive with one of our five senses) or else some more abstract form of knowledge (generally 'received wisdom', or, e.g., in a more specialised sense, a forensic scientist's, or other specialist's, expertise). The danger is of treating instances of 'observation' or 'knowledge' as absolute truths—a fallacy we first discussed in the context of **Chapter 5**. In law, fact-finding is not that simple. We know that one and one make two, but in the courts facts have to be established from a very unscientific source—us! Kohler's famous drawing of the goblet/faces is an example of the kind of difficulty we must deal with (see **Figure 12.2**).

If I tried to describe this I might simply say that I saw the profiled faces of two people, staring at each other from close to. That might be an accurate, and therefore 'true', description, because it might be all that I saw. If another person described accurately a drawing of a goblet she had been shown, would you necessarily realise that each of

Figure 12.2 Kohler's goblet/faces

us was describing the same thing? Two individual perceptions of the same fact may thus be very different, because there may well be equally valid alternative forms of explanation.

This example does not take into account another variable, which is the quality of the observation. Considerable psychological research into skills of observation has emphasised human fallibility. To put it bluntly; we are not particularly good at remembering what we have seen or heard or done. To make matters worse, the more time that passes between the event and the point of recall and the more stress we were under at the time the event happened, the less accurate our recollections are likely to be. Stress or external factors may not be the only cause of unreliability. The internalised values of a particular witness may, consciously or unconsciously, influence testimony; personal expectations or prejudices may well play an important part. For example, Mr Brown lives in a wealthy suburb of town which has suffered a recent spate of burglaries. One day he sees two cars drive slowly down his road. The first is driven by Mrs Smith, the second by Mr Jones. He informs the police about Mr Jones, but does not mention Mrs Smith because he does not think it relevant. Why? Because Mr Brown may be influenced by his own value judgements of what is suspicious behaviour. He may assume that a woman is less likely to be engaged in criminal activity than a man; if Mrs Smith is well dressed and in a smart car, while Mr Jones is badly dressed and in a battered old car, he may be more likely to consider Mr Jones's behaviour deviant, and so on. In recent decades, some scientists and social scientists have come together to argue that we too easily disregard the extent to which what we call 'knowledge' is not wholly objective, but socially constructed. This is what Hanson means by his observation: 'seeing is a theory-laden undertaking' (1958: 19). This applies not just to lay witnesses, but also to expert evidence.

Expert evidence is quite commonly used in court to establish technical evidence outside the competence of lawyers and ordinary witnesses—the cause of an accident, the handwriting on a letter, the ballistics of a particular gun are all likely subjects of expert testimony. Given the adversarial nature of proceedings, each side may have its own experts, whose opinions may well be diametrically opposed. This is because expert testimony, which may reflect on not only what has happened, but also a version of how or why, will depend heavily upon the individual's perspective on his or her subject. Courtrooms can often become a point at which different 'world views' meet head-on.

This is a tendency which is exacerbated by the manner in which such evidence is used in the trial process. To explain this, let us consider an example from a real, American, case, which is of some notoriety.

On 30 March 1981, John Hinckley attempted to assassinate the US President, Ronald Reagan. The assassination attempt failed, though four people, including the President, received bullet wounds from Hinckley's gun. Hinckley was arrested on the spot and subsequently put on trial for attempted murder (see Low *et al.*, 1986). His (successful) defence was one of insanity, and it was the facts that would be used to establish that defence which, even more than the celebrity of his intended victim, caught the public attention. It soon emerged that Hinckley was obsessed with the actress Jodie Foster, then a student at Yale University. He had written to her, phoned her, and followed her repeatedly, and, a fact that was to take on major significance in the trial, watched her in the film *Taxi Driver* over fifteen times.

Taxi Driver became a key piece of evidence in establishing Hinckley's insanity. It was alleged that Hinckley had been particularly influenced by a leading character in the film, the lonely and mentally unstable taxi driver Travis Bickle, who was befriended by the young prostitute portrayed by Jodie Foster. Of critical importance was the fact that, in the film, Bickle was stalking and preparing to assassinate a politician who employed a woman with whom Bickle had unsuccessfully tried to form a relationship. Using *Taxi Driver* as evidence, the defence sought to show that Hinckley's behaviour was consistent with schizophrenia. It was argued that there were clear links between the actions of Bickle and the formulation of Hinckley's bizarre plan to assassinate Reagan and thereby 'rescue' Foster. In essence, it was argued that Hinckley had adopted the persona of Bickle, and turned the fantasy into his own 'reality'. Conversely, the prosecution sought to show that although he may have held certain false beliefs or delusions, this proved only that Hinckley was a 'dreamer'—an essentially ordinary man—and not that he was mentally ill. In an intriguing re-evaluation of the case, Rosanne Kennedy (1992) has focused on the ways in which expert explanations of Hinckley's behaviour and beliefs were polarised by the advocates into sets of binary images: rational–irrational; real–imaginary; mad–bad. As she concludes:

> Over and over, the trial lawyers force essentially indeterminate medical testimony into categories of truth or falsity, thereby masking the undecidability on which the insanity defence is based. (1992: 21)

The role of the advocate in creating an image of the 'facts' of a case, therefore, should not be overlooked. It is worth thinking back to the quotation from Paul Wangerin, cited earlier in this chapter. What Wangerin is stressing is not just an analytical technique, but a *rhetorical* device. It is a creative use of fact whereby the statement of facts is constructed so as to support the legal argument and persuade an adjudicator of its correctness. Do not forget that this is a technique used not only by advocates. Judges may also use the statement of facts as a rhetorical device, as we have seen from Lord Denning's judgment in *Miller* v *Jackson* in **Chapter 5**.

This limited objectivity in fact-finding has important implications in the legal context. It means that there is often something to be said both supporting and denying the existence of a supposed fact, to the extent that it may be difficult to establish that one party's assertion constitutes fact at all. It is hardly surprising that many cases revolve around disputed testimony from witnesses about their observations. The uncertainties of fact-finding in law led some legal theorists to become what have been described as 'fact-sceptics'—theorists who have used the uncertainty of the fact-finding process to challenge the rationality of legal decision-making—the most famous of these was the American Jerome Frank, who once, succinctly if provocatively, argued that 'facts are guesses' (1947). Although such fact-scepticism may seem negative, it provides an important insight into the legal process. By recognising that 'truth' in the courtroom is established by the court arriving at an agreed view of events, rather than by discovering an absolute reality, we are recognising both the extent to which facts have to be created in court, and the extent to which that means that inferences drawn upon legally established facts may be based upon uncertain foundations. This much has been admitted extra-judicially by the Australian judge, Fox J. when he said:

> When it is said that the rules of evidence tend to the ascertainment of truth, the most that can be meant is that by their application a particular piece of evidence may be more reliable, or may be the more correctly assessed by the tribunal. This may or may not be the effect in relation to a particular

> piece of evidence, but one cannot by any process of aggregation of those pieces have any assurance that what is seen as the resultant situation (the ultimate proposition, or finding on the issue) accords with the truth. (1982: 152)

The extent to which facts are established according to rules of evidence and procedure may itself set a further limit on the value of logic to empirical reasoning. The point is that the application of such rules may not accord with strict logic, but with other values endorsed by the legal system. As Fox J. points out, these rules frequently depend upon the demands of expediency, such as expense or delay to proceedings, or upon substantive claims of public policy (for example the assumption, only recently challenged, that the evidence of young children is inherently unreliable, and therefore insufficient by itself to ground a criminal conviction), rather than any devotion to the ascertainment of truth. We thus concur with Professor Julius Stone in his description of the limits of logic:

> The outcomes of 'pure' logical procedures do not correspond to what necessarily is (or will become) law of any actual community. They may be invaluable for criticising existing legal propositions by reference to a hypothetical model of internal logical consistency or … to test the extent to which a legal system can be conceived as a logically consistent set of legal propositions … These are all legitimate outcomes of logical analysis; but they must always be carefully distinguished from erroneous uses of these outcomes. (1985: 45–6)

The various forms of uncertainty we have discussed suggest that the best that *we* can try to achieve is to ensure that our arguments or decisions are essentially rational in the way they are structured, and that they take into account the considerations of legal principle and/or public policy that seem to apply. In this final section which follows, we suggest a practical technique for structuring legal decisions that you will be able to use.

12.3 The Decision Analysis Method

The technique we are about to describe is derived from techniques of decision analysis in business decision-making. The idea of decision analysis is a useful one. Keeney and Raiffa summarise its aims succinctly:

> The major role of formal analysis is 'to promote good decision-making' … As a process, it is intended to force hard thinking about the problem area: generation of alternatives, anticipation of future contingencies, examination of … effects, and so forth. (in Moore and Thomas, 1988: 245)

Do not be put off by this; the model we have adopted is a much simplified version of the original, which has been adapted to fit the legal context more closely. It also builds on the basic techniques of problem solving that we have already discussed. The method involves six steps:

(i) *Structure the problem:* make sure you know who you are and for whom you are acting; in practice, begin to establish the parameters of your theory of the case (in a 'law school' problem, simply identify your relevant facts).

(ii) *Identify alternative courses of action:* e.g. do the facts disclose an action in contract and/or tort (e.g. the possibility of an action on the basis of both negligent misrepresentation and negligent misstatement); civil and/or criminal proceedings; multiple or alternative grounds for proceeding (e.g. theft and handling of stolen goods; innocent or negligent misrepresentation); a court action or some alternative form of resolution (e.g. a common law action for wrongful dismissal and an unfair dismissal claim before an industrial tribunal)?

(iii) *Determine your objectives:* what does the 'client' want—compensation; some other remedy (e.g. injunction, specific performance); or just advice as to his or her liability?

(iv) *Assess the consequences:* will each of your alternative courses of action achieve the objectives you have identified? For example, it may be little consolation advising X that he might be able to sue Y for trespass (by Y stealing fruit from his orchard), if X is concerned at his own liability to Y for the injuries that Y suffered being chased off the land by X's Doberman dog! Discard any alternatives that are clearly incompatible with your objectives. By this stage you should have a clearer idea of the facts that will be material to your case.

(v) *Identify and account for uncertainty:* what are the main uncertainties you face—are there gaps in the facts, or alternative arguments that may be constructed from the same facts; contradictory precedents; ambiguous wording in the Act creating liability, etc. (in which case, can you create rational arguments supporting your case)? Are there strong policy arguments which might sway a court one way or another, or support or undermine a particular aspect of your reasoning? Determine which of these uncertainties you can resolve and which you cannot.

(vi) *Evaluate your remaining alternatives:* taking into account the uncertainties you face, decide which alternative(s) come(s) closest to achieving your objective(s).

This technique is not foolproof—none is! Ultimately it can only be as good as your initial preparation. Do bear in mind that a decision-making technique such as this is dependent upon your doing sufficient thorough research into the issues first—it cannot make a poorly prepared argument look good!

 CHAPTER REFERENCES

ALEXY, R. (1989), *A Theory of Legal Argumentation* (trans. R. Adler and N. MacCormick) (Oxford: Clarendon Press).

ANDERSON, T. and TWINING, W. (1991), *Analysis of Evidence* (London: Butterworths).

BERGEL, J.-L. (2001), *Méthodologie Juridique* (Paris: PUF).

BINGHAM, LORD (2010), *The Rule of Law* (London: Penguin).

BREWER, S. (1996), 'Exemplary Reasoning: Semantics, Pragmatics and the Rational Force of Legal Argument by Analogy', 109 *Harvard Law Review*, 923.

DAWSON, M., DE WITTE, B., and MUIR, E. (eds) (2013), *Judicial Activism at the European Court of Justice* (Cheltenham: Edward Elgar).

DEVLIN, LORD (1981), *The Judge* (Oxford: Oxford University Press).

Dickson, B. (2015), 'Activism and Restraint within the UK Supreme Court' 21 *European Journal of Current Legal Issues*, No. 1. Available at http://webjcli.org/article/view/399/515.

Duxbury, N. (2008), *The Nature and Authority of Precedent* (Cambridge: Cambridge University Press).

Dyson, Lord (2013), 'Where the Common Law Fears to Tread', 34 *Statute Law Review*, 1.

Esser, J. (1972), *Vorverständnis und Methodenwahl in der Rechtsfindung* (Frankfurt: Athenäum).

Farrar, J. (1997), 'Reasoning by Analogy in Law', 9 *Bond Law Review*, 149.

Fox, Mr Justice R. (1982), 'Expediency and Truth-Finding in the Modern Law of Evidence', in E. Campbell and L. Waller (eds), *Well and Truly Tried* (Sydney: Law Book Co).

*Frank, J. (1947), 'Words and Music: Some Remarks on Statutory Interpretation', 47 *Columbia Law Review*, 1267.

—— (1973), *Courts on Trial* (Princeton, NJ: Princeton University Press).

Golding, M. (1984), *Legal Reasoning* (New York: Alfred Knopf).

Griffith, J. (1997), *The Politics of the Judiciary* (5th edn, London: Fontana Press).

*Hanson, N. (1958), *Patterns of Discovery: An Inquiry into the Conceptual Foundations of Science* (Cambridge: Cambridge University Press).

Ivainer, T. (1988), *L'interprétation des faits en droit* (Paris: Librairie générale de droit et de jurisprudence).

Kennedy, R. (1992), 'Spectacular Evidence: Discourses of Subjectivity in the Trial of John Hinckley', 3(1) *Law and Critique*, 3.

Kirby, Justice M. (2006), 'Judicial Activism: Power without Responsibility? No, Appropriate Activism Conforming to Duty' 30 *Melbourne University Law Review*, 576.

Leith, P. and Hoey A. (1998), *The Computerised Lawyer* (2nd edn, London: Springer-Verlag).

Levi, E. (1949), *An Introduction to Legal Reasoning* (Chicago, Ill.: University of Chicago Press).

*Llewellyn, K. (1960), *The Bramble Bush* (New York: Oceana Pub).

Low, P. et al. (1986), *The Trial of John W. Hinckley, Jr: A Case Study in the Insanity Defence* (New York: Foundation Press).

MacCormick, N. (1978), *Legal Reasoning and Legal Theory* (Oxford: Clarendon Press).

Maris, C. (1991), 'Milking the Meter: On Analogy, Universalisability and World Views', in P. Nerhot (ed.), *Legal Knowledge and Analogy: Fragments of Legal Epistemology, Hermeneutics and Linguistics* (Dordrecht: Kluwer).

Maughan, C. and Webb, J. (2005), *Lawyering Skills and the Legal Process* (2nd edn, Cambridge: Cambridge University Press).

Moore, P. and Thomas, H. (1988), *The Anatomy of Decisions* (2nd edn, London: Penguin Books).

Paterson, A. (2013), *Final Judgment: The Last Law Lords and the Supreme Court* (Oxford: Hart).

*Pirsig, R. (1974), *Zen and the Art of Motor Cycle Maintenance* (London: Bodley Head).

Scrutton, Lord Justice (1923), 'The Work of the Commercial Courts', 1 *Cambridge Law Journal*, 6.

Sedley, S. (2012), 'Judicial Politics', *London Review of Books*, 23 February, 15–16. Available at http://www.lrb.co.uk/v34/n04/stephen-sedley/judicial-politics.

Shaw, P. (1981), *Logic and Its Limits* (London: Penguin).

Stone, J. (1985), *Precedent and Law: Dynamics of Common Law Growth* (Sydney: Butterworths).

Sumption, J. (2011), 'Judicial and Political Decision-Making: The Uncertain Boundary', F.A. Mann Lecture 2011. Available at http://www.legalweek.com/digital_assets/3704/MANNLECTURE_final.pdf.

VILLEY, M. (1975), *La formation de la pensée juridique moderne* (4th edn, Paris: Les Editions Montchretien).

WANGERIN, P. (1986), 'Skills Training in Legal Analysis: A Systematic Approach', 40 *University of Miami Law Review*, 409.

ZACCARIA, G. (1991), 'Analogy as Legal Reasoning: The Hermeneutic Foundation of the Analogical Procedure', in P. Nerhot (ed.), *Legal Knowledge and Analogy: Fragments of Legal Epistemology, Hermeneutics and Linguistics* (Dordrecht: Kluwer).

Index

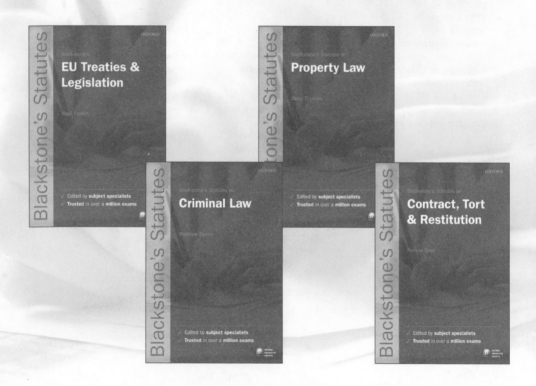